# Biology for CXC

## M. B. V. ROBERTS
*formerly Head of Biology, Marlborough College and Cheltenham College*

## JUNE MITCHELMORE
*formerly Education Officer (Science) Ministry of Education, Jamaica*

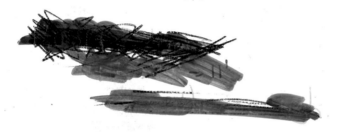

GW00801882

Nelson

*This book is dedicated to Naomi,*
*Sylvia, Catherine, Philip and Anna.*

Thomas Nelson and Sons Ltd
Nelson House   Mayfield Road
Walton-on-Thames   Surrey
KT12 5PL   UK

51 York Place
Edinburgh
EH1 3JD   UK

Thomas Nelson (Hong Kong) Ltd
Toppan Building 10/F
22A Westlands Road
Quarry Bay   Hong Kong

ISBN 0-17-566306-8
NCN 50-RSY-5888-03

© M.B.V. Roberts and June Mitchelmore 1985
First published by Thomas Nelson and Sons Ltd 1985
Reprinted 1985, 1986 (with minor amendments)

Illustrations by
The Pen and Ink Book Company Limited, London
Milne Stebbing Illustration
Picture research by Michael Spillard and Dianne
Ceresa
Cover design and layout by
The Pen and Ink Book Company Limited, London
Cover photograph Oxford Scientific Films Ltd
Printed in Great Britain by Bulter & Tanner Ltd.,
Frome, Somerset

**Publisher's note**
Some of the material in this book appears in
*Biology for Life*, by M.B.V. Roberts, published by
Thomas Nelson and Sons Ltd.

# Preface

This book has been prepared especially to cover the Caribbean Examination Council (CXC) syllabus in Biology. It has been written with the same emphases as the syllabus so that:

**1** Every opportunity has been taken to relate biological studies to the environment; there has been a stress on ecological work, and biological principles have been illustrated by Caribbean examples. There is a glossary of the common and scientific names of the Caribbean flowering plants used in the text, together with alternative names used in the region.

**2** There is a stress on the effect of science on society and vice versa, especially in the studies of disease and the environment. These topics also serve to show the dynamic nature of science, both in the development of scientific ideas and in man's effect on the environment.

**3** The relationship between structure and function has been continually highlighted. *How* things work as related to the structure is a recurring theme. Numerous diagrams and photographs have been used so as to aid understanding.

**4** A practical approach has been used throughout, with an introductory topic to assist students with particular techniques. Each topic has full instructions for practical work, which is seen as integral to the whole teaching process. Assignments for each topic are arranged in order of increasing difficulty and will help with the development of enquiry skills.

Section A of the syllabus *'Living organisms in the environment'* has been treated in the first part of this book (pp. 2 – 43). It is recommended that teachers go through Section A first so as to introduce students to work outside the classroom and to provide an overview of topics which will be developed in greater depth during the rest of the course.

Section B of the syllabus *'Life processes'* has been treated in 'Maintaining Life' (pp. 70 – 187) and 'Responding to Stimuli' (pp. 190 – 245).

Section C of the syllabus *'Continuity and variation'* has been treated in 'The Continuation of Life' (pp. 248 – 321).

Section D of the syllabus *'Diseases and man'* is mainly treated in 'How Organisms affect Humans' (pp. 324 – 353), but there are additional references on p. 313 (sickle cell anaemia) and pp. 76–9 and 142–5 (deficiency diseases).

Section E of the syllabus *'Environment and Man'* is dealt with in 'Living Things and their Environment' (pp. 356 – 399).

As with the syllabus, the major emphasis of the book has been to illustrate the life processes largely in man and flowering plants. However, the material on pp. 46 – 67 ('Life Forms') has been included mainly as a reference to other organisms and especially to illustrate the tendency for specialisation of structure with increase in size and complexity. There are also comparative topics within the third and fourth parts ('Maintaining Life' and 'Responding to Stimuli') to show how these specialisations are related to the manner in which various life processes are carried out in a variety of organisms.

As well as covering the CXC syllabus, this book contains additional topics which expand on certain ideas or are added for completeness. These are for reference only. They are marked with an asterisk * on the Contents page.

Teachers are referred to the CXC syllabus for the estimated time allocation for the various sections. Five 40-minute periods weekly, over the two-year period in Forms IV and V (Grades 10 and 11), are recommended. These should include at least one double period each week to allow for meaningful practical work.

The syllabus is not presented in a teaching sequence although it is expected that Section A will be taught first. This book is divided up into a large number of short topics so that, within reason, they can be studied in any order. This will enable individual teachers to weave the topics together into their own sequence.

Many people have assisted in the production of this book. We are particularly grateful to Dr James Parkyn, Dr Llywelyn Roberts, Mrs Gill Williams and Mr Malcolm Ashby for advice on medical matters and health education; to Mr David Alford for his constructive comments on the first draft; and to Drs Nikolas and Justine Coupland for their invaluable advice on language and readability. In addition we would like to thank Mr John Barker, Mr Peter Fry and Dr John Land for their useful comments, and the numerous teachers and pupils who have patiently read through and commented on the text, investigations and assignments.

We would like to express our thanks to Professor Ivan Goodbody and the staff of the Zoology Department and to Professor George Sidrack and the staff of the Botany Department at Mona, UWI, for their assistance with the choice of Caribbean examples to be used in the book; to Dr C.D. Adams, formerly Reader in Botany, UWI, who assisted with the plant names given in the Glossary; and to Professor Graham Serjeant, head of the Sickle Cell Unit, MRC laboratories, Mona, UWI, for information on sickle cell anaemia.

Particular thanks are expressed to the members of the CXC Biology panel and CXC staff for the dedicated work which was put into the development of the original syllabus, and especially to the Convener, Dr Joyce Glasgow of the School of Education, Mona, UWI. Considerable inspiration for the writing of this book can be traced back to the influence of members of that Biology panel.

Finally it is a pleasure to thank our publishers, Thomas Nelson and Sons Ltd. It was they who first suggested that this book be written, and they have never failed to give us every support.

June Mitchelmore
M.B.V. Roberts

*November 1983*

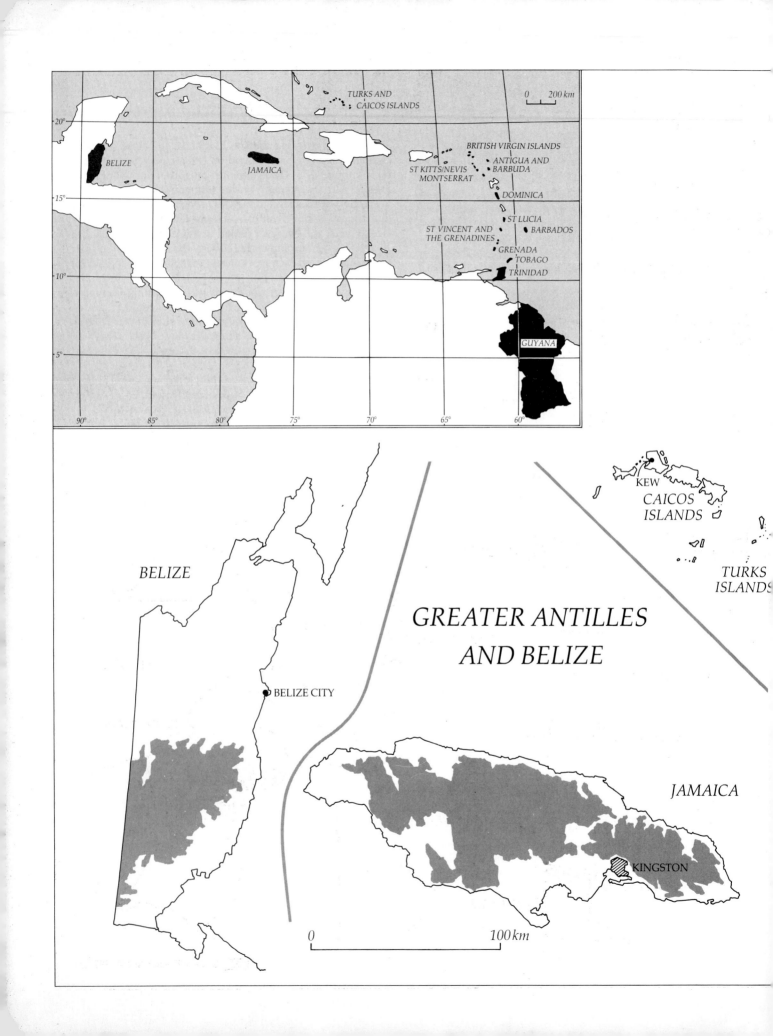

TURKS AND
CAICOS ISLANDS

0    200 km

BELIZE

JAMAICA

BRITISH VIRGIN ISLANDS

ST KITTS/NEVIS
MONTSERRAT

ANTIGUA AND
BARBUDA

DOMINICA

ST LUCIA

ST VINCENT AND
THE GRENADINES

BARBADOS

GRENADA
TOBAGO
TRINIDAD

GUYANA

BELIZE

BELIZE CITY

KEW

CAICOS
ISLANDS

TURKS
ISLANDS

GREATER ANTILLES
AND BELIZE

JAMAICA

KINGSTON

0                    100 km

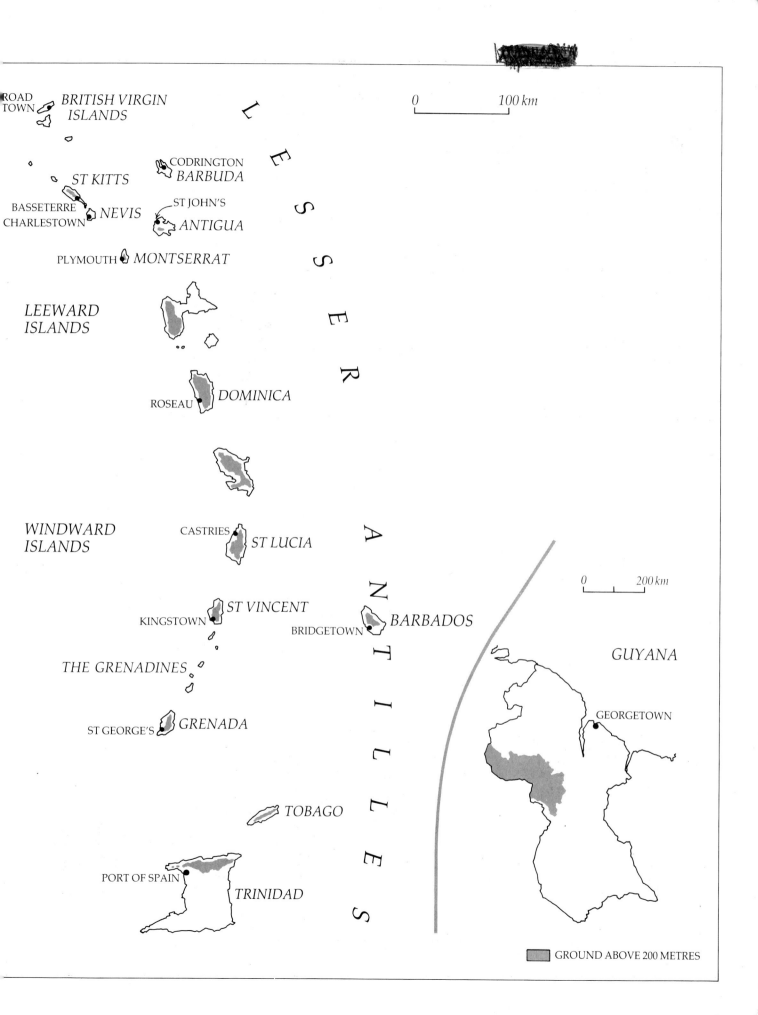

ROAD TOWN

BRITISH VIRGIN ISLANDS

CODRINGTON
BARBUDA

ST KITTS

BASSETERRE
CHARLESTOWN NEVIS

ST JOHN'S
ANTIGUA

PLYMOUTH MONTSERRAT

LEEWARD
ISLANDS

ROSEAU DOMINICA

L E S S E R

WINDWARD
ISLANDS

CASTRIES ST LUCIA

ST VINCENT
KINGSTOWN

THE GRENADINES

ST GEORGE'S GRENADA

BARBADOS
BRIDGETOWN

A N T I L L E S

0        100 km

0        200 km

GUYANA

GEORGETOWN

TOBAGO

PORT OF SPAIN

TRINIDAD

GROUND ABOVE 200 METRES

# Contents

*These sections are included mainly for background information and reference.

# Introducing biology

*Biology is the
study of life and living
things. In the first series of Topics
we shall introduce the subject
and look at some of its
basic principles.*

# Studying living things

*This Topic will show you how we can investigate living things.*

Figure 1 A young biologist carrying out an experiment.

| Temperature °C | Breathing rate (cm³ oxygen/kg)/h |
|---|---|
| 5 | 10 |
| 10 | 25 |
| 15 | 50 |
| 20 | 100 |
| 25 | 150 |
| 30 | 200 |
| 35 | 215 |
| 40 | 225 |

Table 1 Table showing the rate of breathing of a goldfish at different temperatures. The breathing rate is expressed as cubic centimetres of oxygen taken up by one kilogram of body mass in one hour.

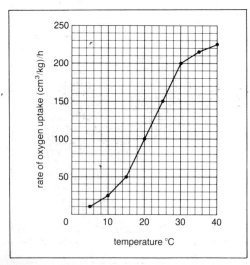

Figure 2 Line graph of the results shown in Table 1.

## How do we find out about living things?

Biology is the study of living things, or **organisms** as we call them. We find out about living things by observing them and asking questions about them. What is that structure for? How does it work? Why is the animal behaving like this? Why are weeds growing here but not there?

## Testing hypotheses

Suppose we want to know why a certain type of plant grows well in place A but badly in place B.

The first thing to do is to put forward a *possible* reason. Scientists call this a **hypothesis**. A hypothesis explaining why plants grow better in one place than another might be that they differ in the amount of light they get. The next step is to test this hypothesis to find out if it is true or not. This is done by carrying out an **experiment**.

Scientists often investigate things by first thinking of a hypothesis, and then testing it by doing experiments (Figure 1). This procedure is sometimes called the **scientific method.**

## Doing experiments

Suppose we want to test the hypothesis that light is needed for the leaves of a young plant to become green.

We obtain a plant and put it in the dark. If the green colour fails to develop, we will conclude that light is needed for it. However, there is something more that we must do: we must obtain a second plant and put it in the light. We need this second plant in order to provide a standard with which to compare the first plant. The second plant is called the **control**.

In carrying out this experiment it is essential that the two plants should be kept in exactly the same conditions, except for the light they receive. To put it in a general way: *we must keep all the variables constant except for the one whose effect we want to investigate.*

## Writing up experiments

You should write up your experiments under these headings:

*Aim*   Why did you do the experiment? What question were you trying to answer? What hypothesis were you testing?

*Method*   What did you do, and how did you do it? Give the names of the organisms you studied, and describe any apparatus and chemicals you used. Give labelled diagrams where these help to explain what you did. Remember to include details of the control. *Another person should be able to follow your instructions and come to the same conclusions.*

*Results*   What happened? What did you find out? As you carried out your experiment, you observed things and perhaps made measurements or took readings. These are your **results**. You can summarise them in various ways. It is also often useful to put the results together in the form of a **table** or a **graph.**

*Interpretation*   This is where you look carefully at your results and answer the questions: What do they mean? Do they show any kind of pattern? Graphs and charts are particularly good at showing up patterns.

*Conclusions*   Do your results answer your original question? Do they support your hypothesis?

## Graphs

A graph is a diagram of a set of results. There are several different kinds of graph, each suited to a particular situation.

### Line graphs

A **line graph** helps us to see at a glance how two sets of numbers are related to each other. As an example let's take the results in Table 1 and present them as a line graph.

The graph is shown in Figure 2. It has two **axes** at right angles to each other. The horizontal axis carries the numbers which you varied in the course of the experiment, i.e. the temperature. We call this the **independent variable**. The vertical axis carries the measurements which you made at each temperature. This is called the **dependent variable**, because the readings depend on something which you were varying, namely the temperature. Notice that the axes begin at zero, and a suitable scale has been chosen so that the graph fits neatly into the available space. The readings are recorded as dots which in this case are joined up by straight lines. Whenever you draw a line graph, give it a title and make sure the axes are labelled fully. Now compare the graph in Figure 2 with Table 1. Can you see a pattern more clearly in the graph?

### Bar charts

Suppose we measure the heights of forty students. Table 2 shows the measurements as a table. The heights are arranged in groups in the left-hand column, and the numbers of students falling into each group are on the right.

Results of this kind are best shown as a **bar chart** (Figure 3). The height groups are put on the horizontal axis, and the number of students on the vertical axis. The number of students in each height group is shown by the length of the bars.

Can you see a pattern in Figure 3? What does the bar chart suggest about the way the students' heights vary? This kind of bar chart is called a **histogram**, and it's very useful in biology.

### Pie charts

Suppose we want to compare the amount of land in a certain country which is taken up by towns, farmland, forests and desert. One way would be to express them as percentages as in Table 3. But how much better it would be to show them as a diagram. One way of doing this is to represent the whole country as a circle, and the different parts by sectors. We call this a **pie chart** (Figure 4).

How do you construct a pie chart? Well, the angle at the centre of a circle is 360°. We have to find what part of this corresponds to each sector. Now suppose the amount of land taken up by towns is ten per cent. Ten per cent of 360° is $\frac{10}{100} \times 360 = 36°$. So we draw a sector with an angle of 36° to show how much of the country consists of towns.

### Diagrams

A diagram shows how things relate to each other rather than what they actually look like. For example, the diagram of the human blood system on page 134 shows the general plan of the circulation, but it does not show the individual blood vessels and where each one goes.

In diagrams arrows are often used to show relationships, and colour may be used to emphasise certain parts.

When you draw a diagram of a piece of apparatus, draw it as if you were looking at a section of it. The edge can be shown by a single line. Tubes that allow things to pass through should be shown by two lines with a space in between (Figure 5). Diagrams must always have a title and be fully labelled.

### Drawings

A drawing differs from a diagram in that it must look like the real thing (Figure 6). The idea is to make an accurate record of the object exactly as you see it. In biology you will sometimes draw specimens: they may be whole organisms, dissections, or thin slices seen under the microscope. Here are a

| Height groups (cm) | Number of students in each group |
|---|---|
| 120–124 | 2 |
| 125–129 | 7 |
| 130–134 | 10 |
| 135–139 | 11 |
| 140–144 | 6 |
| 145–149 | 4 |

**Table 2**  The number of students in each group of heights.

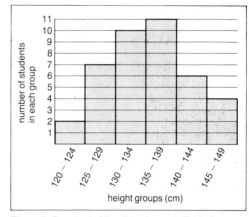

**Figure 3**  Bar chart of the data shown in Table 2.

| Part | Percentage area |
|---|---|
| Town | 10 |
| Farmland | 18 |
| Forest | 17 |
| Desert | 33 |
| Other | 22 |

**Table 3**  Table showing the relative amounts of town, farmland, forest and desert in a certain country.

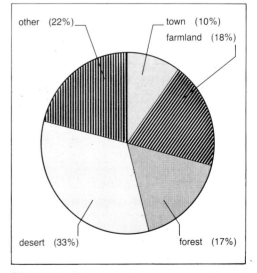

**Figure 4**  Pie chart showing the information in Table 3.

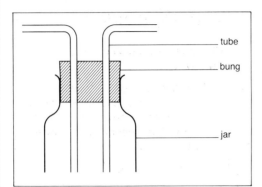

**Figure 5** When you draw a diagram of a piece of apparatus draw it in section as shown here.

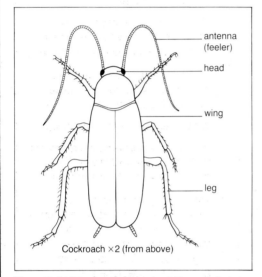

Cockroach ×2 (from above)

**Figure 6** A biological drawing should be realistic but simple. There is no need to shade it.

**Figure 7** This teacher is showing his students how to use a light microscope.

few suggestions about making drawings and labelling them.

1 Use a sharp pencil, *not* a pen or coloured crayon.
2 Make the drawing large, but leave enough space on both sides for labels.
3 Make a faint outline first. The parts on the drawing should be in the same proportion as the corresponding parts on the specimen. Don't draw a big head on a small body!
4 Draw your final lines as single continuous lines, not as a collection of little lines. Draw them smoothly, making them straight or curved as the case may be.
5 Do not shade your drawing. It rarely helps and sometimes it may hide things.
6 Draw clear label-lines with a ruler. The lines should come off the drawing on either side, and must not cross.
7 Label in pencil: you may make a mistake and want to rub it out later!
8 Write down how many times larger your drawing is than the real specimen. If your drawing is twice as large as the specimen, the magnification is ×2. If you draw it life-size, it is ×1.
9 Give your drawing a title: include the name of the specimen and say whether it is viewed from above, below or the side.
10 If necessary make brief notes on any points which you cannot show in your drawing. Such annotated drawings can be very useful.

## Looking at small things

In biology we often have to look at small organisms. A **hand lens** can help us. A typical hand lens has a magnifying power of ×10: this means that we see the object ten times larger than it really is. Hold the lens close to your eye, then bring the object towards the lens until a sharp image is seen.

What do we do if the object is too small to be seen with a hand lens? The answer is that we use a **light microscope** (Figures 7 and 8). If you have not used a microscope before, you should do Investigation 1 very carefully. When looking at an object under the microscope it is important to appreciate how much it has been magnified. Investigations 2 and 3 will help you with this.

If you were to measure the width of a coin you would probably express it in millimetres. However, for small objects seen down the microscope we use a smaller unit called the **micrometre** (μm). A micrometre is one thousandth of a millimetre. For really tiny objects we use an even smaller unit called a **nanometre** (nm). A nanometre is one millionth of a millimetre.

What about objects that are too small to be seen with a light microscope? To see these we must use an **electron microscope** (page 32).

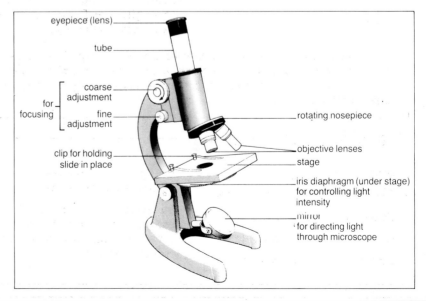

**Figure 8** The main parts of a typical light microscope.

# Investigation 1

## Learning to use the microscope

1  Study your microscope carefully and compare it with Figure 8. Yours may be slightly different. Make sure you understand it before you use it.

2  Objects to be viewed under the microscope are first placed on a glass slide and covered with a thin piece of glass called a coverslip. Your teacher will give you a specimen which has been mounted in this way.

3  Place the slide on the stage of your microscope: arrange it so the specimen is in the centre of the hole in the stage.

4  Fix it in place with the two clips.

5  Rotate the nosepiece so the *small* objective lens is immediately above the specimen: the nosepiece should click into position.

6  Place a lamp in front of the microscope, and set the angle of the mirror so the light is directed up through the microscope.

7  Look down the microscope through the eyepiece. Adjust the iris diaphragm so the field of vision is bright but not dazzling.

8  Look at the microscope from the side. Turn the coarse adjustment knob in the direction of the arrow in Figure 8. This will make the tube move downwards.

9  Continue turning the knob until the tip of the objective lens is close to the slide.

10  Now look down the microscope again. Slowly turn the coarse adjustment knob in the other direction, so the tube gradually moves upwards. The specimen on the slide should eventually come into view.

11  Use the coarse and fine adjustment knobs to focus the object as sharply as possible.

12  If necessary re-adjust the iris diaphragm so the specimen is correctly illuminated. You will get a much better picture if you *don't* have too much light coming through the microscope.

You are now looking at the specimen under low power, i.e. at low magnification.

13  Rotate the nosepiece so the *large* objective lens is immediately above the specimen. The nosepiece should click into position, as before.

14  If the specimen is not in focus, focus it with the fine adjustment knob. *Be careful that the tip of the objective lens does not touch the slide.*

15  Re-adjust the illumination if necessary.

You are now looking at the specimen under high power. Do you agree that it is now much more enlarged?

Always treat the microscope with the greatest care: it is an expensive precision instrument. Always carry it with both hands, and keep it covered when you are not using it. Make sure the lenses never get scratched or damaged: if they need cleaning tell your teacher.

# Investigation 2

## The magnifying power of the microscope

1  Place a transparent ruler on the stage of your microscope. Arrange it so that a line on the millimetre scale is immediately below the low power objective lens.

2  Focus onto the line.

3  Using the ruler, count how many millimetre divisions fit across the low power field of view.

What is the diameter of the low power field of view (a) in millimetres (mm) and (b) in micrometres ($\mu$m)?

4  Now rotate the nosepiece so the high power objective is immediately above a line on the ruler.

What does the line look like now?

What is the approximate diameter of the high power field of view in (a) millimetres and (b) micrometres?

5  The magnifying power of your microscope is the magnifying power of the eyepiece lens, multiplied by the magnifying power of the objective lens. The magnifying power of the eyepiece and objectives is engraved on them.

Work out the low and high power magnifications of your microscope.

# Assignments

1  Look at Table 1 on page 73. Illustrate the information by means of a bar chart.

2  Look at the bar chart on page 393 (Figure 2). Make a table of data from which this bar chart could have been made.

3  Look at page 74, Figure 5. Construct a pie chart to show the relative amounts of different nutrients in dried fish.

4  A certain specimen is 0.5 mm long. What is its length in (a) micrometres, and (b) nanometres? Which of these two units would it be best to express its length in, and why?

# Investigation 3

## Seeing is believing

1  Cut the letter 'e' out of a newspaper.

2  Place it on a slide in a drop of water.

3  Carefully lower a coverslip onto it.

4  Look at the slide under low power.

What does the 'e' look like?
What is its approximate width?

If you drew the 'e' on a piece of paper and gave it a width of one centimetre, what would the scale of your drawing be?

# The characteristics of living things

*If we examine the things organisms do, and the processes which take place inside them, we find certain features that are common to them all.*

Figure 1 The gymnast is showing one of the basic properties of life: movement.

## Living things move

This is obvious in the case of a human being (Figure 1). We move our arms and legs by means of **muscles**, and they are controlled by our **nerves**. Most animals can move in a similar way, at least at some period of their lives.

However movement is not so obvious in a plant. To see movement in a plant you must look inside it, under a microscope. Then you may see things moving about, though it is not always easy (Investigation 1).

## Living things respond to stimuli

If you sit on a drawing pin, you jump up quickly. The pricking of your bottom is called the **stimulus** (plural: stimuli). Your jumping is called the **response**.

Living things respond to different kinds of stimuli. The main ones are touch, chemicals, heat, light and sound. For example, when we see something we are responding to light entering our eyes, and when we taste things we are responding to chemicals in the mouth. Structures such as eyes which detect stimuli are called **receptors**.

At first sight you might think that plants are an exception to the rule that all organisms respond to stimuli. After all, if you hit a tree, it doesn't move away. However, plants *do* respond to certain stimuli, but much more slowly than animals. They do not have muscles. Instead they respond by *growing* in a particular direction. For example, most plants grow towards light (Figure 2).

There are a few plants which respond quickly to touch, like animals do. For example, the leaves of certain sensitive plants close up when you touch them (Investigation 2). However, there are no nerves or muscles in the leaves: the response is brought about by the leaf cells changing shape.

## Living things grow

As an animal or plant develops, it gets larger. In other words, it **grows**. In this process its volume and mass increase.

Growth takes place by substances being taken into the organism from outside. These substances are then built up into the structures of the body: they become part of the organism.

Figure 2 This plant is growing towards the light.

Figure 3 All organisms feed. This lizard is eating a cricket.

A plant, such as a tree, goes on growing throughout its life. Animals usually stop growing when they reach a certain age. For example, humans stop growing at about the age of eighteen.

Even when growth stops, the materials of the body are constantly replaced by new substances coming in from outside. This process of renewal goes on throughout life. It has been worked out that in about seven years all the chemicals in the human body are replaced by new ones.

## Living things feed

We have just seen that in order to grow, an organism must take substances into its body. This is achieved by **feeding (nutrition)**. All organisms need food.

Animals and plants feed in quite different ways. Animals feed on complex organic substances which are often in solid form (Figure 3). In man the food is taken into the mouth. It is then broken down into a soluble form: this process is called **digestion** and it is carried out in the gut.

Any food which cannot be digested passes out of the body through the anus. Meanwhile the digested food is absorbed and used.

In contrast to animals, plants make their own food. They take in simple things like carbon dioxide and water and build them up into complex organic substances. Energy is needed for this: it comes from sunlight. The green pigment **chlorophyll** enables the plant to use sunlight in this way: this is why plants are usually green. The process by which plants make food is called **photosynthesis** (Figure 4).

Organisms like green plants which make their own organic food are called **autotrophs**. Organisms like animals which require ready-made organic food are called **heterotrophs**.

Heterotrophs get their food from various sources. Those that feed on plants are called **herbivores**. Those that feed on animals are called **carnivores**. And those that feed on both plants and animals are called **omnivores**. Some heterotrophs feed on *living* organisms, harming them in the process: they are known as **parasites**. And finally some feed on dead material: we call them **saprotrophs**[1]. You will meet all these different feeding types in later Topics.

Are there different kinds of autotrophic feeding too? Most autotrophs feed by photosynthesis, getting their energy from sunlight. However, certain bacteria can make organic food by using energy from special chemical reactions: this is called **chemosynthesis**.

## Living things produce energy

Living things need energy to move, grow, replace worn-out structures, and so on. They obtain this energy by burning food. The food is not really burned, but it comes to the same thing chemically: the food is broken down into carbon dioxide and water. This process is called **respiration**.

Respiration normally requires oxygen. Organisms get this vital gas from the air or water around them. We call this process **breathing**. For example, in man air is sucked into a pair of lungs (Figure 5). In fish, water flows over the surface of gills. As well as taking up oxygen into the body, lungs and gills get rid of carbon dioxide.

Not all organisms have lungs or gills. Some just let oxygen 'seep' into the body across the surface or through small holes. This is called **diffusion**. It's a slow process, but it's good enough for small or inactive organisms (including plants) which don't need much energy.

Many animals are able to carry oxygen quickly round the body. In man this job is done by the **blood system**: the blood is pumped by the heart through a system of blood vessels. The blood system is also used for transporting dissolved food substances.

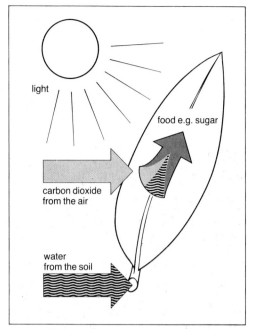

Figure 4 Plants feed by photosynthesis. The plant takes up carbon dioxide and water and turns them into complex food substances such as sugar. This process is carried out mainly in the leaves. In a typical land plant water is absorbed by the roots and transported to the leaves via the stem.

Figure 5 Don Quarrie in a 200 metre race. An athlete in a race has to breathe very deeply. His muscles do a lot of work and they need plenty of oxygen.

[1] In older systems of classification these used to be called **saprophytes**.

**Figure 6** Reproduction is one of the basic features of all living things. Here a new generation of piglets are being suckled by their mother.

## Living things get rid of poisonous waste

In many ways an organism is like a chemical factory. Substances are constantly being broken down to produce energy, or built up to make structures such as bones and muscles. This is called **metabolism**.

Some of the by-products of metabolism are poisonous. They must not be allowed to pile up in the body, or they will kill the organism. So the body must get rid of them. This is called **excretion**.

In animals one of the most poisonous waste substances is **ammonia**. It is so poisonous that most animals quickly turn it into a less poisonous substance. This is then expelled from the body, along with water, in the form of a liquid called **urine**.

Plants get rid of waste substances in a different way. They turn them into harmless substances which they store within the body out of harm's way.

## Living things produce offspring

Organisms produce offspring (Figure 6). This is known as reproduction. Usually it involves the union of two individuals, a male and a female. We call this **sexual reproduction**.

In animals such as humans the male produces sperms, and the female produces eggs. We call these **gametes**. Sperms are much smaller than eggs.

The male and female usually come into close contact, and the male's sperms are put into the female's body. The sperms then unite with the eggs, one sperm per egg. This is called **fertilisation**. The fertilised egg then becomes an **embryo** which develops into a new individual. In flowering plants the male gamete is inside the pollen.

Some organisms can reproduce on their own without the help of another individual. This is called **asexual reproduction**. At its simplest, the organism merely splits in two. In good conditions asexual reproduction may take place very quickly and sometimes a very large number of offspring are produced.

The series of events which take place from the time an organism reproduces to the time its offspring reproduce is called the **life cycle**.

Some animals have a free-living young stage in the course of the life cycle. We call this a **larva**. An example is the tadpole of frogs and toads.

## Living things die

The life of an individual animal or plant does not go on for ever. Eventually all the processes which have been described in this Topic stop and the organism dies.

Some organisms live much longer than others. One of the longest living animals is man: there are many cases of people living to over 100 years. The only other animals to come anywhere near this are tortoises, whales and elephants, and perhaps certain fishes. At the other extreme, adult mayflies live only a few hours: just long enough to find a mate and reproduce.

With plants it is a different story altogether: they can live much longer than animals. The record is held by certain pine trees in California: some of them are estimated to be well over 4000 years old.

## Animals and plants compared

How do you differ from a plant such as a tree? Table 1 summarises the differences between a typical animal and plant. The main difference is in their methods of feeding, and all other differences stem from this. The tree can make its own organic food by photosynthesis, and so it does not need a mouth and a gut. It does not need to move around and find food, so it does not have nerves, muscles and receptors like eyes and a nose. On the other hand the tree needs chlorophyll in order to photosynthesise, and it must be able to take up simple substances from its surroundings. These jobs are carried out by its leaves and roots.

| Typical animal | Typical plant |
| --- | --- |
| Feeds on ready-made organic food (heterotrophic feeding) | Makes its own organic food by photosynthesis (autotrophic feeding) |
| Has feeding structures such as mouth and gut | Lacks feeding structures |
| Lacks chlorophyll | Has chlorophyll |
| Is not rooted to the ground | Is rooted to the ground |
| Moves around | Does not move around |
| Has nerves and muscles | Lacks nerves and muscles |
| Has receptors such as eyes and ears | Lacks receptors |

**Table 1** The differences between a typical animal and plant.

# Investigation 1

**Detecting movement inside a plant**

Movement is difficult to see in most plants, but here is an exception.

1 Obtain a sprig of the water plant Canadian pondweed (*Elodea*) which has been kept in the light for several hours.

2 Cut off one of the leaves and put it in a drop of water on a microscope slide.

3 Cover the leaf with a coverslip so as to keep the leaf flat. Try not to get any air bubbles trapped under the coverslip.

4 Look at the leaf under a microscope. (If you don't know how to use a microscope, look up page 5).

   Can you see lots of small green objects inside the leaf?

   These are chloroplasts (see page 157).

   If they are moving, describe their movement as fully as you can.

The chloroplasts don't *always* move, so don't be disappointed if you see nothing happening.

# Investigation 2

**Getting a plant to respond to touch**

Few plants respond quickly when you touch them, but certain sensitive plants do, for example *Mimosa pudica*.

1 Obtain a potted specimen of a sensitive plant.

2 Gently touch the top side of a leaf with a needle. What happens?

3 Gently touch other parts of the plant, including the lower side of the leaves, and the stem.

   Describe what happens in each case.

4 Pipette a drop of water onto one of the leaves. What happens?

Of what use do you think this response is to the plant?

How do you think the response might be brought about?

How would a similar response be brought about in an animal?

Can you think of an animal that shows this kind of response?

# Investigation 3

**Recognising the characteristics of life in organisms**

1 Make a list of the characteristics of life given in this Topic, starting with 'living things move' and finishing with 'living things reproduce'.

2 Examine a set of organisms such as the following and for each one write down the particular characteristics of life which you can see it shows:

   Yeast growing in sugar solution
   Mould growing on moist bread
   A seedling of a flowering plant
   Leaves of leaf of life
   Flowering plant such as coleus
   An earthworm
   A caterpillar
   A cockroach
   A bony fish
   A frog or toad
   Yourself

*Note* Don't write down the characteristic unless you can actually see it. After doing this, you will realise that some of the characteristics of life are difficult to see in organisms.

How could you find out if an organism possesses a characteristic of life which you cannot actually see?

# Assignments

1 Name three different activities for which we need food.

2 Of all the characteristics of living things mentioned in this Topic, which ones are most important in each of the following?

   The number of characteristics which you should mention in each case is given in brackets.
   a) a person watching television (1)
   b) a footballer kicking a ball (2)
   c) a lion stalking a zebra (2)
   d) germs spreading through your body when you are ill (1)
   e) a plant bending towards the light (1)
   f) a person panting after a race (1)
   g) a bean plant climbing up a bamboo cane (2)

3 Which of the following activities are shown by all animals and plants?

   Respiration, feeding, sexual reproduction, growth, escaping from enemies.

4 Explain in your own words what is meant by a stimulus.

   What sort of stimuli does a named potted plant respond to?

5 If you blow up a balloon and then hold it in front of a stove, it increases in size.

   Is the balloon growing in a biological sense?

   Give reasons for your answer.

6 What is the difference between an object which is dead and one which is non-living?

7 A visitor to our planet from outer space says he thinks motor cars are alive.

   In order to put him straight, make a list of ways in which a motor car is similar to living organisms, and another list of ways in which it is different.

8 Table 1 shows the main differences between a typical animal and a typical plant.
   a) Explain the reason for each of the differences listed in the table.
   b) Some of the features listed in the table have exceptions. For instance, not all plants are rooted to the ground. Write down as many exceptions as you can.
   c) Do the exceptions make the table useless?

# Classifying, naming and identifying

*About one and a half million kinds of organisms have been described. With so many we must have some way of classifying, naming and identifying them.*

| | |
|---|---|
| Kingdom ANIMAL | All animals |
| Phylum VERTEBRATES | Animals with a backbone |
| Class MAMMALIA | Backboned animals with hair |
| Order PRIMATES | Mammals with grasping hands and feet |
| Family HOMINIDAE | Ape-man and primitive man as well as modern man |
| Genus HOMO | Primitive man and modern man only |
| Species SAPIENS | Modern man only |

**Table 1** This figure shows how man is classified.

**Figure 2** *Blighia sapida*. These fruits are called ackees in Jamaica.

**Figure 3** *Melicoccus bijugatus*. These fruits are called ackees in Barbados, but they are called guineps in Jamaica.

## How do we classify living things?

Scientists classify living things by arranging them into groups. Each group is then split into smaller groups, and these groups into even smaller groups and so on. The members of each group have certain features in common which distinguish them from other groups.

Living things are first split into **kingdoms**, such as the animal and plant kingdoms. These kingdoms are then split up into a large number of smaller groups called **phyla** (singular: phylum). All the members of a phylum have certain things in common. Each phylum is broken down into **classes**, classes into **orders**, orders into **families**, families into **genera** (singular: genus), and genera into **species**. Each of these groups contains progressively fewer and fewer kinds of organisms. Thus a phylum contains a wide variety of organisms: they all have certain basic features in common, but there are a lot of differences between them. However, the organisms belonging to a genus are all very similar, and those belonging to the same species are identical in general appearance. This is illustrated in Figure 1, which shows how man is classified.

## What's in a name?

When naming animals and plants we often give them what are called **common names**. These are the names we use in everyday language: cat, dog, rose and so on.

The trouble is that common names can be misleading. One reason is that they are often based on superficial resemblances between living things. For example, termites are usually called 'white ants' because they look something like ants and also live in colonies. However, their actual structure is different from ants and they have a very different kind of life cycle (see page 375).

When we look at plants the situation is even more confusing. Usually the same plant will have been given more than one common name in the different Caribbean countries, and even within the same country. An interesting example is the ackee and the guinep. In Jamaica the name 'ackee' refers to the tree *Blighia sapida* (Figure 2). However, in Barbados the name 'ackee' is given to the tree *Melicoccus bijugatus*. That already causes problems, but in Jamaica this same *Melicoccus bijugatus* is called a guinep tree! (Figure 3).

## A standard system for naming organisms

Biologists use a standard system in which every organism is given two names. The first is the name of the **genus** to which the organism belongs. It shares this name with a number of other closely related organisms. The organism's second name is the name of the **species** to which it belongs. This name is possessed by only one kind of organism: it does not share it with any other organisms in the genus.

It is customary to start the genus name with a capital letter, and the species name with a small letter, and to print both names in *italics*.

Now for an example. The fruit we call soursop is given the full name of *Annona muricata*: *Annona* is the genus name, and *muricata* is its species name. However, the genus *Annona* also includes several other similar juicy fruits belonging to their own separate species. For example, *Annona squamosa* (sweetsop, sugar apple or pomme canelle), *Annona reticulata* (custard apple, golden apple, cashimar, bullock's heart or coeur de boeuf), and *Annona glabra* (alligator apple, bobwood or corkwood).

This system of naming organisms was developed by the 18th-century naturalist Carl Linnaeus (1707–78). Because it involves giving organisms *two* names, it is known as the **binomial system**.

The names just described are called **proper names** or **scientific names**. They are written in Latin. The trouble is that they are often long and difficult to remember. For example, there is a certain kind of worm which is called *Haploscoloplos bustorus*! To make things easier we often call animals and plants by their simpler common names, provided we are sure that there won't be any confusion. Common names usually start with a small letter and are written in ordinary writing, not italics.

## How do we identify living things?

We identify living things by using a **key**. The key tells us what the different animals or plants are like. Then we match our own specimens to the descriptions. When we make a key it is useful to divide the whole group into two smaller groups, and then these into two smaller groups and so on.

This idea has been used in Figure 4 where the leaves were first separated into those with a single leaf blade and those with a divided leaf. The single leaf ones were then further separated into those with a long leaf and those with a broad leaf etc.

Look at the pictures in turn and see how all the separations have been made. Because of its shape it is called a **spider key**. The same information is shown in the **numbered key** in Figure 5. Follow through the various steps in the key so that you can see how it works.

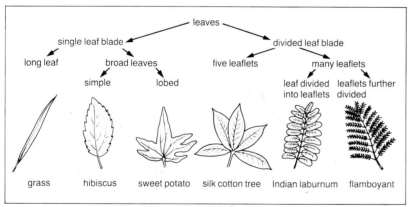

Figure 4 A spider key showing the classification of six selected leaves.

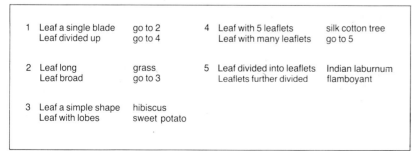

| 1 | Leaf a single blade | go to 2 | 4 | Leaf with 5 leaflets | silk cotton tree |
| | Leaf divided up | go to 4 | | Leaf with many leaflets | go to 5 |
| 2 | Leaf long | grass | 5 | Leaf divided into leaflets | Indian laburnum |
| | Leaf broad | go to 3 | | Leaflets further divided | flamboyant |
| 3 | Leaf a simple shape | hibiscus | | | |
| | Leaf with lobes | sweet potato | | | |

Figure 5 A numbered key for the same leaves shown in Figure 4. (Remember that this key was made specially for this set of leaves and cannot work with just any collection of leaves.)

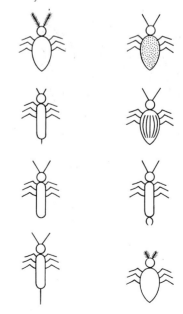

# Collecting living things

*We are surrounded by living things. In this Topic you will find out different ways to collect them.*

## Where can we find living things?

Living things are found almost everywhere in the world: on land and in the air, in water and underground. They are all around us in the soil, under logs and stones, in grass and in trees. Several household pests share our homes with us, and there are also parasites which live on or in other living things.

The place where an organism lives is called its **habitat**. An example of a habitat is a pond or a wood. Within a habitat organisms may live in a particular place such as under a stone or a log. We call such places **microhabitats**. The conditions which exist in a habitat make up the **environment**. Every organism is suited or **adapted** to live in its particular environment. For example, the mangroves are adapted in various ways to life in sea water and mud. Many animals are camouflaged, or can move very quickly so as to escape from their enemies. Organisms can survive only if they are suitably adapted, but this can sometimes make them difficult to find.

Figure 1 shows some of the things you need to take with you if you go on a collecting trip. Table 1 gives you some advice to follow as you collect organisms. The method of collection depends on the kinds of organisms which you are trying to find. Slow-moving animals like snails can be collected by hand. However, most animals are obtained by capturing them in some way.

Some methods for capturing animals are shown in Figure 2. You can use some of them to explore a habitat and find out which particular animals live there (Investigation 1). For some animals, such as those living in the soil, special methods have to be used (see page 386). As you make your collections find out as much as you can about each organism's way of life and try to see how it is adapted to its environment.

### When collecting organisms

1. Only take what you need.
2. Pick up and transport them with care.
3. Replace stones and logs as you found them.
4. Label bags and bottles clearly.
5. Keep animals with the plants they were found on.
6. Whenever possible put organisms back when you have finished with them.

**Remember:** The habitat is the home of the organisms, so respect it.

Table 1 Some points to remember as you collect organisms.

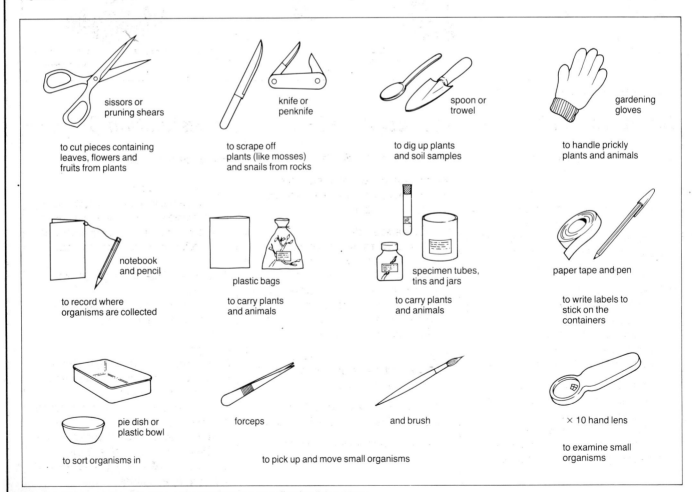

Figure 1 Things you need to take with you when you go collecting living things.

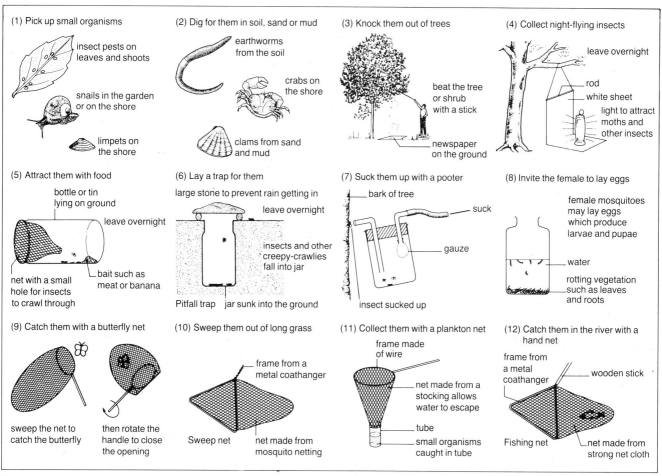

**Figure 2** Different ways of collecting animals.

# Investigation 1

### Collecting and examining living things

1 Use one or more of the methods described in this Topic to collect organisms from a habitat. Put the organisms in containers. Label the containers, noting where the organisms were collected.

2 Examine each organism, using a hand lens or microscope if necessary. Describe or draw the organism, indicating its size. How does it move and feed? How is it adapted to its environment?

3 Use the classification on pages 14–19 to find out what group each organism belongs to. Does your collection tell you anything about how numerous each type of organism is in the habitat?

# Investigation 2

### How to preserve animals

Animals are usually returned to their habitats, but sometimes we preserve them for future study.

1 *Insects and spiders*
   Put them for a few minutes into a bottle with cotton wool soaked in chloroform. This will kill them. Take them out and pin them onto a board with a pin through the body. Spread out the wings of insects and hold them down with paper strips.

2 *Snails, sea urchins and crabs*
   Let the soft inside parts decay. Wash out the shell and keep it.

3 *Soft invertebrates, and tadpoles*
   Store in 70% alcohol or 4% formalin.

*Note* Adult vertebrates should be killed only by the teacher.

# Investigation 3

### How to preserve plants

1 *Flowering plants*
   Lay the plant on a newspaper. Cover it with more newspapers and books. Leave it until it's dry and pressed flat. Stick it onto white paper and label it.

2 *Mosses, lichens, many fruits and seeds*
   Keep them until they become dry. Display and label them.

3 *Algae*
   For hard calcareous red algae from the seashore, keep them until they become dry. Display and label.
   For soft algae, let them float in water so that they are nicely spread out. Then carefully push a piece of paper into the water underneath the alga. Slowly lift up the paper and the alga and let it dry out. Display and label.

# Who's who in the world of living things

*In this Topic we shall look at the main groups of living things. This will give you a glimpse of the variety that is found amongst organisms.*

## Introduction

There are several different ways of classifying living things. In this book we will divide them up into six kingdoms: the **virus kingdom,** the **bacteria kingdom,** the **protist kingdom,** the **fungus kingdom,** the **plant kingdom** and the **animal kingdom**. The first four kingdoms contain mainly very small organisms which you can only see with a microscope. They are very important because many of them cause diseases.

Most living things belong to the plant and animal kingdoms. It is here that we find the greatest number of species and the greatest variety of form. In the lightning tour that follows we can only touch on the tremendous variety that really exists.

## Virus kingdom

Can only be seen with the electron microscope. About 100 nm wide. No cell structure. Can reproduce only inside other organisms, and cause diseases.

## Bacteria kingdom

Can only be seen with the high power of the light microscope. About 1.0 $\mu$m wide. Consist of a single cell without a proper nucleus. Occur in air, water, soil or inside other organisms. Many of them cause diseases.

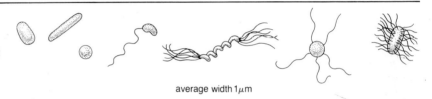

average width 1 $\mu$m

## Protist kingdom

Can be seen with the low power of the microscope. About 10 $\mu$m − 1 mm wide. Consist of a single cell. Some are plant-like and others animal-like. Live mainly in water or inside other organisms.

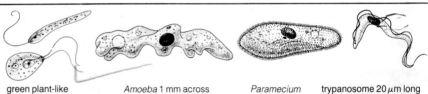

green plant-like organisms 10 $\mu$m wide    *Amoeba* 1 mm across    *Paramecium* 200 $\mu$m long    trypanosome 20 $\mu$m long (causes sleeping sickness)

## Fungus kingdom

Consist of fine threads which may be interwoven to form mushrooms or toadstools. Live in soil or inside other organisms, especially plants.

pin mould (grows on bread etc.)    mushroom 5 cm wide    yeast each cell 5 $\mu$m wide (single cells or short chains)    potato blight (growing out of a potato leaf)

## Lichens

Consist of an alga and a fungus combined together. Flat, like patches of paint, or bushy. Grow on rocks and tree trunks. Very resistant to drying.

Lichens are classified as fungi, but they are so numerous and widespread that they are almost a group in their own right.

shrubby lichen 10mm high    leafy lichen (flat)

## Plant kingdom

Stationary organisms which contain the green substance chlorophyll and make their own food by photosynthesis.

### Algae

Simple plants which do not have roots, stems or leaves. Usually green, but sometimes brown or red. Live in water.

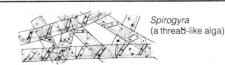 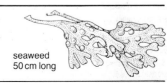

*Spirogyra* (a thread-like alga)

seaweed 50 cm long

## Mosses and liverworts   (Bryophytes)

Have simple leaves or leaf-like form. Found mainly in damp places.

moss 10 mm high

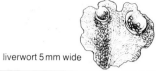

liverwort 5 mm wide

## Ferns   (Pteridophytes)

Have proper roots and stems, and leaf-like fronds. Found mainly in damp places. Reproductive spores are formed on the undersides of the fronds.

staghorn fern (growing on a tree)

common fern 40cm high

tree fern 10 m high

## Conifers   (Gymnosperms)

Large plants with cones for reproduction. Good at surviving in dry or cold climates. Most of them keep their leaves throughout the year.

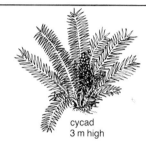

cycad 3 m high

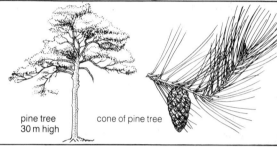

pine tree 30 m high

cone of pine tree

## Flowering plants   (Angiosperms)

Wide range of plants with flowers for reproduction. Range from small herbs to massive trees. Divided into dicotyledons and monocotyledons.

| Dicotyledons | Monocotyledons |
|---|---|
| Seed contains an embryo with two seed-leaves (cotyledons) | Seed contains an embryo with one seed-leaf (cotyledon) |
| Broad leaves with branched veins forming a network | Narrow leaves with straight, parallel veins |
| One main root (taproot) | Bunch of slender roots (fibrous roots) |

## Important dicotyledonous families

**Pride of Barbados family** (Caesalpiniaceae)
Examples: Pride of Barbados, Indian laburnum, dandelion, senna, flamboyant, logwood, tamarind, butterfly flower, coubaril

**Peas and beans family** (Papilionaceae)
Examples: Rattleweed, blue shak shak, gungo pea, sea bean, groundnut, sweethearts, kidney bean, cow-itch, W. Indian ebony, indigo, soya bean, black-eyed pea, crab's eye vine

**Mimosa family** (Mimosaceae)
Examples: Sensitive plant, acacia bush, woman's tongue, black bead shrub, rain tree

**Hibiscus family** (Malvaceae)
Examples: Hibiscus, blue mahoe, red sorrel, ochra (okra), seaside mahoe, cotton, broomweed

**Coleus family** (Labiatae)
Examples: Coleus, French thyme, mint, penny-royal, mosquito bush

**Poinsettia family** (Euphorbiaceae)
Examples: Poinsettia, crown-of-thorns, spurge, croton, cassava, castor oil, sandbox, physic nut, manchineel

**Breadfruit family** (Moraceae)
Examples: Breadfruit, breadnut, jackfruit, marijuana, fig, bearded fig, strangling fig

**Morning glory family** (Convolvulaceae)
Examples: Morning glory, seaside ipomoea, sweet potato, love bush (vine)

**Tomato family** (Solonaceae)
Examples: Tomato, Irish potato, egg plant, tobacco, thorn apple, sweet peppers and chillies

**Sunflower family** (Compositae)
Examples: Sunflower, Spanish needle, railway weed, lettuce, consumption weed, sow thistle, goatweed, fleabane, chrysanthemum

**Cucumber family** (Cucurbitaceae)
Examples: Cucumber, water melon, pumpkin, gourd, cho-cho, cerasee, loofah

**Cactus family** (Cactaceae)
Examples: Prickly pear, night blooming cactus, turk's cap cactus, Barbados gooseberry, old man's beard

## Important monocotyledonous families

**Grass family** (Gramineae)
Examples: Seashore crabgrass, maize, rice, sugar cane, bamboo, Job's tears, bur grass, Guinea grass, reed, Bahama grass, sourgrass

**Sedge family** (Cyperaceae)
Examples: Sedge, nutgrass, rush, star grass

**Palm family** (Palmae)
Examples: Coconut palm, royal palm, oil palm, date palm, sea coconut, thatch palm, raffia

**Onion family** (Amarillidaceae)
Examples: Onion, garlic, scallion, spider lily, easter lily, rain lily

**Cocoyam family** (Araceae)
Examples: Cocoyam, dasheen, caladium, climbing coco, water lettuce, maraval lily

**Water grass family** (Commelinaceae)
Examples: Water grass, Moses-in-the-bulrushes, wandering Jew

# Animal kingdom   Organisms that usually move around and feed on other organisms.

## Animals without backbones   (invertebrates)

### Coelenterates

Body bag- or umbrella-shaped, based on a circular pattern (radial symmetry). Have tentacles with stinging cells. Live singly or in colonies, either attached or floating. May produce an external coating (e.g. corals). Most live in the sea, a few in fresh water.

*Hydra*
(lives in ponds) 10mm long

jellyfish
10 cm wide

sea anenome
50 mm tall

coral

### Flatworms   (Platyhelminthes)

Body long(ish) and flat. Some live in fresh water, but most are parasites of animals. Parasitic tapeworms and flukes have special hooks or suckers at their front ends.

fresh-water flatworm
10 mm long

tapeworm
5 m long

liver fluke
2 cm long

blood fluke
15 mm long

### Roundworms   (Nematodes)

Body long and thread-like, round in cross-section, not segmented. Some live in soil but most are parasites of plants or animals.

eelworms
less than 10 mm long

*Ascaris* 30 cm long
(human roundworm)

hookworm
10 mm long

### Ringed worms   (Annelids)

Body long and usually round in cross-section, divided by rings into a series of segments. Most are aquatic (live in water), but some live in the soil. Some are external parasites.

earthworm 15 cm long
(burrows in soil)

leech 5 cm long
(sucks blood)

ragworm 15 cm long
(swims in the sea)

tube worm 10 cm long
(lives in a tube in the sea)

### Molluscs

Body soft and unsegmented, in most cases covered by a shell which may be in one, two or many parts. Most are aquatic, some live on the seashore and on land.

snail
3 cm high

octopus  10 cm wide
(excluding tentacles)

mussel
5 cm long

slug
10 cm long

squid 30 cm long
(including tentacles)

### Echinoderms

Body star- or ball-shaped or slightly elongated; based on a pattern of five parts. With a tough skin, often with spines. All live in the sea.

starfish
15 cm wide

brittle star
10 cm wide

sea urchin
10 cm wide

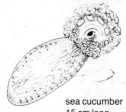
sea cucumber
15 cm long

## Arthropods

Have a hard cuticle and jointed limbs. Divided into four groups, mainly on the basis of the number of legs.

woodlouse
1 cm long

### Crustaceans

Quite a lot of legs.
Two pairs of antennae (feelers).
Front part of body usually protected by a shield-like cover.
Mainly aquatic, breathe with gills.

ghost crab
3 cm wide

shrimp
2 cm long

water flea
1.5 mm long

barnacles 1 cm high
(attatched to rocks etc.)

### Myriapods

Lots of legs.
One pair of antennae.
Body long and clearly segmented.
Live on land.

centipede
25 mm long

millipede
2 cm long

Flattened, with one pair of jointed legs to each segment. With poison glands. Carnivorous and pursue their prey.

Rounded, with two pairs of jointed legs to each segment. Eat dead plant material. Curl up into a ball if disturbed.

### Arachnids

Four pairs of legs.
No antennae.
Mouthparts with pincers.
Body parts joined together.
Live on land; some are ectoparasites.

spider
1 cm wide

scorpion
10 cm long

tick
2 mm long

mite
0.25 mm long

### Insects

Three pairs of legs. One pair of antennae.
Body divided into three parts: head, thorax and abdomen. Usually two pairs of wings.

grasshopper
5 cm long

butterfly
5 cm long

**Incomplete metamorphosis**
(egg → nymph → adult)

**Complete metamorphosis**
(egg → larva → pupa → adult)

**Grasshoppers** (Orthoptera). Hind legs enlarged for jumping. Two pairs flying wings. Eat plants.
Examples: Grasshoppers, locusts, crickets, katydids.

**Butterflies and moths** (Lepidoptera). Two pairs large coloured wings. Suck nectar through a proboscis. Larva is a caterpillar.
Examples: Swallowtail and lemon butterflies, hawk moths.

**Bugs** (Hemiptera). Piercing and sucking mouthparts. Feed on plant and animal juices. Part of wings hard.
Examples: Cotton stainers, aphids, scale insects, bed bugs.

**Ants, wasps and bees** (Hymenoptera). With 'waist' and sting. Many live in colonies with different forms.
Examples: Sugar ants, driver ants, red ants, wasps, honey bees.

**Termites** (Isoptera). Different forms: Queen, King, soldiers, workers and reproductives. Build nests. Eat wood.
Examples: Tree and mound termites ('white ants').

**Flies** (Diptera). One pair of wings, and balancers. Some larvae are aquatic. Land larva is a maggot.
Examples: Houseflies, mosquitoes, tsetse flies.

**Cockroaches** (Dictyoptera). Bodies flattened (roaches) or elongated (mantises). Produce characteristic egg cases.
Examples: Cockroaches, praying mantises.

**Beetles** (Coleoptera). Forewings hard or leathery and meet together on the back.
Examples: Rhinoceros beetles, dung beetles, water beetles, weevils.

# Animals with backbones    (vertebrates)

## Fish

Have a covering of scales. Live in water and have gills for breathing. Muscular body and fins for swimming. Skeleton of cartilage or bone. Shape varied. Eggs usually laid and develop in the water. Cold-blooded.

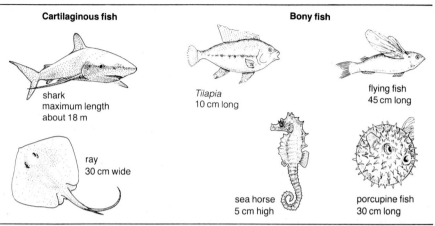

**Cartilaginous fish**

shark
maximum length
about 18 m

ray
30 cm wide

**Bony fish**

*Tilapia*
10 cm long

flying fish
45 cm long

sea horse
5 cm high

porcupine fish
30 cm long

## Amphibians

Have a moist skin without scales. Tadpole (larva) lives in water and has gills for breathing. Adult lives on land and has lungs for breathing. Can swim, walk or hop. Eggs laid and develop in the water or in moist places. Cold-blooded.

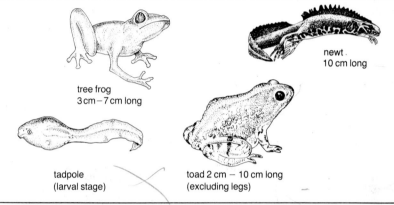

tree frog
3 cm – 7 cm long

tadpole
(larval stage)

newt
10 cm long

toad 2 cm – 10 cm long
(excluding legs)

## Reptiles

Have a dry, waterproof skin with scales. Most live on land and have lungs for breathing. Most have four legs for walking and some can swim. Others have reduced legs and slide along the ground. Eggs have a leathery shell and are laid on land. Cold-blooded.

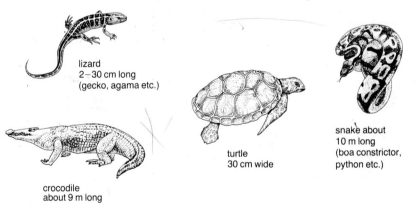

lizard
2 – 30 cm long
(gecko, agama etc.)

crocodile
about 9 m long

turtle
30 cm wide

snake about
10 m long
(boa constrictor,
python etc.)

## Birds

Have a covering of feathers. Live on land and in the air. Have lungs for breathing. Have wings for flying and a beak for feeding. Eggs have a hard shell and are laid in nests. Warm-blooded.

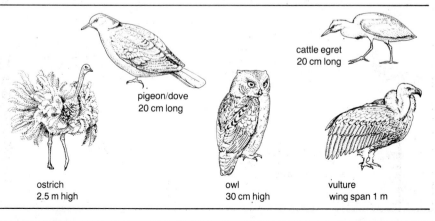

ostrich
2.5 m high

pigeon/dove
20 cm long

owl
30 cm high

cattle egret
20 cm long

vulture
wing span 1 m

## Mammals

Have hair. The young usually develop inside the mother and after birth are fed on her milk. Live on land, in water and in the air. Walk, swim or fly. Have lungs. Warm-blooded.

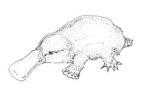

duck-billed platypus
40 cm long

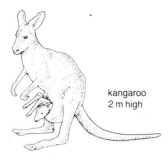

kangaroo
2 m high

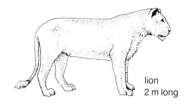

lion
2 m long

*Egg-laying mammals*
Young develop inside an egg which is laid by the mother.

*Pouch-mammals*
Young born at an early stage and finish their development inside a pouch, where they feed on the mother's milk.

*Placental mammals*
Young develop inside the mother, attached to a placenta.

## The main groups of placental mammals

| Name of group | main features | Examples |
|---|---|---|
| **Rodents** | Small mammals with a pointed nose. Have chisel-like front teeth for gnawing at mainly plant food such as nuts, and man's food. | Rats, mice, gerbils, hamsters, squirrels, (Rabbits and hares are close relatives but are put in a separate group.) |
| **Carnivores** | Meat-eaters. Have sharp claws for bringing down prey, and strong jaws and pointed teeth for eating it. Good hunters. | Cats (including lions and tigers), dogs, wolves, foxes, bears. |
| **Ungulates** | Eat plants, particularly grass. Have hooves on their feet. Cheek teeth have a flat ridged surface for grinding food. | Cattle, sheep, pigs, deer, camels, giraffes, hippopotamus, horses, zebras, rhinoceroses. |
| **Proboscideans** | Very large, with legs like pillars. The two upper front teeth form a pair of tusks and the nose is lengthened into a trunk. Have huge cheek teeth for grinding up tough plant food. | Elephants. (Some specimens weigh over 10 tonnes.) |
| **Chiropterans** | Have wings for flying and small pointed teeth for feeding on insects, fruit etc. | Fruit-and insect-eating bats. The vampire bat sucks blood. |
| **Cetaceans** | Streamlined and fish-like in appearance for swimming. Have sharp pointed teeth for feeding on fish, squid etc. Some whales feed on plankton. | Whales, dolphins, porpoises. (The Blue Whale can be over 30 m long and weigh more than 150 tonnes.) |
| **Primates** | Eyes at front of head. Grasping fingers and toes. Tend to stand on hind legs and become upright. | Lemurs, monkeys, apes, man. |

**Figure 1** The lion, a typical carnivorous mammal.

## The main groups of living things at a glance

If you are feeling confused after our lightning tour of the world of living things, the summary below may help you to see how the various groups fit together.

*Note*  In older classifications only two kingdoms were recognised, namely the animal and plant kingdoms. The single-celled animal-like organisms were called protozoa and put in the animal kingdom; the single-celled plant-like organisms were included with the algae in the plant kingdom. Fungi and bacteria were usually included with plants, and viruses were not considered as living organisms at all.

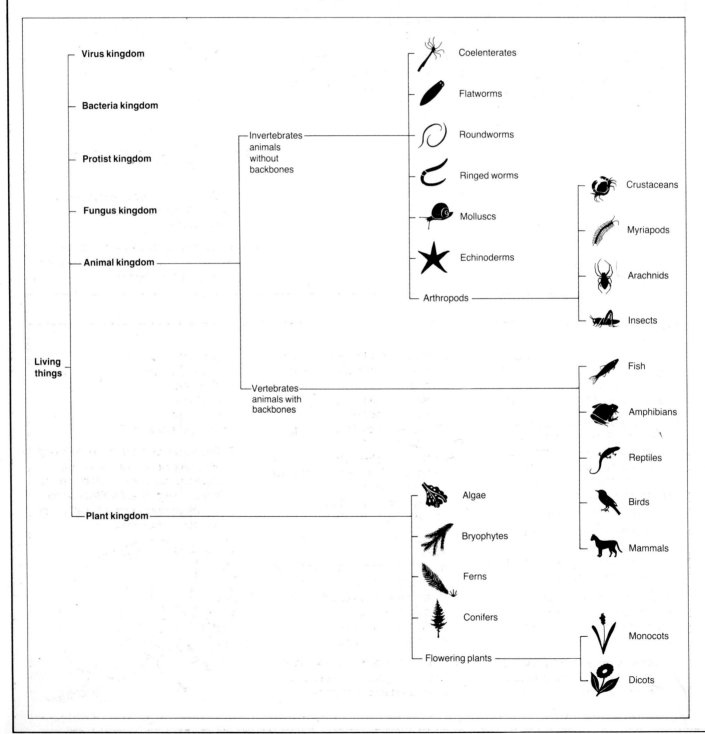

# Investigation 1

### Putting some familiar animals and plants into groups

1 Examine various organisms, or pictures of organisms, provided by your teacher. All of them are featured in the classification on pages 14–19.

2 Write down the name of the group to which each organism belongs. Use the classification on pages 14–19 to help you.

3 Look carefully at each organism.

From its structure, what can you say about the sort of place where it lives, and the kind of life it leads?

# Investigation 2

### Putting some unfamiliar animals and plants into groups

1 Examine various organisms which are *not* illustrated in the classification on pages 14–19.

2 Write down the name of the group to which you think each organism belongs. Do this by relating the characteristics of the organism to the information given on pages 14–19.

3 Which specific animal or plant illustrated on pages 14–19 does each organism resemble most closely?

# Investigation 3

### Collecting and naming organisms

1 Collect organisms from a habitat near your school or home.

2 If any of the organisms are small, rapidly moving land animals such as insects, anaesthetise them by placing them in an ether bottle for a few seconds.

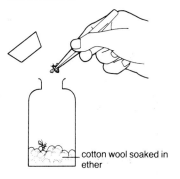

cotton wool soaked in ether

3 Examine each organism, using a hand lens or microscope if necessary.

4 Use the classification on pages 14–19 to find out what group each organism belongs to.

# Assignments

1 What group does each of these organisms belong to: moss, jellyfish, turtle, tapeworm, whale, mushroom, mould, tube worm, seaweed, newt?

2 What would be the easiest way of telling the difference between:
a) an arthropod and a vertebrate,
b) an insect and an arachnid,
c) an amphibian and a reptile,
d) an alga and a fungus,
e) a conifer and a flowering plant?

3 From books, try to find out the largest member of each of the following plant groups: Algae, Ferns, Conifers, Flowering plants.

In each case give the proper name and common names of the organism, and state its approximate size.

4 Give the name of an animal which:
a) is shaped like an umbrella and has sting cells,
b) lays eggs with a leathery shell,
c) has a pouch in which the young develop,
d) is shaped like a star,
e) has two pairs of wings,
f) lives on land but lays its eggs in water,
g) has a long flat body,
h) has long tentacles and belongs to the same group as snails,
i) has four pairs of legs,
j) has scales and gills.

5 Give the name of an organism which:
a) reproduces by means of flowers,
b) has frond-like leaves,
c) consists of only one cell and is coloured green,
d) causes a disease,
e) has no chlorophyll.

6 Which of the following features are possessed only by insects, and which ones belong to other arthropods as well:
a) hard cuticle,
b) joints,
c) 6 legs,
d) feelers,
e) 2 pairs of wings?

7 The picture below is of a small insect which lives in the soil. Name two important structures, typical of most insects, which it lacks. Why do you think this insect does not need these particular structures?

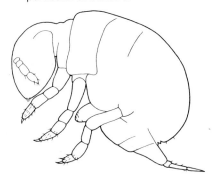

# Feeding relationships

*In the natural world, animals feed on plants and on other animals. This is an essential part of the balance of nature.*

**Figure 1** The larva of the great diving beetle is one of the most savage carnivores found in ponds. It sinks its fang-like teeth into its prey and then sucks up its juices.

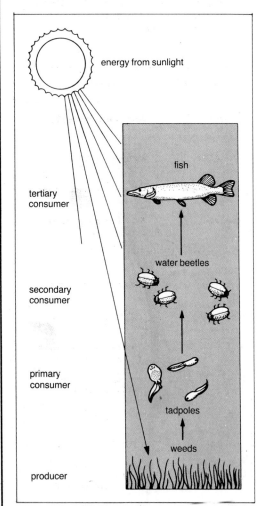

energy from sunlight

fish

tertiary consumer

water beetles

secondary consumer

primary consumer

tadpoles

weeds

producer

**Figure 2** The main steps in a typical food chain. The plants are the **producers** of food, by using energy from the sun. They are eaten by the tadpoles, the **primary consumers**. These in turn are eaten by the water beetles, the **secondary consumers**; and they in turn are eaten by the fish, the **tertiary consumer**.

## Food chains

Suppose we put some weeds, tadpoles and a couple of water beetles into a jar and watch what happens (Investigation 1). We find that the tadpoles nibble at the weeds, and the water beetles eat the tadpoles. We can sum up the feeding relationship between the three organisms like this:

$$\text{weeds} \rightarrow \text{tadpoles} \rightarrow \text{water beetles}$$

We call this a **food chain**, and it is a basic feature of most habitats. Tadpoles feed only on plants and are therefore herbivores. In contrast, water beetles feed on other animals and are carnivores. In fact, some species of water beetle (and their larvae) are extremely voracious (Figure 1).

There are only three links in the food chain shown above. However, in a pond there might be some fish. The fish feed on water beetles amongst other things, so the food chain would be:

$$\text{weeds} \rightarrow \text{tadpoles} \rightarrow \text{water beetles} \rightarrow \text{fish}$$

## Producers and consumers

Let's think about this food chain in a bit more detail. The weeds make their own food by photosynthesis, and they get the necessary energy for doing this from the sun. Because they *make* food (i.e. manufacture organic substances), we call them **producers**. In contrast, the animals in the chain get their food by eating other organisms. For this reason we call them **consumers**. In this particular chain there are three levels of consumers (Figure 2). Producers, primary, secondary and tertiary consumers etc. are called the feeding or **trophic** levels in the food chain.

## Energy and pyramids

In the food chain shown in Figure 2 the weeds use the sun's light energy to make their own food. But only a very small fraction of the sun's energy that falls upon the weeds ends up in their food stores. These food stores are in the leaves which the tadpoles eat. When a tadpole eats the weed only about one tenth of the energy in the plant becomes built up into the body of the tadpole. The rest is released in the tadpole's respiration, much of it as heat. The same is true when the tadpoles are eaten by the water beetles, and again when the water beetles are eaten by the fish. In other words at each step of the food chain a lot of energy is lost.

The result of this is that as you go along the food chain, the number of organisms which can be supported at each level gets less and less. Thus a given number of tadpoles will feed a relatively smaller number of beetles, and these beetles will feed a relatively smaller number of fish (Figure 3). This drop in numbers at each level in a food chain is called the **pyramid of numbers**.

For the same reason there is also a drop in the total mass of living material at each level of a food chain. This is called the **pyramid of biomass**. On the other hand the size of the individual animals at each level tends to increase. This is because carnivores, being predators, are generally larger than their prey.

## Food webs

Let's go back to the jar with which we started this Topic. Suppose we remove the tadpoles, what will happen to the beetles? They will die, because we have taken away their only source of food.

However, if the tadpoles were to disappear from a pond or lake, the beetles would probably survive. This is because there would be other sources of food available to them. For example, it's quite likely that the pond would contain some small young fish which the water beetle could eat. Similarly, if the beetles were to disappear, the fish would still survive because they could eat other things.

By finding out what all the organisms in a habitat feed on, you can build up a diagram summarising their feeding relationships (Investigation 1). This is called the **food web**. In a natural habitat such as a pond, it would be unusual for the organisms to be linked together in a simple chain. Food webs are much more common, and if the habitat contains a large number of different species, the web may be very complex.

## Food chains and food webs on the school compound

You are now ready to explore a habitat close at hand: the school compound.

Let's imagine some students have done this. Whenever they saw an animal, they tried to watch it to find out what it ate. If they could, they collected it and took it back to the laboratory with part of what it was feeding on. Some of the animals, like the humming bird and the hawk, they couldn't collect and they just made a note about what these animals were eating. They made a table of their findings (Table 1).

When they looked carefully at their table they could identify 7 producers, 8 primary consumers, 3 secondary consumers and 2 tertiary consumers. Can you?

After this they made up two food chains using their organisms. One of the food chains started with the nectar of flowers and the other started from grass, and each had at least three animals in it. See if you can find out these food chains.

Then they decided to try to make a diagram of all the feeding relationships. They arranged their organisms in the different trophic levels with the producers at the bottom. Then they linked together all the food chains to make a food web. Can you do this? When you have tried, look at Figure 4.

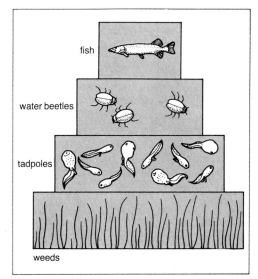

**Figure 3** The diagram shows how the numbers of organisms decrease as you go along a food chain. It is called a pyramid of numbers. The total mass of living matter also decreases at each level, and so does the total amount of energy contained in the bodies of the organisms.

| What we found on the school compound | |
| --- | --- |
| *Animal* | *What it was feeding on* |
| Grasshopper | Eating the grass. |
| Praying mantis | Devouring a grasshopper. |
| Caterpillar | Munching away at some citrus leaves. |
| Woodlice and beetles | Eating bark of a tree. |
| Small birds | Eating all kinds of insects. |
| Humming bird | Sucking nectar from a hibiscus flower. |
| Snail | Eating holes in the leaves of a potted plant. |
| Butterfly | Sucking nectar from a periwinkle flower. |
| Lizard | Eating a praying mantis. |
| Small birds | Eating snails. |
| Aphids (greenfly) | Sucking juices from the young shoots of a rose. |
| Hawk | Seen swooping down on birds and lizards. |

**Table 1** Record made by students of animals seen on the school compound, together with how they feed.

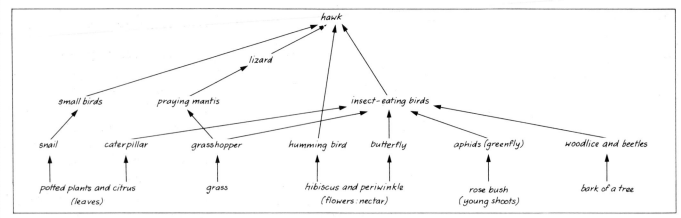

**Figure 4** The food web that has been made from the information collected on the school compound (Table 1). The arrows show 'who eats who'.

**Figure 5** The egrets benefit from their close association with the cattle: an example of commensalism.

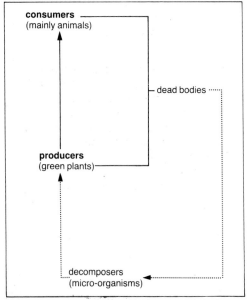

**Figure 6** Decomposers enable the materials in the bodies of the producers and consumers to be used again.

## Another feeding relationship

The students on the school compound also observed the cattle egret with some cattle (Figure 5). At times the egret would ride around on the cow's back and appear to be pecking its skin. At other times the bird would follow behind and be seen putting its head down amongst the grass. The egret was feeding. It gets ticks and lice from the cow's skin and it gets insects from the grass which the cow has disturbed as it walks along. The egret is obviously benefiting from its relationship with the cow. This is an example of **commensalism**. The cow may also benefit from being warned of approaching danger when the egret flies away.

## Food chains in the service of man

Food chains provide us with food. Look at Figure 2 again. The fish that ate the water beetles that ate the tadpoles that ate the weeds might be caught by a fisherman for his supper. The food chain would then be:

weeds → tadpoles → water beetles → fish → man

From man's point of view, some of the most important food chains occur in the sea. In the surface waters where light can penetrate there are millions of microscopic organisms called **plankton**. Some of these organisms are like green plants and carry out photosynthesis, while others are like animals and eat the plant-like ones. So a food chain in the sea would go like this:

plant plankton → animal plankton → fish → man

## Decomposers

When the animals and plants in a habitat die their bodies decay. This is because they are broken down by bacteria and other microbes which feed on them. These microbes are called **decomposers**. As a result of their activities, simple substances are released from the dead bodies, and these can be used again by plants, i.e. by the producers (Figure 6). The decomposers thus play an important part in keeping life going in a habitat (see page 389).

## Ecosystems

We have seen that a habitat such as a pond or the school compound contains three types of organisms: producers, consumers and decomposers. All three are influenced by physical features of the environment such as temperature and rainfall, and together they make up what biologists call an **ecosystem**. Every habitat has its own community of organisms. Within the community each species occupies a particular position in the food web. We call this its **ecological niche**.

# Investigation 1

## Building up a food web

1 Set up an aquarium in your laboratory.

Use a large transparent container. Wash it thoroughly, then put in some clean sand to a depth of about 2 cm. Root some water weeds in the sand. Slowly pour in some pond water until the container is approximately three-quarters full. Put in some floating plants like duckweed and *Spirogyra*. Now add as large a variety of animals from a local pond or stream as you can. If possible include water beetles and their larvae, dragonfly and caddis fly nymphs, mosquito larvae and pupae, shrimps, water snails and a few small fish. Don't put in so many carnivores that they eat up all the other animals!

2 Using a simple identification key find out the names of the animals and plants in the aquarium.

3 Observe the animals, and see if you can find out what each one feeds on. If necessary use books to help you.

4 Write down the names of:
   a) the producers,
   b) the herbivorous consumers,
   c) the carnivorous consumers. Which of the carnivorous consumers are *not* eaten by any other organism?

   What do you think would happen if you removed the consumers from the aquarium?

5 Construct a food web similar to the one in Figure 4, showing the feeding relationships of the animals in your aquarium.

# Investigation 2

## A food web in a natural habitat

1 Choose a habitat. It might be a fresh-water pond, a patch of grass, or a rock pool on the seashore.

2 Find as many animals and plants in the habitat as you can.

   Whenever you find an animal, try to see what it feeds on.

   Write down the name of each animal and its food in your notebook.

3 Construct as many food chains as you can for your habitat.

4 Now try to construct a food web for the habitat.

   If you are not sure what a particular animal eats, try to find the answer in books.

# Assignments

1 In Figure 2 which organisms are:
   a) herbivores
   b) carnivores
   c) predators
   d) prey?

2 Fill in the missing organism in each of the following food chains:
   a) grass → ? → man
   b) grass → grasshopper → ?
   c) plankton → ? → man
   d) aphid (greenfly) → ladybird → ?

3 The following is a food chain that ends up with man:

   plant → bee → man

   Explain precisely how plants provide food for bees, and how bees provide food for man.

4 List the processes involved in the transfer of energy from the sun to that used by an animal for movement.

5 Study the food web in Figure 4, then answer these questions:
   a) Give the name of an organism which is a secondary consumer only.
   b) Give the name of an organism which is a secondary and tertiary consumer.
   c) Give the name of an organism which is a herbivore, and one which is a carnivore.
   d) Give the name of an organism which is a prey, and one which is a predator.
   e) This food web does not include the rotting leaves of plants. Write down a food chain which might lead from rotting leaves.

6 Energy from the sun passes through food chains. However, only a small proportion of the sun's energy gets into the bodies of the final consumers. What happens to the rest?

7 The following figures show the total mass of body material, measured as dry mass, from one square metre of grassland during one year:

   | | |
   |---|---|
   | plants | 470.0 g |
   | herbivores | 0.6 g |
   | carnivores | 0.1 g |

   Explain why the mass of body material decreases at each step of the food chain.

8 In this Topic it is stated that as one proceeds along a food chain, each organism tends to be larger than the one before.
   a) Give an example of a food chain which illustrates this.
   b) Why do you think this is true?
   c) Give an example of a food chain which is an *exception* to this.

# The wheel of life

*One of the most important aspects of nature is that materials circulate. This means that they can be used over and over again.*

## The cycling of water

Suppose there is a heavy shower of rain. The rain sinks into the ground and drains into rivers, lakes and the sea. When the sun comes out some of the water evaporates, and the water vapour rises into the atmosphere. The hotter and drier the weather, the faster will be the rate of evaporation. Later the water vapour may condense to form clouds and, in the right conditions, it may fall as rain or snow – which brings us back to where we started. So water goes round and round in nature. We call this the **water cycle** (Figure 1).

Where does biology come into the water cycle? Well, some of the water which sinks into the ground is taken up by plants. It is drawn into the roots, rises up the stems and evaporates from the leaves. The evaporation of water from the leaves of a plant is called **transpiration**. Animals also take up water and return it to the environment.

The water cycle is very important, particularly to farmers. It ensures that a constant supply of water is available to crops and other plants. Sometimes the water evaporates from the land more quickly than it can be replaced. The soil becomes dry and a **drought** may result. Many of the plants and animals die unless they are specially adapted to survive such conditions. In areas where there is a low rainfall, it may be necessary to irrigate the land with water piped from dammed rivers.

As water flows along a river, it gathers minerals from the surrounding rocks. By the time it reaches the sea there are lots of minerals in the water. This is why **sea water** tastes salty. When water evaporates from the sea, the minerals are left behind. So the rain that falls on the land and fills our lakes and ponds has no salts in to begin with: we call it **fresh water**.

The difference in the amount of salt in fresh water and sea water makes them very different as environments for organisms. Some organisms are adapted to live in sea water, others are adapted to live in fresh water.

**Figure 1** Summary of the water cycle. To keep the diagram simple, evaporation is shown taking place only from the ocean. In practice it also takes place from rivers, lakes and ponds, and from the surface of the soil. Transpiration takes place from the above-ground parts of many other plants besides trees. Animals also play a part in the water cycle.

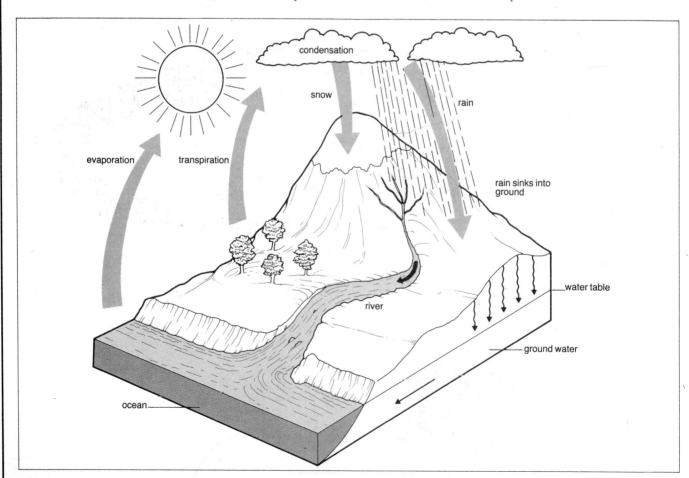

## The cycling of carbon

The air around us contains a small amount of carbon dioxide. This is constantly being absorbed by plants which use it for **photosynthesis**. The carbon dioxide diffuses into the leaves, and is built up into sugar and other complex carbon compounds.

Now when a plant is eaten by an animal the sugar gets into the cells in the animal's body. Here it is broken down into carbon dioxide and water to produce energy (**respiration**). As a result carbon dioxide is put back into the atmosphere.

When the animals and plants die they decay. In this process bacteria and other decomposers feed on them. They too respire, and so once again carbon dioxide is put back into the atmosphere.

We can sum up by saying that *carbon dioxide is taken out of the atmosphere by photosynthesis, and put back into it by respiration and decay.* This is known as the **carbon cycle** and it is summarised in Figure 2.

If you look at this diagram you will see that carbon dioxide is also released into the atmosphere when coal is burned (**combustion**). Coal is formed by the fossilisation of dead plants. If it wasn't for man burning coal the carbon contained in coal would never be returned to the atmosphere, and the arrow pointing downwards in Figure 2 would be a dead end taking carbon out of the cycle for ever.

Coal is a **fossil fuel**. Other fossil fuels include oil and natural gas, and of course they give us energy when they are burned. Vast amounts have been laid down deep in the ground over millions of years. However, it's a slow process and at present we are using them up about one hundred thousand times faster than they are formed. Scientists estimate that at this rate we shall run out of them within a few hundred years unless we go over to other ways of getting energy.

**Figure 2** Summary of the carbon cycle. The main cycle is shown at the top of the diagram. The line leading to coal only happens if oxygen is absent, for example in bogs and swamps: the bacteria that cause decay cannot live without oxygen, and so the dead plants pile up, forming soft, black peat. In the course of time the peat gets buried and hardens to form coal. The other fossil fuels, oil and natural gas, are formed in a similar way from tiny marine organisms that have sunk to the bottom of the sea.

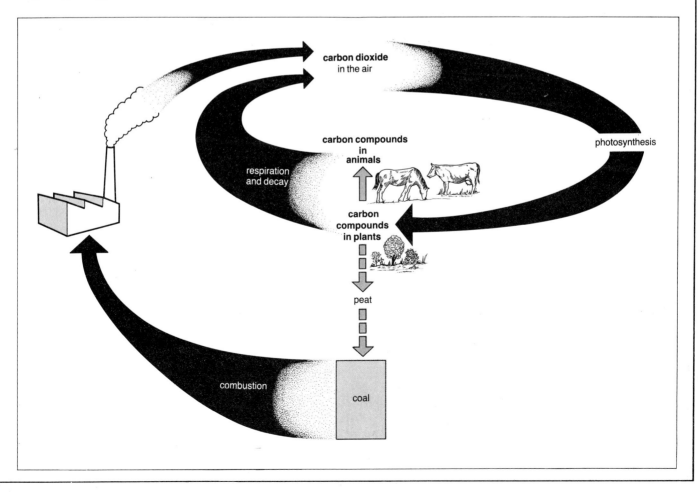

carbon dioxide
in the air

photosynthesis

carbon compounds
in
animals

respiration
and decay

carbon
compounds
in plants

peat

combustion

coal

## The cycling of nitrogen

In the soil there are inorganic nitrogen compounds called nitrates which are dissolved in the soil water. These are absorbed by the roots of plants which then build them up into complex proteins.

Now think what happens when a plant is eaten by an animal. The nitrogen in the plant protein gets into the animal's body and becomes part of its protein.

When the animals and plants die they decay. The microbes which cause decay break the proteins down into ammonia. Ammonia is also formed from the animals' excreta. Now in the soil there are certain bacteria which turn ammonia into nitrites, and others which turn nitrites into nitrates. The effect is to return nitrates to the soil, which can then be used again by plants. Because they enrich the soil in nitrates, they are known as **nitrifying bacteria**. You will now understand why compost and manure improve the soil for plant growth.

This circulation of nitrogen is known as the **nitrogen cycle** and it is illustrated in Figure 3. In this diagram you will see that certain bacteria release nitrogen from nitrates. Obviously they *lower* the nitrate content of the soil, and so we call them **denitrifying bacteria**.

Plants cannot make use of atmospheric nitrogen. However, certain bacteria can absorb nitrogen and build it up into nitrates and protein. They are called **nitrogen-fixing bacteria**, and they are found free in the soil and also inside the roots of plants belonging to the pea and bean family (Figure 4). The nitrogen-fixing bacteria in the roots give some of their nitrogen compounds to the host plant, while they in turn get protection. The relationship is therefore helpful to both organisms, and is an example of **symbiosis** (see page 372). What's more, some of the nitrogen compounds are released into the soil which thus becomes more fertile.

**Figure 3** Summary of the nitrogen cycle. The diagram shows how nitrates can be formed by the action of bacteria on animal and plant protein. Some nitrates can also be made by the action of lightning on the nitrogen in the air. Note that denitrifying bacteria remove nitrates from the soil. There are other kinds of denitrifying bacteria besides the ones shown here. They can convert nitrates into nitrites or ammonia.

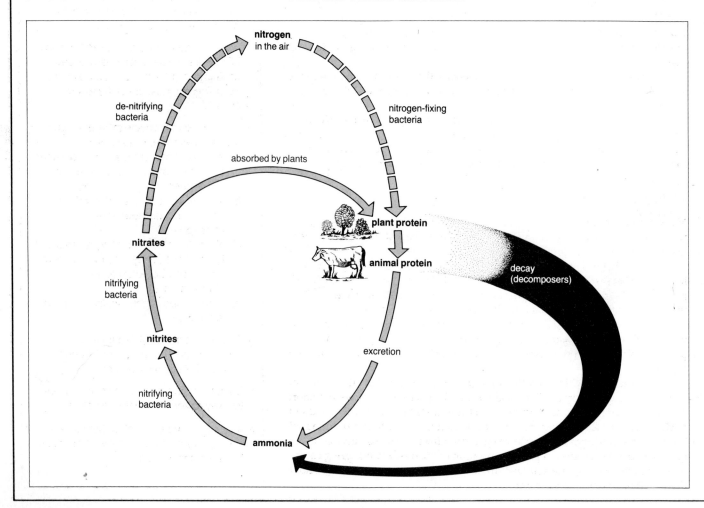

**Figure 4** The roots of this plant have swellings on them called root nodules. Nitrogen-fixing bacteria live in these nodules. They are found in members of the legume family, for example peas and beans.

## The bacteria in the nitrogen cycle

Look at Table 1. This summarises the various bacteria which play a part in the nitrogen cycle. They can be divided into two kinds: helpful and unhelpful. The helpful ones are those that increase the amount of nitrates in the soil. Plants need nitrates as food, and so these bacteria help plants to grow. They are the decay bacteria, nitrifying bacteria and nitrogen-fixing bacteria in Table 1.

The unhelpful bacteria are those that decrease the amount of nitrates in the soil. Obviously they hinder plant growth. They are the denitrifying bacteria in Table 1.

Why do bacteria carry out the various chemical changes shown in Figure 3? They do it to obtain energy for themselves. For example, when the nitrifying bacteria oxidise ammonia or nitrites, energy is produced which the bacteria use for making organic food. This is an example of **chemosynthesis** (see page 7).

## The nitrogen cycle and farming

Many farmers depend on growing crops for their living. For crops to grow well, the soil must be good. Good soil contains the helpful bacteria mentioned in the last section, but not the unhelpful ones.

Now the helpful bacteria need oxygen for their respiration, so it is important that the soil should contain plenty of air; this means keeping it well ploughed. As the roots of legumes contain nitrogen-fixing bacteria, it is useful to plough these plants into the soil from time to time.

In Figure 3 you will see that nitrites are formed between ammonia and nitrates. Nitrites are poisonous to most plants. However, in good soil that has plenty of air in it the nitrites are turned into nitrates as quickly as they are formed.

One of the worst things that can happen to the soil is that it gets full of water, that is **waterlogged**. Such soil has no air spaces and is therefore short of oxygen. Denitrifying bacteria thrive in these conditions because they don't need oxygen for their respiration. We have seen that they take nitrates out of the soil, so waterlogged soil lacks oxygen *and* nitrates. The soil may be made even worse if it contains a high concentration of nitrites. Waterlogging can be prevented by keeping the soil well drained. Sometimes pipes are laid under fields to take away excess water.

**Bacteria in the nitrogen cycle**

HELPFUL

**Decay bacteria (decomposers)**
break down amino acids (from proteins) to ammonia

**Nitrifying bacteria group 1**
oxidise ammonia to nitrites
e.g. *Nitrosomonas*

**Nitrifying bacteria group 2**
oxidise nitrites to nitrates
e.g. *Nitrobacter*

**Nitrogen-fixing bacteria**
build up nitrogen into nitrates and proteins
e.g. *Clostridium* in soil
*Rhizobium* in roots of legumes

UNHELPFUL

**Denitrifying bacteria**
reduce nitrates to nitrites, ammonia or nitrogen

**Table 1** Summary of the various bacteria which play a part in the nitrogen cycle.

## Assignments

1 Explain the part played by each of the following in the water cycle:
   a) mountains   c) leaves of plants
   b) the soil      d) the sea.

2 Figure 1 shows the part played by plants in the water cycle, but it does not say anything about animals. How do animals, including humans, affect the water cycle?

3 Study the carbon cycle in Figure 2 and then answer these questions:
   a) What is photosynthesis and how does it remove carbon dioxide from the atmosphere?
   b) What is respiration and how does it add carbon dioxide to the atmosphere?
   c) Name the main kind of organisms that bring about decay, and explain how they put carbon dioxide into the atmosphere.
   d) What happens chemically when coal is burned?

4 Farmers often plough leguminous plants into the soil. Why is this a good thing to do? Explain your answer fully.

5 Construct a diagram which summarises the way *oxygen* circulates in nature.

6 'Materials can be recycled, but there is only a one-way transfer of energy.' What does this statement mean?

# Cells, the bricks of the body

*An organism is made of cells in much the same way as a house is made of bricks. This Topic is about cells: how we study them, what they look like, and what goes on inside them.*

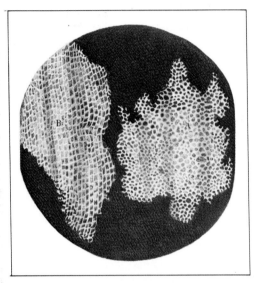

**Figure 1** The first drawing of cells ever made. These cells were observed in a piece of cork by Robert Hooke. This drawing was published in Hooke's famous *Micrographia* in 1665.

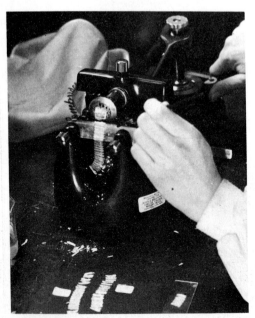

**Figure 2** A technician cutting sections with a microtome. The specimen has been embedded in a wax block. When cut, successive sections stick together in ribbons.

## How were cells discovered?

Cells were discovered in 1665 by the English inventor and scientist, Robert Hooke. Hooke examined a piece of bark which he stripped from a tree. Near the surface of bark is a layer of cork: Hooke cut a thin slice of the cork and placed it under a microscope which he had made himself. Hooke described the cork as being made up of hundreds of little boxes, giving a kind of honeycomb appearance (Figure 1). He called these little boxes **cells**.

As more and more organisms were examined under the microscope, it became clear to scientists that virtually all living things are made of cells. And so cells came to be regarded as the basic unit of which organisms are made. We call this the **cell theory**.

## How can we see cells?

The human body consists of about one hundred million million cells, and each one is very small. Because they are so small, we usually express their size in **micrometres**. A micrometre is one thousandth of a millimetre, and is given the symbol μm. A typical cell is about 20 μm wide.

Objects this size are too small to be seen with the naked eye, or even with a magnifying glass. To see them you must use a light microscope such as the one shown on page 4.

For cells to be seen under the microscope, they must be spread out flat. They must not be on top of each other, otherwise light cannot get through them and no image will be formed.

One of the easiest places to get cells from is inside your cheek. If you scrape the inside of your cheek, the cells will come away and you can put them on a glass slide. Adding a drop of dye will stain the cells and make them show up under the microscope (Investigations 1 and 2).

Sometimes scientists want to look at the cells in the middle of a thick solid organ such as the liver or kidney. To do this it is necessary to cut thin slices of the organ. This is done with an instrument which works rather like a bacon-slicer. It is called a **microtome** (Figure 2). The slices, or **sections** as they are called, are then stained with a dye which makes the cells show up.

## Inside a typical animal cell

Figure 3 shows the structure of a typical animal cell. The cell is bounded by a thin **cell membrane**. In the centre is a tiny ball, the **nucleus**. This is surrounded by a material called the **cytoplasm**.

### The nucleus

It is possible to take the nucleus out of certain cells. If this is done, the cell dies. From this experiment we conclude that the nucleus is essential for the life of the cell. It controls the various processes which go on inside it.

The nucleus contains a number of thread-like bodies called **chromosomes**. However, these can only be seen clearly when the cell is about to split in two (see page 304). The chromosomes determine the organism's characteristics such as the colour of the eyes.

### The cytoplasm

The cytoplasm is told what to do by the nucleus. The cytoplasm produces energy, makes things, and stores food. Hundreds of chemical reactions take place inside it. Together, these reactions make up **metabolism** (see page 43).

Scattered about in the cytoplasm are small granules. Seen under the light microscope, these look like little dots. The larger ones are **mitochondria** (singular: mitochondrion). The mitochondria have been described as the 'powerhouse of the cell': their job is to release energy for the cell.

The smaller granules in the cytoplasm are tiny bits of stored food. Many of them consist of a substance called **glycogen**.

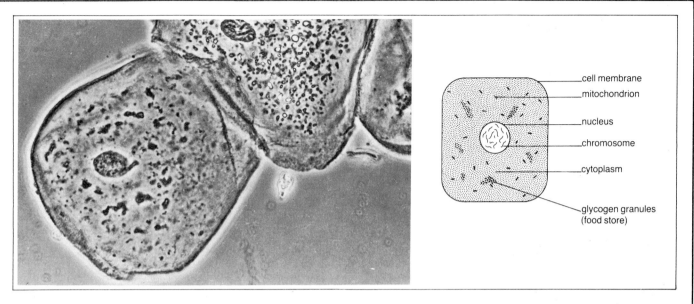

## Inside a typical plant cell

A typical plant cell is shown in Figure 4. It differs from animal cells in the following ways:

1 In addition to the cell membrane, the plant cell has a **cell wall**. It is made of **cellulose**, a rubbery material which helps to make plants tough.

2 In the centre of the cell there is a large cavity called the **vacuole**, which is filled with a watery fluid called **cell sap**. This means that the cytoplasm is pushed towards the edge of the cell. The nucleus is usually found in this layer of cytoplasm. However, in some plant cells the nucleus is suspended in the middle of the vacuole by fine strands of cytoplasm.

3 The cytoplasm contains **starch grains**. This is how plants store food. The starch grains are equivalent to the glycogen granules in animal cells.

4 Many plant cells possess **chloroplasts**. These are located in the cytoplasm, and they contain the green pigment **chlorophyll** which is used in **photosynthesis**. Chloroplasts only occur in the green parts of the plant which are exposed to the light. Roots and other underground structures lack them.

Chloroplasts and starch grains are both examples of **plastids**. These are small bodies in the cell containing a chemical substance. In the case of chloroplasts the chemical substance is chlorophyll; in the case of starch grains it is starch. In the cells of petals the plastids contain pigments which give the petals their colours.

**Figure 3** This diagram shows a typical animal cell. On the left are some cheek cells as they actually appear under the light microscope.

**Figure 4** This diagram shows a typical plant cell. On the left are some leaf cells as they appear under the light microscope.

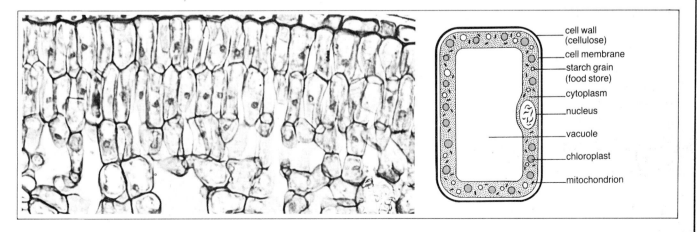

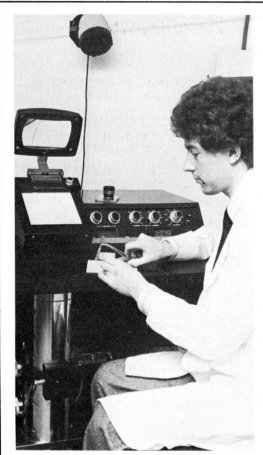

**Figure 5** A scientist about to view a specimen in an electron microscope. The specimen is carefully prepared beforehand and placed in a chamber containing a vacuum. Its image shows up on the fluorescent screen to the left.

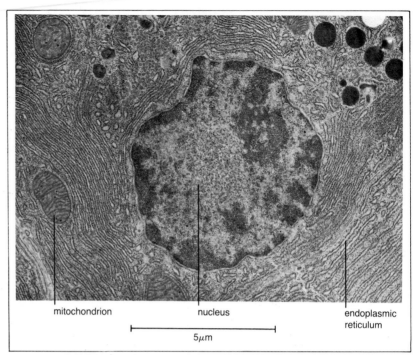

mitochondrion        nucleus        endoplasmic reticulum

5µm

**Figure 6** This is a cell from the pancreas as seen in the electron microscope. It is magnified about 10 000 times. The black blobs are substances which the cell produces.

## A new look at the cell

In the late 1930s a new kind of microscope was invented: the **electron microscope** (Figure 5). It uses a beam of electrons instead of light rays and is much more powerful than the light microscope. It is able to magnify things as much as *half a million times*. Enlarged to this extent, a pinhead would cover ten football pitches side by side.

Figure 6 shows part of an animal cell as it appears in the electron microscope. We can now see much more detail. For example, the cytoplasm appears to consist of a network of membranes and channels. This is called the **endoplasmic reticulum**. Scientists think that it helps to transport material inside the cell.

Stuck to the membranes of the endoplasmic reticulum are minute granules called **ribosomes**. They play an important part in the process by which cells make proteins. The mitochondria show up as hollow sausage-shaped bodies with partitions inside them. These and many other intriguing structures have been revealed by the electron microscope.

## How are new cells formed?

New cells are formed by **cell division**. The cell divides into two **daughter cells**. These then grow to full size after which each may divide again. Cell division enables organisms to grow, to reproduce, and to repair damaged or worn-out parts.

## Different cells for different jobs

Practically all cells contain a nucleus and cytoplasm. However, they vary tremendously in their shape and form. In the human body there are at least twenty different types of cell, each with a particular job to do. Three are shown in Figure 7.

There is thus a **division of labour** between cells. It's rather like a factory or an office in which each person has his or her own job to do. This is more efficient than if each individual tried to do everything.

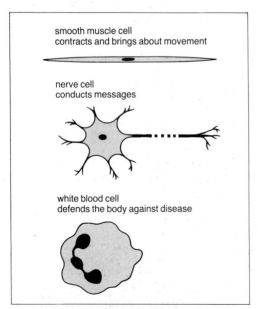

smooth muscle cell
contracts and brings about movement

nerve cell
conducts messages

white blood cell
defends the body against disease

**Figure 7** Three types of cell found in the human body.

# Investigation 1

## Looking at cheek cells

1 Obtain a blunt instrument such as a spatula. It must be clean.

2 Gently scrape the inside of your cheek with the instrument.

3 Put the scrapings onto the surface of a microscope slide.

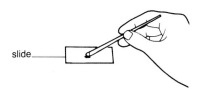

slide

4 Add a drop of methylene blue to the scrapings on the slide. This will stain the cells and help you to see them.

5 Cover with a coverslip. Lower it carefully onto the slide. The stain will spread out beneath it.

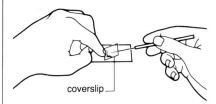

coverslip

6 Examine the slide under the microscope. First use low power to find some of the scrapings, then look at one of the cells under high power.

Which of the structures shown in Figure 3 can you see?

7 Draw the cheek cell and label it as fully as you can.

# Investigation 2

## Looking at plant cells

1 Slice an onion in two lengthways.

2 Take out one of the thick 'leaves' from inside it.

3 With forceps pull away the thin lining from the inner surface of the 'leaf'.

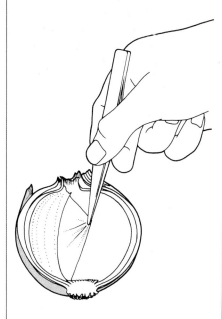

4 With scissors cut out a small piece of the lining, about 5 mm square.

5 Place the piece of lining on a slide and add a drop of dilute iodine.

This will stain the cells and make their nuclei easier to see.

6 Put on a coverslip as shown in Investigation 1.

7 Examine the slide under the microscope, first under low power, then high power.

Which of the structures shown in Figure 4 can you see?

8 Draw one of the onion cells and label it as fully as you can.

9 Place a single leaf of moss or pondweed in a drop of water on a slide and put on a coverslip.

What structures, absent in the onion cells, can you see inside the moss or pondweed cells?

# Assignments

1 A typical cell is 20 micrometres wide.

Suppose that cells of this size were placed side by side.

How many would there be in a row that was the same length as the second line of this assignment? 24000

2 Each word in the left-hand column below is related to one of the words in the right-hand column.

Write them down in the correct pairs.

glycogen        inheritance
chloroplast     energy
mitochondrion   sunlight
chromosomes     elastic
cellulose       storage

3 Which of the structures listed below are found (a) in animal cells only, (b) in plant cells only, and (c) in both animal and plant cells?

cytoplasm
chloroplasts
starch grains
nucleus
vacuole
glycogen granules —
cell wall
chromosomes —
cell membrane
mitochondria

4 Which of the following structures can be seen with a light microscope and which ones can only be seen with an electron microscope?

nucleus
endoplasmic reticulum
ribosomes
chromosomes
chloroplasts

5 The picture below shows a group of cells from a certain organ of the human body. The cells were obtained by cutting a very thin slice (section) of the organ with a microtome.

Why do some of the cells appear not to have a nucleus?

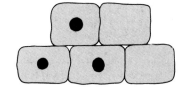

# Tissues, organs and organisation

*In an organism like man the different kinds of cells are arranged in a precise way. The health and well-being of the individual depend on this.*

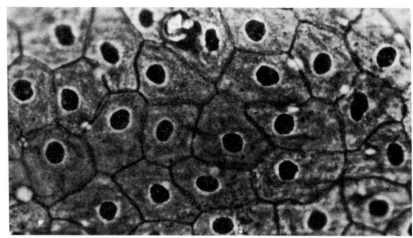

**Figure 1** A simple type of epithelium seen under the microscope. It comes from one of the thin membranes inside the body.

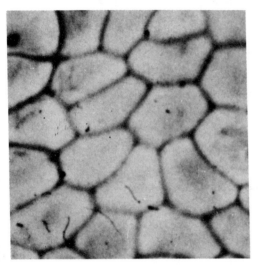

**Figure 2** Plant epidermis from the surface of a leaf seen under the microscope.

## Cells are grouped into tissues

Cells don't normally float around on their own. Usually large numbers of them are massed together into a **tissue** (Investigations 1 and 2).

One of the simplest tissues is shown in Figure 1. It is called **epithelium**. It consists of a sheet of cells. The cells fit neatly together, like paving stones. This kind of tissue forms the lining of spaces and tubes inside the body and is also found on the surface of the skin. Plants have a similar surface tissue called **epidermis** (Figure 2).

In Figure 3, an epithelial tissue is compared with two other kinds of tissue: smooth muscle and nerve tissue. **Smooth muscle** consists of lots of slender muscle cells packed together. You find this tissue in the wall of the gut, amongst other places. Its job is to squeeze the food along. **Nerve tissue**

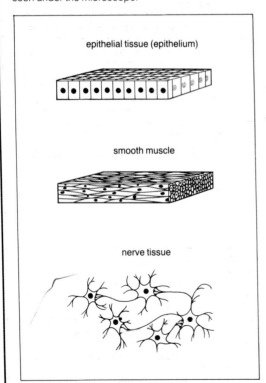

**Figure 3** Three types of tissue found in the human body.

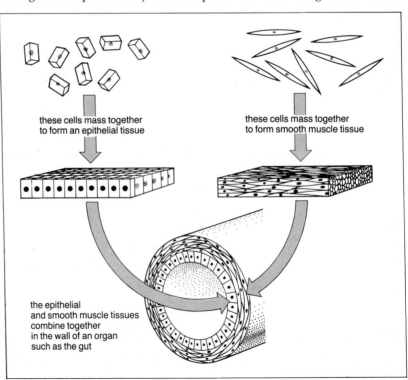

**Figure 4** This diagram shows in a simplified way how cells combine to form tissues and how tissues combine to form organs.

consists of a network of nerve cells connected with one another. This kind of tissue occurs in the brain. It carries messages from place to place, as in a complicated telephone system.

The main tissues of animals and plants are summarised in Tables 1 and 2. Some of them consist of just one type of cell. However, most of them contain two or three types of cells mixed together.

## Tissues are combined into organs

In most animals, including man, tissues are combined together to form **organs** (Figure 4). An organ is a complex structure which has a particular job to do. The main organs in the human body are shown in Figure 5. Look at some organs obtained from the butcher (Investigation 3), and examine thin sections of them under a microscope (Investigation 4).

Some organs do just one job. For example, the only job the heart does is pump blood round the body. Other organs do more than one job. For example, the kidneys get rid of poisonous waste substances and control the amount of water in the body. The organ with the greatest number of jobs is the liver: scientists have worked out that it does about 500 jobs altogether.

## Organs are grouped into systems

In the human body certain tasks are carried out by several different organs working together. These organs all belong to a **system**. An example is the digestive system. This consists of the gut, together with the liver, pancreas and gall bladder. Its job is to digest and absorb food.

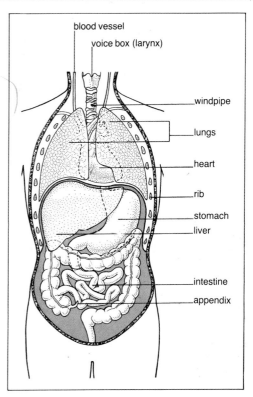

**Figure 5** This diagram shows some of the main organs in the human body as seen from the belly (ventral) side.

## Animal tissues (based on human)

| Name of tissue | What it consists of | Main functions |
| --- | --- | --- |
| Epithelial tissue | Sheets of cells | To line tubes and spaces and form the skin |
| Connective tissue | Tough flexible fibres | To bind other tissues together |
| Skeletal tissue | Hard material | To support the body and permit movement |
| Blood tissue | Runny fluid containing loose cells | To carry oxygen and food round the body |
| Nerve tissue | Network of threads with long cable-like extensions | To conduct and coordinate messages |
| Muscle tissue | Bundles of elongated cells | To bring about movement |

**Table 1** Summary of the main tissues found in animals.

## Plant tissues (based on flowering plant)

| Name of tissue | What it consists of | Main functions |
| --- | --- | --- |
| Epidermal tissue | Sheets of cells | To line the surface of the plant |
| Photosynthetic tissue | Cells with chloroplasts | To feed the plant |
| Packing tissue | Round balloon-like cells | To fill in spaces inside the plant |
| Vascular (conducting) tissue | Long tubes | To transport water and food substances |
| Strengthening tissue | Bundles of tough fibres | To support the plant |

**Table 2** Summary of the main tissues found in plants.

## Systems in the human body

| Name of system | Main organs in the system | Main functions |
| --- | --- | --- |
| Digestive system | Gut, liver and pancreas | To digest and absorb food |
| Respiratory system | Windpipe and lungs | To take in oxygen and get rid of carbon dioxide |
| Blood (circulatory) system | Heart, blood vessels | To carry oxygen and food round the body |
| Excretory system | Kidneys, bladder, liver | To get rid of poisonous waste substances |
| Sensory system | Eyes, ears, nose | To detect stimuli |
| Nervous system | Brain and spinal cord | To conduct messages from one part of the body to another |
| Musculo-skeletal system | Muscles and skeleton | To support and move the body |
| Reproductive system | Testes and ovaries | To produce offspring |

**Table 3** Summary of the systems in the human body.

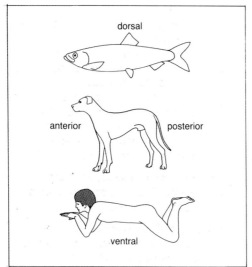

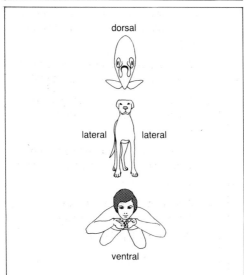

**Figure 6** Most animals have an anterior and posterior end, and dorsal and ventral sides. They are also bilaterally symmetrical: the two sides of the body are mirror images.

The various systems found in the human body are summarised in Table 3. Some organs belong to more than one system. The liver, for example, belongs to the digestive and excretory systems.

### Division of labour

In most organisms we see a division of labour between different kinds of cells. We also see a division of labour between different tissues, and between different organs. They all work in harmony. This is essential for the smooth running of a complex animal like man.

Division of labour is only possible in an organism whose body is made up of many cells. Such organisms are described as **multicellular**.

There are a few multicellular plants whose cells are all identical. And there are some simple organisms which consist of only one cell. In these simple organisms there is obviously no division of labour between cells: all jobs have to be carried out within the one cell.

### The shapes of living things

A plant such as a tree has a rather irregular shape, with branches sticking out all over the place. Animals, on the other hand, are more regular and compact.

Most animals move with one end of the body in the lead. This is the front or **anterior end**. The other end is the **posterior end**. In most animals there is some kind of head at the anterior end.

The lower side of the body, that is the side closest to the ground, is known as the **ventral side**. The upper side is known as the **dorsal side** (Figure 6).

Most animals, man included, have more or less symmetrical right and left sides. Many of the structures on one side are repeated on the other so that the two sides of the body are mirror images of one another. We call this **bilateral symmetry**. You can see this kind of symmetry in Figure 6.

In contrast, some animals have their structures arranged all round a central point, rather like the spokes of a wheel. Sea anemones and jellyfish are examples (see page 107). We call this **radial symmetry**. Plants tend to be radially symmetrical too; think, for instance, of the way the petals and sepals are arranged in a typical flower. If you look at the internal structure of the stem and root of many plants, you will see that they, too, are radially symmetrical.

There are a few organisms which have no symmetry at all. They are **asymmetrical**. Can you think of an example?

# Investigation 1

## Looking at epithelium

1 Put a drop of stain on the surface of a microscope slide.

2 Your teacher will provide you with a piece of frog's skin.

3 With a knife or scalpel gently scrape the surface of the frog's skin. This will remove the epithelium.

4 Dip the knife in the drop of stain. The epithelium will come off the knife and float in the stain.

5 Cover it with a coverslip.

6 Examine your slide under the microscope: low power first, then high power.

How does the tissue compare with the one shown in Figure 1?

Draw a small group of cells, showing how they fit together.

What job does this tissue do?

# Investigation 2

## Looking at plant packing tissue

1 Obtain a soft fruit such as a tomato.

2 Cut the fruit in half.

3 With a knife remove a small piece of the soft pulpy material from inside. This is packing tissue.

4 Put the tissue on a slide and spread it out.

5 With a pipette add a drop of water to the tissue.

6 Cover it with a coverslip.

7 Examine your slide under the microscope: low power first, then high power.

How does the tissue compare in appearance with the epithelial tissue in Investigation 1?

Draw a small group of the cells.

What job does this tissue do?

# Assignments

1 Explain each of these words: tissue, organ, muscle, epithelium, multicellular.

2 Each of the tissues listed in the left-hand column is related to one of the words in the right-hand column. Write them down in the correct pairs.

photosynthetic tissue — transport
epithelial tissue — protection
connective tissue — messages
blood tissue — feeding
nervous tissue — strength

3 What kind of tissue:

a) fills spaces inside a plant stem, *Packing*
b) carries oxygen round the human body, *Blood tissue*
c) brings about movement in animals, *muscle*
d) supplies a plant with food, *Photosynthetic*
e) transports water in a plant,
f) supports your body, *skeletal*
g) lines the surface of a leaf *epidermal*
h) conducts messages from one part of your body to another, *Nerve*
i) binds other tissues together, *connective*
j) lines an animal's body cavity? *epithelial*

4 Why is it an advantage to have a division of labour between different organs in the body?

5 Why is photosynthetic tissue not found in animals, and why is muscle tissue not found in plants?

6 Name two organs in Figure 5 which occur in pairs and two which occur singly. *Windpipe Plungs & Ribs & Appendix*

Why is it an advantage to have pairs of organs rather than single ones?

7 Make a list of all the functions you can think of which are performed by your head.

Why is it an advantage to an animal to have its head at the anterior end of its body?

8 What is the difference between bilateral and radial symmetry? Give one example of each.

# Investigation 3

## Looking at organs

1 Examine some or all of the following organs obtained from a butcher: lungs, stomach, intestine, tongue, liver, pancreas, heart, kidney, muscle, brain and eye.

2 Try tearing, or cutting, each organ to see how tough it is.

3 Cut open each organ with a sharp knife in order to see its inside.

4 Describe what each organ looks and feels like.

5 Find out what each organ has to do in the body.

In what ways does the structure of each organ suit it to its job?

6 For each organ write down the main tissues which are found in it.

How would you relate the presence of the particular tissue to the job which the organ has to do?

# Investigation 4

## Examining the inside of an organ

Your teacher will give you a thin section of an organ which has been cut with a microtome, mounted on a microscope slide, and stained to show up the cells.

1 Look at your section under the low power of the microscope.

2 Firstly try to see the cells of which the organ is composed.

You should be able to recognise them from their nuclei which will be darkly stained.

3 Make a list of particular kinds of tissue which you think you can see in your section.

4 Find out the main function of the organ from which your section was obtained.

Make a list of the ways the internal structure of the organ seems to be suited to carrying out its function.

# Molecules in motion

*In this Topic we shall see how molecules and other tiny particles move about, and why this is important in biology.*

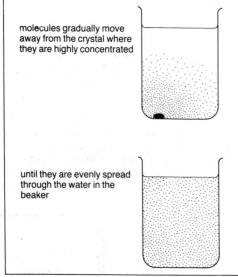

molecules gradually move away from the crystal where they are highly concentrated

until they are evenly spread through the water in the beaker

**Figure 1** An example of diffusion in a liquid: this is what happens when you drop a crystal of potassium permanganate in water. If you are doing chemistry you may know that potassium permanganate molecules split up into potassium and permanganate *ions*, and it's really these which diffuse rather than the whole molecules.

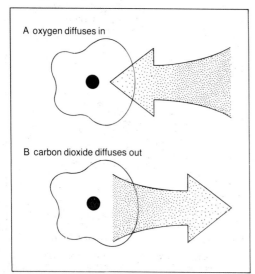

A oxygen diffuses in

B carbon dioxide diffuses out

**Figure 2** *Amoeba* takes in oxygen and gets rid of carbon dioxide by diffusion. Many other cells and organisms carry out gas exchange this way.

## Diffusion

Suppose you are sitting at one end of a room. A lady wearing a lot of perfume comes in and sits down at the other end. Before long the smell of her perfume fills the room and reaches your nose. Why does this happen?

Molecules in a gas or liquid are constantly moving about freely, bumping into one another and bouncing this way and that. This takes place randomly, and it results in the molecules being spread out evenly. We call this kind of movement **diffusion**. It is *the tendency for molecules to become distributed evenly throughout the space they occupy.*

The way a smell spreads through a room is an example of molecules diffusing through air, i.e. through a gas. However, diffusion also takes place in liquids, and this is its main importance in biology.

### Diffusion in a liquid

You can watch diffusion taking place in a liquid by dropping a crystal of potassium permanganate into a bowl of water. Gradually the purple colour of the permanganate spreads through the water until eventually all the water is the same shade of purple.

What exactly has happened? In the crystal, the permanganate molecules are packed tightly together, i.e. they are very concentrated. However, to begin with, the surrounding water contains no permanganate molecules at all. As a result the permanganate molecules move away from the crystal until they are evenly distributed throughout the water (Figure 1). In actual fact the permanganate molecules move randomly in all directions. However, at any given moment more of them will be moving away from the crystal than towards it. In other words there is a *net* movement away from the crystal.

*So diffusion is a net movement of molecules from a region where they are highly concentrated to a region where they are less concentrated.* The difference in concentration between the two regions before diffusion occurs is known as the **diffusion gradient**. Provided such a gradient exists, molecules (or particles derived from them) will always tend to diffuse in this way.

### An example of diffusion in biology

In an animal such as an amoeba, oxygen is continually being used up. The result is that oxygen molecules are less concentrated inside the body than in the surrounding water. As a result, oxygen molecules constantly diffuse in (Figure 2A) and in this way the amoeba gets all the oxygen it needs for respiration.

Meanwhile carbon dioxide is continually being formed. The result is that carbon dioxide molecules are more concentrated inside the body than in the surrounding water. As a result carbon dioxide molecules constantly diffuse out (Figure 2B) and in this way the amoeba gets rid of carbon dioxide.

In order for molecules to diffuse like this, the cell membrane must let them pass through without hindrance – in other words the membrane must be **permeable** to them. Moreover, for diffusion to take place, the molecules must first go into solution, and so the membrane must be moist.

### How fast is diffusion?

Diffusion is a rather slow process. However, it can be speeded up by raising the concentration of the substance which is diffusing – in other words by making the diffusion gradient steeper. Diffusion can also be speeded up by moving the molecules in some way. For example, stirring or heating the contents of the beaker would help to spread out the permanganate molecules, and a gentle breeze would help to spread a lady's perfume around the room. The size of the molecule is also important: small molecules such as oxygen diffuse more rapidly than large molecules such as glucose.

## *Diffusion and surface area*

Imagine that the box below is an organism. It is a cube whose sides are all one centimetre long:

Its surface area is 6 cm², and its volume is 1 cm³.
Now suppose we double the size of the box like this:

By how much have we increased its volume and its surface area? Well, its volume is now 2 cm³, twice what it was. However, its surface area is 10 cm², which is less than twice what it was.

In other words we have doubled its volume, but its surface area is *less* than doubled. This is because, in the process of doubling the volume, we have lost part of the original surface (the part shaded in the first diagram), so we can make this statement: *as an object increases in size the amount of surface area relative to volume (the surface area to volume ratio) gets smaller.*

This is extremely important to organisms which take things in by diffusion. Think of it this way. A small organism, like an amoeba, has a large surface to volume ratio, and so it can take in all the oxygen it needs by diffusion across the body surface. However, a large organism, like a mammal, has a much smaller surface to volume ratio, so it cannot get all the oxygen it needs in this way. Such large organisms need special respiratory organs such as lungs for taking in oxygen. These respiratory organs consist of a sheet of tissue which is folded many times so that it provides a large surface area across which oxygen can be absorbed (Figure 3). The idea of organisms creating a large surface area for absorption is one that we shall meet again and again.

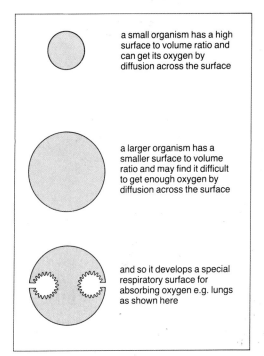

a small organism has a high surface to volume ratio and can get its oxygen by diffusion across the surface

a larger organism has a smaller surface to volume ratio and may find it difficult to get enough oxygen by diffusion across the surface

and so it develops a special respiratory surface for absorbing oxygen e.g. lungs as shown here

**Figure 3** These diagrams show how a large organism can overcome the problem of having a small surface to volume ratio.

## Osmosis

Carry out Investigation 1. This involves making a bag out of a thin membrane, filling it with sugar solution and suspending it in a beaker of water. After a short time, water enters the bag from the beaker, passing through the membrane.

To understand why this happens, look at Figure 4. The sugar molecules are larger than the water molecules. The bag itself has tiny holes in it which are large enough to let the small water molecules through, but too small to let the larger sugar molecules through. Such a membrane is described as a **semi-permeable** membrane.

Now the presence of the sugar molecules in the bag means that there isn't as much room for water molecules there. So the water molecules inside the bag are less concentrated than in the beaker outside. As a result, water molecules *diffuse* into the bag.

This movement of water is called **osmosis**. *Osmosis is the net flow of water through a semi-permeable membrane.* It's really a special case of diffusion, in which only the water molecules move from one region to another. A real-life example of osmosis is explored in Investigation 2.

### *Strong and weak solutions*

Look at Figure 4 again for a moment. For water to move into the bag from outside, the fluid in the beaker doesn't *have* to be water. It could be another sugar solution. All that's necessary is that the solution inside the bag should

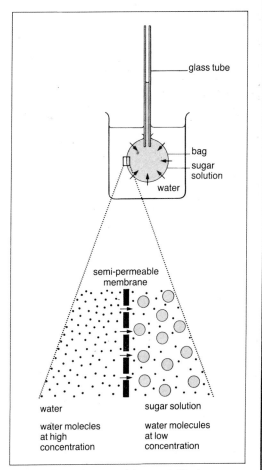

glass tube

bag
sugar solution

water

semi-permeable membrane

water

sugar solution

water
water molecles at high concentration

water molecules at low concentration

**Figure 4** Osmosis, a special case of diffusion.

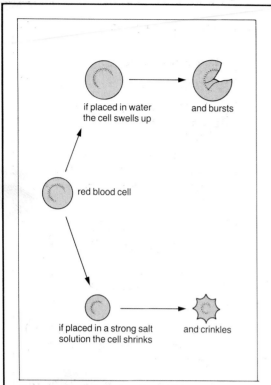

**Figure 5** These diagrams show what happens if you put a red blood cell in water or a strong salt solution.

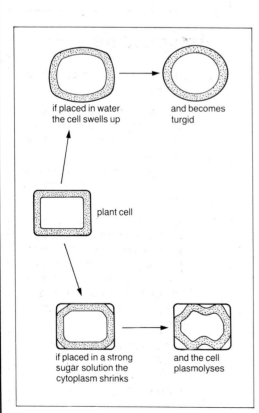

**Figure 6** These diagrams show what happens if you put a plant cell in water or a strong sugar solution.

have a greater concentration of sugar molecules, i.e. be stronger, than the solution in the beaker.

What would happen if the situation was reversed, and the solution in the beaker was stronger than the one in the bag? The answer is that osmosis would occur in the other direction, and water would flow *out* of the bag. As a result it would lose mass and volume and go flabby.

## Osmosis and animal cells

The effect of osmosis on an animal cell can be investigated by putting red blood cells in solutions of different strengths (see page 129).

As with other types of animal cells, red blood cells contain a solution of salts and other substances. These are enclosed inside the cell membrane which is semi-permeable.

If a red blood cell is put in water, water enters the cell by osmosis. The cell swells up and eventually bursts, just as a balloon would do if you blew too much air into it.

However, if you put a red blood cell in a salt solution which is stronger than that inside the cell, water leaves the cell by osmosis. As a result the cell shrinks and crinkles (Figure 5). This is sometimes called **exosmosis**.

This is very important in our bodies. It means that the fluid part of the blood (the plasma), in which the cells float around, must have just the right strength to prevent osmosis occuring in either direction. In a later Topic we shall see how this is achieved.

## Osmosis and plant cells

Now consider what happens if you put a plant cell in solutions of different strengths.

A plant cell has a cellulose wall as well as a cell membrane. In the centre of the cell there is a vacuole which contains a solution of salts and so on. The thin layer of cytoplasm surrounding the vacuole acts as a semi-permeable membrane. The cellulose wall, however, is fully permeable to salts, as well as water.

If you put a plant cell in water, water enters by osmosis and the cell swells up. However, it doesn't burst. This is because the cellulose wall is tough, like elastic: it stretches but does not break. Eventually the cellulose cannot stretch any more and so the cell stops swelling. It's like trying to blow up a football into which no more air can be pumped. When this point is reached, we say the cell is **turgid**. Turgidity, or turgor as it's called, is very important in plants because it helps to make them firm.

Now what happens if you put a plant cell into a solution which is stronger than that in the vacuole (Investigation 3)? In this case water is drawn out of the vacuole and the cell shrinks: it loses its turgor and becomes flabby or flaccid. If the external solution is strong enough, the cytoplasm eventually pulls away from the cellulose wall as shown in Figure 6. We call this process **plasmolysis**.

In this Topic we have seen how molecules move as a result of diffusion and osmosis. You will find many examples of these processes in action in other parts of this book.

# Active transport

In living things molecules and ions are sometimes pumped across the cell membrane. This is called **active transport**. No one knows exactly how it takes place, but it needs energy from respiration. Active transport can move chemicals from a region of low concentration to a region of *higher* concentration; that is, *against* the concentration gradient. For example, this is how plant roots obtain some of their mineral salts from the soil (see page 169).

# Investigation 1

**Watching osmosis**

 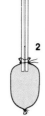 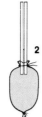 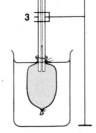

1 Cut a length of visking tubing about 8 cm long.

2 Wet it thoroughly with water.

3 Tie one end with strong thread, so that it forms a bag.

4 Fill the bag with a 20 per cent solution of sucrose (Illustration 1).

5 With a piece of thread, tie the bag to the bottom of a capillary tube (Illustration 2).

6 Clamp the capillary tube to a stand, and lower the bag into a beaker of water (Illustration 3).

7 Mark the level of the sucrose solution in the capillary tube.

8 Five minutes later, with a ruler, measure the distance which the sucrose solution has risen from the original mark. Write down the distance in millimetres.

9 Re-measure the distance every five minutes for about half an hour. In each case write down the distance the sucrose has risen from the original mark.

10 Plot your results on graph paper: put the distance the sucrose has risen on the vertical axis, and time on the horizontal axis.

Why does the sucrose solution rise in the capillary tube?

What property of the visking tubing makes this happen?

# Investigation 2

**Osmosis in a potato**

1 Peel a potato and cut it in two.

2 With a knife or scalpel make a cup-shaped cavity in one half of the potato.

3 Half fill the cavity with a strong solution of sugar and stand the potato-cup in a dish of water (see illustration).

4 Mark the level of the sugar solution by sticking a pin in the side of the potato-cup.

What happens to the level of the sugar solution in the next 30 minutes? Explain your observations.

# Investigation 3

**The effect of osmosis on a plant cell**

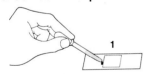 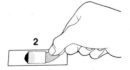

1 Obtain a stem of rhubarb or a leaf of *Rhoeo* (Moses-in-the-bulrushes).

2 With forceps, strip off a piece of the coloured epidermis.

3 Trim the piece of epidermis with scissors so that it is about one centimetre square.

4 Put the piece of epidermis in a drop of water on a slide, and cover it with a coverslip.

5 Look at your slide under the low power of the microscope. Can you see the cells clearly? Notice that each cell is filled with a coloured substance: this is inside the vacuole.

6 With a pipette, place a drop of strong sucrose solution against one side of the coverslip (Illustration 1). The sucrose solution will flow under the coverslip by capillary action.

7 Put a piece of filter paper against the other side of the coverslip, and draw the sucrose solution across. (Illustration 2).

8 Look at the epidermal cells under the microscope.

How does their appearance change?

What happens to the coloured substance inside them?

Explain your observations.

# Assignments

1 Suggest an explanation for each of the following:

 a) If certain kinds of lettuces get floppy, they can be made firm and crisp by putting them in cold water for a while.

 b) If you sprinkle sugar on a bowl of strawberries, the juice comes out of them.

2 A pupil in a school carried out the following experiment. He cut out a rectangular piece of potato 20 mm long, and put it in a dish of strong sucrose solution. Four hours later he found that the piece of potato had shortened so that it was now only 16 mm long.

 a) Suggest an explanation for this result.

 b) What should the control be in this experiment?

# The chemistry of life

*Organisms are like chemical factories. What are the chemicals and what happens to them?*

## What are living things made of?

All living things, including humans, are made of chemical substances. Some of the substances are very complex and contain lots of carbon atoms. We call them **organic substances**; they are a very important ingredient of all living things. The other substances are simpler, and usually lack carbon. They are called **inorganic substances**.

Look at Figure 1. The pie chart shows substances which make up the human body, and their relative amounts. You may be surprised to see that we consist mainly of water! The three main *organic* substances are **carbohydrate, fat** and **protein**. Let's look at each of these in turn.

### Carbohydrate

Carbohydrate contains the elements carbon, hydrogen and oxygen. One of the simplest carbohydrates is **glucose**, which is a type of sugar. Its chemical formula is $C_6H_{12}O_6$. It is typical of a carbohydrate that it contains twice as many hydrogen atoms as oxygen atoms.

Glucose occurs in practically all living things. It dissolves very easily in water, in other words it is very soluble. It is present in your cells and is circulating in your bloodstream at this very moment. It is the main substance from which living things obtain energy.

Another well known carbohydrate is **starch**. It is solid, and if you try to dissolve it in water you get a paste-like suspension. Starch consists of lots of glucose molecules linked together in a chain, like a string of beads. When glucose molecules join together like this, water is taken away from them. This kind of chemical reaction is called **condensation**.

The reverse can also occur: starch is broken down into glucose. This is like breaking a string of beads so that all the beads fall apart. For the glucose molecules to be separated from one another water has to be added. This kind of reaction is called **hydrolysis**.

Glucose is known as a **single-sugar** or **monosaccharide**. Starch, with its many glucose molecules linked together, is called a **multi-sugar** or **polysaccharide**. Some carbohydrates consist of *two* single-sugar molecules linked together: we call them **double-sugars** or **disaccharides**. Ordinary table sugar is a double-sugar called **sucrose**. These three kinds of carbohydrate are illustrated in Figure 2.

### Fat

Fat is like carbohydrate in that it contains carbon, hydrogen and oxygen. However, fat contains much more carbon and hydrogen relative to oxygen.

A fat molecule consists of two parts. The main part is called **glycerol**. Attached to the glycerol are chains called **fatty acids**. The fat can be split into its glycerol and fatty acid parts by adding water (hydrolysis). And these parts can be linked together by taking water away (condensation).

Different kinds of fat contain different fatty acids (see page 73). Their main job is to give us energy. In mammals fat under the skin helps to keep the body warm.

### Protein

Protein contains carbon, hydrogen and oxygen, but it also contains nitrogen and sometimes sulphur too.

A protein molecule is composed of lots of building blocks linked together in chains. The building blocks are called **amino acids** and the links between them are called **peptide links**. About twenty amino acids exist in nature. The particular amino acids present, and the order in which they occur, vary from one protein to another (Figure 3).

Proteins can be split into their amino acids by adding water (hydrolysis). This takes place in two steps: first the protein is broken down into shorter chains called **polypeptides**. Then the polypeptides are broken down into separate amino acids. If water is removed (condensation), the amino acids link together to form polypeptides and eventually protein.

Some proteins are tough and fibre-like. They form the main structures of

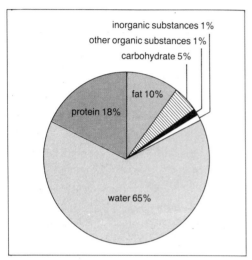

Figure 1 This pie chart shows the relative amounts of the main substances which make up the human body. There is much variation between different individuals – these are average figures. The 'other organic substances' include a number of important substances derived from vitamins. These and all the other substances in this chart come from the food we eat.

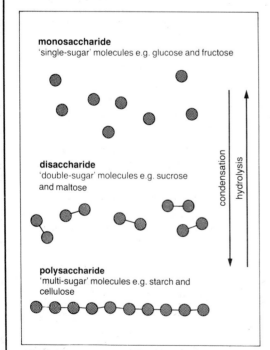

**monosaccharide**
'single-sugar' molecules e.g. glucose and fructose

**disaccharide**
'double-sugar' molecules e.g. sucrose and maltose

condensation ↕ hydrolysis

**polysaccharide**
'multi-sugar' molecules e.g. starch and cellulose

Figure 2 The three kinds of carbohydrate which occur in nature, with examples of each.

the body: bones, muscle, skin and so on. Others exist in solution, for example in the blood and in our cells. These soluble proteins include a very important group of chemicals called **enzymes**.

## Enzymes

Earlier it was said that starch can be broken down into glucose by adding water (hydrolysis). However, if you mix starch and water in a test tube, no reaction can be seen. What do we need to make the reaction go? Well, one way would be to boil it with an acid. However, we could do the same thing more quickly and at a much lower temperature by adding an enzyme.

Enzymes are catalysts. They speed up the chemical reactions which go on inside living things (Investigation). Without them the reactions would be so slow that life would grind to a halt!

Enzymes have seven important properties (Table 1). Notice that they are affected by conditions such as temperature and pH. For this reason the conditions inside our cells must not be allowed to vary very much.

Enzymes are found in plants, for example in germinating seeds where food stores are being hydrolysed (page 82), and in pawpaw leaves from which papain (a protein-digesting enzyme) can be extracted as a meat tenderiser.

## Chemical reactions in the human body

Chemical reactions occur in two main places: in the gut and in the cells. The reactions occurring in the gut are concerned with digesting our food. For example, solid starch is hydrolysed into soluble glucose which can then be absorbed into the bloodstream and taken to the cells.

The reactions occurring inside the cells are called **metabolism**. Some of the reactions build things up: for example, glucose is built up into a multi-sugar called glycogen for storage, and amino acids are linked together to form proteins for body-building. Other reactions break things down: for example glucose is broken down into carbon dioxide and water to produce energy.

All these chemical reactions are catalysed by enzymes. Within reason the warmer it is, the faster the reactions go. However, if it gets *too* hot the enzymes are destroyed and the reactions stop.

Within the cells the reactions take place in a watery solution. Water is the medium through which the chemical substances move and in which they are dissolved. This is one reason why we need plenty of it.

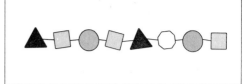

**Figure 3** Part of a protein molecule showing how it is made up of a chain of amino acids. The different shapes represent different kinds of amino acids.

| Property | Notes |
|---|---|
| 1 They are proteins | This is one reason why we need proteins in our food. |
| 2 They are specific | Each enzyme controls one particular reaction, or type of reaction. |
| 3 They can be used over again | This is because they are not destroyed by the reaction. |
| 4 They are destroyed by heat | Most enzymes stop working if the temperature reaches more than about 40°C. |
| 5 They are sensitive to the degree of acidity or alkalinity (pH) | Each enzyme works best at a particular pH. |
| 6 They are inhibited by poisons | This is why poisonous substances such as cyanide and arsenic are lethal. |
| 7 They are helped by vitamins and minerals | This is one reason why these substances are so important in our food. |

**Table 1** Seven important properties of enzymes are summarised in this table.

## Investigation

**Watching an enzyme in action**

1 Obtain two test tubes.
Pour hydrogen peroxide solution into one of them to a depth of about 2 cm. Pour water into the other test tube to serve as a control.

2 Drop a small piece of liver into each test tube.
Watch carefully and describe what happens.

Liver contains a powerful enzyme called **catalase**. This breaks down hydrogen peroxide into water and oxygen.
Do your observations agree with this statement?

3 Take another piece of liver and put it in a beaker of boiling water for about three minutes.

4 Drop the piece of boiled liver into a test tube containing fresh hydrogen peroxide.
What happens?
Explain the result.

5 Carry out experiments to find out if catalase occurs in other things, e.g. kidney, pawpaw leaves and Irish potato.
How could you find out if the gas that is given off really is oxygen?

Describe an experiment which you could do to find out if catalase prefers acid or alkaline conditions.

## Assignments

1 Give *two* functions in the human body of each of the following: fat, protein, enzymes, water.

2 What is the difference between condensation and hydrolysis? Why are they important in biology?

3 The graph shows the effect of gradually increasing the temperature on the rate of a certain metabolic reaction.

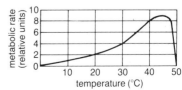

Explain the reason for the shape of the curve.

# Life forms

*These clown anemone
fish are living on a coral reef.
Fish are one of the many groups of organisms
we shall look at briefly in
the next part of the book.*

# Amoeba and other protists

*If you take a drop of water
from a pond or ditch and look
at it under a microscope, you will
see little organisms which consist of
only one cell. These one-celled
organisms are protists.*

## Amoeba

This is one of the largest protists. It can be the size of a pinhead. This makes it easy to see under the microscope.

*Amoeba* lives in ponds where it moves around on the surfaces of stones and weeds. Some species live in damp soil.

With a microscope you can look either at live specimens, or at dead specimens which have been stained so as to show up the structures inside the cell (Investigation 1). You really need to do both if you are to build up a complete picture of this little organism.

*Amoeba* is a single cell (Figure 1). It has a **nucleus** and **cytoplasm**. The cytoplasm is bounded by a very thin **cell membrane**, and is divided into two parts: the outer part is clear and jelly-like and is called the **ectoplasm**; the inner part is granular and runny and is called the **endoplasm**. Various structures float around in the endoplasm. These include **food vacuoles** which contain tiny organisms which the amoeba has eaten, and a **contractile vacuole** which collects unwanted water from inside the cell and every now and again discharges it to the outside. The amoeba is small enough for gas exchange and excretion to take place by simple diffusion.

The animal constantly changes shape. This is because the cell membrane is thin and elastic, and the fluid endoplasm flows around inside it. If you examine a live amoeba under the microscope, you will probably think its insides look chaotic. Linnaeus, the famous eighteenth-century naturalist, thought so too. When he first saw an amoeba, he named it *Chaos chaos*!

The amoeba's ability to change shape provides it with a special method of locomotion: it simply oozes its way around. It reproduces by splitting in two; the two amoebas then grow to their full size and may split again (see page 248).

## Euglena

Countless millions of green protists live in the surface waters of lakes, seas and ponds where there is plenty of light for photosynthesis. These organisms are too tiny to be seen individually, but sometimes there are so many of them that the water looks green.

One such organism is *Euglena* which lives in fresh-water ponds. The largest specimens are not more than a tenth of a millimetre long (100 μm). With a microscope you can see them swimming about in the water (Investigation 2).

The structure of *Euglena* is shown in Figure 2. The cell is bounded by a tough, elastic 'skin' called the **pellicle**. Inside there is a **nucleus** and **cytoplasm**, just as in any other normal cell.

One of the most noticeable features of this little organism is its bright green colour. This is caused by the presence of **chloroplasts** in the cytoplasm. Its chloroplasts enable it to feed by photosynthesis, though it can absorb soluble substances across its pellicle as well. The cytoplasm also contains **food storage granules** similar to starch.

At the front end there is a little **reservoir** into which opens the **contractile vacuole**. The contractile vacuole does the same job as the amoeba's. It collects water from inside the cell and every now and again discharges it to the outside via the reservoir.

From the reservoir springs a long whip-like **flagellum**. This is used for swimming. Waves pass along the flagellum, driving the organism through the water in a kind of corkscrew motion.

At the base of the flagellum there is a **light-sensitive swelling**, and to one side of it a red **pigment spot**. These structures guide the organism towards light when it is swimming.

If the water dries up, *Euglena* stops using its flagellum and wriggles around like a little worm.

As with *Amoeba*, gas exchange and excretion take place by diffusion. *Euglena* reproduces by splitting into new individuals.

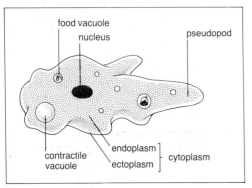

**Figure 1** Diagram of an amoeba. The various internal organs are not in fixed positions but move around as the organism changes shape.

food vacuole
nucleus
pseudopod
contractile vacuole
endoplasm
ectoplasm
cytoplasm

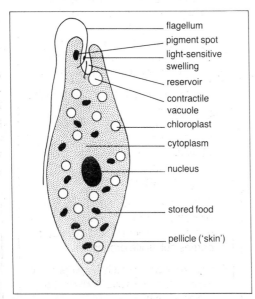

**Figure 2** *Euglena*, showing its structure. In this case the internal structures are in definite positions.

flagellum
pigment spot
light-sensitive swelling
reservoir
contractile vacuole
chloroplast
cytoplasm
nucleus
stored food
pellicle ('skin')

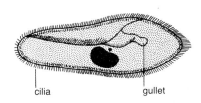
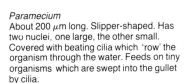

cilia      gullet

*Paramecium*
About 200 $\mu$m long. Slipper-shaped. Has two nuclei, one large, the other small. Covered with beating cilia which 'row' the organism through the water. Feeds on tiny organisms which are swept into the gullet by cilia.

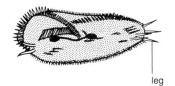

leg

*Stylonichia*
About 100 $\mu$m long. Looks spiky. Groups of cilia are stuck together to form little 'legs' which are used for a rather jerky kind of movement.

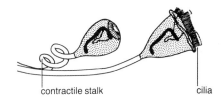

contractile stalk      cilia

*Vorticella*
Can be 1 mm long. Shaped like a bell. Attached to pieces of weed and so on by flexible stalk which can contract like a spring if the organism is disturbed. The cilia are used for sweeping food into the gullet.

**Figure 3** Three common single-celled organisms which you might see under the microscope. They are all found in ponds and ditches. The black objects are the nuclei.

## Other protists

Many other one-celled organisms live in ponds and streams. Figure 3 shows some of them. They vary in size and shape, and in the way they move and feed (Investigation 2).

Some of them swim by means of tiny hairs called **cilia** which beat like the oars of a boat. Others use a whip-like **flagellum** which lashes to and fro. A few of them don't swim at all, but are attached to weeds or stones by a stalk.

Many of them feed by sweeping tiny organisms into a **gullet** by means of beating cilia. Others feed like plants: they contain the green pigment chlorophyll and feed by photosynthesis.

Some protists live as parasites inside the bodies of other organisms and cause serious diseases (see pages 340–3).

# Investigation 1

## Looking at Amoeba

1 Examine a prepared slide of an amoeba under the microscope.

2 Which of the structures shown in Figure 1 can you see?

Draw a specimen, and label it as fully as you can.

3 Your teacher will give you a slide with a live amoeba on it.

4 Examine it under the microscope: using low power first, then high power.

5 Watch the amoeba moving.

6 Make outline drawings of it at one minute intervals to show its changes in shape.

How would you describe the process by which movement takes place?

# Investigation 2

## Looking at Euglena and other protists

1 Obtain a jar of dirty pond water which has been standing in the laboratory for some weeks.

2 Suck up a little of the water into a pipette and put a drop onto a slide.

3 Cover the drop with a coverslip.

4 Examine your slide under the microscope.

5 Look out for protists in the water.

If you see any green ones they may be *Euglena* or one of its relatives.

You may see the ones illustrated in Figure 3, and possibly some others as well.

6 How does each one move?

7 If you see *Paramecium*, look for a contractile vacuole: you may see it filling up and collapsing.

# Assignments

1 Make a list of those structures shown in the diagram of *Amoeba* in Figure 1 which are not found in a typical animal cell.

2 Each word in the left-hand column below is related to one of the words in the right-hand column. Write them down in the correct pairs.

| | |
|---|---|
| contractile vacuole | runny |
| flagellum | reproduction |
| food vacuole | digestion |
| endoplasm | water |
| splitting | movement |

3 What do each of the following pairs of structures have in common:
a) light-sensitive swelling and pigment spot,
b) ectoplasm and endoplasm,
c) food vacuole and chloroplast,
d) cell membrane and pellicle?

4 What structures in an amoeba do the same job as:
a) your lungs,
b) your skin,
c) your kidneys,
d) your legs,
e) your intestine?

5 Write down five ways in which *Amoeba* is simpler than a human, either in its structure or in the way it carries out its life processes.

6 List two ways in which *Euglena* is like a plant, and two ways in which it is like an animal.

# Bacteria

*Bacteria are
very small organisms
with a simple cell structure
and remarkable powers
of survival.*

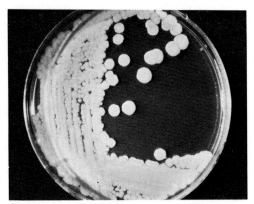

**Figure 1** Bacterial colonies growing on an agar plate. The colonies differ in size, shape and colour.

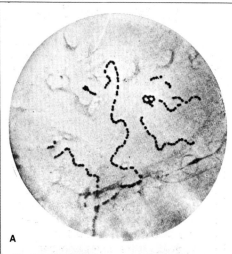

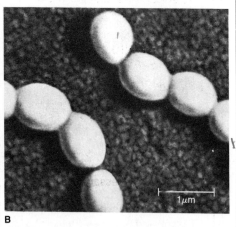

**Figure 2** A shows streptococcal bacteria as seen with a light microscope. B shows the same kind of bacteria as seen with an electron microscope.

## What are bacteria?

Bacteria are amongst the smallest organisms. They were discovered in the seventeenth century by a Dutch draper, Antonie van Leeuwenhoek. He was a skilful amateur biologist, and he saw them under a microscope which he had made himself.

Bacteria occur almost everywhere: in air, water, soil, and inside other organisms. They like warmth, but some can survive at the tops of high mountains such as the Alps where it is very cold. Others live in hot springs at near-boiling temperatures. Many of them are saprotrophs, feeding on dead animals and plants and making them decay. Others are parasites and cause serious diseases.

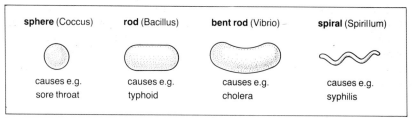

**Figure 3** Different types of bacteria have different shapes. This is one way scientists can tell them apart.

## How can we grow bacteria?

Scientists must be able to grow bacteria in the laboratory. This is necessary if we are to investigate them, and find ways of fighting the diseases they cause.

To grow them, bacteria must be given moisture, warmth and plenty of food. Many years ago it was discovered that they will grow on the surface of a jelly-like material obtained from sea weed. This is called **agar**. Various food substances are added to the agar: this makes it an ideal **nutrient medium** in which to grow, or **culture**, bacteria (Investigation).

The agar is usually put in a shallow **petri dish**. This must be sterilised beforehand and kept covered, otherwise moulds may grow on the agar. To speed up their growth the bacteria should be kept warm: this is best achieved by putting the petri dish in an **incubator**, a warm box in which the temperature can be kept constant.

Now suppose you put some bacteria on the surface of some nutrient agar. In the course of the next day or two the bacteria multiply into **colonies**. Each colony consists of thousands of bacteria clumped together. The individual bacteria are too small to be seen with the naked eye, but the colonies are clearly visible (Figure 1).

Bacterial colonies vary in size, shape and colour, according to the type of bacteria present. How many types can you see in Figure 1?

## What size are bacteria?

A typical bacterium is about a thousandth of a millimetre wide. This is far too small to be seen with the naked eye.

Look at Figure 2. Both pictures show streptococcal bacteria, which can cause sore throats. The top picture shows the bacteria as you would see them under a good light microscope. They are enlarged about 500 times.

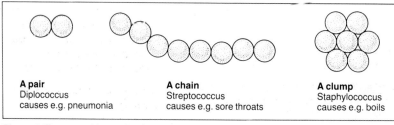

**Figure 4** The coccal bacteria often occur in pairs, chains or clumps.

The bottom picture shows the same kind of bacteria as they appear in the electron microscope. Here they are enlarged about 12 000 times. If a pinhead was magnified to the same extent, it would easily cover a tennis court, with plenty of room to spare.

Bacteria are small enough for gas exchange and excretion to be carried out by diffusion.

### The structure of bacteria

Bacteria vary in their shapes (Figure 3). In some cases they are linked together in chains or small groups (Figure 4). Some have whip-like **flagella** which lash from side to side, propelling the body along.

Thanks to very careful work using the electron microscope, we now know that bacteria are single cells, but the cell is simpler than those of most other organisms (Figure 5). The body is surrounded by a thin **cell membrane**. Beyond this is a protective **cell wall**. In addition some bacteria are surrounded by a slimy **capsule**. This gives them extra protection and prevents them drying out.

### How do bacteria survive bad conditions?

Many bacteria are very good at surviving bad conditions such as poisons, drought and heat They do this by forming a thick protective coat round themselves. They are then known as **spores**. Inside the spore the bacterial cell becomes **dormant** and may remain so for a long time.

When conditions become satisfactory again, the spore bursts open and the bacterial cell is released (Figure 6). It then resumes its normal life. The spores of some bacteria can survive for more than 50 years.

In good conditions bacteria reproduce extremely quickly by splitting in two again and again. Their spores and rapid reproduction can make the disease-causing bacteria very difficult to get rid of.

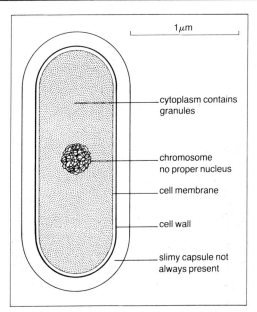

Figure 5  Diagram of a typical bacterial cell.

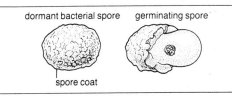

Figure 6  On the left is a bacterial spore with a thick protective coat. On the right the coat has split open and the bacterial cell is coming out.

## Investigation

### Culturing bacteria

1 Obtain a petri dish containing sterile nutrient agar. Keep the lid on whenever possible.

2 Your teacher will give you a petri dish containing a colony of bacteria.

3 Sterilise a wire loop by passing it quickly through a small bunsen flame.

4 Scoop up a small piece of the colony on the end of the wire loop.

5 With the wire loop make a zig-zag streak on the surface of the agar in the new petri dish.

6 Replace the lid on the petri dish and fix it firmly with sellotape.

7 Place the petri dish upside down in an incubator at 37°C.

8 After a day or two examine the dish.

Have the bacteria grown?

---

CARE   Work with bacteria can be dangerous and should be carried out under strict supervision by the teacher.

**Always wash your hands after working with bacteria.**

## Assignments

1 List two ways in which a bacterial cell differs from a typical animal cell.

2 How many bacteria could be fitted side by side in a row the same length as the second line of this question? (Assume that the bacteria are spherical with a diameter of one micrometre.)

3 Give three ways by which a scientist can tell the difference between different kinds of bacteria.

4 Write down two ways in which bacteria feed, and two ways by which they survive bad conditions.

5 In medical research it is important to be able to grow particular kinds of bacteria on their own. Why do you think this is necessary? (Hint: use the index!)

# Viruses

*It used to be thought that bacteria were the smallest organisms. We now know that there are even smaller ones. These are viruses. Viruses cause many diseases such as colds and influenza.*

## How were viruses discovered?

Towards the end of the nineteenth century a way was found of getting rid of bacteria from a liquid. You filter the liquid by passing it through a very fine sieve made of unglazed porcelain. The sieve holds back the bacteria, so the liquid is freed of them.

In 1900 a Dutch professor called Beijerinck did an experiment on some tobacco plants. These plants had a disease in which the leaves became spotted: it is called mosaic disease (Figure 1).

Beijerinck got some juice out of the leaves. He filtered the juice so as to remove any bacteria present. He then rubbed the juice onto the leaves of a healthy plant. Although the bacteria had been removed, the leaves soon went spotty and developed the disease.

How can we explain this? One possible explanation is that the disease is caused by organisms which are smaller than bacteria. Being smaller, they pass through the sieve which holds back bacteria.

We now know that this is the correct explanation. But at the time no one could actually *see* these organisms: the electron microscope had not yet been invented, and there were no other microscopes powerful enough. In fact Professor Beijerinck did not think the infection was caused by an organism at all, but by an infectious fluid. He called this fluid *virus*, a Latin word which means 'poison'. However, later experiments showed that the filtered fluid definitely contained organisms of some kind.

In the early 1940s, the electron microscope started to be used. Juice obtained from diseased tobacco plants was examined in this powerful microscope. The fluid turned out to contain tiny objects like those in Figure 2. For the first time viruses could actually be seen.

## The structure of viruses

Viruses are so small that we have to express their size in a unit called the **nanometre** (nm). A nanometre is one millionth of a millimetre. A typical virus is about 100 nm wide. It is difficult to imagine anything so small, but you can look at it this way: if you lined them up in a row across this page, there would be over two million of them.

Viruses have various shapes. Some are rod-shaped. Others look spherical, though on close examination they turn out to be many sided (Figure 3). Most viruses have a simple shape. However, the last one in Figure 3 has quite a

**Figure 1** This tobacco plant is suffering from mosaic disease. Notice the spots on the lower leaves. Studies carried out on this disease led to the discovery of viruses.

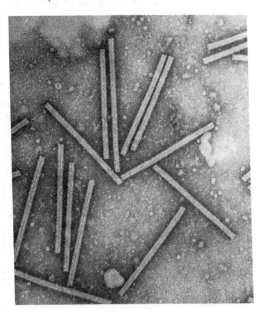

**Figure 2** These viruses, seen here in the electron microscope, cause mosaic disease in tobacco plants. In this picture they are magnified 85 000 times.

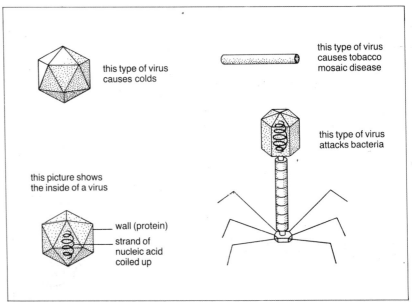

this type of virus causes colds

this type of virus causes tobacco mosaic disease

this type of virus attacks bacteria

this picture shows the inside of a virus

wall (protein)

strand of nucleic acid coiled up

**Figure 3** These diagrams show the structure of viruses. They are not drawn to the same scale.

complex body.

Viruses are simpler than any other organisms, including bacteria. There is no nucleus or cytoplasm, so we cannot call them cells. There is a **wall** which is made of protein; inside is a coiled up strand of **nucleic acid** (see page 306).

## How do viruses reproduce?

The way viruses reproduce is remarkable, and it explains why they are so harmful. They can only reproduce inside the cells of a living organism.

One way in which they reproduce is shown in Figure 4. First the virus attaches itself to the surface of the cell. Then it injects its strand of nucleic acid into the inside, rather like a doctor injects a person with a hypodermic needle. The nucleic acid then multiplies into lots of separate strands. Round each strand a new virus is formed. The materials for making the new viruses come from inside the cell. So the virus is a thief, robbing the cell of its contents. Eventually, the cell bursts open, and the new viruses are set free.

The whole process takes about half an hour. Thousands of new viruses may be released from a single cell, and then they attack more cells. No wonder we feel ill when we have got flu!

Different viruses attack different cells. For example, the common cold virus attacks cells in the nose and throat. The much more serious poliomyelitis virus attacks nerve cells in the spinal cord, which is why the disease often leaves people paralysed.

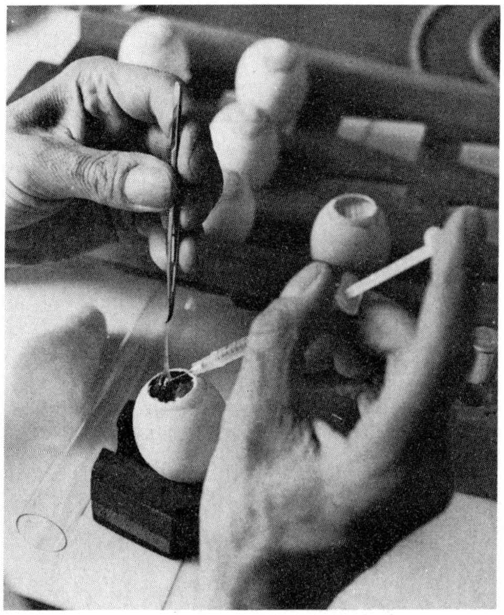

## Growing viruses

Scientists need to be able to grow (or culture) viruses in the laboratory. This is necessary for understanding them, and for developing ways of protecting people against them (see pages 335–6).

Unfortunately, you cannot grow viruses on agar jelly as you can bacteria. This is because they need living cells in order to multiply. So you have to grow them on living tissue. Fertile hens' eggs are sometimes used for this purpose. The virus which you want to cultivate is injected into the eggs, where it proceeds to multiply (Figure 5).

Nowadays it is possible to take a few cells out of an animal or a plant, and grow them on their own in the laboratory. This procedure is called **tissue culture**. It provides a convenient source of cells for growing viruses.

**Figure 5** Influenza viruses being injected into a chicken embryo for growing in the laboratory. Viruses can only be grown inside living cells.

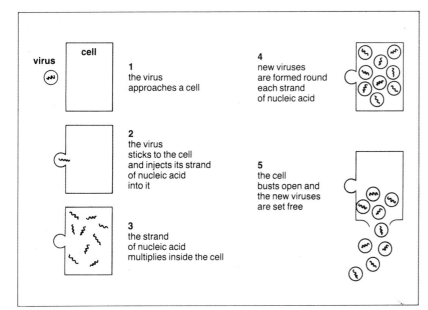

**virus**    **cell**

**1**
the virus
approaches a cell

**2**
the virus
sticks to the cell
and injects its strand
of nucleic acid
into it

**3**
the strand
of nucleic acid
multiplies inside the cell

**4**
new viruses
are formed round
each strand
of nucleic acid

**5**
the cell
busts open and
the new viruses
are set free

**Figure 4** Viruses can only reproduce inside a living cell. Here a virus attacks and destroys a cell.

## Assignments

1  Name four diseases of humans, and one disease of plants, which are caused by viruses.

2  What fraction of a millimetre is (a) a micrometre, and (b) a nanometre?

   Why is it better to express the size of viruses in nanometres rather than micrometres?

3  What part did (a) tobacco plants and (b) unglazed porcelain play in the way viruses were discovered?

4  Why do you think viruses are always harmful?

5  The virus shown at the top of Figure 3 (the one which causes colds) is approximately 70 nanometres wide. How many could be fitted side by side in a row the same length as the fifth line of this assignment?

6  Your friend says that viruses are not really living organisms. What do you think?

# Pin mould

*Pin mould is
one of many moulds
which grow on food.
It is a fungus.*

**Figure 1** Pin mould growing on a piece of stale bread.

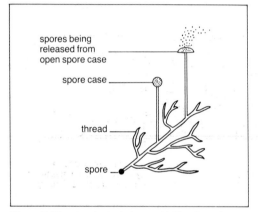

spores being
released from
open spore case

spore case

thread

spore

**Figure 2** The structure of pin mould. The threads have grown from the spore on the left, and new spores are being released from the spore case on the right.

Look at Figure 1. This is what a piece of damp bread looks like after it has been left lying around for a few days. It looks as if it's covered with cotton wool: this is pin mould. To understand how the bread got like this we must study the life cycle of the mould.

Fungi produce **spores**. These are small and light, like specks of dust, and they float through the air. For a spore of pin mould to develop, it must land on a damp surface (Investigation 1).

After the spore has landed, it bursts open and a thread grows out (Figure 2). The thread grows over the surface of the bread, branching this way and that. Eventually the bread becomes covered by a tangled mass of fine silvery threads. The threads are called **hyphae**, and the whole mass of threads is called a **mycelium**. You can see the way the threads branch by looking at them under the microscope (Investigation 2).

After a time short branches grow upwards. The tip of each branch swells up into a little knob. These knobs are **spore cases**. They are known as **sporangia** (singular: sporangium). Inside each one hundreds of spores are formed. Eventually the spore case opens, and the spores are released. They are then carried away by wind or in some cases by people's fingers or small animals such as insects. If one of the spores lands on a suitable surface, a new mould develops and the cycle is repeated.

Scientists have looked at the insides of the threads under the microscope. They contain **cytoplasm** and many **nuclei**, but they are not divided up into separate cells. There is a **vacuole** in the centre.

The mould feeds on the bread, soaking up its goodness. The threads produce digestive enzymes which break down the solid starch into liquid sugar. This is then absorbed by the threads. Pin mould can live on many other things besides bread: jam is a great favourite, and even old football boots will do. The threads always stay near the surface. This is because they need oxygen for respiration. Oxygen diffuses into them, and carbon dioxide diffuses out. You may have noticed that when jam goes mouldy the mould is only at the surface; this is because of its need for oxygen.

Pin mould and many other fungi are saprotrophs and help to make things decay. In a later Topic we shall see that some fungi are parasites, particularly of plants (pages 348–9).

We have seen that pin mould can reproduce by means of spores. This is its asexual method. It can also reproduce sexually by a process called conjugation: the tips of two threads come together and their contents fuse (page 250).

## Investigation 1

**To find out if pin mould needs moisture to grow**

1 Obtain two slices of dry bread.

2 Put one slice in a dish. Sprinkle a little water on it. Put a lid on.

3 Put the other slice in another dish. Leave it dry. Cover it as before.

4 Place the two dishes side by side.

5 Look at the dishes a week later.

Compare the two pieces of bread.

Which piece has the most mould on it?

Is moisture needed for the mould to grow?

## Investigation 2

**Looking at pin mould**

1 Examine pin mould at various stages in its growth.

Can you see the structures shown in Figure 2?

2 With forceps pick up a few threads of pin mould.

3 Put them on a slide with a drop of water. Put on a coverslip.

4 Look at the threads under the microscope: low power first, then high power.

5 Make a drawing of a few threads to show how they branch.

## Assignments

1 Pin mould is a saprotroph. What does this mean?

2 If a piece of bread is kept completely dry it will not go mouldy. Why?

3 Fungi usually produce very large numbers of spores. Why is this necessary?

4 In some classifications fungi are regarded as plants. Write a short essay arguing for or against regarding pin mould as a plant.

5 Draw a diagram of a short length of a hypha of pin mould on a very large scale.

# *Spirogyra*

*In a pond, you may see slender green threads floating about. These are likely to be Spirogyra or one of its close relatives.*

*Spirogyra* is a green alga. It is one of the simplest plants to be made up of many cells (Investigation).

The threads are long unbranched filaments, cylindrical in shape. They are coated with a thin layer of **slime** which prevents them getting tangled. Each filament is made up of a chain of cells. The cells are all identical, so this is an example of an organism in which there is *no* division of labour between cells (see page 32). Figure 1 shows some filaments under the microscope.

The structure of one of the cells is shown in Figure 2. It is bounded by a cellulose **cell wall**. There is a large **vacuole**, and the **nucleus** is suspended in the centre by slender strands of cytoplasm. *Spirogyra* feeds entirely by photosynthesis, for which purpose it has a **chloroplast**. This is shaped like a ribbon, and runs in a spiral round the inside of the cell. **Starch grains**, produced by photosynthesis, are stored in the chloroplast in special bodies called **pyrenoids**. Gas exchange takes place by diffusion.

The filaments of *Spirogyra* often get broken up into fragments. In good conditions these can grow into new filaments: the cells divide across the middle. In this way the filaments gradually increase in length. This process is called **fragmentation** and it is a form of asexual reproduction.

*Spirogyra* also reproduces sexually by a process of conjugation which is described on page 250.

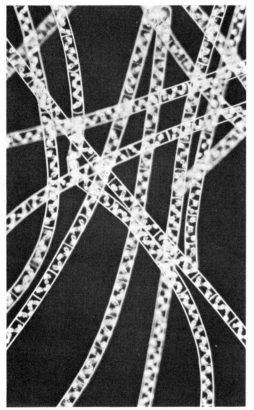

**Figure 1** *Spirogyra* seen under the light microscope. magnified about 250 times.

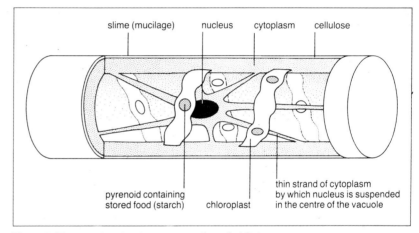

slime (mucilage)   nucleus   cytoplasm   cellulose

pyrenoid containing stored food (starch)    chloroplast

thin strand of cytoplasm by which nucleus is suspended in the centre of the vacuole

**Figure 2** Diagram showing the structure of a cell of *Spirogyra*.

# *Investigation*

### Looking at Spirogyra

1 Obtain a jar of water containing *Spirogyra*.

What does *Spirogyra* look like?

2 With forceps lift a little *Spirogyra* out of the jar, and put it on a slide with a little water.

3 Cover it with a coverslip, then look at it under the microscope: low power first, then high power.

4 Notice that *Spirogyra* consists of slender filaments which are made up of cells.

Are all the cells identical?

5 Look at one cell in detail.

Which of the structures shown in Figure 2 can you see?

How many chloroplasts are there in each cell?

6 With a pipette put a drop of iodine to one side of the coverslip. It will immediately flow under it.

7 Draw the iodine across by pulling water from the other side of the coverslip with a piece of filter paper.

8 As the iodine moves across, it will stain any starch blue-black.

Where is starch located in *Spirogyra*? How do you think the starch gets there?

# *Assignments*

1 What do each of the following pairs have in common:
   a) chloroplasts and pyrenoids,
   b) cell wall and cellulose,
   c) gas exchange and diffusion,
   d) fragmentation and reproduction?

2 Describe how you would measure the width of a *Spirogyra* filament.

3 Make a plasticine model of a cell of *Spirogyra* showing the structures in Figure 2 except the cytoplasm.

4 In what ways is a cell of *Spirogyra*
   a) similar to, and
   b) different from, the plant cell in Figure 4, page 31?

# Hydra

*Hydra is one of the simplest animals that is made of many cells. In many respects its body works like ours but more simply.*

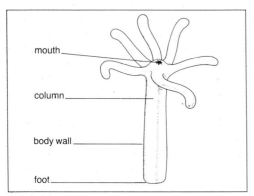

**Figure 1** *Hydra*, one of the simplest many-celled animals.

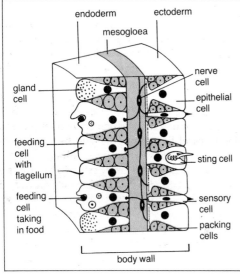

**Figure 2** The body wall of *Hydra*, showing the different kinds of cells.

*Hydra* lives in ponds and ditches (Figure 1). It gets its name from a legendary monster which had many heads: every time its heads were cut off, new ones grew in their place. *Hydra* is similar: if you cut it into pieces, each piece can grow into a new hydra.

You can discover a lot about these animals by looking at them under a hand lens or low-powered microscope (Investigation).

The structure of *Hydra* is shown in Figure 1. Its body consists of a cylindrical **column**. At the top of the column is the **mouth**, surrounded by about six **tentacles**. At the bottom is the **foot**. The foot is sticky and is used for attaching the hydra to stones or weeds.

The tentacles are armed with special **sting cells**. The tentacles wave around and are used for catching water fleas and other small animals which are unfortunate enough to swim into them. The sting cells contain a poison which paralyses the prey. *Hydra's* sting cells could never hurt a human. However, one of its relatives, the Arctic jellyfish, has tentacles ten metres long with sting cells that can kill a human.

The mouth opens into a large **digestive cavity.** Here food is broken down. The mouth is the only opening into this cavity.

The body wall is made of two layers of cells: the **ectoderm** towards the outside, and the **endoderm** towards the inside. In between is a thin layer of jelly-like material called the **mesogloea**. The endoderm lines the digestive cavity. As the body wall is quite thin, gas exchange and excretion can take place by diffusion.

The body wall is composed of seven different types of cells (Figure 2). Each cell has a particular job to do. As well as the sting cells already mentioned, there are **sensory cells** which react to touch, **nerve cells** which transmit messages from one part of the body to another, and **gland cells** which shed enzymes into the digestive cavity. The surface of the body is lined with **epithelial cells** which fit together to form a protective skin. The inner ends of these cells are drawn out into slender **muscle tails** which enable the hydra to move. Finally **packing cells** fill the spaces between the other cells; they can develop into the other kinds of cells if the hydra is damaged. It's largely because of these remarkable cells that small pieces of a hydra can grow into new individuals.

In a one-celled animal like *Amoeba*, all jobs have to be carried out by one cell. But in *Hydra* different jobs are carried out by different types of cells. Each type of cell is specialised to perform a particular task. In other words, *Hydra* shows **division of labour** between its cells.

*Hydra* reproduces asexually by budding off new hydras from the side of its body. It can also reproduce sexually by producing eggs and sperms as described on page 250.

## Investigation

**Looking at Hydra**

1 Obtain a watch glass containing a hydra. Wait for the hydra to open out.

2 Look at the hydra through a hand lens.

 Can you see the parts of the body shown in Figure 1?

 Does the hydra change its shape?

3 Gently poke one of the tentacles with a needle.

 How does the hydra respond?

How do you think the response is produced?

4 Put the watch glass on the stage of a microscope, supporting it underneath with a glass slide.

5 Look at it under *low power*. (Don't try using high power.)

 Can you see the difference between the two layers of cells which make up the body wall?

 Can you see any sting cells in the outer layer?

## Assignments

1 What job do *Hydra's* epithelial cells do besides forming its 'skin'?

2 Although most of *Hydra's* sensory cells are in its outer layer of cells, there are a few in the inner layer as well. What do you think their job is there?

3 *Hydra's* packing cells are sometimes called 'reserve cells'. Why do you think they are given this name?

# The earthworm

*You may come across earthworms if you are digging the garden. They live in burrows in the soil.*

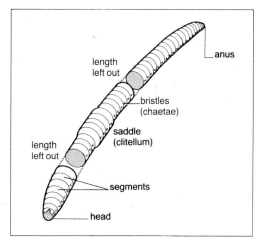

**Figure 1** This diagram shows the external structure of the earthworm.

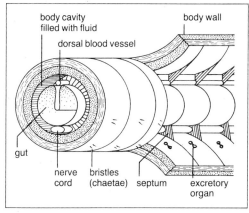

**Figure 2** This diagram shows the main structures and organs inside the earthworm.

A full-grown earthworm is about 15 cm long. Its external structure suits it well to burrowing through the soil (Investigation). The body is elongated and has a streamlined shape. The skin is soft and covered in **mucus** (slime). There are no sense organs or other structures sticking out which might get in the way as it pushes through the soil.

The outside of the body is marked by a series of **rings** (Figure 1). These divide the body up into **segments**. Sticking out of each segment are four pairs of stiff bristles called **chaetae**. The worm can push these out, or pull them in. They enable the worm to grip the sides of its burrow as it moves along.

There is a **mouth** at the front end, and an **anus** at the back end. The **head** is barely distinguishable from the rest of the body, except that it is rather darker in colour. About a third of the way back there is a region where the skin is thicker than in other places. This is called the **saddle** or **clitellum**. It plays an important part in reproduction.

Figure 2 shows the internal structure of the earthworm in simplified form. Much of the inside is taken up by a large **body cavity**. This contains a watery fluid. The body cavity is divided up into segments by a series of partitions, called **septa** (singular: septum). They correspond to the rings on the outside of the worm.

The body cavity is surrounded by the **body wall**. This is made of muscle: when the muscles contract the worm changes its shape. Movement takes place by means of 'bulges' which pass down the body from one end to the other.

Running down the centre of the body cavity is the **gut**. Worms eat soil, and the gut has a special region called the **gizzard** which grinds it up (page 385).

Beneath the gut is the **nerve cord**: this is continuous with a very small **brain** at the extreme front end. From the nerve cord, slender **nerves** pass out to the body wall muscles in each segment.

Gas exchange takes place all over the moist body surface. However, the animal is too bulky for oxygen to diffuse to the innermost tissues quickly enough and so the earthworm has a **blood system** which contains red blood similar to man's. The main blood vessel lies above the gut: because of its position on the top side of the body, it is called the **dorsal blood vessel**.

Nearly all the segments contain a pair of **excretory organs**. Each one is a little tube which runs from the body cavity to the outside. It gets rid of poisonous nitrogenous waste. The earthworm is too large for excretory waste simply to diffuse across the surface as it does in smaller organisms.

In parts of Asia, Australia and South America there are huge 'giant earthworms'. Some of them may be three or four metres long. They too live in the soil, and people say that you can hear rumbling and gurgling sounds as they move through their burrows underground.

## Investigation

### Looking at the earthworm

You will be given a live earthworm in a dish.

1 Observe the structure of the worm.

Can you see the structures shown in Figure 1?

2 Put the worm on a piece of paper. Let it crawl forward.

Can you hear a scratching noise? What is it caused by?

3 Put a coin in its way.

What does the worm do when its head touches the coin?

4 Tap the worm's head with a blunt instrument such as a pencil.

What does the worm do?

5 With a pipette place a drop of vinegar (acetic acid) on the worm's head.

What does the worm do this time?

What part do these responses play in the normal life of the worm?

## Assignments

1 What does the earthworm use the following structures for:

chaetae, mucus, clitellum, body wall, circular muscle?

2 List five ways in which the earthworm is adapted for burrowing.

3 The earthworm is much larger than an animal like *Hydra*. What effect does this have on:
a) the way its organs get oxygen,
b) the way it gets rid of waste substances?

# Insects

*Nearly a million different species of insects have been discovered. They are one of the most successful groups of animals.*

**Figure 1** This dragonfly illustrates the basic design of insects.

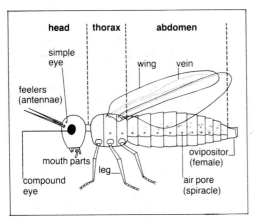

**Figure 2** This diagram shows the external structure of a typical insect.

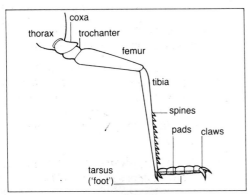

**Figure 3** The leg of an insect. This diagram is based on the hind leg of a locust.

## The structure of an insect

You can study a typical insect by examining a locust, grasshopper or cockroach (Investigations 1 and 2).

The body consists of three main regions: the **head, thorax** and **abdomen** (Figure 2). Each is divided into segments, which are clearly visible in the abdomen. The whole body is covered with a tough **cuticle**.

All insects have three pairs of legs, one pair on each segment of the thorax. Each leg has a series of **joints** where they bend. The foot or **tarsus** has claws and sticky pads which enable insects like flies to walk on a smooth wall, or upside down on a ceiling (Figure 3).

Most insects have two pairs of **wings** which are attached to the second and third segments of the thorax. These wings are supported by a network of tough veins, rather like a leaf.

On each side of the thorax and abdomen there is a row of tiny holes called **spiracles**. These let air into a system of branching tubes through which oxygen passes to all parts of the body. The head has various sense organs. A pair of jointed feelers, called **antennae**, stick out in front. The insect sees with a pair of large **compound eyes**. There are also several smaller **simple eyes** which register changes in light intensity.

Round the mouth there are feeding structures called **mouth parts**. The mouth parts of different insects are adapted for feeding on different kinds of food (see page 108). At the rear end of the abdomen is the anus through which undigested food and excretory substances are passed.

Close to the anus is the **reproductive opening**. In the male there is a device by which sperms are put into the female. In the female the reproductive opening is flanked by various plates and valves which form an egg tube (**ovipositor**). The eggs pass down this tube when they are laid.

Insects are generally rather small. Why is this? One reason is their cuticle. If insects got larger, the cuticle would be so heavy that they would have difficulty holding themselves up and moving around.

Another thing that limits the size of insects is their method of breathing (see page 121). This depends mainly on **diffusion** which is a slow way of getting oxygen to the tissues, and is effective only over short distances.

## The cuticle

The insect's cuticle is made of a tough material called **chitin**. It consists of two layers (Figure 4). The outer layer is hard and rigid; the inner layer is soft and flexible. On the surface is a thin layer of **wax** which makes the cuticle waterproof and enables insects to live in dry places.

In certain parts of the body the hard outer layer of the cuticle is absent, leaving only the flexible inner layer. At these points the cuticle can bend. These joints enable the insect to move: they work like the joints in a suit of armour. Muscles are attached to the inside of the cuticle, and they bring about movement.

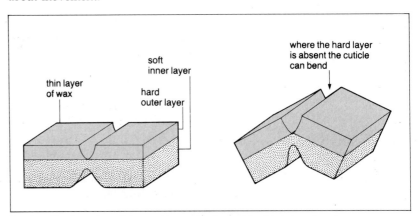

**Figure 4** The insect's cuticle provides protection but is able to bend.

**Figure 5** This picture taken with a scanning electron microscope, shows the compound eyes and feelers on the head of a fly.

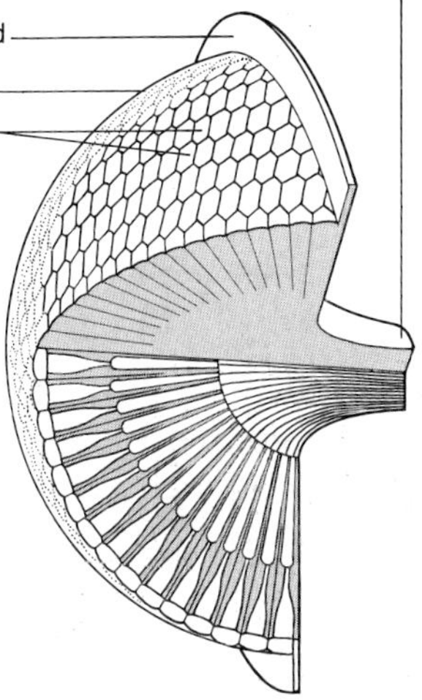

nerve to brain

side of head

surface of eye

ommatidia

**Figure 6** The insect's compound eye is made up of numerous ommatidia.

## The compound eye

The compound eye is composed of numerous little eyes called **ommatidia** (Figures 5 and 6). Each ommatidium forms an image of the world immediately in front of it. The whole eye forms an image which looks rather like a picture made out of lots of dots. The insect's view of the world is probably blurred and indistinct. However, it has a very large field of vision, because the eyes cover a large area of the head. This makes them very good at detecting movement.

## Investigation 1

**Looking at insects**

1  Obtain a dead grasshopper or cockroach.

2  Look at its external structure.

   Can you see all the structures shown in Figure 2?

3  Examine the hind leg in detail.

   Do your observations agree with the diagram in Figure 3?

4  Draw a side view of your insect.

   Label its parts as fully as you can, using Figures 2 and 3 to help you.

5  Obtain the following insects: beetle, housefly, wasp, ant.

6  Examine them carefully.

7  In each case write down the main ways the insect differs from the grasshopper or cockroach.

## Investigation 2

**Looking at live insects**

1  Look at live adult grasshoppers or cockroaches in a container with their usual food.

2  Watch them moving: observe the action of the legs.

3  Can your insect climb and hold onto things?

   How does it do it?

4  Watch your insect feeding.

   What are its mouth parts doing?

   Do the legs play any part in feeding?

5  Look at the insect's abdomen.

   Can you see any pulsating movements of the abdomen?

   What might be the function of these movements?

Make brief notes, with sketches, on your observations.

## Assignments

1  Give the common name, and briefly explain the function, of each of the following:
   a) ovipositor,    c) tarsus,
   b) antenna,      d) spiracle.

2  Write down five ways in which an insect's body differs from yours.

3  An insect's cuticle is described as an exoskeleton. Why?

4  How does a fly manage to walk upside down on a ceiling?

5  Suggest two reasons why it is an advantage to an insect to be small.

6  Three hundred million years ago there were some very large insects. For example a certain dragonfly had a wing span of nearly a metre. Why do you think these large insects died out?

7  Why is it an advantage to an insect to have eyes covering such a large area of its head?

# Fish

*Many organisms live in water, but the greatest experts at this are fish. In order to survive under water, they have many special features.*

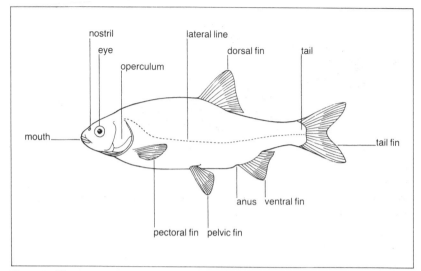

Figure 1   These diagrams show the structure of a typical bony fish.

Figure 2   A typical bony fish.

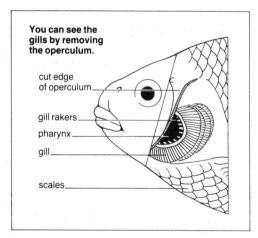

**You can see the gills by removing the operculum.**

cut edge of operculum
gill rakers
pharynx
gill
scales

Figure 3   The gills of a bony fish. The operculum has been removed.

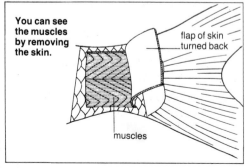

**You can see the muscles by removing the skin.**

flap of skin turned back

muscles

Figure 4   The muscles in the tail region of a bony fish.

## Bony fish

As the name implies, these fish have a skeleton made of bone. They include sea water fish such as the flying fish, and *Tilapia* of fresh water (Investigation). Figures 1 and 2 will help you to identify the parts of the body.

The skin is covered with **scales** which overlap each other like the tiles on the roof of a house. They protect the fish, and prevent water passing through the skin. The body is streamlined, enabling the fish to move quickly and smoothly through the water.

On either side of the head there is a flap of skin, which is stiffened by bones. This is called the **operculum**. Underneath the operculum there are four feathery **gills** side by side — they are used for breathing (Figure 3).

At the posterior end of the body there is a **tail**. Underneath the skin there are muscles, which are arranged in a series of W-shaped blocks. These muscles play an important part in swimming, and they are the part of the fish that people eat (Figure 4).

At various points there are **fins**. Each fin consists of a thin flap of skin supported by slender spines. Some of the fins are arranged in pairs and stick out from the sides of the body. We refer to them as **paired fins**: they include the pectoral fins just behind the head, and the pelvic fins a little further back. The fins help with movement and keep the body stable.

The other fins are single and are attached to the mid-line of the fish. We call them the **median fins**. The median fins include the dorsal, ventral and tail fins. Some fish have more than one dorsal fin, and there is a good deal of variation in their exact positions.

Fish have good sense organs. The **nostrils** are used for smelling, but they play no part in breathing. The **eyes** can see very well under water. Running along each side of the body is a **lateral line** just beneath the surface of the skin; it contains sense organs which detect movements of the water.

Inside the mouth are rows of identical teeth. They are constantly falling out throughout life and are replaced by new ones which grow in their place. The anus is on the ventral side of the body, about two thirds of the way back.

Most bony fish feed on small organisms such as worms, crabs and plankton (see page 24). As the food passes through the pharynx, it is prevented from getting between the gills by the **gill rakers**: these are slender bars which stick out from the bases of the gills. You can see them in Figure 3.

Most bony fish possess a **swim bladder**. This is a bag of air, rather like a balloon, which is found towards the upper side of the body cavity. It helps to keep the fish floating in the water.

Bony fish usually reproduce by the males and females letting out their sperms and eggs into the surrounding water where fertilisation takes place.

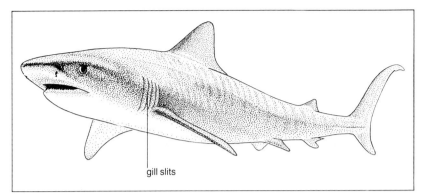

**Figure 5** Cartilaginous fish lack an operculum. In this drawing of a tiger shark, notice the five separate gill slits.

## Cartilaginous fish

These fish have a skeleton made of cartilage (gristle). They include dogfish, sharks and rays.

One of the main differences between bony and cartilaginous fish concerns their gills. In bony fish the gills are covered by the operculum shown in Figure 1. However, in cartilaginous fish there is no operculum; instead a series of **gill slits**, five in all, open separately on either side of the head (Figure 5).

Another difference is that in cartilaginous fish the male has a pair of claspers for putting his sperms into the female's reproductive opening. The eggs are fertilised inside the female and each one is enclosed inside a horny case before it is laid.

Sharks and rays do not have a swim bladder, so their only way of staying up in the water is by swimming. If they stop swimming they sink.

## The shapes and sizes of fish

There is a lot of variation in the shape of fish. Some are long and thin, like the eel. Others are flat, like the plaice: it is flattened from side to side and lies on the sand at the bottom of the sea. Some have strange shapes, such as the sea-horse; and the mud-skipper has pectoral fins like little legs: it lives in mangrove swamps (Figure 6).

Fish also vary greatly in size. The largest fish in the world is the whale shark, which can be twice as long as a bus. However, it feeds on plankton and is quite harmless. The largest flesh-eating fish is the great white shark which lives in some of the warmer seas of the world. It can be over 11 metres long and is a menace to swimmers. At the other end of the scale, certain tropical fish are a mere centimetre or two in length.

**Figure 6** Two unusual fish. Left: the mudskipper; its leg-like pectoral fins enable it to walk over the mud. Right: the sea horse; it swims by waving its dorsal fin and clings to weeds with its tail.

# Frogs and toads

*Frogs and toads
are amphibians.
They live in two different
environments: in water
and on land.*

**Figure 1** An amphibian.

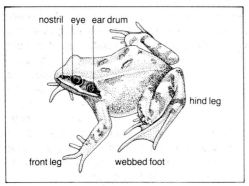

**Figure 2** This diagram shows the external structure of a typical amphibian.

**Figure 3** A frog catching an insect. It's all over in a tenth of a second

You can learn a lot about these fascinating animals by looking at their external structure (Investigation).

The **skin** is moist. This is because it contains glands which produce slime (mucus) all over the surface. The lungs aren't very efficient, so gas exchange takes place across the skin as well. For this to be possible the skin must be moist. The skin has patches of colour, particularly green, black or brown, which help to camouflage and protect the animal.

The front legs are short and stumpy. The hind legs are much longer and there is skin between the toes; in other words the feet are **webbed** (Figure 2), which makes them good for swimming.

Just above the mouth there is a pair of **nostrils**: these open into the mouth cavity and air is drawn in through them when the animal breathes. The **eyes** are high up on the head and bulge out: they give the animal good all-round vision, enabling it to detect movement quickly and escape from danger. The **eardrum** is on the surface of the head and there is no flap of skin behind the ear as there is in man.

Between the back legs there is an opening which leads into a small chamber inside the body. This chamber is called the **cloaca**. Urine, faeces and sex cells (eggs and sperms) all pass out of the body via this chamber. Amphibians mate in water and the eggs are fertilised by the male's sperms as they leave the body. The way they develop is explained on page 284.

If you look inside the mouth of a frog or toad you will see its **tongue**. This differs from the human tongue in that it is attached at the front of the mouth and points backwards. The tongue is used for feeding on insects. When an insect flies past, the frog or toad flicks out its tongue and catches it (Figure 3). The insect is carried to the back of the throat, then quickly swallowed.

Having to have a moist skin means that amphibians always run the risk of drying out. For this reason they must live in damp places.

Amphibians are **cold-blooded**, that is, their body temperature is the same as that of their surroundings. In cold weather they hibernate.

## Investigation

**Looking at a frog or toad**

1 Obtain a preserved frog or toad.

2 Look at its external structure.

Can you see the structures shown in Figure 2? What job does each structure do?

Why are its back legs so much longer than its front legs?

3 Open the mouth and look inside.

How does the tongue differ from yours? What part does the tongue play in feeding? Can you see, or feel, the teeth? What part do they play in feeding?

4 Watch a live frog or toad breathing and moving.

How does it carry out these two functions?

### Note
A typical frog has a smoother skin, a smaller and lighter body, longer hind legs, and more fully webbed feet than a typical toad.

## Assignments

1 Amphibians tend to be restricted to wet parts of the world. Why?

2 It has been suggested that amphibians are so good at breathing through their skin that they do not need to use their lungs.

Can you think of some evidence that would support this statement?

3 In a dry atmosphere frogs and toads lose water very quickly.

a) Why is this so?

b) Suggest an experiment which you could carry out to find out exactly how quickly a frog or toad loses water.

# Lizards

*Although turtles and crocodiles live in water, most reptiles live entirely on land. We can see how they are able to do this by studying lizards.*

Figure 1 A lizard. Notice the scaly skin, and the ear drum behind the eye.

As with amphibians, you can discover much about the lizard's life-style by examining its external structure (Investigation).

The skin is covered with **scales** rather like the tiles on the roof of a house, and it is completely dry: there are no mucous glands opening onto the surface. The scales are made of a tough protein called **keratin** and they help to protect the body. The lizard's lungs are more efficient than the amphibian's and it does not have to breathe across the skin. Like amphibians, reptiles are well camouflaged, and some can actually change colour. For example the chameleon can be yellow, green or brown, depending on its background.

Other features such as the eyes, nostrils and eardrums are similar to those of amphibians. Although chameleons catch insects with their tongue, most lizards grasp their prey with their jaws and then swallow it whole. Some lizards can move their eyes independently, giving them a better view of their surroundings. Some of them can climb up walls (Figure 2).

Lizards have a cloaca like the amphibian's. When they reproduce the male puts his sperms into the female's cloaca and fertilisation takes place inside her body. The fertilised eggs are coated with a shell before they are laid. The shell is soft, rather like paper, and there is **yolk** inside to feed the embryo as it develops. Eventually the shell breaks open and the young lizard clambers out. Amphibians ignore their eggs, but lizards incubate their eggs and some look after the young when they hatch out.

As well as protecting the embryo, the shell helps to prevent the eggs from drying out, and it means that the eggs can be laid on land.

Like fishes and amphibians, reptiles are cold-blooded. However, they can regulate their body temperature by their behaviour: they bask in the sun to raise their temperature and hide under stones when it gets too hot.

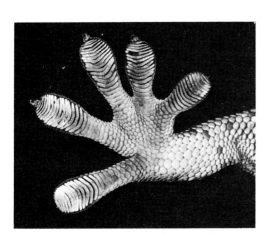

Figure 2 Hind foot of gecko showing parallel ridges and grooves. These help it to climb up walls.

## Investigation

**Looking at lizards**

1 Look at the external structure of a lizard.

Make a list of the ways it is (a) similar to, and (b) different from an amphibian such as a frog or toad. How do the differences relate to the places where they live?

2 Watch live lizards out of doors or in a vivarium.
How do they move and breathe?

If possible watch one feeding. Describe its behaviour.

3 Observe their behaviour at different times of the day.

At what times are they most active and least active?
Explain your observations.

## Assignments

1 Give two reasons why it is useful for a lizard to have a good view of its surroundings. How do reptiles in general achieve this?

2 Reptiles tend to live mainly in warm parts of the world. Why is this?

3 Suggest five ways in which lizards are better suited than frogs and toads for living on dry land.

# Birds

*Apart from insects and bats, birds are the only animals to have developed the power of active flight. It has turned them one of the most successful groups of animals.*

## The structure of birds

The external structure of a typical bird is shown in Figure 1. Most of the body is covered with **feathers**. They are made of the protein keratin, the same material that hair and reptiles' scales are made of. The legs are covered with scales.

The front limbs take the form of a pair of **wings**, which most birds use for flying. The legs are quite different from the wings. The feet have four **toes**, each ending in a **claw**. Generally, three of the toes point forward and one backwards. This enables the foot to grasp objects such as tree branches when the bird is at rest.

All birds have a **beak**. Like the feathers, this is made of keratin. Towards the base of the beak there is a pair of **nostrils** through which the bird breathes. The nostrils open into a cavity rather like the inside of our nose. This is used for smelling. However, birds' sense of smell is rather poor. Their eyesight is much more acute. There is an eardrum as in amphibians and reptiles.

The eyes have the usual upper and lower lids, plus a **third eyelid**. This works like a transparent shutter: it slides over the eye from side to side and protects the eye from dust without stopping it from seeing.

Some birds have special features which are related to the way they live. Take the feet, for example. Most birds use their feet for standing, hopping and holding onto the branches of trees. However, in some cases they are adapted to do other jobs (Figure 2).

Birds have no teeth; they peck at their food, and swallow the pieces whole. The beaks of different birds are adapted for feeding on different kinds of food. In each case, the shape of the beak fits in with the kind of food which the bird eats. This is particularly well shown by the vulture, which uses its curved beak for tearing at flesh (Figure 3). Three other examples are shown in Figure 4.

Because the food is unchewed, birds have a special stomach for breaking it up, called the **gizzard**. Seed-eating birds such as pigeons keep small stones in their gizzard: these rub against the seeds and help to grind them up.

Birds reproduce by the male putting his sperms into the cloaca of the female. The egg shell is much harder and tougher than that of reptiles and the adults take even more care of their young (see page 287).

In keeping with their active life style, birds have very efficient lungs. Leading off the lungs are a number of **air sacs** which make the body lighter and help to cool it during active flight.

## Feathers

Young birds are covered with small fluffy feathers. We call these **down feathers**. As the bird grows, its down feathers fall out and their place is taken by longer and straighter **flight feathers**. An adult bird may keep some of its down feathers, particularly round the tops of the legs.

If you look at a flight feather you will see that there is more to it than appears at first sight (Investigation). Running down the centre is the **quill**. The base of the quill is rooted in the skin: muscles are attached to it so the feather can be moved. The flat part of the feather is called the **vane**. This is composed of numerous hair-like structures called **barbs**. The barbs have further branches which interlock with one another as shown in Figure 5.

If you put your finger between the barbs, you will find that it is easy to break the connections between them. They can be connected up again by gently stroking the feather with your finger. If the connections are broken in real life, the bird puts them together again by rubbing its feathers with its beak. This is called **preening**. The bird also uses its beak to spread oil over the feathers and to remove any parasites which might be crawling amongst them. The oil is produced by a gland on the bird's back, close to the tail: the bird rubs its beak in this oil before it preens itself.

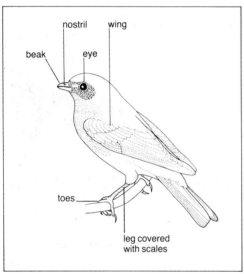

**Figure 1** The external structure of a typical bird.

nostril wing
beak eye
toes
leg covered with scales

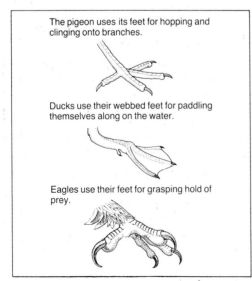

The pigeon uses its feet for hopping and clinging onto branches.

Ducks use their webbed feet for paddling themselves along on the water.

Eagles use their feet for grasping hold of prey.

**Figure 2** In some birds, the feet are adapted for jobs other than clinging to branches and hopping on the ground.

**Figure 3** These vultures are about to feed on the zebra, tearing at its flesh with their strong curved beaks.

## What jobs do feathers do?

The feathers make up the bird's **plumage**. In many ways they are like a person's clothes. They do four main jobs:

### 1 *They are needed for flight.*
Some of the largest feathers are attached to the wing. They give the wing a large surface area which helps to keep the bird up in the air (see page 235).

### 2 *They keep the bird warm.*
They do this by trapping a layer of air against the skin. Air is a poor conductor of heat, so this layer of air holds heat inside the body. Birds are therefore **warm-blooded** and can control their body temperature.

### 3 *They keep water out.*
This is because they are oily. Water tends to run straight off an oily surface without wetting it. This is particularly useful to water birds such as ducks.

### 4 *They enable birds to recognise each other.*
This is due to their characteristic colours. Birds are good at seeing colours, particularly red. Plumage is especially important in enabling the males and females to recognise one another (see page 286).

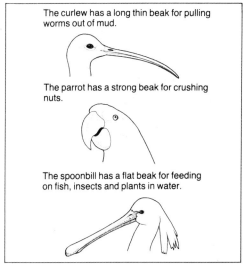

The curlew has a long thin beak for pulling worms out of mud.

The parrot has a strong beak for crushing nuts.

The spoonbill has a flat beak for feeding on fish, insects and plants in water.

**Figure 4** The beaks of different birds are adapted for feeding on different kinds of food. Here are three examples.

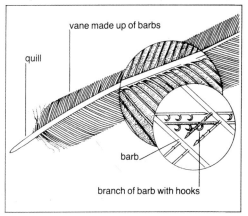

vane made up of barbs

quill

barb

branch of barb with hooks

**Figure 5** A feather is more complicated than it appears at first sight.

## Investigation

### Looking at feathers

1 Obtain a flight feather and a down feather.

  How do they differ?

2 Take the flight feather and put your finger between the barbs.

  Do the barbs separate from each other easily?

3 Put the feather between your thumb and forefinger and stroke it gently.

  Do the barbs join up again?

4 With scissors, cut out a small piece of the vane, about 5 mm square, from the flight feather.

5 Put the piece on a slide.

6 With a pipette add a drop of clove oil or olive oil and cover with a coverslip.

7 Look at it under the microscope, using low power.

  What can you see?

  How do your observations help to explain what happened when you separated and rejoined the barbs?

8 Pipette a few drops of water onto the flight feathers.

  Does the water run off the feather or pass through it?

  Why is this important to the bird?

## Assignments

1 Make a list of five ways a bird's body is adapted for flight.

2 Name one feature of birds which is important in each of the following:
  a) keeping warm,
  b) making the body lighter,
  c) digesting food,
  d) attracting the opposite sex,
  e) producing lots of energy.

3 Look at Figure 4. Choose two kinds of food *not* mentioned in this illustration, give the name of a bird which feeds on each one, and draw its beak.

# Mammals

*Mammals can be found leading active lives almost everywhere, from tropical forests to frozen wastelands in the Arctic. This is the group of animals to which man belongs.*

**Figure 1** This picture shows the main external features of a cat. Which of the structures in bold print on this page can you see in this picture?

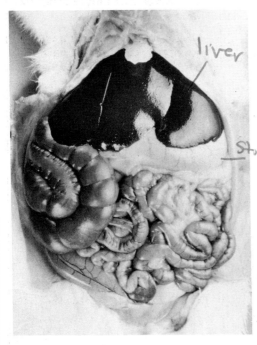

**Figure 2** A rabbit dissected from the belly (ventral) side. Try to identify the organs from the diagram in Figure 3.

## The main features of mammals

Let's take the cat as a typical mammal (Figure 1). Other mammals will be mentioned as we go along.

The slim, agile body is covered with **hair**, which is made of the protein keratin. The hair keeps the body warm, so mammals, like birds, are warm-blooded and are able to keep their body temperature constant.

Like most mammals, the cat walks on four legs, so it is known as a **quadruped**. The feet have five **digits** (toes). Each digit has a claw at the end and a pad underneath. We have nails instead of claws, and some mammals have hooves.

The head contains the main sense organs and feeding structures. The **mouth** is bounded above and below by **lips** which are muscular and can move in various ways. The mouth is opened and closed by powerful **jaws**.

Just inside the mouth are the **teeth**. These are not all the same, as they are in lower vertebrates, but are of different kinds with particular jobs to do.

The mouth opens into the **buccal cavity**. Attached to the floor of the buccal cavity is the **tongue** which, like the lips, can be moved by muscles.

Just above the mouth is a pair of **nostrils**; most mammals have a very good sense of smell and the cat is no exception. On either side of the nose are the **whiskers**; these are sensitive to touch and enable the cat to prowl in total darkness without bumping into things. The **eyes** are positioned high up on the head. On each side of the head is an opening leading into the **ear**. Behind this opening is a flap of skin called the **pinna**. The ear is used for hearing, and the pinna directs sound waves into the opening.

At the hind end there is the **tail**. This helps with balance. The kangaroo uses its tail to support itself when resting, rather like a 'shooting stick', and certain monkeys use it for swinging from trees.

Just below the tail is the **anus**, and below that are the genital organs. The male genital organs consist of a **penis** and a pair of **testes** which make sperms. The testes hang from the body in a bag called the **scrotal sac**. The female has a reproductive opening which leads, via a tube called the **vagina**, to the **uterus** (womb).

On her underside the female cat has two rows of **teats**. After the young have been born, they suck the mother's teats and obtain milk from them. This is called **suckling**, and it nourishes the young until they are able to eat solid food i.e. until they are **weaned**. The milk is produced by special **mammary glands** from which mammals get their name.

A characteristic feature of mammals is that the parents take great care of their young. This reaches its peak in the human species. The young learn quickly. The brain is better developed in mammals than in any other group.

## Man as a mammal

Man differs from the mammal just described in three main ways.

Firstly, he learns to stand upright on his hind legs: he is **bipedal**. His front legs take the form of arms, with hands and fingers at the ends. The hands are used for grasping and holding things. Monkeys and apes are similar.

Secondly, man has very little hair. In consequence our ability to keep warm in cold weather is very poor compared with other mammals, and this is why we wear clothes.

Thirdly, in the human female there are only two teats: they are called **nipples** and are located on the **breasts**. The breasts contain mammary glands which, as in other mammals, produce milk for feeding the young.

Figures 2 and 3 show the inside of the body of a mammal. You can see the various organs by **dissecting** a dead mammal such as a rat or guinea pig (Investigation). Dissection is one of the main ways of finding out about the anatomy of animals. Students training to become vets dissect all manner of animals such as dogs, cats, sheep and even horses, and medical students dissect the human body.

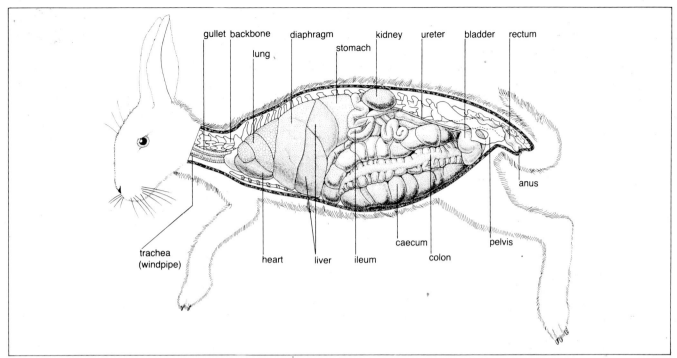

**Figure 3** This illustration shows some of the main structures found inside the body of a rabbit, as seen from the side.

# Investigation

**Dissecting a mammal**  Your teacher will probably do this as a demonstration.

1  Obtain a mammal such as a rat or guinea pig which has been killed with chloroform.

2  Pin the animal through its legs to a board so its belly side is upwards.

3  With scissors cut through the skin in a line running up the middle of the body.

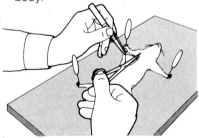

4  Free the skin from the underlying body wall and pin it back.

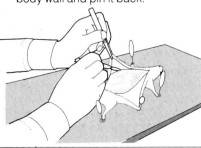

5  Now do the same with the body wall so you can see into the abdomen.

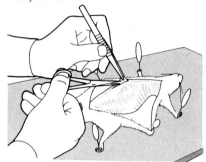

6  With scissors carefully remove the rib cage so you can see into the thorax.

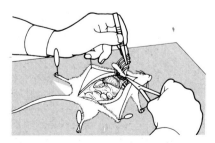

7  Study the internal anatomy of the animal, pushing the organs this way and that to see everything.

# Assignments

1  Make a list of five characteristics of mammals, not possessed by other animals, which have helped make them so successful.

2  Make a list of all the functions you can think of which are performed by your lips.

  In each case, say whether or not the lips perform the same function in other mammals.

  Do you think lips have helped to make mammals successful?

3  Choose one mammal. Find out as much about it as you can, and then write a short essay on it.

4  Write down as many ways as you can think of in which mammals care for their young.

5  What functions, if any, are performed by the following structures?
  a) the pinna of a cat
  b) the tail of a dog
  c) the tongue of a human
  d) the nipples of a human male

# Flowering plants

*Of all the kinds of plants which have been described, well over two thirds are flowering plants.*

## External structure of a flowering plant

The plant is made up of two main parts: the **shoot** and the **roots**. Figure 1 shows the shoot of a typical dicotyledon like coleus, balsam or a bean plant.

At the top of the shoot is an **apical bud** where growth takes place. The main part of the shoot is the **stem. Leaves** stick out from the sides of the stem. They are flat and green and their job is to make food by photosynthesis. The green colour of the leaves and the stem is due to the presence of **chlorophyll**.

The leaves have a network of **veins** which stiffen them and help to prevent them drooping. In some plants the leaves and stem are hairy or have spines which help to protect them from attack by insects and other animals.

Each leaf is attached to the stem by a short **leaf stalk**. The leaves are positioned at regular points along the stem: we refer to these points as **nodes**. The length of stem between one node and the next is called an **internode**. At each node you can usually see a small bud: this is called an **axillary bud** because it is at an angle, or axil, between the leaf stalk and the stem.

The plant shown in Figure 1 is in flower. You will notice that there is a clear sequence from the top downwards. Right at the top there is a cluster of unopened flower buds with the apical bud in the middle. Further back you can see the **flowers**. Further back still **fruits** are visible. This sequence reflects how the plant develops: as the stem grows upward new buds are formed, they open into flowers, and the flowers give rise to fruits. The fruits contain the **seeds** which will give rise to new plants.

Eventually, the apical bud develops into a flower. When this happens the main stem stops growing. Axillary buds are either dormant, or they may sprout into side branches, giving rise to a bushy kind of plant.

Figure 2 shows a typical monocotyledonous plant such as a grass. It has long, slender leaves with parallel veins.

Roots are shown in Figure 3. Dicotyledons usually have a main **taproot** which gives off shorter side roots. Most monocotyledons have a bunch of thin **fibrous roots**.

Each root has a **root cap** at the tip, and further back a covering of fine **root hairs**. The roots anchor the plant and absorb water and mineral salts from the soil. The root hairs increase the surface area for absorption.

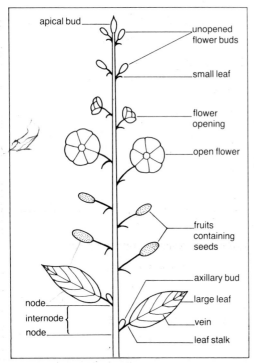

**Figure 1** A typical dicotyledon. In other dicotyledons there are different arrangements of flowers.

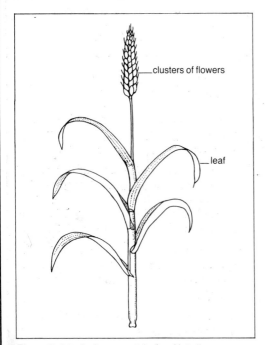

**Figure 2** A typical monocotyledon. Not all monocotyledons have clusters of flowers like this; some have a single flower, for example lilies.

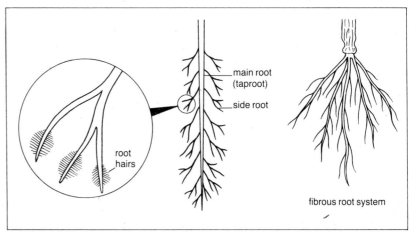

**Figure 3** The roots of (left) a typical dicotyledon and (right) a typical monocotyledon.

## Herbs, shrubs and trees

**Herbs** do not contain much wood; they generally range in height from a few centimetres to about a metre. They include plants such as mint and thyme whose leaves are used for flavouring food, as well as many weeds and leafy plants such as cabbage and lettuce.

**Shrubs** are larger. They contain a good deal of wood and may reach several metres in height. They branch close to the ground and so usually have a bushy appearance. Examples are hibiscus and bougainvillea.

**Trees** are larger still. They have an extremely woody main stem or **trunk**, which is very strong and can hold up tremendous weights. The trunks of certain trees provide man with timber for furniture and building.

## Annuals, biennials and perennials

Some plants get through their life cycle – that is they grow, produce seeds, then die – within one year. Such plants are called **annuals**. Many garden plants are annuals, for example sunflowers, peas and beans, and so are many weeds and also cereals such as maize and rice.

Some plants complete their life cycle so quickly that three or four generations are produced within one year. Such is the case with sweethearts and spurge, tiresome weeds which reproduce and spread very quickly. We call them **ephemerals**. Many desert plants grow up and complete their life cycle in a few days during the brief rainy season.

Some plants take two years to complete their life cycle. They are called **biennials**. In the first year they send up a leafy shoot, but they do not produce flowers and seeds until the second year, after which they die. Examples are carrots and onions.

Some plants go on and flower year after year. They are called **perennials**. There are two kinds: in **herbaceous perennials** the shoot produces flowers and seeds, then dies down. However, the underground part of the plant lives through the winter or dry season and sends up new shoots the following year (Figure 4). Nutgrass and other plants with underground storage organs, such as bulbs and corms, are examples.

In shrubs and trees the shoot contains much wood. It does not die down but continues to live producing flowers and fruits every year. We call these plants **woody perennials**. Hibiscus, mango and guava are examples.

## Deciduous and evergreen plants

Many plants in the tropics drop their leaves in the dry season and form new ones in the following wet season. (The corresponding seasons in cooler parts are winter and summer.) Such plants are called **deciduous**, for example trees like *Delonix* and the boabab tree. Many trees and shrubs, however, such as mango, hibiscus and bougainvillea, keep their leaves throughout the dry season. They are called **evergreens**.

Being evergeen does not mean that the plant never drops its leaves. Eventually the leaves do die and fall off and are replaced by new ones, but not all at the same time. If you look under an evergreen tree you will see plenty of dead leaves lying on the ground.

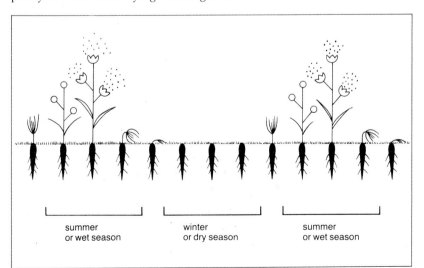

| summer or wet season | winter or dry season | summer or wet season |

**Figure 4** A perennial plant like the one shown here produces flowers and seeds every year. The underground parts of the plant remain dormant in the soil during the winter or the dry season.

# Maintaining life

*This cat has just caught
a sparrow. Feeding is just one
aspect of maintaining life, which
is the subject of the next
series of topics.*

# The air around us

*What is it about the atmosphere surrounding the earth which makes it capable of supporting life? In this Topic we will look into this question.*

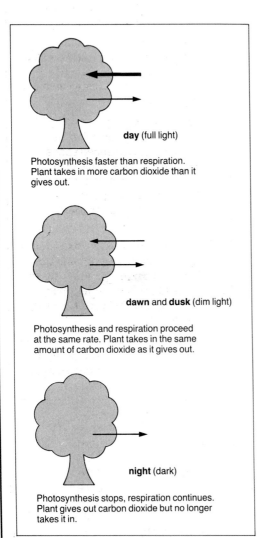

**day** (full light)

Photosynthesis faster than respiration. Plant takes in more carbon dioxide than it gives out.

**dawn** and **dusk** (dim light)

Photosynthesis and respiration proceed at the same rate. Plant takes in the same amount of carbon dioxide as it gives out.

**night** (dark)

Photosynthesis stops, respiration continues. Plant gives out carbon dioxide but no longer takes it in.

**Figure 1** Whether a plant takes up, or gives out, carbon dioxide depends on how light it is. The arrows show the movement of carbon dioxide into and out of the tree.

**Figure 2** Carbon dioxide is put into the atmosphere by animals all the time, and by plants at night. It is removed from the atmosphere by plants during the day.

## What does the atmosphere consist of?

The earth's atmosphere contains oxygen and carbon dioxide in amounts which never vary very much (see p. 110).

This is just as well, because a change in the amounts of oxygen and carbon dioxide in the atmosphere could make our air unfit for breathing. For example, suppose the amount of carbon dioxide was to go up and up? You would feel drowsy, get a headache, become very hot and faint. Your brain would stop working properly and eventually you would die. This is why places where people live and work must be well ventilated. In a well ventilated room there is plenty of oxygen, and carbon dioxide does not build up to a harmful level.

## How is the composition of the atmosphere kept constant?

When living things breathe (respire) they use up oxygen and give out carbon dioxide. However, when green plants photosynthesise they use up carbon dioxide and give out oxygen. In other words *respiration removes oxygen from the atmosphere and adds carbon dioxide to it, whereas photosynthesis removes carbon dioxide from the atmosphere and adds oxygen to it.*

In the world as a whole, respiration and photosynthesis are in balance with each other. The result is that the amounts of carbon dioxide and oxygen are kept constant.

Another process, besides respiration, takes oxygen out of the atmosphere and adds carbon dioxide to it. This is combustion (burning). What happens if we put some extra carbon dioxide into the air by, for example, burning coal in a factory or making a bonfire? If the amount isn't too great, plants simply respond by using it up more quickly. In this way the level of carbon dioxide in the atmosphere stays more or less the same.

## A more detailed look at carbon dioxide

Try the Investigation. Your results should enable you to draw certain conclusions about the effect of plants, animals, and the two together, on the amount of carbon dioxide in the atmosphere.

Whether a plant gives out, or takes up, carbon dioxide depends on the time of day (Figure 1). Animals, on the other hand, give out carbon dioxide all the time. So they are always adding carbon dioxide to the atmosphere (Figure 2).

The *overall* effect of animals and plants living together in a normal environment is to keep the level of carbon dioxide in the atmosphere more or less constant.

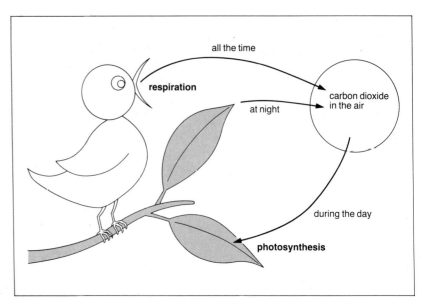

all the time

**respiration**

at night

carbon dioxide in the air

during the day

**photosynthesis**

# Investigation

**How do organisms affect the amount of carbon dioxide in the atmosphere?**

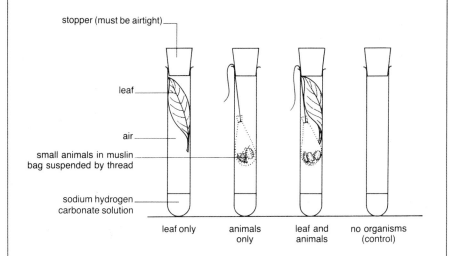

stopper (must be airtight)

leaf

air

small animals in muslin bag suspended by thread

sodium hydrogen carbonate solution

| leaf only | animals only | leaf and animals | no organisms (control) |

In this experiment we will make use of a hydrogen carbonate indicator. This changes colour according to how much carbon dioxide is present.

1 Label four test tubes A to D. Pour a little indicator into the bottom of each tube. Notice that the indicator is reddish-orange: this is its colour when it is in contact with ordinary atmospheric air.

2 Set up the four test tubes as shown in the illustration. Seal all the tubes with a stopper so there is no chance of air getting in or out.

3 Set up four more test tubes exactly like the first four, and label them E to H.

4 Put test tubes A to D in the light. (But do not use a lamp that is liable to heat them up.)

5 Put test tubes E to H in the dark. (A good way is to put them under a cardboard box.)

6 After about an hour give each test tube a quick shake.

Now compare the colour of the indicator in the test tubes. It is best to look at the colours against a plain white background.

The colour tells you how much carbon dioxide is present in the test tube compared with ordinary atmospheric air.

**Yellow** means there is more carbon dioxide than in atmospheric air.

**Purple** means there is less carbon dioxide than in atmospheric air.

**Reddish-orange** means there is the same amount of carbon dioxide as in atmospheric air.

Write down the colour of the indicator in each test tube.

For each test tube, say whether carbon dioxide has been added to, or removed from the air, and explain the reason.

# Assignments

1 Why is it a good idea to open classroom windows whenever possible?

2 A scientist measured the carbon dioxide content of the air in a part of the northern hemisphere with a temperate climate. He found that the content in March was 0.02971 per cent, whereas in September it was 0.02905 per cent. Explain the difference. Would you expect the same to be true in the tropics?

3 Imagine there is a catastrophe in which all the plants of the world are suddenly destroyed. Describe in detail the effects which you think this might have.

4 It has been suggested that a suitable atmosphere might be maintained in a manned space capsule by having some plants inside. Do you think this is feasible? What problems might be encountered in putting it into practice?

5 At an agricultural research station, a group of scientists measured the amount of carbon dioxide in the air in the middle of a wheat field every three hours for 24 hours. Here are their results:

| Time | Percentage of carbon dioxide in the air |
|---|---|
| 24 (midnight) | 0.042 |
| 3 | 0.037 |
| 6 | 0.031 |
| 9 | 0.029 |
| 12 (noon) | 0.028 |
| 15 | 0.030 |
| 18 | 0.032 |
| 21 | 0.035 |
| 24 (midnight) | 0.042 |

a) Plot these results on graph paper.
b) Explain them as fully as you can.
c) How would you expect oxygen to change during the same period?

# Food and diet

*In the course of a lifetime, a person may eat as much as 100 tonnes of food. The next two Topics are all about food: what it is, and what it does for us.*

**Figure 1** A person may eat 100 tonnes of food in his or her lifetime.

**Figure 2** A balanced diet should contain many different kinds of food such as the ones shown here.

## Why do we need food?

We need food for four main reasons:

1  It serves as fuel, giving us energy and warmth.
2  It enables us to grow and repair and replace our tissues.
3  It provides us with important substances which control our metabolism.
4  It keeps us healthy, helping us to fight disease.

These functions of food apply not just to man, but to other organisms too.

## Our diet

The food we consume each day makes up our diet. This includes things we drink as well as those we eat. Whatever we choose to eat, our diet must include the following substances: carbohydrates, fats, proteins, water, minerals and vitamins. A diet which contains all these substances in the right proportions is called a **complete** or **balanced diet** (Figure 2).

Now let's look at each substance in turn. We will deal with the ones we need in bulk in this Topic, and the ones we need in only small amounts in the next Topic. Their chemistry is dealt with on page 42.

# Carbohydrates

Carbohydrates include sugar, starch and cellulose.

### Sugar

Different kinds of sugar occur in different foods. In fruit the sugar is fructose or glucose, in milk it is lactose. Ordinary table sugar is sucrose, obtained from sugar cane and sugar beet. Normally sugar tastes sweet, which is why it is so popular. Sugar gives us energy, so we call it an energy food.

In its natural state, sugar is normally liquid – think of the sugar in orange juice for example. However, when sugar loses water, it forms crystals. This is what happens when table sugar is made. Juice is extracted from sugar cane or beet and then it is purified (refined). After that, water is evaporated from it, so sugar crystals are formed. The crystals quickly dissolve if placed in water – as you know when you put sugar in a cup of tea.

Brown sugar is less refined than white sugar: it contains various impurities which make it brown and slightly sticky. These impurities do us no harm, indeed they make the sugar better for making cakes, biscuits and toffee.

### Starch

Starch is found in bread, potatoes, cereals and many other plant foods. It exists naturally in the form of small granules called **starch grains** (see page 31). We can digest starch easily once it is cooked. Each starch grain is enclosed within a membrane and cooking causes the starch grains to swell up and burst. Like sugar, starch gives us energy.

### Cellulose

Cellulose forms the cell walls of plants, and is very tough. For this reason, plants are often difficult to chew, but cooking softens the cellulose and makes it easier to eat.

Man cannot digest cellulose – we don't have the necessary enzymes in our gut for breaking it down. This means that we cannot get energy from it, but it still performs a useful function: together with other indigestible matter, it forms **roughage** (fibre). Roughage keeps food moving along the gut and prevents constipation (see page 96).

In industrialised countries people tend to eat a lot of highly refined foods which contain little or no roughage. Unrefined foods such as wholemeal bread, bran cereals and fresh fruit and vegetables contain plenty of roughage. This is one reason why such foods are good for us.

# Fats

Fats occur in both animals and plants. Butter, lard and dripping are all animal fats obtained from pigs and cattle. These fats are solid at room temperature, though if you heat them they go into liquid form. Plant fats, on the other hand, are normally in liquid form at room temperature. We call these **oils**. Two well known examples are sunflower oil and corn oil, both of which are used a lot in cooking.

Margarine, in contrast to butter, consists of mainly vegetable oils. These oils are obtained from groundnuts, soya beans etc., and are then turned into solid fat by chemical treatment. Other treatments give it the right colour, make it easy to spread, and are supposed to make it taste like butter.

The main function of fats is to give us energy, so – like carbohydrates – they are energy foods. In man and other animals fat is stored under the skin: this helps to keep the body warm, as well as serving as an energy store.

There are many different kinds of fat. Each contains particular **fatty acids** (see page 42). Now some fatty acids are described as **saturated**, others as **unsaturated**. A saturated fatty acid is one which cannot possess any more atoms: the molecule is full up, like a saturated sponge full of water. An unsaturated fatty acid, on the other hand, has room for more atoms.

Foods vary in the amount of saturated and unsaturated fat they contain. In general animal foods contain mainly saturated fat, whereas plant foods contain mainly unsaturated fat. Some scientists claim that the more unsaturated, as opposed to saturated, fat we eat, the healthier we are likely to be. Margarine, being a vegetable fat, contains more unsaturated fat than butter, so it is thought to be better for us (see page 137).

# Proteins

A certain amount of protein is present in most foods, but it is particularly abundant in milk, eggs and meat. In milk and eggs the protein is in liquid form, in meat it consists of solid thread-like fibres.

Proteins form the main structures of our body. We therefore need protein for growth and body-building, and for repairing worn-out or damaged tissues. We also need protein to make enzymes. In addition proteins give us a certain amount of energy, but they are not as important in this respect as carbohydrates and fat.

How much protein do we need? Doctors recommend about 70 grams per day. In fact we could probably manage with a lot less than this. In rich countries people tend to eat much more protein than they need. On the other hand, in poor countries many people get hardly any.

Proteins are composed of **amino acids**. Certain amino acids can be made by our bodies, so we do not need them in our diet. Others cannot be made so we must get them in our diet. These are called **essential amino acids**. They are vital for good health and absence of just one can have severe consequences.

Now look at Table 1. This shows how useful the proteins are in different foods. As you will see, animal proteins come out on top, so they are particularly good for us; plant proteins come lower down, so they are less useful.

# Water

Water is essential for life, so it must regularly be included in our diet. One can go without other foods for several weeks without being permanently harmed, but a person can die in a few days from lack of water.

We take in water mainly by drinking. However there is plenty of water in most solid foods: 90 per cent of a lettuce or cabbage is water, and even bread contains about 40 per cent. Some animals get all their water from solid food and never drink, but human beings normally need to drink about a litre of liquid every day.

Shortage of water in our environment (drought) is one of the main causes of famine. It kills domestic animals, and causes crops to fail.

**Figure 3** These foods contain the proteins needed for a healthy life.

| Type of protein | Marks out of 10 |
| --- | --- |
| Mother's milk | 10 |
| Eggs | 10 |
| Fish | 8 |
| Meat | 8 |
| Cow's milk | 7½ |
| Potatoes | 7 |
| Liver (beef) | 6½ |
| Rice | 5½ |
| Soya beans | 5½ |
| Maize | 5½ |
| Wheat (white flour) | 5 |
| Peas | 4½ |
| Beans | 4½ |

**Table 1** In this table each food is given marks out of ten depending on how good it is at giving us the amino acids we need. A high mark means that the protein contains all the essential amino acids in the right proportions for human beings. A low mark means that it is short of certain amino acids. You will see that soya bean protein is one of the best plant proteins, and is not far behind meat itself. Also the total amount of protein in soya beans is greater than in most plants. Soya beans are therefore used a lot for manufacturing artificial meat. Potato protein is also valuable, but unfortunately the total amount of protein in a potato is very small.

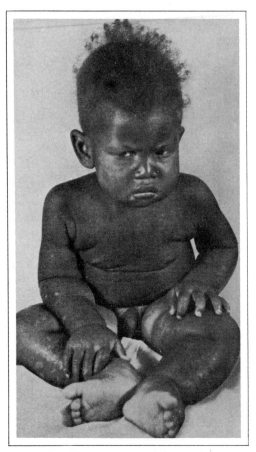

**Figure 4** This child is suffering from lack of protein (kwashiorkor). The child looks fat because of fluid in the tissues (see page 141).

## Malnutrition

A person whose diet is inadequate suffers from **malnutrition**. Shortage of particular nutrients gives rise to **deficiency diseases**. Here are two important ones:

**Marasmus**   This is a general wasting of the body resulting from an all-round shortage of nutrients, particularly energy foods. It is explained further on page 86.

**Kwashiorkor**   This is a disease of children resulting mainly from lack of protein. A child suffering from this disease is miserable, listless and weak (Figure 4). Kwashiorkor is an African word meaning 'the rejected one' and it is one of the commonest types of malnutrition in poorer countries. It is often seen in babies who are being breast-fed by an undernourished mother, particularly if she is pregnant.

Specific deficiency diseases also arise when people don't get enough minerals or vitamins, as we shall see in the next Topic.

## Finding out what is in our food

Various tests can be done to find out which particular chemical substances are present in different foods. Simple tests which you could do yourself are described in the Investigation.

More complicated experiments can be done to find out how much of each chemical substance is found in different foods (Figure 5). This information is valuable because it tells us what each kind of food is useful for. For example, maize contains a lot of carbohydrate and is a good energy food, whereas meat contains a lot of protein which makes it useful for growth and body-building.

## Vegetarians

A **vegetarian** is a person who eats plant foods but not meat. The diet may include animal products such as milk, eggs and butter, but not the animals themselves. Some very strict vegetarians, known as **vegans**, don't even eat animal products.

A varied vegetarian diet can provide all the nutrients needed for a healthy life, particularly if dairy products are included. Plants are our only source of roughage and also provide lots of vitamins as we shall see in the next Topic.

**Figure 5** This chart shows the relative amounts of different nutrients in some well known foods. The numbers alongside each bar are the percentages.

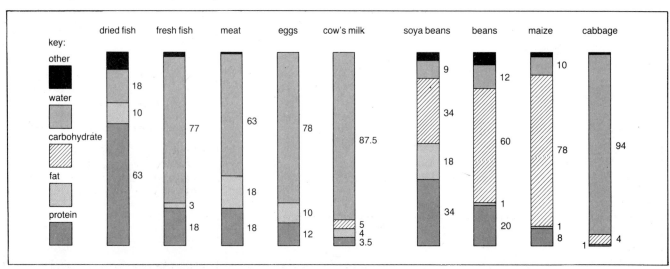

# Investigation

**To find out what substances are present in various foods**

You can do this by carrying out the following tests. Try them on orange juice, banana, bread, milk, egg white, butter or margarine, a breakfast cereal and baby food.

**Sugar**  *Simple reducing*

1 If the food is not already in liquid form, mash it up with a pestle and mortar, and add a little water to make a suspension.

2 Pour about 2 cm³ of the food into a test tube.

3 Add about 2 cm³ of Benedict's or Fehling's solution to the test tube, and shake.

4 Boil some water in a beaker over a bunsen burner.

5 Put the test tube in the beaker of boiling water, and leave it there for a minute or two.

If a precipitate develops, sugar is present. (The precipitate is usually green or brown.)

**Starch**

1 Obtain a small quantity of the food: it can be in liquid or solid form.

2 With a pipette add 2 or 3 drops of dilute iodine to the food.

If a blue-black colour develops, starch is present.

### Additional notes on testing for sugar

Benedict's and Fehling's solutions contain copper sulphate. The sugar reduces the copper sulphate on heating, forming a precipitate. Sugars which do this include glucose, fructose and lactose: we call them **reducing sugars**.

Sucrose (cane sugar) is not a reducing sugar. It will give a precipitate with Benedict's or Fehling's solution only if you first break it down into its reducing sugars (glucose and fructose). To do this, boil it with a few drops of dilute hydrochloric acid for several minutes. Add a few drops of sodium or potassium hydroxide to neutralise the solution, and then carry out the Benedict's or Fehling's test as described above.

(Fehling's solution consists of two separate solutions, A and B. These should be mixed together in equal amounts immediately before use.)

## Fat

*Simple test*

1 Rub the food onto a piece of thin paper.

2 Hold the paper in front of a light, so light shines through it.

If the food has left a translucent mark on the paper, fat is present.

*More complicated test*

1 Pour about 1 cm³ of absolute ethanol into a test tube.

2 Add a small amount of the food to the ethanol. (If the food is a liquid, just add one or two drops; if it is solid, cut it up into very small pieces first.)

3 Shake the test tube.

4 Add about 1 cm³ of water to the test tube.

If a cloudy white precipitate develops, fat is present.

**Protein**

1 If the food is not already in liquid form, mash it up with a pestle and mortar, and add a little water to make a suspension.

2 Pour about 2 cm³ of the food into a test tube.

3 Add a little sodium or potassium hydroxide till the solution clears.

4 Add a few drops of dilute copper sulphate, and shake.

If the solution goes purple, protein is present.

# Assignments

1 Give four reasons why we need food.

2 In what kind of food is each of the following substances found:

a) lactose, b) sucrose, c) cellulose, d) sunflower oil, e) liquid protein?

3 What effect does cooking have on each of the following:

a) starch, b) cellulose, c) butter, d) sunflower oil, e) liquid protein?

4 Explain each of the following statements.

a) A child suffering from shortage of protein does not grow as quickly as he should.

b) Eggs are better for body-building than bread.

5 Look at Figure 5, then answer these questions.

a) Which food contains most protein?

b) Which food contains most carbohydrate?

c) Which food contains most water?

d) Which food would you recommend for a child suffering from kwashiorkor, and why?

e) Which plant food would be best for a vegetarian, and why?

6 Each of the foods in the left-hand list is closely related to one of the words in the right-hand list. Write them down in the correct pairs.

wholemeal bread     protein
sugar                insulation
butter               artificial meat
eggs                 roughage
soya beans           energy

7 'The amount of protein present in a particular food, and how good that protein is for body-building, are two quite different things.'

Explain what this statement means.

8 Vegetarians can get all the nutrients they need provided that the diet is varied. Why must the diet be varied? (Hint: Look at Table 1, page 73.)

# Minerals and vitamins

*We need these substances in only small amounts. They come from the sort of foods shown in Figure 1. We shall see why we need them, and what happens if we don't get them.*

**Figure 1** Some foods which are particularly rich in minerals and vitamins.

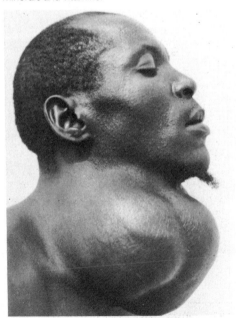

**Figure 2** This person is suffering from goitre caused by iodine deficiency.

## Minerals

Minerals contain certain chemical elements. All these elements have particular jobs to do. Some of them give the blood its correct composition. Others belong to important structures such as bones and teeth. Others help to control the chemical reactions which occur in the body. Here are some of the most important ones:

### Sodium

We take in sodium when we eat salt, for common salt is sodium chloride. Salt is present in most foods, though some are saltier than others.

Our blood must contain the right amount of salt. It helps our nerves to transmit messages and our muscles to contract. If a person runs short of it, he gets a sharp pain in his muscles: we call this cramp. People lose salt when they sweat. Miners, and other people who work in hot places, eat salt tablets to make up for the salt they lose by sweating. However, it's important not to take too much because it may cause high blood pressure.

### Calcium

Calcium is needed for hardening our bones and teeth. When a baby is born, its bones are soft. To become hard they must take up calcium salts. These salts are calcium phosphate and carbonate, and the process is called calcification. A similar process causes hardening of teeth.

Calcium occurs in foods such as milk, cheese and fish. If a child does not get enough calcium, his bones remain soft and become deformed. This condition is known as **rickets**. Calcium is also needed for making muscles contract, and it helps blood to clot when you cut yourself.

### Phosphorus

The main calcium salt in bone and teeth is calcium phosphate, so we need phosphorus as well as calcium in our diet. Phosphorus also occurs in cell membranes and is a constituent of many important chemical substances in the body. Fortunately it is present in most foods.

### Iron

Iron is present in haemoglobin, the red pigment in blood. Haemoglobin carries oxygen round the body, so iron is very important in the diet.

Iron occurs in a number of foods, especially liver and kidneys. Small amounts occur in most drinking water, and we get quite a lot of it from metal utensils used in cooking: the amount of iron in a piece of beef can be doubled by mincing it in an iron mincer.

Shortage of iron results in the blood containing too little haemoglobin. This is a type of **anaemia**. The oxygen-carrying power of the blood is cut down, resulting in tiredness and lack of energy. People who are anaemic may need to take iron tablets.

### Iodine

Some elements are needed in only the tiniest quantities. These are called **trace elements**. One such element is iodine.

Iodine is present in most drinking water and in sea foods. We need iodine for making the hormone **thyroxine**. This is produced by the thyroid gland which is situated close the the 'adam's apple' in the neck.

Thyroxine speeds up chemical reactions in the body, making us more active (see page 239). If we do not get enough iodine, the thyroid gland cannot produce thyroxine. As a result the gland enlarges, causing the neck to swell. This condition is called **goitre** (Figure 2).

There are places where the drinking water lacks iodine. One such place is Derbyshire in the middle of England. In the old days it was common for people in that area to have enlarged thyroid glands, so the condition was called 'Derbyshire neck'. Nowadays, iodine is added to the salt, so the condition no longer occurs. Old portraits, such as the one in Figure 3, show people with swollen necks: almost certainly this was caused by too little iodine in the water.

## *Fluorine*

Fluorine is another important trace element. No one knows for certain what it does, but it seems to prevent **tooth decay** (see page 101). Small amounts of fluorine occur in most drinking water. Nowadays dentists encourage children to clean their teeth with fluoride toothpaste, and to suck fluoride tablets. In some places where it does not occur naturally, fluorine is put into the drinking water.

# Vitamins

In the early 1900s a famous English scientist, Sir Frederick Gowland Hopkins, fed some rats on a special food mixture. The mixture contained plenty of carbohydrate, fat, protein and minerals – all the things thought to be necessary for healthy life. After a few weeks the rats were dead. However a second group of rats was given exactly the same food mixture, plus a very small amount of milk. They flourished. Apparently the milk contained something extra which the rats needed. We now know that this extra 'something' was vitamins (Figure 4).

Vitamins are a collection of organic substances which are needed in the diet. Each has a specific job to do, but their overall function is to help control the chemical reactions which take place in the body. Each one occurs in particular kinds of food. If any of them are missing from the diet, we become ill and may die.

Vitamins are known by letters: A B C etc. This way of naming them was introduced before their chemical structure was known. It is still used, though we can now give them proper chemical names.

For vitamins to do their job they must be in solution. Some of them dissolve in water, others dissolve in fat. This is one reason why we need water and fat in our diet.

Now let's look at some of the most important vitamins in detail.

## *Vitamin A    (fat soluble)*

Vitamin A (**retinol**) is important for our eyes. It protects their surface, and helps us to see in dim light.

The best source of this vitamin is fish liver oil. We can also get it by eating carrots: the orange pigment in carrots (called carotene) is turned into vitamin A inside our bodies. Red peppers and mangoes are also good sources.

Shortage of vitamin A makes it hard to see in dim light. This is known as **night-blindness**. Severe lack of it causes the cornea to become thick and dry, a condition known as **xerophthalmia**. In extreme cases this can lead to total blindness.

## *The B vitamins    (water soluble)*

In 1916 an American doctor, Joseph Goldberger, came across some convicts who had a strange disease. They had swollen tongues, skin rashes, upset stomachs and headaches. Some of them were mentally ill.

Now this disease might have been caused by germs, but Goldberger suspected it was due to their diet. To prove this he carried out a brave experiment. He took some blood from one of the convicts and injected it into

**Figure 3** The person in this portrait by Leonardo da Vinci may have lived in an area where there was no iodine in the water.

**Figure 4** The two rats at the top were fed on a full diet including vitamins. The two rats at the bottom were given a full diet minus vitamins.

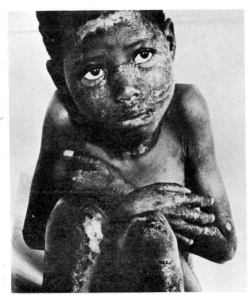

**Figure 5** This child is suffering from pellagra caused by lack of the vitamin niacin (nicotinic acid).

himself. He ate the skin rash of one of the others and swallowed some discharge from the intestine of another. Goldberger reasoned that if the disease was caused by a germ, he should catch it. On the other hand, if it was caused by poor diet, he should remain healthy. Goldberger did not get the disease. We now know that these convicts were suffering from lack of the vitamin niacin (**nicotinic acid**). There is plenty of this vitamin in liver, meat and fish – just the kind of food which the unfortunate convicts were not getting. The disease resulting from its absence is called **pellagra** (Figure 5).

Niacin belongs to a group of vitamins called the B vitamins. All the B vitamins assist the process by which energy is produced in our bodies.

One of the most important B vitamins is vitamin $B_1$ (**thiamine**). This vitamin was discovered by a Polish scientist called Casimir Funk. It occurs in yeast and cereals. Lack of it causes a serious disease called **beri-beri**. This word means 'I cannot'. It starts with stomach trouble and weakness of the muscles; in the end the person becomes paralysed and may die.

There is a lot of vitamin $B_1$ in rice: it occurs in the husk, the tough coat surrounding the grain. When rice is prepared, the husk is usually stripped off and the grain polished, but this removes the vitamin. Beri-beri is therefore common in places where people live on polished rice.

Another important B vitamin is vitamin $B_2$ (**riboflavin**). It is found in a number of foods, particularly leafy vegetables, eggs and fish. Lack of it causes sores in the skin and round the mouth, and poor growth.

## Vitamin C   (water soluble)

In the 1740s Anson, the famous British Admiral, led a fleet into the Pacific to fight the Spanish. In the course of the voyage, 626 of his 961 men died of a disease called **scurvy**. In this disease bleeding occurs in various parts of the body, particularly the gums (Figure 6).

Scurvy is caused by lack of vitamin C (**ascorbic acid**). This vitamin is abundant in green vegetables such as spinach, and citrus fruits such as oranges, lemons and limes (Investigation). If people eat this kind of food, they will not get scurvy. Admiral Nelson realised this, and he always insisted that his ships should carry an ample supply of limes. This is why British sailors were called 'limeys'.

One snag about vitamin C is that it is destroyed by heating. As a result a lot of it can be lost during cooking and while the food is being kept hot afterwards. In restaurants and canteens, where the food is kept hot for a long time, over 90 per cent of the vitamin C may be lost.

## Vitamin D   (fat soluble)

We have seen that as a child grows, his bones become hard by taking up calcium salts. For this to happen vitamin D (**calciferol**) is needed. If the child does not get enough vitamin D he will develop **rickets**, the same disease that occurs if he doesn't get enough calcium.

Vitamin D occurs in fish liver oil. A certain amount of vitamin D can be made by the body itself; it is made in the skin provided sunlight is present. In a sunny climate an adult can get all the vitamin D he needs this way.

Vitamin D is one of the few vitamins that you can have too much of. Very large doses can cause tissues other than the bones to become calcified, for example the kidneys and lungs.

## Vitamin E   (fat soluble)

This vitamin is found in milk and egg yolk and in many plant foods including lettuce. Lack of it in animals can cause the ovaries and testes to wither so that eggs and sperms cannot be produced (sterility).

## Vitamin K   (fat soluble)

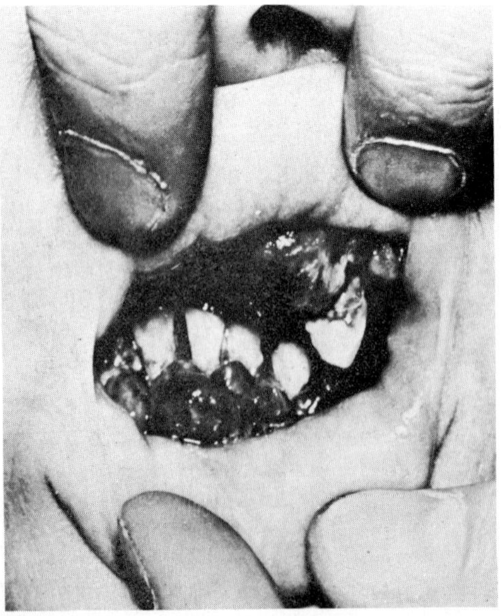

In the 1930s some chickens in America were being fed on a diet of pellets.

**Figure 6** Lack of vitamin C causes scurvy which is characterised by bleeding gums.

Unfortunately they died from internal bleeding. It was found that this could be prevented by including vegetables in their diet. Scientists later discovered that vegetables, particularly spinach, contain a chemical substance which helps the blood to clot. This is vitamin K.

You will now realise how important vitamins are, and how serious it can be if we don't get enough of them. Unfortunately vitamin deficiency diseases are common in poor countries. Even in rich countries they occur from time to time. Those at risk include pregnant women, old people living alone, and people who refuse to eat certain kinds of food – vegetarians for example. It's a good idea for such people to take vitamin tablets.

# *Investigation*

## Testing food for vitamin C

1 Obtain a lemon, and squeeze some of its juice into a beaker.

2 Pipette one drop of blue DCPIP solution onto a white tile*.

3 With a pipette or syringe add lemon juice to the DCPIP solution, drop by drop, and stir with a needle. Count how many drops of lemon are needed to make the DCPIP solution turn colourless.

The disappearance of the blue colour tells us that vitamin C is present in the lemon juice.

4 Use this test to compare the vitamin C content of different foods. In each case get some juice out of the food. Then find out how many drops of the juice are needed to decolorise one drop of DCPIP solution.

Do you think this is an accurate way of comparing the vitamin C content of different foods?

How could you make the experiment more accurate?

Why can't this test be done with blackcurrant juice?

5 Boil some lemon juice in a test tube and then test it for vitamin C with DCPIP solution.

What effect does boiling have on vitamin C?

* DCPIP is short for 2, 6-dichlorophenol indophenol.

# *Assignments*

1 Each of the diseases in the left-hand column is caused by lack of one or more of the substances in the right-hand column. Which causes which?

| | |
|---|---|
| night-blindness | iron |
| rickets | vitamin A |
| anaemia | calcium |
| goitre | vitamin D |
| xerophthalmia | iodine |

2 Explain the reason for each of the following statements.
a) Carrots are good for you.
b) A person who has been sun-bathing all day eats a salt tablet.
c) A mother may give her child orange juice.
d) Old people who live alone tend to get scurvy towards the end of the winter.

3 Read how Goldberger discovered the cause of pellagra on pages 77-8, then answer these questions.
a) Does the fact that Goldberger did not get the disease *prove* that it was caused by a poor diet? Explain your answer.
b) Suggest one way in which Goldberger might have confirmed his conclusions.

4 Describe an experiment which could be done to find out if the husk surrounding the rice seed contains a substance which prevents beri-beri.

5 A scientist carried out an experiment to find the effect of cooking a finely shredded cabbage on the amount of vitamin C in it. He put the cabbage in boiling water and continued to boil it for 10 minutes. He estimated the vitamin C content at intervals, expressing it as a percentage of the amount in the uncooked cabbage.

Here are his results:

| Time after putting the cabbage in the water | Vitamin C content |
|---|---|
| 0 min | 100% |
| ½ min | 66% |
| 1 min | 55% |
| 4 min | 49% |
| 7 min | 43% |
| 10 min | 37% |

a) Plot these results on graph paper.
b) Suggest reasons why the vitamin C content of the cabbage falls.
c) What experiments could you do to test your suggestions?
d) What advice would you give to a chef about cooking vegetables?

6 The following table shows the daily amount of vitamin D required by different people. The figures are in 'international units' (iu).

| | |
|---|---|
| Woman during first half of pregnancy | 400 iu |
| Woman during second half of pregnancy | 600 iu |
| Woman breast feeding her baby | 800 iu |
| Child 1–3 years old | 400 iu |

Explain (a) what each of these people needs vitamin D for, and (b) why a woman's requirement goes up in the second half of pregnancy and when she is breast feeding her baby.

# How are substances stored?

*The carrot shown is
one of the largest ever grown.
It weighs nearly 3.5 kilograms! Why
should the carrot plant produce
a structure like this?*

**Figure 1** A giant carrot. This record-winning carrot weighed 3.5 kg (7lb 11½ oz).

## Why do organisms store substances?

We know that plants and animals use their food for providing energy and doing various other jobs. But any food left over is stored in their bodies. This enables them to survive when food is unavailable or scarce. In fact, by using the food stores in his body, a man can live for several weeks without eating anything. Many animals, particularly hibernating ones, can survive for much longer than this and many of them get through the winter or dry season in this way.

## Where are substances stored?

Organisms store substances all over their bodies to some extent. However, most of it is packed away in special places. In man one of the main storage places is the liver.

In plants food is often stored in special storage organs which are formed by part of the plant swelling up. Storage organs may be formed from the roots, stems or leaves. The carrot in Figure 1 is a swollen root, and so is the radish. The potato, on the other hand, is a swollen stem, and the onion is a mass of swollen leaves.

A plant's storage organs can survive the winter or dry season and give rise to new plants the following year (see page 300). When a new plant sprouts from a carrot, potato or onion, food moves into it from the storage organ, giving it nourishment until it can make its own food by photosynthesis.

Plants also store substances in their seeds and fruits. When a seed germinates, food passes from it into the new growing plant, giving it nourishment until it can support itself.

The same thing applies to the eggs of animals. Birds' eggs, for instance, contain a rich store of food in the yolk which is used by the growing chick before the egg hatches.

## In what form do plants store substances?

Green plants make **glucose** by photosynthesis. Some of this is used straight away. The rest is usually turned into **starch**. The starch is converted back into glucose when it's needed:

$$\text{GLUCOSE} \rightleftharpoons \text{STARCH}$$

Some plants turn their surplus glucose into other substances, such as oil, and some store it in the form of sugar itself. You can find out what kind of food is present in a particular plant by doing chemical tests on it (see page 75). Although other substances are often present, starch is the main storage

**Figure 2** Plants store food in various places, for example in leaves (onion), roots (sweet potato and turnip), stems (yam), and fruits (plantain).

substance of plants. Starch gives a blue-black colour with iodine and this is an easy way of showing where it occurs.

## What is needed for glucose to be turned into starch?

What do you think happens if you mix a small amount of glucose with some potato juice? (Investigation 1). The answer is that the glucose is turned into starch.

Obviously, then, the potato juice contains something which turns glucose into starch. Scientists have discovered that this 'something' is an **enzyme**.

The same enzyme is also present in leaves. You can show its action by putting a piece of de-starched leaf into a glucose solution and keeping it in the dark (Investigation 2). The leaf takes up the glucose and turns it into starch.

## How is glucose turned into starch?

The glucose in a plant is in solution. Starch, on the other hand, is in the form of solid grains (Investigation 3). When glucose is turned into starch, the glucose molecules join up to form a long chain like a string of beads (condensation), and this chain curls up like a spring. In this way thousands of glucose molecules get packed together into a solid grain of starch (Figure 3).

When starch is converted back into glucose, the chain uncoils and the glucose molecules separate (hydrolysis).

## How do animals store substances?

Animals get glucose from the food they eat. What do they do with surplus glucose which they do not need straight away? They turn it into a substance called **glycogen**. The glycogen is converted back into glucose when it's needed:

$$\text{GLUCOSE} \rightleftharpoons \text{GLYCOGEN}$$

Glycogen is equivalent to starch in plants – in fact it is sometimes called 'animal starch'. Both are carbohydrates. Like starch, glycogen is made by glucose molecules joining together. Glycogen takes the form of tiny granules which are stored in the body's cells, particularly in the liver. Animals also store food as fat which is laid down beneath the skin, where it performs the additional function of keeping the body warm.

## Mobilising food stores

When food is stored it is usually in a solid form, but when the stored food is needed, it must first be hydrolysed. This is under the control of enzymes

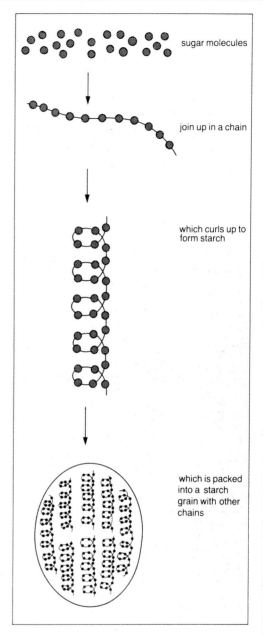

sugar molecules

join up in a chain

which curls up to form starch

which is packed into a starch grain with other chains

**Figure 3** Starch is a convenient way of storing sugar molecules.

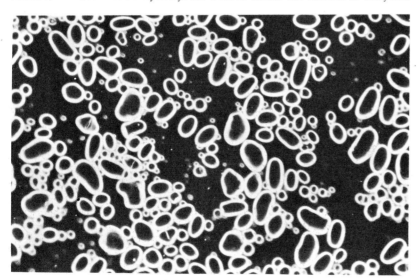

**Figure 4** Starch grains from inside the cells of a potato seen under the microscope. The larger grains are about 3 micrometres wide.

**Figure 5** This diagram shows what happens to the stored food when a new plant sprouts from a storage organ such as a potato tuber.

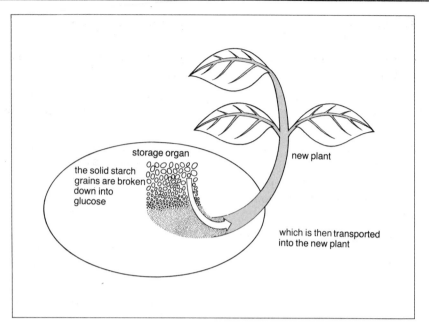

**Figure 6** Potatoes being harvested.

**Figure 7** Rice growing in a field. The rice grains are an important source of food for humans.

(page 43). Starch and glycogen are broken down into soluble glucose; fat is broken down into soluble acids. Only then can the stored food be moved to places where it is needed (Figure 5).

When stored food is changed into a form which can be moved, we say the food is being mobilised. It's rather like mobilising an army so it can be moved into action.

## Why are food stores important to man?

When an organism stores food, the food substances are usually packed together in one place, often in concentrated form. Any part of an organism where food is stored can therefore be a rich source of food for man.

Take Irish potatoes for example. We have seen that they contain starch, which make them a useful energy food; they also contain small amounts of other important nutrients. Potatoes are an important food crop. Each plant bears about six to eight potatoes (Figure 6). These can be eaten or planted so as to grow new potato plants.

Even more important are maize, wheat and rice, which are three of the most widely grown crops in the world. Here starch, protein and a number of other useful nutrients are packed into the ripe seeds (the grains) which are clustered at the tops of the stems (Figure 7).

Maize, wheat and rice are a more concentrated food than potatoes, because the grains contain less water — in fact one kilogram of wheat has more food in it than three kilograms of potatoes. It is a general rule that seeds, being drier, are a more concentrated form of food than storage organs.

Another important food plant is sugar cane. This is a giant grass, like bamboo, and may grow to a height of six metres. Sugar, in the form of sucrose, is stored in its thick stem. Much of the world's sugar comes from sugar cane, but it will only grow in hot countries (see pages 153 and 325). Sugar beet, on the other hand, will grow in cooler climates. This stores sugar in large swollen roots. Sugar beet is becoming more and more important as a source of sugar for man, particularly in temperate countries.

What about animal food stores – to what extent do we use them as a source of food? Two of the most valuable animal foods are eggs and liver, which both contain many useful nutrients.

Many other examples could be given, but the important principle is that any localised store of food in an organism can provide us with a valuable source of food (page 324).

# Investigation 1

**To see if potato juice will turn glucose into starch**

1 Put a few pieces of potato pulp (not the skin) in a mortar. Add a pinch of washed sand and a little water.

2 Grind up the potato pulp with a pestle.

3 Filter the contents of the mortar into a test tube. This is your potato juice.

4 Put a drop of the potato juice onto a white tile. Test it for starch by adding a drop of iodine solution. (There should be no starch present in the potato juice.)

5 Put six drops of 0.5 per cent glucose-1-phosphate, side by side on a white tile.
(Glucose-1-phosphate is an activated form of glucose.)

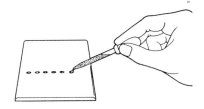

6 To each drop of glucose-1-phosphate add a drop of potato juice and mix.

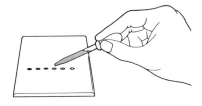

7 To each drop of the mixture in turn, add a drop of iodine solution after 2, 4, 6, 8, 10 and 12 minutes.

What happens to the colour of each drop?

If it turns blue-black it means there is starch present. In which drops has starch been formed?

What is present in potato juice which turns glucose into starch?

Should this experiment have any further controls?
If so, what should they be?

# Investigation 2

**To see if a leaf will turn glucose into starch**

1 Detach a leaf from a potted plant which has been kept in the dark for at least three days.

2 Test a small piece of the leaf with iodine to be certain there is no starch present (see page 147).

3 Place several small pieces of the leaf in a dish of 5 per cent glucose solution. Label this A.

4 Place several more pieces of leaf in a dish of water. Label this B: it is your control.

5 Put the dishes side by side in a dark place.

6 After several days test the two groups of leaf-pieces for starch (see page 147).

Has either group of leaf pieces turned black? If they have, starch has been formed.

What is present inside the leaf which turns glucose into starch?

# Investigation 3

**Looking at starch in a potato**

1 Slice open a potato to expose the white pulp.

2 Scrape off a little of the pulp and place it on a slide.

3 Put a drop of iodine solution onto the tissue.

4 Cover the tissue with a coverslip.

5 Examine it under the microscope.

Can you see starch grains? (They should have stained blue-black with the iodine solution.)

Can you see that they are located inside the cells?

Approximately how many are there inside the cells?

In what respect do they differ from one another?

# Assignments

1 Where, and in what form, do the following store food?

a) man, b) a potato plant, c) a rice plant, d) sugar cane, e) sugar beet.

2 Give two reasons why it is useful for organisms to be able to store food.

3 Which is best as a source of food for man: grain or storage organs? Give reasons for your answer.

4 When a potato sprouts into a new plant, the starch has to be turned into glucose before it can be moved into the new plant.

a) Why is this necessary?
b) What is present in the potato which enables the starch to be turned into glucose?

5 Describe an experiment which you would carry out to see whether or not the stem of a particular plant is able to convert glucose into starch.

6 The graph below shows the relative amounts of carbohydrate in leaves and tubers of a potato plant towards the end of the growing season.

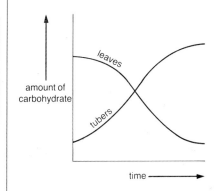

Explain the changes in the potato plant which are illustrated by this graph.

7 Why is food stored in each of the following?

a) a tomato,
b) a hen's egg,
c) a bean,
d) a coconut,
e) a carrot?

# Getting energy from food

*We need energy to move, grow, mend our tissues when they are damaged, and just to keep ourselves alive. We get energy from our food.*

| | kJ/g |
|---|---|
| margarine | 32.2 |
| butter | 31.2 |
| peanuts/groundnuts | 24.5 |
| chocolate (milk) | 24.2 |
| cake (plain) | 18.0 |
| sugar (white) | 16.5 |
| sausages (pork) | 15.5 |
| cornflakes | 15.3 |
| rice | 15.0 |
| bread (white) | 10.6 |
| chips | 9.9 |
| chicken (roast) | 7.7 |
| eggs (fresh) | 6.6 |
| potatoes (boiled) | 3.3 |
| milk | 2.7 |
| beer (bottled) | 1.2 |
| cabbage (boiled) | 0.34 |

**Table 1** How much energy is there in various everyday foods? You can find out by looking at this list.

| | kJ/day |
|---|---|
| New-born baby | 2 000 |
| Child 1 year | 3 000 |
| Child 2–3 | 6 000 |
| Child 5–7 | 7 500 |
| Girl 12–15 | 9 500 |
| Boy 12–15 | 12 000 |
| Office worker | 11 000 |
| Factory worker | 12 500 |
| Heavy manual worker | 15 000 |
| Pregnant woman | 10 000 |
| Woman breast-feeding | 11 000 |

**Table 2** Approximate amounts of energy required daily by different types of people

*The unit of energy used to be the kilocalorie, and in fact this unit is still used in some circles. However, it has now been officially replaced by the kilojoule.

## Does food really contain energy?

How can we show that a piece of bread, for example, contains energy? One way is to burn it. When the food is burned the energy contained inside it is set free as heat.

We can use this to find out how much energy a particular piece of food contains. We set fire to it, and estimate how much heat it gives out. This can be done simply, as in the Investigation, or more accurately by the method shown in Figure 1.

A known mass of food is burned. The heat given out heats up a known quantity of water. From the rise in temperature of the water we can work out the amount of energy released by the food. The energy contained in food can be expressed in **kilojoules** (kJ)*. 4.2 kJ of energy are required to raise the temperature of 1 kg of water through 1°C.

The three main kinds of food are carbohydrate, fat and protein (see pages 72 and 73). If we estimate the amount of energy in each of these, we can compare their **energy values**. Here they are:

| | |
|---|---|
| Carbohydrate | 1 g contains 17 kJ |
| Fat | 1 g contains 39 kJ |
| Protein | 1 g contains 18 kJ |

You will see that fat contains the greatest amount of energy. Carbohydrate and protein contain about half as much as fat.

## How much energy do different foods contain?

Look at Table 1. This tells us how much energy there is in some everyday foods. The amount of energy in a particular food depends on the substances which it contains. Thus margarine and butter contain a lot of energy because they consist almost entirely of fat. At the other extreme, cabbage contains very little energy because it consists of a high percentage of water.

Another thing which determines how much energy a particular food contains is how it is cooked. For example there is three times as much energy in chips as there is in boiled potatoes. Why do you think this is?

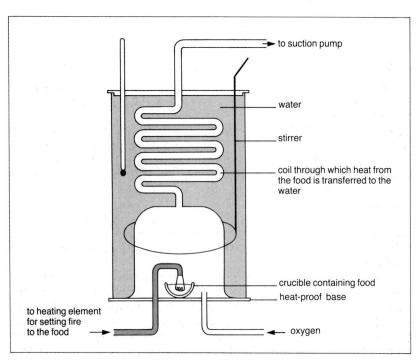

**Figure 1** This apparatus can be used to find out how much energy there is in a sample of food. It is called a food calorimeter.

## How much energy do we need each day?

Imagine someone lying in bed doing nothing. Even in such an inactive state he needs energy to breathe, make his heart beat, and drive all those countless chemical reactions which keep him alive. The rate at which these 'ticking over' processes take place is called the **basal metabolic rate**.

How much energy is needed to maintain the basal metabolic rate? It is difficult to say, because it varies from one individual to another. Very roughly the amount needed is 7 000 kJ per day. This is about the same amount of energy that would be needed to boil enough water for one hundred cups of tea.

This figure applies to a person who is completely at rest. It doesn't even include the energy he needs to feed himself. Scientists have tried to work out how much energy an average person needs to get through the day with the minimum effort, i.e. to get up in the morning, eat and drink and do other essential tasks, but no more. The figure is about 9200 kJ per day. A person could get enough energy to satisfy this need by eating one large white loaf a day, though of course this would not be a balanced diet.

Few of us spend our days like that – most of us do something. Look at Table 2. This tells us roughly how much energy is needed each day by different people. You will see that the amount depends on the person's age, sex and occupation. A person who spends most of his time sitting down needs far less energy than a very active person.

The important thing is that we should eat sufficient food to provide enough energy for our daily activities whatever they may be.

## What happens when we eat too much?

Suppose a person eats more food than he needs for producing enough energy. What happens to the food left over? Most of it is turned into fat and stored beneath the skin. The result is that his body weight* increases, and he runs the risk of becoming fat. Putting on weight is caused by a person's energy input being greater than his energy output.

The most 'fattening' foods are those which provide the most energy, such as bread and margarine, cake and sweets.

How can a person lose weight? The only way is by making his energy input less than his output. This can be done in two different ways:

1  By taking more exercise: this will increase his energy output.
2  By eating less energy-containing food: this will decrease his energy input.

The first method is not very effective – we've tried it! A person has to take a lot of exercise to make much difference to his weight. For example, a man trying to lose weight may play a game of tennis for half an hour. In doing so he loses about 700 kJ of energy. After the game he feels thirsty and has a glass of beer. The result is that he puts back all the energy he has just lost.

The second method is very effective if carried out properly. A person on a well planned weight-reducing diet can lose about 1 kg per week. Such diets contain relatively little high-energy food and a lot of low-energy food; the result of going on such a diet is shown in Figure 2.

The best results can be obtained by combining both methods, i.e. by going on a weight-reducing diet and taking more exercise.

For everyone there is a 'correct' weight. This will depend on his or her age, height and build.

Look at the bar chart in Figure 3. It is based on data obtained in the United States for people between the ages of 15 and 70. It shows that there are more deaths amongst people who are overweight than amongst people of normal weight. In other words, overweight people do not live as long, on average, as people who are the normal weight. An overweight person has a greater chance of having a stroke or a heart attack (see page 137). Other illnesses, too, are connected with overweight. The risk of death is greater for men than for women, and it increases with the amount of overweight.

**Figure 2** Going on a diet can be a good way of losing weight. This particular person reduced her weight from 183.5 kg (28 st 12 lb) to 64 kg (10 st 1 lb) in under a year, a loss of 119.5 kg (18 st 11 lb). By trick photography she is seen in this picture before and after losing weight.

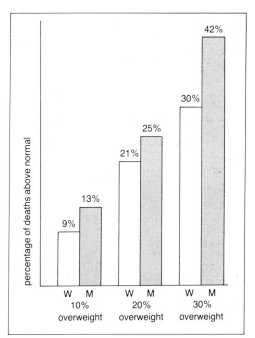

**Figure 3** This bar chart shows the relationship between people's body weight and the death rate in the United States.

¹ Strictly speaking we should call this the body *mass*. However, the word 'weight' is normally used in this context, and so we shall use it here.

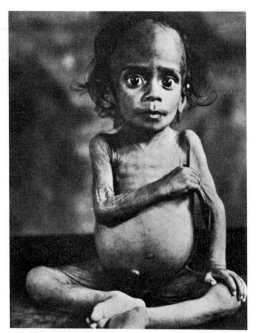

**Figure 4** This little girl is suffering from general starvation (marasmus).

**Figure 5** This map shows the approximate percentage of the population who are starving in different parts of the world. The shaded areas in each pie chart represents the proportion of the population who receive less than 9200 kJ of energy per day from their food.

## What happens when someone starves?

What happens if a person eats nothing at all? To begin with he will get energy from his fat stores, As a result he loses weight.

Eventually all his fat gets used up. In order to stay alive the body then starts getting energy from his tissue proteins, particularly the muscles. As a result he 'wastes away', becoming thin and weak. Death usually occurs after about 60 days. This may happen to victims in concentration camps, and in areas where there is a severe famine. Occasionally it happens to a person who goes on a 'hunger strike' in prison.

Some people suffer from a mental condition in which they lose their appetite and eat very little. This is called **anorexia nervosa**. It sometimes happens to people, particularly young women, who are suffering from emotional stress. Such people often become thin and frail and can die.

There are many countries in the world where people do not get enough to eat. Although they may not die from lack of food, they become thin and weak and find it difficult to work. The wasting of the body resulting from a general lack of food is called **marasmus** (Figure 4). Don't confuse it with kwashiorkor (page 74). A child with kwashiorkor may be getting enough energy food; what it lacks mainly is protein. In practice it is often difficult to distinguish between different types of starvation, because the person may be short of all sorts of different nutrients and the effects may be complex. A person who is not getting enough protein or vitamins may be just as lacking in energy as a person who is not getting enough energy food.

## How many people are starving in the world?

We saw earlier that to get through the day a person needs at least 9200 kJ of energy. Anyone who receives less than this can be said to be starving.

Now look at Figure 5. From this you will see that in many places people get less than this minimum amount of energy. However in other places there are many people who get much more than they require.

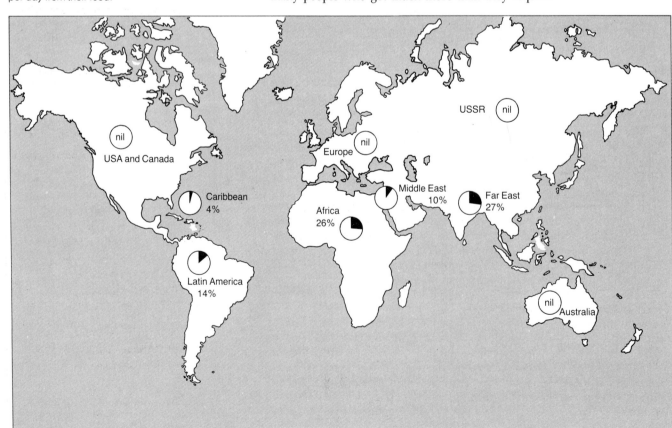

# Investigation

**A simple way to find out how much energy a piece of food contains**

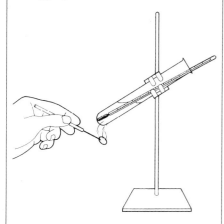

1  Measure out 20 cm³ of water with a measuring cylinder, then transfer it to a large test tube.

2  Clamp the test tube to a stand, and put a thermometer in it, as shown in the illustration.

3  Record the temperature of the water.

4  Weigh a peanut (groundnut), then stick it onto the pointed end of a mounted needle.

5  Hold the nut in a bunsen flame until it starts to burn, then place it under the test tube as shown in the illustration.

6  When the nut stops burning, record the temperature of the water again.

By how much has the temperature of the water risen?

Energy released from the nut in joules (J) = mass of water in grams × rise in temperature in °C × 4.2

Work out the amount of energy in joules released from the nut.

Convert the joules into kilojoules (kJ) by dividing by 1000.

Knowing the mass of the nut, work out how much energy in kilojoules is contained in one gram of peanut.

Compare your figure with others in your class and find the average.

How does the class average compare with the figure given in Table 1?

Do you think this is an accurate way of finding out how much energy there is in a piece of food?

# Assignments

1  What mass of roasted peanuts (groundnuts) would the heavy manual worker referred to in Table 2 have to eat in a day to just satisfy his energy needs?

2  Work out the total amount of energy you take into your body in a particular day. To do this you will need to weigh each item of food before you eat it, then look up Table 1 on page 84 to find out how much energy it contains. Are you getting more, or less, energy than the amount recommended in Table 2?

3  The table below gives the percentages of carbohydrate, fat and protein in three chocolate products.

|  | carbo-hydrate % | fat % | protein % |
|---|---|---|---|
| plain chocolate | 59 | 33 | 4 |
| milk chocolate | 54 | 36 | 8 |
| cocoa powder | 36 | 26 | 19 |

Which one contains the most energy, and which one contains the least?

4  The figures given in Table 1 are the amounts of energy actually present in carbohydrate, fat and protein as measured with a food calorimeter. In practice the amount of energy our bodies get out of each one is slightly less than the figures given. Suggest reasons for this.

5  The data summarised in Figure 3 were compiled by an American life insurance company.
   a)  Explain in full how you think the data were obtained.
   b)  Why should a life insurance company want to compile such data?

6  Give examples of the sort of food you would recommend to (a) someone who is going on a hiking holiday, and (b) someone who wishes to lose weight.

7  The following table shows the approximate amounts of energy used up in different activities by a normal man.

| | |
|---|---|
| sleeping | 4.5 kJ/min |
| sitting | 5.9 kJ/min |
| standing | 7.1 kJ/min |
| washing and dressing | 14.7 kJ/min |
| walking slowly | 12.6 kJ/min |
| walking fairly fast | 21.0 kJ/min |
| walking up stairs | 37.8 kJ/min |
| carpentry | 15.5 kJ/min |
| playing tennis | 26.0 kJ/min |
| playing football | 36.5 kJ/min |
| cross-country running | 42.0 kJ/min |

   a)  From these figures work out the approximate total amount of energy which you yourself use up in 24 hours. Show your working in full.
   b)  Using Table 1 draw up a menu for breakfast, lunch and supper which would give you just enough energy to satisfy your need. Give the amount of each food item which you would need.
   c)  A person who ate the food listed in your menu might still be getting an inadequate diet. Why?

8  The table below shows the daily energy requirements of people of different ages.

| Age (years) | Energy requirements (kJ/day) |
|---|---|
| 1 | 3 000 |
| 2 | 6 000 |
| 6 | 7 500 |
| 12 | 10 000 |
| 15 | 12 000 |
| 18 | 13 000 |

   a)  Plot these figures as a graph.
   b)  How would you explain the shape of the graph?
   c)  What assumptions are made in drawing up figures of this sort?
   d)  What can you say about a person's energy requirements *after* the age of 18?

# How is energy released?

*First we will find out what happens when we burn a piece of food in the laboratory. Then we will see if the same thing happens in our bodies.*

## What happens when food is burned in the laboratory?

When a piece of food is burned, energy is set free (see page 84). However, for the food to burn, certain things are necessary and certain things are produced. Thus food will only burn if oxygen is present. The more oxygen that's present, the better it will burn. One of the best ways of putting out a fire is to stifle it, i.e. to deprive it of oxygen.

In the chemical reaction which takes place when a piece of food burns, a gas is given off. If this gas is bubbled through lime water, the lime water goes milky (Investigation 1). This tells us that the gas is carbon dioxide. So burning food produces carbon dioxide.

We know, too, that burning food produces some water and of course it also produces energy in the form of heat.

So, to sum up, *when a piece of food is burned oxygen is used up, carbon dioxide is given off, water is formed and heat energy is produced.*

## How is energy produced in the body?

We have seen what happens when food is burned in the laboratory. Does the same thing happen in our bodies?

It has been known for a long time that living organisms generate heat (Investigation 2), and that they take in oxygen and give out carbon dioxide (Investigations 3 to 5 for example). But how can we find out if taking in oxygen and giving out carbon dioxide are connected with the breaking down of food?

One way of doing this is to use radio-active tracers (see page 160). In an experiment scientists made some glucose in which the normal carbon atoms were replaced with the radio-active isotope of carbon. In other words, the carbon atoms in the glucose were 'labelled'. They then fed this labelled glucose to a mouse and traced what happened to it (Figure 1). The radio-active carbon was detected by means of a Geiger counter.

**Figure 1** Experiment showing that the carbon dioxide which an animal breathes out comes from its food.

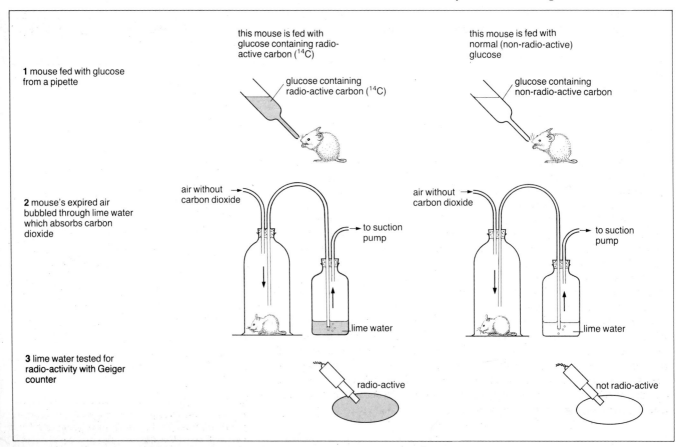

**1** mouse fed with glucose from a pipette

this mouse is fed with glucose containing radio-active carbon ($^{14}C$)

glucose containing radio-active carbon ($^{14}C$)

this mouse is fed with normal (non-radio-active) glucose

glucose containing non-radio-active carbon

**2** mouse's expired air bubbled through lime water which absorbs carbon dioxide

air without carbon dioxide

to suction pump

lime water

air without carbon dioxide

to suction pump

lime water

**3** lime water tested for radio-activity with Geiger counter

radio-active

not radio-active

The scientists found that after a short time the mouse started breathing out radio-active carbon dioxide. They concluded that the carbon dioxide breathed out came from the glucose.

We now know that in our cells glucose is **oxidised** to give carbon dioxide and water. In this process energy is set free, just as it is when a piece of food is burned in the laboratory.

We can summarise what happens like this:

$$C_6H_{12}O_6 \; + \; 6O_2 \; \rightarrow \; 6CO_2 \; + \; 6H_2O \; + \; energy$$

glucose     oxygen     carbon      water
dioxide

This process takes place in practically all living cells. We call it **respiration**. It is vitally important because it gives us energy.

### What is the energy used for?

Here are some of the things that organisms need energy for:
**Animals** need energy for movement (muscle contraction), for sending messages through nerves, for transporting things inside the body, and for keeping warm.
**Plants** need energy for taking up mineral salts from the soil, for opening and closing their stomata, and for transporting food substances.
**All organisms** need energy for growth, for cell division, and just for staying alive.

We can sum up by saying that our food serves as a fuel. The oxidation of the food in respiration drives our bodies, just as the burning of petrol drives a car.

### The chemistry of respiration

You can measure an organism's rate of respiration by measuring how quickly it takes up oxygen: the apparatus is called a **respirometer** (Investigation 6). Now if you measure the rate of respiration at different temperatures, you find that it increases as the temperature rises. In fact a rise of 10°C doubles the rate. This is true of chemical reactions in general, and it shows that respiration is basically an ordinary chemical process.

If the temperature rises much above 40°C respiration slows down rapidly and then stops altogether. This is the temperature at which enzymes are destroyed (see page 43), and it suggests that respiration is a chemical process which is catalysed by enzymes.

We now know that respiration is very complex. Scientists have shown that glucose is not broken down in one jump as the equation given above suggests. It is broken down in a series of small steps, each catalysed by a particular enzyme. The energy is released bit by bit (Figure 2). Why is this important? Think of it this way. A slice of pizza or apple pie contains as much energy as a stick of dynamite. If the energy was set free in one go, as when dynamite explodes, the person's body temperature would shoot up by at least 10°C and he would die.

The energy produced by the breakdown of glucose is not used directly. It is linked to activities such as muscle contraction by another chemical substance known as **adenosine triphosphate**, or ATP for short.

The breakdown of glucose releases energy which is used for making lots of ATP. The ATP then transfers the energy to the muscle, making it contract (Figure 3). It is interesting that if you put a drop of ATP on an isolated muscle fibre, it will contract; but if you put some glucose on it, nothing happens. This shows that glucose, by itself, cannot provide the energy needed for muscle contraction. It's the ATP, made as a result of breaking down glucose, which provides the energy for this and all other biological functions.

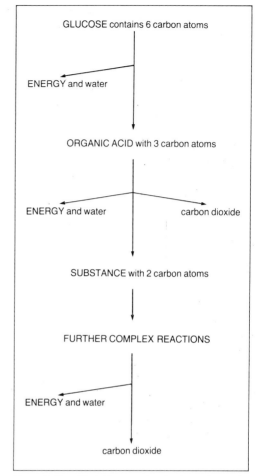

**Figure 2** Simplified diagram showing how glucose is broken down in cells to produce energy.

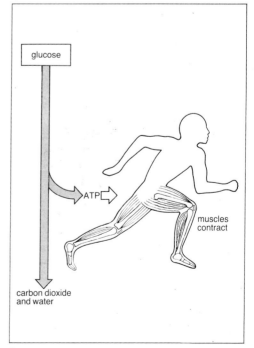

**Figure 3** Adenosine triphosphate (ATP) is thought to be a link between the breakdown of glucose and the contraction of muscles.

# Investigation 1

## To find out if burning food produces carbon dioxide

1 Put one level teaspoonful of sugar (sucrose) into a large test tube.

2 Set up the test tube as shown.

3 Place a bunsen burner under the sugar and heat it with a moderate flame.

If the lime water turns milky, this means that carbon dioxide gas is being given off by the burning sugar.

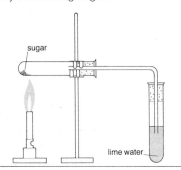

# Investigation 3

## To find out if a person breathes out carbon dioxide

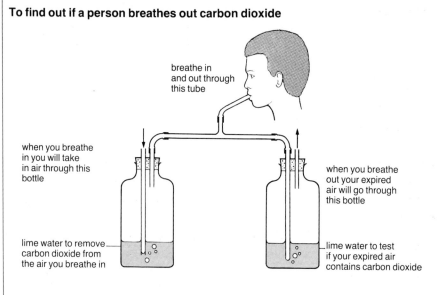

breathe in and out through this tube

when you breathe in you will take in air through this bottle

when you breathe out your expired air will go through this bottle

lime water to remove carbon dioxide from the air you breathe in

lime water to test if your expired air contains carbon dioxide

1 Set up the apparatus shown in the illustration.

2 Breathe in and out of the tube.

What happens to the lime water?

If it turns milky, the air you breathe out contains carbon dioxide.

# Investigation 2

## To find out if germinating peas give out heat

1 Put some moist cotton wool at the bottom of a thermos flask, then fill the flask with germinating peas and set it up as shown in the illustration.

2 Set up a second flask in the same way but use germinating peas which have been killed by boiling.

3 Leave the two flasks side by side for 24 hours, then note the temperature in each flask.

What conclusion do you draw?
Why were thermos flasks used?
Why was the second flask needed?

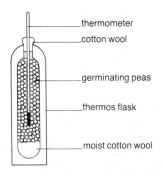

thermometer
cotton wool
germinating peas
thermos flask
moist cotton wool

# Investigation 4

## To find out if a small mammal gives out carbon dioxide
(*This experiment should be done as a demonstration by the teacher.*)

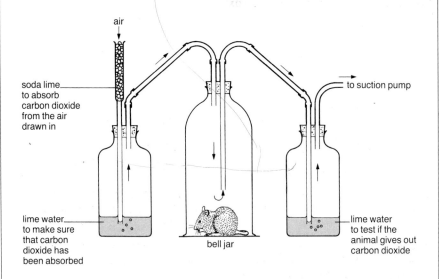

air

soda lime to absorb carbon dioxide from the air drawn in

to suction pump

lime water to make sure that carbon dioxide has been absorbed

bell jar

lime water to test if the animal gives out carbon dioxide

1 Put a small mammal such as a mouse or gerbil on a glass plate under a bell jar.

2 Set up the apparatus shown in the illustration. Use vaseline to make sure the three jars are air-tight.

3 Turn on the suction pump and draw air through slowly.

What happens to the lime water in the right-hand jar?

If it turns milky, the animal has been giving out carbon dioxide.

Where is the control in this experiment?

# Investigation 5

## To find out if small animals and plants give out carbon dioxide

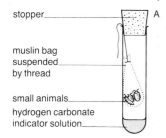

stopper

muslin bag
suspended
by thread

small animals
hydrogen carbonate
indicator solution

1  Put some small animals such as woodlice, or a cockroach, in a muslin bag.

2  Obtain a green leaf.
   Pour a little hydrogen carbonate indicator solution into three test tubes. Notice that the indicator is reddish-orange.
   What has happened to the hydrogen carbonate indicator in each test tube?

4  Set up the three test tubes as shown in the illustration.

5  Put test tube B in the dark, e.g. under a cardboard box.

6  Leave the three test tubes for about an hour.

7  After about an hour give each of the test tubes a quick shake.

What has happened to the hydrogen carbonate indicator in each test tube?

If it has turned from reddish-orange to yellow, it means that carbon dioxide has been given off.

What is the purpose of test tube C?
Why did you put test tube B in the dark?

# Investigation 6

## To find out if small animals take up oxygen

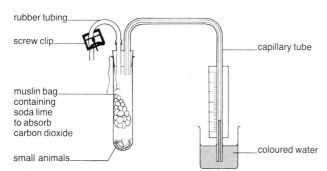

rubber tubing

screw clip

muslin bag
containing
soda lime
to absorb
carbon dioxide

small animals

capillary tube

coloured water

1  Put some small animals, e.g. woodlice, or a cockroach, in a test tube.

2  Set up the test tube as shown in the illustration. Make sure the system is air-tight by sealing the stopper with vaseline.

3  Set up another test tube exactly like the first one but without any animals in it. This is your control.

4  Close the screw clip and find out how far the coloured water rises up the capillary tube in 30 minutes.

Has the water risen in the glass tube? If it has, it could be caused by the animals taking up oxygen.

Can you think of any other possible explanation of your results?

This apparatus is called a **respirometer**. How could you use it to:

a) Compare the rate of respiration of different animals, and

b) find the effect of varying the temperature on the rate of respiration?

# Assignments

1  What would you conclude from each of these observations?
   a) A piece of food will only burn if oxygen is present.
   b) When food is burned a gas is given off which turns lime water milky.

2  Describe a simple experiment which could be done to find out if a piece of burning food produces water.

3  In order to show that the air we breathe out contains carbon dioxide, a teacher blows bubbles through a drinking straw into a glass of lime water.

   Why is this not as good an experiment as the one given in Investigation 3?

4  Your uncle did not do any science at school, and he does not believe that the air he breathes out contains carbon atoms from the food he eats. Write a short letter to convince him.

5  Give two differences between the way a piece of food releases energy when you burn it in a test tube and when it is broken down inside our cells.

6  The graph below shows the effect of temperature on the rate of respiration of a small animal. The respiration rate is expressed as the volume of oxygen consumed per kg of body mass per hour.

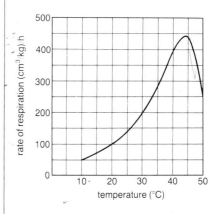

a) What do we call the apparatus that was used in this experiment?

b) What conclusions would you draw from the graph about the general nature of respiration?

# How do we digest our food?

*Have you ever wondered what happens to the food you eat? In this Topic we will follow what happens to an egg sandwich after it has been put in the mouth.*

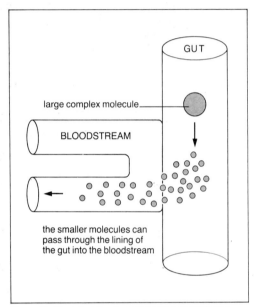

**Figure 2** Digestion involves breaking down large molecules into smaller, soluble ones which can then be absorbed into the bloodstream.

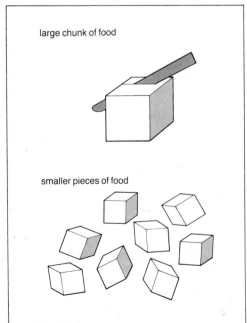

**Figure 3** Chopping up food into small pieces increases its surface area.

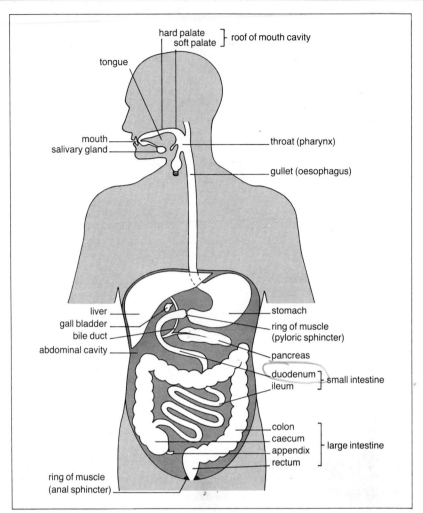

**Figure 1** This diagram shows the main regions of the human gut.

## The structure of the gut

The mouth leads into the gut or alimentary canal. This is really a tube running from the mouth to the anus. It's between 8 and 9 metres in length – that's about four times an average person's height. Being so long, much of it is coiled up and this enables it to fit into the abdominal cavity (Figure 1).

## What happens in the gut?

An egg sandwich contains starch, fat and protein: the starch is in the bread, the fat is in the margarine and the protein is in the egg.

All three of these substances are solids, but as they pass along the gut they are broken down into soluble substances. This process is called **digestion.** The soluble substances are then absorbed through the lining of the gut into the bloodstream, and carried round the body to where they are needed (Figure 2).

Digestion is brought about by two distinct processes which occur in the gut:

1   Breaking the food up into small pieces by chewing it and churning it up. This has no effect on the chemistry of the food; it merely breaks it up physically.
2   Mixing the food with **digestive enzymes** which dissolve it and break it down into a simpler chemical form. Large molecules such as starch are hydrolysed into smaller *soluble* molecules such as glucose.

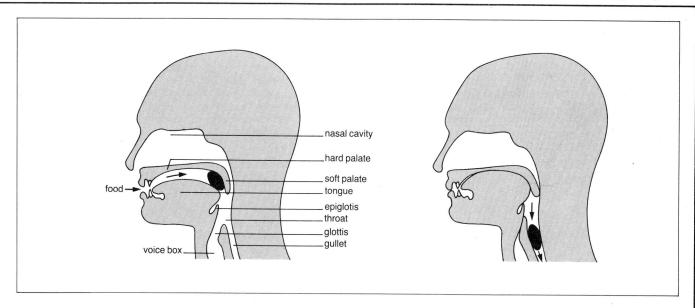

These two processes go on at the same time. Chopping up the food makes it easier for the enzymes to work, because it mixes them with the food and increases the surface area over which they can act (Figure 3). The enzymes are produced by various **glands** which open into the gut.

Now let's look in detail at what happens in each part of the gut.

## In the mouth cavity

You bite off pieces of the sandwich with your front teeth, and chew them with your back teeth. At the same time your mouth waters – in other words it becomes filled with **saliva** or 'spit'. This is produced by several salivary glands, each of which is connected to the mouth cavity by a tube, or duct, and it has the effect of moistening the food.

Actually your mouth starts watering *before* you begin to eat the sandwich. This is because the sight, smell and even the thought of food is enough to start saliva flowing. However, the greatest flow occurs when the food is actually in the mouth.

Saliva contains water together with two other main substances:

### 1 Mucus

This makes the food slippery so it slides easily through the throat when it's swallowed. Swallowing a piece of dry food, such as a digestive biscuit, without moistening it with saliva first, can be an uncomfortable experience!

### 2 Amylase (ptyalin)

This is the first enzyme which the sandwich meets as it travels through the gut. It acts on starch, breaking it down into a type of sugar called maltose (Investigation 1). If you chew a piece of bread for long enough, you can actually taste the sweetness as the maltose is formed.

Saliva also contains a chemical which kills many germs, preventing them getting into the stomach.

## Through the throat and down the gullet

When you swallow, the food is pushed down your throat into your gullet. Figure 4 explains what happens.

Once swallowed, the food passes down the gullet to the stomach. The gullet has muscles in its wall. A ring of contraction moves slowly downwards, pushing the food in front of it. This process is called **peristalsis** (Figure 5). The mucus from the saliva acts as a lubricant so that the food slips down easily.

**Figure 4** These diagrams show how swallowing takes place. Notice how the glottis is closed off so the food is prevented from getting into the windpipe.

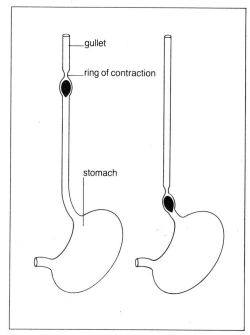

**Figure 5** Food is pushed down the gullet by a ring of contraction called a peristaltic wave.

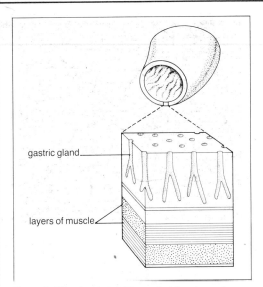

Figure 6  The structure of the wall of the stomach.

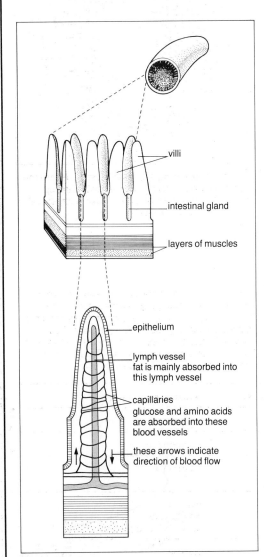

Figure 7  The structure of the wall of the small intestine is well suited to its job of completing the digestion and absorption of food.

## In the stomach

The stomach wall is thick and muscular, and its inner surface has numerous holes which lead into narrow cavities called **gastric glands** (Figure 6).

The gastric glands produce a fluid called **gastric juice**. This contains an enzyme called **pepsin** which helps to dissolve the protein in the egg by breaking it down into simpler substances called polypeptides (see page 42). Pepsin is quite different from saliva in its action: whereas saliva attacks starch, pepsin only goes for protein (Investigation 2).

If you were to cut open the stomach of, say, a rat and test the contents with pH paper, you would find it to be acidic. This is because the gastric glands produce large amounts of **hydrochloric acid**. Pepsin works best in these conditions (Investigation 3). The acid also helps to kill germs.

The wall of the stomach also produces lots of mucus which protects the stomach lining from being damaged by the acid in the gastric juice.

The food spends three or four hours in the stomach. Every now and again a wave of contraction passes along the stomach and churns the food up. As a result of all these actions, the food is turned into a mushy fluid. chyme

Between the stomach and small intestine there is a ring of muscle. Occasionally this opens and a wave of contraction sweeps some of the food into the first part of the small intestine. If there is anything wrong with the food, violent contractions in the other direction shoot it up the gullet and out through the mouth. This, of course, is **vomiting**, and it is an important way of getting rid of germs or poisons from the body.

## In the small intestine

The small intestine, despite its name, is the longest part of the gut and may be over six metres in length. Here the digestion of the egg sandwich is completed, and the soluble products are absorbed into the blood.

The small intestine receives fluids from three different places.

### 1 The liver

This produces a fluid called **bile**. The bile is stored in the gall bladder and after a meal it is squirted, bit by bit, into the duodenum. Bile contains substances called **bile salts**. These act on the fat, breaking it up into small droplets. The same kind of thing happens when washing-up liquid comes into contact with fat. We call this process **emulsification** (Investigation 4).

### 2 The pancreas

This produces a fluid called **pancreatic juice** which flows down the pancreatic duct into the duodenum. It contains three important enzymes:
**Amylase** breaks starch down into maltose, and thus continues the process which was begun by saliva in the mouth cavity.
**Trypsin** breaks down protein into polypeptides, as pepsin does in the stomach.
**Lipase** attacks fat, breaking it down into fatty acids and glycerol. This completes the digestion of the fat. The action of lipase is made easier by the fact that the fat has already been broken up into droplets by the bile.

### 3 Intestinal glands

These glands are situated in the wall of the intestine itself. They produce the enzyme **maltase** which breaks maltose down into glucose, thereby finishing off the digestion of starch. They also produce several enzymes called **peptidases** which complete the digestion of protein by breaking up the polypeptides into amino acids.

If you were to test the contents of the small intestine with pH paper, you would find them to be alkaline. This is because the various fluids which are secreted into the small intestine contain a lot of sodium hydrogen carbonate. This neutralises the acid from the stomach, which is necessary because trypsin and the other enzymes in the small intestine will only work properly in alkaline conditions (Investigation 5).

While all this is going on, wave-like contractions of the small intestine move the food about, and finally sweep it on towards the large intestine.

The egg sandwich has now been more or less completely dissolved. The soluble products of digestion are now absorbed through the lining of the small intestine into the blood vessels within its wall.

The structure of the wall of the small intestine is shown in Figure 7. It is well suited to carry out its jobs. It contains numerous pouch-like glands for producing intestinal juice. Thousands of finger-like projections called **villi** (singular: villus) stick into the cavity, greatly increasing the surface area for absorption (Figure 8). Within the villi there are numerous blood capillaries for taking up the absorbed food. Towards the outside of the wall there are muscles for bringing about the contractions mentioned earlier.

Table 1 summarises the various enzymes and other secretions which have helped to digest the egg sandwich.

## What happens in the large intestine?

The bread which was used for making the egg sandwich contained a certain amount of cellulose. We refer to this as fibre or roughage (see page 72). Human beings don't have an enzyme to break this down, so it cannot be digested. Along with some fluid, it passes on to the colon.

As material passes along the colon, water is absorbed from it, so it becomes more solid. This solid matter then passes on to the rectum where it is stored as **faeces**. The lining of the rectum produces mucus which eases the passage of the faeces along it. Eventually the faeces are voided through the anus by powerful contractions of the wall of the rectum. We call this **defaecation**.

Although there is much variation, it normally takes between 24 and 48 hours from the time the food is eaten to the time when the faeces derived from it are ready to be voided through the anus.

## The caecum and appendix

The caecum and appendix are an offshoot from the first part of the large intestine, a kind of blind alley. They have no function in man, but in grass-eating mammals such as rabbits they contain large numbers of bacteria which can digest cellulose and break it down into glucose (see page 102).

## Things that can go wrong with the gut

In man the appendix occasionally gets infected with germs. As it is an offshoot from the main part of the gut, the germs do not get flushed out by the normal passage of material along the gut. So they multiply there and may cause severe inflammation leading to **appendicitis**. Normally appendicitis is cured by removing the appendix in an operation.

People often complain of 'indigestion'. This is usually caused by eating food too quickly and not chewing it enough. The gastric glands produce extra

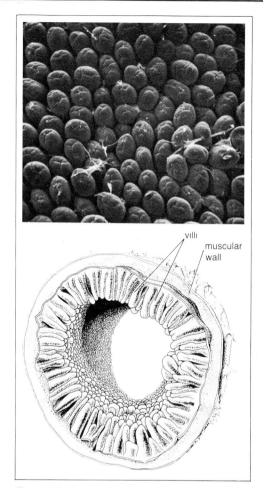

Figure 8 Looking into the small intestine. Notice the finger-like villi projecting into the cavity. The top picture, taken with a scanning electron microscope, shows the villi in surface view.

Table 1 Summary of the main digestive enzymes found in the human gut. Bile salts are included though they are not really enzymes. The stomach of calves produces an additional enzyme called rennin. Rennin turns soluble milk protein into a solid which is then attacked by pepsin. Rennin is not produced by the human stomach.

| Where it comes from | Where it works | Name of enzyme | Food acted on | Substances produced | |
|---|---|---|---|---|---|
| salivary glands | mouth cavity | amylase | starch | maltose | |
| stomach wall | stomach | pepsin | protein | polypeptides | |
| liver | small intestine | bile salts (not enzymes) | fat | fat droplets | |
| pancreas | small intestine | amylase<br>trypsin<br>lipase | starch<br>protein<br>fat | maltose<br>polypeptides<br>fatty acids and glycerol | can be absorbed |
| wall of small intestine | small intestine | maltase<br>sucrase<br>peptidases | maltose<br>sucrose<br>polypeptides | glucose<br>glucose and fructose<br>amino acids | |

large amounts of gastric juice with the result that the stomach contains a lot of acid. If the person belches, some of the acid comes up the gullet giving a burning sensation which is sometimes called 'heartburn'. Indigestion can be counteracted by taking a tablet or drink which will neutralise the acid.

A person who constantly has too much acid in his stomach may get an **ulcer**. The gastric juice starts to eat into the lining of the stomach which becomes raw and painful. Ulcers tend to develop in middle-aged and elderly people, and they often seem to be brought on by overwork and worry.

A doctor can find out if a person has an ulcer by getting him to drink a thick fluid containing barium. This is called a 'barium meal'. The barium is opaque to X-rays, and if the patient is X-rayed the inside of his gut shows up clearly (Figure 9). An ulcer will appear as a bump in the lining.

Most people suffer from **constipation** at some time or another. The faeces move too slowly along the large intestine, with the result that more water is absorbed from them than usual and they become hard and dry. Constipation is often caused by bad bowel habits. People usually feel the need to defaecate after a meal, particularly breakfast: this is a natural reflex arising from stretching of the gut wall. If you persistently suppress this reflex, the faeces are held in the large intestine and constipation may result.

Doctors believe that constipation is also caused by eating over-refined foods which don't contain much roughage. Roughage adds to the bulk of material in the large intestine, stretching its wall. This stimulates the muscles to contract, pushing the faeces along and keeping them moving.

The opposite of constipation is **diarrhoea**. This results from faeces moving too quickly along the large intestine so there isn't time for the usual amount of water to be absorbed. Diarrhoea is often caused by germs which irritate the lining of the gut. This causes the lining to produce a lot of watery mucus and sets up waves of contraction which sweep the contents along very quickly.

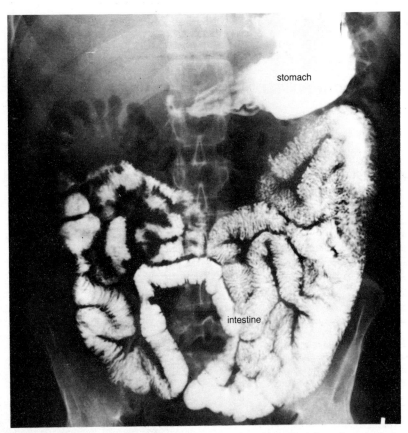

**Figure 9** An X-ray photograph of the human stomach and intestine taken after a barium meal was swallowed.

## Investigation 1

### To find out if saliva breaks down starch

1  Collect your saliva in a test tube to a depth of 2 cm.

2  Half fill another test tube with a 4 per cent starch solution.

3  With a pipette place 15 drops of iodine solution, side by side, on a white tile.

4  With a glass rod lift a drop of the starch solution from the test tube and mix it with the first drop of iodine on the white tile. A blue-black colour indicates starch. This will serve as your control.

5  Pour your saliva into the test tube of starch suspension, and shake quickly.

6  With the glass rod place a drop of the starch-saliva mixture with a drop of iodine on the white tile, and mix them together.

7  Repeat step 6 with the other drops of iodine at half-minute intervals. Note the colour given each time.

Explain the colour reactions as fully as you can.

Approximately how long does it take for your saliva to break down the starch?

## Investigation 5

### To find out if trypsin works best in alkaline conditions

Follow the same instructions as in Investigation 3, but use trypsin instead of pepsin.

What happens to the egg white in each test tube?

Does trypsin work best in acid or alkaline conditions?

How does trypsin compare with pepsin as regards the conditions in which it works best?

# Investigation 2

**To compare the actions of saliva and pepsin**

1 Obtain four large test tubes. Label them A to D.

2 Collect some saliva in a test tube.

3 Obtain some acidified pepsin solution.

4 Obtain some hard-boiled egg white (albumen) and some white bread.

5 Set up the four test tubes like this:

   A  bread covered with saliva
   B  bread covered with pepsin
   C  egg white covered with saliva
   D  egg white covered with pepsin

6 Leave the test tubes in a warm place, for 48 hours.

7 After 48 hours examine the contents of the test tubes.

In which test tubes has the food material disappeared?

Which of the two food materials is acted upon by:

(a) saliva, and (b) pepsin?

What conclusions do you draw from this experiment?

# Investigation 3

**To find out if pepsin works best in acid conditions**

1 Obtain four large test tubes. Label them A to D.

2 Obtain some hard-boiled egg white (albumen) and cut it up into four pieces.

3 Place one piece of the egg white in each test tube.

4 Cover the egg white with one of the following solutions:

   A  pepsin plus acid
   B  pepsin plus alkali
   C  water plus acid
   D  water plus alkali

5 Leave the test tubes in a warm place, for 48 hours.

6 After 48 hours examine the contents of the test tubes.

What has happened to the egg white in each test tube?

What is the point of setting up test tubes C and D?

Does pepsin work best in acid or alkaline conditions?

# Investigation 4

**To find the effect of bile salts on oil**

1 Obtain three test tubes, and label them A, B and C.

2 Pour some corn oil into each test tube to a depth of about 3 cm.

3 To A add a few drops of water.
To B add a pinch of powdered bile salts.
To C add a few drops of washing-up liquid.

4 Shake the test tubes, then let them stand for a while.

What has happened to the oil in each test tube?

How do bile salts help digestion?

How does washing-up liquid help with washing up?

5 Half fill a test tube with water and add a small piece of solid fat. Shake well.

6 Half fill a second test tube with a solution of bile salts and add a small piece of fat. Shake well.

What happens to the fat in each test tube? Explain your observations.

# Assignments

1 Which region of the human gut:

  a) absorbs water from indigestible material, *colon*
  b) receives bile from the bile duct, *duodenum*
  c) contains the enzyme pepsin, *stomach*
  d) is normally acidic? *stomach*

2 Put forward a reason for each of the following:

  a) A piece of food is dissolved by digestive enzymes more rapidly if it is chewed first,
  b) Eating plenty of roughage (fibre) helps to prevent constipation.

3 What job does mucus do in (a) the throat, (b) the stomach, and (c) the rectum?

4 There is a disease of cattle in which the villi in the small intestine are destroyed and the inner lining of the small intestine becomes smooth. As a result the animal gets weak and wastes away. Why do you think the disease has this effect?

5 It has been suggested that saliva produced *during* a meal digests starch faster than saliva produced *before* the meal. Describe an experiment which could be done to find out if this is true.

6 The diagram, right, shows an experiment which is intended to show what happens in the human gut.

After being set up, glucose but *not* starch passes out of the bag into the surrounding water.

  a) How could you show that glucose has leaked out, but starch has not?
  b) How would you explain this result?
  c) To what extent is this similar to what happens in the human gut?

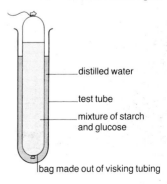

distilled water

test tube

mixture of starch and glucose

bag made out of visking tubing

# Teeth

*Teeth are one of our most valuable possessions. Here we shall look at their structure, and see what happens if we don't look after them properly.*

kc

ll macdonald

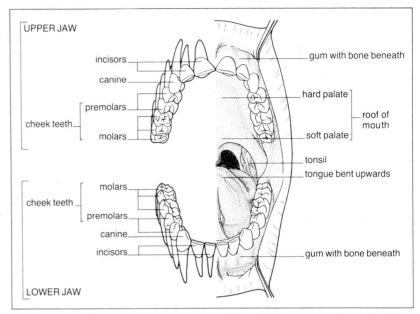

Figure 1 Open wide! Looking inside the mouth of an adult human to see the teeth and other related structures. The roots are shown on the left-hand side.

## What kind of teeth do we have?

Figure 1 shows the inside of the mouth of an adult man with a full set of teeth. Figure 2 shows some of the teeth as a dentist might see them.

On both sides of the upper and lower jaws there are, from the middle outwards:

TWO **incisor teeth** which are shaped like chisels and are used for cutting food;

ONE **canine tooth** which is shaped like a dagger and also cuts food;

FIVE **cheek teeth** which have broad tops with bumpy surfaces and are used for grinding food.

The first two cheek teeth are known as **premolars**, and the last three as **molars**. There are 32 teeth altogether.

Now compare the teeth in Figure 1 with your own teeth (Investigation 1).

When the mouth is closed the upper and lower teeth fit together as shown in Figure 3. This biting action is brought about by powerful muscles which run from the lower jaw to the side of the skull.

## Looking at the outside of our teeth

If you look at teeth which have been extracted by a dentist, you will see that they can be divided into two parts: the **crown** and the **root** (Figure 4). The crown is the part of the tooth which you can see inside the mouth, that is the part above the gums. The crowns of the cheek teeth have several **cusps** like little mountains on them. The premolars usually have two cusps each, whereas the molars have four.

The root is normally buried in a socket in the jaw bone and is therefore hidden from view. The incisors and canines have roots which consist of a single projection, but the cheek teeth, being larger, generally have two or three projections.

## The inside of a tooth

Figure 5 shows the inside of our teeth. The crown is made up of three layers. On the outside is a thin layer of extremely hard **enamel**. Beneath this is a layer of hard ivory-like **dentine**. In the centre is a soft area called the **pulp cavity** which contains small blood vessels and a nerve. Tiny channels

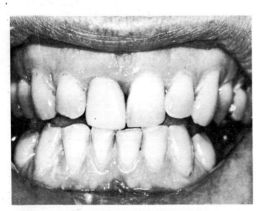

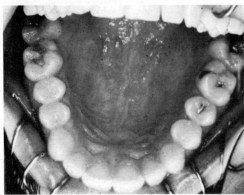

Figure 2 A dentist's view of the inside of a person's mouth. Try to identify the various teeth, using Figure 1 to help you.

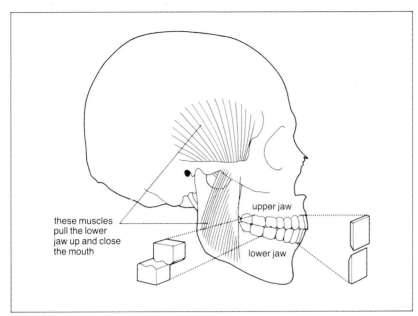

Figure 3  When the mouth closes and you bite something, the teeth fit together as shown in this picture.

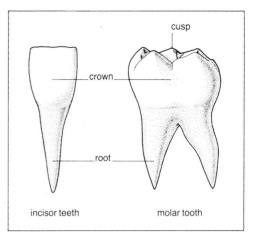

Figure 4  This is what teeth look like after they have been extracted from the jaw.

containing extensions of living cells run out from the pulp cavity into the dentine. This makes the dentine very sensitive. The enamel and dentine both contain calcium phosphate, and it is this that makes them hard.

On the outside of the root is another hard material called **cement**. Attached to the cement are tough fibres which run into the jaw bone. These fibres hold the tooth in its socket, but they permit it to move very slightly and cushion it from excessive jarring when it hits something hard.

## When do we get our teeth?

A baby is born without teeth. During the next few years it develops a set of 20 **milk teeth**. The first tooth breaks through when the baby is about six months old, and usually the set is complete by the age of two or three. There are two incisors and one canine on either side of each jaw, but there are only two cheek teeth as the baby's jaws are too small for any more.

Between the ages of six and twelve the milk teeth fall out, one by one, and are replaced by a set of **permanent teeth**. There are four cheek teeth on either side of each jaw. A fifth cheek tooth may be added after the age of 17. These are known as **wisdom teeth**. The person now has a full set of 32 teeth. This is his final set; if he loses any now, they will not be replaced.

If the person's jaws are small, a wisdom tooth may break through behind the fourth cheek tooth and push it against the third. This is called an impacted wisdom tooth and it can be very painful. Usually the dentist extracts the wisdom tooth together with the tooth immediately in front of it.

## Tooth decay

In developed countries **tooth decay** is a serious problem. In Britain, for example, eight out of ten children have tooth decay by the age of five; and by the age of twenty, three people in ten have lost *all* their teeth and wear 'false teeth' or dentures.

Why do our teeth decay? Saliva is normally slightly alkaline, but after a meal, bacteria in the mouth feed on any sugar present and turn it into acids. The acid eats into the teeth. After an hour or so the saliva neutralises the acid and washes it away, but by then the rot has begun.

If you look at some teeth which have been pulled out by the dentist, you will see what decay can do to them. Decay usually starts in the crevices

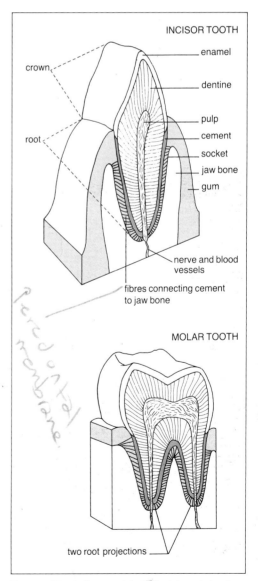

Figure 5  These diagrams show the internal structure of teeth.

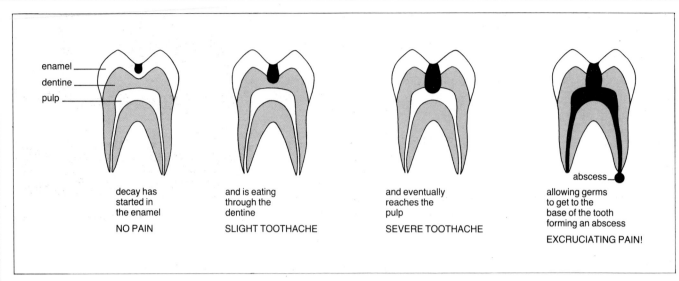

enamel
dentine
pulp

decay has
started in
the enamel
**NO PAIN**

and is eating
through the
dentine
**SLIGHT TOOTHACHE**

and eventually
reaches the
pulp
**SEVERE TOOTHACHE**

abscess

allowing germs
to get to the
base of the tooth
forming an abscess
**EXCRUCIATING PAIN!**

**Figure 6**  The progress of decay in a cheek tooth.

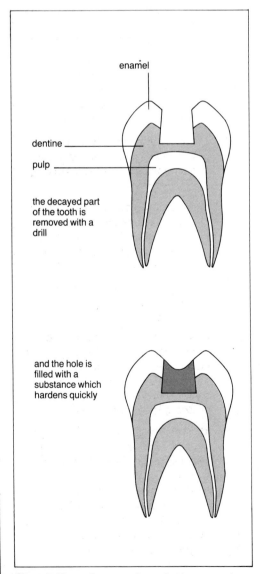

enamel

dentine
pulp

the decayed part
of the tooth is
removed with a
drill

and the hole is
filled with a
substance which
hardens quickly

**Figure 7**  These diagrams show what happens when a dentist fills a tooth.

between the cusps on the surface of the crowns, and also between the teeth. The acid eats through the enamel into the dentine, thereby enabling the bacteria to infect the pulp cavity (Figure 6). This causes **toothache**. In severe cases the pulp may be killed and the infection may spread to the base of the tooth, causing an **abscess**. This can be extremely painful.

Provided the decay hasn't gone too far, the tooth can be repaired by a dentist (Figure 7). The dentist cuts away the decayed part of the tooth with a drill, and fills the hole with a substance which hardens quickly. The hole is always made wider at the bottom than the top: this prevents the filling from falling out.

Normally back teeth are filled with a mixture of metals such as silver and tin, but front teeth are filled with porcelain or a plastic-like material which is the same colour as the teeth.

If the decay has got right into the pulp cavity, the dentist may be unable to save the tooth and he may have to pull it out. Sometimes the dentist will take an X-ray of the person's teeth to find out what state they are in (Figure 8).

Two other common conditions are **gum disease** and **pyorrhoea**. Gum disease, as the name implies, is infection of the gums. In pyorrhoea the fibres which hold the tooth in its socket get infected, with the result that the tooth becomes loose. Pyorrhoea is a major reason why people lose their teeth and have to wear dentures.

## Tooth decay and the diet

Many studies have been made which show that tooth decay is caused by eating sugary foods such as cakes, ice cream and sweets, and by drinking sugary drinks. The amount of tooth decay in children in Britain has greatly increased over the last twenty years – so has the amount of sweet-eating. In contrast, the incidence of tooth decay amongst African tribes who don't eat sweets is low. It's also interesting that during World War 2, when few sweets were available in Britain, tooth decay was much less common than it is today.

## How can we prevent tooth decay?

The bacteria which cause decay form a thin layer of scum over the surface of the teeth. This scum is called **plaque** (Investigation 2). Tooth decay can be prevented by removing this plaque or stopping it being formed. It takes about 24 hours for plaque to be re-formed after it has been removed, so it's essential to remove it at least once a day.

Here are some tips recommended by dentists:

1   Clean your teeth regularly, particularly after breakfast and before going to bed at night. Use **dental floss** as well as a toothbrush.

2 If possible finish your meal with a rough vegetable such as a carrot, then rinse your mouth out with water.

3 Don't eat sweets or drink sugary drinks between meals, and above all don't hold sweets in your mouth and suck them for a long time.

You should visit the dentist every six months, even if you think there's nothing wrong with your teeth. Decay may have started without you realising it. The dentist can then do any necessary fillings *before* the decay gets bad.

There is a growing belief amongst dentists and scientists that fluoride helps to prevent tooth decay by strengthening teeth, particularly when they are forming, and possibly by stopping plaque-formation. Fluoride occurs naturally in the drinking water in some parts of the world, and in these areas the amount of tooth decay is said to be less than elsewhere. In some places very small amounts of fluoride are added to the drinking water, and it's claimed that this has reduced the incidence of tooth decay.

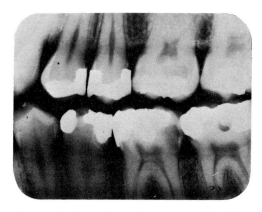

**Figure 8** An X-ray picture of human teeth. The white areas are fillings.

# Investigation 1

## Looking at human teeth

1 Look at the inside of your mouth with a mirror.

Which structures shown in Figure 1 can you see?
How many teeth have you got altogether?
Identify your incisors, canines and cheek teeth.
Which of the teeth shown in Figure 1 have you *not* got?
Which of your teeth are permanent and which ones, if any, belong to your milk set?

2 Examine healthy human teeth in detail.

Using Figure 1 to help you, decide whether each tooth is an incisor, canine or cheek tooth.

Draw each type of tooth, showing as many of the structures in Figure 4 as you can see.

3 Examine a human skull and lower jaw.

Whereabouts does the lower jaw move against the upper jaw?

Where would the muscles which close the mouth be attached?

4 Examine decayed teeth which have been extracted by the dentist.

Compare them with healthy teeth. Whereabouts is the decay?

Why do you think the decay is situated where it is?

# Investigation 2

## To see the plaque on your teeth

This can be done using plaque-staining tablets available from a pharmacy.

1 Chew a tablet and spread it over your teeth with your tongue. Then spit it out. (These tablets are not meant to be swallowed, but it will do you no harm if you swallow them.)

2 Rinse your mouth with water.

3 Look at your teeth in a mirror. Any plaque will be stained pink. Where is the plaque located?

4 Brush your teeth with toothpaste in the usual way, then rinse your mouth out with water.

5 Look at your teeth in the mirror again.

Has all the plaque been removed? If not, where is it still left?

6 Brush your teeth again. Work the toothbrush this way and that, and try hard to remove all traces of plaque. Then rinse your mouth out with water.

7 Look at your teeth in the mirror again.

Has all the stained plaque been removed now?

8 If there is still some plaque between your teeth, try removing it with dental floss. This is a thread-like material which can be pulled backwards and forwards between the teeth.

Does dental floss remove the plaque?

# Assignments

1 Each structure in the left-hand column below is related to one of the words on the right.
Write them down in the correct pairs.

enamel          crushing
pulp            sharp
tooth fibres    hard
canine          sensitive
molar           pyorrhoea

2 In about a hundred words, give advice to the general public on how to clean their teeth so that all plaque is removed from them.

3 You are employed by a research organisation to test the claim that small amounts of fluoride in drinking water help to prevent tooth decay. How would you tackle this problem?

4 The 'dental formula' of an adult human is

$$i\frac{2}{2} \quad c\frac{1}{1} \quad pm\frac{2}{2} \quad m\frac{3}{3}$$

i stands for incisors, c canines, pm premolars, m molars. The top figures denote the number of teeth on *one* side of the upper jaw, the bottom figures denote the number of teeth on *one* side of the lower jaw.

a) What is your own dental formula at the moment?

b) Which teeth, if any, do you lack and why?

c) What was your dental formula likely to have been when you were 5 years old?

d) Explain what has happened to your teeth since you were 5.

# Feeding in other mammals

*All mammals digest their food in basically the same way as man does. However, the structure of the gut and teeth vary according to the kind of food each animal eats.*

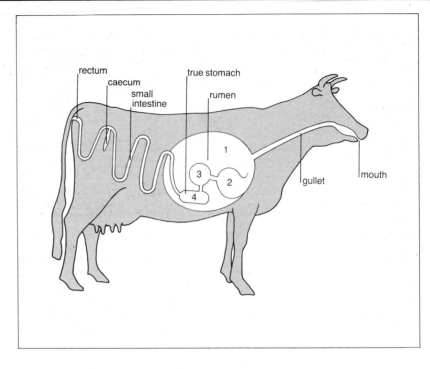

**Figure 1** The stomach of a ruminant has four chambers. In the first chamber (the rumen) cellulose is broken down by microbes; in the second chamber the food is filtered; in the third chamber water is absorbed from it; and in the fourth (the true stomach) it is digested by pepsin in the usual way.

**Figure 2** Tigers have large canine teeth for tearing the flesh of their prey. The tiger is the largest and fiercest of the great cats. It can bring down antelopes, cattle and water buffalo.

## Who eats what?

Animals can be split into carnivores, herbivores and omnivores. **Carnivores** eat other animals: examples include dogs, cats, lions, tigers and wolves. **Herbivores** eat plants: they include rabbits, cows, sheep and horses. **Omnivores** eat other animals and plants: man and pigs are examples.

## Differences in the structure of the gut

Omnivorous and carnivorous mammals have guts which are similar to man's: there is no need for them to be different. Herbivores, however, have a problem because much of their food consists of cellulose which is tough and difficult to digest. Mammals do not possess the necessary enzyme for breaking down cellulose – in fact the only organisms to possess this enzyme are certain microbes.

Herbivorous mammals have three special features which enable them to digest cellulose:

1  They have a very long small intestine – as long as 40 metres in the case of the cow. Digestion is slower than in other mammals, and having a long intestine ensures that digestion is complete before the food reaches the end.

2  They have a large caecum and appendix which contain numerous bacteria capable of breaking cellulose down into sugar. Some of the sugar is used by the bacteria, but the rest is absorbed by the herbivore. This is an example of two organisms helping one another: the microbes get shelter and protection, and in return the herbivore gets sugar from cellulose. This kind of partnership is called **symbiosis** (see page 372).

3  Some herbivorous mammals have a special kind of stomach. Such mammals are called **ruminants** and they include cows and sheep. The stomach consists of four chambers, the first of which is called the **rumen** and is very large (Figure 1). The animal eats grass and swallows it into the rumen without chewing it first. After a while it stops eating, and regurgitates the grass, a little at a time, into the mouth cavity where it is chewed. This is called chewing the cud. In the rumen the food is churned up by contractions of the muscles, and the cellulose is broken down by microbes. The food is then passed on to the other chambers where it is further processed, before entering the small intestine.

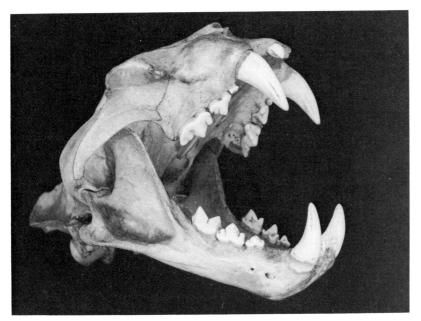

**Figure 3** The skull of a lion. Notice the large dagger-like canines. They can cut right through the neck of a zebra or antelope. In Africa more humans have been killed by lions than by any other wild animal. In one area a pair of lions terrorised the local people for nearly a year before being shot. During this time they killed and ate numerous people, including 28 workmen who were building a new railway.

## Differences in the teeth

The structure of the teeth is closely related to the diet (Investigation). Thus lions and tigers have large dagger-like canines for killing their prey and tearing its flesh (Figures 2 and 3). Dogs have an extra-large cheek tooth on either side of each jaw for scraping flesh off bones (Figure 4). Rabbits, mice

**Figure 4** These diagrams show the structure and action of the teeth of a carnivore such as the dog.

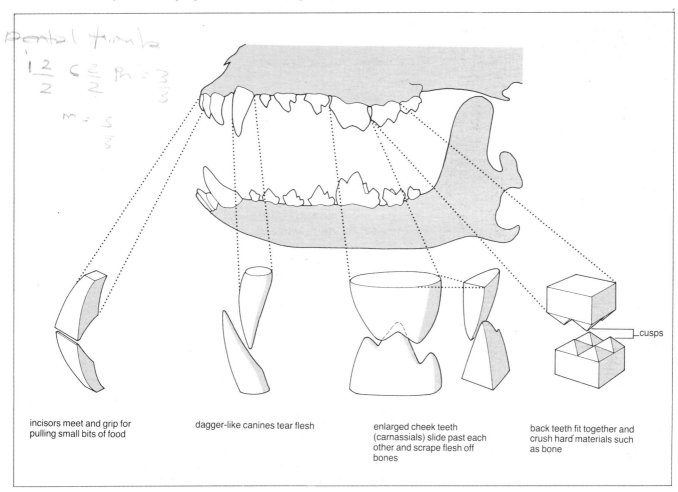

incisors meet and grip for pulling small bits of food

dagger-like canines tear flesh

enlarged cheek teeth (carnassials) slide past each other and scrape flesh off bones

back teeth fit together and crush hard materials such as bone

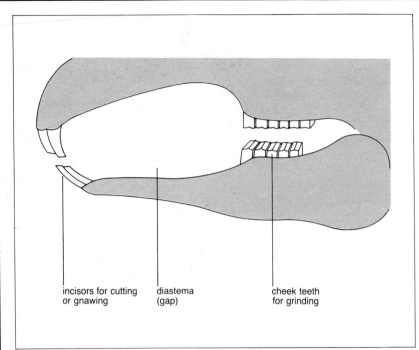

**Figure 5** The teeth of a rabbit are used for gnawing and grinding plant food. The diastema provides a space in the mouth cavity where food can be held before being ground up.

incisors for cutting or gnawing

diastema (gap)

cheek teeth for grinding

**Figure 6** These diagrams show the structure and action of the teeth of a herbivore such as the sheep.

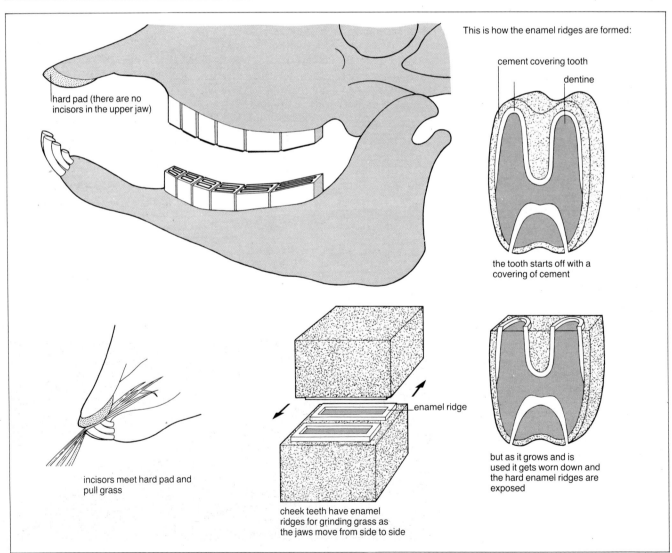

hard pad (there are no incisors in the upper jaw)

This is how the enamel ridges are formed:

cement covering tooth

dentine

the tooth starts off with a covering of cement

but as it grows and is used it gets worn down and the hard enamel ridges are exposed

incisors meet hard pad and pull grass

enamel ridge

cheek teeth have enamel ridges for grinding grass as the jaws move from side to side and squirrels have sharp chisel-like incisors for cutting or gnawing, and a row of file-like cheek teeth for grinding their food; they have no canines: instead there is a gap called the **diastema** (Figure 5). Horses, sheep and cows have blunt incisors for cropping grass, and cheek teeth with ridges on the surface for grinding it up. The ridges result from the teeth gradually being worn down: the enamel wears down more slowly than the other materials, so it stands up above the rest of the tooth (Figure 6).

If you watch a sheep chewing its food, you will see that its lower jaw moves from side to side. The same is true of many other herbivores such as cows and deer. This fits in with the structure of the cheek teeth whose enamel ridges run longways along the length of the jaw as shown in Figure 6. Obviously the grinding effect will be greatest if the jaw moves from side to side.

Certain herbivores, such as the rhinoceros, have enamel ridges which run transversely across the cheek teeth. For them the best grinding effect will be achieved if they move the lower jaw backwards and forwards – and that's exactly what they do.

One of the most efficient herbivores is the horse. The enamel ridges on its cheek teeth form a complicated pattern and are very good at grinding up grass (Figure 7).

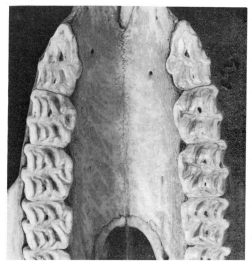

**Figure 7** Notice the enamel ridges on these teeth belonging to a horse.

# Investigation

### Comparing the teeth of different animals

1 Examine the skull of a carnivore such as a dog. Identify the incisors, canines and cheek teeth.

  How do the teeth differ from yours? What job does each type of tooth do?

2 Repeat the above with the skull of a herbivore such as a sheep or rabbit.

  How do its teeth differ from (a) a human's, and (b) a dog's?

3 Look at the skulls of other animals which your teacher gives you. In each case look carefully at the teeth, and suggest what kind of food the animal feeds on.

4 Write down the dental formula of each animal (see page 101). Are any types of teeth (incisors, canines, etc.) missing?

  How do you think the animal manages without them?

5 When you get an opportunity, watch various mammals eating. Observe the action of the jaws and relate it to the structure of their teeth.

# Assignments

1 Why is it that:
   a) man cannot digest cellulose,
   b) herbivores have a particularly long small intestine,
   c) a sheep's jaw moves from side to side when it chews,
   d) the cow has a hard pad at the front of its upper jaw?

2 In what way does (a) chewing the cud, and (b) the grinding up of grass by the teeth, help digestion in a herbivore such as the cow?

3 What is it about the structure of:
   a) a lion's canine teeth that enables it to tear flesh,
   b) a dog's carnassial teeth that enables it to scrape all the flesh off a bone,
   c) a dog's back molar teeth that enables it to break a stick in two,
   d) a horse's cheek teeth that enables it to eat grass?

4 Mammals other than humans rarely suffer from tooth decay. Why do you think this is?

5 Many animals use their teeth for purposes other than feeding. Write down the names of two such animals, and in each case suggest *one* use of the teeth apart from feeding.

6 The photograph below shows the front part of the skull of a certain mammal.
   a) What kind of mammal do you think it is?
   b) What do you think it feeds on?
   c) What do you think it uses its teeth for?

Give reasons for your answers.

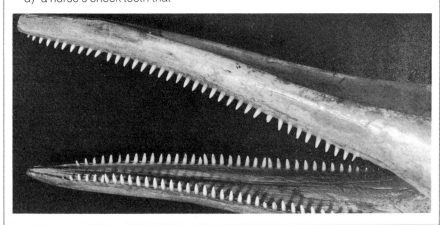

# How do other organisms feed?

*Having studied feeding in mammals, we will now see how it occurs in a variety of other oganisms.*

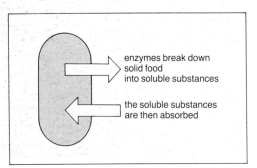

Figure 1 Some bacteria feed like animals. Complex food substances which may be in solid form, are broken down into a liquid and then absorbed.

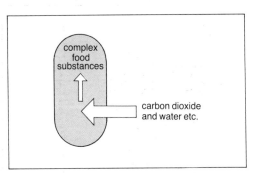

Figure 2 Some bacteria feed like plants. Simple substances such as carbon dioxide and water are built up into complex food substances.

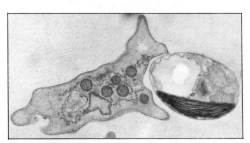

Figure 3 *Amoeba*. Left: seen in section under the microscope, taking in a larger piece of food than it can manage! Right: what happens during feeding.

## How do bacteria feed?

Bacteria have two quite different ways of feeding: some feed like animals, others like plants. Through their feeding activities these bacteria play an important part in the cycling of elements in nature (see page 28).

### Bacteria that feed like animals

These bacteria feed on ready-made organic food. They get their food from the bodies of living or dead animals and plants. Those that feed on dead material are **saprotrophs**; they help to bring about decay. Those that feed on living organisms are generally **parasites** and cause disease.

To feed on solid material, bacteria must first break it down into soluble substances. They do this by shedding **digestive enzymes** through their body surface. These enzymes break the food down outside the bacteria. This is called **extra-cellular digestion**. They then soak it up (Figure 1). A large population of bacteria can eventually turn a solid object into a liquid. This is what happens when things decay.

### Bacteria that feed like plants

These bacteria make their own organic food from simple substances like carbon dioxide and water (Figure 2). Many of them get the necessary energy from sunlight just as green plants do, by a type of **photosynthesis**, and they possess a special kind of **chlorophyll** for carrying it out.

Some bacteria which can make their own food do not get energy from sunlight. Instead they produce energy by special chemical reactions which take place inside their bodies. We call this **chemosynthesis**. Many of these bacteria put useful nitrogen compounds into the soil which plants need (see page 29).

## How do fungi feed?

Fungi feed on ready-made organic food. They get their food from two sources. Some of them feed on dead material: these are **saprotrophs**. They make food go mouldy and help to bring about decay.

Other fungi feed on living organisms: they are **parasites**. Some of them do a lot of harm, damaging crops and killing trees.

## How does Amoeba feed?

*Amoeba* feeds on tiny organisms in the water, mainly bacteria and green protists. Suppose a little organism of this kind comes close to an amoeba. The amoeba's cytoplasm flows round it, forming a cup (Figure 3). Eventually the prey becomes completely trapped in the cavity. We call this a **food vacuole**. Here the prey is killed and digested, and the soluble products are absorbed into the surrounding cytoplasm. Any bits and pieces that cannot be digested are got rid of across the cell membrane.

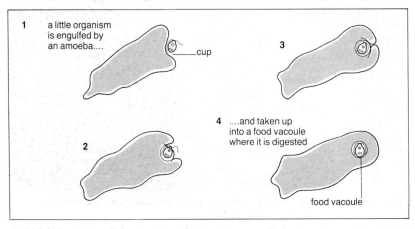

## How does Euglena feed?

When the sun is shining and there is plenty of light, *Euglena* feeds like a plant. Using its chloroplasts, it makes its own food by photosynthesis.

To help it do this, *Euglena* always swims towards well-lit places. The mechanism which guides it towards light is described on page 46.

When it's dark, or the light is dim, *Euglena* can feed by taking in organic substances from the surrounding water. It cannot take in solid food, but it can absorb dissolved substances across its surface.

## How does Hydra feed?

*Hydra* feeds on small animals like water fleas. When the animal bumps into the hydra's tentacles, it is in for trouble (Figure 4). You can watch what happens by putting a water flea in a dish with a hungry hydra (Investigation 1).

The moment the water flea touches the tentacle, the **sting cells** leap into action. Each one shoots out a **thread**, like a harpoon (Figure 5). The thread has a pointed tip which pierces the prey's skin. A drop of **poison** then oozes out of the tip: this paralyses the water flea, stopping it moving. Other similar cells have a long coiled thread which wraps itself round the water flea's bristles, holding it firm.

Meanwhile the tentacles close round the unfortunate animal, and pull it towards the mouth. It is then forced into the **digestive cavity**.

Inside the digestive cavity, the prey is broken down into pieces by **digestive enzymes** produced by the gland cells. The pieces are then taken up by the absorptive cells which engulf them rather like the amoeba does. When the cell has done this, it develops a flagellum. This waves about and stirs up the digestive fluid.

Finally bits which cannot be broken down are forced out of the mouth.

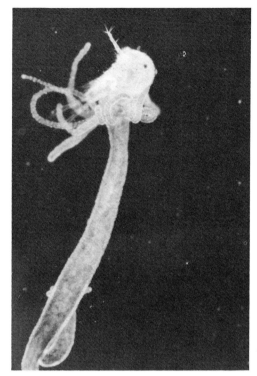

**Figure 4** There is no escape for this water flea which swam into the hydra's tentacles.

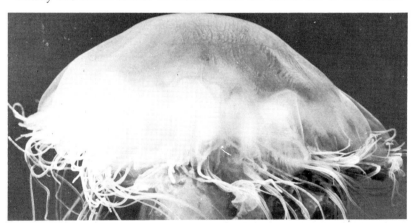

**Figure 6** The jellyfish (top) and sea anemone are relatives of *Hydra*. They possess tentacles and sting cells and feed in a similar way.

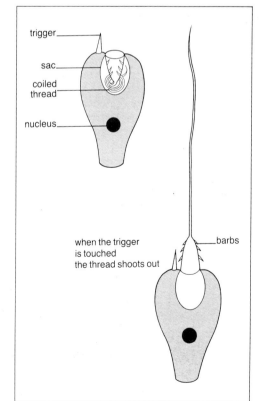

**Figure 5** The sting cell of a hydra before and after its thread is shot out.

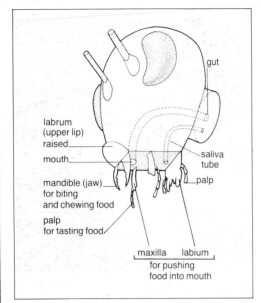

Figure 7 The mouth parts of an insect such as the locust, cockroach or grasshopper. In reality, the mouth parts are closer together than shown here, but they have been separated to show them clearly.

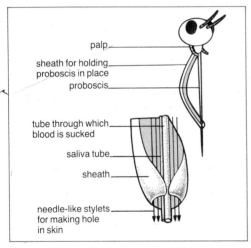

Figure 8 The mouth parts of a mosquito.

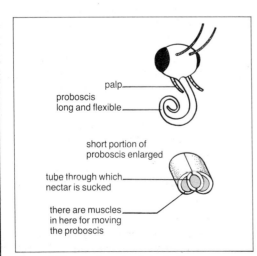

Figure 9 The mouth parts of a butterfly.

## How do insects feed?

For feeding, insects have special structures round the mouth. These are called **mouth parts**. Different insects have mouth parts which are adapted for feeding on different foods (Investigation 2). Here are four examples.

### The locust chews plants

The locust's mouth parts include a pair of powerful jaw-like **mandibles** (Figure 7). These cut off pieces of leaf, and grind them up. Behind the mandibles are structures which push the food into the mouth. Sensitive finger-like **palps** hang down on either side: with these the insect tastes the food to see if it is suitable for eating. While the food is being chewed, it is moistened with saliva, which comes from a pair of salivary glands in the thorax.

### The mosquito sucks blood

The mosquito's mouth parts take the form of a needle-like **proboscis** (Figure 8). When a mosquito lands on a person's body, it pushes its proboscis through the skin. The proboscis is protected by a sheath which holds it in place when it is being driven into the skin. It then injects a drop of saliva into the wound. This stops the blood congealing, otherwise it might block the proboscis. The mosquito then sucks blood through its proboscis.

### The butterfly sucks nectar

The butterfly has a long proboscis like a tongue (Figure 9). It pushes this into flowers in order to suck up the nectar. It coils its proboscis up when not in use.

### The housefly sucks solids

The housefly has a probosics which acts like a vacuum cleaner (Figure 10). It has a pair of swollen pads at the end. The pads are covered with narrow grooves which are connected with a tube that runs up the middle of the proboscis to the gut. Flies can feed on solid things like lumps of sugar. The fly puts its pads in contact with the sugar. A drop of saliva flows down the proboscis. This dissolves the sugar and then the fly sucks it up. The narrowness of the grooves prevents any solid matter getting into the proboscis.

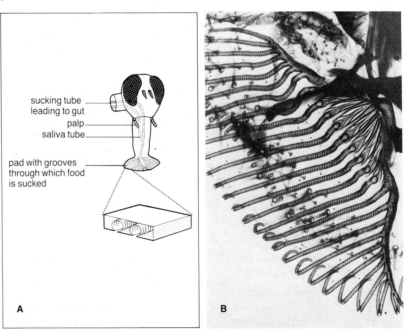

Figure 10 A The mouth parts of a housefly; B Photograph, taken down the microscope, of part of one of the pads at the end of the proboscis. Notice the food grooves.

## How do fish feed?

Most fish feed on small organisms such as plankton (see page 24) worms and crabs (Investigation 3). As the food passes through the pharynx, it is prevented from getting between the gills by the **gill rakers**: these are slender bars which stick out from the bases of the gills (see page 58).

Some fishes eat much larger prey, which they bite into pieces or swallow whole (Figure 11). Scientists have opened up the stomachs of sharks and found such surprising objects as buckets and old petrol cans. The stomach of a large specimen, caught in the 18th century, is said to have contained an entire suit of armour!

For hunting down their prey, sharks use their excellent sense organs. Take the great white shark for example. This huge fish is extremely sensitive to movements of the water: it can detect a moving object, such as a swimmer, over a kilometre away. As the shark moves closer to its prey, its sense of smell takes over. As it closes in for the kill, it depends mainly on its eyes. Finally, when it is almost on top of its prey, it closes its eyes and opens its mouth: it now relies on an 'electrical' sense which works rather like radar. As soon as the shark feels the pressure of the prey on its teeth, its jaws automatically snap shut.

Figure 11 The huge dagger-like teeth of this Great White shark are used for biting the prey into pieces.

## Investigation 1

**Watching hydra feeding**

1 Obtain a watch glass containing a hydra which has been starved for several days.

2 Obtain a jar containing water fleas.

3 With a pipette transfer one or two water fleas from the jar to the watch glass.

4 If a water flea bumps into the tentacles, the hydra may catch it and eat it.

   If this happens, watch the hydra's feeding behaviour.

5 Make drawings every now and again to show what happens.

Someone has suggested that hydra must suffer from severe indigestion. Why should this be?

## Investigation 2

**Examining the mouth parts of insects**

1 Obtain a preserved locust, grasshopper or cockroach.

2 With a needle lift up the labrum ('upper lip').

   Can you now see the mandibles (jaws)?

3 Now try to find the other feeding structures shown in Figure 7.

4 Look at the mouth parts of other insects, such as the mosquito, butterfly and housefly, under a microscope.

   Which of the structures shown in Figures 8 to 10 can you see?

   How are the mouth parts suited to dealing with the kind of food which each insect eats?

## Assignments

1 Describe how an amoeba ingests its food. What happens to the food after it has been ingested?

2 Give the name of an organism which has two alternative methods of feeding. What are the advantages of having two methods?

3 How is the nutrition of bread mould
   a) similar to, and
   b) different from
   that of a mammal?

4 How do:
   a) fishes stop bits of food getting into their gills,
   b) houseflies liquify their food before ingesting it,
   c) mosquitoes prevent blood from clotting inside the proboscis,
   d) sharks locate their prey?

5 Describe an experiment which you could do to find out if a sea anemone prefers to eat shrimps or small fish.

6 When a water flea bumps into a hydra's tentacles, the sting cells send out their threads. However, when the hydra touches the ground with its tentacles while it is moving, the sting cells do not send out their threads.

   Put forward explanations of why the sting cells respond differently to the water flea and to the ground.

## Investigation 3

**Examining the gut of a fish**

1 Obtain a bony fish, preferably one which is used as food by humans.

2 Slit open the ventral (belly) side and remove the gut. This is called 'gutting', and it has to be done before a fish is cooked for eating.

3 Identify the main regions of the gut. How does it differ from a mammal's gut?

4 Cut open the stomach and examine its contents. What has the fish been eating?

# How do we breathe?

*Breathing is the process by which we draw air into our bodies. It is an essential part of respiration. If a person is prevented from breathing, he is likely to die within a few minutes.*

## What happens to the air we breathe in?

Air is a mixture of gases which include oxygen and carbon dioxide. What happens to these gases when we breathe in? You can find out by comparing the air we breathe in (inhaled air) with the air we breathe out (exhaled air) (Investigation 3). Table 1 shows the results of an accurate comparison. You will see that exhaled air contains less oxygen and more carbon dioxide than inhaled air.

## The lungs

When we breathe in, air is sucked into our **lungs**. The lungs are the main organs of our respiratory system. The butcher calls them 'lights'. If you examine them you will see why (Investigation 1). They are light and soft, and are riddled with spaces like a sponge. These spaces contain air. From this air oxygen is taken up into the blood, while carbon dioxide passes in the opposite direction. We refer to this movement of gases as **gas exchange**.

We have two lungs, situated side-by-side in the chest or **thorax**. The sides of the chest are bounded by the **ribs**, which are joined to the backbone (vertebral column) at the back and the breastbone (sternum) at the front. Between the ribs are muscles called **intercostal muscles**. The thorax is separated from the abdomen below by the **diaphragm**. This is a sheet of muscular tissue, shaped like a dome, which is stretched across between the bottom-most ribs. You can see some of these structures in Figures 1 and 2.

Each lung is surrounded by two thin sheets of tissue, called the **pleural membranes**. The inner one covers the lungs, and the outer one lines the inside of the thorax. Between them is a narrow space containing a fluid. This fluid serves as a lubricant, allowing the membranes to slide over each other smoothly as we breathe in and out.

## The route by which air reaches the lungs

Air is sucked into the lungs through a series of cavities and tubes which together make up the **respiratory system** (Figure 3).

**Table 1** The percentage composition of inhaled and exhaled air of a resting human.

|  | Inhaled air | Exhaled air |
| --- | --- | --- |
| Oxygen | 20.93 | 16.4 |
| Carbon dioxide | 0.03 | 4.1 |
| Nitrogen (and argon) | 79.04 | 79.5 |

**Figure 1** The lungs are located inside the chest cavity as shown in this diagram.

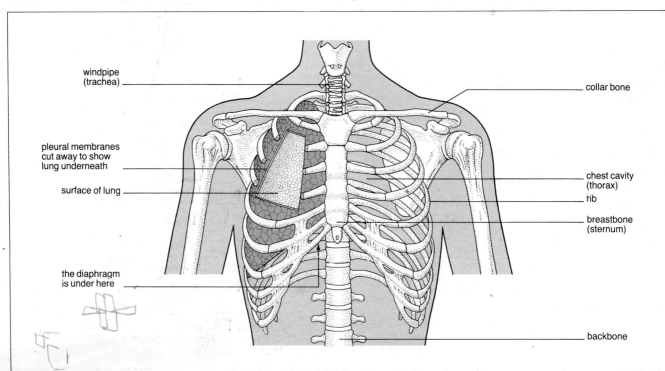

windpipe (trachea)

pleural membranes cut away to show lung underneath

surface of lung

the diaphragm is under here

collar bone

chest cavity (thorax)

rib

breastbone (sternum)

backbone

Here are some notes on the main structures which make up the respiratory system.

*The nose*

Air is drawn into the nose through the **nostrils**. The inside of the nose is moist and warm. It is moist because its lining produces mucus. It is warm because there are numerous blood vessels close to the surface. If you've ever had a nose-bleed you will know what a lot of blood there is in the lining of the nose.

At the back of the nose there is a large space called the **nasal cavity**. This is divided up by several bony partitions which give it a large surface area rather like the radiator of a car. The air is warmed and moistened as it passes over these surfaces, and it is cleaned at the same time. Dust and germs get caught in the mucus and are wafted towards the throat by beating cilia. The mucus, like saliva, contains a substance which kills germs. The mucus is then swallowed or coughed up – unless of course you expel it beforehand by blowing your nose. The lining of the nose is also very sensitive to touch, and this may make you sneeze. These are all ways of preventing germs getting into the lungs.

In the lining of the nasal cavity there are sensory cells sensitive to smell. Our sense of smell tells us whether or not the air is suitable for breathing. It therefore enables us to test the air before we take it into our lungs.

We can sum up the functions of the nose by saying that it warms, moistens, cleans and tests the air we breathe in. It protects the lungs from germs and harmful substances which might injure them or start an infection.

You can, of course, breathe through your mouth. If you do this the protective functions of the nose are not carried out and the risk of infection is increased. We all breathe through our mouths when we have a cold in the nose, but in general it is a bad habit.

Leading from the nasal cavity at the front of the skull are a number of cavities called **sinuses**. The sinuses produce mucus which normally drains into the nasal cavity. However, the holes connecting the sinuses with the nasal cavity are small, and if the person has a cold they get swollen and blocked. The sinuses then fill up with fluid, and the pressure may cause a headache.

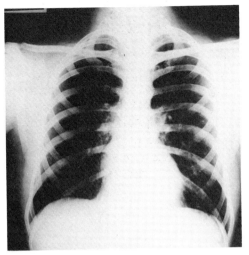

**Figure 2** X-ray of the human chest. How many of the structures shown in Figure 1 can you see in this photograph?

**Figure 3** The respiratory system of man. The lungs are located in the chest cavity or thorax. There are really far more alveoli than are shown in this simplified diagram.

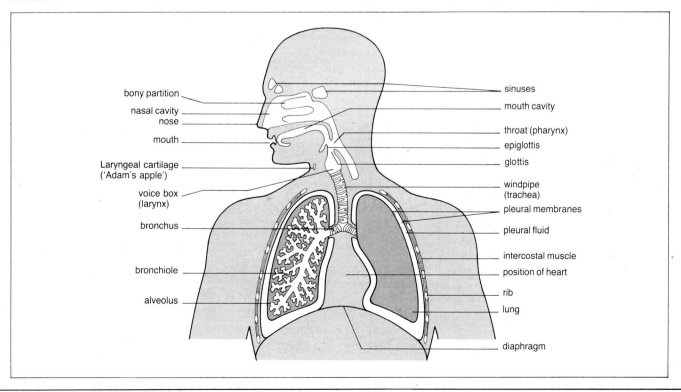

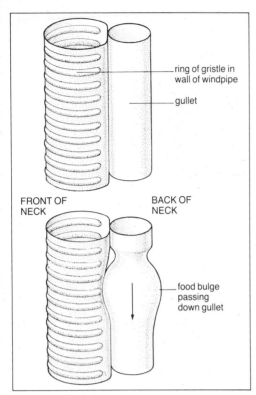

**Figure 4** The rings of gristle keep the windpipe open even when food passes down the gullet.

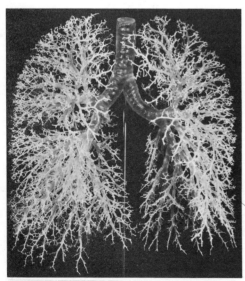

**Figure 5** A corrosion preparation of the human lungs. All the lung tissue except the bronchial tubes has been dissolved away.

### The throat

The throat, or **pharynx**, belongs to both the respiratory and alimentary systems (see page 92). Food passes from the mouth cavity into the gullet and thence to the stomach. Air, on the other hand, passes from the nasal cavity into the windpipe and so to the lungs.

The air enters the windpipe through a small hole called the **glottis**. Obviously it is important that food should not get into this hole. This is prevented by the **epiglottis**, a small flap of tissue stiffened with gristle. When we swallow, the glottis becomes closed off by the epiglottis, and breathing stops. Despite this mechanism, a piece of food may sometimes get stuck in the glottis: we say it has gone down the wrong way. It can usually be dislodged by coughing, helped if necessary by a pat on the back.

### The voice box

The glottis opens into the voice box or **larynx**. This shows up at the front of your neck as your 'Adam's apple'. It feels hard because there are pieces of gristle in its wall. The voice box enables us to talk, sing and shout. Thin membranes, formed from its lining, are stretched across the cavity. They are called **vocal cords**. When air is forced through the voice box the cords vibrate, producing sounds in much the same way that a piano produces sounds when the strings vibrate.

### The windpipe

If you put your finger below your 'Adam's apple', you can feel your windpipe or **trachea**. It is a straight tube, about 12 cm long, situated just in front of the gullet.

For air to pass freely to and from the lungs, it is important that the windpipe should be open all the time. To keep it open, its wall is stiffened by rings of gristle. These rings are like a pile of C's which face towards the centre of the neck so the open side of the C is next to the gullet: this allows the gullet to expand when food passes down it (Figure 4).

The inner lining of the windpipe produces mucus and is covered with cilia. Some of the dust particles and germs which have escaped being caught in the nasal cavity, get caught in this mucus. The cilia waft the mucus upwards to the glottis so that it can be either swallowed or coughed out. The windpipe thus helps to prevent germs and harmful substances getting to the lungs.

### The bronchi

After the windpipe has entered the chest, it splits into two short tubes called **bronchi** (singular: bronchus), one to each lung. The bronchi are similar to the windpipe, except that they are narrower.

### The bronchioles

Within each lung the bronchus splits into numerous branches, like a tree: the whole structure is called the **bronchial tree** (Figure 5). The branches are called **bronchioles**, and they get very narrow towards the ends. Their walls are not surrounded by rings of gristle; instead they contain smooth muscle which allows them to widen or get narrower depending on circumstances.

### The alveoli

Each bronchiole leads to a bunch of tiny sacs called **alveoli** (singular: alveolus). The alveoli are surrounded by a network of blood capillaries, rather like a string bag (Figure 6). The capillaries are in close contact with the alveoli, and the membrane separating them is extremely thin. Across this membrane gas exchange takes place: oxygen diffuses from the alveoli into the blood, and carbon dioxide diffuses from the blood into the alveoli. The lining of each alveolus is covered by a thin layer of fluid and the oxygen dissolves in this before it passes through into the blood (Figure 7).

There are about 150 million alveoli in each lung, and altogether they cover a very large surface area. Someone has worked out that if you were to open them out and flatten them like a sheet, they would cover an area as large as a tennis court! It is very important that the lungs should have a large surface area, because it means that more oxygen can be taken up by the blood every time we breathe in.

The alveoli always contain air, even when we breathe out as hard as we can. If there was no air inside them, their walls would cave in and stick together. Their surface area would then be reduced and gas exchange would be impossible.

## How does air get into the lungs?

Breathing takes place by movements of the chest. The chest works rather like a pair of bellows, sucking air in and then forcing it out.

We can divide breathing into two parts:

**Inspiration:** this is the sucking of air into the lungs, and it is brought about by the chest expanding.

**Expiration:** this is the forcing of air out of the lungs, and it is brought about by the chest contracting.

This is how inspiration is brought about (Figure 8):

1  The ribs swing outwards and upwards. This is brought about by contraction of the intercostal muscles. This increases the size of the thorax in the side-to-side direction. At the same time the breast bone moves forward slightly, so the size of the thorax is increased in a front-to-back direction as well.

2  The diaphragm moves downwards, so that instead of being dome-shaped, it becomes flattened. This is brought about by contraction of muscles in the diaphragm itself. This increases the size of the thorax in a top-to-bottom direction.

All these movements result in a negative pressure – a suction force – being developed inside the thorax. The result is that the walls of the lungs are pulled outwards and air is drawn into them (Investigation 2).

Expiration is brought about by the reverse process: the ribs swing downwards and inwards, the breastbone moves back slightly, and the diaphragm bows upwards. A positive pressure is developed inside the thorax. The result is that air is forced out of the lungs.

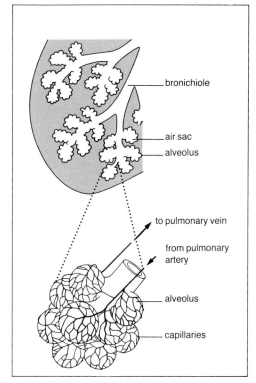

**Figure 6** These diagrams show the detailed structure of part of a lung and its blood supply.

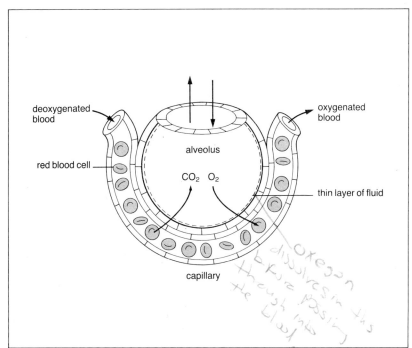

**Figure 7** As the red blood cells go past an alveolus, they give up carbon dioxide and pick up oxygen. These gases move in and out by diffusion.

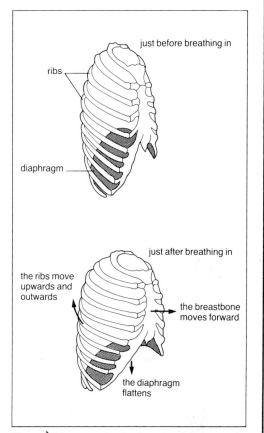

**Figure 8** Diagrams showing how the chest expands when we breathe in.

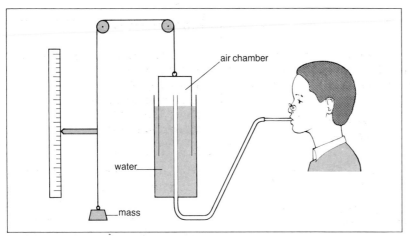

**Figure 9** A spirometer measures the amount of air you can take into your lungs. You take the deepest possible breath in, and then exhale as completely as possible into the air chamber. The major divisions on the scale are litres.

How much air do we take into our lungs when we breathe in? About half a litre when we are at rest. However, this is only a fraction of the amount we *can* take in if we want to. You can find out how much air you can take into your lungs by means of a **spirometer** (Figure 9). The maximum amount for an adult male is usually between 4 and 5 litres, though a trained athlete can often take in more than this. The total amount of air which a person can breathe in is called the **vital capacity**.

## How is our breathing controlled?

When we take exercise certain changes take place in our breathing. The most noticeable change is that we breathe more quickly. This is because our muscles are working harder so they need more oxygen. Also the extra carbon dioxide which they produce must be removed quickly, otherwise it might build up and poison our tissues.

You do not have to think about this; it happens automatically. It is brought about by a reflex: the brain senses that there is too much carbon dioxide in the bloodstream, and this automatically causes us to breathe faster.

In fact we do not just breathe faster – we breathe more deeply as well. In this respect there is a difference between fit and unfit people: fit people tend to breathe more deeply when they take exercise; unfit people tend to breathe more quickly, keeping their breathing rather shallow.

There are many other ways in which our breathing changes: for example, when we cough, sneeze, gasp, yawn or talk. Yawning, for example, occurs when we feel tired: we take a long deep breath in, which has the effect of getting more oxygen into the body. Some of these changes are brought about by involuntary reflexes: we cannot help them happening. Over other activities such as talking, we have voluntary control.

Another situation in which our breathing changes is when we go up to a high altitude. As one goes higher the atmospheric pressure decreases and the air gets thinner. This makes oxygen more difficult to obtain. Now suppose you have been living in a low-lying area and you move to a city such as Nairobi which is about 2000 metres above sea level. At first you get out of breath very quickly. However, you gradually adjust by breathing faster and more deeply, and your blood system gets more efficient at carrying oxygen. In this way you become **acclimatised** to the greater height.

Jet airliners fly at heights of 10 000 metres or more. At such heights the atmosphere is so thin that the aircraft must have its own air supply with oxygen at the normal pressure. Such aircraft are said to be **pressurised**. The same applies to spacecraft which operate in places where there is no atmosphere at all.

## Investigation 1

**Looking at the lungs of a mammal**

1   Examine the lungs of a pig or sheep obtained from the butcher.

2   Press the lung with your finger.
    What does it feel like?
    How would you explain how it feels?

3   Look at the windpipe.
    How is it attached to the lungs?

4   Squeeze the windpipe with your fingers.
    What does it feel like?
    How would you explain how it feels?

5   Attach a pair of bellows to the cut end of the windpipe. Make sure the joint is airtight. Pump air in and out of the lungs.

6   Look at a prepared slide of a section of lung under the microscope.

In what ways does its microscopic appearance suit its function?

## Investigation 2

**A working model of the chest**

1   Assemble the model as shown in the illustration. Make sure the bell jar is air-tight.

2   Grasp the rubber diaphragm and move it downwards and upwards.

    What happens to the balloons when you move the diaphragm?

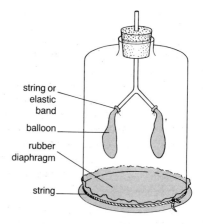

Explain your observations.

How does the action of this model differ from your own chest?

# Investigation 3

**Comparing the composition of inhaled and exhaled air**

*Analysis of atmospheric (inhaled) air*

1 Immerse the end of a J-tube in a beaker of water, then draw a column of water approximately 5 cm long into the tube.

2 Remove the tube from the water and draw in approximately 10 cm of air. Then draw in water again until the column of air occupies the straight part of the J-tube. Wait for one minute, then measure the length of the air column with a ruler.

syringe

J-tube

3 Expel all but about 1.0 cm of the water from the J-tube and then draw in concentrated potassium hydroxide. Keeping the tip of the J-tube in the hydroxide, shuttle the potassium hydroxide backwards and forwards so the air sample comes into contact with the sides of the tube which have been wetted with the hydroxide. The hydroxide will absorb carbon dioxide from the air sample. Wait for a further minute, then re-measure the length of the air column. In fact you will probably find that the decrease is very small and difficult to measure.

4 Now expel all but the last 5 cm of the hydroxide and draw in pyrogallol. Shuttle backwards and forwards as before. The pyrogallol will react with the potassium hydroxide still in the tube forming potassium pyrogallate

which will absorb oxygen from the air sample. Wait for one minute, then measure the length of the air column again.

5 Calculate the percentage of carbon dioxide and oxygen in the air sample.

$$\text{Percentage of } CO_2 \text{ in the air sample} = \frac{a - b}{a} \times 100$$

$$\text{Percentage of } O_2 \text{ in the air sample} = \frac{b - c}{a} \times 100$$

*a* is original length before hydroxide added.
*b* is new length after hydroxide added.
*c* is new length after pyrogallol added.

*Analysis of exhaled air*

1 Collect exhaled air in a test tube by the method shown below.

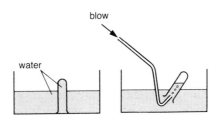

blow

water

2 Insert the tip of the J-tube into the test tube and draw in a sample of your exhaled air just as you did for your inhaled air.

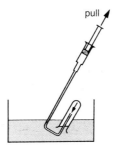

pull

3 Analyse first the carbon dioxide and then the oxygen in the sample of exhaled air exactly as you did for inhaled air.

Make a table like the one on page 110 (Table 1) to compare your samples of inhaled and exhaled air.
How would you explain the differences?

# Assignments

1 What function is carried out by each of the following:
a) the epiglottis;
b) the intercostal muscles;
c) the diaphragm;
d) the pleural fluid?

2 Why is it desirable to:
a) breathe through your nose rather than your mouth;
b) stop talking when you swallow;
c) breathe as deeply as possible;
d) blow your nose when necessary?

3 Table 1 on page 110 shows the percentage volumes of oxygen and carbon dioxide in the air inhaled and exhaled by a man. Explain how the change in composition of the air is brought about in the lungs.

4 Explain each of the following in terms of breathing in and out: a cough; a gasp; a sneeze; a sigh; a laugh.

5 An experiment was carried out on a young man in which the volume of air taken in at each breath, and the number of breaths per minute, were measured at rest and after running. Here are the results:

| | volume of air per breath | breaths per minute |
|---|---|---|
| at rest | 450 cm³ | 20 |
| after running | 1000 cm³ | 38 |

a) What is the total volume of air breathed in per minute at rest and after running?
b) 20 per cent of the air breathed in consisted of oxygen, but only 16 per cent of the air breathed out consisted of oxygen. Assuming that these figures remain constant, work out the volume of oxygen entering the blood per minute at rest and after exercise.
c) Why does the amount of oxygen taken up into the blood increase after exercise?
d) How is the increase in the rate of respiration brought about?

# Breathing and health

*If our lungs become damaged or diseased, or if air is prevented from getting to them, our lives are in danger. In this Topic we will see how this can happen.*

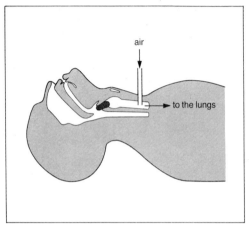

**Figure 1** If a person's glottis is completely blocked a tracheotomy may save his life.

**Figure 2** Artificial respiration by mouth-to-mouth resuscitation, otherwise known as the kiss of life.

## What happens if the respiratory tract becomes blocked?

It all depends where the block occurs. If you have a heavy cold, extra mucus is secreted in the nose which may become blocked. However, this isn't serious. You can blow your nose or breathe through your mouth, and if necessary you can clear your nose with nasal drops.

Occasionally a piece of food gets stuck in the glottis so firmly that it cannot be moved. If this happens an emergency operation called a **tracheotomy** may be necessary. A small cut is made into the windpipe below the Adam's apple. A tube is then inserted into it, through which the person can breathe until the obstruction has been cleared (Figure 1).

## Artificial respiration

If a person has an accident, he may go unconscious and stop breathing. Sometimes it is possible to keep the person alive by **artificial respiration**. This must be carried out as soon as possible, otherwise the brain cells may be damaged so badly by lack of oxygen that they never recover. This may happen within a few minutes after the person stops breathing, so speed is essential.

One of the best methods of artificial respiration is the 'kiss of life', known as mouth-to-mouth resuscitation (Figure 2). First you lay the person on his back. You then take a deep breath in, and breathe out into his mouth. As you are forcing your own exhaled air into his lungs, you might think this would do more harm than good. However, there is enough oxygen in your exhaled air to keep him alive. What's more, the carbon dioxide in your exhaled air may stimulate him to start breathing again.

After some accidents the person's brain is so badly damaged that he cannot start breathing for himself. He may then be kept alive by means of a **resuscitator**. He is connected by a tube to a machine which regularly forces air or oxygen into his lungs and then sucks it out. A system of valves ensures that fresh air is sent to the lungs each time. An unconscious person can be kept alive for many weeks or even months on a machine like this. Sometimes the brain recovers sufficiently for the person to start breathing again. On the other hand he may not recover, and the family and doctors have to decide whether to keep him alive on the machine or to switch it off and let him die. Obviously this is an agonising decision to have to make.

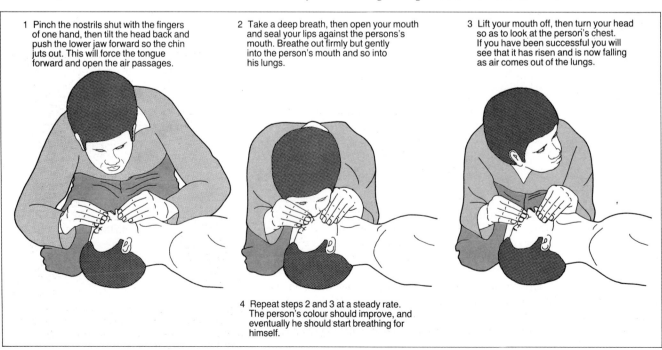

1 Pinch the nostrils shut with the fingers of one hand, then tilt the head back and push the lower jaw forward so the chin juts out. This will force the tongue forward and open the air passages.

2 Take a deep breath, then open your mouth and seal your lips against the persons's mouth. Breathe out firmly but gently into the person's mouth and so into his lungs.

3 Lift your mouth off, then turn your head so as to look at the person's chest. If you have been successful you will see that it has risen and is now falling as air comes out of the lungs.

4 Repeat steps 2 and 3 at a steady rate. The person's colour should improve, and eventually he should start breathing for himself.

## Respiratory diseases

Despite the mechanisms in the nose for keeping germs out, there are times when most of us get an infection in some part of the respiratory system. The area becomes inflamed and sore, we cough a lot, and a large amount of mucus may be produced which makes it difficult to breathe. Any part of the respiratory system can become infected. Thus **pharyngitis** is inflammation of the pharynx (throat), **tracheitis** is inflammation of the trachea (windpipe), and **bronchitis** is inflammation of the bronchial tubes. **Laryngitis** is inflammation of the larynx (voice box), and this may cause us to become hoarse and lose our voice. Sometimes the pleural membranes surrounding the lungs become inflamed. This is called **pleurisy** and it can make breathing painful.

Sometimes the lungs themselves become inflamed. For example, chronic inflammation may occur if you breathe in dust over a long period. In the past this has happened to workers in certain industries where a lot of dust is generated. The general name for the condition is **pneumoconiosis**. If it is caused by asbestos dust it is called **asbestosis**; if it is caused by silica dust it is called **silicosis**.

Severe inflammation of the lungs may give rise to **pneumonia**, which is caused by a type of bacteria. Fluid collects in the alveoli: this cuts down the area over which gas exchange can take place, so the patient gets short of breath.

Another serious disease of the lungs is **tuberculosis**, or TB for short. This is caused by bacteria which destroy the lung tissue. Doctors can find out if a person has got TB by doing a chest X-ray which shows up the diseased areas of the lungs. At one time TB, or consumption as it was called, was one of the most common causes of death. Thanks to modern medicine it is now rare.

Today **lung cancer** has taken over from TB as the major killer (Figure 3). In lung cancer a growth develops in the wall of the bronchial tubes. This blocks them, so breathing becomes more and more difficult. Unless the growth is discovered, and destroyed, in time the cancer may spread to other neighbouring organs such as the liver or spine.

Doctors can find out if a person has got cancer of the lungs by doing a chest X-ray (Figure 4). If a growth is visible, the person may have an operation in which the diseased part of the lung is removed, or the growth may be destroyed by radiation treatment. However, these measures are not always successful and unfortunately many patients die.

What causes lung cancer? We don't know for certain, but breathing in asbestos dust over a long period is known to cause it, and the link with smoking is now well established.

## How does smoking affect the lungs?

Most people who smoke inhale the smoke right down into their lungs. What effect does this have on them?

One way of finding the answer is to take two groups of people of the same sex and age. One group are smokers and the other group are non-smokers. You then study each group over a period of many years, and see what happens to their health. If a certain disease is developed by many of the smokers, but not by the non-smokers, this suggests that smoking may cause this particular disease.

In the last thirty years several surveys of this kind have been carried out in Britain by the Royal College of Physicians, and similar surveys have been carried out in other countries. The results all show one thing: amongst people who smoke there are more cases of lung cancer than amongst people who don't smoke. In other words, smoking seems to be associated with lung cancer.

This conclusion is supported by laboratory experiments on animals. These experiments have shown that cigarette smoke contains chemical substances which cause cancer. We call these substances **carcinogens**. The main carcinogens in cigarette smoke are a group of sweet-smelling chemicals which are usually referred to as 'tar'.

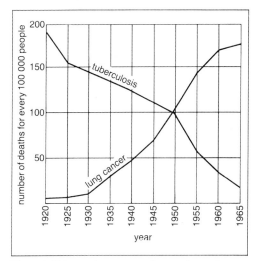

**Figure 3** This graph compares the numbers of people dying each year from tuberculosis and lung cancer between 1920 and 1965.

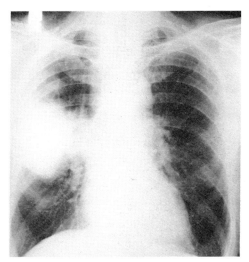

**Figure 4** X-ray of a human chest taken from the front, showing lung cancer. The cancer is the white area on the left. Compare this X-ray with the X-ray of the normal chest on page 111.

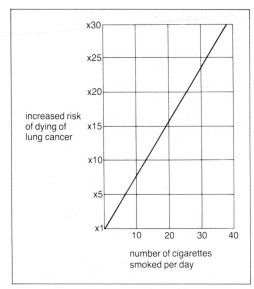

x30
x25
x20
increased risk
of dying of       x15
lung cancer
x10
x5
x1

10   20   30   40

number of cigarettes
smoked per day

**Figure 5** This graph shows the relationship between the number of cigarettes smoked per day and the risk of dying of lung cancer.

This is what the alveoli look like in a normal lung:

alveoli

and this is what they look like in the lung of someone with severe emphysema:

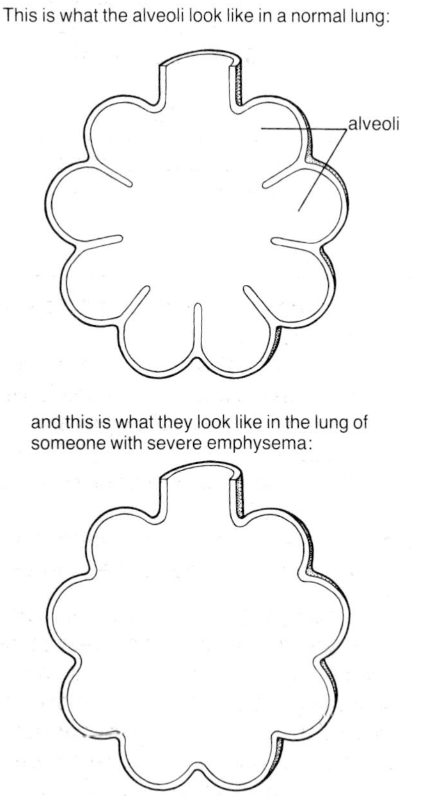

**Figure 6** These diagrams show how emphysema affects the lungs.

Now here is an important point. Being a smoker doesn't mean that you are *bound* to get lung cancer; nor does being a non-smoker ensure that you won't get it. All we can say is that you are more *likely* to get it if you smoke.

Look at Figure 5. This shows that the more cigarettes a person smokes, the greater is the chance of his getting lung cancer. A man who smokes twenty cigarettes a day is about fifteen times more likely to die of lung cancer than a non-smoker; and if he smokes thirty a day, he is about 25 times more likely to get it.

The surveys which have been carried out indicate that a smoker is *less* likely to get lung cancer if he:

1  doesn't inhale,
2  smokes cigars or a pipe rather than cigarettes,
3  takes fewer puffs per cigarette,
4  smokes filter-tips,
5  smokes 'low-tar' cigarettes.

But the best thing is to give it up altogether. If a heavy smoker stops smoking, the risk of his getting lung cancer gradually falls until after a few years it is about the same as for a non-smoker.

## Other diseases caused by smoking

When a person smokes, tiny particles in the smoke get caught on the lining of the windpipe and bronchial tubes. Extra mucus is produced and the cilia stop beating: smoking one cigarette is said to stop the cilia beating for about an hour. The mucus collects in the bronchial tubes and this gives rise to a 'smoker's cough'. If the tubes become infected, the person may get **chronic bronchitis**. 'Chronic' means long-lasting: instead of clearing up, the disease persists.

Further unpleasant effects may follow. Repeated coughing may cause the delicate walls of the alveoli to break down into larger air spaces. This cuts down the surface area over which gas exchange can take place, so the person gets very short of breath. Doctors call this condition **emphysema** (Figure 6).

Although smoking mainly affects the lungs, it can also cause cancer of other organs such as the mouth, throat, oesophagus and bladder. It is also associated with heart disease and stomach ulcers, and a woman who smokes while she is pregnant is more likely to have a spontaneous abortion or stillbirth or to give birth to an under-sized baby.

Scientists have shown that the number of cases of heart disease is much greater among smokers than among non-smokers. The effect of smoking on the heart is mainly due to nicotine, a chemical substance which gets into the blood when tobacco smoke is inhaled. Nicotine is a habit-forming drug, which is why people get 'hooked' on smoking and find it hard to give up. Nicotine stimulates the brain and relaxes the muscles. This in itself isn't harmful; but nicotine also raises the blood pressure and increases the amount of fatty substances in the blood. It is this that can lead to heart disease.

## Smoking and society

In Britain between 60 and 70 thousand people die of lung cancer, chronic bronchitis and emphysema every year. This is over eight times as many as are killed in road accidents. The same trend is true in the Caribbean.

The connection between smoking and these diseases is now so firmly established that in many countries cigarette commercials on television have been banned, and every packet of cigarettes has to carry a government health warning. Smoking has been prohibited in many public buildings and in cinemas special areas are often reserved for non-smokers. The trouble is that governments get a lot of money from taxes on tobacco; this has made some countries reluctant to campaign too hard against smoking.

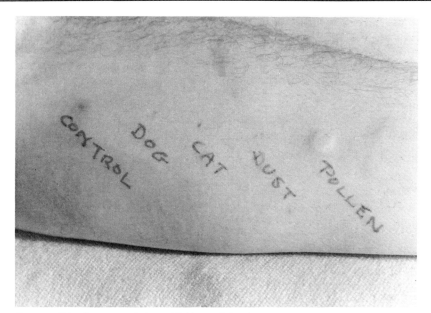

**Figure 7** Skin allergy test. A drop of fluid containing the substance to be tested is placed on the skin, then the skin is pricked through the drop. If the person is allergic to the substance, a 'blister' develops. This particular person was found to be allergic to certain kinds of pollen. What do you think the control drop consists of, and why is it included in the test?

Despite the warnings, more and more cigarettes are bought each year. Only amongst doctors has smoking decreased. They understand the risks too well, and they also know how unpleasant it is to die of lung cancer.

Scientists have shown that lung cancer is more common amongst people who live in towns than amongst those who live in the country. There is evidence that it can be brought on by motor car exhaust fumes, industrial smoke and dust, and radio-active materials. However, these causes are insignificant compared with smoking. It is claimed that if everyone gave up smoking, deaths from lung cancer would fall to a tenth of what they are at the moment.

## Hay fever and asthma

Many people suffer from **hay fever**. This is usually caused by a reaction to pollen, and is therefore particularly common when flowers are open. The lining of the nasal cavity becomes sensitive and inflamed and produces a large amount of mucus, so the nose runs and the person sneezes a lot. The eyes may be affected in the same way, becoming itchy, sore and weepy. When a person reacts adversely to a substance in this kind of way, we say he is **allergic** to it.

People can be allergic to all sorts of things besides pollen. In treating a patient the doctor must first discover the particular substance to which the person is allergic. This may involve doing a **skin test** of the kind shown in Figure 7.

**Asthma** is more serious. The muscles in the walls of the bronchioles contract, so the tubes get narrower. This makes it difficult to breathe and the person wheezes. The attacks are often brought on by pollen or dust, or occasionally by some kind of food to which the person is allergic. With some people the attacks are made worse by nervousness or worry. Asthma can be treated with drugs which make the bronchial muscles relax, so the tubes widen allowing air to be breathed in and out of the lungs more easily.

## Assignments

1 Briefly state the cause and symptoms of each of these diseases: bronchitis, pleurisy, tuberculosis, emphysema and asthma.

2 What is meant by mouth-to-mouth resuscitation? Under what circumstances would it *not* be possible to carry it out?

3 Explain why each of these remarks is unscientific:
   a) 'My dad smokes like a chimney so he's bound to get cancer.'
   b) 'All that stuff about smoking and cancer is nonsense: my uncle died of lung cancer and he never touched a cigarette all his life.'

4 In 1952 two British scientists carried out a survey in a large hospital. They selected two groups of patients, both the same sex and roughly the same age. The patients in group A all had lung cancer, whereas those in group B had other diseases. The scientists then found out how many patients in each group smoked. Here are the results:

| | Percentage of patients who smoked more than 15 cigarettes per day |
|---|---|
| Group A | 25 |
| Group B | 13 |

| | Percentage of patients who were non-smokers |
|---|---|
| Group A | 0.5 |
| Group B | 4.5 |

   a) What do you think the scientists were trying to find out?
   b) Group B is called the control group. Why was it necessary to investigate this group of patients as well as Group A?
   c) What conclusion would you draw from the results?
   d) Suggest one other way the scientists might have carried out their survey.

5 It has been suggested that smoking and lung cancer appear to be connected, not because smoking *causes* cancer, but because people who need to smoke are the kind of people who get cancer. What sort of investigations would have to be carried out to show that this is *not* the correct explanation?

# How do other organisms breathe?

*Humans have
lungs and a blood system
for getting oxygen. We will now see how
other organisms carry out
this process.*

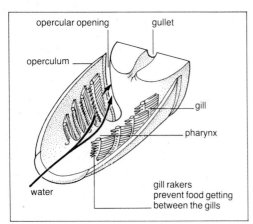

**Figure 1** The head of this fish has been sliced horizontally so we can see into its pharynx. The gills lie on either side. Water flows between the gills as indicated by the arrows.

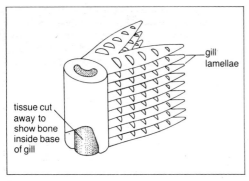

**Figure 2** Part of one gill in detail. Notice the large surface area created by the many gill lamellae.

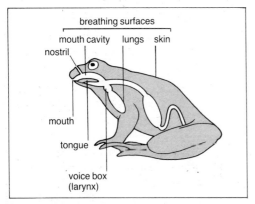

**Figure 3** This diagram of the inside of an amphibian shows its three breathing surfaces.

## Plants and simple organisms

Small organisms like *Amoeba* and *Hydra* breathe by diffusion. Oxygen diffuses passively into the animal from the surrounding water. Carbon dioxide diffuses out. There are no special organs such as gills to aid this. Nor is there a circulatory system for transporting things within the body. Plants manage in the same kind of way.

The earthworm is a bit more complicated. It breathes through its moist skin by diffusion and there are no special organs for helping with this. However, the animal is too large for oxygen to get to all parts of the body by diffusion, and so the worm has a blood system which carries oxygen to the various organs. The blood contains the red pigment **haemoglobin** just as ours does: this carries the oxygen (see page 126).

In more advanced animals there are special respiratory surfaces such as lungs and gills. A respiratory surface has three essential features:

1  It has a large surface area.
2  It is permanently moist.
3  It has a very good blood supply.

In addition there is usually a special mechanism for bringing the surrounding air or water in contact with the respiratory surface.

## How do fish breathe?

Fish use their **gills** for breathing. Figure 1 shows how the gills of a bony fish are arranged. Notice that there are holes in between them: these connect the pharynx with the outside (Investigation 1).

The fish sucks water in through its mouth. The water flows between the gills and passes out of the fish by the opercular opening as indicated by the arrows in Figure 1. In this way a continuous stream of water is kept flowing past the gills; this stream is maintained by flapping movements of the operculum and the opening and closing of the mouth.

The gills have a large surface area (Figure 2) and blood continuously passes through them. As water flows over the gills, oxygen is taken up by the blood and carbon dioxide diffuses out.

## How do amphibians breathe?

Amphibians breathe in three different ways: through their **skin**, through the lining of the **mouth cavity**, and by means of **lungs**. Oxygen and carbon dioxide diffuse across these three surfaces (Figure 3).

In order to serve as a breathing surface, the skin must be kept moist: gases will only diffuse through it if this is so. Amphibians' skin contains many **glands** which secrete a watery slime (mucus) onto the surface. This is why amphibians are always moist and slimy. However, there is a grave disadvantage in having a moist skin: water readily evaporates from it and the animal is liable to dry up. This is the main reason why frogs and other amphibians are normally found only in damp places. The skin has other features which make it suitable as a breathing surface: for example, it is thin and has a good blood supply.

If you watch a frog or toad you will notice that sometimes its throat moves up and down. These movements pump air in and out of the mouth cavity through the nostrils. When this happens, gas exchange takes place through the moist lining of the mouth cavity.

When the animal is active and needs a lot of oxygen, it takes a large gulp of air and forces it down into its lungs. The lungs consist of a pair of simple thin-walled sacks situated in the chest region.

## How do insects breathe?

In man oxygen is carried from the lungs to the tissues by the blood. Insects have a very different system. They have hundreds of breathing tubes through which oxygen passes to all parts of the body. This is called the **tracheal system** (Figure 4) (Investigation 2).

Air enters the tracheal system through the **spiracles**, which are tiny holes in the cuticle. In some insects the spiracles are fitted with **valves** which can open and close like sliding doors.

The spiracles open into tubes called **tracheae** (singular: trachea). These are lined with hard cuticle which is thickened into a spiral. This prevents their walls from caving in.

The tracheae branch like a tree. The ends of the branches are fine tubes called **tracheoles**. These have thin walls which are not lined with cuticle. They contain a watery fluid. The tracheoles are wrapped round, and penetrate, all the organs and tissues, bringing oxygen to them.

In most insects oxygen passes through the tracheal system by diffusion. However, in large and active insects like the locust, air is pumped through the tracheal system by muscular movements of the abdomen. If you watch a locust, you can sometimes see these movements. The spiracles open and close in such a way that air is sucked in through the front spiracles and expelled through the back ones. When the insect is active, the spiracles open more frequently, and the pumping movements are more vigorous than when the insect is resting.

Insects have a **blood system** but it is very different from ours. The blood is a colourless fluid. It does not contain a red pigment, and it plays no part in carrying oxygen round the body. Its main job is to transport food substances and waste matter.

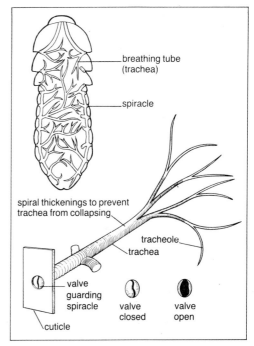

**Figure 4** The tracheal system consists of breathing tubes which carry oxygen to the organs and tissues.

---

## Investigation 1

**Looking at gills**

1 Obtain a large dead bony fish.

2 Remove the operculum by cutting round it with scissors.

3 Look at the gills underneath.

   How many are there?

4 Observe the structure of one gill in detail.

   How is it suited to its job?

   How is water made to flow past the gills?

5 Show the route taken by water by passing a piece of thread through the mouth and out between the gills. The thread should follow the course of the arrow in Figure 1.

When a bony fish breathes, why does water flow past the gills and not into the gullet?

## Investigation 2

**Examining the tracheal system**

1 Cut open a dead cockroach.

2 Observe the breathing tubes (tracheae).

3 With forceps pull out a small piece of muscle from the thorax.

4 Mount the muscle in a drop of water on a slide, and put on a coverslip.

5 Look at your slide under the microscope: low power first, then high power.

6 Draw part of the tracheal system, showing how the breathing tubes branch.

What function is carried out by the tracheal system?

How is the same function carried out in humans?

## Assignments

1 Why is it difficult for a large organism to get the oxygen it needs by diffusion alone?

2 The three essential features of a respiratory surface are that it should have a large surface area, be permanently moist, and have a good blood supply. Why must it have these features?

3 List three reasons why it is an advantage to an insect to have valves guarding its spiracles.

4 Insects have no red pigment in their blood. How do they manage without it?

5 A certain insect is said to suck air into its body through its thoracic spiracles and expel air through its abdominal spiracles.

   Can you think of an experiment which could be done to test the suggestion?

# Living without oxygen

*What makes dough
rise and beer alcoholic?
It is because of an organism
which can respire
without oxygen.*

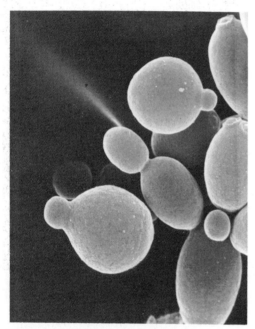

**Figure 1** Yeast cells greatly magnified. Wild yeast lives in places where there is plenty of sugar, on the surface of fruit for example.

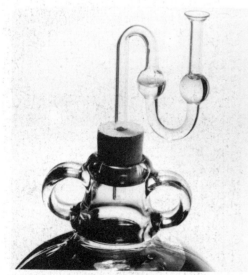

**Figure 2** In making wine the jar is fitted with a valve which allows carbon dioxide to escape but prevents bacteria from getting in.

## Respiration without oxygen

Organisms obtain energy by respiration. Normally sugar (glucose) is broken down in the presence of oxygen into carbon dioxide and water (see page 89):

$$\text{glucose} + \text{oxygen} \rightarrow \text{carbon dioxide} + \text{water} + \text{energy}$$
$$C_6H_{12}O_6 \quad 6O_2 \qquad 6CO_2 \qquad\quad 6H_2O \quad (2880 \text{ kJ})$$

For sugar to be broken down like this oxygen is essential. For this reason we call it **aerobic respiration**.

Now what happens if no oxygen is available? Usually the organism will suffocate. However in some cases sugar may still be broken down and energy released (Investigation 1). Oxygen is not needed for this, so we call it **anaerobic respiration** – respiration without oxygen.

Anaerobic respiration occurs in several kinds of organisms. The end products vary, as we shall see.

## How does yeast respire without oxygen?

Yeast respires without oxygen by converting **sugar** into **ethanol (alcohol)** and carbon dioxide gas.

$$\text{glucose} \rightarrow \text{ethanol} + \text{carbon dioxide} + \text{energy}$$
$$C_6H_{12}O_6 \quad 2C_2H_5OH \quad 2CO_2 \qquad\quad (210 \text{ kJ})$$

We call this process **alcoholic fermentation** (Investigation 2). As with aerobic respiration, this reaction does not take place in one go, but in a series of steps.

Compare the amount of energy produced by the two equations above; it is given in kilojoules at the end of each equation. Notice that anaerobic respiration does not produce as much energy as aerobic. In aerobic respiration the sugar is broken down completely; in anaerobic respiration it is only partly broken down – a lot of energy is still locked up in the ethanol. This can be shown by burning some ethanol; the energy in it is then released as heat. Though inefficient, alcoholic fermentation is a useful way of getting energy when oxygen is scarce.

Fresh yeast bought from a shop looks like putty. But it is really a fungus consisting of millions of tiny living cells (Figure 1). Wild yeast grows on the surface of fruit, feeding on sugar. In the right conditions it multiplies rapidly by budding: each cell pinches off new ones. A large number of cells can be formed in a short time.

For centuries man has used yeast for making alcohol and bread.

### Making alcohol

Basically all you need for making alcohol is sugar, yeast and water. But to make a pleasant alcoholic drink it is not quite so simple, as any wine-maker will tell you.

Wine is usually made from grapes. The grapes are crushed and the juice is extracted. The juice contains sugar and wild yeast. The yeast ferments the sugar and gradually turns it into alcohol.

Wine-making is an art which has been practised for over 4000 years. Although the alcohol is always the same, every wine has its own flavour. This depends on the type of grapes used and the conditions in which fermentation is carried out. Other plants besides grapes can be used for making wine. For example, in West Africa wine is made from the sap of oil palm trees, which is usually taken from the flowering shoots. Home-made wine can be made in a special glass jar. The jar is fitted with a valve which allows carbon dioxide to escape but prevents bacteria from getting in (Figure 2). If bacteria do get in they may turn the alcohol into vinegar.

Beer is made from barley. The process is known as **brewing**. The grain, which contains malt sugar, is mashed with water, and the resulting liquid is given the right flavour by boiling with hops. Then yeast is added and fermentation commences (Figure 4). The sugar is gradually converted into alcohol.

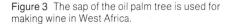

Figure 3 The sap of the oil palm tree is used for making wine in West Africa.

One problem is that alcohol is poisonous in large amounts. If the concentration of alcohol in fermenting wine or beer gets more than about 14 per cent it kills the yeast and fermentation stops. This is why beer and wine never contain more than this amount of alcohol. The only way to produce a stronger alcoholic drink is to **distil** it after fermentation is complete. The fermented liquid is heated to a certain temperature in a special flask: the alcohol vaporises and condenses on the cool sides of the flask. The drops of alcohol are then collected. This is how spirits such as whisky, gin and rum are made. Rum is distilled mainly from the fermented juice of sugar cane and is produced on a large scale in the Caribbean. Whisky is distilled mainly from fermented barley. These distilled spirits contain a lot of alcohol. If they have more than 57 per cent by volume they are called 'over proof'.

Exporting rum earns foreign exchange for the Caribbean, but drinking too much alcohol can also cause problems. For the benefits (and the problems!) which we gain from alcohol we have to thank the tiny yeast organism.

Figure 4 Beer fermenting in fermentation tanks in a brewery.

### Making bread

Imagine you are a baker. You mix some flour and water with a small amount of sugar and yeast. This makes **dough**. (Investigation 3). You then leave the dough for an hour or so in a warm place. During this period the living yeast cells multiply and give off carbon dioxide gas. The gas should make the dough rise, more or less doubling its size (Figure 5). Then you bake the dough in a hot oven: the heat kills the yeast and evaporates the alcohol. Result? A crisp golden loaf if you're lucky – or a brick if you're not.

### How do animals respire without oxygen?

If there is no oxygen available, animals break glucose down through a series of small steps into **lactic acid**. In this case carbon dioxide is *not* given off.

$$\text{glucose} \rightarrow \text{lactic acid} + \text{energy}$$
$$C_6H_{12}O_6 \qquad 2C_3H_6O_3 \qquad (150 \text{ kJ})$$

Animals which live in places where there is little or no oxygen respire anaerobically. Here are some examples: worms living in mud at the bottom of stagnant lakes; diving mammals such as whales and seals which can stay under water for long periods; and parasites like the tapeworm which live in the gut. And we can do it too.

If we take strenuous exercise our muscles need extra oxygen. Unfortunately we cannot breathe fast enough, nor pump our blood sufficiently quickly to get oxygen to our muscles. So the muscles produce energy by making lactic acid.

Figure 5 In making bread yeast causes the dough to rise.

**Figure 6** A sprinter can hold his breath while running a hundred metres.

Think of running a 100 metre sprint (Figure 6). During the race lactic acid builds up in your body. Lactic acid is a mild poison and it causes our muscles to ache (Investigation 4). When the race is over we have to get rid of it. This is done by breaking it down into carbon dioxide and water. Oxygen is needed for this, and it is why we pant immediately after the race. The oxygen required to get rid of the lactic acid is called the **oxygen debt**. If we incur an oxygen debt during a race, we must pay it off immediately afterwards. Because the muscles can work for a short time without oxygen, a sprinter can hold his breath while running a hundred metres.

In a long distance race lactic acid builds up to begin with, but later it is removed while the athlete is actually running. When this happens we say that the person has got his 'second wind'.

Anaerobic respiration produces far less energy than aerobic and it cannot go on indefinitely. However, it can make the difference between life and death. An antelope fleeing from a cheetah may owe its life to the fact that for a short time its muscles can produce energy without oxygen.

### How do bacteria respire without oxygen?

Many kinds of bacteria can live without oxygen. They ferment sugar but the end products vary. Some produce alcohol, others lactic acid. Some of them are useful to humans. For example, the ones that produce lactic acid are used for making butter, yoghurt and silage (see pages 326 and 389). Certain bacteria convert alcohol into acetic acid (ethanoic acid), and so are used for making vinegar.

Some anaerobic bacteria produce the gas methane (formula $CH_4$). When this gas is burned heat energy is released. This 'biogas' is used as a fuel in sewage works, and in the future it may become more widely used as an energy source. There are several pilot projects in the Caribbean.

### How long can organisms respire without oxygen?

For man the time is very short – a matter of seconds. Some lower animals and plants can respire anaerobically for much longer periods, but eventually they must return to aerobic respiration.

Certain bacteria and parasites can respire anaerobically all their lives. They can live permanently in places where there is no oxygen. In fact some of them are actually poisoned by oxygen.

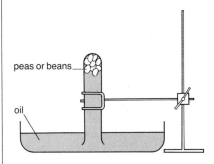

# Investigation 2

**Finding out about the products of alcoholic fermentation**

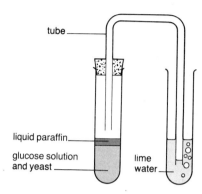

tube

liquid paraffin

glucose solution
and yeast

lime
water

1 Put some 10 per cent glucose into a
large test tube to a depth of 2 cm.

2 Boil the glucose to expel any oxygen
present in it.

3 Cool it, then add a little yeast.

4 Pour a thin layer of liquid paraffin on
top of the glucose to stop oxygen
getting to the yeast.

5 Set up the test tube as shown in the
illustration.

6 Set up a second test tube exactly
like the first one but do not add any
yeast to the glucose. This is your
control.

7 Leave the test tubes in a warm place
for at least an hour. Then examine
them.

Has the lime water gone cloudy? If it
has, carbon dioxide has been given
off.

Sniff the contents of the test tubes.
Does either smell of alcohol?

Feel the two test tubes. Is one warmer
than the other?

What conclusions do you draw from
this experiment?

How might the experiment be
improved?

# Investigation 3

**To find out if yeast makes dough rise**

1 Make a small amount of dough as
follows. To 50 g of flour add water a
little at a time and mix with a knife.
Don't add too much water.

2 Put some yeast in a test tube and
shake it up with some warm water.
Add about 10 g of sugar and shake
again.

3 Divide the dough into two portions.
To one portion add the yeast
suspension and mix it in well with
your hands. Do not put any yeast
into the second portion.

4 Grease the inside of two beakers.
Into one beaker put the dough which
contains yeast.

5 Into the second beaker put the
dough which does not contain yeast.
This is your control.

6 Leave both beakers in a warm place
for about an hour.

7 After an hour compare the
appearance of the dough in the two
beakers.

Has either risen? If so which one – and
why?

Why was it necessary to put some
sugar with the yeast before adding it to
the dough?

Design, and if possible carry out, an
experiment to find out the effect of
temperature on the rising of dough.

# Investigation 4

**To show the effect of lactic acid in
our muscles**

1 Raise one arm above your head.

2 Clench and unclench your fist twice
a second for as long as you can.

3 Notice the feeling in your arm as you
exercise your muscles.

4 When you can continue no longer,
rest your arm on your lap and follow
what happens to the feeling.

How would you describe the feeling in
your arm during and after the exercise?

Does your experience fit in with the
idea that lactic acid builds up in the
muscles during exercise and is
removed afterwards?

# Assignments

1 A wine maker always makes sure that
his equipment is absolutely clean
before he starts. Why do you think
this is important?

2 Mr Smith and Mr Brown both make
their own wine. Mr Smith leaves his
to ferment in a sunny place whereas
Mr Brown puts his in a shady place.
Whose would you expect to ferment
first and why?

3 A housewife makes some
marmalade and stores it in jars in a
cupboard in the kitchen. When she
opens one of the jars several months
later the marmalade looks frothy and
smells of alcohol. What do you think
has happened, and why? How might
she prevent this occurring in the
future?

4 Why does anaerobic respiration
produce less energy then aerobic
respiration?

5 The following animals are all able to
respire anaerobically:

a) whales, b) the beef tapeworm,
c) threadworms.

Find out where each of these
animals lives, and then explain why it
is useful to it to be able to respire
anaerobically.

# Blood, the living fluid

*An average sized man contains about five litres of blood – that's nearly a bucket full. In this Topic we will deal with the main components of blood and what they do.*

*hare*

*biconcare disc*

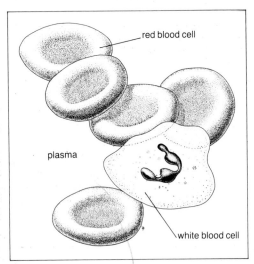

Figure 1  Human blood cells highly magnified.

*carboxyhaemoglobin*

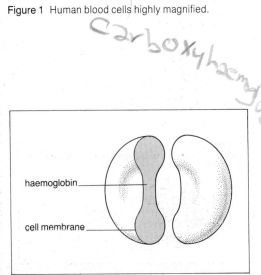

Figure 2  A human red blood cell sectioned to show its characteristic shape.

## What does blood consist of?

To the naked eye blood looks like a simple liquid. However, if you look at some blood under the microscope, you can see that there is more to it than that (Investigation 1). In fact it is a very special kind of tissue in which numerous cells float about in a fluid (Figure 1).

The cells are of two types: **red blood cells** (erythrocytes) and **white blood cells** (leucocytes). The fluid part of the blood is called **plasma**.

## Red blood cells

The red blood cells are extremely numerous: a single drop of blood contains millions of them. Their job is to carry oxygen and carbon dioxide around the body (Investigation 2).

The red blood cell has a very distinctive shape: it is a disc which looks as if it has been pressed in on either side, like the wheel of a car (Figure 2). This gives it a large surface area so it can take up more oxygen.

Another peculiar feature of red blood cells is that they do not have a nucleus. The inside is filled with the red pigment **haemoglobin** – this is what makes blood look red. Haemoglobin is a remarkable substance, and is responsible for carrying the oxygen.

### How does the blood carry oxygen?

When a red blood cell passes through the lungs, the haemoglobin readily takes up oxygen. However, when it reaches the tissues it gives it up equally readily (Figure 3). The movement of oxygen in and out of the red blood cells takes place by diffusion.

How does haemoglobin work? When it combines with oxygen it is turned into a compound called **oxyhaemoglobin**. In this form the oxygen is carried by the blood from the lungs to the tissues. Once it has reached the tissues, the oxyhaemoglobin releases the oxygen and is turned back into haemoglobin. Haemoglobin contains iron, and this plays an important part in the way the oxygen is carried. This is why we need iron in our food.

### How does the blood carry carbon dioxide?

As the red blood cells pass through the tissues they pick up carbon dioxide. Most of the carbon dioxide combines, not with the haemoglobin, but with water to form carbonic acid. There is an enzyme inside the red cell which causes the carbon dioxide to combine with the water extremely quickly. Once the carbonic acid has been formed it splits into two parts. About 70 per cent of the part containing the original carbon dioxide leaks out of the red blood cells into the plasma; the rest remains in the red cells.

### Red blood cells and carbon monoxide poisoning

Carbon monoxide is a gas which is given off by burning fuel. It is poisonous because it affects our blood. It combines with haemoglobin about three hundred times more readily than oxygen does. The result is that if we breathe it in, it displaces the oxygen from the red blood cells, so oxygen can't be carried to the tissues. Breathing concentrated carbon monoxide gas for more than a few minutes can be fatal.

Carbon monoxide is present in coal gas, but not in natural gas such as is now used in many countries. It is also present in motor car exhaust fumes, which is why it is dangerous to run a car engine in a closed garage. Small amounts of it are also present in cigarette smoke, which is why a person who is not used to smoking feels faint when he smokes a cigarette.

### How are red blood cells produced?

Red blood cells live for only about four months, after which they are destroyed. To keep up the full number in our bloodstream, new ones are constantly being produced. They are made in the bone marrow, the soft tissue in the centre of certain bones (see page 222). About two million are manufactured every second!

In certain circumstances red blood cells are produced at an even faster rate, so the number in the blood increases. This happens, for example, when people live at high altitudes where there is not so much oxygen in the air. Their extra red blood cells help them to get enough oxygen to their tissues. This is an important aspect of acclimatisation (see page 114).

If a person's blood does not contain enough red blood cells, or enough haemoglobin, he suffers from **anaemia**. An anaemic person is tired and pale. Anaemia can be caused by not getting enough iron in our food, or by losing a lot of blood.

## White blood cells

There is roughly one white cell for every 700 red cells. They do not contain haemoglobin and they have a nucleus just like most other kinds of cell. Their job is to kill germs which get into the body, so they help to defend us against disease.

There are two main kinds of white blood cell in our bodies: **phagocytes** and **lymph cells**. Phagocytes are produced in the bone marrow, whereas antibody-producing cells are produced in the lymph glands (see page 141). In both cases extra cells are produced when we are ill and need a good supply.

### Phagocytes

Phagocytes are remarkable cells. They move and feed like *Amoeba* (see page 106). When a phagocyte comes into contact with a germ, it engulfs it and takes it into its body. The germ is then killed and digested (Figure 4A.)

Phagocytes are the policemen of the body. They patrol the bloodstream and tissues, waiting for germs to arrive. If the body becomes infected they wriggle to the site of the infection and attack the germs. It's like a battle, and the place where it happens becomes red, swollen and painful. We call this **inflammation**. As in a real battle, there are casualties on both sides: the remains of dead bacteria and phagocytes accumulate to form **pus**. Sometimes the inflamed area swells up into a **boil**. Pressure builds up inside the boil, so that eventually it bursts.

### Lymph cells

Suppose you are attacked by the virus which causes measles. When the virus gets into your bloodstream it is detected by your **lymph cells** (lymphocytes).

When a lymph cell detects the viruses, it produces a chemical substance which kills them (Figure 4B). Not all the viruses are killed instantly. Some of them multiply and damage your tissues, and this makes you feel ill. But gradually your lymph cells overcome them and you begin to feel better.

What causes the lymph cells to behave in this way? Germs contain chemical substances which we call **antigens**. When antigens get into your body they stimulate the lymph cells to produce chemical substances called **antibodies**. The antibodies then combine with the antigens, and this kills the germs.

Exactly how the germs are killed varies from one kind of antibody to another. Some antibodies make the germs burst; others stick to the surface of the germ, making it easier for phagocytes to engulf it; and there are some which make the germs clump together, after which they may be eaten up by phagocytes. In the case of germs which release poisonous substances, the antibodies combine with the poison making it harmless. Such antibodies are called **antitoxins**.

Some unfortunate people develop a disease known as **leukaemia**, a sort of cancer of the blood. The number of white blood cells increases greatly, and they start destroying the red blood cells. There are different kinds of leukaemia, some more serious than others. Some kinds can be treated quite successfully with certain drugs.

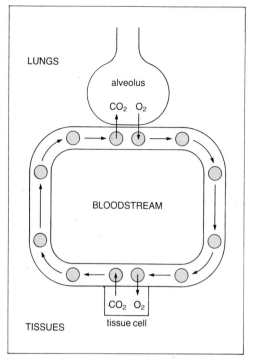

**Figure 3** Blood carries oxygen from the lungs to the tissues, and carbon dioxide from the tissues to the lungs.

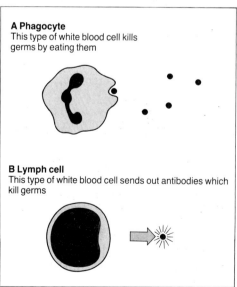

**A Phagocyte**
This type of white blood cell kills germs by eating them

**B Lymph cell**
This type of white blood cell sends out antibodies which kill germs

**Figure 4** The two main types of white blood cell found in the human bloodstream. The dark object in each of the cells is the nucleus.

## Plasma

This is the fluid part of the blood in which the cells float around (Investigation 3). It consists mainly of water, but many important substances are dissolved in it. They include salts, food substances such as glucose, excretory substances such as urea, hormones, and an important group of substances called **plasma proteins**. There are three kinds of plasma proteins and each has a particular job to do:

### 1 *Albumen*

This is the same protein as is found in the 'white' of an egg. It makes the blood thick and viscous.

### 2 *Globulin*

This kind of protein is produced by the lymph cells for destroying germs. It constitutes the antibodies. Certain types of globulin are also needed for the clotting of blood.

### 3 *Fibrinogen*

This protein plays an important part in the clotting of blood which is discussed in the next Topic.

Fibrinogen can be taken out of the plasma by allowing it to clot and then removing the clot. What's left is a colourless fluid called **serum**.

It's essential that the plasma should contain just the right amount of water and salt and other substances. If these are allowed to vary, the blood cells may gain or lose water as a result of osmosis, and this could damage them (Investigation 4).

Floating in the plasma are small bodies called **platelets**. They are formed from certain bone marrow cells, and they play an important part in the clotting of blood.

## Summary of the functions of blood

Blood does three different kinds of job: transport, protection and regulation.

*Transport*
1. It carries oxygen from the lungs to the tissues and carbon dioxide from the tissues to the lungs.
2. It carries dissolved food substances from the gut to the various parts of the body.
3. It carries unwanted substances to the kidneys which then get rid of them.
4. It carries hormones from one part of the body to another.
5. It carries antibodies from place to place.

*Protection*
1. By clotting it prevents fluid being lost from cuts and wounds.
2. It protects us against disease by killing germs.

*Regulation*
1. It helps to control the amount of water in the tissues.
2. It helps to regulate the amounts of various chemical substances in the tissues.
3. It helps to keep our body temperature constant by spreading warmth evenly around the body.

Many of these functions are discussed in more detail in later Topics.

# Investigation 1

### Looking at blood

This experiment involves drawing your own blood. *This must be done under proper supervision in strictly hygienic conditions to avoid any possibility of transmitting infection. Alternatively use blood from a blood bank, or a prepared slide.*

1. Put an elastic band round one of your fingers.
2. Clean the skin of your finger by rubbing it with cotton wool soaked in ethanol.
3. With a sterile lancet prick the tip of your finger with a firm jab, so a drop of blood comes out.

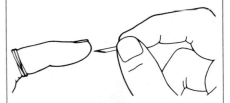

4. Place the drop of blood at one end of a microscope slide.

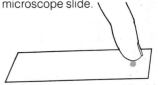

5. With another slide spread the blood over the surface of the slide so it forms a smear.

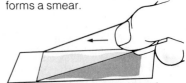

6. Let the blood smear dry, then examine it under the microscope: low power first, then high power.

   Can you see red blood cells?

   White blood cells will only show up if they are stained.

7. Cover the smear with Leishman's stain and leave it for five minutes. Then gently wash the stain off with tap water.

8. Let the slide dry, then examine it under the microscope again.

   Can you see any white blood cells like those in Figure 4?

# Investigation 2

**The effect of gases on blood**

Use blood from a blood bank or slaughter house. The blood has been prevented from clotting by having sodium oxalate added to it.

1 Pour equal amounts of blood into two small flasks.

2 Bubble oxygen through the blood in one flask, and carbon dioxide through the other.

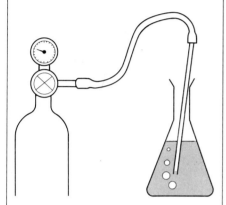

How do they differ in colour?

3 Bubble oxygen through the blood which has just had carbon dioxide put into it.

What happens to its colour?

4 Bubble carbon dioxide through the blood which had oxygen put into it. What happens to its colour?

5 Draw air out of the oxygenated blood with a vacuum pump. What happens to its colour?

What do we learn from this experiment about the functions of blood?

# Investigation 3

**Separating the components of blood**

This investigation involves using a centrifuge, a machine in which a liquid can be spun round and round very rapidly.

1 Take some blood which has been obtained from a blood bank.

2 Fill two centrifuge tubes with the blood.

3 Spin the tubes for five minutes in the centrifuge. This will throw any solid objects to the bottom of the tubes.

4 Stop the centrifuge and take out the tubes. Notice the clear fluid towards the top of the tube, and the red sediment at the bottom.

What is the clear fluid?
What does the sediment consist of?

Approximately what percentage of the blood is made up of red blood cells?

# Investigation 4

**The effect of osmosis on red blood cells**

This experiment involves drawing your own blood. *This must be done under proper supervision in strictly hygienic conditions to avoid any possibility of transmitting infection.*

1 Label three microscope slides A, B and C.

2 Obtain a drop of blood from your finger or thumb with a sterile lancet (see Investigation 1).

3 Place a small drop on each slide.

4 To A add a drop of distilled water.
To B add a drop of 0.75 per cent salt solution.
To C add a drop of 3.0 per cent salt solution.

5 Put a coverslip on each slide.

6 Examine each slide under the microscope at regular intervals.

What happens to the red blood cells?

Explain your observations.

# Assignments

1 Write down three ways red and white blood cells differ in their structure. What job does each do?

2 Why is it dangerous to breathe in motor car exhaust? Explain the reason for your answer.

3 There are approximately 5 million red blood cells in a cubic millimetre of human blood, and the total volume of blood in the whole body is about 5 litres. Each red blood cell has a surface area of about 120 square micrometres.
a) How many red blood cells are there in the entire bloodstream?
b) What will be the total surface area of all the red blood cells? Give your answer in square metres.

4 In the lungs there is a steep diffusion gradient favouring the passage of oxygen from the alveoli into the blood.
a) What do you understand by the term 'diffusion gradient'?
b) How is this steep diffusion gradient maintained?

5 In what form is carbon dioxide carried in the blood? Laboratory experiments have shown that the greater the amount of carbon dioxide present in the blood, the less firmly haemoglobin holds onto oxygen. Why do you think this is important in the body?

6 A scientist investigated the number of red blood cells possessed by people living at sea level and in a mountainous region at a height of 5860 metres. Here are his results:

Sea level          5.0 million per mm$^3$
5860 metres     7.4 million per mm$^3$

Why do you think they differ?

7 A human red blood cell has a diameter of about 8.0 micrometres. What is the approximate magnification of the blood cells in Figure 1 on page 126?

8 When a doctor injects a fluid into a person's bloodstream, he always uses a fluid which has the same concentration as the blood. Why?

# More about blood

*In this Topic
we will look in
detail at how our blood helps
to protect us, particularly
from disease.*

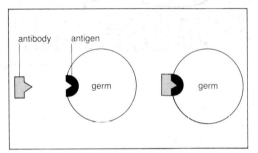

**Figure 1** Why will a particular antibody attack only one kind of germ? The antigen on the surface of this germ has a shape which will only allow an antibody with a corresponding shape to fit into it.

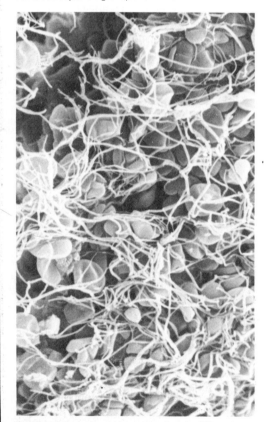

**Figure 2** When blood clots a meshwork of fibres is formed as shown in this photograph which was obtained by means of an electron microscope. The objects which look like deflated footballs are red blood cells greatly magnified.

## Becoming immune to diseases

Once you have had a disease like measles you are protected against getting it again. A doctor would say that you have now developed **immunity** against the disease.

We can explain immunity like this. The first attack taught your lymph cells how to make antibodies against measles. Once your lymph cells have learned how to do this, they will make antibodies more quickly in future. When a second attack comes, the lymph cells leap into action so quickly that the germs are destroyed before they have a chance to do any damage.

Having a particular disease will protect you against that disease in the future, in some cases for life. However, it won't protect you against other diseases. This is because the antibodies you produce against, say, measles will act only against the measles germs – they will not act against any other kinds of germs. The reason for this is explained in Figure 1.

Sometimes people get a mild attack of a disease when they are young – so mild they don't even notice it. However, it causes them to make antibodies, so they are protected from this particular disease when they are grown up. This is how many people gain immunity to diseases such as tuberculosis.

Babies are protected against some diseases by getting antibodies from the mother, either across the placenta or from her milk. However, antibodies picked up from another person like this are destroyed after a short time and so protection does not last very long. Nevertheless it helps to get the baby through the first few weeks of life, while it makes its own antibodies.

Some diseases – mumps for example – are mild in children but severe in adults. It's a good thing to get such diseases when we are young. This enables us to build up immunity, so we don't get the disease again later.

There are a few diseases which we seem never to become immune to – the common cold for instance. This is because colds are caused by many different types of viruses, and one type is constantly changing into another. When you get a cold, it may give you immunity against that particular virus in the future. However, your next cold will probably be caused by a different type of virus, against which you have no protection. Much the same applies to flu.

Sometimes people make antibodies against things which are harmless, such as pollen. The antibodies attack the pollen grains in the tissues lining the nose and eyes. This makes the person sneeze and his eyes run. We call it hay fever. When a person reacts in this kind of way to a substance, we say that he is **allergic** to it (see page 119). Some people are allergic to some kinds of food or to substances on the skin such as cosmetics.

## Blood clotting

Normally when you bleed from a cut, the blood soon hardens and the bleeding stops. The hardening of the blood is called **clotting**. Clotting is important because it stops too much blood being lost through cuts and wounds, prevents germs entering and is the first step towards healing.

### How does clotting take place?

The damaging of a blood vessel, or the exposure of blood to air, triggers off a chain reaction. In the last step of this process, the plasma protein **fibrinogen** is turned into a meshwork of solid fibres called **fibrin** (Figure 2). For this to happen a substance called **thrombin** has to be formed in the blood first.

Many different chemical substances are needed in our blood to make it clot. We are born with some of them; others we get from our food – **calcium** and **vitamin K** for example. Vitamin K is found in cabbage and spinach and after being eaten it is stored for a short time in the liver. Also important are the small bodies found in the blood called **platelets**.

Occasionally a person is born without one of the substances needed for blood-clotting. This may result in bleeder's disease or **haemophilia** in which the blood takes an exceptionally long time to clot, so that the person may lose a great deal of blood from even a small cut. This is an inherited disease and runs in families. At one time the royal families of Europe suffered from it.

It is obviously desirable that blood should clot when we are cut or wounded. However, it would be fatal if this happened while the blood is flowing through the blood vessels. To prevent this, our blood vessels contain substances called **anti-coagulants**, which prevent clotting. Anti-coagulants are also added to blood which is kept in hospitals (Investigation 1).

## What happens if we lose a lot of blood?

Despite the clotting process, a person may lose a lot of blood after an accident, or if one of his blood vessels bursts. Losing blood is called a **haemorrhage**. A person can lose a litre or two of blood without ill effects, but if more than this is lost he is in danger for two reasons:

1 His blood pressure is reduced, and this slows down the flow of blood round the body.
2 The number of red blood cells is reduced, so the oxygen-carrying power of his blood is lowered.

All sorts of consequences follow, but the main one is that not enough oxygen gets to the brain, so the person may go unconscious and eventually die. However, his life may be saved by giving him a **blood transfusion**.

## Blood transfusions

During a blood transfusion the person is given blood which has been taken from other people. The blood is put into a vein in his arm through a narrow tube (Figure 3). Usually 'whole blood' is given, but sometimes plasma alone is used. This restores the blood pressure, so the blood will move round at its normal speed. Over the next few weeks the patient makes new red blood cells to replace the ones that he has lost.

### Do blood transfusions always work?
Blood transfusions were first carried out during the First World War. In some cases they worked, but in many cases the results were disastrous: the red blood cells in the transfused blood stuck together, blocking the patient's blood vessels and causing death. This sticking together of the red blood cells is called **agglutination**.

We now know that for a blood transfusion to be successful, the two lots of blood must be able to mix without sticking together. In practice this means that they should belong to compatible **blood groups**.

## What are blood groups?

Everyone's blood belongs to one of four different groups which we call A, B, AB and O. The letters A and B refer to certain substances which are present in the red blood cells: AB means that both are present, and O means that neither is present. If bloods of different groups are mixed together, agglutination of the red blood cells may occur. The reason for this is explained in Figure 4.

In addition to the A and B substances, there is another substance in red blood cells called the **Rhesus factor**, so-called because it was first discovered in a type of monkey known as the Rhesus monkey. People who have this substance in their blood are described as Rhesus positive; people who don't have it are Rhesus negative. If Rhesus positive blood is given to a Rhesus negative person, agglutination will occur.

Before a blood transfusion is carried out, doctors always make sure that the patient's blood is compatible with the transfused blood, with respect to both the ABO and Rhesus systems. The blood groups are determined by means of a simple compatability test (Investigation 2).

We inherit our blood groups from our parents (see page 312). The percentages of people with different blood groups vary from one country to another. The commonest groups are usually O, A and Rhesus positive. The

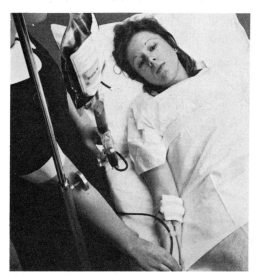

Figure 3 This girl is being given a blood transfusion.

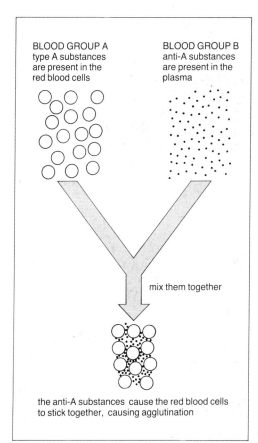

Figure 4 Diagram showing why agglutination occurs when blood of different blood groups are mixed together.

rarest is AB. This information is important to doctors because it tells them which particular blood groups are likely to be needed most for blood transfusions.

There is a special problem with the Rhesus system. If a Rhesus negative mother bears a Rhesus positive baby, the baby's blood may agglutinate. The reason is explained in Figure 5. The baby's life may be saved by giving it a transfusion of Rhesus negative blood while it is still in the womb.

## Giving blood

Hospitals always need a supply of blood for use when needed. Many people give blood at Blood Donation Centres. They are known as **blood donors**. A blood donor must be healthy and aged between about 18 and 65. First a drop of his blood is tested to find out what group he belongs to. Then about half a litre of blood is taken from a vein in the arm and drained into a bottle. He then needs to rest for a little while. After that he can resume his normal activities. The blood which he has lost will soon be replaced by his own body.

Meanwhile an anti-coagulant is added to the blood which the donor has given, to stop it clotting. The blood is then stored at a temperature just above freezing in a **blood bank**. The blood is normally kept for about a month. It cannot be used for transfusions after that because too many red blood cells will have died by then.

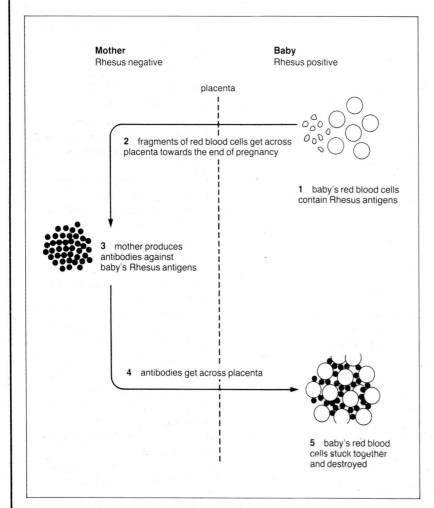

**Figure 5**  This diagram shows what may happen if a Rhesus negative mother has a Rhesus positive baby. In the first baby only a small proportion of the red blood cells are destroyed, but second and subsequent babies, if Rhesus positive, may suffer from massive destruction of their red blood cells.

## Investigation 1

### To find out how long blood takes to clot

This investigation involves drawing your own blood. *This must be done under proper supervision in strictly hygienic conditions to avoid any possibility of transmitting infection.*

1  Prick the tip of a finger with a sterile lancet and squeeze out a little blood (see Investigation 1, page 128).

2  Place two drops of blood side by side on a white tile.

3  To one drop of blood add a very small drop of sodium citrate solution.

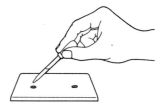

4  To the other drop of blood add a very small drop of water.

5  Stir each drop with a needle, and keep stirring until the blood begins to clot.

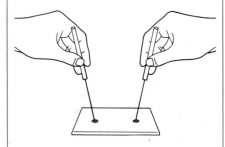

How long does it take for the blood to clot?

What effect does the sodium citrate have on clotting?

When a person gives blood at a blood donation centre, a small amount of citrate is added to the blood: why?

# Investigation 2

## Finding your blood group

Use a blood group test card: examine it carefully first. You will need to get a drop of blood from your finger or thumb. *This must be done under proper supervision in strictly hygienic conditions to avoid any possibility of transmitting infection.*

1 Pipette one drop of water onto each of the test panels.

2 Mix the water and reagent in each panel with the flat end of a plastic stick. *Clean the stick thoroughly between finishing one panel and moving to the next.*

3 Obtain a drop of blood from your finger or thumb with a sterile lancet (see Investigation 1, page 128).

4 Place the blood on the flat end of the plastic stick as shown.

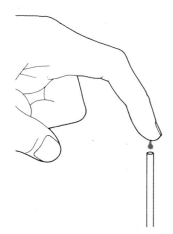

5 Mix the blood with the reagent in the left-hand test panel, spreading it evenly over the whole panel.

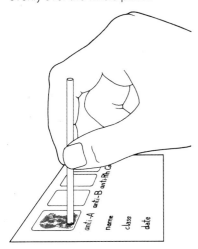

6 Wipe the stick, then mix another drop of blood with the reagent in each of the other panels. Wipe the stick between each one.

7 Tilt the card backwards and forwards so as to mix the blood thoroughly with the reagents in the test panels.

In which test panel or panels has the blood agglutinated?

8 Find your blood group from this table:

---

Agglutination in anti-A panel means you are group A

Agglutination in anti-B panel means you are group B

Agglutination in both panels means you are group AB

Agglutination in neither panel means you are group O

Agglutination in anti-Rh panel means you are Rh positive

No agglutination in anti-Rh panel means you are Rh negative.

---

9 Write down the blood groups of everyone else in your class and work out the percentage of students belonging to each group.

Compare the percentages with those given for Britain.
In each case indicate whether your class figures are higher or lower than these figures:

*ABO system*

| Group | percentage |
|-------|------------|
| O | 47% |
| A | 41% |
| B | 9% |
| AB | 3% |

*Rhesus system*

| | |
|---|---|
| Rh + | 85% |
| Rh − | 15% |

# Assignments

1 Give two reasons why it is dangerous to lose more than two litres of blood.

2 Explain the reason for each of the following:

a) Not more than half a litre of blood is normally taken from a blood donor.

b) After a person has given blood he or she is advised to sit down quietly for about half an hour.

c) A little sodium citrate is usually added to blood which has been given at the blood donation centre.

d) Complete blood is only kept for about a month after it has been obtained from a blood donor, but plasma may be kept much longer.

3 The poison of certain snakes causes the blood of their victims to clot inside the blood vessels, thereby blocking the vessels. Suggest two different ways by which this effect might be brought about.

4 In trying to find their own blood groups, four pupils in a school mixed drops of their blood with different kinds of serum:
John got agglutination with anti-A serum but not with anti-B;
David got agglutination with anti-B serum but not with anti-A;
Susan got no agglutination with either serum; and Tim got agglutination with both sera.
a) Which blood group does each pupil belong to?
b) Whose blood group is needed most in blood donation centres, and why?
c) What causes agglutination?

5 A scientist fed chickens on a diet of synthetic pellets, and he found that the chickens died of bleeding as a result of their blood clotting extremely slowly. However, when he fed his chickens on a diet which included cabbage, the chickens did not suffer from this condition.

How would you explain these observations?

# How does blood move round the body?

*Blood constantly flows round the body, and this is called the circulation. The various structures through which the blood flows all belong to the circulatory system.*

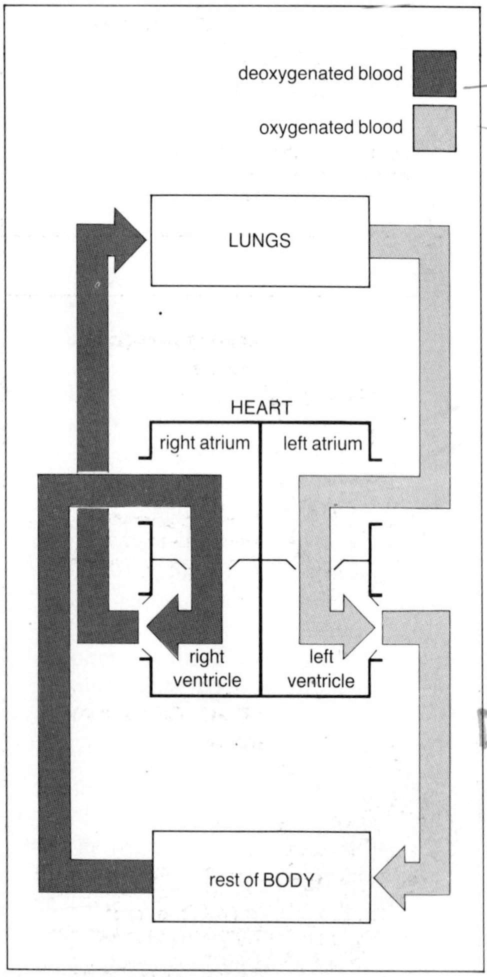

## The general plan of the human circulation

The main organ in our circulatory system is the **heart**, which is situated in the chest between the lungs. The heart is hollow and its wall contains muscles: its job is to pump the blood round the body.

The blood flows round the body in tube-like **blood vessels** which eventually lead back to the heart. The blood vessels which carry blood away from the heart are called **arteries**. Those that bring blood back to it are called **veins**. The arteries and veins are connected by narrow, thin-walled vessels called **capillaries**.

As blood flows through the capillaries, oxygen and other useful substances pass out of them to the surrounding cells, and unwanted substances pass in the reverse direction. In this way the capillaries bring life to the cells and maintain them in a state of health and repair.

The capillaries are extremely numerous and every organ contains thousands of them: no cell is more than a twentieth of a millimetre from the nearest one. If a person's capillaries were laid end to end, they would stretch round the world 2½ times!

## A closer look at the circulation

If you look at Figure 1, you will see that there are really two circulations: one serves the lungs and the other serves the rest of the body. The heart is divided by a partition into left and right halves. Blood is pumped from the right side of the heart to the lungs where it takes up oxygen. The oxygenated blood is taken back to the left side of the heart and is then pumped to the rest of the body. The oxygen is taken up by the various organs as the blood passes through them. The deoxygenated blood then returns to the right side of the heart, and the cycle is repeated.

Each side of the heart consists of two chambers: an **atrium** (plural: atria)* and a **ventricle** (Investigation 1). Both have muscles in their walls, but the walls of the ventricles are much thicker and more muscular than those of the atria. The ventricles play the most important part in pumping blood round the body. A detailed diagram of the human heart and circulation is shown in Figures 2 and 3.

## The heart as a pump

The heart contracts approximately 70 times a minute throughout our life: that's over 100 000 times a day. This is made possible by the muscles in its wall. Heart muscle differs from other kinds of muscle in that it does not get tired. Try clenching your fist at the rate of 70 times per minute and your hand muscles will soon give up. Heart muscle, however, has no difficulty in working at this rate.

Each contraction of the heart is followed by relaxation during which the heart wall returns to its original position. When it relaxes, blood is sucked into it from the veins. When it contracts, the blood is pumped out of the heart into the arteries. So blood flows through the heart in only one direction. This is made possible by **valves** which prevent the blood flowing backwards (Figure 4).

Every time the heart beats it sets up a wave of pressure which travels along the main arteries. This is called a **pulse wave**, and if you put your finger on your skin just above the artery in your wrist you can feel it as a slight throb (Investigation 2). Doctors and nurses often feel a patient's pulse to see if the heart is beating at its normal rate. It is also possible to *hear* the heart by putting your ear, or better still a stethoscope, against a person's chest (Invesgation 3).

In order to contract repeatedly and powerfully throughout life, the heart muscles must have a good supply of oxygen. They get this through a system of arteries which spread over the heart wall. These are called the **coronary vessels**.

deoxygenated blood

oxygenated blood

LUNGS

HEART

right atrium | left atrium

right ventricle | left ventricle

rest of BODY

**Figure 1** General plan of the human circulation. It is usual to show pictures of the human anatomy from the ventral (belly) side, so in this diagram the right side of the heart is on the left, and the left side of the heart is on the right.

*The atria are also known as **auricles**.

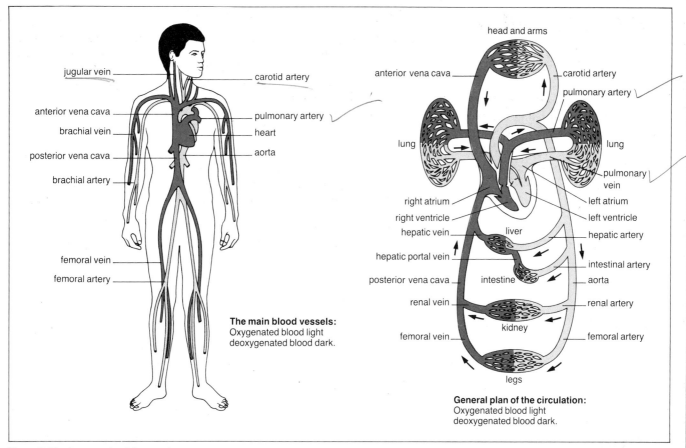

jugular vein

carotid artery

anterior vena cava

brachial vein

pulmonary artery

heart

posterior vena cava

aorta

brachial artery

femoral vein

femoral artery

**The main blood vessels:**
Oxygenated blood light
deoxygenated blood dark.

head and arms

anterior vena cava

carotid artery

pulmonary artery

lung

lung

pulmonary
vein

right atrium

left atrium

right ventricle

left ventricle

hepatic vein

liver

hepatic artery

hepatic portal vein

intestinal artery

posterior vena cava

intestine

aorta

renal vein

renal artery

kidney

femoral vein

femoral artery

legs

**General plan of the circulation:**
Oxygenated blood light
deoxygenated blood dark.

Figure 2 The human circulatory system.

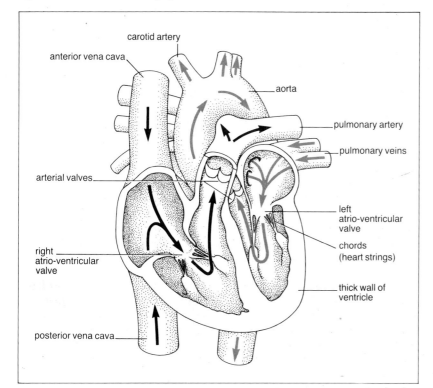

carotid artery

anterior vena cava

aorta

pulmonary artery

pulmonary veins

arterial valves

left
atrio-ventricular
valve

chords
(heart strings)

right
atrio-ventricular
valve

thick wall of
ventricle

posterior vena cava

Figure 3 The heart in detail. Note how the aorta and pulmonary artery twist round each other. The atrio-ventricular valves consist of flaps which are attached to the sides of the ventricles by tough chords, the heart strings. The arterial valves are like little pockets. Oxygenated blood, light arrows; deoxygenated blood, dark arrows.

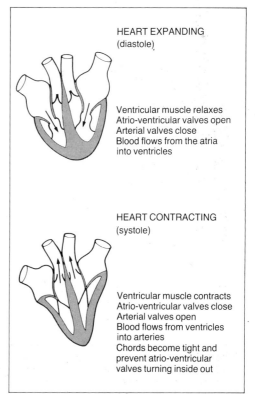

HEART EXPANDING
(diastole)

Ventricular muscle relaxes
Atrio-ventricular valves open
Arterial valves close
Blood flows from the atria
into ventricles

HEART CONTRACTING
(systole)

Ventricular muscle contracts
Atrio-ventricular valves close
Arterial valves open
Blood flows from ventricles
into arteries
Chords become tight and
prevent atrio-ventricular
valves turning inside out

Figure 4 These diagrams show how blood flows through the heart. The valves prevent the blood flowing backwards.

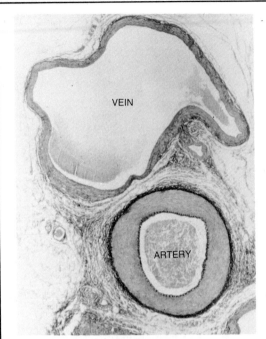

**Figure 5** Section of an artery and vein as seen under the microscope. Note that the artery is narrower than the vein and has a thicker wall.

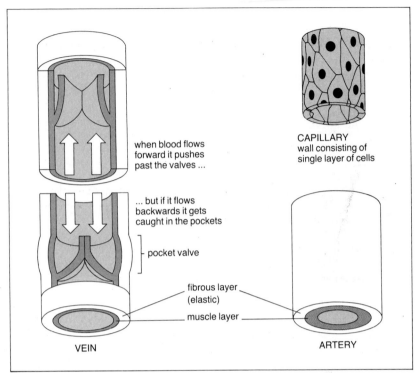

**Figure 6** The three types of blood vessel found in the circulatory system.

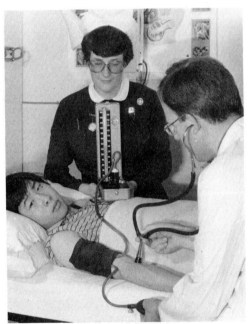

**Figure 7** A doctor taking a patient's blood pressure. The pressure is registered by the mercury manometer. The doctor has wrapped an inflatable band round the upper arm and is listening to the pulse with a stethoscope. He pumps up the arm band until it is so tight it stops the blood passing down the main artery of the arm; this makes the pulse disappear. He now lets the air very slowly out of the arm band. As he does so there comes a moment when he can just hear the patient's pulse again. At this point the blood manages to pass the arm band every time the heart contracts (**systolic pressure**). The doctor continues to let air out of the arm band until a moment is reached when the pulse gets very much quieter. At this point the blood passes the arm band continuously even when the heart is relaxing (**diastolic pressure**).

## The blood vessels

Figures 5 and 6 show the structure of an artery, vein and capillary. Their structure suits them to their particular jobs.

The arteries have a narrow cavity and tough elastic walls containing smooth muscle (see page 34). The walls press back against the blood as it flows through them. This helps to force the blood along quickly, much as water is forced along a narrow hosepipe.

The capillaries are only just wide enough to allow the red blood cells to pass along in single file. Their walls are very thin, consisting of a single layer of flattened cells. This enables oxygen and other substances to diffuse through easily.

By the time the blood gets through the capillaries into the veins, the pressure pushing it along is greatly reduced, and it is now mainly moving against gravity. This makes it difficult for the blood to get back to the heart. However, the veins are wider and have thinner walls than the arteries, so they have more 'give' and let the blood along more easily. Also they contain valves which prevent the blood slipping back. Movement and exercise also help to keep the blood going because the contraction of the leg muscles squeezes the blood along the veins.

## Blood pressure

The pumping action of the heart, combined with the narrowness of the smaller vessels, results in a considerable pressure being built up in the arteries. This is what we mean when we talk about 'blood pressure'. It's important that our blood pressure should be reasonably high because it keeps the blood on the move.

A person's blood pressure varies according to what he is doing. In general anything which makes the heart beat faster, or the arteries get narrower, will increase the blood pressure. For example, anger, excitement and exercise all have this effect.

The blood pressure goes up and down as the heart beats. It is highest when the heart contracts (**systolic pressure**), and lowest when the heart relaxes (**diastolic pressure**). If a person goes to the doctor feeling tired and run down, one of the first things the doctor does is to measure his blood pressure (Figure 7). He measures both the systolic and diastolic pressures and expresses them as a fraction. For example, a healthy person's blood pressure should be around 120/70. This means that his systolic pressure is 120 millimetres of mercury and his diastolic pressure 70 millimetres.

## The circulation during exercise

Suppose you run a race. During the exercise your heart beats faster (Investigation 4). What makes this happen? The answer is that extra carbon dioxide is produced by your muscles and this starts to build up in your bloodstream. The brain senses this is happening, and it sends nerve impulses to the heart making it beat faster. This is an automatic reflex: it happens without you having to think about it.

The result of the heart beating faster is that more blood can be sent to the muscles. The arteries serving the muscles widen, whereas those serving less needful organs get narrower. The result is that extra blood is diverted to the structures that need it most.

## What can go wrong with the circulation?

One of the most common defects of the circulation is high blood pressure, or **hypertension**. We all develop high blood pressure at one time or another, when we take exercise for example, but some people have it all the time. This puts an extra strain on the heart, and may lead to **heart failure**. It also pushes out the walls of the arteries, and may burst them – just as a balloon will burst if you blow it up too much. The risk of this happening is greatest in old people whose arteries have become fragile. Sometimes an artery bursts inside the brain, and the spillage of blood kills the cells in that part of the brain. This results in a **stroke**, and it may leave the person partly paralysed and unable to speak properly. A severe stroke can be fatal.

What causes high blood pressure? We don't know, but it is frequently associated with the stress and tensions of modern life, overeating and drinking too much alcohol.

Another defect of the circulation is **hardening of the arteries**. This is caused by fatty substances being laid down in the walls of the vessels, making them narrower and slowing the flow of blood through them. Where this happens, a blood clot may occur inside the artery, completely blocking it. The structures served by that particular artery will no longer receive any oxygen. If this happens in one of the coronary vessels, the part of the heart deprived of oxygen stops contracting and the result is a **heart attack**. If only a small area of the heart is affected, the person may recover, but if a large part is involved, the attack may be fatal. The person's life may be saved by massaging the heart (Figure 8).

Sometimes a blood clot gets lodged in one of the arteries serving the brain, and this is another cause of a stroke.

What causes hardening of the arteries? There is some debate about this, but eating large amounts of animal fat appears to increase the chances of it happening (see page 73). So does smoking (see page 118).

The defects mentioned so far are all serious, but other less serious things may go wrong with our circulation. For example, the flow of blood through some of the veins may become sluggish and the valves may not work properly. The back-pressure of blood stretches the walls of these veins which become flabby, like thin bags. These are called **varicose veins**, and they are particularly liable to develop just under the skin at the back of the legs. Sometimes the same thing happens in the wall of the rectum where it gives rise to piles or **haemorrhoids**.

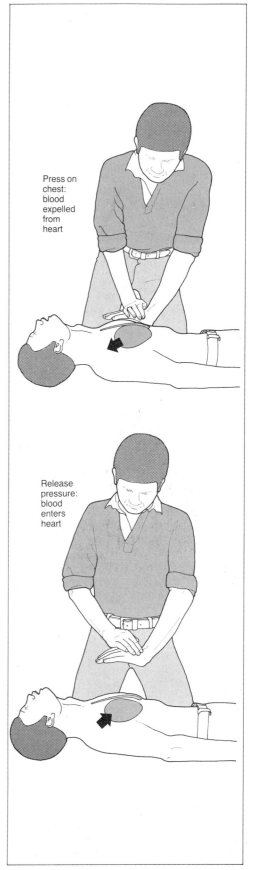

Press on chest: blood expelled from heart

Release pressure: blood enters heart

**Figure 8** A person who has had a heart attack can sometimes be saved by cardiac massage.

# Investigation 1

**Looking at the heart**

1 Look at the heart of a mammal such as a pig or sheep obtained from the butcher. The heart has been cut open, so you can look inside.

2 Decide which side of the heart is dorsal, and which side is ventral. The more rounded (convex) side is the ventral.

3 Identify the two atria, and the ventricles.

How do they differ in size and shape?

4 Feel the atria and ventricles with your fingers.

How do they differ in the way they feel?
Explain the reason for the difference.

5 Look at the large blood vessels attached to the heart.

Can you recognise the vessels shown in Figure 3?
Which ones are arteries and which ones are veins?
How do the arteries and veins differ from each other?

6 Observe the narrow blood vessels ramifying over the surface of the ventricles, and notice where they come from. These are the coronary vessels.
What is their function?
What would happen if one of them became blocked?

7 Look at the cut which has been made in the wall of the ventricles.

What is the wall made of?
Has one of the ventricles got a thicker wall than the other?
Why do you think they differ in this way?

8 Look inside one of the ventricles.

Which structures shown in Figure 3 can you see?
In particular notice the valves.
What are their functions?

In what ways is the heart suited to its job of pumping blood round the body?

# Investigation 2

**Finding how fast your heart is beating**

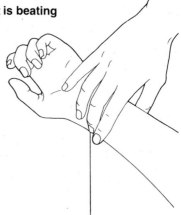

feel pulse with this finger

You can find how fast your heart is beating, that is your heart rate, by feeling your pulse.

1 Sit down comfortably in a chair with the palm of your hand facing upwards.

2 Gently place the middle finger of your other hand on your wrist as shown in the illustration. Can you feel your pulse as a repeated throb? If necessary change the position of your finger, until you can feel your pulse really well.

3 Count the number of heart beats in one minute.

4 Repeat step 3 four times.

Write down the number of beats per minute each time.
Work out your average heart rate. As this is your heart rate when sitting down, it is called the resting heart rate.

5 Stand up for one minute.

6 Still standing, take your pulse another five times.

Work out your average heart rate in beats per minute. This is called your standing heart rate.

How do your resting and standing heart rates differ?

Why do you think they are different?

# Investigation 3

**Listening to the heart**

Work in pairs, one person acting as the subject. The subject should sit down comfortably.

1 Put the bell of a stethoscope against the chest wall and listen.

Can you hear regular thud-like sounds?

2 Listen with the bell of the stethoscope in different positions.

Where is the best place to put the stethoscope for the sounds to be loudest?
What kind of information do you think the doctor can get about a patient's heart by listening to it with a stethoscope?
What do you think causes the heart sounds?

3 Learn how to feel the pulse (see Investigation 2).

4 Now feel the pulse, and listen to the heart sounds at the same time.

Notice that there is a time lag between the heart sounds and the pulse.

What is the time lag caused by?

In what circumstances would you expect the time lag to be shorter?

# Investigation 4

## To find the effect of exercise on the heart rate

1 Measure your standing heart rate by feeling your pulse (see Investigation 2). Write down your heart rate in beats per minute.

2 Do steady walking on the spot for 3 minutes.

3 Immediately after walking, measure your heart rate again. Write down your new heart rate in beats per minute.

How does it differ from the standing heart rate?
How would you explain the difference?

4 Stand still and wait until your heart rate returns to its normal standing rate.

5 Do some hard exercise for 3 minutes. Stepping exercises are suitable, such as stepping up onto a stool and down again at a steady rate.

6 Immediately after the exercise, measure your heart rate every minute until it returns to the normal standing rate. Write down your heart rate in beats per minute for each minute.

How does your heart rate immediately after the hard exercise differ from the standing rate?

How would you explain the difference?

How long did it take for your heart rate to return to its normal standing rate?

# Assignments

1 A person's blood pressure can be recorded continuously by means of an electronic pressure gauge placed inside one of the arteries.

Here is a recording obtained in this way:

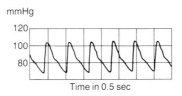

mmHg

Time in 0.5 sec

a) Why do you think the pressure goes up and down all the time?
b) Give two circumstances in which you would expect the frequency of the waves to increase.

2 Suggest a reason for each of the following:

a) the right atrium is larger than the left atrium;
b) the left ventricle has a thicker, more muscular wall than the right ventricle;
c) arteries have more muscle in their walls than veins;
d) capillaries have very thin walls;
e) veins contain valves.

3 Devise an experiment which you could do to test the suggestion that veins have more stretchable walls than arteries.

4 The average speed of the blood in the arteries is 45 cm/s, but the average speed in the capillaries is only 0.5 mm/s.

a) Give the speed in the capillaries as a percentage of the speed in the arteries.
b) What do you think causes the difference?
c) Why is it desirable for blood to flow through the capillaries comparatively slowly?

5 The chart below shows the pulse rate of a hospital patient measured at four hourly intervals every day.
a) Can you detect a regular pattern in the way the pulse rate changes? If so, describe the pattern.
b) Do you have any criticisms of the way the pulse rate is graphed in the chart?
c) What were the highest and lowest values of the pulse rate during the period in question and when were they recorded?
d) Give possible reasons why the pulse rate reached these particular values.

6 The blood system has been likened to a bus route. In this comparison, each of the items listed on the left below is equivalent to one of those on the right. Write them down in the correct pairs.

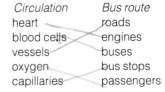

| Circulation | Bus route |
| --- | --- |
| heart | roads |
| blood cells | engines |
| vessels | buses |
| oxygen | bus stops |
| capillaries | passengers |

In your town which bus route is most like the human blood system?

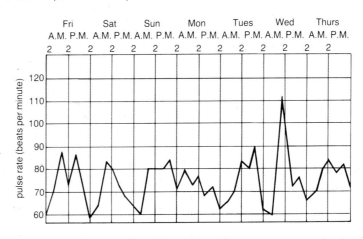

# Tissue fluid and lymph

*Our bodies contain other important fluids besides blood. These include tissue fluid and lymph.*

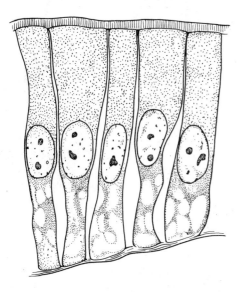

**Figure 1** Mammalian cells in a tissue, showing spaces between the cells. The spaces contain tissue fluid.

## Tissue fluid

In between our cells there are narrow spaces filled with a watery fluid. This is **tissue fluid** (Figure 1).

Tissue fluid is extremely important. It bathes the cells and keeps them in the right condition. The cells get all the substances they need from the bloodstream, *via* the tissue fluid. The tissue fluid is therefore an essential link between the bloodstream and the cells, and it comprises the immediate surroundings of the cells.

## How is tissue fluid formed?

Tissue fluid is formed from the blood (Figure 2). As blood flows along the capillaries, a certain amount of fluid leaks through the capillary walls into the spaces between the cells. Once it has left the capillaries, it becomes the tissue fluid.

The process by which tissue fluid is formed involves a kind of filtration: the blood cells and plasma proteins are too large to go through the capillary walls, so they stay in the bloodstream. What passes through is therefore a colourless fluid consisting of blood plasma minus the proteins.

## Lymph

Once formed, the tissue fluid seeps around amongst the cells. If there is too much of it, it either returns to the capillaries, or is drained into a system of narrow channels called **lymph vessels**. The fluid in these vessels is called **lymph**.

The body is permeated by lymph vessels: some of them can be seen in Figure 3. They eventually lead to the veins, so sooner or later lymph gets back into the bloodstream. The lymph vessels contain valves, which help to keep the lymph flowing in the right direction.

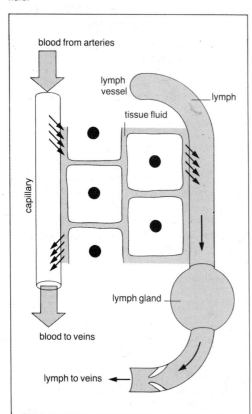

**Figure 2** This diagram shows how tissue fluid and lymph are formed.

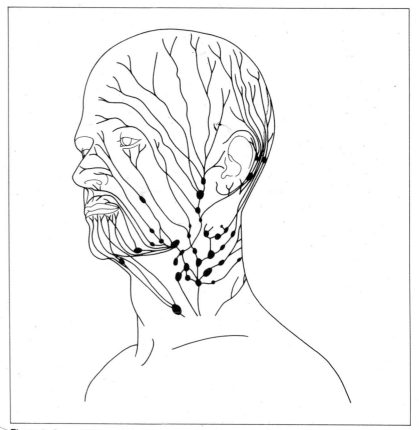

**Figure 3** Some of the main lymph vessels and glands in the head and neck.

Occasionally tissue fluid is formed faster than it can be drained away in the lymph vessels. The result is that fluid builds up in the tissues, causing them to swell up. This is called **oedema**. It tends to occur in the legs, particularly of old people, pregnant women and people who stand a lot (Figure 4).

## Lymph glands

If you look at Figure 3 you will see that there are little swellings at intervals along the length of the lymph vessels. These are called **lymph glands** or **lymph nodes**.

Each lymph gland is full of tiny spaces like a sponge, and the lymph has to filter through these spaces before it can continue on its journey back to the bloodstream.

The lymph glands help us to fight disease. They contain cells which attack and destroy germs in the lymph as it filters through. These cells are the same as the white blood cells mentioned on page 127. Some of them are phagocytes and eat up the germs; others produce antibodies against them.

The positions of our main lymph glands are shown in Figure 5. The largest ones are located in the neck, armpits and groin.

Suppose you have a severe throat infection. The germs get trapped in the nearby lymph glands in your neck where your phagocytes and lymph cells do their best to kill them and prevent them getting into the rest of your body. This causes the glands to swell up and become tender and painful. Lymph tissue is also found in the **tonsils** and **adenoids** in the throat. Sometimes these organs get repeatedly infected and swollen, making it difficult to breathe. This may make it necessary for them to be removed in an operation. At one time children had their tonsils and adenoids out almost as a matter of course but nowadays it is only done if it is really necessary. After all, these are useful organs which help to defend us against disease, and it's best to keep them if we can.

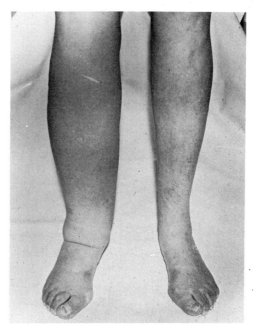

Figure 4 The legs of this person are swollen as a result of tissue fluid accumulating in them.

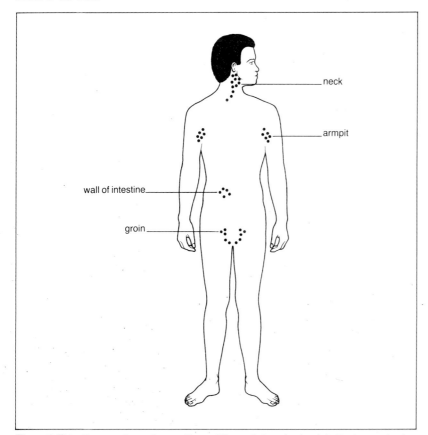

Figure 5 This diagram shows the positions of the main lymph glands in the human body.

## Assignments

1 In what respect do blood, tissue fluid and lymph differ in what they contain? Explain the reason for the differences.

2 State two functions which are performed by the lymph system.

3 A person cuts his foot and the cut goes septic. Within a short time his groin hurts whenever he touches it. Explain the reason for the pain.

4 At the arterial end of a capillary, the blood pressure is high, but the salt concentration of the blood is low. However, at the venous end, the blood pressure is low, but the salt concentration is high.
   a) Why do you think the blood pressure is higher at the arterial end than at the venous end?
   b) Why do you think the salt concentration is higher at the venous end than at the arterial end?
   c) What part do you think these differences play in the formation and movement of tissue fluid?

5 Sometimes elderly people get tissue fluid accumulating in their feet and legs which consequently become swollen. Suggest two possible reasons why this may happen.

# What do plants need to live?

*When a gardener or a farmer puts manure or fertiliser in the soil, he is giving his plants essential materials which they need for healthy growth.*

**Figure 1** The effect of depriving barley seedlings of certain major elements. The plants in Jar A were grown in Knop's solution; those in B were deprived of potassium, in C of nitrogen, and in D of phosphorus.

**Table 1** The main mineral elements needed by plants, why they are needed and what happens if they don't get them. One of the main signs of lack of mineral elements is that the leaves go yellow. This is known as *chlorosis*.

## Plants need certain major elements

It has long been known that plants need the elements carbon, hydrogen, oxygen, nitrogen, phosphorus, sulphur, magnesium, potassium, calcium and iron. These ten elements are needed in quite large amounts by all green plants. For this reason we call them 'major elements' or **essential elements**.

Think of a plant growing in your garden or in a park. It obtains carbon and oxygen from the air. It obtains hydrogen from water in the soil, which it absorbs through its roots. The other elements are also absorbed by the roots. They are present in the soil in the form of mineral salts, such as calcium nitrate and potassium phosphate.

One of the first people to realise that plants need these mineral elements was a German scientist called Willhelm Knop. In 1865 he made up a solution which appeared to be ideal for plant growth. Knop's solution contained salts of all the mineral elements listed above. All he had to do was to suspend the roots of a young seedling in his solution, and it grew. However, if he left out one of the major elements, the seedling would not grow properly (Figure 1). You can repeat Knop's experiment for yourself (Investigation).

The reasons why plants need these elements, and what happens if they don't get them, are summarised in Table 1.

## Some minor elements are needed too

We know that most plants need, in addition to the major elements, certain other elements as well. These are required in only tiny amounts, so we call them **trace elements** or minor elements. These elements include boron, zinc, copper, aluminium, molybdenum, sodium, chlorine, silicon, manganese and cobalt. As with the major elements, they are obtained in the form of mineral salts. Plants absorb them through their roots.

If any of these minor elements is absent from the soil, plants may show poor growth. Look at Figure 2: this shows the effect of depriving tomato plants of the element molybdenum. In certain parts of Australia crops grew very badly until it was discovered that there was no molybdenum in the soil. The soil was then sprayed with a very dilute solution of molybdenum, and this made all the difference – the plants grew splendidly. Very little molybdenum was needed: one teaspoonful was enough for an area the size of a tennis court. Putting on too much of a trace element may have a damaging effect on plants.

## What makes soil short of minerals?

Think of a natural plant community – a forest if you like, or a field. When plants die they rot: the various chemicals in their bodies are set free and put back into the soil. They can then be absorbed and used again by new plants.

Now think what happens in a field with a crop in it, such as wheat or rice. The crop is harvested and the plants are taken away. The chemicals are not returned to the soil, and so the soil becomes poor. The soil is made even

| Element | Why needed | Deficiency effects |
|---|---|---|
| Nitrogen | Contained in proteins | Poor growth, yellow leaves |
| Phosphorus | Contained in important chemicals | Poor growth, leaves dull green with curly brown edges |
| Potassium | Increases hardiness | Yellow edges to leaves, die early |
| Sulphur | Contained in proteins | Yellow leaves |
| Calcium | Needed for cell formation | Poor buds, stunted growth |
| Magnesium | Contained in chlorophyll | Yellow leaves |
| Iron | Needed for chlorophyll formation | Yellow leaves |

worse if heavy rain washes useful chemicals out of it. This often happens when soil becomes eroded (see page 381).

How can we overcome this problem? One way is to grow crops on one piece of land for several years and then move somewhere else. This is what nomadic tribes do in certain parts of the world. It is called **shifting cultivation**. But it can't be done where land is short. A better solution is to make sure that the soil does not become poor in the first place. This can be achieved in two ways: by rotating the crops or putting on a fertiliser.

Figure 2 The tomato plants on the left were given everything they need. The ones on the right were deprived of the trace element molybdenum.

## Rotation of crops

A farmer does not usually grow the same crop in a field year after year. For a year or two he may grow cassava, then maize perhaps, then yams — and so on. This is known as **rotation of crops**, and it has been carried out since Roman times.

This is a good idea because some plants take more of certain chemicals out of the soil than others. If the same crop is grown in a field year after year, a particular element – nitrogen say – may eventually be removed altogether. Rotating crops helps to prevent this.

Every now and again a farmer may grow a crop of beans, peas or some other leguminous plant in his field. The roots of these plants contain nitrogen-fixing bacteria, so they make the soil richer in nitrates (see page 28). They therefore have a good effect on the soil.

It isn't only farmers who rotate crops – a gardener may do it too. He plants his various vegetables in different places each year. The vegetables take different nutrients from the soil. The rotation also helps to avoid the spread of diseases which may have been left in the soil.

## Fertilisers

The best way of preventing the soil from becoming poor is to put back into it what the plants take out. This can be achieved by putting fertilisers into the soil.

A fertiliser is any substance containing chemical elements needed for plant growth. We can divide them into two groups: **organic fertilisers** and **inorganic fertilisers**. Let's take each in turn.

One of the most natural organic fertilisers is farmyard manure. This consists of the dung and urine produced by farm animals, mixed with straw. It is spread on the ground where it decays. As it rots, nitrates and other inorganic nutrients are released from it into the soil. These can then be used by plants.

Another natural organic fertiliser is compost. This consists of the rotting remains of vegetable matter: old cabbage stalks, grass cuttings, and so on. Many people make compost heaps in their gardens (see page 389). As with farmyard manure, the decay process releases inorganic nutrients into the soil which can then be used by plants.

Because of their colour, farmyard manure and compost are referred to as **brown manure**. Sometimes, however, a farmer will grow a crop of green plants and then plough them into the soil. This is called **green manure**. Once ploughed in, it rots and the nutrients are set free. Plants such as peas, beans and clover make good green manure because they enrich the soil with nitrates.

Organic fertilisers have one disadvantage: they have to decompose first before the inorganic nutrients can be released. This makes them slow to act, though in some cases this may be a good thing.

Quicker results can be achieved by using inorganic fertilisers. These contain mineral nutrients which can be absorbed by plants straight away. General fertilisers contain nitrogen, phosphorus and potassium (N, P, K). They are manufactured in fertiliser factories, either from natural materials such as bone and horns, or by special chemical processes.

Figure 3 Bean plants enrich the soil in nitrates because their roots contain nitrogen-fixing bacteria.

Figure 4  The rice plants on the left were given a fertiliser; those on the right were not.

**Figure 5** The Broadbalk Field at Rothamsted Experimental Research Station, showing one of the strips of wheat.

## Do fertilisers work?

Look at Figure 4. This shows the result of a trial with rice that was carried out in the Middle East. The soil on the left had a fertiliser added to it containing nitrogen and phosphorus; the soil on the right was unfertilised. The results speak for themselves.

In England there is an experimental research station at Rothamsted. Here there are strips of soil where wheat is grown each year (Figure 5). In one strip wheat has been planted and harvested every year for over a hundred years. During this time no fertiliser has ever been added to the soil. Since the first crop was harvested way back in 1843, the annual yield of grain has fallen to less than half what it was originally.

In other strips, however, different kinds of fertiliser have been added to the soil. In some of these strips the yield has more than doubled (Figure 6). So fertilisers certainly help.

Which is better, natural manure or artificial fertiliser? The Rothamsted results suggest that it does not matter much: equally high yields have been obtained with both. However, what applies to wheat at an experimental research station may not apply to the onions in Mr Smith's back garden. Some gardeners swear by farmyard manure. Others feel that artificial fertilisers are better and a lot easier to use. An undoubted advantage of manure is that it improves the texture of the soil, aerating it and helping the soil particles to stick together.

Artificial fertilisers are sprayed onto the soil in liquid form. Alternatively they may be scattered as pellets or powders which are then dissolved and washed into the soil by the rain. It is important that they should not be too concentrated, otherwise water may be drawn out of the plants' roots by osmosis.

Without doubt artificial fertilisers have revolutionised agriculture. Thanks to them, a rigid rotation of crops is no longer necessary, and the plants grow well even if they are very close together. In other words the land can be used much more intensively. This allows farmers to grow more food for more people.

Despite the advantages, there are snags with growing crops very intensively. For example, diseases can spread more quickly through them. Can you think of any other problems and how they may be overcome?

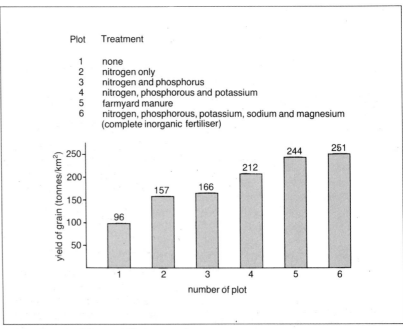

**Figure 6** This bar chart shows the average yearly yield of grain given by six of the plots of wheat in the Broadbalk Field at Rothamsted Experimental Station between 1852 and 1967.

# Investigation

## To find out which elements are needed for plant growth

In this experiment we will grow plants in a series of solutions. This is called **water culture**. One of the solutions contains all the chemical elements believed to be needed for plant growth. This serves as a control. The other solutions each lack one particular element.

1 Obtain 8 bottles, and label them A to H.

2 Fill each bottle with the following solutions:

  A Complete solution: this contains all the necessary elements.*
  B Complete solution minus nitrogen.
  C Complete solution minus phosphorus.
  D Complete solution minus sulphur.
  E Complete solution minus magnesium.
  F Complete solution minus potassium.
  G Complete solution minus calcium.
  H Complete solution minus iron.

3 Obtain 8 identical seedlings of e.g. wheat, maize, barley or broad bean.

4 Put one seedling in each bottle as shown below.

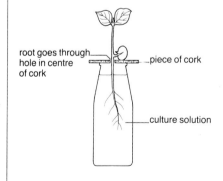

root goes through hole in centre of cork — piece of cork — culture solution

5 Wrap a sheet of black paper round each bottle to shield it from light.

  This will prevent algae growing inside.

6 Put the bottles in a warm, light place, e.g. close to a window or in a greenhouse.

7 Observe the seedlings at intervals over the next 2–3 weeks.

*Note* You may need to bubble air into the solutions from time to time to make sure the roots get enough oxygen. Do this as shown below.

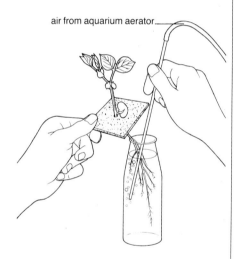

air from aquarium aerator

After 2–3 weeks, how do the eight seedlings differ in appearance? Can you explain the differences?

*Other similar investigations*

1 As an alternative to water culture, seedlings may be grown in sand which has been washed beforehand in distilled water. This is known as **sand culture**. After planting the seedlings the sand should be watered regularly with the solutions listed in step 2 above.

2 Try growing seedlings of, e.g., maize in distilled water and in distilled water plus a general fertiliser at a series of different concentrations, below and above the recommended level.

*Either Knop's or Sach's solution can be used. For a suitable recipe see Nuffield Revised Biology. Text 2, *Living Things in Action*.

# Assignments

1 Gardening shops sell a special liquid medium which can be used for growing pot plants. Make a list of the major chemical elements which you think it should contain.

2 Give two reasons why soil may become poor in mineral nutrients.

3 Why is it a good idea:
  a) to plant your vegetables in a different part of the garden each year,
  b) to dig compost into the soil,
  c) to give a potted plant some 'plant food' every week or so?

4 Give two advantages which farmyard manure has over artificial fertilisers, and two advantages which artificial fertilisers have over farmyard manure.

5 The maize in a certain area of Jamaica is giving a lower yield of grain than would be expected. You have been called in to find out the cause. What would you do?

6 Look at Figure 6, then answer these questions:
  a) Express the yield of grain given by plots 2 to 6 as a percentage increase over that given by plot 1.
  b) From the data it might be concluded that artificial fertiliser is better than farmyard manure. Do you think this conclusion is justified? Give reasons to support your answer.

7 At Rothamsted Experimental Station scientists have investigated the effect on the annual yield of wheat grain of leaving a field bare (fallow) every fifth year. Here is a sample of their results: the yield is expressed as a percentage of what it is when wheat is grown continuously.

| Years after fallow | 1 | 2 | 3 | 4 |
|---|---|---|---|---|
| Percentage increase | 101 | 65 | 48 | 50 |

  a) Explain in words what is meant by an increase of 101 per cent.
  b) Suggest reasons why the yield increases and then gradually decreases after the fallow year.

# How do plants feed?

*What sort of organic substances do plants contain and where do they get them from?*

**Figure 1** This plant contains organic food substances. How did they get there?

**Figure 2** Mount Everest, the highest mountain in the world. Its peak is well over 8000 metres above sea level. Imagine a pile of sugar that high!

## What sort of organic substances do plants contain?

You can answer this by testing a plant for sugar. This can be done with Benedict's or Fehling's solution (Investigation 1). The plant must be given all the things it needs beforehand, such as plenty of light and well watered soil.

What about starch? You can find out if a plant contains starch by testing it with iodine (Investigation 2). Again it is important that the plant should be given all the things it needs beforehand, such as plenty of light and well watered soil.

These two experiments, and many others besides, tell us that plants contain organic substances such as sugar and starch (Figure 1). Normally plants convert sugar into starch for storage.

## Where do plants get their organic substances from?

It is possible that plants might obtain sugar from the soil. How could you find out if this is so? One way would be to test a small sample of soil to see if there is any sugar there (Investigation 3).

You will find that no sugar can be detected in the soil. In fact neither the soil enveloping the roots of a plant, nor the air surrounding its leaves, contains sugar.

So plants contain sugar, but they do not take it in. How, then, does sugar get there?

## Van Helmont's experiment

In 1692 a Dutchman called Van Helmont did an interesting experiment which helps us to answer this question. He weighed a young willow tree and planted it in a pot containing a known mass of soil. He then left the tree to grow, giving it nothing but water. After five years he weighed the tree, and the soil, again. He found that the tree had gained 74 kg in mass, but the soil had only lost 56 g. Try to explain the results of Van Helmont's experiment before you read further.

Although Van Helmont did not realise it at the time, the willow tree had absorbed simple substances from the air and soil and had built them up into food. We now know that all green plants can do this provided they are kept in the light. It is their method of feeding, and we call the process **photosynthesis**. It is a remarkable process and for over 100 years man has tried to repeat the process in the laboratory, but with very little success. Yet it happens naturally in the leaves of a green plant.

## Why is photosynthesis important?

Think of it in this way. Animals cannot make complex food substances for themselves. The only way an animal can get these substances is by eating plants – or by eating animals which have eaten the plants – or by eating animals which have eaten the animals which have eaten the plants.

So animals are dependent on plants for their food. When you eat a chunk of beef, you are able to do so only because the cow ate grass. We can sum this up by saying that plants manufacture food which can then be consumed by animals.

To give you an idea of the importance of this, here are some facts and figures: a hectare (nearly 2½ acres) of maize can make more than 20 000 kg of sugar in a year. If it was in the form of ordinary table sugar, this would be enough to sweeten well over a million cups of tea.

Or looking at it another way: if the food made by all the world's plants was amassed in the form of sugar for three years, it would form a heap the size of Mount Everest (Figure 2).

The next five topics are all about photosynthesis. We shall see how, when and where this important process takes place.

# Investigation 1

### Testing a plant for reducing sugar

Try this test on an onion, both the green leaves and the bulb.

1 Put a few pieces of onion into a mortar. Add a pinch of sand and cover with water.

2 Grind up the pieces of onion with a pestle.

3 Filter the contents of the mortar into a test tube to a depth of about one centimetre.

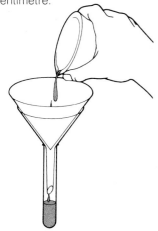

4 Pour the same amount of Benedict's or Fehling's solution (see page 75) into the test tube. Stand the tube in a beaker of boiling water until its contents boil.

5 Repeat step 4 on some water in a test tube to serve as a control.

What happens to the solution in the test tubes?

A green, brown or red colour means there's reducing sugar present.

Is there any reducing sugar in the onion?

# Investigation 2

### Testing a plant for starch

Try this test on a geranium or hibiscus leaf.

1 Dip your leaf into a beaker of boiling water for about ten seconds. This will kill it and make it soft.

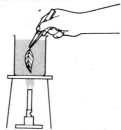

2 **Turn out the bunsen.**
Put the leaf into a test tube of ethanol. Stand the test tube in the beaker of hot water for about ten minutes. The ethanol will boil and this will decolorise the leaf.

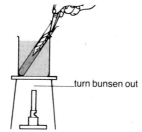
turn bunsen out

3 Wash the leaf by waving it to and fro in the beaker of water.

4 Put the leaf in a petri dish and cover it with dilute iodine solution.

A black colour shows that starch is present.
Is there any starch in the leaf?

# Investigation 3

### Testing soil for reducing sugar

1 Put a small sample of soil in a mortar. Add a little water.

2 Grind up the soil with a pestle.

3 Filter the contents of the mortar into a test tube.

4 Pour a little Benedict's or Fehling's solution into the test tube.

5 Heat to boiling in a beaker of water over a bunsen flame.

6 Repeat steps 4 and 5 on some tap water in a test tube: this will serve as a control.

A green, brown or red colour means there is reducing sugar present.

Is there any reducing sugar in the soil?

# Assignments

1 How does a tree differ from a human being in the way it feeds?

2 Plants are generally rooted to the ground and do not move about. How does this fit in with their method of feeding?

3 'When you eat a chunk of beef, you are able to do so only because the cow ate grass.' Explain the reason for this.

4 Using the index, find out what substances are present (a) in the air, and (b) in the soil. List them, and put a tick against those which you think the plant uses for making food.

5 Someone has worked out that the total amount of organic matter made by all the world's plants in a year is 125 thousand million tonnes. But the total amount of food consumed by the earth's human population is only 1/200th of this. If plants make more food than man needs, why are people starving?

# Photosynthesis

*Plants make
their own organic
food such as starch,
but how do they
do it?*

## Finding out what plants need in order to produce starch

One way of discovering how plants make food is to find out what they need in order to produce starch. Just from a general knowledge of plants we can say that the following might be necessary: light, carbon dioxide, chlorophyll, and water.

We can do experiments to find out if these four factors are required for starch formation.

The principle behind the experiments is quite simple. First we remove all the starch from the plant's leaves. This can be done by putting it in the dark for a few days. To make sure it has been completely de-starched, we do an iodine test on one of its leaves.

We then give the plant everything it needs except the one factor we want to investigate. After a time we again do an iodine test on one of the leaves to find out if it has been making starch. If it has not made any starch, we can conclude that this particular factor is needed for starch formation.

As with other biological experiments we must have a control with which to compare the result. The control plant is given everything it needs, including the factor which we are investigating.

Now let's look at the individual experiments in detail.

## Do plants need carbon dioxide to make starch?

We can investigate this by removing carbon dioxide from the air surrounding one plant, while another plant, the control, is given air containing plenty of carbon dioxide (Investigation 1). Later a leaf from each plant is tested with iodine to see if it has made any starch.

## Do plants need chlorophyll to make starch?

The ideal way of investigating this would be to remove the chlorophyll from a leaf and see if this stops it making starch. However, it is impossible to remove the chlorophyll without killing the leaf!

So what can we do? Luckily nature comes to our aid. It so happens that the leaves of certain plants are green in some places but yellow in others: chlorophyll is present in the green areas, but absent from the yellow areas. Such leaves are described as **variegated**. Good examples are hibiscus, coleus, and certain types of ivy (Figure 1).

To find out if chlorophyll is needed for starch-formation, all we have to do is to carry out a starch test on a variegated leaf (Investigation 2).

## Do plants need light for making starch?

We can investigate this by putting one plant in the dark and another plant, the control, in the light (Investigation 3, method a). After a few days each one is tested for starch.

Another way is to take a plant and cover part of one leaf with a piece of black paper. We then leave the plant in the light (Investigation 3, method b). Later we test the leaf with iodine to see if the covered area has been prevented from making starch.

## Do plants need water to make starch?

There is no simple experiment which can be done to answer this question. You certainly cannot do it by depriving the plant of water because it is impossible to take all the water out of a plant without killing it. The importance of water has been investigated by more complicated methods involving the use of isotopes. This is described on page 160.

## What do these experiments tell us?

The results of these and many other experiments tell us that plants need

Figure 1 A coleus plant with variegated leaves.

carbon dioxide, water, light and chlorophyll in order to make starch. If the plant is deprived of any of these essential factors, it cannot make starch. Even if a single leaf, or just part of the leaf, is deprived, starch is not made in that region. This is seen most strikingly in the experiment where part of a leaf is covered with black paper to prevent light getting to it (Investigation 3, method b). On testing the leaf with iodine you get the characteristic black colour only where the leaf was uncovered. This is called a **starch print** and a nice example is shown in Figure 2.

## What does photosynthesis produce?

We have seen that photosynthesis produces food substances such as starch. But is anything else formed in the process?

Figure 3 illustrates an experiment which helps us to answer this question. A lighted candle is placed in a sealed chamber. After a while it goes out.

A sprig of mint is then introduced into the chamber without any air being let in. It is then left in the light. After about ten days the candle, on being lit, burns again.

This experiment was first carried out by Joseph Priestley in 1771. He did not understand why the mint should enable the candle to be re-lit. However, we now know that the burning candle had used up all the oxygen. Putting the mint into the chamber had the effect of putting oxygen back into the air, so that the candle could burn again. This was the first demonstration that plants give out oxygen.

A more direct way of finding out if plants give out oxygen is to use a water plant such as Canadian pondweed or its close relative *Hydrilla* (Figure 4). These plants obligingly produce bubbles when put in the light (Figure 5). The bubbles can be collected and tested for oxygen (Investigation 4).

There is now a lot of evidence that *all* green plants give off oxygen in the light. The observation that they will do this only in the light strongly suggests that it has something to do with photosynthesis.

**Figure 2** A starch print made on a geranium leaf. The top picture shows the black cover on the leaf. The bottom picture shows the same leaf after staining with iodine.

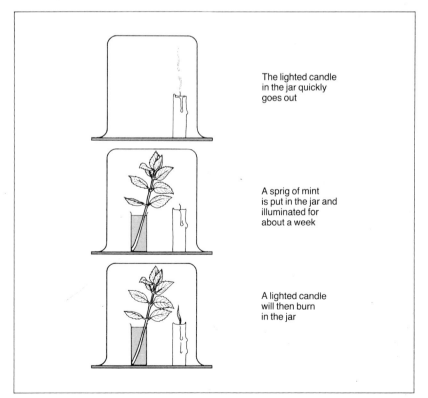

The lighted candle in the jar quickly goes out

A sprig of mint is put in the jar and illuminated for about a week

A lighted candle will then burn in the jar

**Figure 3** The principle behind the experiment which was carried out by Joseph Priestley in 1771.

**Figure 4** Canadian pondweed and *Hydrilla* belong to a group of plants which live in ponds and slow-flowing streams.

## What happens during photosynthesis?

The experiments in this Topic tell us that plants need carbon dioxide, water, light and chlorophyll in order to make food; and starch and oxygen are produced.

Carbon dioxide and water are the **raw materials** of photosynthesis. They react in some way to produce starch and oxygen, the **products**. We now know that this is not a simple reaction, but takes place in a series of steps. The reactions need energy, and this comes from the light. The chlorophyll enables the plant to use light energy in this way. Light and chlorophyll are therefore essential 'helpers' in the process.

Although starch is made in the end, it is not the first substance to be formed. Glucose is formed first and this is then turned into starch.

Photosynthesis is therefore a complicated process. However, it is usually summed up by this simple equation:

$$6CO_2 + 6H_2O \xrightarrow{\text{light \& chlorophyll}} C_6H_{12}O_6 + 6O_2$$

carbon dioxide    water               glucose     oxygen

$\underbrace{\qquad\qquad\qquad\qquad}_{\text{raw materials}}$        $\underbrace{\qquad\qquad\qquad}_{\text{products}}$

In later Topics we will explore some of the details of this reaction.

**Figure 5** When brightly lit, pieces of Canadian pondweed and *Hydrilla* give off bubbles. The bubbles contain oxygen.

## Investigation 1

**To find out if a plant needs carbon dioxide in order to make starch**

1 You will need two potted plants which have been de-starched. Balsam or coleus will do.

2 Put a dish of dampened soda lime on the soil beside one of the plants. Cover the plant with a polythene bag as shown in the upper illustration. The soda lime will absorb carbon dioxide from the air inside the bag, so this plant will be deprived of carbon dioxide.

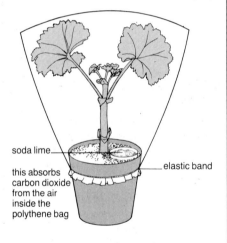

soda lime

this absorbs carbon dioxide from the air inside the polythene bag

elastic band

3 Put a dish of saturated sodium hydrogen carbonate solution on the soil beside the other plant. Cover the plant with a polythene bag as shown in the lower illustration. The sodium hydrogen carbonate will slowly give out carbon dioxide into the bag, so this plant will have plenty of carbon dioxide.

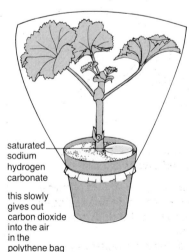

saturated sodium hydrogen carbonate

this slowly gives out carbon dioxide into the air in the polythene bag

4 Place both plants side by side in a well lit place for about 48 hours.

5 After about 48 hours take a leaf, or part of a leaf, from each plant. Test them for starch (see page 147).

Which plant contains starch?

Is carbon dioxide needed for starch formation?

## Investigation 2

**To find out if a plant needs chlorophyll to make starch**

1 You will need a potted plant with variegated leaves, e.g. coleus. The plant should have been put in the light for several days.

2 Detach one of the leaves and draw its upper side, making a clear distinction between the green and non-green areas.

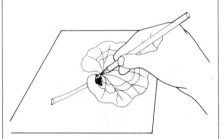

3 Now carry out a starch test on the whole leaf (see page 147).

Which parts of the leaf turn black when treated with iodine?
Indicate your answer in your drawing by writing B in the black areas.

Where is the control in this experiment?
Is chlorophyll needed for starch formation?

# Investigation 3

**To find out if a plant needs light in order to make starch**

### Method a

1 You will need two potted plants which have been de-starched.

2 Place one of them in the dark, and the other in the light. The plant in the light is your control plant.

3 After several days take a leaf (or part of a leaf) from each plant. Test them for starch (see page 147). Don't forget which leaf is which!

   Has either plant formed starch?
   Is light needed for starch formation?

### Method b

1 You will need a potted coleus plant which has been de-starched.

2 Attach a strip of black paper or foil to the upper and lower sides of a leaf, as shown in the illustration.

3 Put the plant in a well-lit place.

4 After several days detach the leaf and test it for starch (see page 147). Make a drawing of the leaf to show your result.

This is called a 'starch print'. What conclusion do you draw?

# Investigation 4

**To find out if a water plant gives off oxygen**

1 Put some Canadian pondweed or *Hydrilla* into two separate beakers of water.

2 Cover the weed with an upturned funnel and test tube, as shown in the illustration.

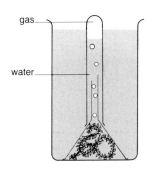

3 Place one of the beakers in the light and the other one in the dark.

4 After a few days compare what has happened in the two cases.

   Has the illuminated pondweed produced some gas?
   Has the darkened one done so?

5 Test the gas for oxygen with a glowing splint:

   Remove the test tube from the beaker. Quickly insert a glowing splint to the far end as shown in the illustration. If it flares up, oxygen is present.

Has the illuminated pondweed produced oxygen?

Unfortunately the amount of oxygen in the gas, compared with nitrogen, is so small that the glowing splint test seldom works.
Can you think of a better way of testing the gas for oxygen?

# Assignments

1 Explain how the starch print in Figure 2 was made.

2 Some people feel that from a scientific point of view a starch print is not a good way of finding out if a plant needs light for making starch. What do you think?

3 In Investigation 1 the plants should be de-starched first.
   a) How are they de-starched?
   b) Why is this necessary?
   c) How could you make sure they have been completely de-starched before you begin the experiment?

4 Elizabeth wants to find out if a potted plant needs carbon dioxide in order to make starch. She is not very satisfied with the method given in Investigation 1, so she tries a different way. She selects two leaves on the plant and, *without cutting them off*, she encloses each one in a small polythene bag. In one bag she puts some soda lime, and in the other bag some saturated sodium hydrogen carbonate solution. Make a diagram of the set-up. Do you think Elizabeth's method is as good as the one in Investigation 1? Give reasons for your answer.

5 One way of showing that carbon dioxide is necessary for starch formation is illustrated below. Study the picture, then answer the questions underneath it.

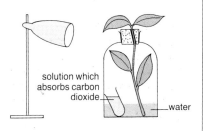

solution which absorbs carbon dioxide

water

   a) What should be done to the plant beforehand, and why?
   b) Where is the control in this experiment?
   c) At the end of the experiment, how would you find out if the plant has made starch in its leaves?
   d) Is this a satisfactory experiment? Give reasons for your opinion.

# What controls the rate of photosynthesis?

*Photosynthesis occurs rapidly or slowly, depending on circumstances, and this will determine how much food is made in a certain period of time. This is important for man because we depend on plants for our food.*

**Figure 1** Ferns are able to photosynthesise efficiently in shady places such as this forest.

**Figure 2** The lettuces on the left were grown in an atmosphere containing more carbon dioxide than those on the right.

## What factors affect the rate of photosynthesis?

Four factors have a particular effect on the rate of photosynthesis: light, carbon dioxide, temperature and water. We will look at them in turn.

### Light

We can find out the effect of light on photosynthesis by using one of those water plants which produce bubbles in the light. If the brightness of the light affects the speed of photosynthesis, we would expect the plant to produce more bubbles the brighter the light. We can do an experiment to test this (Investigation).

This and other experiments tell us that, up to a point, the brighter the light the faster the rate of photosynthesis.

How does light affect plants in their natural surroundings? Light varies from day to day and from place to place. On a bright sunny day plants photosynthesise faster than on a dull day. And a plant growing in an open meadow photosynthesises more quickly than a plant growing in the shade.

This is important to gardeners. If a gardener wants his vegetables to do well, he plants them in a place which gets the sun. Sometimes bright lights are shone on indoor plants to increase their rate of photosynthesis. However some plants, such as ferns, thrive in shady places such as a wood (Figure 1). They can photosynthesise even in dim light.

As with many other things in life, it is possible to have too much of a good thing: in *very* bright sunshine photosynthesis actually slows down. Very bright sunshine contains a lot of ultraviolet light which can damage plants. Moreover, a shady place is likely to be cooler and more moist, which is a particular advantage in the tropics.

### Carbon dioxide

Experiments have shown that the more carbon dioxide there is in the air surrounding a plant the faster the plant photosynthesises. How does this affect plants in their natural surroundings? The amount of carbon dioxide in the atmosphere is about 0.03 per cent and it does not vary very much. Even so, there are slight differences from place to place which may affect the rate of photosynthesis. For example, the concentration of carbon dioxide close to the ground in a dense forest is higher than in an open field. Why do you think this is?

Extra carbon dioxide is sometimes pumped into greenhouses, or produced by a 'burner' so as to increase the rate of photosynthesis. This is useful to gardeners, as well as to scientists, who want to increase the speed at which plants make food (Figure 2).

## Temperature

Up to a certain point, the higher the temperature, the faster a plant will photosynthesise. Normally a rise of 10°C doubles the rate. This is true of any normal chemical process, and photosynthesis is no exception.

In the natural world there are tremendous variations in temperature, both from place to place and at different times of the day and year. One of the main reasons why plants do so well in a greenhouse or a sheltered garden is because of the warmth there (Figure 3).

Raising the temperature up to about 40°C increases the rate of photosynthesis. However if the temperature gets above this, photosynthesis slows down and soon stops altogether. This is because the heat destroys the enzymes which are responsible for the chemical reactions.

## Water

Plants need water for photosynthesis and if they do not get enough of it they will not photosynthesise so quickly. A plant which is beginning to droop through lack of water may photosynthesise at only half the normal rate. This is mainly because its air pores (stomata) are closed. Water is needed for many other purposes besides photosynthesis, and the effect of water-shortage on photosynthesis may be indirect.

## Which places provide the best conditions for photosynthesis?

The answer is the tropical rain forests of the Caribbean, South America, Central Africa and South East Asia. Lots of sunshine, warmth and a high rainfall ensure maximum photosynthesis and prolific growth of plants (Figure 4).

Crop plants grown in places where light, temperature and moisture are at their most suitable for photosynthesis, make particularly large amounts of food. This is true of sugar cane, for example, which has the highest yield of all crop plants (Figure 5).

Sugar cane needs a hot, moist climate with temperatures averaging around 21°C (71°F) and an annual rainfall of about 1500 mm. This it gets in places such as the Caribbean and South East Asia. When grown in drier places like North America and Southern Africa, water must be supplied by irrigation.

In some parts of the world plants are grown in special air conditioned greenhouses in which all the factors affecting photosynthesis and plant growth are carefully controlled. In this way scientists can make sure that the plants are given exactly what they need.

**Figure 3** The warm conditions inside the greenhouse enabled this excellent crop of melons to be produced. In the tropics they are grown out of doors.

**Figure 4** The tropical rain forest has been described as a vegetative frenzy. Notice the dense vegetation in this photograph of the Everglades in Florida, USA.

**Figure 5** Sugar cane, being harvested by a farmer in the Caribbean. It is one of the largest members of the grass family, reaching heights of six metres or more. Most of the world's sugar comes from sugar cane. Plants like sugar cane are particularly good at absorbing carbon dioxide and turning it into carbohydrate.

## Which places provide the worst conditions for photosynthesis?

The answer is dark or dimly lit places, particularly if they are cold as well. For example, grass may be lush in an open meadow, but in a corner which is always in the shade it may be sparse. Have you ever noticed how bare the soil is under certain trees? This is because the leaves of the tree don't let much light through (see page 162). The soil is even barer under overhanging rocks and in caves. However, you have only to provide an artificial light and a few green plants will soon pop up if there's enough moisture for them. Some plants will even grow in disused wells and dungeons (Figure 6).

In general, temperate and Arctic regions are less good for photosynthesis than the tropics. Why do you think this is?

## How do the factors influence each other?

Look at the graph in Figure 7. This shows the results of an experiment which was designed to find the effect of raising the light intensity on the rate of photosynthesis – like the experiment in the Investigation.

First look at curve A. Notice that as the light intensity is gradually raised, the curve rises, i.e. the rate of photosynthesis increases.

However, there comes a point when the curve flattens out – in other words the rate of photosynthesis does not increase any more, however much the light intensity is raised. Why do you think the rate of photosynthesis stops increasing? The answer is that some factor other than light is preventing photosynthesis from going any faster. We say that this factor is now **limiting** the rate of photosynthesis.

What might this factor be? Well, it could be carbon dioxide. How could we find out if it is carbon dioxide? One way would be to raise the amount of carbon dioxide in the atmosphere surrounding the plant and repeat the experiment.

The result of doing this is shown in curve B. This time a much higher rate of photosynthesis is achieved. What does this tell us? It tells us that carbon dioxide must have been limiting the rate of photosynthesis when the curve flattened out in the first experiment.

From experiments of this kind we can draw this general conclusion. The rate of photosynthesis is controlled by several different factors. At a particular moment the rate is determined by whichever factor is closest to its minimum value. This is called the **law of limiting factors**, and is of great importance to plants.

In a particular place, a wheat field for instance, different factors limit photosynthesis at different times of the day. At the beginning and end of the day, when the light is dim, light limits the rate of photosynthesis. In the middle of the day, when the light is good, carbon dioxide limits photosynthesis.

The same kind of thing applies to the seasons. Take the British summer and winter for example. In summer, when the light is good, carbon dioxide limits photosynthesis most of the time. In winter, on the other hand, light is the limiting factor most of the time.

What about a small plant growing in a forest? Here the light is dim but the concentration of carbon dioxide is high. Result? Light limits photosynthesis all the time.

In the tropics light is rarely a limiting factor, except in very shady places. In the dry season water is the most important limiting factor. The same applies to temperate regions where there is a drought. In a prolonged drought many plants die altogether, not just because they can't photosynthesise but for other reasons as well. Can you think of these other reasons?

We have already seen that in the closed atmosphere of a greenhouse extra carbon dioxide can increase the rate of photosynthesis. However, the law of limiting factors must always be born in mind. It is no use pumping extra carbon dioxide into a greenhouse if the light is poor. It simply will not make any difference.

**Figure 6** This photograph was taken in the dungeon of an old castle. A shaft of sunlight enabled these ferns to grow on one of the walls.

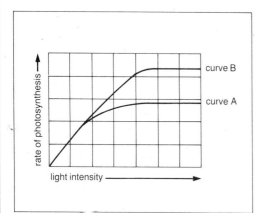

**Figure 7** This graph shows how a plant's rate of photosynthesis is affected by the light intensity at two concentrations of carbon dioxide. Curve A was obtained with the plant in a low concentration of carbon dioxide. Curve B was obtained at a higher concentration of carbon dioxide.

# Investigation

**To see if raising the light intensity increases the rate of photosynthesis**

For this experiment use *Elodea* (Canadian pondweed) or *Hydrilla*.

paper clip     heat shield

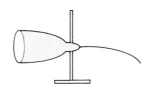

1 Darken the room so the light from the windows does not vary.

2 Cut off a piece of the weed about 5 cm long.

3 Attach a paper clip to the top end to weigh it down.

4 Put it in a beaker or jam jar of water as shown in the illustration.

5 Add a pinch of potassium hydrogen carbonate to the water or blow bubbles through it with a straw: this will ensure that the pondweed has a good supply of carbon dioxide.

6 Place a lamp to one side of the jar.

7 Fill a narrow aquarium tank with water and place it between the jar and the lamp. This will serve as a heat shield and will prevent the pondweed from heating up.

8 Illuminate the weed with the lamp placed a long way away (say 50 cm).

9 Wait a few minutes, then count the number of bubbles given off during a one minute period. Do this three times and work out the average.

10 Now bring the lamp closer, wait a few minutes, then count the number of bubbles again. Do this three times and work out the average.

How many bubbles are given off per minute (a) with the lamp a long way away, and (b) with the lamp close?

Do you find that the closer the lamp, the greater is the rate at which bubbles are given off?

Does raising the light intensity increase the rate of photosynthesis?

# Assignments

1 Mr Smith plants his onions in a shady place whereas Mr Jones plants his in the sun. Whose onions would you expect to do best, and why?

2 Mr Jones left a bucket on his lawn for several weeks. When he lifted it up he found that the grass underneath was yellow and dead. What might have killed the grass and why was it yellow?

3 Someone observed that wheat grows taller, and gives a higher yield of grain, close to a certain coal-burning factory than further away. Suggest a reason for this. What investigations would you carry out to find if your suggestion is right?

4 The following figures give the total annual amounts of organic matter produced per hectare by plants in different parts of the world:

| | |
|---|---|
| sugar cane (Java) | 87 tonnes |
| tropical rain forest | 59 tonnes |
| pine forest, England | 16 tonnes |
| birch forest, England | 8.5 tonnes |

Can you account for the differences?

5 An experiment was carried out to investigate the effect on a plant's rate of photosynthesis of increasing the amount of carbon dioxide in the air. The light intensity and temperature were kept constant throughout the experiment. The results are shown in this graph:

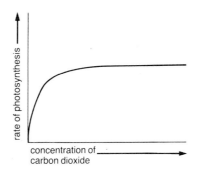

a) Say in your own words what the graph shows.

b) Why does the curve rise to begin with?

c) Suggest reasons why the curve eventually flattens out.

d) What experiments would you do to find out which of your reasons in (c) is correct?

6 A scientist grew some cereal plants in a field. During the course of one day he took several plants every four hours and measured the amount of sugar in the leaves. The sugar concentrations, expressed as a percentage of the dry mass of the leaves, are given below:

| Time of day | Sugar concentration |
|---|---|
| 4 am | 0.45 |
| 8 am | 0.60 |
| 12 noon | 1.75 |
| 4 pm | 2.00 |
| 8 pm | 1.4 |
| 12 midnight | 0.5 |
| 4 am | 0.45 |

a) Plot the data on graph paper, putting sugar concentration on the vertical axis.

b) What is the probable concentration of sugar in the leaves at (a) 10 am and (b) 2 am?

c) At what time of the day is sugar probably at a maximum in the leaf?

d) Explain the changes which occur in the sugar concentration over the 24 hour period.

# Chlorophyll – the miracle molecule

*The green colour of plants is caused by the chemical substance chlorophyll which occurs inside them. Chlorophyll does a remarkable job, as we shall see.*

Figure 1 In a rainbow the light is split up into its separate colours by drops of water in the atmosphere.

Figure 2 In many seaweeds the green colour of the chlorophyll is masked by other pigments, as in bladder wrack, a brown seaweed which grows on the seashore.

## What is chlorophyll?

To find out what chlorophyll is, we can extract it from leaves and make a solution of it (Investigation 1). By doing this we can see that it's a green substance. Coloured substances of this sort are called **pigments**.

Scientists have analysed this pigment. It turns out to be a complex organic substance containing magnesium (see page 142).

Chlorophyll plays a vital part in photosynthesis. To understand what it does, we must first examine its effect on light.

## What does chlorophyll do to light?

We can investigate this by observing what happens to light as it passes through a solution of chlorophyll (Investigation 2).

Ordinary white light, such as sunlight, is made up of different colours or wave-lengths. We don't normally see these colours except, for example, when there's a rainbow (Figure 1). However, in the laboratory light can be split up into its colours by means of a prism. The colours form a series which we call a **spectrum**.

Now when light passes through chlorophyll, certain colours disappear. Which ones? If you do Investigation 2 you will see that the colours which disappear are **blue** and, to a lesser extent, **red**.

These two colours disappear because they are absorbed by the chlorophyll. Other colours, particularly green, pass straight through it or are reflected. The reason why leaves look green is that chlorophyll reflects the green part of the spectrum.

## What colours are used in photosynthesis?

Chlorophyll absorbs blue and red light. It would therefore seem likely that these two colours are used in photosynthesis.

Can you think of an experiment which could be done to test this suggestion? One way would be to shine different coloured lights onto plants. We could then find out which colours are most suitable for photosynthesis. As an indication of how much photosynthesis had been going on with each colour, we could measure either the volume of oxygen given off or the amount of starch formed.

Experiments of this kind show that the two colours which are best for photosynthesis are blue and red – the very same colours that are absorbed. A plant which is deprived of these two colours cannot photosynthesise properly and doesn't make much starch. Sunlight provides these two colours in the right proportions.

## Other pigments

Leaves contain several pigments besides chlorophyll. They can be separated from each other by a process called **chromatography** (Investigation 3). In addition to chlorophyll there are yellow and grey pigments.

Separating the pigments like this is useful because after they have been isolated each one can be investigated on its own. In this way scientists can find out what each one does.

Careful experiments of this sort have shown that they all play a part in photosynthesis, but the most important is the green chlorophyll.

Certain plants which are known to photosynthesise are not green. How can we explain this?

Take seaweed, for example. Most seaweeds are brown. This is because they possess a brown pigment called **fucoxanthin**. Chlorophyll is present too, but the brown pigment is so abundant that it completely masks the green colour of the chlorophyll. Both are used in photosynthesis. Some seaweeds contain a red pigment in addition to chlorophyll.

Many plants have purple leaves – copper beech, for instance, and the tropical plant *Rhoeo*. Their cells contain a purple substance called **anthocy-**

**anin**. There are several different anthocyanins, and they help to give flowers and fruits their characteristic colours, but they play no part in photosynthesis.

## Where does chlorophyll occur?

If you look at a simple leaf under the microscope (Investigation 4), you will see that its cells contain lots of small green bodies (Figure 3). These bodies are called **chloroplasts**. They are packed together in the cytoplasm round the edges of the cells. Each one is filled with chlorophyll. It's here that photosynthesis takes place and starch is formed.

## Inside the chloroplast

Chloroplasts are extremely small: about ten thousand of them would fit onto the full stop at the end of this sentence. They are therefore invisible to the naked eye, but under the light microscope each one can be detected individually. However, the light microscope does not magnify them enough for us to see any detail inside them. With an electron microscope, however, we can see much more.

Figure 4 shows a chloroplast as seen in the electron microscope. It is magnified about 30 000 times. If a whole moss leaf was magnified to this extent, it would be the size of a tree.

You will notice that the chloroplast is filled with rows of thin membranes. The way they are arranged is shown in Figure 5. By careful analysis scientists have shown that millions and millions of chlorophyll molecules are attached to these membranes.

The chlorophyll molecules are laid out on the chloroplast membranes rather like library books are stacked on shelves. In this way a great many chlorophyll molecules are packed together inside a small space.

Think of a large tree. It has a large number of leaves. Inside each leaf are numerous chloroplasts; within each chloroplast are numerous membranes; and covering each membrane are numerous chlorophyll molecules. So there is a lot of chlorophyll in a single plant like a tree and it covers a huge surface area. This is very important in view of the job it has to do.

## What does chlorophyll do?

Chlorophyll absorbs light energy and enables it to be used by the plant for building up sugar. The overall effect is that energy is transferred from sunlight to sugar molecules.

The energy contained inside molecules is called chemical energy. So chlorophyll's job is really to convert light energy into chemical energy.

There is nothing particularly mysterious about this in itself: it is a well known law of physics that one form of energy can be changed into another.

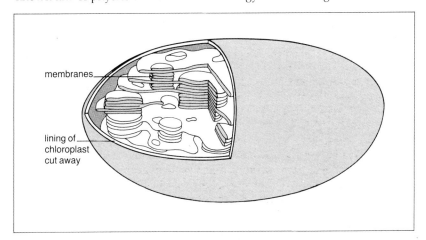

membranes

lining of
chloroplast
cut away

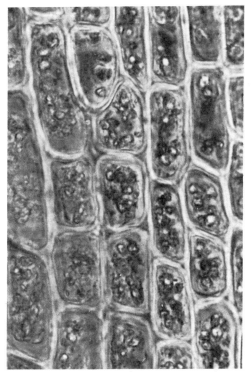

Figure 3 Part of a moss leaf as seen under a light microscope. Notice the numerous chloroplasts in the cells.

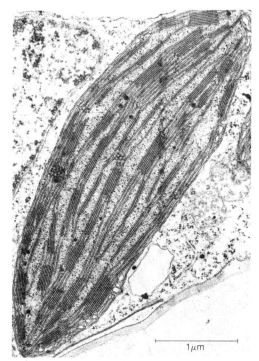

1 μm

Figure 4 A single chloroplast seen in section in the electron microscope. It is magnified 30 000 times.

Figure 5 This drawing shows the structure of a chloroplast based on its appearance in the electron microscope.

# Investigation 1

### How to make a solution of chlorophyll

There are several ways of doing this. Here is one of the simplest methods:

1  Cut up a few green leaves into small pieces.

2  Put them in a mortar with a pinch of washed sand.

3  Cover them with a solvent (ethanol or acetone), and grind them up with a pestle. This will break open the cells, and the chlorophyll will dissolve in the solvent.

4  Filter the fluid into a beaker (see illustration). The green chlorophyll solution will pass through the filter paper, leaving any bits of leaf behind.

5  If necessary add some water to the chlorophyll solution to make it less concentrated.

What colour is the chlorophyll?

Does its colour differ from that of the leaf from which it was obtained?

If so, in what way does it differ, and why?

# Investigation 2

### To find the effect of chlorophyll on light

1  Prepare a solution of chlorophyll as instructed in Investigation 1.

2  Pour the solution into a narrow transparent container as shown in the upper part of the illustration.

3  Set up a projector, prism and screen as shown in the lower part of the illustration. The prism splits the light into its different colours.

What colours can you see?

4  Now place your chlorophyll solution between the projector light and the prism (see arrow in the illustration).

Do you find that certain colours disappear?

If so, which ones?

What effect does chlorophyll have on the light from the projector?

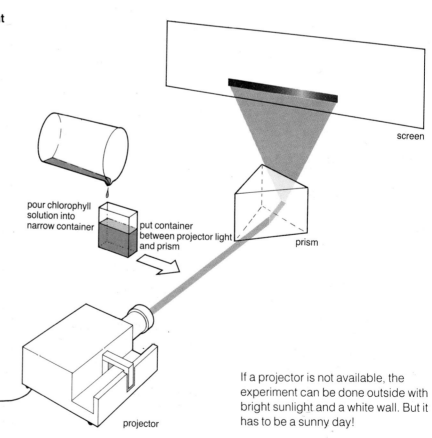

screen

pour chlorophyll solution into narrow container

put container between projector light and prism

prism

projector

If a projector is not available, the experiment can be done outside with bright sunlight and a white wall. But it has to be a sunny day!

# Investigation 3

**To separate the pigments present in a leaf**

*First method*

1 Prepare a solution of leaf pigment as instructed in Investigation 1. The solution should be as strong as possible.

2 Dip a stick of white blackboard chalk into the solution so the end of the chalk goes thoroughly green.

3 Let the chalk dry. Meanwhile, pour a little solvent (ethanol or acetone) into the bottom of a small beaker.

4 Stand your piece of chalk, green end downwards, in the solvent.

What happens?

Can you see that the solution is made up of at least two different pigments?

What colours are these pigments?

*Second method*

This method is called **paper chromatography**.

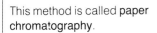

1 Pour some solvent (ethanol or acetone) into a large test tube to a depth of about 2 cm. Put a stopper in the end of the tube and leave it.

2 Cut a strip of filter paper the same length as the test tube.

3 With a pin place a drop of concentrated chlorophyll solution about 3 cm from the end of the strip of paper, and let it dry.

4 Keep adding more drops of chlorophyll solution, letting each one dry before putting on the next one. The idea is to build up a really concentrated spot of chlorophyll on the paper.

5 Hang the paper in the test tube as shown in the illustration.

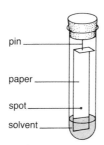

6 The solvent should rise up the strip of paper, carrying the chlorophyll pigments with it.

7 When the solvent has risen about 8 cm, take the paper out of the test tube and dry it.

How many different colours can you see?
What has separated them, and why?

# Investigation 4

**Looking at chloroplasts in a moss leaf**

1 With a pair of tweezers, carefully detach one small leaf from a moss plant.

2 Put the leaf in a drop of water on a slide, and cover it with a coverslip.

3 Examine the leaf under a microscope.

Where is the green pigment?
Look at Figure 3. Can you see the various structures shown in this picture in your own moss leaf?

4 Lift up the coverslip and put a drop of iodine on the leaf.

5 Put the coverslip back.

6 Examine the leaf under the microscope again.

A black colour indicates starch. Is there any starch in the cell? If there is, where is it?

What conclusions would you draw from this experiment about the function of chlorophyll?

# Assignments

1 Why do leaves generally look green?

2 Describe *in detail* an experiment which you would do to find out which colours of the spectrum a potted plant uses in photosynthesis.

3 A man works in a windowless office lit by a single light bulb. To cheer himself up he puts a potted plant in the room. After a few weeks the plant dies. Suggest explanations.

4 Observe the leaves of various indoor and outdoor plants. Are they always green? If they are not, can you suggest why they are some other colour?

5 If you put a green plant in the dark for a week or so, the leaves turn yellow. Several days after returning the plant to the light the leaves turn green again.
a) Suggest an explanation for this.
b) How would you find out if yellowing of the leaves prevented them from photosynthesising?
c) What do you think would happen to the plant if you left it in the dark for ever, and why?

6 The following diagram shows light being shone onto a screen from a slide projector.
a) What colour would you expect the light to be on the screen?
b) What would happen if you put a prism in the beam of light at A?
c) What effect would be produced if you then put a glass jar containing a solution of chlorophyll at B?
d) What conclusions can be drawn from this experiment?

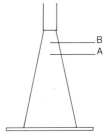

# More about photosynthesis

*In recent years scientists have discovered a lot about the chemical reactions which take place during photosynthesis thanks to the use of isotopes*

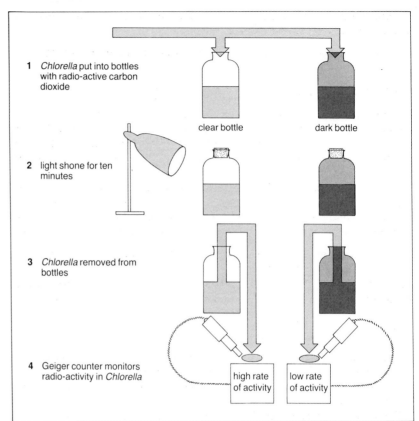

1. *Chlorella* put into bottles with radio-active carbon dioxide

clear bottle    dark bottle

2. light shone for ten minutes

3. *Chlorella* removed from bottles

4. Geiger counter monitors radio-activity in *Chlorella*

high rate of activity    low rate of activity

**Figure 1** This diagram summarises an experiment which scientists have carried out with *Chlorella*.

**Figure 2** A scientist, wearing protective gloves, transferring some radio-active hydrogen carbonate solution into a bottle containing *Chlorella*. The hydrogen carbonate solution contains radio-active carbon atoms. This provides the plant with a source of labelled carbon dioxide.

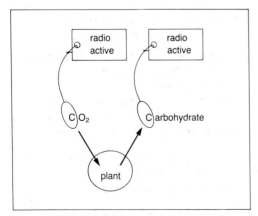

radio active    radio active

$C$ $O_2$    $C$ arbohydrate

plant

**Figure 3** If *Chlorella* is supplied with carbon dioxide whose carbon is radio-active, the radio-active carbon gets into the carbohydrate which the plant makes.

## What are isotopes?

Consider the element carbon. The normal form of carbon has an atomic mass of 12 ($^{12}C$). However, there is another kind of carbon which has an atomic mass of 14 ($^{14}C$), and is **radio-active**. These two forms of carbon are known as **isotopes**. The radio-active form can be detected by means of a **Geiger counter**. This has a probe: when the probe is brought close to a radio-active substance it clicks repeatedly.

One of the first places to use isotopes for studying photosynthesis was Berkeley, California. There in the Lawrence Radiation Laboratory, scientists have used radio-active carbon to study photosynthesis in *Chlorella*. *Chlorella* is a single-celled organism which is easily grown in the laboratory.

## Tracing what happens to carbon dioxide in photosynthesis

Here is a simplified account of what the Berkeley scientists did. First they made some carbon dioxide whose normal carbon had been replaced by its radio-active isotope. By substituting the radio-active isotope for the normal carbon, they were able to 'label' the carbon dioxide and follow what happened to it.

The labelled carbon dioxide was supplied to *Chlorella*, and a Geiger counter was used to detect it. A simplified version of the experiment is summarised in Figure 1, and one of the steps is illustrated in Figure 2.

The Berkeley scientists found that in the light the radio-active carbon was taken up by the plant. However, they went further than this. They carefully extracted the chemical compounds from the plant and tested them for radio-activity. They found that the radio-active carbon had got into the carbohydrate (sugar) which the plant had made (Figure 3). From this experiment it was concluded that the carbon in the carbohydrate made by plants comes from carbon dioxide:

Carbon dioxide + $H_2O$ ⟶ Carbohydrate + Oxygen

## Tracing what happens to oxygen

Carbon dioxide contains oxygen as well as carbon. What happens to the oxygen? Labelling experiments have given us the answer to this too. There is a rare isotope of oxygen whose atoms are slightly heavier than those of normal oxygen. They can be detected by a machine called a **mass spectrometer**.

Scientists have given plants carbon dioxide whose normal oxygen has been replaced by this heavy isotope. What happens? The heavy oxygen gets into the carbohydrate which the plants make. This tells us that the oxygen in the carbohydrate made by plants comes from carbon dioxide:

Carbon diOxide + $H_2O$ ⟶ CarbOhydrate + Oxygen

The conclusion from these experiments is that in photosynthesis carbon dioxide is somehow converted into carbohydrate.

## How is carbon dioxide converted into carbohydrate?

If you compare the formulae of carbon dioxide and a carbohydrate, you will find that the carbohydrate contains hydrogen whereas carbon dioxide does not. Where does the hydrogen in the carbohydrate come from? There is really only one possible answer: water.

The formula of water is $H_2O$. It is possible to label the oxygen in water by replacing it with its heavy isotope. If such water is given to an illuminated plant, the heavy oxygen is given off as a gas. This tells us that the oxygen which plants give off during photosynthesis comes from water:

Carbon dioxide + $H_2O$ ⟶ Carbohydrate + Oxygen

The water must therefore be split into its constituent hydrogen and oxygen atoms. Careful experiments have confirmed that this really does happen in photosynthesis, though the details are very complicated.

## Photosynthesis occurs in two stages

We now know that photosynthesis occurs in two stages (Figure 4). In the first stage water is split into oxygen and hydrogen. In the second stage hydrogen combines with carbon dioxide to form carbohydrate.

Scientists have discovered an interesting thing about these two stages: only the first requires light; the second can occur in the dark. So we call these the **light** and **dark stages** respectively.

The job of the light stage is to split water and provide hydrogen atoms for the dark stage. Energy for this comes from sunlight and is trapped by the chlorophyll. Neither light energy nor chlorophyll are needed for the dark stage.

## How do plants make other things besides carbohydrate?

The scientists who did the experiment with *Chlorella* (Figure 1) found that radio-active carbon quickly got into carbohydrates, but later on it got into other more complex compounds such as fats and protein. The plant makes carbohydrate first and then converts some of this into other things.

To make proteins a plant needs the extra elements nitrogen and sulphur, in addition to carbon, hydrogen and oxygen. It obtains these extra elements from its surroundings in the form of mineral salts.

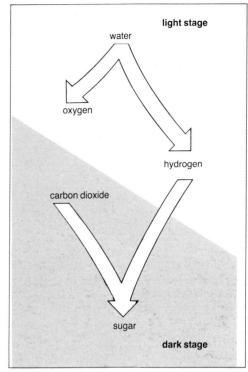

**Figure 4** Photosynthesis occurs in two stages. First water is split into oxygen and hydrogen. Then the hydrogen combines with carbon dioxide to form sugar (carbohydrate).

# Assignments

1 How has heavy oxygen helped scientists to understand photosynthesis?

2 If you transfer a green plant from the light to total darkness, do you think it stops making sugar straight away? Explain your answer.

3 A farmer gives his crops a nitrogen fertiliser. Why is this desirable?

4 What criticisms, if any, do you have of the experiment illustrated in Figure 1?

5 Experiments with isotope tracers enable us to say the following about photosynthesis:
a) The carbon and the oxygen in the sugar come from carbon dioxide.
b) The hydrogen in the sugar comes from water.
c) The oxygen gas that's given off comes from water.
d) Some water is formed.

Give a balanced chemical equation for photosynthesis that takes all these observations into account.

# The leaf: organ of photosynthesis

*This Topic is about
the structure of leaves, and how
it fits their job of feeding the plant.
We shall concentrate on the leaves
of dicotyledonous plants.*

## The external structure of leaves

You can learn much about leaves simply by looking at them from the outside (Investigation 1). The leaf is attached to the stem or branch by a leaf stalk or **petiole**. The leaf stalk is continuous with the veins (Figures 1 and 2).

Here is a summary of the leaf's main adaptations for photosynthesis which you can see from the outside.

### Leaves have a large surface area

Leaves come in all manner of shapes and sizes, but they are generally flat, sometimes large, and usually numerous. The result is that they cover a large surface area (Investigation 2). This makes them good at absorbing carbon dioxide from the air, and light energy from the sun.

### Leaves are arranged in the best way

Leaves are usually positioned in such a way that they get the maximum amount of light. Moreover, they may fit together snugly so very little light passes through to the ground below. This is why it is so dark under many trees and shrubs.

In a large tree with a lot of leaves there is always a risk that the leaves at the top may shade those lower down. This is avoided by having leaves which are divided into leaflets, or have jagged edges, so light can get between them. Another way is by the leaves at the top arranging themselves so their edges are directed towards the sun. This allows light to pass between them to the leaves lower down (Figure 3).

### Leaves have pores

A leaf's 'skin' (the **epidermis**) is pierced by tiny air pores known as **stomata** (singular: stoma). They occur mainly on the lower side of the leaf. They allow gases to pass in and out of the leaf. Some leaves have a very large number of stomata (Figure 4). They are discussed in more detail on page 166.

### Leaves are thin

Leaves are usually less than a millimetre thick. This cuts down the distance through which carbon dioxide has to diffuse after it has entered the leaf.

But there's a problem. Being so thin, leaves would be liable to droop, but this is prevented by the **veins** which serve as a kind of skeleton holding the leaf out flat (Figure 5).

**Figure 1** Leaves are the main place where plants make food.

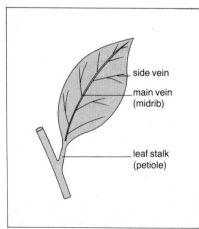

**Figure 2** The main parts of a typical leaf.

side vein

main vein
(midrib)

leaf stalk
(petiole)

**Figure 3** Some plants have their leaves arranged like this.

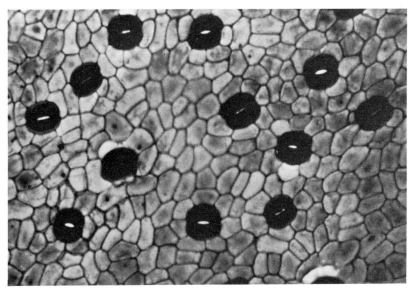

Figure 4  Stomata on the lower side of a leaf, seen under a light microscope.

Figure 5  Underside of a leaf showing the branching veins.

## The internal structure of leaves

You can study the inside of a leaf by cutting thin sections of it and examining them under a microscope (Investigation 3).

Figure 6 shows the inside of a dicotyledonous leaf as it appears under the microscope. The leaf is lined above and below by the **epidermis**. In between are lots of cells which together make up the **mesophyll**. The mesophyll is divided into the **palisade mesophyll** on the upper side and the **spongy mesophyll** below. The cells of the palisade mesophyll are shaped like bricks and are arranged neatly side by side. The spongy mesophyll cells are rounded and appear haphazard in their arrangement.

In the middle of the leaf in Figure 6, there is a small vein. This consists of two main tissues: **xylem** towards the top and **phloem** below. The xylem contains pipe-like **vessels**, and the phloem contains elongated cells called **sieve tubes** (see page 166).

Figure 6  Cross-section of part of a leaf as seen under a light microscope.

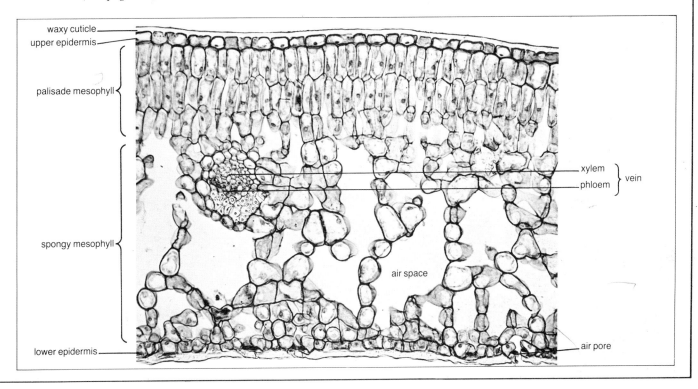

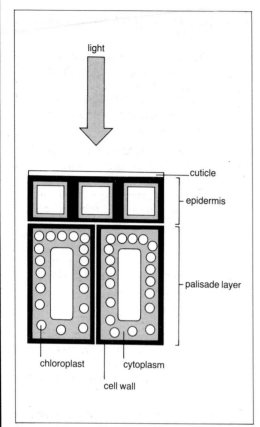

**Figure 7** The surface cells of a leaf showing the palisade layer. Notice how the chloroplasts are bunched up towards the top of the cells where the greatest amount of light is.

**Figure 8** The food-making mesophyll cells in the leaf take up carbon dioxide which diffuses in through the stomata, and water and minerals which come to them from the roots via the vessels. They give out oxygen which escapes through the stomata, and they make sugar some of which is carried away in the sieve tubes.

Here are the main adaptations for photosynthesis which you can see inside the leaf.

### The mesophyll cells contain chloroplasts

The palisade and spongy mesophyll cells all contain chloroplasts and can photosynthesise. However, most of the chloroplasts are located in the palisade layer, so it is here that photosynthesis mainly takes place (Figure 7).

### The photosynthetic cells are mainly on the upper side of the leaf

The palisade cells, where most of the photosynthesis takes place, are near the surface of the leaf on the side which gets most light. Inside these cells, the chloroplasts – as if greedy for light – are often clustered towards the upper side.

### There are air spaces between the mesophyll cells

The cells making up the spongy mesophyll are loosely packed, with large air spaces in between. Carbon dioxide diffuses readily through the stomata into these spaces. It then circulates freely inside the leaf, passing through the moist cell walls into the cells.

### The leaf contains transport tissues

As well as giving strength, the veins serve as the leaf's transport system. The vessels carry water and mineral salts from the roots to the leaves. The sieve tubes carry sugar and other food substances which have been made by photosynthesis, from the leaves to other parts of the plant.

The dense network of veins, typical of most leaves, ensures that none of the leaf cells is far away from the transport system.

### What happens to the sugar which a leaf makes?

Some of the sugar is broken down straight away to provide energy for the leaf's own needs. Some of it is converted into starch and stored. The rest is sent to other parts of the plant, either to supply energy there or to be stored.

As the plant's food-manufacturing device, the leaves must be as extensive as possible and in full communication with the rest of the plant (Figure 8).

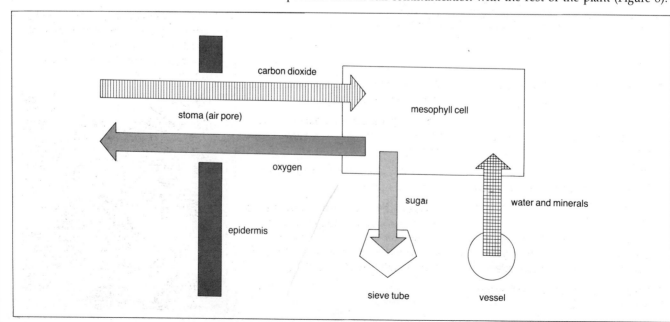

# Investigation 1

## Looking at leaves

1 Examine a leaf of a dicotyledonous plant. Which of the structures shown in Figure 2 can you see?

2 How does the colour of the upper side of a leaf differ from the lower side? Why the difference?

3 Look at leaves from different trees. Can you explain their different shapes?

4 Examine the veins of different leaves. What sort of pattern do they form?

5 Tear leaves in two. Does this tell you anything about the function of the veins?

A method for looking at the air pores of a leaf is described in Investigation 5 on page 171.

# Investigation 2

## Finding the leaf area of a plant

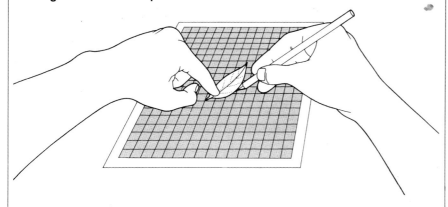

1 Select a large plant (tree or shrub) whose leaves are approximately equal in size.

2 Detach a leaf. Lay it on squared paper and trace round it with a pencil.

3 From the number of squares which the leaf covers, work out the surface area of the leaf.

4 Count the number of leaves on the plant. (If your plant is a tree, you will have to make a rough estimate.)

5 Multiply the area of one leaf by the number of leaves.

What is the total surface area of the leaves of your plant?

How does the area compare with the floor of the room where you are working?

Why is it useful to the plant to have a large leaf area?

(A quick way of estimating the area of a leaf is to measure its length and maximum width in millimetres. Its approximate area in square millimetres is the length × width × 0.75.)

# Investigation 3

## Looking inside the leaf

You will need either a prepared slide, or a thin section of a leaf which you can mount on a slide yourself. If you are mounting a section, proceed as follows:

1 Put a drop of water on a microscope slide.

2 Carefully transfer the leaf section to the drop of water on the slide.

3 Cover the section with a coverslip.

4 Examine it under the microscope.

Can you see the structures shown in Figure 6? (You may be looking at a different kind of leaf from the one shown in the figure, so watch out for differences.)

In what respects is the inside of the leaf adapted for photosynthesis?

# Assignments

1 Make a list of all those features of green plants in general which help the leaves to get as much light as possible. (It may help you to do this if you observe plants living around your home or school.)

2 Each word in column A, below, is related to one or more words in Column B.
   a) Against each word in column A write down the appropriate word, or words, from column B.

| A | B |
|---|---|
| stomata | carbon dioxide |
| vessels | light |
| chloroplasts | water |
| air spaces | chlorophyll |

   b) What do the four words in column A have in common?
   c) What do the four words in column B have in common?

3 Why is the lower side of a leaf often a paler green than the upper side?

4 Why do the palisade mesophyll cells contain more chloroplasts than the spongy mesophyll cells?

5 What part is played by each of these structures in photosynthesis:
   a) the xylem,
   b) the stomata, and
   c) the air spaces in the spongy mesophyll?

6 The photograph below shows part of a tree with the leaves in their natural position. In what way might the positioning of the leaves help the tree to survive?

# Uptake and transport in plants

*The inside of a plant is the scene of much activity. Substances are constantly being moved from one place to another. To understand how this occurs, we must first look at the structures inside the plant.*

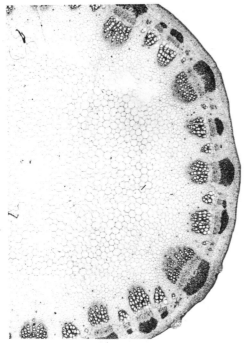

**Figure 1** Transverse section of a sunflower stem.

**Figure 2** Experiment to show that water evaporates from the leaves of a plant. After 24 hours a lot of water will have condensed on the inside of the left-hand bell jar. The right-hand bell jar is the control and will show no condensation.

## Inside the plant

A flowering plant consists of three main parts: the roots, stem and leaves. To find out about the internal structure of the plant, you need to cut thin sections of it and look at them under the microscope (Investigation 1). The internal structure of a flowering plant is shown in Figures 1, 3 and 4. You will see that it is composed of different kinds of tissues. These are the main ones:

**Epidermis**: this is the outermost layer of cells and forms a kind of skin. The epidermis of the leaves and stem is covered with a waxy **cuticle** which prevents water evaporating through it, and it is pierced by a variable number of air pores or **stomata** (singular: stoma). The root does not have a cuticle or stomata, but the cells towards the tip have extensions called **root hairs**.

**Packing tissue**: this is composed mainly of rounded cells packed close together. This makes up the bulk of the inside of the plant.

**Xylem**: this contains long tubular **vessels**. These are dead structures, and their walls contain a hard substance called lignin (see page 173). They are narrow, like capillary tubes (Figure 4A).

**Phloem**: this contains elongated living cells with cellulose walls. They are called **sieve tubes** because the end walls between one cell and the next are perforated by tiny holes, like a sieve (Figure 4B).

The xylem and phloem together make up the plant's **vascular tissue**, which plays a very important part in transporting substances within the plant.

## Transpiration

A simple experiment can be done to show that water evaporates from the leaves of a plant (Figure 2). As quickly as it is lost from the leaves, more water is taken up by the roots and passed up the stem (Investigations 2 and 3). The evaporation of water from the above-ground parts of the plant is called **transpiration**, and the flow of water – or sap as it's called – through the plant is called the **transpiration stream.** Experiments have shown that this movement of water occurs in the xylem vessels (Investigation 4).

In keeping the water moving, the stomata have an important part to play, for they provide the main route by which water can escape from the plant into the atmosphere.

## The stomata

You can find out about the stomata by looking at the surface of a leaf under the microscope (Investigation 5). In most plants, the stomata are mainly on the undersides of the leaves: there may be as many as four hundred of them in a square millimetre. Because of this, water generally evaporates more quickly from the lower side of the leaf than from the upper side of the leaf (Investigation 6).

The structure of a stoma is shown in Figure 5. It is bounded by a pair of sausage-shaped **guard cells**. How does the stoma open? The guard cells take in water by osmosis from the neighbouring epidermal cells. As a result, the guard cells swell up (become **turgid**) and bend, so a gap develops between them. The bending is accentuated by the fact that the inner wall of the guard cell is thicker and less elastic than the outer wall. The stoma closes by the reverse process: water is drawn *out* of the guard cells by osmosis, so they become less turgid and straighten.

The stomata of most plants open during the day and close at night. When they are open, water vapour can escape from inside the leaf, and oxygen and carbon dioxide can diffuse in and out.

## How does water move through the plant?

Figure 6 summarises how water passes through a plant. Water is drawn into the root from the surrounding soil. The root hairs help by increasing the surface area. The concentration of salts in the root hairs is greater than that in

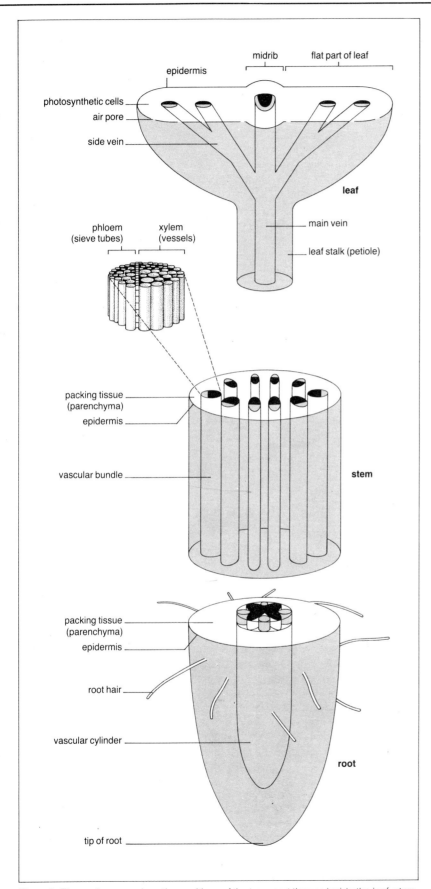

Figure 3 These diagrams show the positions of the transport tissues inside the leaf, stem and root of a flowering plant, xylem black, phloem grey.

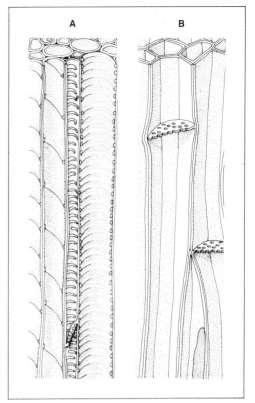

Figure 4 Vessels (left) and sieve tubes (right) inside a plant stem as they appear in a thin section cut longways and viewed under a microscope.

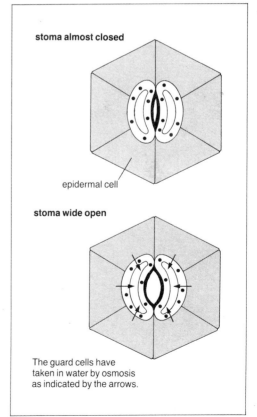

Figure 5 Stomata (air pores), greatly enlarged, as they appear in a surface view of a leaf.

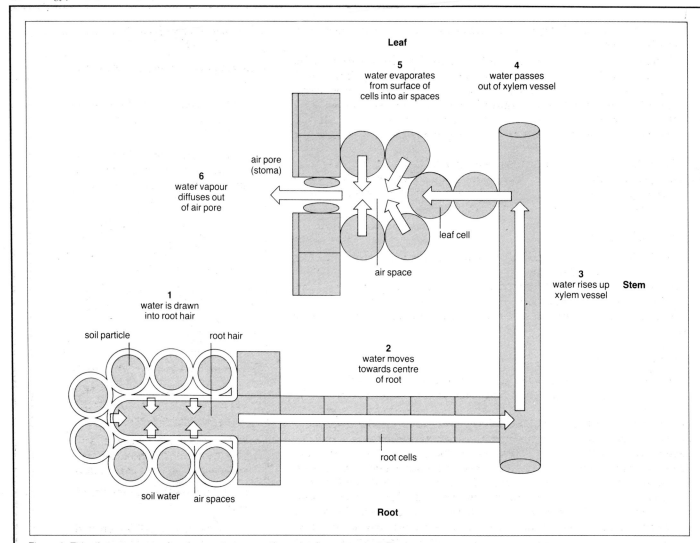

**Leaf**

**5** water evaporates from surface of cells into air spaces

**4** water passes out of xylem vessel

air pore (stoma)

**6** water vapour diffuses out of air pore

leaf cell

air space

**3** water rises up xylem vessel

**Stem**

**1** water is drawn into root hair

soil particle    root hair

**2** water moves towards centre of root

root cells

soil water    air spaces

**Root**

**Figure 6** This diagram summarises how water passes through a flowering plant. There are three different pathways through which water may be transported in the root and leaf. Most of it flows along the cellulose cell walls; some travels in the cytoplasm of the cells; and the rest passes from vacuole to vacuole.

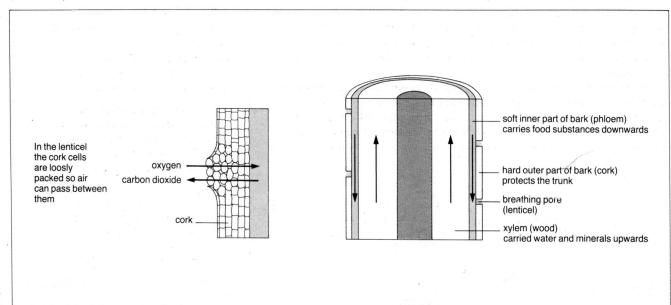

In the lenticel the cork cells are loosly packed so air can pass between them

oxygen

carbon dioxide

cork

soft inner part of bark (phloem) carries food substances downwards

hard outer part of bark (cork) protects the trunk

breathing pore (lenticel)

xylem (wood) carried water and minerals upwards

**Figure 7** The main structures in a tree trunk, showing the movement of materials within it.

the soil water, so water is drawn into them by osmosis. The water then moves towards the centre of the root.

Water rises in the xylem vessels partly because they are very narrow. This is called **capillarity** and can be demonstrated by standing capillary tubes in water. The water is moved up the stem partly by being pushed from below, and partly by being pulled from above. The pushing force can be shown by cutting a stem near its base: provided there is plenty of water in the soil, water will ooze out of the stump for a long time. This is known as **root pressure**.

The pull from above is created by the evaporation of water from the leaf. If you stop this pulling force by, for example, cutting off the leaves, the passage of water up the stem is slowed down. This is why little water is taken up by deciduous trees when they drop their leaves.

## Uptake of mineral salts

Mineral salts are drawn into the roots along with the water. They are taken up partly by passive diffusion.

However, they can be absorbed by the roots even when they are more dilute in the soil than they are inside the root cells. In these circumstances they are taken up by **active transport** which requires energy from respiration (see page 40).

## Transport of food substances

If you turn to page 160, you can read about an experiment in which scientists gave a plant carbon dioxide containing radio-active carbon. Eventually the radio-active carbon got into the sugars and other food substances which the plant made during its photosynthesis. Scientists have traced what happens to the radio-active food substances later on. They have shown that some of them move out of the leaves to other parts of the plant such as the growing points, storage organs and roots. They travel in the sieve tubes which, as we saw earlier, belong to the phloem tissue. This process is called **translocation**.

The importance of the phloem in transporting food substances can be seen in trees (Figure 7). In a tree trunk, the phloem tissue is located in the soft inner part of the **bark**. If a ring of bark is cut out from right round a tree trunk, food substances cannot get down the trunk (Figure 8), so the roots are starved and eventually the tree dies. Now suppose this is done with a tree whose leaves are given radio-active carbon dioxide. The radio-active substances spread down the trunk but get stuck above the ring.

Many other experiments and observations indicate that the phloem is the pathway by which food substances are transported inside the plant. However, no one knows for certain *how* it takes place except that it definitely requires energy from respiration and if the sieve tubes are killed it stops immediately.

The phloem must therefore have an adequate supply of oxygen. The corky part of bark is impervious to gases, but scattered around are breathing pores called **lenticels** which allow oxygen to diffuse into the phloem and carbon dioxide to diffuse out. A lenticel is shown on the left-hand side of Figure 7.

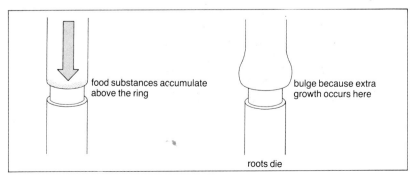

food substances accumulate above the ring

bulge because extra growth occurs here

roots die

**Figure 8** The effect of removing a ring of bark from a tree trunk.

---

## *Investigation 1*

### Looking at the transport tissues in a stem

1 Obtain a short length of a non-woody stem, about 6 cm long. It must be fairly stiff.

2 With a sharp razor blade, cut very thin slices of the stem as shown in the illustration. These slices are transverse sections.

3 Float the sections in a dish of water.

4 Pour some phloroglucin stain into a watch glass and add three drops of concentrated hydrochloric acid.

5 With a paint brush, transfer one of your thinnest sections into the stain, and leave it there for three minutes.

6 Put a drop of water in the centre of a slide.

7 Lift the section out of the stain, and place it in the water on the slide.

8 Cover the section with a coverslip, and examine it under the low power of the microscope.

Which structures shown in Figure 3 can you see?
(The phloroglucin should have stained all woody structures red, including the xylem vessels.)

9 Try cutting sections longways as shown in the illustration below. Stain them with phloroglucin as before. This will enable you to see the transport tissues in side view.

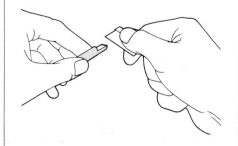

# Investigation 2

**Measuring the uptake of water by a plant**

1 Obtain a leafy twig of a tree or shrub.

2 With the cut end of the shoot under water, attach it to a capillary tube by means of a short length of rubber tubing.

3 Clamp the capillary tube to a stand, with the bottom end in a beaker of water as shown in the illustration.

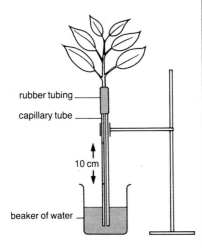

rubber tubing

capillary tube

10 cm

beaker of water

4 Make two marks on the capillary tube 10 cm apart.

*The apparatus which you have set up is called a* **potometer**. *You can use it to measure the rate at which the plant takes up water as follows:*

5 Lift the capillary tube out of the beaker, touch the end of it with blotting paper, and then put it back. An air bubble will have been introduced into the capillary.

6 Time how long it takes for the air bubble to travel from the first to the second marks on the capillary tube.

7 When the air bubble has passed the second mark, push it out of the capillary tube into the beaker of water by squeezing the rubber tubing.

8 Repeat the experiment with plants in different conditions, and try it with different kinds of plants.

Explain your results.

# Investigation 3

**To find out how much water a plant loses and gains**

1 Obtain a leafy, non-woody plant and wash its roots carefully.

2 Stand it in a 20 cm³ measuring cylinder.

3 Pour water into the measuring cylinder up to the top mark.

4 Carefully run a little oil into the measuring cylinder so that it forms a thin layer over the surface of the water. This will prevent water evaporating from the measuring cylinder.

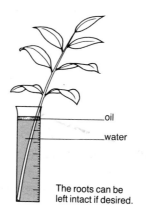

oil

water

The roots can be left intact if desired.

5 Weigh the plant and measuring cylinder together.

6 Leave the plant for about 24 hours.

7 After about 24 hours, weigh the plant and measuring cylinder again. Write down their mass in grams.

8 Read off the new level of the water in the measuring cylinder.

How much mass has been lost?

What volume of water has been taken up?

One cm³ of water weighs one gram: from this work out the mass of water which has been taken up by the plant.

Does this figure equal the loss in mass?

What do you think happens to the water which the plant takes up?

Are there any other reasons why the plant might lose mass besides losing water?

# Investigation 4

**Showing the passage of water through a plant**

1 Obtain a plant with its leaves and roots intact.

2 Wash the soil off the roots.

3 Stand the plant in a jar of water containing a coloured dye such as eosin or red ink, for about 4 hours.

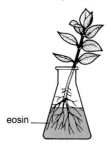

eosin

4 After 4 hours, cut the stem in two with a sharp knife.

Whereabouts is the dye?

Compare the appearance of the stem with that of a plant which has been standing in water.

Explain your observations.

5 Cut the stem longways so as to find out more about where the dye is within the stem.

6 Stand a balsam plant ('Busy Lizzie') in a jar of dye, and leave it for 24 hours. This plant has a transparent stem, and you will be able to see where the dye is inside it.

7 Obtain a plant with white flowers, such as hibiscus or periwinkle, and stand it in a jar of dye for several days.

Does the dye eventually reach the flowers?

# Investigation 5

**Looking at the stomata in a leaf**

1  Cut a green leaf off a plant.

2  With a paintbrush apply a thin layer of clear nail varnish to a small area on the lower surface of the leaf.

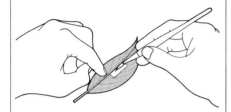

3  When the nail varnish is dry, peel it off with a pair of forceps. The nail varnish will have made an exact replica of the leaf surface.

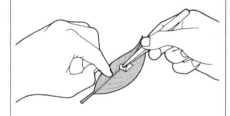

4  Put the nail varnish in a drop of water on a slide, and cover it with a coverslip.

5  Examine it under the low power of the microscope.

Can you see the stomata? Approximately how many stomata are visible in the field of view?

6  Now look at a single stoma under the high power.

Can you see the guard cells?

7  Repeat the experiment on the upper surface of the leaf.

How many stomata are visible in the field of view this time?

Which side of the leaf has the greater number of stomata, the upper side or lower side?

Why do you think the two sides of the leaf differ in this respect?

# Investigation 6

**To see how quickly the two sides of a leaf lose water**

1  Obtain two small pieces of dry cobalt chloride or thiocyanate paper. This is blue when dry, but turns pink when moist.

2  Obtain a leafy twig of a tree or shrub and stand it in water.

3  With sellotape stick one piece of the cobalt thiocyanate paper to the upper side of a leaf. Completely cover the piece of paper with the sellotape.

4  Stick the other piece of cobalt thiocyanate paper to the lower side of a different leaf in the same way.

5  Note the time, and observe the two pieces of cobalt thiocyanate paper at intervals.

How long does it take for the first trace of pink to appear on each piece of paper?

How long does it take for each piece of paper to go completely pink?

Which side of the leaf loses water faster, the upper side or the lower side?

Why do you think one side loses water faster than the other?

# Assignments

1  Before going to bed, a lady placed a potted plant on the windowsill and pulled the curtains. It was a chilly night. The following morning she found that the glass behind the plant was covered with drops of moisture. Explain fully.

2  Suggest a reason for each of the following:
   a) On a hot day it is best to water plants in the evening.
   b) Before transplanting a plant it is a good idea to remove some of the leaves.
   c) Water moves up a stem more quickly on a hot dry day than on a cool wet day.
   d) When a greenfly feeds on a plant it sticks its proboscis into the phloem.

3  How could a five-year old child kill a tree with a penknife? Explain fully.

4  In order to show how the stomata of a plant open, a student makes an artificial stoma as follows. He fills two short lengths of visking tubing with a 20 per cent solution of sucrose (sugar) and ties the ends together as shown in the left-hand diagram above. He then places the artificial stoma in a dish of distilled water and leaves it there for three hours. At the end of the three-hour period it looks like the right-hand diagram.

   a) What structures does the visking tubing represent?
   b) Explain how the change in appearance is brought about.
   c) Mention two ways in which the working of this artificial stoma differs from a real one.

5  A scientist investigated the uptake of mineral salts by the roots of young cereal plants. This is what she found:
   a) Salts were taken up even when they were more dilute in the soil-water than inside the root.
   b) The rate of uptake was increased by raising the temperature, so long as it did not exceed 40°C.
   c) Uptake stopped if the roots were treated with a poison that prevented metabolism.
   d) Uptake was much slower if the soil was waterlogged.

What conclusions can be drawn from each of these findings? How might they help farmers?

# How do plants support themselves?

*The tree below is
over 80 metres tall and has a
mass of over 600 tonnes. How can
such a huge structure stand up?
In this Topic we shall see how
plants support
themselves.*

**Figure 1** The General Grant Tree, a giant conifer, in California, is estimated to be 3500 years old and at 60 m above the ground the trunk is 3 m thick.

## Why do plants need to stand upright?

There are two main reasons:

1 It puts the leaves in the best position to get plenty of light for photosynthesis. This is particularly important in a forest where plants are competing with one another for light.
2 It lifts the flowers into a high position from which pollen, fruits and seeds can be scattered over a wide area. This helps the species to reproduce and spread to new places.

The main way plants stand upright is by having a strong stem (Investigation 1).

## What makes the stem strong?

In general, strength is achieved by the stem containing three different structures, namely packing cells, cellulose strands, and wood. Let's look at each of these in turn.

### Packing cells

If you look at the inside of the stem of a herbaceous plant like a sunflower under the microscope you will see that it is full of large rounded cells (Figure 2). These are packing cells, they are full of a watery fluid and are blown up like balloons. The epidermis or 'skin' of the stem holds the packing cells in place, and causes them to press against one another, making the whole stem firm yet flexible. Similar cells inside the leaf help to keep that firm too.

What keeps the packing cells full of fluid? The packing cells draw in water by osmosis which makes them **turgid** (see page 40). However, this will only happen if the plant has a good supply of water from the soil.

If the packing cells don't get enough water they become flabby or flaccid, just as a balloon does if you let air out of it. When this occurs the whole plant droops (Figure 3). We call this **wilting**. It happens on hot dry days when water evaporates from the leaves more rapidly than it can be replaced by the roots.

### Cellulose strands

A plant like a sunflower contains strands of cellulose just beneath the

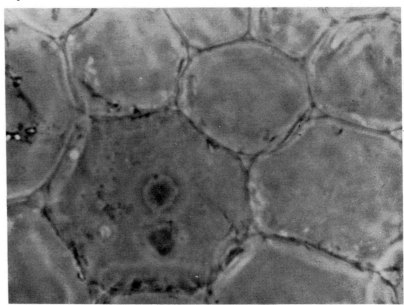

**Figure 2** Packing cells seen in a transverse section of a plant stem, magnified 300 times.

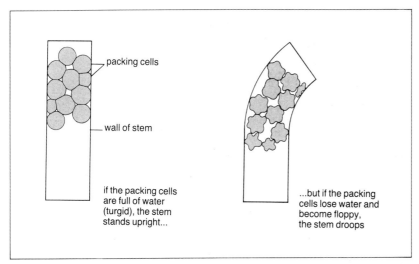

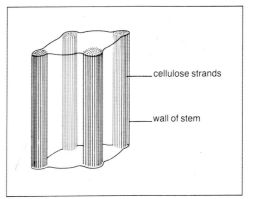

Figure 4 In this stem the cellulose strands are concentrated at the corners, making it strong and helping it to stand upright.

Figure 3 These diagrams show how the packing cells in a stem help it to stand upright.

epidermis in the stem. These strands are formed by the thick cellulose walls of living cells which lengthen as the stem grows. The cellulose strands are tough and rubbery, and they help to make the stem strong and flexible.

In the stems of such plants as deadnettle and coleus, which look square in cross section, the cellulose strands are concentrated at the corners. The corners thus serve as buttresses, strengthening the stem and helping it to stand erect (Figure 4).

## Wood

When a plant grows, certain cells in the stem lengthen, and a substance called **lignin** is added to the cellulose in their walls. Lignified cells are wood. As lignin won't let water through, the cells die, so all that's left in the mature stem are long strands of wood. These strands are of two types. Some of them are narrow tube-like **vessels** and their job is to carry water and minerals through the plant as well as to provide support (see page 166). Others, known as **fibres**, do not transport anything and their job is only to support the plant.

Plants vary in the amount of wood their stems contain (Investigation 2). In herbaceous plants that only last one year, there is not much wood and it is confined to special regions called the vascular bundles (Figure 5). On the other hand, in shrubs and trees, which go on year after year, the wood more or less fills the entire stem, and more is added every year (see page 254).

Wood makes stems strong and rigid. Think of a tree, for example. The branches and leaves, which together make up the canopy, are held up by a single trunk. This may be very tall: some of the giant conifers in California are over a hundred metres high (Figure 1).

As a tree gets taller, its trunk gradually broadens, helping it to support the increasing weight of the canopy. Some of the giant conifers have trunks up to eleven metres wide, and there is a cypress tree in Mexico whose trunk is over 34 metres wide: twelve buses could be lined up side by side behind this tree-trunk without being seen.

## Inside a tree trunk

If you look at the cut end of a felled tree trunk you may see that there is a dark region towards the centre and a lighter region further out. The dark central region is called the **heartwood** and the lighter region the **sapwood** (Figure 6).

The heartwood is extremely dense and hard and its only job is to support the tree. The sapwood is less dense and therefore softer than the heartwood. It provides support too, but it also carries water and mineral salts (sap) up the trunk. It is therefore much wetter than the heartwood.

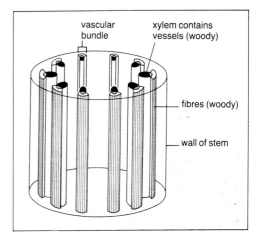

Figure 5 This diagram shows the positions of the woody tissue in the stem of a herbaceous plant such as a sunflower.

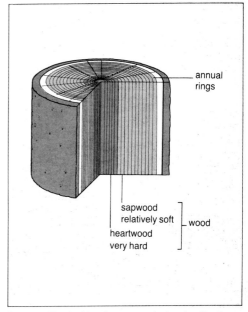

Figure 6 The inside of a tree trunk showing the two kinds of wood.

**Figure 7** A sawmill. These tree trunks have been transported down the river, and they will be cut up into planks.

**Figure 8** How do plants with weak stems manage to support themselves and get to the light? **A** A climber, which attaches itself to a tree trunk. **B** Morning glory, which twines round a support, **C** An epiphytic bromeliad growing on a tree.

## Wood and the timber industry

Wood is extremely strong for its weight, and so it has been used for building and similar purposes for centuries. Its main disadvantage is that it's liable to be attacked by fungi or insects. For example 'dry rot' is caused by a fungus.

For building, heartwood is better than sapwood because it is stronger, drier and more resistant to decay. Also being drier, it is less likely to shrink.

Every type of tree has its own particular kind of wood which varies in appearance and strength. The arrangement of the cells gives the wood its characteristic grain. Generally the wood of coniferous trees, such as pine, is softer than the wood of flowering trees such as oak or mahogany.

Different trees have different uses. For example, the wood of the ash tree is strong and springy, which makes it ideal for the handles of tennis racquets. On the other hand the oak has very hard and durable wood, which makes it more suitable for building, and mahogany, with its beautiful grain, is ideal for furniture.

In temperate regions, the trees most often used for their wood are conifers such as pine, spruce and fir. They grow comparatively quickly and their wood is hard enough for most purposes. The seeds are sown in nurseries, and when the seedlings are large enough they are transplanted to plantations in the country. They are usually grown in areas which are unsuitable for other kinds of crops, such as steep mountain slopes. Conifers do not grow well in the Caribbean, except in the higher, cooler areas. We depend more on the wood of flowering trees such as W. Indian ebony, cedar and elm, as well as lignum vitae and blue mahoe. As we cut down our timber trees, we also need to plant more trees in reafforestation programmes.

After felling, the trunks are sawn up (Figure 7). Before it can be used the wood must be allowed to dry out, that is **seasoned**. In this process its mass may be halved. If wood isn't seasoned it is likely to shrink and warp later.

## Other methods of support

Many plants have floppy stems; they don't have the efficient strengthening devices mentioned earlier. Some simply lie on the ground. Others get round the problem in the following ways:

1 Some attach themselves to vertical surfaces such as walls, and climb up them.
2 Some wind themselves round sticks or the stems of other plants.
3 Some float in ponds, lakes, rivers or the sea, where they are supported by the water.
4 Some hang on the branches of trees, rooting themselves in humus that has collected in crevices in the bark. We call such plants **epiphytes**.

Some examples of these kinds of plant are shown in Figure 8.

# Investigation 1

**To find how strong a stem is**

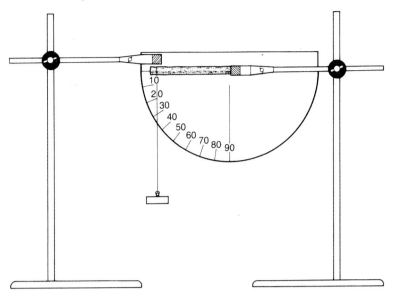

1 Cut off a 5 cm length of a stem which is approximately 5 mm wide.

2 Clamp a protractor to a stand as shown in the illustration.

3 Clamp the stem horizontally to another stand in front of the protractor.

4 Hang a 10 g mass on the end of the stem.

5 From the protractor, note the angle through which the stem bends.

6 Repeat this experiment on the stems (or branches) of different plants. They should all be the same length and thickness, and the same mass should be used for all of them.

What are the advantages and disadvantages to a stem of being able to bend?

# Investigation 2

**To find out how much wood there is in a stem**

1 Obtain a short length of the stem of a plant such as a sunflower.

2 Cut one end cleanly with a knife.

3 Pour some phloroglucin stain into a watch glass and add three drops of concentrated hydrochloric acid. Acidified phloroglucin stains wood red.

4 Dip the cut end of the stem into the stain and leave it for five minutes.

5 Take the stem out of the stain and look at the cut end. Draw the cut end to show where wood is situated.

Approximately what proportion of the cut end of the stem is taken up with wood?

6 Repeat this investigation on the stems or branches of different plants. In each case try breaking the stem or branch with your hands before you stain it.

How do the stems or branches of the various plants which you have examined differ in the amount of wood that they contain?

What do you think makes a stem or branch difficult to break?

# Assignments

1 Mention three structures which help stems to stand erect.

2 It was a hot dry day. By midday the plants in the flowerbed were drooping. That evening the gardener watered the soil, and within an hour the plants were standing up straight.

 a) Explain in detail what caused the plants to droop, and then stand up straight again.
 b) Despite the hot, dry weather some of the plants did not droop at all. Give possible reasons.

3 Find out about the use of one timber tree grown in your country.

4 How do heartwood and sapwood differ in their properties and in their functions in a mature tree?

5 Give one reason each why:
 a) heartwood is preferred to sapwood for building purposes;
 b) bullet wood is used for buildings;
 c) mahogany is used for furniture;
 d) lignum vitae is used for ornamental pieces.

6 If you cut the end of a piece of celery or paw-paw stem longways, and put it in water, the ends bend outwards as shown in the illustration below.

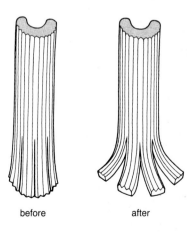

before          after

 a) Why do you think this happens?
 b) What sort of solution could you put the stem in to make the ends bend inwards again?

# The skin and temperature control

*We usually think of the skin as just a covering which holds the body together and keeps the things inside from falling out. However, there's much more to the skin than that, as we shall see.*

Porche 944 S2

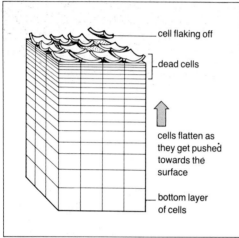

**Figure 2** Diagrammatic view of the epidermis of human skin.

- cell flaking off
- dead cells
- cells flatten as they get pushed towards the surface
- bottom layer of cells

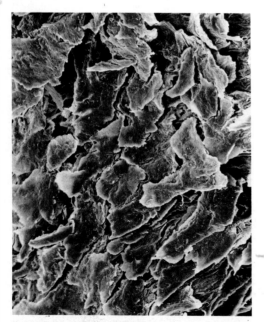

**Figure 3** This picture shows the surface of the skin greatly magnified in the scanning electron microscope. The structures which look like dead leaves are epithelial cells flaking off.

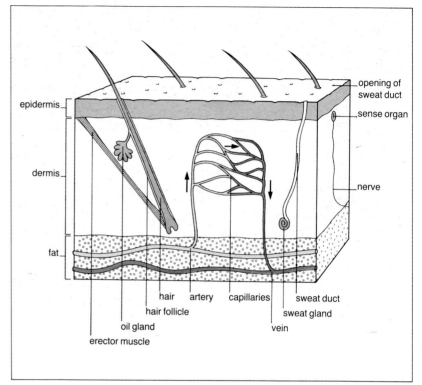

epidermis

dermis

fat

opening of sweat duct

sense organ

nerve

hair    artery    capillaries

hair follicle

oil gland

erector muscle

sweat duct

sweat gland

vein

**Figure 1** The main structures found in the skin of a mammal.

## The skin

The detailed structure of the skin is shown in Figure 1. It is divided into two main layers: a thin **epidermis** at the surface and a thicker **dermis** beneath.

The epidermis is made up of layers of cells like a brick wall (Figure 2). New cells are constantly being formed by the bottom-most layer and they push the older ones towards the surface. As the cells get pushed upwards, they become flat and hard and eventually die, forming a dead layer at the surface. The cells right at the top are like overlapping tiles and are constantly flaking off (Figure 3). These cells contain the protein keratin, the same substance that the scales of reptiles and feathers of birds are made of. It makes the skin waterproof and protective.

The epidermis of human skin contains a dark pigment called **melanin**. Black-skinned people have a lot of melanin, and oriental people have an additional pigment called carotene which gives their skin a yellowish colour. White-skinned people don't have much melanin, though the amount can be increased by the action of ultraviolet light on the skin, which is why they go brown when they sunbathe.

The dermis is composed of a network of tough connective tissue fibres. In amongst the fibres are blood capillaries and sense organs. Towards the bottom of the dermis there are **sweat glands** from which narrow sweat ducts run to the surface of the skin.

Sticking out of the skin are **hairs**. Each hair projects from a deep pit called the hair follicle, and its root is situated deep in the dermis. Hairs are made of keratin, as are other skin structures such as nails and claws.

Opening into the hair follicles are glands which produce oil. This keeps the hair supple and helps to make the skin waterproof.

A slender muscle runs from the side of each hair to the base of the epidermis. When this **erector muscle** contracts, the hair stands upright. When it relaxes, the hair lies down flat. This is important in temperature control, as we shall see presently.

Below the dermis is a layer of cells containing fat which varies in thickness from one part of the body to another.

Figure 4 The spines of this West African crested porcupine protect it from attack.

Figure 5 The tiger's stripes camouflage it by breaking up its surface.

## What does the skin do?

We will answer this mainly in relation to man, with occasional reference to other animals.

### 1 It protects the body

The keratinous layer of the skin, and the hairs, play the most important part in this. In some mammals the hairs are thickened up into sharp spines or flat plates which protect the animal from attack (Figure 4), and in animals like the rhinoceros the horns are made of lots of hairs all fused together. The skin also protects the body from germs, and the melanin pigment stops harmful ultraviolet rays from entering the body.

To a certain extent unwanted nitrogen can be got rid of via the skin (see page 182). This is another aspect of the skin's protective function.

### 2 It camouflages the animal

In many mammals the hairs vary in colour and pattern, camouflaging the animal in its natural surroundings (Figure 5).

### 3 It keeps water in

The keratinous layer of the skin is waterproof, and this prevents the body drying out. It also stops water getting in by osmosis when, for example, we go swimming.

### 4 It is sensitive to stimuli

The skin is sensitive to touch, pain, temperature and pressure. Sense organs in the skin are responsible for detecting these stimuli (page 200).

### 5 It keeps the body warm

The hair plays a very important part in this. Of course, humans have very little hair and that's why we wear clothes. But other mammals have plenty of hair. In birds the same thing is achieved by the feathers.

The fat under the dermis also helps to keep the body warm. Animals such as whales and seals which live in cold water have a specially thick layer of fat called **blubber** (Figure 6).

Although the skin certainly keeps the body warm, it does more than that: it helps to *control* the body temperature, keeping it constant.

Figure 6 This sea lion has a thick layer of fat, or blubber, in its skin to help keep it warm.

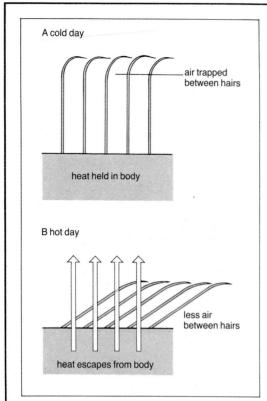

**Figure 7** These diagrams show the part played by the hairs on the skin in controlling the body temperature of a mammal.

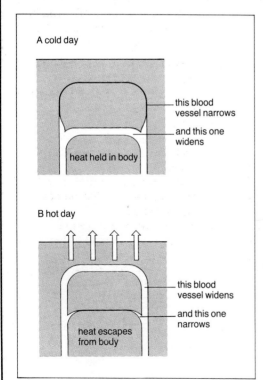

**Figure 8** These diagrams show the part played by the blood vessels in the skin in controlling the body temperature of a mammal.

## Temperature control

Except when we're ill, the body temperature stays at just under 37°C all the time. This is the temperature at which our body functions best; indeed, if the body temperature gets much above 40°C, death is likely to occur.

**If it's cold, the following things happen which keep the body warm:**

### 1 *The hairs are raised*
You may have noticed that on cold days a cat's hairs are ruffed up. This is brought about by contracting the erector muscles. As a result, the hairs stand up and a layer of air is trapped between them (Figure 7A). Air is a poor conductor of heat, so this helps to insulate the body and prevents heat being lost from it (Investigation). Of course, this response is not much use to man with his sparse covering of hair; nevertheless our erector muscles still contract in cold weather, giving rise to goose pimples.

### 2 *Blood is held back from the surface of the skin*
Instead of flowing through the capillaries just under the epidermis, the blood is diverted through blood vessels deeper down. This prevents heat being lost from the blood as it flows through the skin. This response is brought about by the surface blood vessels getting narrow so blood can't flow through them so easily (Figure 8A). This is why white people tend to go pale in cold weather.

### 3 *More heat is made by the body*
In cold weather our metabolic rate increases and we produce extra heat. The liver plays an important part in this. Also we shiver and may run about so as to keep warm. Shivering is caused by an involuntary contraction of our muscles.

**If it's hot, various things happen which keep the body cool:**

### 1 *The hairs are lowered*
This is brought about by relaxing the erector muscles. As a result, the hairs lie down flat: a layer of air is no longer held between them, so heat is lost more easily from the body (Figure 7B).

### 2 *Blood flows close to the surface of the skin*
In warm weather, the surface blood vessels widen so that more blood flows through them, and heat is lost as it flows close to the surface (Figure 8B). This is why white people go pink in warm weather.

### 3 *Sweating or panting occur*
In hot weather, our skin gets covered with sweat, which is secreted by the sweat glands. When the sweat evaporates, it cools the skin and the blood flowing through it.

Evaporation occurs more quickly in dry air than in wet, humid air. That's why we feel hot and sticky on a humid day. Movement of the air helps to evaporate the sweat, so a gentle breeze has a cooling effect.

Not all mammals sweat. Dogs, for example, have sweat glands only on the pads of their paws, and they cool themselves mainly by panting. When a dog pants, water evaporates from its mouth and tongue.

The various heating and cooling mechanisms just mentioned happen without our having to think about them. They are controlled by a special centre in the brain. In addition to these automatic responses, we can of course take deliberate steps to control our temperature by, for example, putting on more clothes if it's cold, or bathing in cool water if it's hot.

The warmth of our clothing depends on the fact that it traps a layer of air against the skin. As we have seen, air is a poor conductor of heat, so this helps to prevent heat being lost from the body. Woolly clothes are particularly warm because air gets trapped in the meshes.

Animals which can keep their body temperature constant, irrespective of the temperature of their surroundings, are described as **warm-blooded** (or homoiothermic). They include all mammals and birds.

All other animals are described as **cold-blooded** (or poikilothermic): their body temperature is the same as that of their surroundings. The only way that such an animal can control its body temperature is by making sure that it is always in a place where the temperature is suitable.

Adjusting the body temperature so that it is kept constant is an example of what biologists call **homeostasis**. It is explained on page 244.

# Investigation

### To see the effect of insulation on heat loss

1 Obtain two identical tin cans with press-on lids.

2 Make a hole in the centre of each lid.

3 Put a wad of cotton wool on top of the lid of one can, and wrap another wad round the sides. Leave the second can uncovered.

4 Pour hot water into the two cans, the same amount into each.

5 Put a thermometer into each can, and take the temperature of the water at one minute intervals for at least fifteen minutes.

6 Plot the temperatures on graph paper, putting temperature on the vertical axis and time in minutes on the horizontal axis. Use the same sheet of graph paper for both cans, so you can compare them easily.

Which can loses heat fastest?

How does the cotton wool help to prevent heat being lost?

What structures in a mammal are equivalent to the cotton wool?

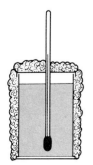 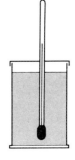

# Assignments

1 A small girl remarked that her cat looked larger on cold days than on warm days. How would you explain this?

2 What is the dark colour of a black person's skin caused by, and why is it useful?

3 Explain each of the following:
 a) You feel cooler on a hot dry day than on a hot humid day.
 b) Dogs pant when they're hot.
 c) The metabolic rate of a naked human increases if the surrounding air temperature is lowered.
 d) On a cool day on the beach you feel warmer after a swim in the sea even though the temperature of the sea is lower than that of the air.
 e) While you are asleep at night your body temperature falls by about 2°C.

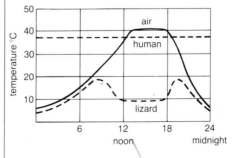

4 A scientist carried out an experiment which showed that in cold conditions the amount of heat lost per unit mass from a small mammal was greater than that from a large mammal, although their insulation mechanisms were equally efficient and their body temperatures stayed the same.
 a) Why do you think the small mammal lost more heat than the large mammal?
 b) How do you think the small mammal managed to keep its body temperature as high as the large mammal?
 c) The small mammal ate more than its own mass in food each day, whereas the large mammal ate only a small fraction of its mass in food. How would you account for this difference?

5 The graph on the left shows how the air temperature and the body temperature of a human and a lizard varied in the course of 24 hours in the desert.
 a) Explain what the lizard was probably doing at 8 am, 2 pm and 6 pm.
 b) How was the human's body temperature controlled between 12 noon and 6 pm?
 c) What do these results tell us about the way warm-blooded and cold-blooded animals control their body temperature?

# The liver

*'Is life worth living? It all depends on the liver.' The liver performs many functions which affect our day-to-day health.*

*most blood from gut*

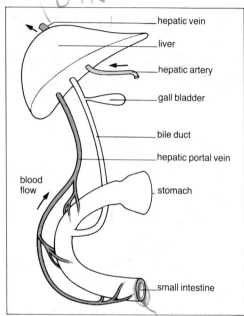

**Figure 1** The liver showing its blood supply and connections with the gut.

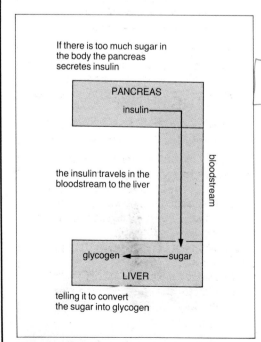

**Figure 2** A simple scheme to show how the hormone insulin controls the amount of sugar in the body.

## The structure of the liver

The liver is the body's largest organ, weighing well over a kilogram. It is situated at the top of the abdominal cavity just under the diaphragm; you can feel it as a hardish area just below your bottom rib. Leading from the liver to the small intestine is the **bile duct**, attached to which is the **gall bladder** (see page 94).

The liver has a very good blood supply: about a litre of blood flows through it every minute – this is more than is sent to any other organ. Much of its blood comes from the **hepatic portal vein** which brings blood to it from the gut (Figure 1). All the food which is absorbed into the bloodstream from the gut is taken straight to the liver in this vein. This is because one of the liver's main jobs is to 'process' the food before it goes on to the rest of the body.

The liver itself is composed of masses of small cells, and the whole organ is riddled with narrow passages and blood vessels which give it a soft spongy texture.

## What does the liver do?

The liver does many jobs. These are the main ones:

### 1 It helps with digestion
It does this by producing **bile** which is held in the gall bladder before being sent to the small intestine. Bile contains bile salts which emulsify fat, breaking it up into tiny droplets (see page 94).

### 2 It produces heat
Many chemical reactions take place in the liver, and this makes it produce a lot of heat. As blood flows through the liver, it is warmed up and this keeps the inside of the body warm.

### 3 It gets rid of poisons
Suppose you eat some food which happens to contain a mild poison: when the poison gets to the liver, the liver turns it into a harmless substance. We call this process **detoxification**. Poisonous substances are constantly being formed in our bodies as by-products of the many chemical reactions which take place inside our cells. The liver detoxifies these too.

### 4 It makes urea
Most people eat more protein than they need. The liver cannot store the unwanted protein. Instead, it breaks it down, getting some energy from it in the process. The nitrogen part is removed from the amino acids in a process called **deamination**. It is then turned into ammonia. This is very poisonous and would kill you if it was allowed to build up. So the liver quickly converts it into a less poisonous substance called **urea**. This is carried by the blood to the kidneys, and is then expelled in the urine.

### 5 It destroys old red blood cells
After about four months, red blood cells wear out and stop working properly. The liver then breaks them up and any unwanted haemoglobin is converted into coloured substances which pass out with the bile. In the intestine these **bile pigments** are turned into a brown substance which gives the faeces their characteristic colour.

### 6 It stores food substances
After a meal, glucose is carried to the liver by the hepatic portal vein, and the liver turns any unwanted glucose into **glycogen**. This is stored inside the liver cells in the form of tiny granules. The glycogen can be turned back into glucose when the body needs it. The liver also stores many other food substances, including various vitamins (e.g. vitamin K) and minerals such as iron.

## 7 It controls the amount of sugar in the blood

We have just seen that the liver stores surplus glucose. By storing surplus glucose, the liver ensures that there is never too much sugar in the blood. This is most important because, if sugar was to build up in our bloodstream our cells would be unable to work properly. What makes the liver turn sugar into glycogen? The answer is a hormone called **insulin** which is secreted into the bloodstream by special cells in the pancreas: insulin is a protein, and the cells which produce it occur in little groups called the Islets of Langerhans. Figure 2 summarises the process. It is an example of **homeostasis** (see page 244).

## Diabetes

Some people have too much sugar in their blood. They are suffering from **diabetes** and are known as diabetics. The extra sugar in their blood makes them tired and thirsty. If nothing is done about it, the person loses weight and may eventually die. The kidneys try to get rid of the extra sugar, so one of the signs of diabetes is that sugar is present in the urine. In the old days, doctors used to tell whether or not a patient had diabetes by tasting his urine to see if it was sweet. Nowadays, a simple chemical test is used.

Diabetes is caused by the pancreas not producing enough insulin. The result is that the liver does not turn as much sugar into glycogen as it normally would. A person may inherit this condition or he may develop it as he gets older. It cannot be cured, but it can be controlled by:

1   following a restricted diet: the aim is to eat foods which do not contain much carbohydrate, so you don't get too much sugar in your blood.
2   taking tablets: certain tablets have the effect of lowering the amount of sugar in the blood.
3   insulin treatment: the diabetic takes a certain amount of insulin every day. This makes the liver turn his blood sugar into glycogen.

Unfortunately insulin cannot be taken by mouth, because it is broken down by digestive enzymes in the gut. So it must be injected through the skin with a hypodermic needle. Diabetics are taught to do this for themselves (Figure 3).

The trouble is that it's sometimes difficult to get the dose exactly right. What sometimes happens is that the diabetic gives himself too much insulin with the result that his blood sugar falls too low. This can produce all sorts of effects such as trembling, sweating and weakness. The diabetic learns to recognise these signs and, if they come on, he eats a few lumps of sugar or glucose tablets to bring his blood sugar up to the right level.

With proper medical help, the diabetic can learn to control his affliction and to work, play games and lead a full and active life. Some leading sportsmen are diabetics.

## Gallstones and diseases of the liver

Normally the various substances present in the bile are in solution, but sometimes they solidify in the gall bladder or bile duct forming **gall stones**. These may block the bile duct and stop the bile getting into the intestine. One effect of this is that the skin and the whites of the eyes go yellow. This is a type of **jaundice** and is caused by the bile pigments getting into the bloodstream.

Jaundice can also be caused by the liver not working properly as happens in certain diseases such as cancer of the liver and viral hepatitis (see page 339). A serious liver disease is **cirrhosis**, which can be caused by drinking too much alcohol over a long period. The alcohol kills the liver cells, which become replaced by useless fibrous tissue. It is the usual cause of death in alcoholics.

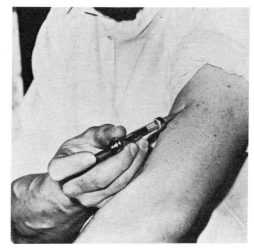

Figure 3  A diabetic injecting himself with insulin.

## Assignments

1   Which functions of the liver listed in this topic:
   a)  help in temperature regulation,
   b)  assist the action of a digestive enzyme,
   c)  make bile coloured,
   d)  help the body to get rid of nitrogenous waste,
   e)  make liver a useful food?

2   Look at Figure 1. Which of the various tubes in this illustration would you expect to:
   a)  contain a lot of glucose after a meal,
   b)  carry the hormone insulin,
   c)  contain an emulsifying agent,
   d)  contain digestive enzymes?

3   A person who is suspected of having diabetes is asked to produce a sample of urine. The urine is then tested for sugar.
   a)  Describe a suitable test which could be carried out.
   b)  What would be the cause of sugar being present in the urine?

4   Insulin cannot be taken by mouth because it would be broken down by digestive enzymes in the gut.
   a)  Give the names of two digestive enzymes which would attack the insulin.
   b)  What would these enzymes break the insulin down into?
   c)  How is insulin taken by a diabetic?
   d)  Mention one danger of taking insulin this way.

# How do we get rid of waste substances?

*Like a chemical factory, the body produces many waste products, some of which are poisonous. The body must get rid of these unwanted substances. This is known as excretion.*

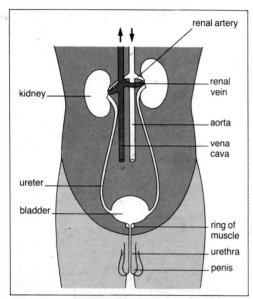

**Figure 1** The excretory system of a human male. The arrows indicate the direction of flow of blood.

| Substance | Quantity (g/100 cm³) | |
|---|---|---|
| | Blood | Urine |
| Water | 92 | 95 |
| Proteins | 7 | 0 |
| Glucose | 0.1 | 0 |
| Chloride (salt) | 0.37 | 0.6 |
| Urea | 0.03 | 2 |

**Table 1** This table compares the quantities of five different substances in the blood and urine of the human.

## Excretion

Excretion is any process which gets rid of unwanted products of the body's chemistry. This includes getting rid of carbon dioxide in the air we breathe out. There is unwanted nitrogen in sweat, nails and hair, and that too can be regarded as an aspect of excretion. In addition to these processes the body has a special system for getting rid of waste substances. This is the **excretory system**.

Don't confuse excretion and defaecation. Defaecation is getting rid of the part of our food which we cannot digest.

## The excretory system

The main organs in the excretory system are the **kidneys**. We have two; they are reddish bean-shaped organs situated towards the back of the abdominal cavity just above the waist. If you put your hands on your hips, your kidneys are just about where your thumbs are.

Figure 1 shows how the kidneys are connected with the rest of the excretory system. A narrow tube called the **ureter** runs from each kidney to the **bladder**, a muscular bag situated towards the bottom of the abdominal cavity. Leading from the bladder is a tube called the **urethra** which runs down the middle of the penis in the male, and opens close to the vaginal opening in the female (see page 267).

The kidneys have a good blood supply: blood is carried to each one by the **renal artery** and away from it by the **renal vein**.

The kidneys produce a watery fluid called **urine** which contains substances which the body does not want. The urine trickles down the ureters to the bladder which gradually expands like a balloon as more and more urine collects inside it.

How is the bladder emptied? If you look at Figure 1 you will see that the top of the urethra is surrounded by a ring of muscle. Normally this muscle is tightly contracted, so urine cannot get out of the bladder. When the bladder is emptied this ring of muscle relaxes, and at the same time the muscles in the wall of the bladder contract, so urine is forced out of the body. This process is called **urination**.

## How is urine formed?

Look at Table 1. You will see that some substances are more plentiful in the urine than in the blood plasma. These are the waste substances which the body does not want. The main waste substance in urine is **urea** (see page 180). The figures in Table 1 show that there is about sixty times more urea in our urine than there is in the blood. The explanation is that as the blood passes through the kidneys, urea is taken out of it and passed into the urine.

However, the kidneys do more than simply cleanse the blood of urea. They also regulate the amount of water and salt in the blood (Investigation 1).

Suppose you drink a lot of water quickly. The water is absorbed from your gut into the bloodstream, and it has the effect of *diluting* the blood. The diluted blood reaches the kidneys which take the water out of it and pass it into the urine.

Salt is dealt with in the same kind of way. Suppose you have a very salty meal. The salt is absorbed into your blood, which thus becomes very concentrated. The salty blood reaches the kidneys which remove the salt from it and pass it into the urine.

The relative amounts of water and salts in the blood give the blood a particular concentration, and this is turn determines its osmotic properties (see page 40). By regulating the water and salt, the kidneys make sure that the concentration of the blood stays more or less the same all the time. The name for this process is **osmo-regulation** and it is an example of homeostasis (see page 244). If the concentration of the blood was allowed to fluctuate wildly our cells would not work properly.

## Inside the kidney

The kidney is divided into two areas: a light outer area called the **cortex**, and a darker inner area called the **medulla** (Investigation 2). The medulla is connected to the ureter as shown in Figure 2.

Inside the kidney there are about a million microscopic devices called **uriniferous tubules** or **nephrons**. The structure of an individual nephron, together with its blood supply, is shown in Figure 3. It consists of a little cup-like **capsule** which is connected to a narrow **tubule**. The tubule twists and turns, doubles back on itself and eventually leads to a **collecting duct**. About twelve nephrons share the same collecting duct, and all the collecting ducts open into the ureter.

The nephron's blood supply comes from a branch of the renal artery. This enters the capsule and splits up into a little bunch of capillaries called the **glomerulus**. These then join up again to form a vessel which leaves the capsule and splits up into further capillaries which are wrapped round the tubule. These then join up to form a vessel which leads to the renal vein.

In Figure 3 notice the shape of the tubule as it runs from the capsule to the collecting duct. It consists of three regions: after leaving the capsule it is coiled up (**first convolution**), then it becomes U-shaped (the **loop of Henle**), and finally it is coiled up again (**second convolution**).

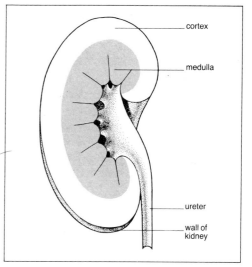

**Figure 2** A kidney sliced horizontally to show the inside.

**Figure 3** The structure of a nephron. The black arrows indicate the direction of blood flow; the open arrows indicate the direction in which the urine flows.

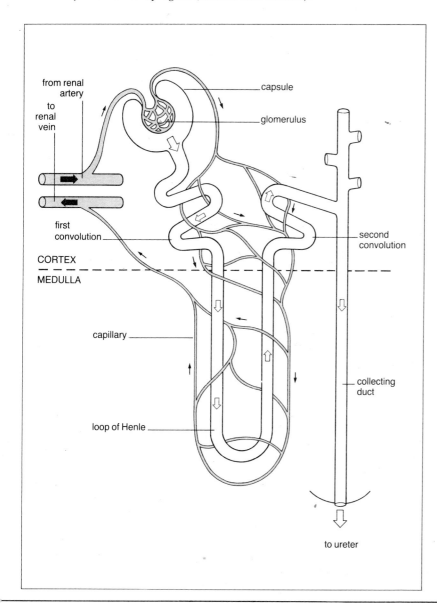

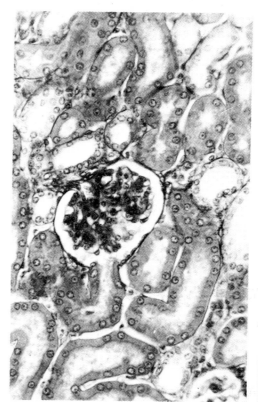

**Figure 4** Part of the inside of the kidney as seen under the light microscope, highly magnified. The round structure in the centre is a capsule, and you can see the tubule leading from it. The rest of the section consists of tubules cut in various planes.

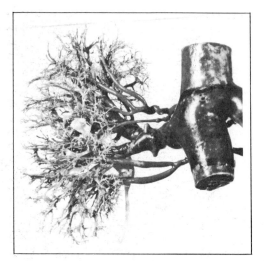

**Figure 5** A corrosion preparation of the kidney. All the tissues except the main blood vessels have been dissolved away. The two kidneys contain about 16 km of tubules and 160 km of blood vessels.

## How do the nephrons work?

The kidney is full of blood vessels, some of which are shown in Figure 5. This good blood supply is essential if the nephrons are to do their job.

Figure 6 will help you to understand how the nephron works. The blood which reaches the glomerulus is under high pressure. This is because the vessel which leaves the capsule is narrower than the one which enters it. As a result, the fluid part of the blood is forced through the walls of the capillaries into the space inside the capsule. The fluid which goes through contains urea, glucose, water and salt. However, the blood cells and proteins are too large to go through, so they stay in the capillaries. In this way the blood is *filtered* as it passes through the glomerulus.

The filtered fluid, or filtrate, then trickles along the tubule. The urea remains in the tubule and eventually passes via the collecting duct into the ureter. However, all the glucose, most of the water and some of the salts are taken back into the capillaries wrapped round the tubule. Just enough water and salts are taken back to give the blood its correct composition.

So the kidneys work by first filtering the blood, and then reabsorbing back into it those substances which the body needs.

Most of the reabsorption takes place in the first convolution and is finished by the time the fluid reaches the loop of Henle. However, water is an exception. The final portion of the water is reabsorbed in the collecting duct, according to the body's needs, and the loop of Henle helps with this. Mammals can live in dry places largely because of this part of the nephron.

Reabsorption of water is an extremely important function of the kidney. If the kidneys stopped reabsorbing water, the body would become completely dehydrated in less than three minutes.

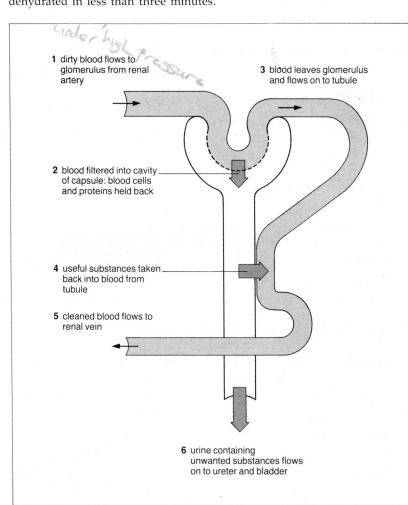

1 dirty blood flows to glomerulus from renal artery

3 blood leaves glomerulus and flows on to tubule

2 blood filtered into cavity of capsule: blood cells and proteins held back

4 useful substances taken back into blood from tubule

5 cleaned blood flows to renal vein

6 urine containing unwanted substances flows on to ureter and bladder

**Figure 6** This diagram shows very simply how the nephron cleans the blood and makes urine.

## What happens if the kidneys fail?

Occasionally one or both kidneys stop working properly. This may happen if they become infected, or sometimes after a severe shock such as a car accident.

A person can manage with only one kidney, but if both fail the blood soon becomes full of urea and other waste substances, and if nothing is done about it the person will die.

One way of saving the person's life is to attach him to an **artificial kidney** (Figure 7). This is a machine which filters and cleans the blood. A tube is connected to an artery in the patient's arm. His blood is then drawn off and made to flow over the surface of a thin sheet of cellophane on the other side of which is a watery solution. Urea and other unwanted substances in the blood pass through the cellophane into the solution on the other side, while larger components of the blood, including the blood cells, are held back. The blood is then returned to the patient by a tube inserted into one of his veins. As well as cleansing the blood of urea, the kidney machine adjusts the amount of salt in the blood before it is returned to the patient.

A person with complete kidney failure needs to spend about twelve hours on a kidney machine twice a week, either in hospital or at home. He can then lead a more or less normal life.

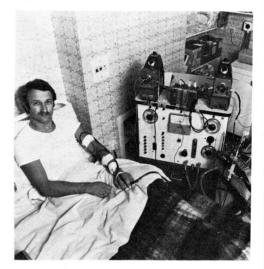

**Figure 7** A person connected to an artificial kidney (kidney machine).

## Investigation 1

**To find the effect of drinking on urine production**

1 Urinate as completely as possible, preferably after going for a long time without drinking.

2 Fifteen minutes later urinate again into a measuring cylinder, and estimate the volume of urine produced.

3 Fill a test tube with a sample of the urine, then throw the rest away.

4 Now drink a litre of water.

5 Fifteen minutes later urinate and measure the volume of urine, as before.

6 Fill a second test tube with a sample of this new lot of urine, then throw the rest away.

7 Repeat steps 5 and 6 at fifteen minute intervals for as long as possible. Do not drink any more water during the experiment. Compare the volume of urine produced in each case, and also its colour.

8 Plot your results on graph paper. Put volume of urine on the vertical axis, and time on the horizontal axis.

How do the urine samples differ in colour?

Why do they differ in this way?

How would you explain the volume differences?

What organ is responsible for controlling the water content of the body?

## Investigation 2

**Looking at the kidney**

1 Obtain a kidney of a mammal such as the pig, obtained from a butcher.

2 With a sharp knife slice the kidney across the middle as shown in the illustration.

3 Which of the parts shown in Figure 2 can you see?

Whereabouts does urine leave the kidney?

Where does the urine go after it has left the kidney?

## Assignments

1 What effect, if any, would you expect each of the following to have on the quantity and composition of the urine?
   a) Eating a large quantity of salty food.
   b) Having a bath.
   c) Drinking a lot of beer.
   d) Playing a hard game of squash.
   e) Eating two bars of chocolate.

2 Explain the meaning of the terms excretion and osmo-regulation. What job does the kidney do
   a) as an excretory organ, and
   b) as an organ of osmo-regulation?

3 Which of the substances listed in column A are found in each of the fluids listed in column B?

   Column A     Column B
   protein      blood entering kidney
   glucose      blood leaving kidney
   urea         fluid filtered into capsules
   water        urine leaving kidney

4 It has been suggested that in hot weather a person passes less urine than in cold weather.
   a) Describe an experiment which could be done to find out if this is true.
   b) How would you explain it?

# Water balance and waste removal in other organisms

*Organisms
lose or gain water for
various reasons, and this can affect
the way they get rid of waste
substances.*

## How does Amoeba control its water content?

Water constantly enters an amoeba's body from outside. The cell membrane is semi-permeable and water passes across it because of **osmosis** (see page 39).

What would happen if the amoeba did not control this intake of water? It would gradually get bigger and bigger, and eventually it would burst. So the organism must get rid of the water as quickly as it comes in. It's rather like a boat with a leak in the bottom: if the boat is to be prevented from sinking, the water must be bailed out as fast as it enters.

The amoeba gets rid of water by means of its **contractile vacuole** (Figure 1). This is a tiny sack situated in the cytoplasm. The sack gradually fills up with water, getting larger and larger like a balloon. When it is full, it empties its contents to the outside. The contractile vacuole then becomes tiny again, and the process is repeated. The contractile vacuole empties once every few minutes. If you're lucky you may see it happening.

Excretion takes place in a simple way. Poisonous waste substances, such as **ammonia**, diffuse passively across the cell membrane into the surrounding water.

## How do fishes control their water content?

The answer depends on whether the fish lives in fresh water or sea water. If it's a fresh-water fish like a goldfish or guppy, water comes into the body by osmosis, just as it does in *Amoeba*. It doesn't pass across the skin because the scales won't let water through, but it does pass across the thin lining of the mouth cavity and gills. However, as quickly as water enters, it is got rid of by the kidneys. The nitrogenous waste, **urea**, is excreted in large amounts of watery (dilute) urine.

Now suppose you are a sea-water fish such as a flying fish. In this case the sea water is more salty than the blood. The result is that water is drawn out of the fish by osmosis. This would make the blood very salty were it not for special cells in the gills which get rid of the excess salt, passing it from the blood to the surrounding sea water. This is a case of active transport, as the movement is occurring against a concentration gradient. The kidneys help by getting rid of as little water as possible. The urea is excreted in small quantities of more concentrated urine.

Figure 2 summarises the way fresh-water and sea-water fish control their water content.

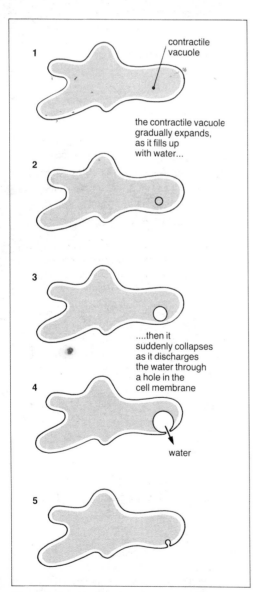

1

contractile vacuole

2

the contractile vacuole gradually expands, as it fills up with water...

3

....then it suddenly collapses as it discharges the water through a hole in the cell membrane

4

water

5

**Figure 1** *Amoeba* uses its contractile vacuole to get rid of water.

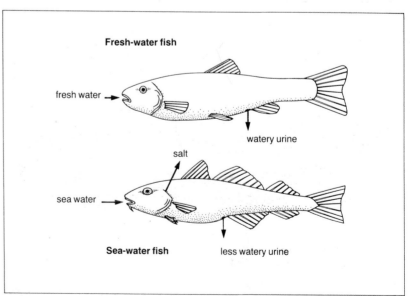

**Fresh-water fish**

fresh water →

watery urine

salt

sea water →

**Sea-water fish**

less watery urine

**Figure 2** These diagrams compare how fresh-water and sea-water fish control their water and salt content.

## Land-dwelling animals

An animal living on land constantly runs the risk of losing water by evaporation from the body surface, particularly if it lives in a hot, dry place. Insects show us how this can be avoided. Liquid waste matter is released from the tissues into the blood. It is then taken up by the excretory tubules (Figure 3). Inside the tubules the waste matter is turned into a solid substance called **uric acid**. Water is removed from it and absorbed back into the blood. Meanwhile the solid waste passes out of the body through the anus.

Insects get rid of their excretory waste in solid form so as not to lose water. It enables them to live in hot, dry places without drying out. Insects have other ways of preventing water being lost. For example, the **cuticle** is waterproof. This prevents water evaporating from the surface of the body. The cuticle is made waterproof by a thin layer of wax on its surface.

The only problem is that water may evaporate through the spiracles. To keep this to a minimum, the spiracles are kept closed as much as possible. So we see that insects are very good at saving water.

What about other animals? Well, land animals such as reptiles have a waterproof surface, as do many plants. It's also interesting that reptiles and birds save water by excreting their waste matter in solid form, as insects do. You have probably noticed that bird droppings are a mixture of black and white sludge. The black part is the bird's faeces, the remains of food which it hasn't been able to digest. The white part is uric acid, its nitrogenous waste.

## Storing waste

All the organisms mentioned so far get rid of waste substances from the body. However, this is not the only way of dealing with waste substances. Another way is to store them inside the body, out of harm's way. This is what plants do — and some animals too.

If you look at plant cells under the microscope, you often see crystals inside them. Usually these crystals are made of calcium carbonate or oxalate, and they are the plant's way of disposing of excess calcium (Figure 4).

The nitrogenous waste products of plants are tannins and alkaloids. Tannins accumulate in the bark and contribute to its brown colour. Alkaloids accumulate in the leaves and are lost when the plant sheds its leaves (page 364).

The same kind of thing is done by the earthworm. At least part of its nitrogenous waste is stored in the walls of the excretory organs (see page 55). And unhatched chicks do it too: their excretory waste is stored as uric acid in a special bag inside the egg, where it remains until hatching takes place.

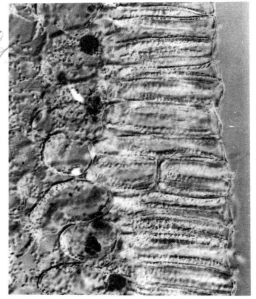
**Figure 4** Section of a Begonia leaf seen under the microscope. The white objects inside the cells are crystals of calcium oxalate.

## Assignments

1 Look up osmosis on page 39. Write a brief explanation of why water enters *Amoeba's* body, using these words: semi-permeable membrane, osmosis, concentration, salts.

2 List three ways in which insects prevent water being lost from their bodies.

3 Plants that live in dry places have ways of saving water. In what respects are their ways of saving water similar to those of insects?

4 A scientist put a specimen of *Paramecium* (see page 47) into (a) distilled water and (b) sea water, and counted the number of times the contractile vacuole emptied each minute. Here are his results:

| Medium | Number of emptyings |
| --- | --- |
| Distilled water | 6 |
| Sea water | 1 |

a) Explain these results.
b) What further experiments would you do to test your explanation?

5 Ammonia requires less energy to produce than urea, and urea requires less energy than uric acid. So why do insects, reptiles and birds excrete uric acid?

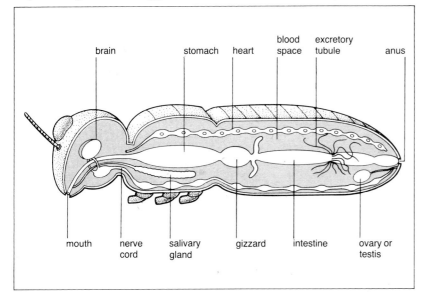
**Figure 3** Looking inside an insect from the side. The main organs are shown. Notice the bunch of excretory tubules attached to the intestine at the hind end.

# Responding to stimuli

*The sense organs
in the tips of the tentacles
of the sea anemone are sensitive
to changes in the surroundings which cause
the animal to respond. The way
organisms respond to stimuli
is the subject of the next
group of topics.*

# The nervous system and reflex action

*If you put your hand on a hot plate, you pull it away quickly. This response is brought about by messages which are sent at high speed through the nervous system.*

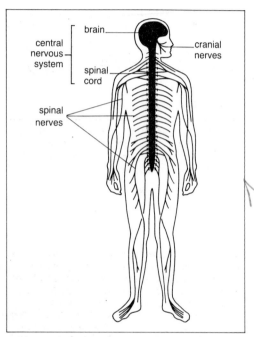

**Figure 1** The main parts of the human nervous system.

brain
central nervous system
cranial nerves
spinal cord
spinal nerves

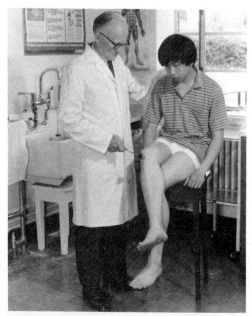

**Figure 2** This doctor is testing a patient's knee jerk.

## General plan of the nervous system

The nervous system consists of two parts: the **Central Nervous System (CNS)**, and a series of **nerves** which link the CNS with the various organs (Figure 1).

The CNS is divided into two parts: the **brain** and the **spinal cord**. The brain is enclosed within the **cranium** or brain case which is part of the skull. The spinal cord runs down the centre of the backbone. The whole of the CNS is therefore protected by a covering of bone.

The nerves are of two kinds. Some of them come out of the brain, and go mainly to structures in the head such as the eyes and jaws: these are called **cranial nerves**. Others come out of the spinal cord, and go to the arms, legs and various structures in the trunk. They are known as **spinal nerves**.

## Nerve messages

The main job of the nervous system is to carry messages from one part of the body to another. Scientists have carried out experiments to find out about these messages, and they have discovered that they consist of tiny pulses of electricity which travel rapidly through the CNS and along the nerves. We call these messages **nerve impulses**.

## Reflex action

If you put your hand on a hot plate, you pull it away quickly. This is an example of a **reflex action**. *A reflex action is an immediate response of the body to a stimulus.* Many other reflexes are shown by humans and other animals (Investigation 1). For example, if you tap your knee in a certain place, your leg gives a little kick. This is called the **knee jerk**, and it is often used by doctors to find out if the patient's spinal cord is working properly (Figure 2). Another well known reflex is the scratching movement of the hind leg of a dog when you tickle its tummy.

Let's consider what happens when you pull your hand away from a hot object. First of all, sensory endings in your fingers are stimulated by the heat. This causes impulses to pass up the nerve in your arm to the spinal cord and brain: the actual feeling of pain occurs when the impulses reach the brain. Further impulses then pass back down the arm to the muscles, causing them to contract. The contraction of the muscles has the effect of pulling your arm away from the unpleasant stimulus (Figure 3). The whole response only takes a fraction of a second and this shows how quickly the impulses travel through the nervous system (Investigation 2).

## The reflex arc

Scientists have worked out the route by which impulses travel through the nervous system in bringing about a reflex action. This comprises what we call a **reflex arc**.

The structure of the reflex arc involved in pulling your hand away from a hot object is shown in Figure 4. It is made up of five distinct parts:

1  A **receptor** which receives the stimulus. In this reflex the receptors are the sensory endings in the skin.
2  A **sensory nerve fibre** which carries impulses from the sensory endings to the spinal cord.
3  An **intermediate nerve fibre** which carries the impulses from the upper to the lower side of the spinal cord.
4  A **motor nerve fibre** which carries the impulses from the spinal cord to the muscle.
5  An **effector** which responds when impulses reach it. In this reflex the effector is the muscle in the arm.

The three nerve fibres are thread-like extensions of **nerve cells** which are located in, or close to, the spinal cord. They are connected to each other by junctions inside the grey matter of the spinal cord. These junctions are called **synapses**.

When an impulse travels through a reflex arc it has to cross these synapses. They will only let the impulses pass in one direction, and this ensures that the impulses always go the right way, i.e. *from* the sensory endings *to* the spinal cord and on to the muscles.

All three nerve fibres must be working properly if the impulses are to get through to the muscle. If one of the fibres dies the reflex cannot occur. In the disease **poliomyelitis** ('polio') a certain kind of germ (a virus) attacks some of the motor nerve cells in the spinal cord. As a result, impulses cannot reach the muscles and the person becomes paralysed. Which particular muscles are affected depends on what part of the spinal cord is attacked by the virus. Polio victims often lose the use of their legs. Fortunately people can now be immunised against this disease (see page 335).

A few reflexes do not involve the brain and can occur in an animal whose brain has been completely destroyed. The knee jerk is an example. However, most reflexes involve the brain as well as the spinal cord. The messages travel into the spinal cord, and then up to the brain. They then travel back down again, and out to the muscles. This is important for two reasons. Firstly, it means that you feel pain when the reflex occurs – you can feel sensations only if impulses go to your brain. Secondly, it means that you could leave your hand on the hot object if you wanted to, or you could pull it away with extra force; in other words you can exert *voluntary control* over the reflex.

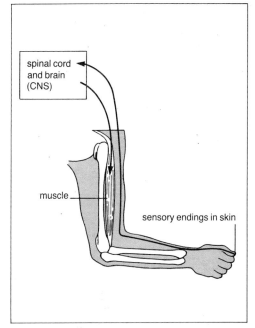

**Figure 3** When you pull your hand away from a hot object, the arm muscle (biceps) contracts when it receives messages from the sensory endings in the skin of the hand.

## Voluntary and involuntary responses

Scratching your head, crossing your legs or walking across the room are all voluntary actions which you can do or not do as you wish. They are brought about by muscles attached to the skeleton, and the part of the nervous system which controls them is known as the **voluntary system**. In contrast, various processes are constantly occurring in our bodies over which we have no voluntary control – for example, the beating of the heart and the movements of the gut. We cannot *make* these things happen, nor can we stop them of our own free will. These activities are brought about by muscles which are controlled by the **involuntary** or **autonomic nervous system**.

**Figure 4** The reflex arc involved in pulling your hand away from a hot object. The dorsal root ganglion contains the cell bodies of many other sensory fibres besides the one shown; that's why it is swollen. The grey matter in the spinal cord contains mainly cell bodies and synapses; the white matter contains long nerve fibres which run up and down the spinal cord; they connect this reflex arc with other reflex arcs and with the brain.

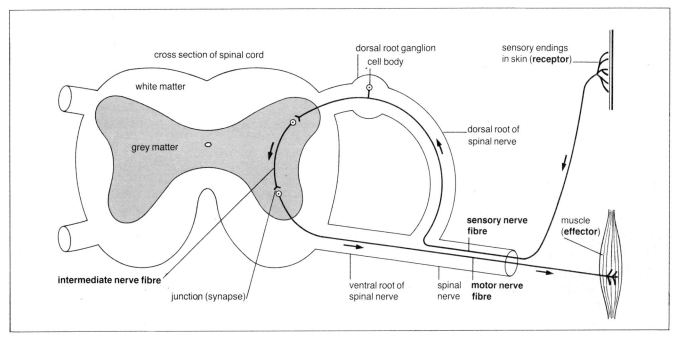

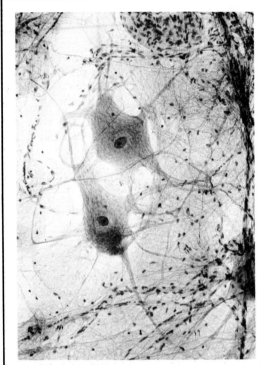

**Figure 5** This is a thin section of the spinal cord seen under the microscope. The section has been stained to show up the nerve cells and fibres in the grey matter.

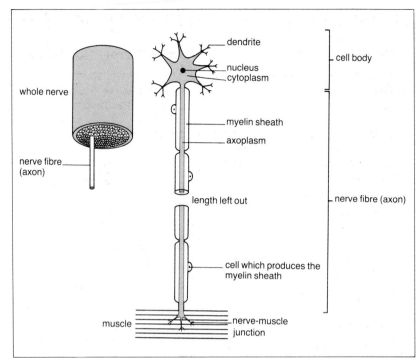

**Figure 6** The structure of a motor nerve cell. Notice the long nerve fibre (axon) extending from the cell body. A whole nerve contains numerous nerve fibres, as shown in the left diagram.

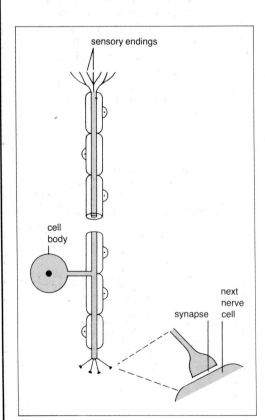

**Figure 7** The structure of a sensory cell.

As an example of an involuntary response, let's take the heart. The heart receives two nerves: when messages reach it through one of these nerves, the heart beats faster, when messages reach it through the other nerve, the heart slows down. Many other involuntary organs have a double nerve supply of this kind and in general the two nerves produce opposite effects.

There are some actions which we cannot control early in life, but we gradually learn to control them as we get older. The emptying of the bladder and bowels are two examples.

Finally some activities, such as breathing, are partly voluntary and partly involuntary: we breathe automatically without thinking about it, and yet we can alter the rate of our breathing if we want to.

## Nerve cells

Look at Figure 5. This shows two motor nerve cells in the spinal cord as you would see them under the microscope. Now look at the diagram in Figure 6. This shows a complete motor nerve cell. The cell is made up of two parts: a **cell body** and the long thread-like **nerve fibre** or **axon**. The cell body is situated in the CNS, and the nerve fibre extends out into a nerve.

The cell body has a number of branches protruding from it. These are called **dendrites**. They link up with other nerve cells to form a complex network. This enables impulses to be sent in many different directions within the nervous system.

The nerve fibre is enveloped by a layer of fat called the **myelin sheath** which speeds up the impulses and prevents them leaking out. If the myelin sheaths don't work impulses cannot be transmitted properly, so the person gradually loses the use of his muscles. This happens in the disease **multiple sclerosis**.

Figure 7 shows a sensory nerve cell. Notice that it differs from the motor nerve cell in the shape and position of the cell body. Notice the fine branches at the lower end of the nerve fibre. Each branch ends up as a little knob which makes a synapse with another nerve cell in the CNS.

# Investigation 1

## Some human reflexes

Work in pairs, one person acting as the subject.

1  *The knee jerk*

   Sit on a table with your legs hanging loosely. With a heavy instrument such as a metal rod, your partner should gently tap your knee just below the knee cap.

   What happens?

2  *The ankle jerk*

   Kneel on a chair and let your feet hang loosely. Your partner should tap the back of your foot just above the heel.

   What happens?

3  Repeat the above reflexes but this time make a conscious effort to *prevent* them taking place.

   Do you succeed?

   What conclusions do you draw?

4  *The blink reflex*

   Open your eyes and look straight ahead. Your partner should suddenly wave his hand in front of your eyes.

   What happens?

5  *The swallowing reflex*

   Swallow the saliva in your mouth, then immediately try swallowing again.

   Is it difficult to swallow the second time?

   Suggest an explanation.

6  Repeat the above experiment, but this time swallow your saliva and then swallow a mouthful of water.

   What difference does this make?

   What conclusions do you draw?

Choose one of the reflexes which you have investigated and say why it is useful to humans.

# Investigation 2

## Measuring your reaction time

Hold a metre rule vertically. Your partner should place his hand at the bottom of the rule in readiness to catch it. Find out how far it falls before being caught by your partner.

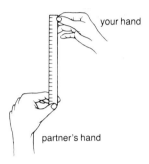

your hand

partner's hand

Here is another thing you can do:

1  Divide into two teams, with the same number of people in each.

2  Stand in a row, holding hands.

3  When your teacher says 'go' the first person should squeeze the hand of the second person, and so on. Your teacher will time how long it takes for the chain reaction to reach the front.

Trace the nervous pathway through which the impulses pass in bringing about the above responses.

# Investigation 3

## Looking at nerve cells in the spinal cord

1  Obain a prepared transverse section of the spinal cord, which has been specially stained to show up the nerve cells.

2  Examine the slide under the low power of the microscope. Identify the grey and white matter.

   Can you see nerve cells in the grey matter similar to the ones in Figure 5?

3  Go over to high power, and focus on a single nerve cell. Draw the nerve cell to show its shape.

   What part of the nerve cell shown in Figure 5 does your drawing correspond to?

# Assignments

1  A person walks across a room in bare feet and treads on a drawing pin. He lets out a cry. Explain what happens in his nervous system in bringing about this response.

2  Explain the reason for the following:
   a) If you tickle a dog's tummy it 'scratches' with its hind leg.
   b) Messages travel through a reflex arc in only one direction.
   c) In multiple sclerosis the person gradually becomes weak.
   d) In 'polio' the patient may lose the use of his legs.

3  The diagram shows the pathway through which messages travel in bringing about the knee jerk. When the tendon is tapped, receptors in the muscle are stretched and this causes the messages to be sent off.
   a) Which structure is stimulated by the hammer?
   b) Which structure carries impulses away from the spinal cord?
   c) Which structure shortens as a result of the reflex?
   d) What would be the approximate length of structure E in a human?
   e) Assuming that the impulses travel at 100 metres per second, how long would it take for an impulse to travel through this reflex arc?
   f) How does the structure of this reflex arc differ from the one in Figure 4 (page 191)?

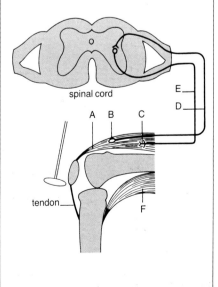

spinal cord

A  B  C

E

D

tendon

F

# The brain and behaviour

*We all have to think and make decisions every day: this comes into almost every aspect of our lives. The organ which enables us to do these things is the brain*

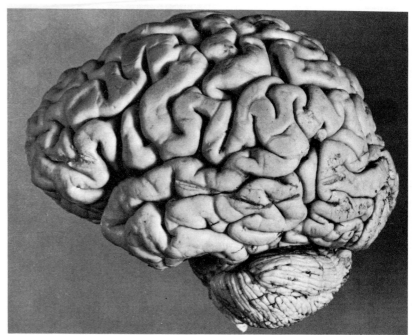

Figure 1 Human brain viewed from the side.

## What does the brain consist of?

Figure 1 shows a human brain. If you were to slice it open you would not see much, just a soft whitish material. However, if you looked at a thin section of it under the microscope you would see that it's made up of countless millions of **nerve cells** (Figure 2). Scientists have worked out that there are over one thousand million nerve cells in the brain. Each cell may be connected with 25 000 others and the total number of connections in the entire brain is around ten to the power of three million. This number is so enormous that if it was written out fully as a figure it would fill a book as large as the one you are reading at the moment! With so many connections, the brain is like an extremely complex computer with thousands of electrical messages travelling from place to place. But it is much more than a computer because it makes us conscious beings with feelings and emotions.

## The structure of the brain

The brain is shaped like a large mushroom (Figure 3). The cap of the mushroom is called the **cerebrum**, and the stalk is called the **brain stem**. Sticking out of the top side of the brain stem just below the cerebrum is a protuberance rather like a little cauliflower: this is called the **cerebellum**. The rear part of the brain stem is called the **medulla**; it is continuous with the spinal cord.

Notice the pituitary gland on the underside of the brain. Its functions are explained on page 239. The pituitary gland is attached to a part of the brain called the **hypothalamus**.

The entire brain is enclosed within the bony brain case or **cranium** which is part of the skull. Surrounding the brain inside the cranium are two membranes with fluid in between. This is called **cerebro-spinal fluid**, and it is formed from two masses of fine blood capillaries called **plexuses** in the roof of the brain. The cerebro-spinal fluid serves as a shock absorber, so the brain is cushioned from damage when the person jumps around or bangs his head.

If you look at Figure 3 you will see that there is a cavity in the centre of the brain: cerebro-spinal fluid is found in here too. It is also found inside and around the spinal cord whose cavity is continuous with that of the brain.

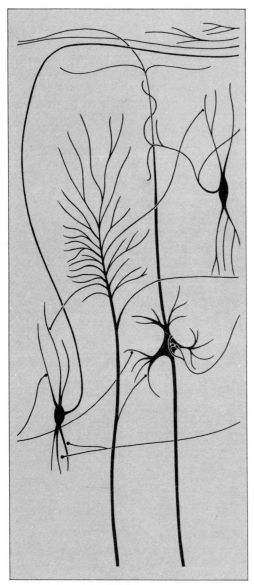

Figure 2 The brain contains millions of nerve cells which are connected with one another in a most complex way. Just a few of them are shown here as they appear in a microscope section of the brain. Only a few nerve cells are included in this picture. In reality there would be at least ten times as many in the small area of the brain shown here.

## What does the brain do?

For our purposes the three main parts of the brain are the cerebrum, cerebellum and medulla. Scientists have discovered what each of these parts does by observing the behaviour of people whose brains have been damaged in accidents. Here is an example:

A motor cyclist has a crash and his cerebellum is badly damaged but the rest of his brain is unaffected. He gradually recovers, but he keeps toppling over when he stands up, and he finds it difficult to make accurate movements with his hands.

From this kind of observation we can say that the cerebellum controls our sense of balance and allows us to make precise and accurate movements. In doing this, it works in conjunction with various sense organs (see page 200).

The cerebrum registers various sensations, such as seeing and hearing, and it makes our legs and arms move. It also enables us to think, speak and remember things. This is such an important part of the brain that we shall study it in more detail in a moment.

The medulla controls various processes which go on without our thinking about them, such as breathing and the beating of the heart.

The hypothalamus contains control centres which help to keep the body temperature and the concentration of the blood constant (see page 244).

**Figure 3**  The human brain seen in its natural position inside the head.

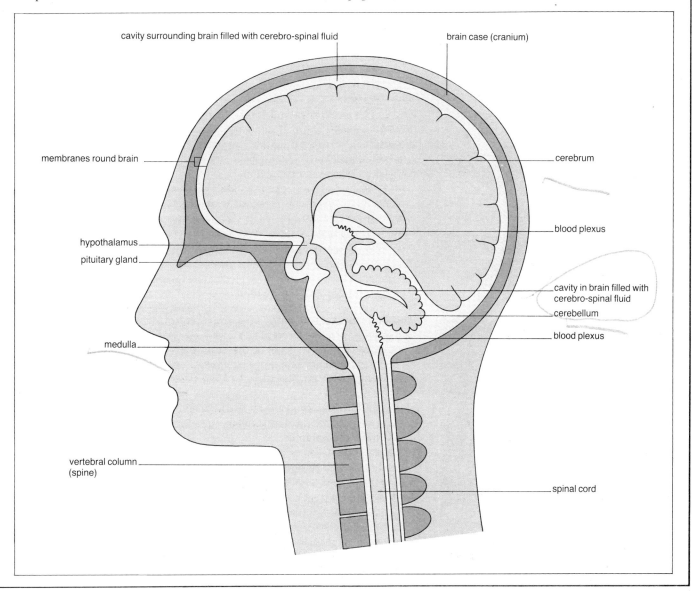

cavity surrounding brain filled with cerebro-spinal fluid

brain case (cranium)

membranes round brain

cerebrum

hypothalamus

blood plexus

pituitary gland

cavity in brain filled with cerebro-spinal fluid

cerebellum

blood plexus

medulla

vertebral column (spine)

spinal cord

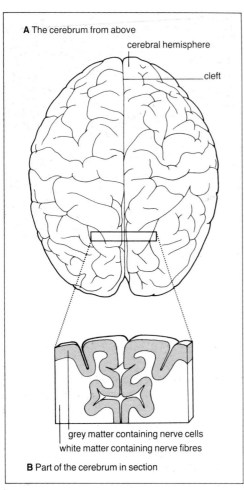

**A** The cerebrum from above

cerebral hemisphere

cleft

grey matter containing nerve cells
white matter containing nerve fibres

**B** Part of the cerebrum in section

**Figure 4** The structure of the cerebrum. Notice the folding of the grey matter. The left hemisphere is connected to the right side of the body and vice versa.

**Figure 5** Who is this?

## A closer look at the cerebrum

If you look at Figure 4A, you will see that the cerebrum is divided into two halves by a cleft which runs down the middle. The two halves are called **cerebral hemispheres**. The two hemispheres are connected by nerve fibres and are very much in communication with one another.

Most of the nerve cells in the brain are situated in the cerebrum, where they are concentrated in a thick layer towards the surface. This is the grey matter or **cerebral cortex**. If you look at a slice of the cerebrum you will notice that the grey matter is folded like a piece of crumpled paper (Figure 4B). This has the effect of increasing the surface area, so a greater number of brain cells can be packed into the brain.

## What does the cerebrum do?

The function of the cerebrum can be illustrated by considering a certain dog called Oliver. Oliver is sitting outside when suddenly he sees a cat at the bottom of the garden. He is just about to chase it when his owner calls him in for his supper. So he delivers a quick menacing bark at the cat and runs indoors.

What has been happening in Oliver's brain? On seeing the cat, impulses were sent from the eyes to the cerebrum. When a moment later he heard his owner calling, impulses were sent from his ears to the cerebrum. Oliver's cerebrum understood that his owner's call meant food, so it sent impulses to the leg muscles and made him run indoors.

We can sum it up like this: the cerebrum receives impulses from various sense organs, it sorts them out and then sends impulses to the particular muscles which are needed.

## Learning

How did Oliver *know* that when his owner called it was supper time? Ever since he was a puppy, his owner had clanked his dish on the floor when calling him for supper. In the course of time Oliver had learned to associate this clanking noise with food.

In the same way he had learned not to urinate in the house: he had come to associate doing *that* with a smack on the backside.

We call this kind of behaviour **conditioning**. It was first described in the early 1900s by a Russian scientist called Pavlov who did some interesting experiments on dogs. Normally a dog's mouth waters when it is given food: this is a straightforward reflex of the kind described on page 190. In one experiment Pavlov rang a bell just before giving the dog its food. After repeating this several times, the dog learned to associate the bell with the food, and it would salivate as soon as it heard the bell, i.e. before the food appeared. Pavlov called this response a **conditioned reflex**. Many examples of this kind of thing are shown by humans and other animals. In general, conditioning can be speeded up if the animal is rewarded for doing the right thing, and punished for doing the wrong thing. This principle is used in training dogs and other animals.

Conditioning is a form of **learning**. We can define learning as a change in behaviour resulting from past experience. Learning is made possible because the cerebrum can store information, or, to put it simply, it can remember things (Investigation 1).

Learning enables us to get to know our surroundings and to respond in the right way to new situations. Learning also enables us to recognise objects, even when they are not very clear (Figure 5). In fact the brain is remarkably good at filling in gaps, provided that it has some idea of what to expect (Investigation 2).

In humans the cerebrum is also the seat of intelligence and artistic functions. In right-handed people speech and mathematical ability are dealt with by the left hemisphere, whereas appreciation of space and form are handled by the right hemisphere.

## Instinct

Returning to Oliver, if it hadn't been for his supper arriving, he would have chased the cat. Oliver hadn't learned to chase cats. He'd done it all his life, and was born with the knowledge of how to do it.

This kind of behaviour is called **instinct**. Instinctive behaviour is inherited and does not need to be learned. All that's necessary is that it is set off by the right kind of stimulus. For Oliver the appearance of the cat was the stimulus, unleashing the chasing behaviour. In fact, dogs will instinctively chase any swiftly moving object they happen to see. This is made use of in greyhound racing in which the dogs run after a dummy hare propelled along a track.

Instinctive behaviour is common in many animals: we see it in the courtship behaviour of birds, for example (see page 286). However it is less obvious in human beings, though in babies sucking the mother's nipples for milk and pushing things into the mouth are probably instinctive.

Many scientists feel that it is wrong to make a sharp distinction between learning and instinct. The behaviour of higher animals, and humans in particular, results from a combination of these and other types of activity. Greyhound racing, though based on instinct, depends to some extent on learning in that the dogs are trained to chase the dummy hare as fast as they can.

**Figure 6**   A greyhound chasing the 'hare'.

## Investigation 1

**Short-term and long-term memory**

*First experiment*

1 Your teacher will give you ten objects to look at for a minute.

2 After the minute is up, write down the names of as many of the objects as you can remember.

3 About half an hour later, try writing them down again.

How many did you get right the first time?

And the second time?

*Second experiment*

1 Make a simple drawing of the front of any building which you know well and see regularly.

2 Compare your drawing with the actual building.

In what respects is your drawing right?

In what respects is it wrong?

Which of these two experiments demonstrates your short-term memory, and which one demonstrates your long-term memory?

## Investigation 2

**Recognising things**

1 Your teacher will give you a box containing ten objects, some well known to you, others less well known.

2 Put your hands in the box, *but do not look inside.*

3 Feel each object in turn and write down what you think it is.

4 When you have finished making your list, look at the objects in the box.

Which ones have you got right?

How much has past experience helped you to recognise these objects?

5 Your teacher will give you various incomplete or fuzzy objects or pictures.

6 In each case write down what you think the object is.

Which ones did you find difficult to recognise? Why?

Which ones are made easier to recognise by looking at them from further away?

What does this experiment tell us about the brain?

## Assignments

1 Give one function which is performed by each of the following:
 a) the cerebro-spinal fluid,
 b) the cerebellum,
 c) the cranium,
 d) the brain stem,
 e) the cerebrum.

2 The ability to learn is associated with certain parts of the cerebrum. How do you think we know this?

3 How do you think scientists know that there are over one thousand million nerve cells in the human brain?

4 A chimpanzee is put in a cage in which there is a lever. Every time the chimpanzee presses the lever, he is given a banana. After a time the chimpanzee realises that if he wants a banana all he has to do is to press the lever.

In what respect is the chimpanzee's behaviour (a) similar to, and (b) different from the behaviour of Pavlov's dogs?

5 What is meant by instinctive behaviour? Describe an experiment which could be done to test the suggestion that a dog chasing a cat is an example of instinct.

# Drugs and mental illness

*The brain is easily affected by outside influences, particularly drugs. In this Topic we will look briefly at how drugs affect the brain, and what happens when the brain does not work properly.*

## Drugs

A drug is any substance which alters the way the body works. Here we will concentrate on drugs that affect the brain. Such drugs fall into four groups:

### 1 *Sedatives*

These drugs slow down the brain and make you feel sleepy. They include tranquillisers and sleeping pills. Tranquillisers have a calming effect and are often given to people suffering from anxiety. An example is valium. Sedatives include a group of chemical substances called **barbiturates** which are so powerful that they are used as anaesthetics. Alcohol is also a sedative.

### 2 *Stimulants*

These drugs speed up the action of the brain and make you more alert. They include 'pep pills' which are sometimes given to people who are suffering from severe depression. Cocaine, obtained from the leaves of certain South American plants, is a particularly powerful stimulant. Coffee and tea contain a mild stimulant called caffeine, as does Coca-Cola. Another mild stimulant is nicotine, the drug found in tobacco.

### 3 *Hallucinogens*

These drugs cause **hallucinations**. An hallucination is something which a person senses but which does not actually exist. Drugs that cause hallucinations include cannabis or marijuana (nicknamed 'pot') and LSD (lysergic acid diethylamide).

### 4 *Pain-killers*

These drugs suppress the part of the brain responsible for the sense of pain. They include two powerful drugs called **morphine** and **heroin** which are obtained from opium, a substance found in a certain type of poppy. Morphine is often given to people suffering from severe pain.

## Why are drugs dangerous?

If taken under doctor's orders certain drugs, such as sedatives and pain killers, can be very helpful to sick people. However, they must be taken in the right amounts at the right times. If taken in the wrong circumstances they may be extremely harmful. There are three main reasons for this:

### 1 *They may impair the person's judgements and make him clumsy.*

Often they lengthen the reaction time, so the person takes longer to respond to a stimulus. Such is the case with alcohol. In an experiment, a group of bus drivers drove their buses between two rows of posts, and then did the same again after drinking some whisky. It was found that after drinking they knocked over more posts than they had done before.

### 2 *The person may become dependent on the drug and crave for it.*

Such is the case with cigarette smoking and cannabis, both of which are habit-forming. Drugs such as heroin get such a grip on the body that if the person has to go without regular doses, he may develop **withdrawal symptoms** such as fever, sickness and severe cramp. People who reach this state are said to be **addicted** to the drug.

It's particularly easy to become dependent on alcohol. Such a person is called an **alcoholic**. What starts as a habit can quickly become an addiction. Once a person becomes addicted to a drug it is very difficult to give it up, as Figure 1 makes only too clear.

### 3 *It may injure the body by damaging the cells.*

For example, in a heavy drinker the alcohol goes to the liver and gradually kills the cells (see page 181). Cannabis is dangerous too: there is evidence that it damages the brain cells.

**Figure 1** An addict injecting himself with a drug: the start of a life of misery and maybe an early death.

# Mental illness

Mental illnesses develop when the brain does not work properly. Some are the result of accidents in which the brain is damaged, others are by-products of diseases such as syphilis; and sometimes a person is born with a mental disorder.

## Types of mental illness

Doctors recognise two main kinds of mental illness:

### 1 Neurosis

Neurotic illnesses are fairly mild and it's not normally necessary for the person to go into hospital. They often involve the person being obsessive about something. For example, he may have an obsession about being clean, or an obsessive fear of being shut into a small space such as a crowded bus. Such fears are called **phobias**. Usually the person realises he has a problem and wants to overcome it.

### 2 Psychosis

Psychotic illnesses are more serious and usually necessitate going to hospital. Often the patient does not realise there's anything wrong with him. He may think that everyone is getting at him, or that he is a famous character such as Napoleon or Hitler, and he will act accordingly. Violent crimes are sometimes committed by psychotic individuals.

There is much variation in the symptoms of mental illnesses and how long they last. For example, in **epilepsy** the patient suffers from occasional 'fits' which may be mild or severe depending on what kind of epilepsy it is.

In epilepsy and many other mental disorders the person may be perfectly normal at times when he is not having an attack of the illness. For example, there is a condition called **schizophrenia**. This word comes from Greek and literally means 'split mind'. A typical schizophrenic has two different personalities: a normal one and an abnormal one. Much of the time he behaves just like anyone else, but at times he becomes psychotic and his behaviour changes accordingly.

## Treating people with mental illnesses

Doctors who specialise in mental illness are called **psychiatrists**, and they can do much to help people overcome even the most severe illnesses.

One of the difficulties is knowing exactly what's wrong with the patient. This can sometimes be found out by recording the electrical waves from the patient's brain with a machine called an **electroencephalograph** or **EEG**. The waves are picked up by electrodes which are placed on the patient's head, and they are recorded on a roll of moving paper by a series of pens (Figure 2).

Everyone has the same kind of brain waves, but if the brain is not working properly the waves are abnormal and this shows up on the paper.

## What is a nervous breakdown?

This is a rather unscientific term, but it usually refers to a type of mental illness which is brought on by stress, worry or overwork. Usually the person is overwhelmed by a feeling of utter despair, a condition which is known as **depression**. Of course we all feel depressed at times, but the kind of depression which occurs in a nervous breakdown is particularly intense and may be accompanied by various obsessions and hallucinations. Sometimes the periods of depression alternate with periods of extreme elation.

Much can be done to help people through such an illness. With proper treatment the patient may be able to return to a normal life within a few months.

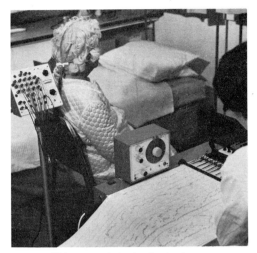

**Figure 2** This person is having her brain waves recorded by an electroencephalograph.

# Assignments

1 Each of the words in the left-hand column is related to one of the words in the right-hand column. Write them down in the correct pairs.

cannabis — stimulant
morphine — tobacco
caffeine — hallucination
barbiturate — anaesthetic
nicotine — pain-killer

2 Make a table summarising the effects, uses, and withdrawal symptoms if any, of these drugs: caffeine, alcohol, nicotine, valium and heroin.

3 Nowadays doctors try to avoid giving people barbiturates except in special circumstances. Why do you think this is?

4 Briefly explain each of the following terms: sedative, hallucinogen, neurosis, nervous breakdown.

5 Some scientists believe that caffeine is a harmful drug. They say that heavy coffee-drinkers can become addicted to it, and that stopping it can cause withdrawal symptoms such as a fall in blood pressure and headaches. How would you investigate the truth of this claim?

6 The number of people attending psychiatric clinics is much greater now than it was fifty years ago. Suggest reasons for this.

# Feeling, smelling and tasting

*We are constantly subjected to all sorts of stimuli. It is vital that we should be able to detect these stimuli and respond to them in the right way.*

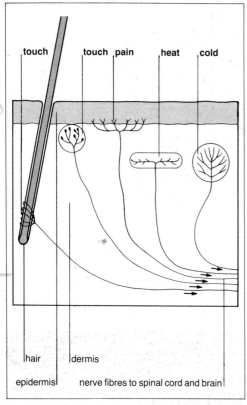

**Figure 1** This diagram shows the main receptors in human skin and the sensations they respond to.

*Labels in figure: touch, touch, pain, heat, cold; hair; dermis; epidermis; nerve fibres to spinal cord and brain*

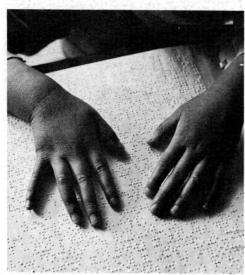

**Figure 2** A blind person reading braille.

## How are stimuli detected?

We have a number of different **receptors** or **sense organs**, and each is sensitive to a particular kind of stimulus: some respond to touch, others to light, and so on.

A receptor is usually composed of a group of **sensory cells**. These link up with nerve fibres which lead to the brain or spinal cord. When a receptor is stimulated, impulses are sent to the brain where they give rise to a corresponding **sensation**. For example, when you put your hand on something warm, impulses pass from certain receptors in your skin to the brain, giving rise to a feeling of warmth.

Now let's look at some everyday sensations and see how they are produced. We will start with the skin, whose receptors are shown in Figure 1.

## Touch

If you place the tip of a needle in contact with your skin, you will feel the sensation of touch. You get the same kind of feeling if you wiggle one of the hairs on the back of your hand. Our sense of touch is explored in Investigations 1–4.

The sense of touch is spread all over the skin, though some areas are more sensitive than others.

If you put on a hairy shirt, it tickles at first but gradually the sensation wears off until eventually you stop noticing it. This is because after a time the touch receptors stop sending impulses to the brain. This is called **sensory adaptation**. Why do you think it's useful?

Most of us don't use our sense of touch as much as we might. This is because we depend more on our eyes for finding out what's round about us. However, blind people develop their sense of touch to a much greater degree, particularly in their finger tips which they use for identifying objects and for reading braille (Figure 2 and Investigation 4).

## Pain

There are special receptors in the body which, when stimulated, give rise to the sensation of pain. In the skin these receptors take the form of free nerve endings. However, pain is also caused by excessive stimulation of other kinds of receptor. Pain also results from muscle spasms, as in cramp, and when an organ is short of oxygen. For example, the pain which is felt by people with heart trouble is caused by the heart muscle not getting enough oxygen.

People with certain kinds of heart trouble get pain in the left arm a long way from the heart itself. This is because impulses from the heart and the left arm go to the same part of the spinal cord. Pain which is felt some distance from its true origin is called **referred pain**.

People who have had a leg amputated often say that they can feel pain in the missing leg. This is called **phantom pain**. It is caused by the severed nerve healing and then sending impulses to the brain again.

## Temperature

In our skin there are receptors for telling us whether it's hot or cold. In fact there are two different receptors, one for detecting heat and the other for detecting cold.

Our temperature receptors are not very good at telling us what the actual temperature is. What they really do is to tell us when the temperature changes, and what we actually feel depends on how quickly the skin gains or loses heat (Investigation 5).

If we *feel* uncomfortably hot or cold we do something to remedy the situation; for instance if it is cold we put on more clothes. This helps us to maintain a constant body temperature (see page 178).

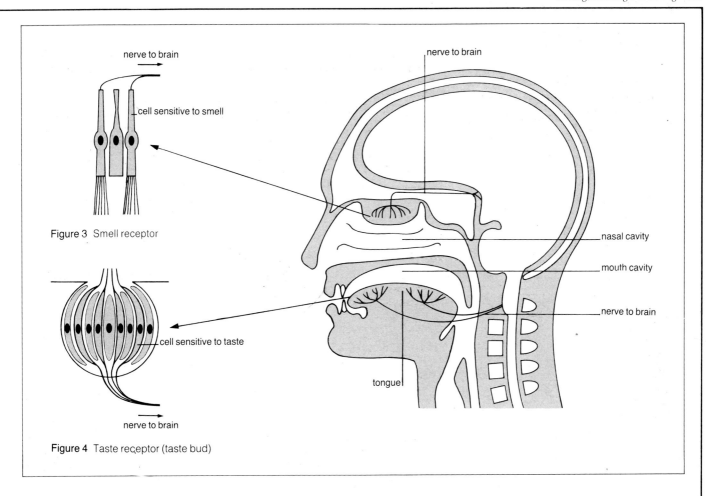

Figure 3  Smell receptor

Figure 4  Taste receptor (taste bud)

## Smell

The receptors responsible for our sense of smell are shown in Figure 3. They consist of groups of sensory cells in the roof of the nasal cavity. The cells have minute bristles like little brushes, and they are stimulated by molecules which float through the air and land on them. For something to be smelled, it must go into solution first, and so the lining of the nasal cavity is covered with a thin layer of fluid. Our nose is sensitive to many different smells, but our sense of smell is very poor compared with that of other mammals such as dogs. Smells which are far too faint to be detected by a man will be picked up by his dog.

## Taste

If you stick your tongue out and look at it in the mirror, you will see that it is covered with hundreds of short hair-like structures towards the front and wart-like bumps towards the back. These contain receptors called **taste buds**, which are sensitive to certain chemicals (Investigation 6). Each taste bud is a tiny flask containing about half a dozen sensory cells (Figures 4 and 5). As with the sense of smell, substances must be in solution before they can be tasted.

Experiments show that the tongue is sensitive to only four kinds of stimuli: sweet, sour, bitter and salt. Each of these stimuli is detected by a different part of the tongue (Investigation 7).

How can we explain the wide variety of taste sensations which we experience when we eat and drink? The answer is that our sense of smell also plays an important part: when you think you're tasting something, you're also smelling it. Have you noticed that if you have a heavy cold and your nose is blocked, your sense of taste is impaired as well as your sense of smell?

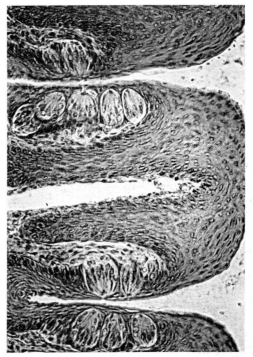

Figure 5  A small part of the tongue seen under the light microscope in vertical section. The flask-like structures are taste buds.

# Investigation 1

**Which parts of the skin are sensitive to touch?**

Work in pairs, one person acting as the subject.

1 With a fine ball-point pen, rule a grid of 25 squares on the back of your partner's hand: the sides of the squares should be 2 mm long so each one will have an area of 4 mm$^2$.

2 Obtain a bristle which has been mounted on a wooden holder.

3 Press the tip of the bristle against the skin in one of the squares until it just bends.

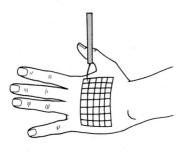

Does your partner feel the bristle?

4 Now touch the skin in the other squares, one by one.

In each case note whether or not your partner feels the bristle.

5 If some of the squares were insensitive, try touching them more strongly with a blunt needle.

Does your partner feel anything now?

6 Repeat this experiment on different parts of the skin, for example on the arm and leg.

Are some parts of the skin more sensitive than others?

How could you find out which parts of the skin are sensitive to other stimuli, such as pain and temperature?

# Investigation 2

**Getting used to a stimulus**

1 With a mounted needle, wiggle a hair on your arm or hand.

What does it feel like?

2 Keep wiggling the hair until you can no longer feel it.

Suggest a possible reason why the sensation disappears. Why is it an advantage to get used to this kind of stimulus?

3 Wiggle another hair and note the sensation.

4 Now rub the skin with your finger for about 15 seconds.

5 Wiggle the hair again.

Can you still feel it?

Suggest an explanation for what has happened.

# Investigation 3

**To find out the localising power of the skin**

Work in pairs, one person acting as the subject.

1 Subject: close your eyes.

2 Partner: touch the skin on the back of the subject's hand with the point of a fine felt pen.

3 Subject: without looking try to touch the skin in exactly the same place with the point of another pen.

How far apart are the two dots on the skin?

What does this experiment tell us about our sense of touch?

# Investigation 4

**Reading with your fingers**

Blind people read by means of 'braille' which was invented in France by Louis Braille. In braille each letter of the alphabet is represented by a character consisting of one to six dots embossed on thick paper.

1 Obtain a braille exercise card.

2 Without looking, put the tip of your finger on one of the characters. Do this with your non-writing hand.

How many dots is the character composed of?

Draw the arrangement of the dots on a piece of paper.

3 Now take your finger off the character and look at the dots.

Is your drawing of the dots correct?

4 Repeat the above with other characters, and try using different fingers.

Do your attempts at feeling the characters correctly improve with practice?

Are certain fingers better at it than others?

Which finger do you find the best? What do you think makes some fingers better at it than others?

Some blind people use another system called 'moon' which was developed by an Englishman called Dr Moon.

5 Carry out steps 2 to 4 on a sheet of 'moon'.

Are the characters easier to tell apart than the braille ones? If so, why?

What does reading in braille and moon tell us about our sense of touch?

What experiment could you carry out to investigate this further?

# Investigation 5

## An interesting aspect of our temperature sense

1 Obtain three bowls: the first should contain ice-cold water, the second hot water, and the third water at room temperature.

2 Place your left hand in the cold water, and your right hand in the hot water for one minute.

3 When the minute is up, place both hands in the room temperature water

What does each hand feel like?

What does this tell us about our temperature sense?

# Investigation 6

## Looking at the tongue

1 Look at the top side of your tongue in a mirror: if necessary shine a torch into your mouth, so as to show it up more clearly.

Can you see any projections sticking up from the surface of your tongue?

How many different kinds of projections can you see?

2 Swallow your saliva, and dry your tongue with a tissue.

3 Place a lump of sugar on your dry tongue.

Can you taste it?

4 Let your tongue get wet with saliva, and then place the sugar lump on your tongue again.

Can you taste it now?

What conclusions do you draw from this experiment about the way we taste things?

# Investigation 7

## Which parts of your tongue respond to different tastes?

All the materials used in this investigation must be clean, and the experiment should be carried out under close supervision.

Work in pairs, one person acting as the subject.

1 Your teacher will give you four small beakers containing respectively a dilute solution of sugar, salt, acetic acid (ethanoic acid) and quinine (a bitter substance). Each beaker should have a small paintbrush with it.

2 Subject: swallow your saliva and dry your tongue with a tissue, then stick your tongue out as far as you can.

3 Partner: draw the tongue in outline on a piece of paper.

4 With the brush put a little sugar solution onto different parts of the subject's tongue and note whether or not the subject can taste it.

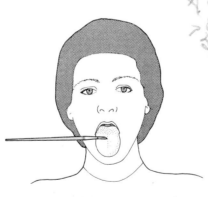

5 Put a cross in your drawing of the tongue to indicate the areas sensitive to sugar.

6 Subject: wash your mouth out with water, and dry your tongue again.

7 Repeat the experiment with the salt, acetic acid (ethanoic acid) and quinine.

Indicate in your drawing of the tongue whereabouts each substance can be tasted.

What conclusions do you draw from this experiment about our sense of taste?

# Assignments

1 What kind of receptors are stimulated when you:
a) move a hair on the back of your hand, *touch*
b) cut your finger with a knife, *pain*
c) read braille, *touch*
d) put clothes on, *touch*
e) place some food in your mouth? *taste*

2 What is meant by sensory adaptation? Give one example of it, and explain why it is useful. *Hair on cloths*

3 Suggest a reason why our sense of pain is useful.

4 Explain the difference between referred pain and phantom pain, and try to explain each.

5 a) Why do you think it is difficult to taste things when you have a cold?
b) It is said that dogs can taste their food as it passes down the gullet (oesophagus). How could you find out if this is true?

6 Occasionally people have been born without any pain receptors. Do you think this would be an advantage or a disadvantage? Explain your answer. *disadvantage*

7 A large number of volunteers were tested to find out the lowest (minimum) skin temperature that causes the sensation of pain. The results are shown below.
a) Explain in words exactly what the graph shows.
b) What conclusions can you draw from the results?

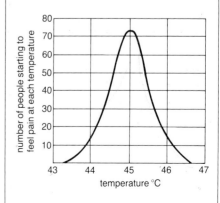

# A look at the eye

*Most people depend more on their eyesight than on any other sense, for it tells us so much about the world around us. The organ of sight is the eye.*

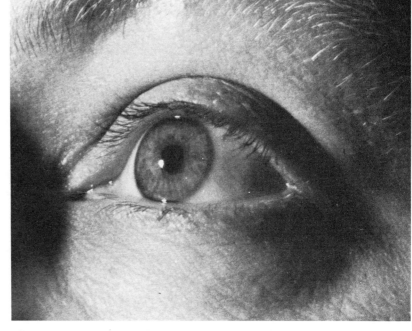

**Figure 1** The human eye.

## The external structure of the eye

Each eye consists of an **eyeball** which is held in a socket in the skull (Figure 2). The eyeball is surrounded by a thick coat (Investigation 1). This is transparent at the front, and white and opaque at the sides and back; it is called the white of the eye or **sclera**. The transparent front part is called the **cornea** and it is covered by a very thin membrane called the **conjunctiva** which is really part of the skin. Occasionally this gets infected and inflamed, resulting in a disease called **conjunctivitis** or **pink-eye**. Though very sensitive to touch, the cornea does not contain any blood vessels: it gets all its nourishment from the fluid inside the eyeball.

Beneath the cornea in the centre of the eye is what looks like a black hole: this is called the **pupil** and it leads to the inside of the eye. The pupil is surrounded by the **iris**, which is the coloured part of the eye.

The eyeball is held in place, and moved, by six muscles. A large **optic nerve** runs from the back of the eye to the brain (Figure 3). When you look at something, messages are sent off in this nerve and as a result you see the object.

**Figure 2** Photograph of a human skull, showing the eye socket (orbit). The hole at the back of the socket is for the optic nerve, which connects the eye with the brain.

**Figure 3** The eyeball in its socket. Only three of the six eye muscles are shown. The remaining ones are on the other side.

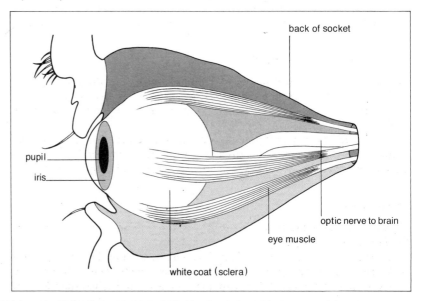

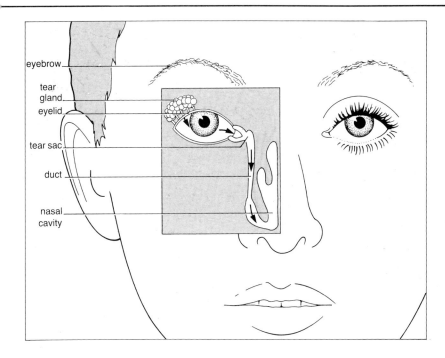

**Figure 4** This diagram shows the main structures that keep the eye clean. The arrows indicate the way tears normally flow.

**Figure 5** These diagrams show how the external eye muscles move the eye in its socket. Only two of the six muscles are shown here.

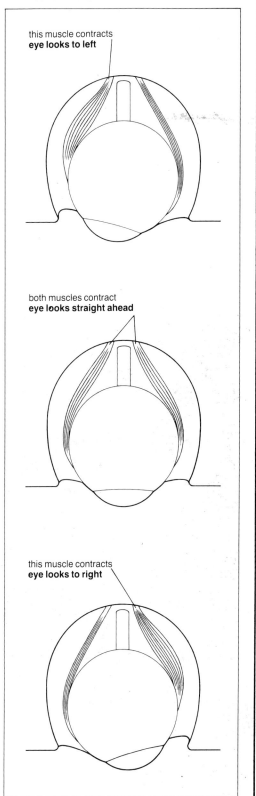

this muscle contracts
**eye looks to left**

both muscles contract
**eye looks straight ahead**

this muscle contracts
**eye looks to right**

## How is the eye protected?

The eye is a precision instrument and must be protected and kept clean. The main structures involved in this are shown in Figure 4. The surface of the eye is kept moist by a lubricating fluid produced by the **tear gland**. When you blink, the fluid is spread over the surface of the eyeball by the eyelids which act rather like windscreen wipers. The fluid contains a substance called **lysozyme** which kills germs. Surplus fluid drains into the duct in the corner of the eye and trickles down to the nasal cavity. When a person cries, so much fluid is produced that it cannot be drained away, and so it rolls down the cheeks as tears.

As well as spreading fluid over the eyes, the eyelids protect them. Thus we blink when something passes close by, and the eyelashes help to stop sweat and dirt running into the eyes. Infection of the eyelids can cause a **stye** in which the edge of the lid becomes red and sore.

Some animals, such as reptiles and birds, have a transparent shutter which can slide sideways over the eye. This **third eyelid** protects the surface of the eye while allowing it to see at the same time.

## How do we move our eyes?

The muscles which move the eyes run from the sides of the eyeball to the back of the socket. Between them, these muscles can rotate the eyes in various planes within their sockets. The action of two of the muscles is shown in Figure 5.

Human beings can only move both eyes together. However, certain reptiles, e.g. the chameleon, can move their eyes independently of one another. What are the advantages and disadvantages of being able to do this?

## Inside the eye

Figure 6 shows the inside of the eye. The two most important structures are the **lens** and the **retina**.

The lens is like a transparent bag. It is held in position by fine ligaments which run from its edge to the surrounding **ciliary body**. The eyeball in front of and behind the lens is filled with a transparent fluid called the **humour**.

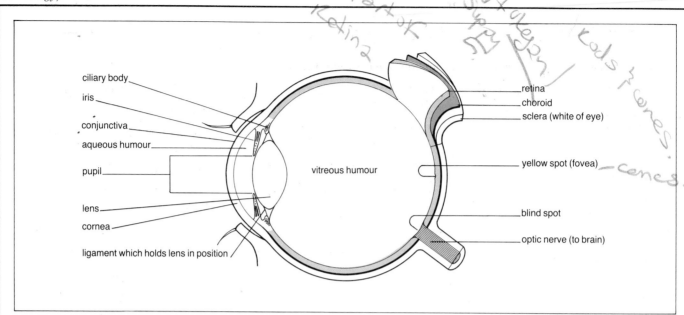

**Figure 6** The internal structure of the human eye. The eyeball is filled with fluid. The fluid behind the lens is like jelly; it is called vitreous humour. It presses on the wall of the eyeball, keeping it spherical. The fluid in front of the lens is more runny; it is called aqueous humour. It maintains the right pressure in the front part of the eye, and it nourishes the cornea which has no blood vessels of its own. Fresh aqueous humour is continually produced by the ciliary body and drains into small veins outside the eye. If the drainage canal becomes blocked, pressure builds up in the eye, a condition known as **glaucoma**. This can cause nerve fibres to die and can lead to blindness. It is treated by the use of special eye drops or an operation which reopens the drainage canal.

The retina is a delicate layer of tissue lining the inside of the eyeball. It contains millions of sensory cells which are sensitive to light entering the eye through the pupil: this is how the eye sees things. The part of the retina responsible for seeing things most clearly is a small area right in the middle, immediately behind the lens. This is called the **yellow spot** or **fovea**.

Beneath the retina is a layer of black tissue called the **choroid**. This absorbs the light and prevents it being reflected back out of the eye. There are numerous blood vessels in the choroid which supply the retina with oxygen and food substances.

The point where the optic nerve leaves the eye is called the **blind spot**. It's the only part of the back of the eye without sensory cells, and so it is incapable of seeing (Investigation 4).

## Controlling the amount of light that enters the eye

If a bright light is shone in your eye, a reflex action occurs (Investigation 3). The pupil gets smaller and this prevents too much light getting into the eye.

The opposite happens in the dark: the pupil gets larger, so more light can enter the eye.

These changes in the size of the pupil are brought about by the iris. In the iris there are muscles which can make it either constrict or open up (Figure 7). This is bound up with the way the eye works, which is the subject of the next Topic.

**Figure 7** Here you can see how the pupil responds to a dim and bright light.

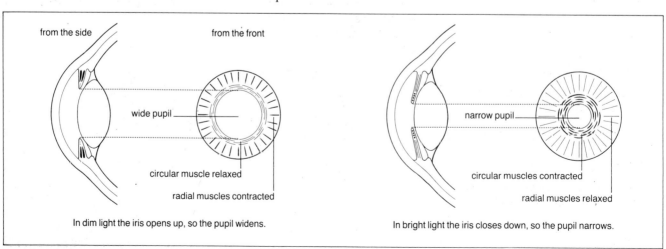

In dim light the iris opens up, so the pupil widens.

In bright light the iris closes down, so the pupil narrows.

## Investigation 1

### Looking at the outside of the eye

1 Look at one of your eyes in a mirror.

   Which structures in Figures 1 and 3 can you see?

2 Move your eyes up and down and from side to side so as to see the 'whites' of your eyes.

   What structures can you see running over the 'whites'?

## Investigation 2

### Dissection of the eye

1 Obtain a cow's or sheep's eye from the butcher.

2 Carefully cut away the muscles from the outside of the eyeball.

   What are the muscles for?

3 With scissors cut a hole in the side of the eyeball.

   What comes out of the hole?

   What effect does making the hole have on the shape of the eyeball?

4 Find the lens and the retina.

5 Cut the lens out of the eye.

   What does the lens feel like?

6 What other structures in Figure 6 can you see?

## Investigation 3

### The pupil reflex

Work in pairs, one person acting as subject.

1 The subject should close his eyes for ten seconds and then open them.

   What happens to his pupils when he opens his eyes?

2 Shine a torch in the subject's eye, and watch the pupil.

   What happens to the pupil?

3 The subject should look at an object in the distance and then nearby.

   What happens to his pupils when he does this?

## Investigation 4

### Demonstrating the blind spot

1 Look at the picture below: hold it about 10 cm from your eyes.

2 Close your left eye, and look at the house with your right eye.

3 Slowly move the picture away from your eyes, keeping your right eye focused on the house all the time

   What happens to the ghost as you move the picture away from you?

   How would you explain this?

4 Repeat the experiment with both eyes open.

   What happens this time?

   How would you explain the difference?

## Assignments

| | |
|---|---|
| optic nerve | protecting the cornea |
| tear gland | sensitivity to light |
| external eye muscle | sending messages to brain |
| retina | moving eyeball |
| iris | preventing too much light entering eye |

1 Each of the structures listed above in the left-hand column is responsible for doing one of the jobs listed in the right-hand column. Write them down in the correct pairs.

2 The pictures below show what a person's eyes look like if he moves them in certain ways. By means of diagrams like the ones in Figure 5, explain how each position is brought about.

3 Explain briefly what causes pink-eye and a stye.

4 If you look at something a long way off and then near at hand, your pupil gets smaller.
   a) How is this change brought about?
   b) Why do you think it happens?

A
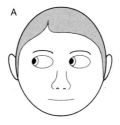

B
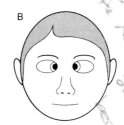

# How does the eye work?

*When you take a photograph, light enters the camera and is focused by a lens onto a light-sensitive film at the back. The eye works in the same kind of way.*

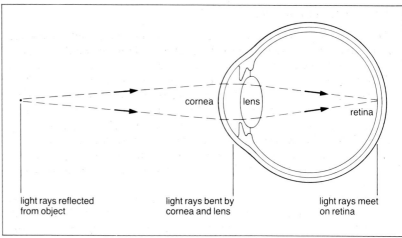

Figure 1 How the eye focuses on a dot.

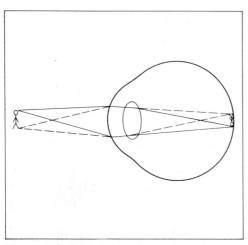

**Figure 2** This diagram shows how an image is turned upside down by the lens in the eye. The same thing is done by the lens in a camera.

**Figure 3** How the eye keeps an object in focus as it gets closer.

## What happens when we look at something?

Suppose you are looking at a dot in the distance. Light rays are reflected from it and enter your eye (Figure 1). The light rays are bent inwards as they pass through the cornea and lens, so they meet on the retina at the back of the eye. Here they produce an accurate image of the dot. *For the image to be clear and in focus the light rays must meet exactly on the retina.* The bending of light rays in this way is called **refraction**, and it plays a very important part in giving us good eyesight.

## Seeing things the right way up

Suppose you are looking at a person. Figure 2 shows how light rays reflected from the person pass through your eye. Notice that the rays coming from the head cross those that come from the feet. The result is that the image is upside down on the retina.

Why, then, don't we see everything upside down? The answer is that the brain comes to the rescue and turns the picture the right way up for us. An experiment has been done in which a man was given a special pair of spectacles which made him see everything upside down. After a while his brain made the necessary correction and he began to see things the right way up again.

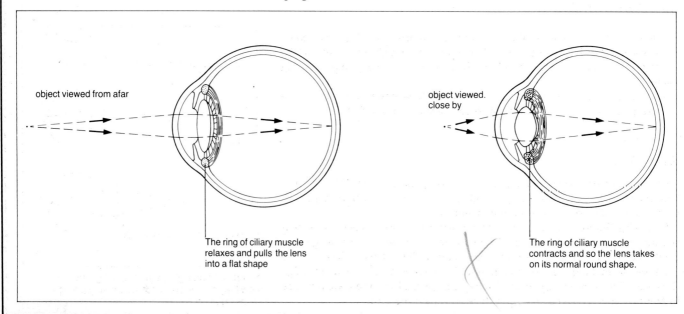

## Seeing things close at hand

Suppose a distant object comes much closer. If the eye did not adjust in some way, the light rays would meet *behind* the retina and the dot would be out of focus. However, the eye does adjust: the lens becomes rounder. This bends the light rays more, so that they meet on the retina as before (Figure 3).

This adjustment of the eye for looking at near objects is called **accommodation** and it is made possible by the fact that the lens is soft and can change its shape. The change of shape of the lens is brought about by the ring of ciliary muscles. When the muscle relaxes, the ciliary ring springs outwards and pulls the lens into a flattened shape. When the muscle contracts, the ciliary ring moves inwards, releasing the tension on the lens which consequently becomes rounder.

In old people the lens sometimes hardens, so accommodation becomes difficult and they find it hard to see things close at hand. This is why grandma holds her book a long way away when she's reading. However, the defect can be remedied by wearing glasses.

Much more serious is when the lens becomes opaque and won't let light through at all. This is known as a **cataract**. The only remedy is to take out the lens in an operation. The person must then wear very strong spectacles or contact lenses. In the latest operations the patient is fitted with an artificial acrylic lens.

## Defects of the eye

### 1 Short-sighted people

A short-sighted person can focus on things close to but not a long way off. This is due to the eyeball being too long, or the lens too strong, with the result that the light rays meet in front of the retina.

Short-sightedness is corrected by wearing glasses which bend the light rays outwards before they reach the eye (Figure 4A).

### 2 Long-sighted people

A long-sighted person can focus on things a long way off but not close to. This is due to the eyeball being too short, or the lens too weak, with the result that the light rays are directed to a point behind the retina. Long-sightedness is corrected by wearing glasses which bend the light rays inwards before they get to the eye (Figure 4B). The same kind of glasses are worn by old people whose lenses have hardened.

Some people have a defect of the eye called an **astigmatism**. This is caused by the cornea and/or lens being unevenly curved, so the light rays meet on the retina in one plane but not in another. This, too, can be corrected by wearing glasses.

Various tests can be carried out to find out how good your eyesight is (Investigation 1). They are normally performed by an optician.

## Seeing in depth

If you look at a solid object such as a book through only one eye, it looks flat. However, if you look at it through both eyes, it appears to have depth. In other words you see it in **three dimensions**.

So seeing things in depth depends on using both eyes. Each eye sees a slightly different aspect of the same object. In our brain the two images are combined to give us a single three dimensional view of the object.

As well as making the world look more interesting, this helps us to judge distances. For example, if you are driving along a road and there are two cars in front of you, you know roughly how far apart they are.

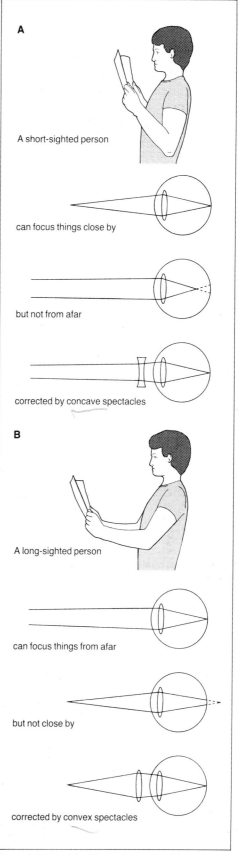

**A**

A short-sighted person

can focus things close by

but not from afar

corrected by concave spectacles

**B**

A long-sighted person

can focus things from afar

but not close by

corrected by convex spectacles

**Figure 4** Short sight (A) and long sight (B) and how they can be corrected by wearing the right kind of glasses.

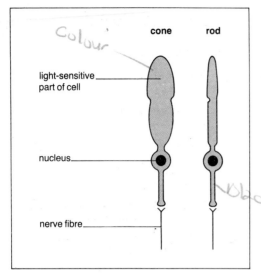

**Figure 5** The two kinds of sensory cell found in the retina. The cones are for seeing things clearly and in colour when it is light; the rods enable us to see things when it is dark or gloomy, but only in black and white.

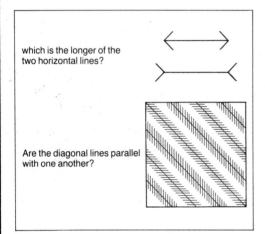

**Figure 6** Is seeing always believing? Here are two well known optical illusions.

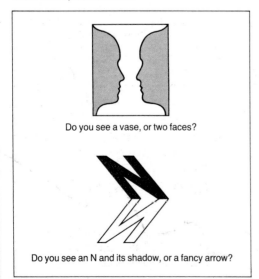

**Figure 7** What do you see?

## What does the retina do?

If you look straight at an object, and then look at it out of the corner of your eye, you will find that its appearance changes. From being clear and sharp it becomes indistinct and fuzzy. Also it is difficult to tell what colour it is.

How can we explain this difference? The retina is divided into two parts. When we look straight at something, we are using the central part immediately behind the lens: the **yellow spot** or **fovea**. This contains sensory cells called **cones** which detect things clearly and in colour. When, however, we look at something out of the corner of the eye, we are using the part of the retina further out towards the edge of the eye. This contains sensory cells of a different kind, called **rods**. They detect things less clearly and in black and white (Figure 5).

## Seeing in the dark

From what's just been said you might have got the idea that the edge of the retina isn't much use. However, it is good at seeing things in dim light (Investigation 2). You can prove this by looking at a faint star: it's much easier to see it out of the corner of your eye than by looking straight at it.

The reason for this is that the rods work better than the cones in the dark. They contain a substance called **visual purple** which is broken down by very small amounts of light. This causes them to send impluses to the brain. No sooner has the visual purple been broken down than it's re-made and is ready to be used again. This happens very quickly and is the reason why a flickering light can sometimes be detected out of the corner of the eye.

Visual purple is made from vitamin A, which is particularly abundant in carrots. A person who hasn't been getting enough vitamin A in his food has difficulty seeing in the dark, a condition called **night-blindness**.

Have you noticed that when you go into a gloomy room from bright sunlight you can't see anything at first but gradually things become visible? This is known as **dark adaptation.** The explanation of it is that all the visual purple has been broken down by the sunlight and it takes a while for the rods to re-make it and start working.

## How do we see colours?

The ability of the eye to detect colours is due to the cones in the central part of the retina. The colour of an object is determined by the wavelength of light reflected from it. Scientists believe there are different kinds of cones for detecting different wavelengths and therefore different colours. However, they only work when the light is good; in dim light you cannot see colours.

Not all animals can see colours. Dogs for example see everything in black and white. Certain people are completely colour-blind and cannot make out colours at all. Others cannot tell the difference between red and green, and this can cause difficulty when looking at warning signs. Various tests can be carried out to find out if a person is colour-blind (Investigation 3).

## Is seeing believing?

What we see depends not only on our eyes, but also on our brain. We have already seen that the brain turns images the right way up. What else does it do?

Briefly it does two things: it fills in gaps, and sometimes it distorts things. The way the brain fills in gaps is dealt with on page 196. The way it distorts things is shown by **optical illusions** (Figure 6). The image registered by the eye is accurate, but the brain plays a trick on us and makes the image misleading.

To some extent this is because we are used to seeing certain things, and are baffled by anything unusual. In other words we tend to see what we *want* to see, or are used to seeing. Figure 7 illustrates this nicely. Can you think of any other examples of this?

## Investigation 1

**How good is your eyesight?**

1  Hang a card on the wall on which there are two parallel lines one millimetre apart.

2  Gradually back away from the card until the two parallel lines appear as one, then stop.

   How far are you from the card?

   Compare your distance with that of other people in the class.

3  Hang an eyesight test card on the wall.

4  Stand facing the card six metres away.

   How many lines can you read?

   At a distance of six metres, a person with normal eyesight should be able to read as far down as line 6.

5  Repeat the eyesight test on each eye separately.

   Can you see better out of one eye than the other?

How does your eyesight compare with others in your class?

## Investigation 2

**Seeing in the dark**

Do this experiment in a dimly lit room.

1  Stare into a bright light for five minutes: a bench lamp will do.

2  Turn the light off.

3  Look straight ahead. Your teacher has placed a certain object at the front of the room.

   Write down the name of the object as soon as you can tell what it is.

   Tell your teacher when you have done this.

   How long did it take you to recognise the object?

   Compare your time with that of others in your class.

   What was happening in your eye:
   a) while you were staring at the bright light,
   b) while you were in darkness afterwards?

What have you learnt about the human eye from this experiment?

## Investigation 3

**Seeing colours**

1  Obtain two cards, one red and the other green.

2  Look at the two cards out of the corner of your eye.

   Can you tell which colour is which?

   How would you explain your observation?

3  Obtain a set of colour-blindness test cards. On each card there are numerous coloured dots. People with normal colour vision can make out certain numbers, whereas colour-blind people can't.

4  Test your eyes with the cards, following the instructions carefully.

   Can you see colours normally or are you colour-blind?

   If you are colour-blind, are you totally colour-blind or are you colour-blind only to red and green?

   How many students in your class, if any, are (a) totally colour-blind, and (b) red-green colour-blind?

People who are red-green colour-blind say that they have no difficulty telling whether the traffic lights are red or green. How would you explain this?

## Assignments

1  The picture below shows a person wearing 'half-moon' spectacles. What sort of eye defect do you think he has, and why are these particular spectacles useful to him?

2  What are the advantages of having two eyes rather than only one?

3  Explain the reason for each of the following:
   a) When you go into a cinema from bright sunshine, you cannot see the seats at first, but gradually they become visible.
   b) If you are trying to see a faint star in the night sky, it is better to look slightly to one side of it rather than straight at it.
   c) When it is getting dark at night, it is impossible to make out the colours of cars on the road.
   d) If you look at a cinema screen out of the corner of your eye, you can see it flickering.

   e) If both your eyes are open and you press the side of one of your eyeballs, you see double.

4  Nocturnal animals, i.e. animals which sleep during the day and come out at night, tend to have wide pupils and lots of rods in their retinas. Suggest a reason for this.

5  With a piece of straight-edged paper cover the top half of the following phrase:

   **HAPPY BIRTHDAY**

   Can you read it?

   Now cover the bottom half of the phrase. Can you read it now? Explain the difference.

# The ear and hearing

*The ear does two jobs: it enables us to hear and it also helps us to keep our balance. In this Topic we will look at the structure of the ear and the way it works in hearing.*

## The structure of the ear

People tend to think of the ear as just a flap on the side of the head, but there's much more to it than that, as you can see in Figure 1. The flap is simply a device for catching sounds and directing them into the hole just in front. The flap itself is called the **pinna** and it contains gristle to keep it stiff.

The hole leads into a short tube called the **external ear channel**. The skin lining the first part of the channel is hairy and secretes wax which catches germs and dust, preventing them from getting into the ear.

Stretched across the inner end of the channel is a tough membrane, the **eardrum**. On the other side of the eardrum is a chamber called the middle ear. This contains three tiny bones called the **ear ossicles**: because of their shapes they are called the **hammer** (malleus), **anvil** (incus) and **stirrup** (stapes). They run from the inner side of the eardrum to a membrane covering a small hole on the other side of the middle ear chamber. This is called the **oval window**, and it leads to the inner ear.

The inner ear consists of a series of chambers and canals filled with fluid. It is made up of two parts which, though connected, do quite different jobs. The two parts are:

### 1 The hearing apparatus

This consists of a tube called the **cochlea** which is coiled like a snail's shell. Inside the cochlea there are sensory cells which are connected to the brain by the **auditory nerve**.

**Figure 1** The structure of the human ear, slightly simplified.

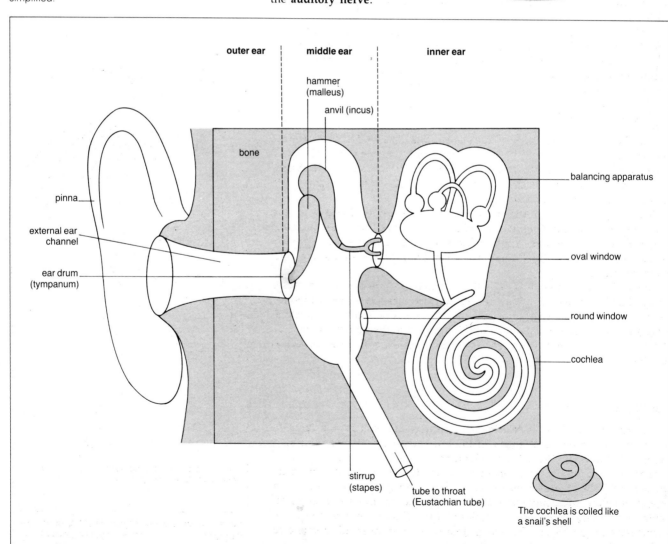

outer ear    middle ear    inner ear

hammer (malleus)

anvil (incus)

bone

balancing apparatus

pinna

external ear channel

oval window

ear drum (tympanum)

round window

cochlea

stirrup (stapes)

tube to throat (Eustachian tube)

The cochlea is coiled like a snail's shell

## 2 *The balancing apparatus*

This is dealt with in the next Topic.

The whole ear is embedded in the temporal bone which forms the side of the skull just above the pinna.

## Why do our ears go pop?

Suppose the pressure in the middle ear chamber was to suddenly increase. This would make the eardrum bulge outwards. Not only would this be painful, but it might even burst the eardrum. So it's important that the pressure in the middle ear should be more or less the same as the atmospheric pressure outside the eardrum (Figure 2). The structure that makes this possible is the **Eustachian tube**. This connects the middle ear with the throat and it allows air to get in and out of the middle ear.

If you go up in an aeroplane, the atmospheric pressure outside the eardrum falls. As a result, the eardrum bulges outwards. You can rectify this by, for example, yawning or swallowing: this opens the Eustachian tube and so equalises the pressure on the two sides of the eardrum. The result is that the eardrum springs back into its normal position, making your ears pop.

The reverse happens when the aeroplane comes down to land, or if you go down a deep mine in a lift. In this case the atmospheric pressure increases causing your eardrum to bulge inwards. You can rectify this by swallowing or yawning as before.

The Eustachian tube is, therefore, an important part of the ear. The trouble is that if you have a heavy cold germs may get up it into the middle ear. The Eustachian tube may then become blocked, and pressure may build up in the middle ear causing earache.

## How does the ear hear?

Suppose you are walking down the street and there's a loud bang. The noise sets off vibrations or sound waves which travel through the air in all directions, rather like ripples in a pond when you throw a stone in it. Within a fraction of a second the sound waves reach your ear, and the pinna directs them into the external ear channel.

Being rather small and pressed back against the side of the head, the human pinna is not much good at catching sound waves. However, the much larger pinna of an alsatian dog or a fox is more efficient, particularly if it's pricked up. Of course the human pinna can be improved by putting your hand behind it.

The sound waves now pass along the external ear channel to the eardrum. When they hit the eardrum they make it vibrate. This in turn moves the ear ossicles backwards and forwards, causing the membrane covering the oval window to vibrate. The vibrations of this membrane then move the fluid in the cochlea. This stimulates the sensory cells which send off messages in the auditory nerve to the brain.

## Getting used to sounds

If you are subjected to a continuous or repetitive noise, you soon get used to it – provided of course that it isn't *too* loud. In fact after a time you may stop hearing it altogether. We call this **adaptation**.

There are two possible explanations of adaptation. One is that after a time the sensory cells in the cochlea stop sending messages to the brain, even though they are still being stimulated. Another is that the messages go on being sent, but the brain takes no notice of them. Either way after a time the sound is no longer heard. This means that we do not constantly respond to background noises that do not really matter.

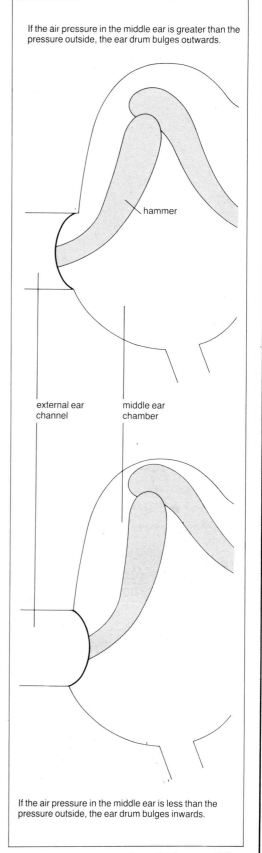

If the air pressure in the middle ear is greater than the pressure outside, the ear drum bulges outwards.

hammer

external ear channel

middle ear chamber

If the air pressure in the middle ear is less than the pressure outside, the ear drum bulges inwards.

**Figure 2** These diagrams show what happens if the air pressure is not the same on the two sides of the ear drum.

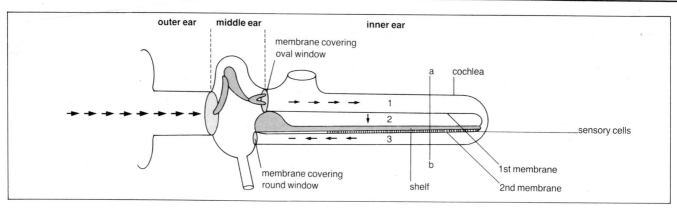

**Figure 3** In this diagram the arrows show the passage of a sound wave through the ear. The cochlea is shown straightened out and its three canals are numbered 1, 2 and 3.

## A closer look at the cochlea

Look at Figure 3. You will see that the cochlea is divided lengthways into three canals. These are numbered 1, 2 and 3 in the diagram. They are separated from each other by delicate membranes which can move up and down. When the membrane covering the oval window is pushed inwards by the stirrup, the fluid in the first canal is moved. This pushes the first membrane downwards, which moves the fluid in the second canal. This, in turn, pushes the second membrane downwards, which moves the fluid in the third canal. This finally presses on the membrane covering the round window, causing it to bulge outwards into the middle ear chamber.

How do these movements cause messages to be sent off in the auditory nerve? Figure 4 shows the sensory cells in the cochlea. You will see that they are attached to the membrane which separates the second and third canals. When this membrane moves up and down, it distorts the sensory cells, and as a result they send off messages in the nerve.

## Loud and soft sounds

If you play a note on a piano, its loudness depends on how hard you hit the key. This in turn determines the distance through which the wire moves up and down when it vibrates: this is called the **amplitude**.

The loudness of a sound is registered by the ear in the same way. Soft sounds vibrate the eardrum, and hence the cochlea membrane, only slightly, whereas loud sounds cause much greater vibrations.

There are many different ways of testing one's ears to find out how sensitive they are. Investigation 1 is a simple method.

## High and low notes

With a piano you make different notes by hitting different keys. The actual note, or pitch, depends on how rapidly the wire vibrates: this is called the **frequency**. Wires that vibrate at high frequency give high notes, whereas those that vibrate at low frequency give low notes.

Although the details are different, the ear works in the same kind of way. It has been found that the cochlea membrane is made of thousands of parallel fibres which run across it. The fibres towards the base of the cochlea are short and stiff: they vibrate very rapidly and are sensitive to high notes. In contrast, the fibres towards the apex are long and more flexible: they vibrate more slowly and are sensitive to low notes.

## What causes deafness?

There are several different types of deafness, depending on which part of the ear is affected.

People sometimes become temporarily deaf because they produce too much hard wax, which consequently blocks up the external ear channel. This is easily removed by the doctor syringing out the ears with warm water.

**Figure 4** This is a simplified cross section of the cochlea, cut in the plane a-b in Figure 3. It shows the three canals and the membranes in between. The canals are numbered as in Figure 3. The shelf is firm, and when the second membrane vibrates it distorts the sensory cells and impulses are sent off in the nerve fibres to the brain. The part of the cochlea where the sensory cells are located is called the **organ of Corti** after the man who first described it.

An explosion, or a blow on the side of the head, may rupture the eardrum, causing deafness. However, the eardrum usually heals quite quickly and then the person gets his hearing back.

A much more serious type of deafness is caused by connective tissue growing into the middle ear chamber. This prevents the ear ossicles moving, in much the same way as a piston may become seized up with rust. If nothing is done about it, the person may become permanently deaf. However, the person's hearing can sometimes be improved by wearing a hearing aid which amplifies the sound waves, and in severe cases an operation may prove helpful.

There are other causes of deafness. For example, it may be caused by damage to the cochlea. If a person is subjected to a repeated loud sound of a particular pitch, the sensory cells may become damaged, making him deaf to that particular note. It's said that some pop singers have become deaf to certain notes because of this (see page 395).

### How can we tell where a sound comes from?

Normally when you hear a sound, you know where it comes from. This is because we have two ears, one on each side of the head. Suppose you hear a noise from the right. Sound waves reach the right ear a fraction of a second before they reach the left ear (Figure 5). So impulses are sent to the brain from the right ear slightly before they are sent from the left ear. From this the brain knows that the sound must have come from the right.

Now suppose you can hear a faint buzz and you want to find where it's coming from. With two ears you can compare the loudness of the sound on each side of the head, and this will guide you towards the source of the sound (Investigation 2).

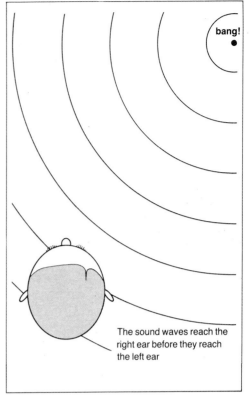

The sound waves reach the right ear before they reach the left ear

**Figure 5** Where did that bang come from?

## Investigation 1

**How well can you hear?**

This experiment must be done in a quiet room.
Work in pairs, one person acting as subject.

1 The subject should sit down and plug one ear with cotton wool.

2 Hold a ticking watch close to the subject's ear and gradually move it away until he can no longer hear it.

At what distance does the subject cease to hear the watch?

3 Hold the watch out of hearing range, then gradually move it towards the subject's ear until he can just hear it.

At what distance does the subject start to hear the watch?

Are the two distances which you have measured the same?
If not, which one is the furthest?
How would you explain the difference?

## Investigation 2

**Finding an object by sound**

This experiment is best done as a class with one person acting as subject.

1 Blindfold the subject outside the room.

2 Place a ticking clock somewhere in the room.

3 Bring the subject in and ask him to find the clock.
(Someone should stand close to the subject to prevent him bumping into the furniture.)

4 Watch the subject's head as he goes about this task.

In what way do you think the movements of his head help him to find the clock?

What do you think he would do if one of his ears was plugged with cotton wool? Find out by repeating the experiment with one of the subject's ears blocked.

## Assignments

1 If a person ruptures his eardrum he finds it difficult to hear until it has healed. Why is this?

2 Why do your ears go pop when you go up in an aeroplane?

3 What jobs are done by each of the following:
(a) the pinna, (b) the ear ossicles, (c) the round window, (d) the Eustachian tube?

4 People who are subjected day after day to a very loud noise of a particular pitch, may eventually become permanently deaf to all sounds of that pitch.
a) What is meant by the word pitch?
b) What do you think might cause this kind of deafness?

5 It is claimed that having two ears enables us to tell where a sound comes from. Devise an experiment to find out if two ears are really needed for this.

# How do we keep our balance?

*Figure 1 shows a tight-rope walker in action. How does he manage to stay upright and stop himself falling over?*

**Figure 1** How does this tight-rope walker keep his balance?

centre of gravity towards the front

centre of gravity towards the back

**Figure 2** The centre of gravity is the point through which the weight (mass) of a body acts. It is indicated by the arrows in these diagrams.

## Centre of gravity

Suppose you balance an empty tray on your finger, so that it is horizontal, like this:

Your finger marks the point where the weight or mass of the tray is concentrated. This point is called the **centre of gravity**. *The centre of gravity is the point through which the mass of a body acts.*

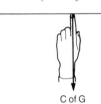

C of G

The mass of an empty tray is spread out evenly all over, so the centre of gravity is in the centre. But suppose there's a cup at one end. This will make the tray heavier at that end, so the centre of gravity will be shifted in that direction.

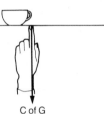

C of G

*So the position of the centre of gravity of an object depends on how the mass is distributed within it.* Figure 2 shows the position of the centre of gravity in a few well-known objects.

## Stability

Imagine a model man standing in an upright position. The centre of gravity is immediately above the part of his body on which the model stands, i.e. the feet:

C of G

With the centre of gravity in this position, the model stays upright and doesn't topple over: we say that it is **stable**.

Now suppose we tilt the model slightly to one side, like this:

C of G

On letting go, the model returns to its original position: in other words it remains stable.

*An object is said to be stable if it returns to its original position when displaced.*

But suppose we tilt the model a bit more, like this:

C of G

This time, instead of returning to its original position when we let go, it becomes **unstable** and falls over.

Why is the model stable when we tilt it slightly, but unstable when we tilt it more? The answer lies with the centre of gravity. Look again at the previous two diagrams. With a slight tilt, the centre of gravity still falls within the area of the body on which it was standing. But with a larger tilt, the centre of gravity falls outside this area. *When displaced, a body becomes unstable and is liable to fall over if its centre of gravity falls outside the area on which it was standing.*

## It's different with people

Now suppose our model is a real man and he leans over as in the last diagram. His centre of gravity now falls outside the area of his body on which he stands. However, in contrast to the model, he can stop himself falling over. This is because various muscles, particularly those in the legs, tighten up, and the body moves in such a way as to bring the centre of gravity back into its original position. So the body, having become unstable, becomes stable again.

This comes into many things we do. Even in a simple action like walking, the body constantly becomes unstable for a moment, only to regain stability immediately afterwards. This is even more true of the tight-rope walker in Figure 1. It also applies to many animals, particularly agile ones like the one shown in Figure 3.

## How do we keep stable?

Stability is maintained by a number of reflexes which are set off by the stimulation of certain sense organs. Let's look at these in turn.

### 1 *Eyes*
The eyes are more important in balance than you may think (Investigation 1). By looking at fixed objects such as the skyline and the sides of buildings, you become aware of the horizontal and vertical planes. This helps you to keep your body in the right position, and it explains why it's difficult to keep your balance in the dark.

### 2 *Pressure receptors*
If you're standing to attention and you lean forward, you can feel the extra pressure on the front of your feet. This makes you lean back again, so you don't fall forward. The feeling comes from receptors in the skin which are sensitive to pressure and they pass messages to the brain (Investigation 3).

### 3 *Stretch receptors*
When you lean forward you can also feel tension in the muscles at the back of your leg. All our muscles have special receptors inside them which are stimulated by being stretched. We call them **proprioceptors**. If a muscle is stretched, as often happens when the body becomes unstable, the body responds in such a way that the stretching is relieved.

### 4 *Ears*
Our ears contain a special balancing apparatus which is shown in Figure 4. It consists of two main parts: the **semicircular canals** and the **ear sac**.

Figure 3 A gibbon leaping from tree to tree in the jungle. This small ape is one of the most acrobatic animals.

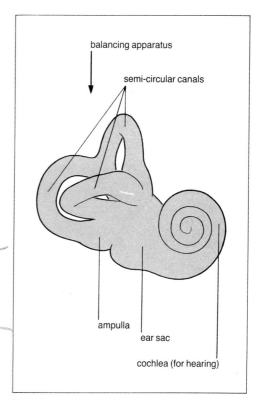

balancing apparatus

semi-circular canals

ampulla

ear sac

cochlea (for hearing)

Figure 4 This diagram shows the balancing apparatus in the ear.

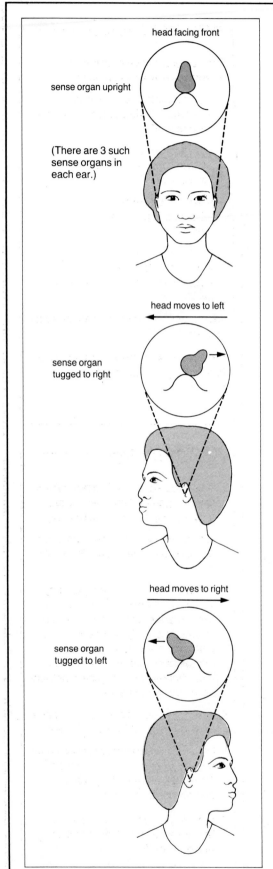

head facing front

sense organ upright

(There are 3 such sense organs in each ear.)

head moves to left

sense organ tugged to right

head moves to right

sense organ tugged to left

**Figure 5** These diagrams show what happens to our semicircular canal organs when we turn our head suddenly.

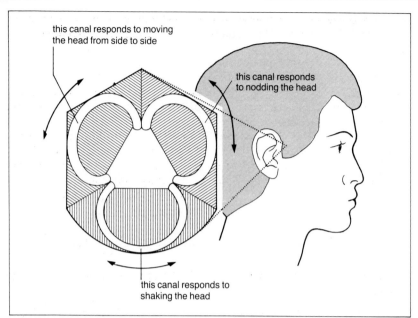

this canal responds to moving the head from side to side

this canal responds to nodding the head

this canal responds to shaking the head

**Figure 6** The three semicircular canals are at right angles to each other, so movement of the head in any plane can be detected by the sense organs.

## The semicircular canals

If you nod or shake your head you can feel your head moving. What's more you know if it's moving quickly or slowly, or if it changes speed. The organs which tell you this are the semicircular canals.

The semicircular canals are filled with fluid, and each one has a little swelling at one end called an **ampulla**. The ampulla contains a sense organ which sticks into it like a little finger. If you suddenly move your head in the same plane as the canal, the fluid tugs on the sense organ (Figure 5). As a result it sends messages to the brain, telling it that the head has moved.

We have three semicircular canals in each ear, and they are situated at right angles to each other. Each one is sensitive to movement in a different plane: one of them responds when you shake your head, another when you nod, and the third when you move it from side to side (Figure 6).

If you are spun round at a constant speed, as, for example, when you go on a roundabout, the fluid in the semicircular canal stays still relative to your

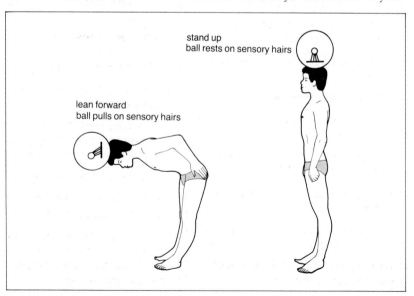

stand up
ball rests on sensory hairs

lean forward
ball pulls on sensory hairs

**Figure 7** These diagrams show what happens to the organs in the ear sac when we change the position of our head.

head (Investigation 2). However, when you stop, it goes on swirling round and round for a while. This stimulates the receptors and makes you feel dizzy.

*The ear sac*

Even when your eyes are closed, you know the position of your head, i.e. whether it's vertical or horizontal. We get this information from the ear sac just beneath the semicircular canals (see Figure 4).

The ear sac is filled with fluid, and it contains a tiny ball of chalk which is attached to a group of sensory cells. If your head is upright, the ball sits neatly on top of the sensory cells. However, if your head is bent forward, the ball pulls on the sensory cells (Figure 7). This causes them to send messages to the brain, telling it that the head is now in this new position.

## Investigation 1

**The importance of the eyes in balance**

1 Stand up with your eyes open.

2 Raise one leg off the floor.

   Do you find it easy to stand on one foot?

3 Now repeat the above with your eyes closed.

   Do you find it harder or easier to stand on one foot now?

4 Stand up with your feet together and your arms at your sides. Look straight ahead. Note the extent to which you sway from side to side.

5 Now close your eyes and continue to stand as before.

   Are your swaying movements greater or less than before?

   Why do you think the swaying movements occur?

   What part is played by the eyes in balance?

6 Sit down and close your eyes.

7 Place the heel of one foot on the toes of the other.

   Is it easier to do this when you're looking at your feet?

8 Put your finger on the end of your nose.

   Can you do this more accurately with your eyes open?

What do you think these experiments tell us about balance?

## Investigation 2

**To see how the semicircular canals work**

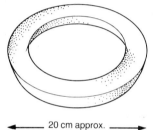

←——— 20 cm approx. ———→

1 Obtain a circular trough of the kind shown in the illustration: a circular cooking mould does nicely.

2 Half fill the trough with water and place it on the turntable of a record player.

3 Float a match on the water, and wait for it to be still: the match will help you to see which way the water moves.

4 Rotate the turntable quickly through a quarter turn.
   What happens to the water?

5 Spin the turntable slowly at a constant speed.

   What happens to the water (a) when you start spinning, and (b) once the spinning has got underway?

6 Stop the turntable suddenly.

   What happens to the water after the turntable has stopped?

What conclusions can you draw about the way the receptors in the semicircular canals are stimulated when the head moves?

## Investigation 3

**The part played by pressure and stretch receptors in balance**

1 Stand up with your feet together. Whereabouts do you feel pressure on your feet?

2 Lean forward as far as you can. Where do you feel most of the pressure now?

3 Now lean backwards. Where do you feel the pressure now?

4 Lean forward again. Which muscles feel tense? What movements stop you falling over?

What does this experiment tell us about balance?

What other part of the body, besides our feet and legs, helps us to keep our balance?

## Assignments

1 When you are sitting in a bus, which sense organs tell you that you are moving? Explain your answer fully.

2 Why do we need *three* semicircular canals in each ear, rather than only one?

3 When you wake up in the morning you know where your leg is in relation to the rest of your body, i.e. whether it is straight or bent or in a particular position. What sort of receptors give us this information, and what part do they play in helping us to keep our balance?

4 Why do you feel dizzy after you have been on a roundabout in a funfair?

5 Describe an experiment which could be done to find out how important the eyes are in enabling human beings to walk straight.

6 Why do you think people lose their balance when they have drunk too much alcohol?

# Introducing the skeleton

*Man, like many other animals, possesses a skeleton which forms a framework inside the body. The next three Topics are about the skeleton and its functions.*

Figure 1  The main parts of the human skeleton.

## The parts of the skeleton

You can discover a lot about the human skeleton just by looking at it (Investigation 1). It is divided into two main parts (Figure 1).

### 1 *Axial skeleton*

Structures which lie in the centre of the body, namely the skull, backbone (vertebral column) and rib cage. The ribs run from the backbone to the breastbone (sternum). The backbone itself is made up of a chain of bones called vertebrae (Figures 2 and 3).

### 2 *Appendicular skeleton*

Structures which lie on either side of the body, namely the limb girdles (shoulders and hips) and the limbs (arms and legs). The limbs are attached to the girdles, the arms to the shoulder girdle and the legs to the hip girdle. The

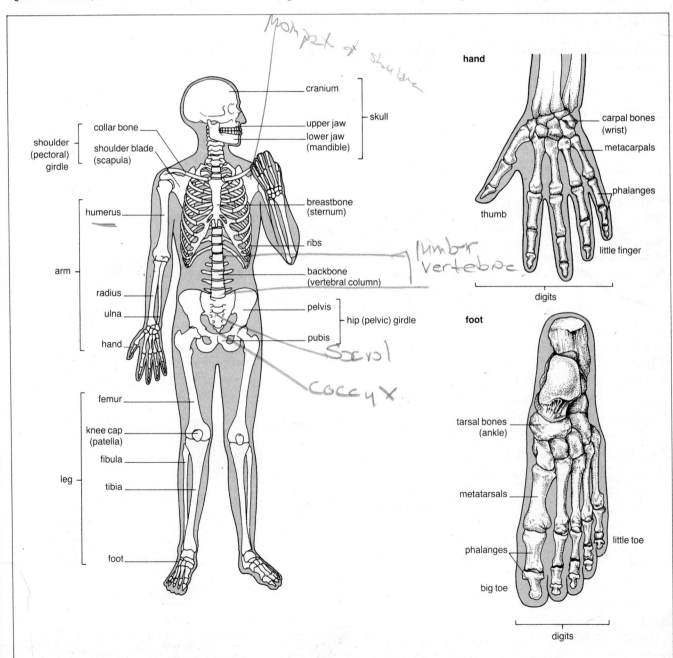

main part of the shoulder girdle is the shoulder blade (scapula). We have two shoulder blades, one on either side of the rib cage and they are completely separate from each other. In contrast the two sides of the hip girdle are fused together.

The various bones that make up the skeleton are connected in such a way that they can move, or **articulate**, with one another. Notice, for example, the articulating surfaces on the vertebrae in Figures 2 and 3. The vertebrae in different regions of the backbone have different structures and functions (see Table 1 overleaf). The bones are held together by **ligaments**: these are tough elastic strands which run from one bone to another across the joints. The most mobile parts of the skeleton are of course the arms and legs (limbs) and in particular the hands and feet.

## What does the skeleton do?

The skeleton does four main jobs:
1 **It supports the body**, giving it shape and form. Without it, the whole body would collapse.
2 **It protects the soft organs**. Thus the cranium protects the brain, and the vertebrae protect the spinal cord. The ribs and breastbone protect the lungs and heart, and the pelvis shields the reproductive organs.
3 **It makes blood cells**. Red blood cells, and certain kinds of white blood cells, are made *inside* certain bones.
4 **It brings about movement**. In doing this the skeleton works with muscles which are attached to it.

## What is the skeleton made of?

The skeleton is made mainly of **bone**, which is hard because it contains minerals. The main mineral is calcium, and this is why growing children need plenty of this element in their food. If you take the calcium out of a bone by treating it with an acid, it becomes soft like rubber (Investigation 2).

Although bone looks dead, it is really very much alive. It is a living tissue containing blood vessels and nerves, and special bone cells which make new bone and repair it when damaged.

Between the bones there is a softer material called **cartilage** (gristle). This acts like a shock absorber, preventing the bones from jarring when we move around. In this respect the cartilage discs between the vertebrae are especially important, and they also help to make the backbone flexible.

The skeletons of different vertebrates vary in the amount of cartilage they contain. In sharks and their relatives the entire skeleton is made of cartilage.

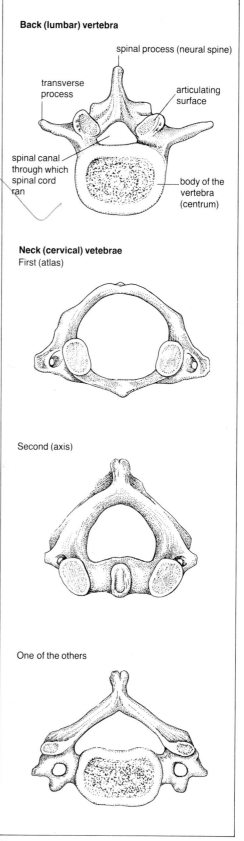

**Back (lumbar) vertebra**

spinal process (neural spine)

transverse process

articulating surface

spinal canal through which spinal cord ran

body of the vertebra (centrum)

**Neck (cervical) vetebrae**
First (atlas)

Second (axis)

One of the others

**Figure 3** Human vertebrae, seen end-on. At the top is a back (lumbar) vertebra in detail to illustrate the basic structure. Beneath it are three neck (cervical) vertebrae for comparison.

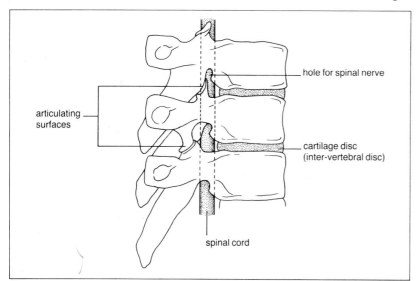

hole for spinal nerve

articulating surfaces

cartilage disc (inter-vertebral disc)

spinal cord

**Figure 2** Part of the backbone of a human showing three lumbar vertebrae from the side. Notice how the vertebrae fit together. The articulating surfaces of one vertebra fit against those of the vertebrae on either side.

**Figure 4** The structure of a typical bone can be seen in this diagram of the femur. The femur has to bear the mass of the body and so it must be strong. This is achieved mainly by the spongy bone: the fibres form a frame like the metal lattice in a crane.

In supporting the body the femur is like a crane

head

spongy bone

marrow cavity

compact bone

shaft

| Vertebrae | Structure related to function |
|-----------|-------------------------------|
| Cervical  | Small and with articulating surfaces to allow nodding and twisting of the head. Two small holes for arteries to the head. |
| Thoracic  | Long neural spines for attachment of upper back muscles. Long transverse processes for articulation with ribs. |
| Lumbar    | Large and stumpy. Neural spine and transverse processes for attachment of lower back muscles. |
| Sacral    | Fused into a single bone (sacrum) which is strong to help transmit forces from the legs to the rest of the backbone. |
| Caudal    | Reduced to small bones (coccyx) without a function in humans. |

**Table 1** The structures and functions of the vertebrae in different regions of the backbone.

**Figure 5** The skeleton of a rabbit.

## Inside a bone

If you saw a bone right down the middle you can see its inside (Investigation 3). Figure 4 shows the structure of a bone such as the femur. The outer part consists of dense **compact bone**. Beneath this at the end of the bone there is a criss-cross network of bony fibres called **spongy bone**. In the centre there is a cavity filled with a soft substance called **marrow**. Yellow marrow consists mainly of fat. Red marrow, which is found in certain bones such as the pelvis and ribs, is where blood cells are made.

## The skeleton of other vertebrates

Man is a peculiar mammal in that he walks on two legs: he is known as a **biped**. Most other mammals walk on all fours and are called **quadrupeds**. You might expect this to make a lot of difference to the skeleton. However, if you compare the human skeleton with that of a quadruped such as a rabbit, you find they are really very similar (Figure 5). The same bones occur in each, though their individual shapes are different. Other vertebrates have basically similar skeletons too, though there are individual variations. These can usually be related to the animal's way of life and how it moves (Investigation 4).

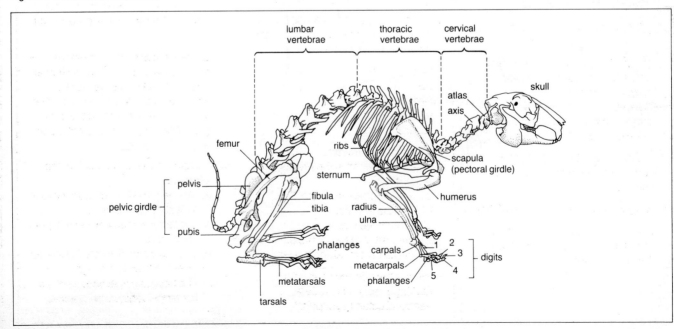

# Investigation 1

**Looking at the human skeleton**

1 Examine a human skeleton.

Which structures shown in Figure 1 can you see?

Which structures:
a) hold the body up?
b) are involved in locomotion?
c) protect the soft organs?

2 Compare the shoulder and hip bones.

What do they have in common?

In what ways do they differ?

Can you explain the differences?

3 Examine the hand and foot in detail.

Which structures shown in Figure 1 can you see?

In what ways are they suited to their jobs?

4 Examine a vertebra in detail.

Which structures shown in Figures 2 and 3 can you see?

What are the functions of the vertebrae?

# Investigation 2

**To find the effect of taking the calcium out of a bone**

1 Your teacher will give you a bone which has had all the flesh and marrow removed.

2 Obtain a 3 per cent solution of hydrochloric acid in which some salt has been dissolved.

3 Put the bone in the acid, and leave it for several days.

4 After several days lift the bone out of the acid with forceps, and wash it in water.

5 Dry the bone with a cloth.

Can you bend the bone?

What effect has the acid had on it? *Softening effect*

What is the function of calcium in the skeleton? *To keep it hard*

In what chemical form does calcium occur in our bodies?

How do we get the calcium that we need? *from food*

# Investigation 3

**Looking inside a bone**

1 Your teacher will give you a fresh bone which has been sawn in half down the middle.

Which structures shown in Figure 4 can you see?

What does the bone marrow feel like?

What do you think the marrow is made of?

How could you test your suggestion?

2 Now look at a dry bone which has been cut in half.

Where is the spongy bone and what job does it do? *at the ends. compact bone it makes it mass/bulk (?)*

# Investigation 4

**Looking at other skeletons**

1 Look at the skeleton of a four-legged mammal such as a rabbit.

Write down five ways in which it differs from the human skeleton, apart from its size.
How would you explain the differences in terms of what the skeleton has to do?

2 Examine the skeletons of other vertebrates such as a bird, frog and fish.

How do they differ from each other?

In each case relate the structure of the skeleton to the kind of life which the animal leads.

# Assignments

1 Each of the words in the left-hand column is related to one of the words in the right-hand column. Write them down in the correct pairs.

tarsals — hip
rib — wrist
pelvis — ankle
carpals — chest
femur — leg

2 Which of the structures in the left-hand column in the previous question:
a) are important in locomotion, *legs*
b) help us to write, *wrist*
c) protect the lungs, *ribs*
d) are part of the axial skeleton, *ribs*
e) play a part in raising the leg? *pelvis*

3 What is the common name for cartilage, mandible, patella, vertebral column, scapula? *gristle, lower jaw, knee cap, backbone, shoulder blade*

4 Most dogs enjoy the marrow part of a bone. Why is the marrow good for them? *Because it consists of fat and some red blood cells are made*

5 Someone has said that from the mechanical point of view the human backbone is like a skyscraper. However, someone else claims that it is more like the leaning tower of Pisa. Who do you think is right, and why? *Because it is straight when erect RATHER than does not lean but can bend because the bones are made*

6 Explain the reason for each of the following:
a) It is easy to slice through the skull of a shark with a knife. *softer*
b) Ligaments stretch when you pull them hard. *Because it*
c) A bone which is treated with acid eventually becomes soft. *Because it*
d) The head of a limb bone such as the femur contains bony fibres. *Because it has mass. To bear the full weight of the body which is delivered mainly by the bone*

# How do we move?

*One of the most important functions of the skeleton is to support the body and enable it to move. In doing this it works with the muscles.*

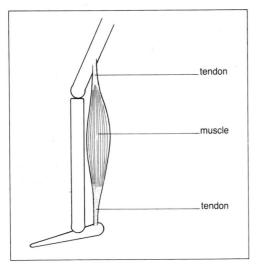

**Figure 2** A muscle is attached to the bones of the skeleton by a tough tendon at each end.

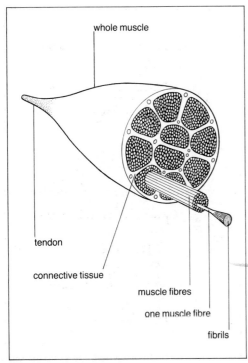

**Figure 3** A whole muscle is made of muscle fibres, which in turn are composed of very fine strands called fibrils.

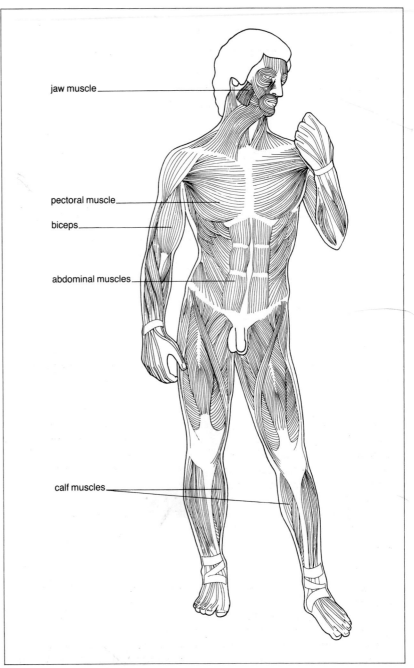

**Figure 1** The main superficial muscles of a human.

## Muscles and the skeleton

The entire skeleton is covered with muscles (Figure 1). This kind of skeleton in which the bones are situated *inside* the muscles is called an **endoskeleton** and it is characteristic of all vertebrates. If you buy a chicken leg, you can see that the meat (muscle) completely envelops the bone.

A structure like the arm or leg contains numerous muscles which move it in different directions (Investigation 1). Each muscle is attached to the skeleton at both ends by a **tendon** (Figure 2). The tendons are very tough and don't stretch much when they are pulled.

Each muscle is composed of hundreds of **muscle fibres** enclosed within a connective tissue envelope. With a pair of needles you can tease out the fibres (Investigation 2). Scientists have discovered that they are made up of even finer strands called **fibrils** (Figure 3).

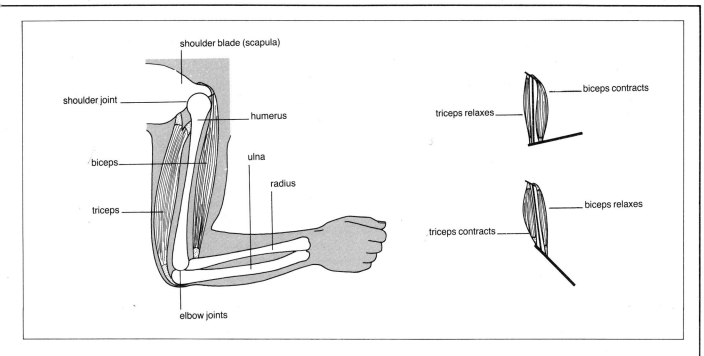

shoulder blade (scapula)

shoulder joint

humerus

biceps

ulna

radius

triceps

elbow joints

triceps relaxes

biceps contracts

triceps contracts

biceps relaxes

Every muscle has a nerve going to it. When it gets into the muscle, the nerve splits up into branches with supply the individual muscle fibres. The point where the nerve joins the muscle fibre is called the **nerve-muscle junction**.

When a message reaches the end of the nerve, it crosses the nerve-muscle junction and then spreads along the muscle fibres making them **contract**. If, for some reason, the nerve isn't working, or if the nerve-muscle junctions are blocked, the muscle cannot contract and becomes paralysed. Certain drugs block the nerve-muscle junctions: an example is curare, which South American natives used to put on their arrowheads to paralyse the animals they were hunting.

When the body is in a fixed position (as in Figure 1 for example), all the muscles are taut: this is called **muscle tone**.

## How do muscles move the skeleton?

To illustrate this, let's consider the arm. Two main muscles move the arm: the **biceps** bends it and the **triceps** straightens it (Figure 4). These two muscles produce opposite effects so they must not contract at the same time, otherwise the arm won't move at all. The nervous system ensures that this does not happen. Each muscle has its own nerve supply, so that when messages are sent to the biceps, telling it to contract, they stop being sent to the triceps, and vice-versa. Muscles which produce opposite effects are described as **antagonistic**.

Muscles such as the biceps which bend a limb are called **flexors**; those like the triceps which straighten it are called **extensors**. Of course we have flexors and extensors in our legs as well as our arms, and they play an important part in walking and running.

For the muscles to be effective, the limb bones must move easily against each other. This occurs at the **joints**.

## Joints

The structure of a joint is shown in Figure 5. It is enclosed within a tough **capsule**. Immediately beneath the capsule is a thin **synovial membrane** which secretes a fluid into the space inside. This **synovial fluid** serves as a lubricant enabling the two bones to slide smoothly against each other. It's like the oil between the moving parts of a machine.

**Figure 4** The biceps and triceps muscles move the arm at the elbow joint. These two muscles produce opposite effects. Such muscles are described as antagonistic.

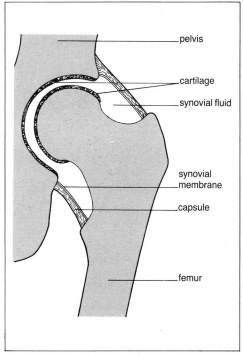

pelvis

cartilage

synovial fluid

synovial membrane

capsule

femur

**Figure 5** The structure of a typical joint is illustrated here by the hip joint between the femur and the pelvis.

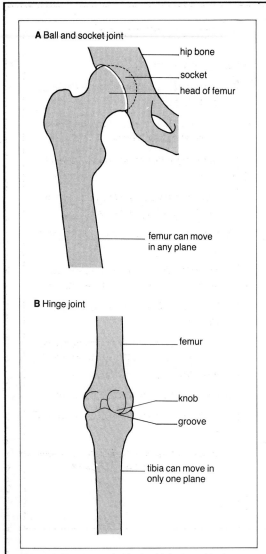

**A** Ball and socket joint

hip bone
socket
head of femur

femur can move
in any plane

**B** Hinge joint

femur

knob
groove

tibia can move in
only one plane

**Figure 6** The two main kinds of joint found in the human body.

**Figure 7** The three different kinds of lever found in the human body.

The ends of the two bones are made of cartilage. Being comparatively soft, this prevents jarring when the two bones move against each other.

Joints are weak points in the skeleton, and it is important that they should be protected. The knees are particularly vulnerable because of their exposed position and complicated structure. To protect them, they are covered by a small bone called the **knee cap**. Behind and in front of the knee cap there are cavities filled with synovial fluid which serve as a cushioning device.

If you move your leg around, you will notice that at the hip you can move it in any direction, whereas at the knee you can only move it backwards and forwards. This difference is due to the kinds of joints which are found in these two places (Investigation 3).

The hip joint consists of a ball at the top of the femur which fits into a cup-like socket in the pelvis. This is called a **ball and socket joint**, and it allows movement in any plane (Figure 6A). However, the knee joint is constructed differently: it consists of two knobs at the bottom end of the femur which fit into two grooves at the top of the tibia. This is called a **hinge joint**, and it allows movement in only one plane (Figure 6B).

The arm works on the same principle as the leg. What kind of joint do you think we have at the shoulder, and the elbow?

*Bones as levers*

Suppose you are trying to force open the lid of a box with an iron bar like this:

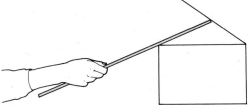

You are using the iron bar as a **lever**. *A lever is a bar which is turned about a fixed point.* The fixed point is called the **fulcrum**. In the lever illustrated above, there is a **load** (the lid) on one side of the fulcrum, and a force or **effort** is being applied by your hand on the other side:

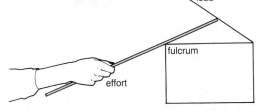

load
fulcrum
effort

Now some of our bones work as levers. There are three kinds of lever, which differ in the position of the fulcrum relative to the effort and load. All three are found in the human skeleton, and Figure 7 gives some examples.

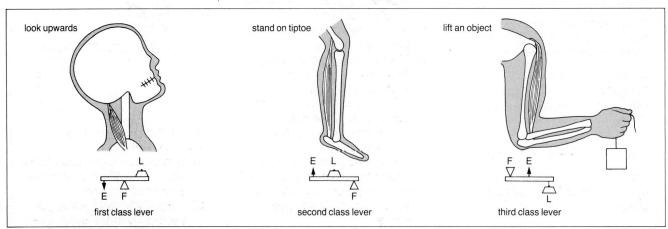

look upwards

L
E   F

first class lever

stand on tiptoe

E   L

F

second class lever

lift an object

F   E

L

third class lever

## Investigation 1

**Looking at muscles in relation to the skeleton**

Your teacher will provide you with a pig's trotter which has been obtained from the butcher.

1 Remove as much of the skin as possible.

2 Pull the various muscles one by one.

   What movement does each one produce?

3 Cut away one of the muscles from its neighbours, and follow it down to the bone.

4 Observe the tendon by which the muscle is attached to the bone.

5 Feel the tendon and test its strength by pulling it.

   How does it differ from the muscle?

6 How is the tendon joined to the muscle?

   Meat that comes from the *end* of a muscle is often tough and gristly.

   Why do you think this is?

## Investigation 2

**Finding out about the structure of a muscle**

1 Your teacher will give you a small piece of muscle from the leg of, e.g., a frog, rat or chicken.

2 Put the piece of muscle on a microscope slide.

3 With needles tease out the muscle fibres, and spread them out on the slide.

4 Add a drop of salt solution (0.75 per cent), and cover with a coverslip.

5 Observe under the microscope (low power).

   Can you see the individual muscle fibres?

   What do they look like?

   Can you see anything inside them?

   At a guess, how many fibres do you think the muscle possesses altogether?

   Why is it an advantage for the muscle to be made up of lots of separate fibres?

## Investigation 3

**Studying joints**

1 Move your arm about at the shoulder and elbow.

   How much freedom of movement is there at each of these joints?

2 Move your leg about at the hip and knee.

   How much freedom of movement is there at each of these joints?

3 Look at examples of the above joints obtained from the butcher.

   Move the bones so as to see what kind of movement occurs at the joint.

   How much freedom of movement is there?

   How does the amount of freedom of movement fit in with the structure of the joint?

4 Examine the structure of the joint.

   Which structures in Figure 5 can you see?

   What enables the two bones to move smoothly against each other?

   *the cartilage disk between them*

## Assignments

1 What job does each of the following structures do:
   a) tendons, *attach the muscle to skeleton*
   b) synovial fluid,
   c) nerve-muscle junction,
   c) spongy bone,
   e) inter-vertebral discs?

2 The following table gives the maximum speeds of four different animals in kilometres per hour:

   cheetah    70
   greyhound  64
   racehorse  64
   man        29

   Suggest reasons why man has the slowest speed of the animals listed.

3 Why is it important that tendons should not stretch when a muscle contracts?

4 The diagram, right, shows some of the muscles, bones and nerves in the human arm.
   a) What will happen to the position of the forearm if muscle X contracts?
   b) What happens to muscle X when muscle Y contracts? *It relaxes*
   c) What happens to muscle X when messages travel down nerve 1? *It contracts*
   d) When messages are travelling down nerve 1, what happens to messages in nerve 2? *messages stop*
   e) If the distance AB is 2 cm and AC is 30 cm, what effort must be exerted by muscle X to lift a bucket weighing 20 kg?
   f) If muscle X was attached to the forearm bone at point D, would it require more or less effort to raise the same load? Explain your answer.

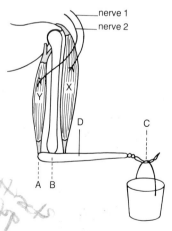

5 Look at the three kinds of lever shown in Figure 7.
   a) Give one further example of each type of lever, in either the human or some other animal.
   b) Suggest possible advantages and disadvantages of each type.

# Aches, pains and broken bones

*In this Topic
we will look at some
of the things that can go wrong
with our skeleton
and muscles.*

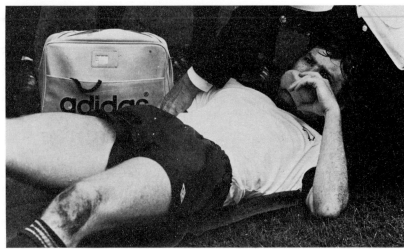
**Figure 1** An injured footballer about to be taken off the pitch.

## Broken bones

A broken bone is called a **fracture**. There are many different kinds of fractures, some more serious than others (Figure 2).

Suppose you break your arm. The first thing the hospital does is to take an X-ray. A machine sends a beam of X-rays through your arm: the rays pass through the skin and muscles, but not through the bones. Behind your arm is a photographic film which goes dark everywhere except where the bones are. So an X-ray photograph will show up the bones in the body, and any breaks can be seen clearly (Figure 3). In hospital X-ray pictures are taken by a specially trained person called a **radiographer**.

## How does a broken bone mend?

A bone mends in three main stages (Figure 4):

1 When the bone is fractured, blood vessels are broken, so much bleeding occurs. The blood congeals around the fracture, forming a clot. This may press on the tissues, causing a lot of pain.
2 Bone cells multiply and move into the blood clot where they lay down new bone tissue. In this way the two separated parts of the bone become joined together again (Figure 5). In the mending process, a ring of new bone tissue is formed round the fracture, so the mended bone is slightly thicker in the region of the fracture − rather like the joint which a plumber makes when he connects two lengths of pipe.
3 The new bone is now re-modelled: any unwanted bits are broken down and reabsorbed, so the final mend is almost undetectable in an X-ray.

For a broken bone to heal neatly, the two ends must be correctly positioned, which means that the arm must be kept still. This is achieved by putting the arm in plaster or holding it in position with a splint (Figure 6).

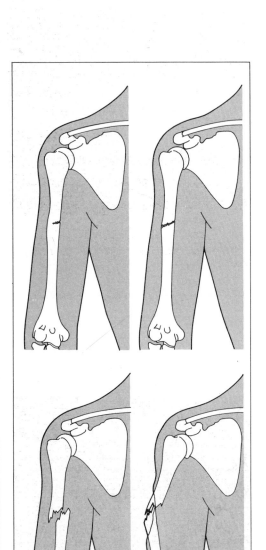
**Figure 2** Four ways the humerus can be fractured.

**Figure 3** An X-ray of a fractured arm.

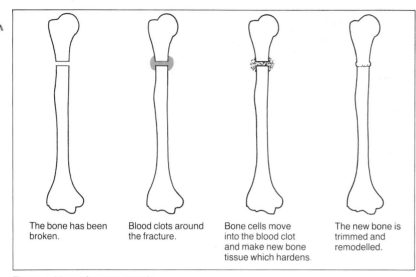

| The bone has been broken. | Blood clots around the fracture. | Bone cells move into the blood clot and make new bone tissue which hardens. | The new bone is trimmed and remodelled. |

**Figure 4** How a fracture mends.

A severe fracture may take many months to heal, much longer than it takes other tissues such as skin. This is because it takes a long time for bone to grow and harden.

## What is a slipped disc?

The cartilage discs between the vertebrae in the backbone are made up of two parts: the outer part is hard and fibrous, whereas the middle part is soft and rubbery.

Now these discs have to carry a heavy load. Sometimes the strain is so great that the outer part of the disc splits open, and the rubbery material bulges out (Figure 7). This may press on a nerve, causing a lot of pain. So the disc doesn't really *slip*: it bursts.

Whereabouts the pain occurs depends on which part of the backbone is affected. If the disc is towards the top of the backbone, the person gets neckache and armache; if it's in the middle, he gets backache; and if it's at the bottom, he gets legache. In this last case it is the sciatic nerve which is pressed and so it is called sciatica.

A person with a slipped disc in his back wears a special corset which holds the vertebrae still and thereby relieves the pain. If the disc is in his neck, he wears a special collar. If the pain is very bad, an operation may have to be performed in which the protruding part of the disc is removed.

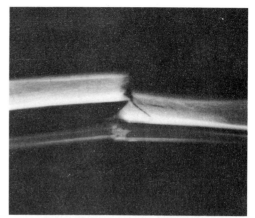

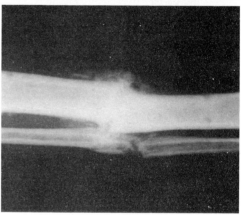

**Figure 5** The top X-ray shows a fractured tibia and fibula just after a car accident. The bottom X-ray shows the same bones six months later, after being splinted.

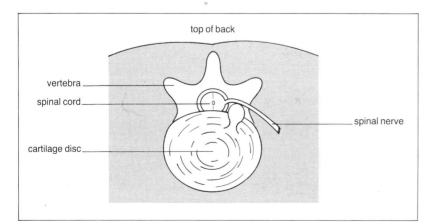

**Figure 7** A slipped disc. The cartilage disc has burst and a rubbery bulge sticks out of it as shown.

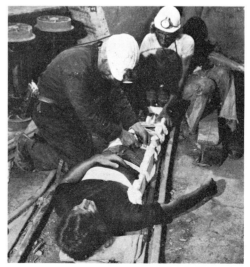

**Figure 6** This injured miner is put in splints before being moved.

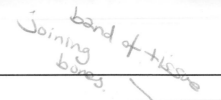

Joining
bones.
band of tissue

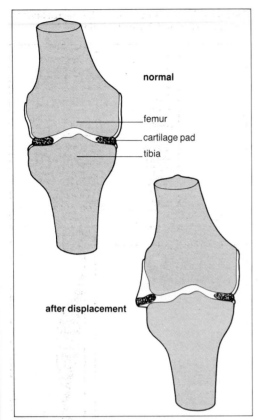

Figure 8  The knee joint has a pair of cartilage pads which sometimes get displaced.

Figure 9  An X-ray of a dislocated hip joint.

## Faulty joints

All sorts of things can go wrong with our joints. One of the most common mishaps is to wrench one of them, thereby tearing a ligament or tendon. This is called a **sprain**. A sprained ankle may be caused by suddenly twisting the foot inwards, which tears the ligament on the outer side. The same kind of thing can happen in the wrist.

You sometimes hear of footballers who need to have a cartilage removed from their knee. Since the knee has to bear a considerable strain, the knee joint contains a pair of cartilage pads, which serve as extra shock absorbers. Now occasionally one of these pads becomes loose and gets pushed out of place (Figure 8). This can be an awful nuisance as well as painful, and on occasions it may 'lock' the knee joint completely so that no movement is possible, highly embarrassing for a footballer if it happens in the middle of a game! The only answer is to remove the cartilage in an operation.

Sometimes a joint becomes swollen and painful because its lining gets inflamed and produces too much synovial fluid. This tends to happen in joints which are used a lot, particularly the knee and elbow. Tennis players often suffer from it, and it's called **tennis elbow**.

Just in front of the knee cap is a small sack containing synovial fluid. This, too, can become inflamed, particularly in people who kneel a lot: it's called **water on the knee**. Usually these conditions are put right by bandaging the joint and resting it.

Sometimes a person is involved in an accident in which the upper arm bone is forced out of the shoulder socket; in fact with some people this can happen remarkably easily. It is called a **dislocated shoulder**. The doctor can usually put the arm back by moving it about in a certain way.

Occasionally a baby is born with the head of the femur outside its socket. This is called a **dislocated hip** (Figure 9). The doctor puts this right by moving the legs about in such a way as to bring the head of the femur back into its socket. The child is then put in plaster with its legs pushed far apart for many months. This may run in families. Nowadays, a simple test is carried out immediately after birth on *all* babies to make sure their hips are all right.

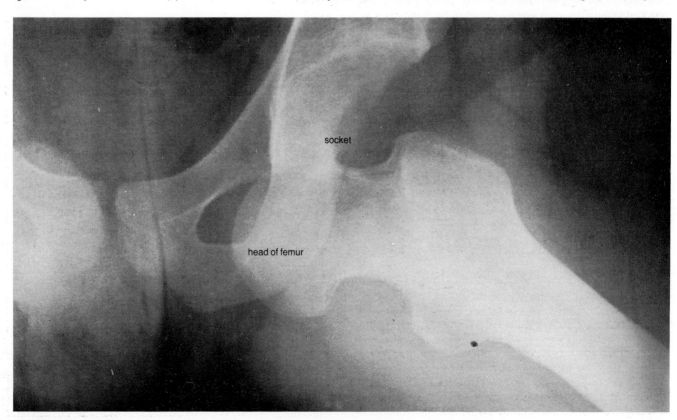

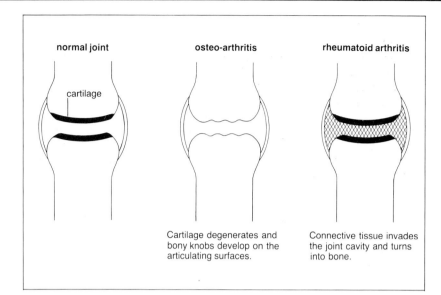

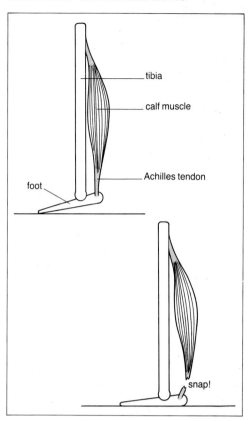

**Figure 10** These diagrams show the main difference between osteo- and rheumatoid arthritis.

**Figure 11** This person has torn his Achilles tendon, with the result that he can no longer stand on tiptoe.

## *Arthritis*

Many people complain of **arthritis**: the joints swell up and hurt, and movement is difficult. There are two kinds of arthritis (Figure 10):

### 1 *Osteo-arthritis*
This occurs mainly in elderly people and is due to wear and tear of the joints. The cartilage gradually breaks down so the joints lose their shock absorbers, and the bones no longer move smoothly against each other.

### 2 *Rheumatoid arthritis*
In this case connective tissue grows into the joints and eventually hardens, so the two bones become fused together, making movement impossible. This kind of arthritis tends to run in families and can start at any age.

Arthritis is a painful and crippling disease, but a lot can be done about it these days. For example, it is possible for the head of the femur to be replaced by a stainless steel 'ball', and the socket to be replaced by a plastic 'cup', so the person is given an artificial hip joint.

## *Muscle troubles*

Many people suffer from aches and pains in their muscles, particularly as they get older. The general name for this is **rheumatism** or **lumbago**.

Doctors aren't certain what causes rheumatism, but it may be caused by inflammation of the connective tissue in the muscle: the tissue swells up and presses on the nerve endings and blood vessels, preventing blood flowing through the muscle and thus causing pain.

Rheumatism tends to be brought on by cold and damp, and there's no doubt that warmth and massage can bring relief. Otherwise, not much can be done about it.

Everyone gets **cramp** from time to time. This is caused by a muscle spasm: the muscle suddenly contracts so powerfully that it hurts. Cramp is brought on by cold, or by using a muscle a great deal. **Stitch** is a type of cramp which occurs in the abdominal muscles, usually after a hard bout of exercise.

Finally, people sometimes tear a muscle or tendon in an accident. In severe cases the muscle or tendon may be torn right across (Figure 11). The two ends must be stitched together before they will heal.

In recovering from bone and muscle ailments people can be greatly helped by **physiotherapy**. This involves exercising the muscles and joints, and treating them with heat and massage.

## Assignments

1 Why is a broken arm usually put in plaster?

2 'My back is killing me.' Give two possible things that might be wrong with this person's back.

3 Why do footballers sometimes have a cartilage removed?

4 Explain each of the following: sprained ankle, water on the knee, dislocated hip, cramp, rheumatism.

5 People sometimes suffer from a painful knee because they spend so much time kneeling. What do you think causes the pain?

6 In an X-ray why do the bones show up but not the skin, connective tissue, blood vessels and nerves?

7 Old people tend to get shorter. Suggest reasons for this.

8 Why is it important that fractures should mend neatly?

# How do other organisms move?

*Organisms move in different ways. Here we shall look at just a few examples to gain some idea of the methods used.*

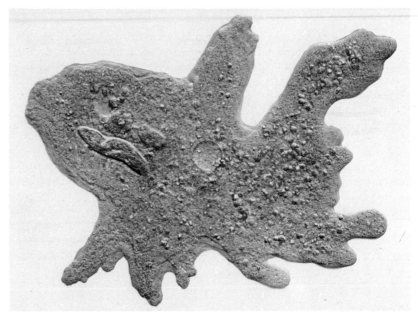

**Figure 1** This photograph of a live amoeba was taken down the microscope while the organism was moving.

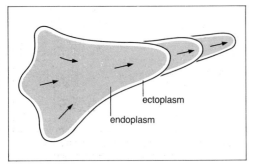

**Figure 2** *Amoeba* moves by the runny endoplasm flowing forward. At the front end the fluid endoplasm changes into the more solid ectoplasm, and at the rear end the reverse takes place.

## How does Amoeba move?

If you watch a live amoeba moving under the microscope, you will see that the runny endoplasm flows towards one end of the cell. As a result a bulge grows out. This is a **pseudopod** or 'false foot'.

Watching an amoeba, it looks as if the soft endoplasm is being squeezed into the pseudopod, rather like toothpaste being squeezed along its tube. In this way the animal 'oozes' slowly from place to place (Figures 1 and 2).

## How does Hydra move?

*Hydra* spends most of its time attached to stones or pieces of weed by its foot. But if the animal is hungry, or if there is something in the water which it does not like, it will go for a 'walk'. It does this by a strange looping or somersaulting motion (Figure 3). The body alternately stretches out, then closes up. This is brought about by contraction of its **muscle tails** (Figure 4).

The muscle tails are also responsible for the writhing movements of the tentacles which help the animal to catch prey.

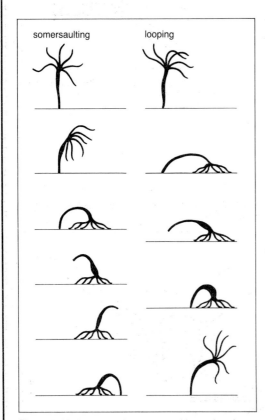

**Figure 3** *Hydra* moves by somersaulting or looping.

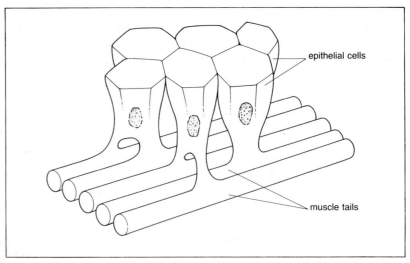

**Figure 4** The epithelial cells in *Hydra's* body wall are drawn out on their inner side to form contractile muscle tails.

## How does the earthworm move?

You can learn a lot about how worms move by watching one crawling on a piece of paper (Investigation 1). Bulges pass backwards along the body like waves (Figure 5). Where a bulge occurs, the bristles stick out. They enable the worm to get a firm grip on the sides of its burrow as it moves forward.

If you watch an earthworm moving, you will see that it constantly changes its shape: one moment it is long and thin, the next moment it is short and fat. These changes in shape are brought about by the muscles in the body wall which press against the fluid inside the body cavity. This is described as a **hydrostatic skeleton**.

The muscles in the body wall consist of numerous slender muscle fibres packed close together. They are arranged in two layers. In the outer layer the muscle fibres run round the worm in a circular direction: these are called **circular muscles**. In the inner layer the muscle fibres run longways: they are called **longitudinal muscles**.

To make the worm long and thin, the circular muscles contract and the longitudinal muscles relax. To make it short and fat, the longitudinal muscles contract and the circular muscles relax.

## How do insects move?

In common with other arthropods, insects have a hard cuticle which also serves as a skeleton. Because it is outside the muscles which work it, it is known as an **exoskeleton**.

Figure 6 shows how the muscles move the leg. At the joint there is a ball and socket **pivot** which works like a see-saw (Investigation 2).

The muscles which straighten the leg are called **extensors**. Those which

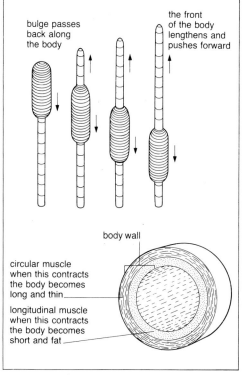

Figure 5 These diagrams show how the earthworm moves by bulges passing back along the body.

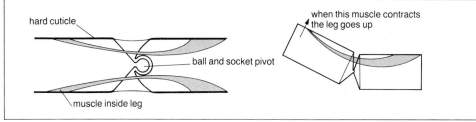

bend it are called **flexors**. These two muscles produce opposite effects: when one contracts, the other must relax, otherwise the leg will simply stay still.

Some insects, such as grasshoppers and locusts, can hop. Hopping is achieved by the third pair of legs. These are longer, stouter and more powerful than the others, and the extensor muscles inside them are particularly well developed.

The **wings** are worked by muscles inside the thorax. When the muscles contract, the wings go up and down (Figure 7). The locust beats its wings about 20 times a second, but certain midges can beat them over 1000 times a second.

Figure 6 These diagrams show how the muscles are arranged inside the leg of an insect and how they make the leg move.

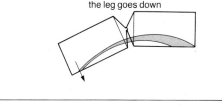

Figure 7 Muscles inside the thorax make the wings go up and down.

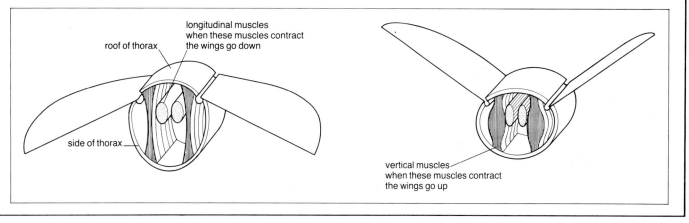

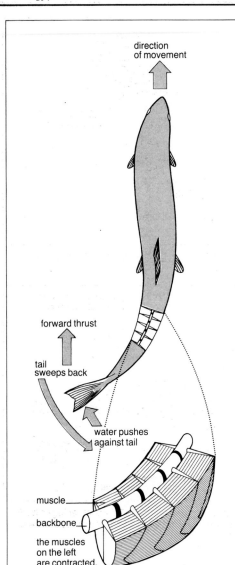

Figure 8  A fish swims by swinging its tail from side to side as shown in this diagram.

## How do fish swim?

You can discover much about how fish swim by watching one swimming in an aquarium (Investigation 3). You will see that it swings its tail from side to side. As the tail sweeps through the water, it drives the fish forward (Figure 8). The **tail fin**, with its large surface area, increases the forward thrust.

The movements of the tail are brought about by contraction of the **muscle blocks**, first on one side and then on the other. In Figure 8 note that the skeleton is internal to the muscles. We call it an **endoskeleton**; it is the kind of skeleton found in all vertebrates. Some fish can swim quite fast: speeds of over 60 km/h are quite common, and certain fish can move at over 100 km/h.

When a boat moves through the water it tends to rock about. In fish this is prevented by the fins, which keep the body steady, rather like the feathers at the back of an arrow or dart (Figure 9).

If you watch a fish swimming in an aquarium, you will see that it constantly changes direction, and sometimes slows down and stops. These steering and braking movements are achieved mainly by movements of the pectoral fins.

Most fish possess a swim bladder which keeps the body up in the water. This is a sausage-shaped bag full of air, rather like a balloon, which is situated towards the upper side of the body cavity.

Sharks and rays do not have a swim bladder, so their only way of staying up in the water is by swimming. If they stop swimming they sink to the bottom.

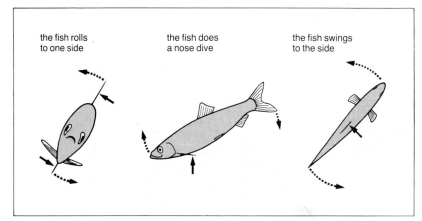

Figure 9  These diagrams explain how a fish is kept on an even keel when it is swimming. If the fish is displaced, the water presses against the fins (solid arrows). The fish then returns to its original position (dotted arrows). Three kinds of instability are shown here: rolling, pitching and yawing. Notice which particular fins stabilise the fish in each case.

Figure 10  The frog jumps by straightening its powerful back legs.

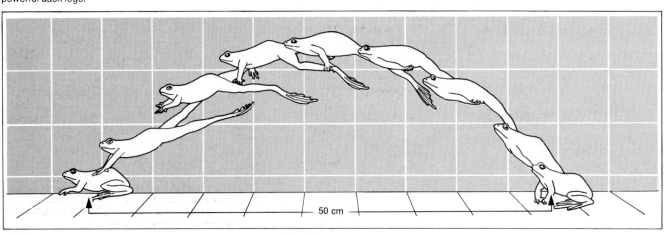

50 cm

## How do frogs and toads move?

Being vertebrates, frogs and toads have an endoskeleton. You can discover how they move by watching them in the laboratory (Investigation 4).

Figure 10 shows what happens when a frog jumps. Frogs are expert hoppers because their back legs are long and have powerful muscles (Figure 11). The same sort of action enables the frog to swim, and the webbed foot gives the frog a good push against the water (Figure 12).

Toads can hop too, at least some species can, but they are not as expert as frogs. They tend to walk rather than hop.

## How do birds fly?

Birds fly by flapping their wings, or by gliding. When fully spread out, the wings have a large surface area (Investigation 5).

The bird's wing is equivalent to the human arm. However, instead of having five equal fingers, there is just one long one. The others are small or absent (Figure 13). The 'thumb' forms the so-called **bastard wing**, which sticks out in front.

When gliding the wing acts as an **aerofoil** (Figure 14A): air flows over it in such a way that the pressure below the wing is raised whilst the pressure above it is lowered. The result is that the bird is given lift. The same principle keeps aeroplanes and gliders in the air. The bastard wing smooths the flow of air over the top of the wing, thereby preventing turbulence which could make it stall (Figure 14B). When gliding, the bird makes use of rising air currents to hold it up in the air.

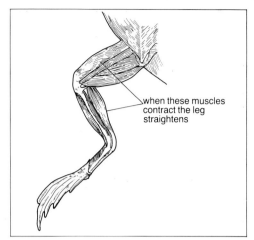

Figure 11 The leg of a frog skinned to show the muscles.

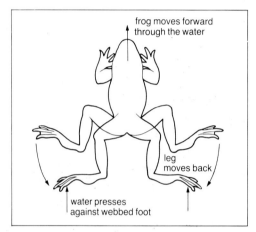

Figure 12 The frog swims by straightening its back legs and pushing its webbed feet against the water.

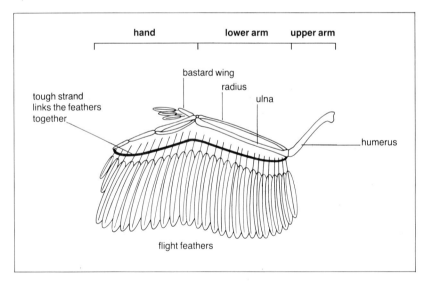

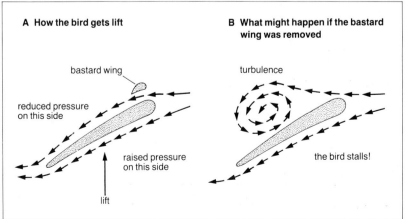

Figure 13 The structure of a bird's wing.

Figure 14 End-on view of the wing of a gliding bird. The leading edge of the wing is to the right, and the arrows indicate the air-flow.

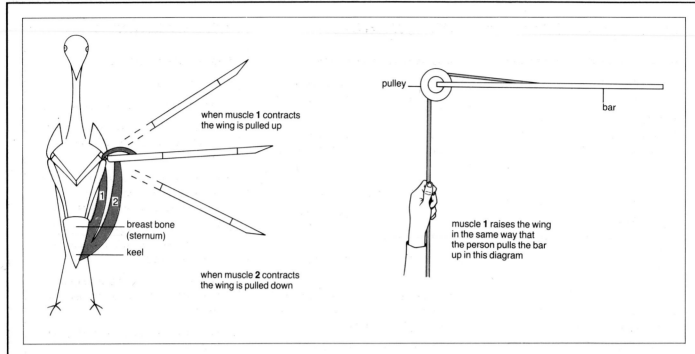

Figure 15  These diagrams show how the muscles work in pulling the bird's wing up and down.

The wings are operated by powerful **flight muscles**, which are attached to the **breastbone** (Figure 15). The breastbone has a deep keel to increase the area for the attachment of these large muscles. They make up the 'white meat' which is so good to eat in a chicken or turkey. There are two flight muscles. One pulls the wing down and the other pulls it up. The muscle which raises the wing has a tendon which runs through a hole at the point where the humerus joins the main skeleton. In pulling the wing up, this muscle works like a pulley.

When the bird flaps its wings, the feathers behave like the slats of a Venetian blind or louvre window: they close when the wing goes down and open when it goes up (Figure 16). In this way the bird is given plenty of lift as the wings are lowered, but it is not dragged downwards when they are raised.

Birds have several other features which help them to fly. They are streamlined and light. To make them light, they have **air sacs** inside their bodies and their bones are hollow. Their tail feathers play an important part in balance, and their muscles help to make them very agile. Can you think of any other ways birds are adapted for flight?

Birds are certainly expert flyers and can achieve high speeds. A racing pigeon can fly at 60 km/h for long periods, and swifts can reach speeds of over 150 km/h in still air.

Figure 16  These diagrams show what happens when a bird flies in a straight line.

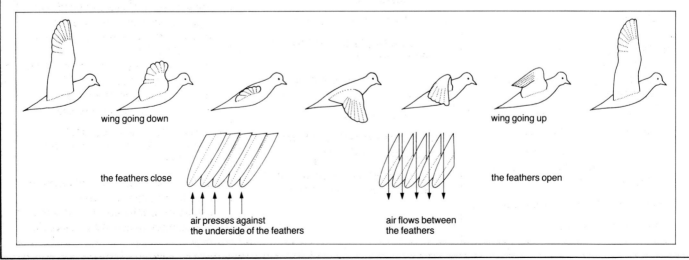

# Investigation 1

## Watching the earthworm moving

For this Investigation you will be given a live earthworm in a dish.

Handle it as little as possible, otherwise it will get tired and you will not be able to see much movement.

1 Put the worm on a piece of rough paper and watch it moving.

What happens to its shape as it moves?

2 Put your ear very close to the worm and listen carefully.

What can you hear?

Explain the sounds.

3 Repeat steps 1 and 2 with the worm on a white tile or a sheet of glass.

Does it move as quickly now?

Can you hear the same sounds?

Explain your observations.

What sort of muscles and skeleton would be needed to bring about the changes in shape which you have observed?

# Investigation 3

## Watching a fish swimming

1 Watch a fish, such as a goldfish or *Tilapia*, swimming in an aquarium tank.

2 As the fish moves along, describe the actions of the tail and the fins.

What makes the fish move forward?

How does it turn left and right?

How does it swim up and down?

How does it stop?

What stops it rolling around in the water?

3 Observe other actions which the fish performs: in particular watch the mouth and operculum.

Explain your observations.

How is the external structure of the fish suited to its method of movement?

# Investigation 5

## Looking at the bird's wing

1 Examine a bird's wing.

How are the feathers attached to it?

2 Lay the wing on a piece of squared paper, and trace round it with a pencil.

3 Count the number of squares within the outline of the wing, and work out its approximate surface area.

4 Now examine a wing of the same size from which the feathers have been removed.

5 Using the squared paper, work out the surface area of the featherless wing.

What is the surface of the wing with feathers?

What is its surface area without feathers?

By how many times do the feathers increase the surface area of the wing?

Why is this important to the bird?

# Investigation 2

## How does the arthropod leg work?

You will need a leg of a large crab such as the shore crab *Carcinus*.

1 With a pointed scalpel blade, cut a rectangular window in the largest section of the leg (the fourth section from the far end).

2 Remove the soft, white muscles from inside the leg, leaving the tendon-like processes to which they are attached.

3 With small forceps, grasp each process in turn and pull gently.

Do you find that one of the processes flexes the leg and the other extends it?

What kind of skeleton has the crab got?

How do the joints work?

# Investigation 4

## Watching a frog or toad moving

In this investigation you will be handling a live vertebrate. When you pick it up, carry it gently but firmly. Try not to frighten it. If you are squeamish or get into difficulties, your teacher will help you.

1 Place a live frog or toad in a cardboard box.

2 Watch it hopping or walking.

What part is played by its hind legs when it hops or walks?

3 Put your frog or toad in a tank of water.

4 Watch it swimming.

How does it differ from a human doing the breast stroke?

In what ways are the animal's hind legs adapted for swimming?

# Assignments

1 Explain the difference between an exoskeleton and an endoskeleton.

2 For the earthworm to move in the way it does (Figure 5), the body must be divided up into a series of separate watertight segments.

Why is this necessary?

3 A student observes an earthworm in the laboratory. He taps its head with a pencil. The worm immediately changes its shape from long and thin to short and fat.
a) Explain how this change in shape is brought about.
b) What use is this response in the worm's natural environment?

4 How do these animals propel themselves forward: a fish, a toad and a bird?

5 Look up the meaning of *antagonistic* muscles on page 225. Give examples of antagonistic muscles in *four* animals mentioned in this Topic.

# Chemical messengers

*Nerves provide one way by which messages can be sent from one part of the body to another. However, there is another way, and that is by means of glands.*

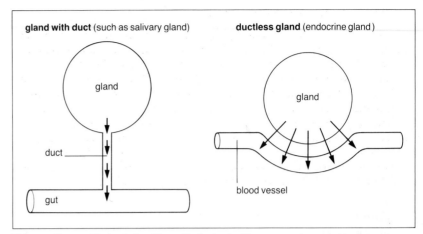

**Figure 1** The two kinds of gland found in the body. The arrows show what happens to the substance (secretion) which the gland produces.

## What are glands?

There are many glands in the body, and their job is usually to produce, or **secrete**, some kind of useful substance.

Many of our glands shed their secretion into a tube or duct which carries it to wherever it's needed. For example, the salivary glands secrete saliva into the mouth cavity via the salivary ducts (see page 93).

In contrast, we also possess a number of glands which shed their secretion not into a duct but into the bloodstream (Figure 1). These are known as **ductless glands** (or **endocrine glands**), and the substances they produce are called **hormones**.

## What do hormones do?

After being shed into the bloodstream, the hormone is carried to all parts of the body. It then produces an effect on certain organs. What the hormone is really doing is to carry a message from one part of the body to another, telling it to respond in a particular way. For this reason hormones are sometimes called **chemical messengers**.

Scientists have investigated the functions of different hormones by injecting them into animals such as mice, and noting the effects. Another approach has been to find out what happens when a particular gland is removed from the body.

The main ductless glands in the human body are shown in Figure 2. Each gland secretes one or more hormones, and their functions are summed up in Table 1. Many of them are discussed in detail in other Topics.

Most hormones produce their effects rather slowly. However, there is one hormone that acts very quickly: this is **adrenaline**.

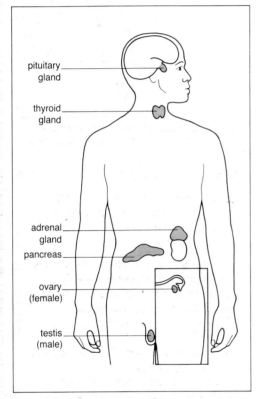

**Figure 2** The main ductless (endocrine) glands in the human body.

**Table 1** Summary of the human body's main hormone-producing glands and their secretions.

| Endocrine Gland | Hormone | Function |
| --- | --- | --- |
| Thyroid | Thyroxine | Controls the metabolic rate |
| Adrenals | Adrenaline | Prepares the body for action |
| Pancreas | Insulin | Regulates the amount of sugar in the blood |
| Ovaries | Female sex hormones | Control sexual development |
| Testes | Male sex hormones | Control sexual development |
| Pituitary | Growth hormone | Speeds up growth |
| | Thyroid-stimulating hormone | Stimulates the thyroid gland to secrete thyroxine |
| | Gonad-stimulating hormone | Stimulate the gonads (ovaries and testes) to secrete sex hormones |

## Adrenaline, the emergency hormone

Have you ever had that sinking feeling just before an important game of football, or an examination? The whole body tenses up, the heart beats faster and we feel ready for action. This effect is brought about by adrenaline.

Adrenaline is secreted by the **adrenal glands**, which are situated close to the kidneys. As with other ductless glands, the hormone passes straight into the bloodstream and is then carried all round the body. The cells respond to it by using up more oxygen and releasing more energy. At the same time the heart beats more quickly and blood is diverted from the less important organs to the really important ones such as the muscles and brain (Figure 3). The overall effect is to prepare the body for an emergency. For this reason adrenaline has been described as the fight or flight hormone.

## The pituitary, master gland

It's obviously important that the right quantity of hormones should be produced at all times. What tells a gland how much hormone it should secrete? The answer in many cases is the **pituitary gland**. This produces hormones which stimulate other glands to produce their secretions. For example, one of the pituitary hormones stimulates the thyroid gland to secrete thyroxine (page 245), and others stimulate the gonads (ovaries and testes) to secrete sex hormones. Because it controls the other glands, the pituitary is sometimes called the **master gland**. This is an important aspect of **homeostasis**, which is explained fully on page 244.

## Thyroxine

Despite the controlling influence of the pituitary gland, things sometimes go wrong and either too much or too little of a hormone is produced.

Take the thyroid gland for example. Some people have a thyroid gland which secretes too much thyroxine. As a result metabolism speeds up, and the person becomes thin, excitable and over-active. The eyes protrude and the thyroid gland swells up, giving a condition called **goitre** (Figure 4A). The person can be cured by removing part of the thyroid in an operation or by destroying some of the thyroid cells by radiation treatment.

Some people have a thyroid gland which does not secrete enough thyroxine. In this case metabolism slows down, and the person becomes fat and sluggish (Figure 4B). The person can be cured by being given doses of thyroxine by mouth or by injection.

If a child is not producing enough thyroxine, growth is slowed down and if nothing is done he may become mentally retarded. This is called **cretinism**.

Thyroxine contains iodine which is normally present in the diet. If drinking water lacks iodine, goitre or cretinism may result (see page 77).

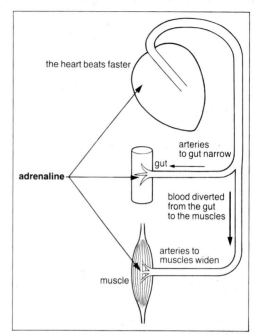

**Figure 3** This diagram shows how the hormone adrenaline affects the circulation in an emergency.

## Assignments

1  Ductless glands such as the thyroid contain a large number of capillaries which are located close to the cells. Why do you think this is?

2  If necessary use the index to answer this question. The pancreas is made up of two parts: part of it secretes insulin and part of it secretes pancreatic juice.
   a) Which part is functioning as a ductless gland?
   b) What is insulin and what effect does it have in the body?
   c) What does pancreatic juice contain?
   d) Where does pancreatic juice go?

3  In Table 1, which hormone:
   a) makes a person more active,
   b) causes the male to start producing sperms,
   c) causes a sinking feeling in the stomach,
   d) is produced by a gland in the neck,
   e) causes breasts to develop in the female?

4  Nerves and ductless glands both provide a way of sending messages from one part of the body to another.

   Write down four differences between the two systems.

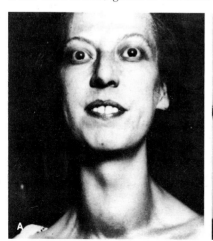 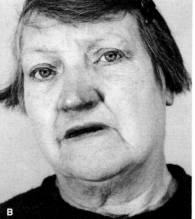

**Figure 4**  A:  the effect of an over-active thyroid.   B:  the effect of an under-active thyroid.

# How do plants respond to stimuli?

*The leaf or stem of a plant does not normally react when you touch it. This might suggest that plants do not respond to stimuli. However they do respond, though more slowly than animals, and in a different way.*

**Figure 1** These seedlings were lit for several days from the right-hand side.

## Growth responses

Plants don't respond to stimuli by moving from one place to another. Instead they normally respond by growing in a particular direction. Such growth responses are called **tropisms**. They are much slower and longer-lasting than the responses given by animals.

Plants respond to three main kinds of stimuli: light, gravity and touch. Let's look at each in turn.

## Light

Look at Figure 1. This shows the effect of lighting some seedlings from one side. This is called **unilateral** stimulation. The seedlings have bent over towards the light. Most plants respond to light in this way, and it ensures that the leaves get plenty of light for photosynthesis. A growth response to light is called **phototropism**. A structure such as a shoot which grows *towards* light is said to be *positively phototropic*.

How is this response brought about? A simple experiment helps us to see how (Investigation 1). A shoot has its tip covered with a little foil cap, and is then lit from one side. Instead of bending towards the light, it grows straight up (Figure 2).

It seems that normally the tip receives the light stimulus, but the bending itself occurs *behind* the tip. This suggests that some kind of message is sent from the tip to the part of the shoot a little further back.

On pages 256–7 some experiments are described which show that a shoot is made to grow by a hormone called **auxin** produced in the tip: the auxin passes down the shoot causing the cells behind the tip to expand. We can explain the shoot's response to light by suggesting that when the shoot is lit from one side more auxin gathers on the dark side than on the light side, so the dark side grows faster.

An experiment can be done to test this idea (Figure 3). The tip of a shoot is cut off and placed on a block of agar jelly which is divided by a thin partition into two halves. The tip is then lit from the right. After a while, the light is turned off and the agar block is placed on the top of the cut shoot. The result is that the shoot bends over to the right.

How can we explain this result? It seems that more auxin from the tip gets into the left-hand side of the agar block than into the right-hand side. So when it is placed on the cut shoot it causes more growth on the left-hand side.

These and other experiments all point to the same conclusion: *lighting a shoot from one side causes more auxin to be present on the dark side than on the light side and this makes the shoot bend towards the light* (Figure 4).

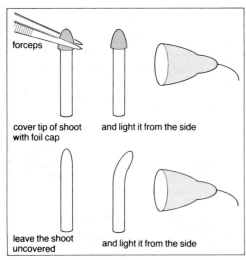

forceps

cover tip of shoot with foil cap — and light it from the side

leave the shoot uncovered — and light it from the side

**Figure 2** An experiment to find out if covering the tip of a shoot affects its response to light.

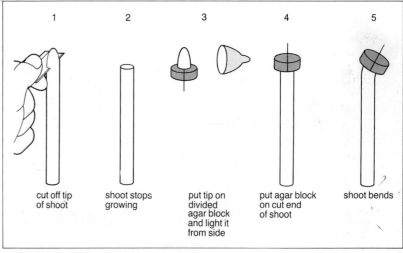

1    2    3    4    5

cut off tip of shoot

shoot stops growing

put tip on divided agar block and light it from side

put agar block on cut end of shoot

shoot bends

**Figure 3** An experiment to find out if a hormone is responsible for making a shoot bend towards light.

What about roots – how do they respond to light? Experiments indicate that the roots of most plants don't respond to light at all. However, some roots grow *away* from light, that is they are *negatively phototropic*.

## Gravity

Look at Figure 5. This shows what happens if you place a newly germinated broad bean seedling in a horizontal position in the dark; it is put in the dark so as to avoid any effects caused by light. The result is that the shoot bends upwards and the root downwards. This is a growth response to gravity, and it is called **geotropism**. If a structure grows towards gravity, we say it is *positively geotropic*; if it grows away from gravity, we say it is *negatively geotropic*. Whatever way up a seed is, the shoot always grows upwards and the root downwards (Investigation 2). This means that if you plant some seeds, you need not worry which way up they are: nature will always make sure that the shoots and roots grow in the right direction.

Now look at Figure 6. Marks are made at equal intervals along the straight shoot and root of a seedling which is growing vertically. The seedling is then placed in a horizontal position. As the shoot bends upwards, the marks on the lower side gradually get further apart. This suggests that growth occurs more quickly on the lower side than on the upper side. However, in the root the marks on the *upper* side get further apart, which suggests that in this case growth occurs more quickly on the upper side than on the lower side. In both instances growth takes place behind the tip where the cells are actively lengthening.

How is this response brought about? One possible explanation is that the auxin which is produced at the tip of the shoot moves to the lower side causing it to grow faster on that side; however, in the root it produces the opposite effect: it causes it to grow more *slowly* on the lower side.

Scientists believe that this is the correct explanation for the shoot. However, the root's response is thought to involve another hormone, produced by the root cap, which *slows down* growth on the lower side (Figure 7).

Look again at Figure 5. Imagine you were to turn the seedling round so that the shoot points downwards and the root upwards. You would expect the shoot and root to change their direction of growth, the shoot bending upwards and the root downwards. This is precisely what happens. Experiments of this sort can be done with an instrument called a **klinostat** (Investigation 3). The results suggest that however much you change the seedling's position, the shoot and root always grow in the right direction.

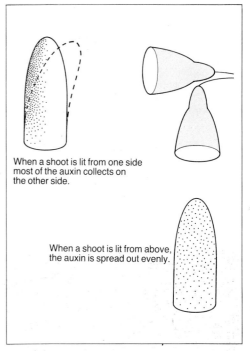

Figure 4 The direction of light affects the distribution of auxin inside the shoot.

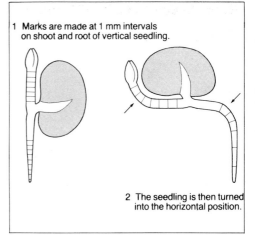

Figure 6 An experiment to show that the shoot and root respond to gravity by growing more quickly on one side than the other. The way the lines get pushed apart suggests that extra growth takes place in the positions marked by the arrows.

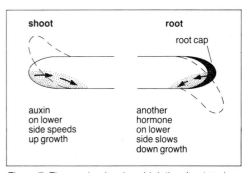

Figure 7 The mechanism by which the shoot and root are thought to respond to gravity.

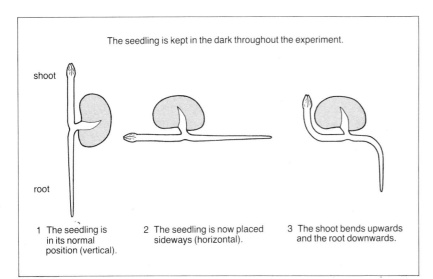

Figure 5 An experiment to see how a bean seedling responds to gravity.

**Figure 8** The tendrils of this plant are twisting round a supporting branch.

## Touch

Coralita, with its pink flowers, is an example of a plant with a floppy stem, so it can't support itself. However, it can grow upwards, clinging to poles and fences by means of tendrils. In this case the tendrils are the modified end of the inflorescence stalk, and when they touch an object they wind themselves round it. The side of the tendril which is touching the object grows more slowly than the other side, so it is made to bend round it.

There are many other climbing plants besides coralita. Some of them, such as passion flower, have tendrils; in others, such as yam and morning glory, the stem winds itself round firm objects such as poles, drainpipes or the stems of other plants (Figure 8; see also page 174).

Some specialised plants respond remarkably quickly to touch. For example, the leaves of the sensitive mimosa plant fold inwards when you touch them (see page 6).

Quick responses are also given by **carnivorous plants**, which feed on small animals such as insects and spiders. An example is Venus' fly-trap, a tropical plant which is often a curiosity in greenhouses. This has a leaf which is divided into two halves by a hinge down the middle. The two 'half-leaves' are set at an angle to each other like an open book (Figure 9). If an insect such as a fly lands on the surface of the leaf, it sets off a response in which the two sides of the leaf suddenly close up together trapping its prey. Rigid spines round the edge of the leaf prevent the insect getting out. Thus imprisoned, the insect's body is broken down by digestive juices which are secreted by special cells in the leaf. It takes up to a week for the insect to be digested and absorbed, after which the leaf re-opens.

This response is rather like an animal reflex. However, the plant has no nerves or muscles, so the mechanism is quite different. No one knows for certain how it is brought about.

## Other responses

Plants respond to water, chemicals and temperature. Thus roots tend to grow *towards* soil which is well watered, contains the right chemicals, and is reasonably warm; and they grow away from poor soil which does not have these qualities.

In temperate regions seeds will not usually germinate unless they are chilled beforehand, which ensures that they do not germinate until after the winter; and for flowering to occur, plants need to be given a certain amount of light beforehand.

## What causes flowering?

Flowering is a good example of plants responding to stimuli. Many plants will only flower after they have been given a certain amount of light each day. The amount needed varies from one kind of plant to another. Some need long days and short nights, others need long nights and short days. In temperate regions long-day plants tend to flower in the summer, whereas short-day plants flower in the spring or autumn. It is possible to play a trick on a plant and get it to flower early (or late) by altering the amount of light it receives.

In the tropics the length of day does not vary very much during the year, and flower growers sometimes have to vary the amount of light artificially. In this way they can get chrysanthemums to flower by giving them short 'days'. Responding to the amount of light received per day is known as **photoperiodism**; scientists have discovered that the stimulus is perceived by the leaves and that it causes the release of a hormone which makes the flower buds open.

Temperature is also important in controlling flowering in temperate regions. In order to flower later on, seeds and bulbs often need to be subjected to a brief period of cold first. This ensures that when a bulb has been formed it won't send up another flowering shoot until next year. However, you can make a bulb flower early by putting it in a refrigerator for a few weeks: in effect you are kidding the bulb that it has been through winter!

**Figure 9** The Venus fly-trap responds quickly to the stimulus of touch.

# Investigation 1

**To find which part of a shoot responds to light**

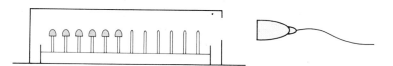

1 Obtain a dish containing about 12 seedlings of e.g. maize or rice. The shoots should be at least 10 mm long.

2 Make six little 'caps' out of aluminium foil.

3 Put a cap on six of the shoots so that it covers the tip, as shown in the illustration.

4 Light the dish from one side, as shown in the illustration, and leave it for several days.

How does the appearance of the covered seedlings differ from the others?

What conclusions can you draw about how shoots respond to light?

# Investigation 2

**To find if a seedling responds to gravity**

1 Obtain six bean seedlings whose roots are just visible.

2 With pins attach them to a sheet of cork in various positions as shown in the illustration.

3 Put the cork in a small aquarium tank with a little water at the bottom, and put a sheet of glass on top.

4 Cover the tank with an upturned cardboard box so as to keep the seedlings dark.

5 After about a week observe the seedlings and sketch their appearance.

What conclusions do you draw regarding the way the shoot and root respond to gravity?

# Assignments

1 Describe an experiment which you would do to find out if a bean root responds to light coming from one side.

2 Mr Lewis spends the morning in the garden. He plants some seeds and puts many of them in the soil upside down.

Does this matter? Explain your answer.

3 A small quantity of auxin is painted onto the shoot and root of a seedling in the positions shown by the arrows in Figure 6. How do you imagine the seedling will appear after 48 hours?

4 A young bean seedling is placed in a klinostat in the position shown in the diagram below. The seedling is then rotated slowly for two days. Draw what you suppose would be the shape of the seedling at the end of the two-day period.

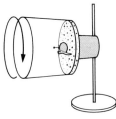

5 Describe one experiment which in your opinion provides the strongest evidence that a hormone is involved in making a shoot bend towards light.

# Investigation 3

**Experiments with a klinostat**

A klinostat is a small cylindrical chamber which can slowly rotate. The chamber contains a piece of cork to which young seedlings can be pinned.

1 Obtain two young bean seedlings whose roots are about 1 cm long.

2 Pin one of the seedlings to the cork in the klinostat as shown in the left-hand illustration.

3 Pin the other one to a piece of cork in a beaker as shown in the right-hand illustration. This is your control.

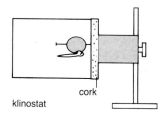 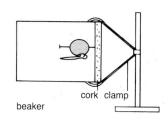

4 Put some moist cotton wool in the klinostat chamber and the beaker so as to keep the seedlings moist.

5 Cover the klinostat and beaker with an upturned cardboard box, and leave the klinostat running for several days.

6 After several days, observe the two seedlings.

How do they differ in appearance? Explain your observations.

# Adjustment and control

*It is vital that the conditions inside the body should not vary too much. Control is achieved by feedback mechanisms.*

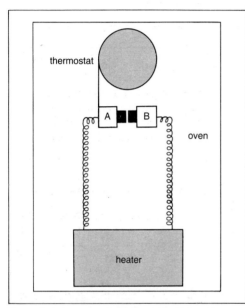

**Figure 1** A thermostatically controlled heater in an oven.

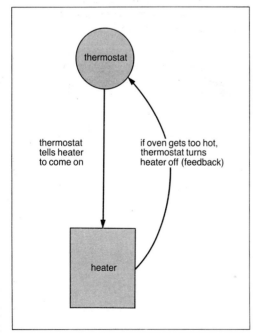

**Figure 2** This diagram shows how the production of heat in an oven is controlled by the thermostat.

## The thermostat, a simple feedback system

Think of an oven. If an oven is to cook things properly it must stay at about the same temperature all the time. This is achieved by means of a thermostat. You set the oven at the desired temperature and the thermostat makes sure that the oven stays at about that temperature.

Figure 1 shows how the thermostat works. A and B are two metal contacts. For the heater to come on, A must touch B. Now if the oven temperature falls, A moves towards B and touches it. This makes the heater come on. The oven temperature now rises, and this makes A move away from B. As soon as A loses contact with B, the heater goes off and the temperature falls. As a result the oven temperature is kept pretty constant, though there will obviously be slight fluctuations.

The thermostat is an example of a **feedback system**. Information about the temperature of the oven is *fed back* to the heater via the thermostat, telling it to come on or go off (Figure 2). In this way a constant temperature is maintained.

## Homeostasis

Feedback systems are very common in biology. They help to keep conditions inside the body constant. This is important because if conditions such as the body temperature were to vary greatly, our enzymes would not work properly and we would die. Keeping conditions constant is called **homeostasis**, a Greek word which literally means 'staying the same'. Now let's look at some examples of it.

## Controlling the body temperature

You probably know how mammals produce heat and keep it in the body (see page 178). A mammal's body is like a thermostatically controlled oven. Suppose the body temperature falls slightly. This is detected by a special centre in the brain. The brain then sends out messages in various nerves, which switch on the mechanisms that warm the body (Figure 3). When the body temperature rises, it switches on the mechanisms that cool the body. The brain centre thus functions as a thermostat, keeping the body temperature more or less constant.

## Controlling blood glucose

It is very important that there should be the right amount of glucose in the bloodstream (see page 181). If there is too much glucose, extra **insulin** is secreted by the pancreas and the amount of blood glucose falls. On the other hand, if there is too little glucose, less insulin is secreted and the amount of blood glucose rises. In this way the amount of glucose in the bloodstream is kept pretty constant.

## Controlling water balance

The amount of water in the bloodstream must be delicately controlled. If your body is short of water, the blood becomes too concentrated with salts and other solutes. This is detected by special cells in the brain which tell the pituitary gland to secrete a **water-regulating hormone**. This hormone passes round the bloodstream to the kidneys and tells them to reabsorb more water into the bloodstream instead of letting it out in the urine. You will also feel thirsty and drink some water. In this way the concentration of the blood is brought down. What do you think will happen if you drink too *much* water?

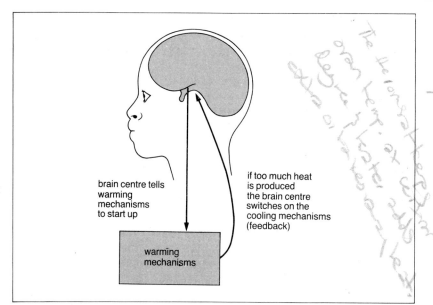

**Figure 3** This diagram shows how the body's warming mechanisms are controlled by the brain.

## Controlling the thyroid gland

Normally the thyroid gland is made to secrete thyroxine by a **thyroid-stimulating hormone** from the pituitary gland. The more thyroid-stimulating hormone that is produced, the greater is the flow of thyroxine. Now suppose the thyroid gland is producing too much thyroxine; the thyroxine itself tells the pituitary gland to secrete less thyroid-stimulating hormone (Figure 4). The amount of thyroxine will then automatically fall. This is exactly like a high temperature in a heated oven switching *off* the heater.

There are many other feedback systems in biology. You may be able to think of some yourself. We also find them in other walks of life such as business and industry. Can you think of one *non*-biological example of a feedback system?

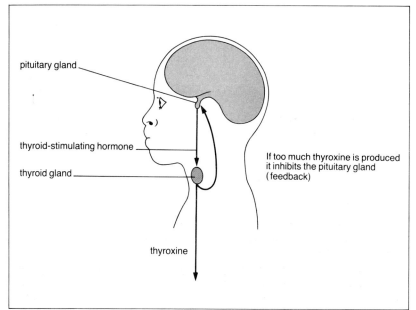

**Figure 4** This diagram shows how the activity of the thyroid gland is controlled by the pituitary.

# Assignments

1 In a thermostatically controlled oven what is the difference between the heater and the thermostat? Why is it an advantage for an oven to be controlled in this way?

2 Explain the meaning of the term feedback.

3 Make a list of the human body's 'warming mechanisms'. When, and how, are they brought into action?

4 Make diagrams, similar to the one in Figure 3, showing how the amounts of (a) blood sugar and (b) water are controlled in the human body.

5 The body temperature of a normal healthy person was taken with a sensitive thermometer placed in one of the blood vessels. The results are shown below:

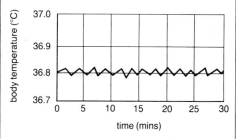

a) Why does the temperature go up and down all the time?

b) If the temperature had been taken with an ordinary clinical thermometer placed in the mouth, these fluctuations would not have been detected. Why not?

6 It is impossible for the amount of glucose in the bloodstream to be kept *absolutely* constant. Why is this?

# Continuation of life

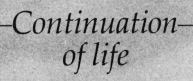

*African elephants, old and young, photographed in Amboseli National Park, Kenya. In the next group of topics we shall see how organisms grow and reproduce.*

# Producing offspring

*Producing offspring involves reproduction. Here we will look at the various ways organisms reproduce.*

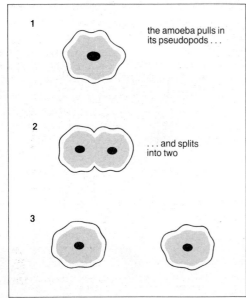

**Figure 1** An amoeba reproduces by splitting into two (binary fission).

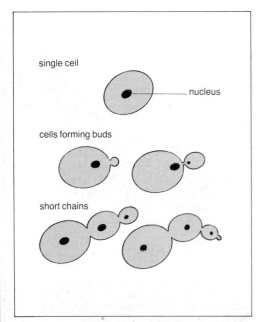

**Figure 2** Diagram of yeast cells budding.

## Asexual methods

Many organisms reproduce on their own without the help of another individual. We call this **asexual reproduction**. This kind of reproduction takes place when there is plenty of food available and conditions are good for growth. These are the main methods.

*Splitting (fission)*
This method is used by single-celled organisms. Take *Amoeba* for example. When it is ready to reproduce it simply splits into two (Figure 1). First the nucleus splits, and then the rest of the body. The two little amoebas then feed and grow. When fully grown, each splits again. In good conditions this may happen about once a day.

We call this process **binary fission**. Binary means 'two', and fission means 'splitting', so the term literally means 'splitting in two'.

Bacteria also reproduce by splitting, but they do it faster than *Amoeba*: that's why there are so many of them. In suitable conditions some bacteria can split once every twenty minutes. This may not seem very fast, but try working out how many bacteria would be formed from one original cell after six hours. It's a large number!

*Budding*
An organism that reproduces by **budding** is yeast (Investigation 1). Yeast is a fungus, but it differs from most fungi in that it usually consists of single cells. When budding occurs the cell sends out a small outgrowth which gets larger and eventually breaks off as a new cell (Figure 2). Sometimes the new cell starts budding before it has broken away from the old cell: this can give rise to chains or clumps of cells.

*Hydra* is another organism which reproduces by budding: a new hydra grows out of the side (Figure 3). To begin with the bud gets food from its parent, but eventually the new hydra breaks away and becomes independent.

*Spores*
A **spore** is a tiny spherical cell that will grow into a new individual. An example of an organism that produces spores is given on page 52. It is pin mould, the fungus that grows on bread and other kinds of food.

Another fungus that produces spores is the mushroom. A mushroom doesn't look much like pin mould. However, in the soil there are lots of fine threads, similar to those of pin mould. The mushroom itself is the spore-forming body (Investigation 2).

Mosses and ferns also produce spores. They are formed inside **spore capsules**. In mosses the spore capsule is at the top of a stalk which sticks out of the leafy part of the plant. In ferns the spore capsules are in groups on the underside of the fronds (Figure 4). When ripe, the capsules open and the spores are scattered.

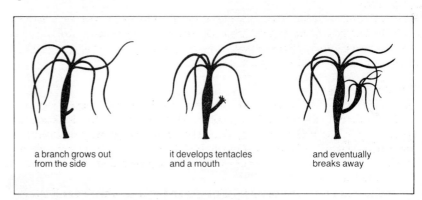

a branch grows out from the side

it develops tentacles and a mouth

and eventually breaks away

**Figure 3** *Hydra* reproduces asexually by budding.

*Vegetative reproduction*
Flowering plants reproduce asexually by a special method which we call **vegetative reproduction**. This is described fully on pages 300-3.

*The pros and cons of asexual reproduction*
The great advantage of asexual reproduction is that a lot of new individuals are produced quickly without the need for a partner. However, all the new individuals are exactly like the parent. In other words *no variety is produced by asexual reproduction*. This is because the new cells are formed by a type of cell division in which the daughter cells are exactly like the parent cells (see page 304).

# Sexual methods

Sexual reproduction involves two individuals, normally a **male** and **female**. It's a complicated process but basically what happens is that chromosomes from the two individuals are brought together. Exactly how this is achieved varies from one species to another.

In many cases sexual reproduction takes place when conditions are not good for growth. It provides a means by which the species survives unfavourable periods such as winter or a dry season.

Now let's look at some examples. We will start with more advanced organisms such as vertebrates and flowering plants. Then we will look at some lower organisms for comparison.

*Fish*
Most bony fish reproduce by the male and female releasing their sperms and eggs into the surrounding water. The sperms then swim to the eggs and fertilise them. We call this **external fertilisation**. Some fish produce vast numbers of eggs. For example, a cod can produce as many as eight million at one time.

The chances of the eggs being fertilised are greatly increased if the male releases his sperms close to the female's eggs. The stickleback or 'tiddler' shows how this can be achieved. In the mating season, the male stickleback develops a red breast and builds an underwater nest out of pieces of weed which he glues together with a substance made by his kidneys. He then lures a ripe female to his nest by showing her his red breast. The female enters the nest and lays her eggs (Figure 5). She leaves the nest through the other side. The male may persuade several other females to lay eggs in the same nest. When there are between 50 and 100 eggs in the nest, he enters and releases his sperms on top of them.

The male now looks after the fertilised eggs, guarding them against other fishes which might eat them, and fanning them with his tail. This stirs up the water and helps to get oxygen to the eggs. After they have hatched, the male looks after the young sticklebacks for a few days until they are able to fend for themselves.

*Amphibians*
Although frogs and toads live on land, they breed in water. The male mates with the female by climbing on her back, and fertilisation takes place in the water. The fertilised egg develops into a larva (the tadpole), which eventually changes into the adult (see page 284).

*Reptiles and birds*
Great advances are shown over amphibians. The males and females mate on land, and the sperms are put inside the female body where they fertilise the eggs. This is called **internal fertilisation**. The fertilised eggs are coated with a protective **shell** before being laid. The embryo is provided with a store of food inside the shell: this is the **yolk**. The embryo grows and develops and eventually hatches.

Reptiles and birds take care of their eggs and young. This helps them to survive and it means that fewer eggs need to be produced (see page 287).

**Figure 4** The upper photograph is of a moss plant showing a ripe spore capsule. The lower one shows the underside of part of the frond of a fern showing groups of spore capsules.

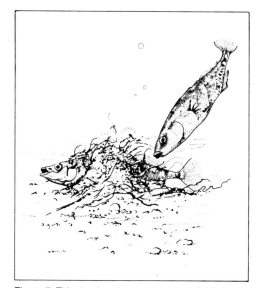

**Figure 5** This drawing shows a female stickleback inside the nest which has been made by the male. The male prods her tail and this makes her lay her eggs.

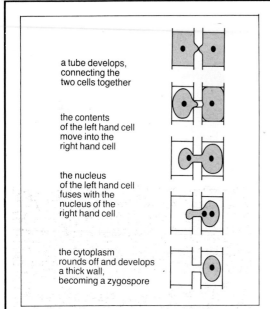

**Figure 6** These diagrams show what happens when two cells of *Spyrogyra* conjugate.

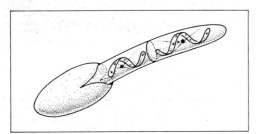

**Figure 7** A zygospore of *Spirogyra* splits open and a new filament grows out.

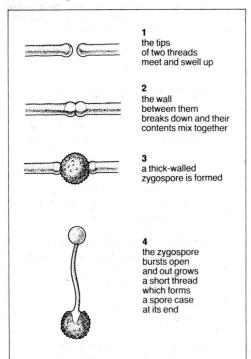

**Figure 8** Pin mould can reproduce sexually. Threads from the two neighbouring moulds conjugate.

## Mammals

Mammals, too, have internal fertilisation. What's more the embryo grows and develops inside the mother and is born at a reasonably advanced stage. Animals which bear live young like this are described as **viviparous**.

Mammals take particular care of their young, feeding them on **milk** and teaching them to fend for themselves. Mammalian reproduction is dealt with in detail on pages 260–75.

## Flowering plants

Sexual reproduction in flowering plants is dealt with on pages 288–99. The problem of bringing the male gamete to the egg is solved by having **pollen grains**. And the problem of dispersal is solved by having **seeds** and **fruits**. Seeds also help the plant to survive unfavourable seasons.

## Spirogyra

*Spirogyra* reproduces sexually by **conjugation**. Two filaments lie side by side. Short tubes grow out from each filament, connecting next-door cells (Figure 6). Through the tubes the contents of one cell move into the other, and their nuclei combine. The cytoplasm then rounds off to form a **zygote**. This develops a thick wall, becoming a **zygospore**. The process just described takes place between an entire row of cells all at the same time. As a result, a zygospore develops in each cell. Eventually the cell walls break open and the zygospores sink to the bottom of the pond. Here they survive the winter or the pond drying up. When conditions improve they burst open and new filaments grow out (Figure 7).

## Pin mould

Pin mould can also reproduce sexually by conjugating (Figure 8). Two threads from different moulds grow towards each other. Their tips meet and swell up. The walls separating them break down, and the nuclei from the two threads fuse together in pairs. A round ball-like zygote is formed. This develops a thick wall and becomes a dormant zygospore. The zygospore can survive for up to a year, even in bad conditions.

When conditions are suitable, the zygospore bursts open and sends out a thread which grows upwards. A spore case is formed at the end. Spores are released from the spore case as described on page 52.

## Hydra

If you look at hydras, you may see bumps sticking out from the side of the body. These are **testes** and **ovaries** (Figure 9).

Each testis contains numerous **sperms**, and each ovary contains an **egg**. The sperms and eggs are formed from packing cells in the ectoderm.

When the testes and ovaries are mature, they burst open. The sperms swim to an open ovary of another hydra, and one of them fertilises the egg. The fertilised egg then divides up into a little ball of cells, the **embryo**. A hard wall is formed round it: this is called a **cyst**. The cyst drops out of the ovary, and sinks to the bottom of the pond. When the winter comes or the pond dries up the parent hydra dies, but the cyst survives. When conditions improve it bursts open, and a young hydra emerges.

The hydra in Figure 9 has a testis *and* an ovary. It is a **hermaphrodite**, producing sperms and eggs. Some species of *Hydra* are hermaphrodites, others have separate sexes.

The eggs of a hermaphrodite may be fertilised by its own sperms: this is known as **self-fertilisation**. But self-fertilisation has disadvantages, and most hermaphrodites have ways of preventing it. *Hydra* prevents self-fertilisation like this: in an individual hydra the testes mature before the ovary, so the sperms are released before the egg is ready to be fertilised. The sperms must therefore swim to an egg in another individual. We call this **cross-fertilisation**.

## The earthworm

Earthworms reproduce sexually by **copulating** with one another. They do

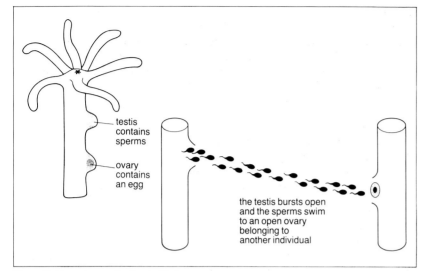

Figure 9  Sexual reproduction in *Hydra*.

this at night on the surface of the ground. The worms come together in pairs as shown in Figure 10. They become glued together by slime (mucus) which is produced by their saddles.

Worms are hermaphrodites. When they copulate, sperms pass from each individual into the other. In this way the eggs in both worms become fertilised and self-fertilisation is avoided. The eggs are then laid in the soil. Eventually they hatch into new worms.

*Pros and cons of sexual reproduction*
Sexual reproduction does not produce lots of new individuals quickly, as asexual reproduction often does. However, it has the great advantage that the offspring differ from their parents and from one another. In other words, *sexual reproduction gives rise to variety*. This is because the gametes are formed by a type of cell division in which the daughter cells differ from the parent cells, and when fertilisation takes place the various characteristics of the parents are brought together in a random manner (see page 316).

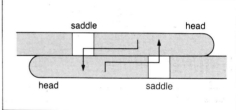

Figure 10  Two earthworms copulating. The diagram shows what happens. Sperms pass from each worm into the other as indicated by the arrows.

# Investigation 1

**Looking at yeast budding**

1  Obtain a jar of fermenting yeast.

2  With a pipette put a drop of the yeast on a slide.

3  Add a drop of a stain such as methylene blue or lactophenol.

4  Cover it with a coverslip.

5  Look at your slide under the microscope: low power first, then high power.

Can you see the yeast cells clearly?

Are any of them budding?

# Investigation 2

**To see if a mushroom produces spores**

1  Obtain a mature mushroom and cut the cap off the stalk.

2  Place the cap, lower surface downwards, on a sheet of paper.

3  Cover it with an inverted dish.

4  After a day or two, remove the dish and lift up the mushroom cap.

What does the paper look like now?

Explain what you see.

5  Place a few spores on a slide and look at them under the microscope.

Why do you think they are so small?

# Assignments

1  In good conditions a bacterial cell splits every 20 minutes. How many would be formed from a single original one after 10 hours?

2  One mushroom may produce ten thousand million spores in a few days. Why so many?

3  Explain the difference between
   a)  internal and external fertilisation,
   b)  self-fertilisation and cross-fertilisation.

4  Why are eggs much larger than sperms?

5  Choose one hermaphroditic organism and explain how it prevents self-fertilisation.

# How do living things grow?

*Growth is the increase in size which takes place as an organism develops. It ensures that the organism is the right size to survive in its environment.*

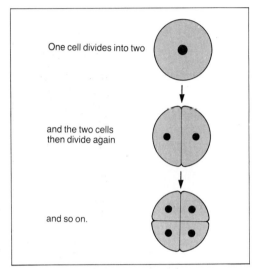

**Figure 1** Cell division is the basis of growth in a multicellular organism.

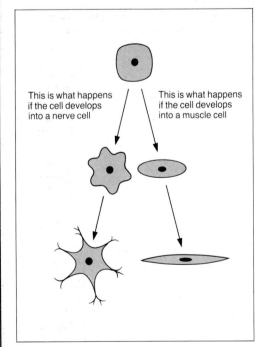

**Figure 2** A cell may change its shape and form and develop into a particular kind of cell with a specific function.

**Figure 3** These diagrams show how different parts of the body increase in size during the first twenty years of a person's life.

## Measuring growth

There are many different ways of measuring growth, depending on the organism in question. Usually we measure some dimension such as height, length or mass at regular intervals of time. Investigations 1 and 2 and Assignment 5 will introduce you to some of the methods and difficulties involved.

## How does growth take place?

Most animals and plants are composed of many cells. However, they usually start off as a single cell, the fertilised egg. This divides into two cells, then into four, eight, sixteen and so on. This process of **cell division** is the basis of growth.

Figure 1 shows what happens when a cell divides. The nucleus divides first, and then the rest of the cell divides across the middle. At first the daughter cells are smaller than the original parent cell, but they soon grow to full size. For this to happen they must take in food substances to provide the necessary materials and energy. This is why a growing organism needs plenty of food.

Eventually the cells change their shape and form and turn into particular types of cell, depending on their position in the body. In the human body, for example, a cell might develop into a smooth muscle cell if it happens to be in the wall of the gut, or into a brain cell if it's in the head (Figure 2). The process by which cells become specialised like this is called **differentiation**, and it plays a vital part in the construction of the full-grown adult organism.

Normally once a cell has become specialised in this way it does not divide any more.

## Growth in humans

In a growing child cell division takes place in all parts of the body. As a result, the child gets steadily larger. However, different parts of the body grow at different rates: this is because cell division occurs more quickly in some places than in others. For example the head grows quickly in the early stages of development and then slows down, whereas the legs and arms grow slowly at first and then speed up later (Figure 3).

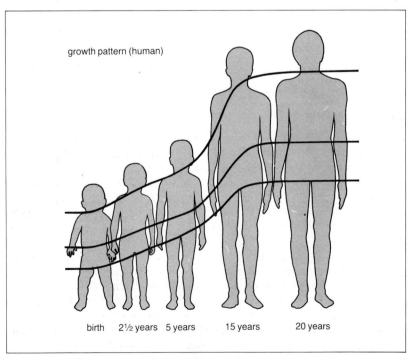

growth pattern (human)

birth    2½ years    5 years    15 years    20 years

Eventually no more cells are added to the body, and so the person stops growing. In humans this happens at the age of about eighteen, though in most other animals it occurs much sooner.

Certain cells need to be replaced, so these go on dividing throughout life: they include the cells at the base of the epidermis in the skin, the cells in the bone marrow from which blood cells are formed, and the cells from which eggs and sperms are formed. Cells will also start dividing again when the body is cut or damaged, to patch up the wound and heal it.

## Growth in insects

You will remember that insects have a hard cuticle that cannot stretch. An insect can only grow if it sheds its cuticle first. This process is called **moulting** or **ecdysis**.

The first thing that happens during moulting is that a fluid is formed underneath the cuticle. This fluid dissolves all but the hard outer layer of the cuticle. The insect then expands, usually by swallowing air, and blows up like a balloon. This causes the old cuticle to split, and the insect struggles free.

Meanwhile a new cuticle has been formed under the old one. This is soft at first and as the body expands, it stretches. When the old cuticle has been cast off, the new one starts to harden. Once the new cuticle has hardened, the insect cannot expand any further until the cuticle is cast off again. An insect such as the locust may moult five or six times before it is fully grown, and the cockroach may moult twelve or thirteen times. So insects do not grow smoothly as humans do, but in a series of spurts (Figure 4).

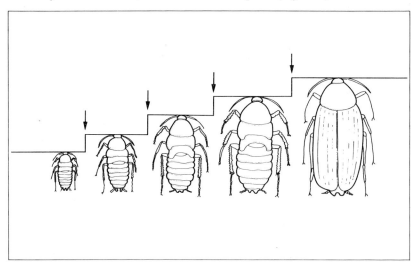

## Growth in plants

We have seen that in a growing child cell division takes place all over the body. This is true of most animals. In a young plant, however, cell division is restricted to certain regions called **meristems**. The main meristems are at the tip of the shoot and root (Investigation 3). If you make marks on a young shoot or root, you can see exactly where growth is occurring (Figure 5).

Consider a growing shoot (Figure 6). In the tip, cells are continually dividing. These young cells draw in water by osmosis and expand. This has the effect of lengthening the shoot, and helps it to thrust its way upwards. The same kind of thing happens in the roots as well, and it helps them to push their way down into the soil. So in plants growth is achieved not just by cell division, but by **cell expansion** as well (Investigation 4).

While the cells are expanding, they differentiate into specialised tissues according to their position in the plant and the task which they have to perform. For example, most of the cells in the shoot develop into packing tissue but in certain regions they develop into transport tissues.

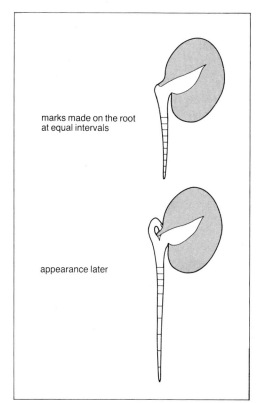

**Figure 5** An experiment to show whereabouts growth occurs in a young bean root.

**Figure 4** (left) A cockroach grows in spurts, increasing in size every time it moults. The arrows indicate when moulting occurs. Many more moults take place than are shown here.

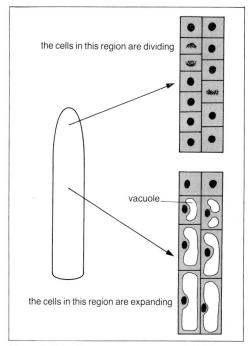

**Figure 6** This diagram shows where cell division and expansion take place in a growing shoot. The same applies to the root.

## *How does a stem get thicker?*

The kind of growth just described makes the stem get longer. However, as you know, stems get thicker too. Think of a tree, for instance, whose trunk gets thicker year by year. As this occurs *after* the stem has increased in length, we call it **secondary growth** or **secondary thickening**.

This is how secondary growth occurs. At the same time as the stem is getting longer, a layer of cells develops inside it called the **cambium**. If you look at a cross-section of the stem, the cambium appears as a ring of cells situated between the xylem and phloem (Figure 7). Now the cambium cells are able to divide long after the other cells have stopped doing so. They divide to form new xylem tissue (wood) towards the inside, and new phloem tissue towards the outside. In fact far more xylem tissue is formed than phloem, so the amount of wood in the stem increases greatly.

Meanwhile another layer of dividing cells is formed just under the surface of the stem. This is called the **cork cambium**, and its cells divide to form the hard corky part of the bark.

Secondary growth takes place mainly in the summer, or in the rainy season in the tropics. In the winter or dry season it slows down or stops. If you cut a tree down, you can see rings of wood corresponding to each year's secondary growth: they are called **annual rings** (Figure 8). By counting the rings you can tell the age of the tree. You can do the same with individual twigs (Investigation 5).

The secondary growth described above occurs in all dicotyledonous shrubs and trees and it enables some of them to get very large. However, it does not occur in monocotyledonous plants, which is why few monocotyledons reach the size of trees. Palms, however, are an exception: they can grow to considerable heights because they develop a lot of wood in their stems.

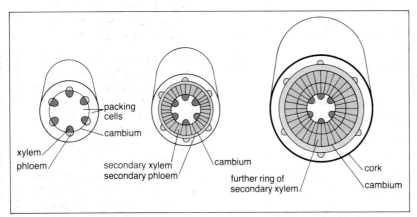

**Figure 7**  Secondary growth enables a stem to get wider year by year.

**Figure 8**  Part of the cut end of the trunk of a felled tree showing the annual rings. This is a temperate species which grew in a part of the world where there was a marked distinction between winter and summer.

## *Investigation 1*

### Measuring the growth of an animal

If you have a young pet, such as a kitten or puppy you can carry out this investigation at home. Alternatively you can do it in the laboratory, using a small mammal such as a mouse or gerbil.

1  With a ruler measure the animal's length from the tip of its nose to the *base* of its tail.

2  Weigh the animal and find its mass.

3  Repeat steps 1 and 2 at regular intervals (at least twice a week) until growth appears to stop.

4  Plot your results on a piece of graph paper, putting length and mass on the vertical axis, and time on the horizontal axis.

   Did the length and mass stop increasing at the same time? If not, can you explain the reason?

5  Work out the percentage increase in size which occurred between your first and last readings.

   percentage increase =

   $$\frac{\text{final size} - \text{initial size}}{\text{initial size}} \times 100$$

## *Investigation 2*

### Measuring the growth of a plant

For this experiment use maize or rice.

1  Soak the seeds in water and sow them in moist soil.

2  When the shoot appears measure its length.

3  Repeat this at regular intervals (every day if possible) for at least a week.

4  Plot your measurements on graph paper, putting length of shoot on the vertical axis and time on the horizontal axis.

5  From your graph work out the rate of growth (increase in length per day) for each day.

How does the rate of growth vary during the week?

# Investigation 3

## To find where growth takes place in a root

1 Obtain a bean seedling with a root at least 2 cm long.

2 With Indian ink, make a series of marks along the length of the root 1 mm apart. Use the special 'pen' shown in the illustration.

3 Pin the seedling to a piece of cork with the root pointing downwards.

4 Put the cork in a jar with a little water in the bottom to keep it moist, and cover it with a sheet of glass.

5 After several days examine the seedling.

Are the marks still the same distance apart?
Where does growth occur in the root?

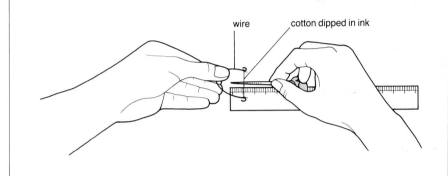

wire      cotton dipped in ink

# Investigation 4

## Examining the inside of a young root

1 Look at a prepared longitudinal section of a young root under the microscope.

2 Observe the cells just behind the tip.

Draw one of the cells in outline to show its shape.

What were these cells doing when the root was alive?

How do you know?

3 Now look at the cells further back.

Draw one of them to show its shape.

How did the cells come to be this shape?

How does the change in shape help the root to grow?

What happens to the various cells after they have changed their shape?

# Investigation 5

## Looking at secondary growth in a plant

1 Obtain prepared transverse sections of a series of twigs of different ages.

Alternatively you can cut your own sections as instructed on page 169. If you do this, stain the sections by putting them in a watch glass full of acidified phloroglucin. This will show up the woody part of the twig by staining it red.

2 Put the sections against a light background and if necessary look at them through a hand lens.

How do they differ in appearance?
Can you tell how old each one is?

3 Look at the cut end of a series of older stems or branches.

How do they differ in appearance?

Can you tell how old they are?

If you look at the annual rings in a felled tree, you sometimes see that some rings are much wider than others. How would you explain this?

# Assignments

1 Fill in the missing words in this passage:

In order for an organism to grow, its cells ____ (a) ____. This process requires ____ (b) ____ which comes from the organism's ____ (c) ____. Later on the cells ____ (d) ____ into different types of cells depending on their ____ (e) ____ in the body.

2 Give three ways in which growth in animals differs from growth in flowering plants.

3 Explain briefly how a growing stem increases in length, and how later it increases in width.

4 With a ruler measure in millimetres the width of the head and the length of the legs in the diagrams in Figure 3. Plot the results on a sheet of graph paper so the curves can be compared.
   a) Which grows more quickly between the ages of 5 and 15 years, the head or the legs?
   b) By how many times does one grow faster than the other?

5 A scientist sows a large number of seeds all at the same time, and he wants to measure the rate of growth of the seedlings. Here are three methods which he might use:
   a) He measures the *heights* of the shoots of fifty plants every day and takes the average.
   b) He digs up five plants every day, removes the soil from their roots, and estimates their *fresh mass* by weighing them.
   c) He digs up five plants every day and dries them by heating them in a hot oven until all traces of water have been driven off. He then weighs them, thereby obtaining their *dry mass*.

Write down the advantages and disadvantages of each method.

In method (c) how could the scientist be certain that all the water had been removed from the plants before he found their dry mass?

# How is growth controlled?

*What makes an organism grow at a certain rate, and to a particular size? In this Topic we will look into this question, and also see what happens when growth goes wrong.*

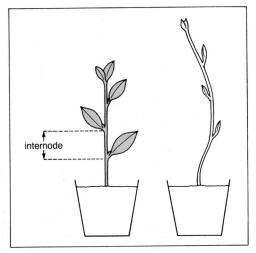

**Figure 1** The seedling on the left was grown in the light; the one on the right was grown in the dark. Notice that the distance between the nodes, the internode, is greater in the seedling grown in the dark. It is etiolated.

**Figure 2** Experiment to find out if the tip of a shoot is needed for growth to occur.

**Figure 3** Experiment to find out if a hormone produced by the tip makes the shoot grow.

## The part played by the environment

For good growth the right conditions are needed. For example, there must be plenty of food and a suitably high temperature. A tadpole will grow more quickly in a warm pond than in a cooler one.

For plants light is important. This can be seen by growing a seedling in the dark (Investigation 1). In an effort to reach the light it grows rapidly, becoming tall and spindly. The leaves don't expand and the plant is yellowish because the green chlorophyll can only be formed in the light. A plant in this state is described as **etiolated** (Figure 1).

## The role of hormones in plants

If you cut off the tip of a shoot, the part behind will stop growing. However, If you put the tip back, the shoot will start growing again (Figure 2). There seems to be something in the tip which stimulates growth to take place (Investigation 2).

What is it? Figure 3 shows an experiment that was done to find the answer. The tip of a shoot was cut off and placed on a small block of agar jelly. Deprived of its tip, the shoot stopped growing. After a few hours the agar block was placed on the cut end of the shoot. The result was that the shoot started growing again.

This experiment suggests that the tip of the shoot produces a chemical substance which passes down the shoot, making it grow. Scientists have managed to isolate this substance and have named it **auxin**. Two other

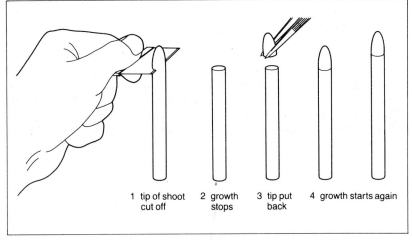

1 tip of shoot cut off    2 growth stops    3 tip put back    4 growth starts again

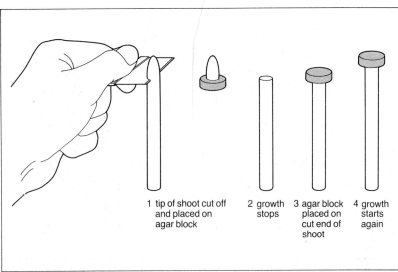

1 tip of shoot cut off and placed on agar block    2 growth stops    3 agar block placed on cut end of shoot    4 growth starts again

experiments supporting the auxin theory are illustrated in Figure 4.

Auxin is produced at the tip of the shoot and then it slowly diffuses down to the roots producing various effects on the plant as it flows along. It therefore functions as a hormone, rather like those found in animals (see page 238).

Auxin doesn't always *stimulate* growth; sometimes it *stops* it. For example, as it passes down the stem, it tends to *prevent* side branches growing out, thus making the plant tall and straight. If you cut the apical bud off such a plant, the flow of auxin stops and side branches will then develop (Investigation 3). Gardeners sometimes cut the tops off plants to make them more bushy (Figure 5): this is the secret behind making a thick hedge.

Since auxin was isolated, scientists have discovered other hormones which play an important part in plant growth. Nowadays these substances, or very similar ones, are manufactured in chemical factories; they are known as **growth substances** and are much used in gardening and horticulture. For example a substance similar to auxin is used for helping cuttings to 'take' (see page 302): the cut stem is dipped in the substance and this stimulates roots to grow out from it (Investigation 4).

## The role of hormones in animals

In man a **growth hormone** is produced by the pituitary gland at the base of the brain, and this speeds up growth. If too little of this hormone is produced during childhood, the person remains short and becomes a dwarf. On the other hand, if too much is produced, the person may grow into a giant (Figure 6).

Another hormone which helps children to grow is **thyroxine**: this is produced by the thyroid gland in the neck (see page 239).

Hormones control growth in other animals too. For example, scientists have carried out experiments which show that in insects growth is brought about by a hormone produced by certain cells in the brain. This is called **moulting hormone** and it stimulates the insect to shed its cuticle and grow. Another hormone, produced by a gland in the thorax, prevents moulting. This is called **juvenile hormone** because it keeps the insect in a young state. Whether the insect moults or not at a given time depends on the balance between these two hormones.

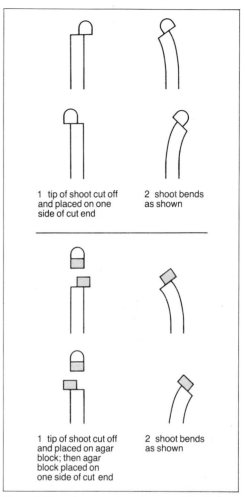

1 tip of shoot cut off and placed on one side of cut end

2 shoot bends as shown

1 tip of shoot cut off and placed on agar block; then agar block placed on one side of cut end

2 shoot bends as shown

**Figure 4** These two experiments support the theory that the growth of a shoot is stimulated by a chemical substance produced in the tip.

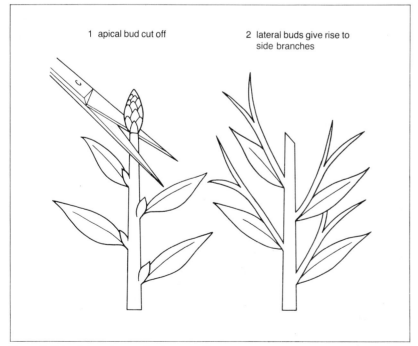

1 apical bud cut off

2 lateral buds give rise to side branches

**Figure 5** This picture shows what happens if you cut the apical bud off a plant.

**Figure 6** A pituitary giant and dwarf side by side.

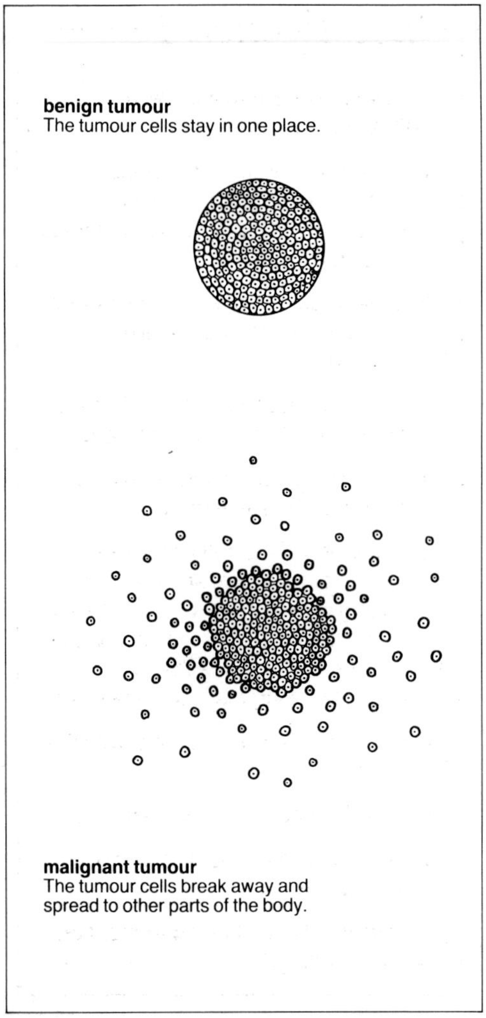

**benign tumour**
The tumour cells stay in one place.

**malignant tumour**
The tumour cells break away and
spread to other parts of the body.

**Figure 7**  Two kinds of tumour which can occur in
man and other animals.

## When growth goes wrong

We have seen that growth takes place by cell division, and that in animals there comes a time when it stops. Some kind of control process prevents the cells dividing any more.

On occasions this control process may break down in some part of the body and the cells start dividing again. This results in the formation of a disorganised mass of simple cells which don't perform a useful function. Doctors call this a **growth** or **tumour**.

There are two kinds of tumour: **benign** and **malignant** (Figure 7). A benign tumour stays in one place and does not harm the surrounding tissues except by pressing on them. In contrast a malignant tumour spreads: cells become detached from it and are carried by the lymph or blood to other parts of the body where they invade and destroy the tissues and grow into new tumours. Tumours which spread like this are known as **cancer** (carcinoma).

Cancer is second only to heart disease as a cause of death, and people are very frightened of it. However, there are many cases of people being cured of it and better methods of diagnosis and treatment are constantly being devised. The surest remedy is for a surgeon to remove the tumour before it has a chance to spread, but cancer can also be treated by drugs and radio-active rays (radiotherapy). Such treatment kills the tumour cells or at least stops them dividing (Figure 8).

The success of the treatment depends partly on how soon the tumour is discovered. A person who has a complaint that won't go away should go to the doctor. A persistent cough, chronic indigestion, a lump under the skin, bleeding from the anus – any of these *might* be a sign of cancer if they don't clear up. A quick test can often be carried out to see if it's serious. For example, a chest X-ray will show up cancer of the lung, and a doctor can find out if a woman has cancer of the womb by taking a smear from the neck (cervix) of the womb: this is called a **cervical smear** or **Pap smear**. He then looks at the smear under the microscope to see if there are any abnormal cells there. If cancer is developing, it may be necessary to remove the womb. This operation is called a **hysterectomy**.

What causes cancer? There are many possible causes, and a great deal of research is going on into this question. You cannot catch it from other people, but it can be brought on by environmental hazards such as atomic radiation, asbestos dust and smoking.

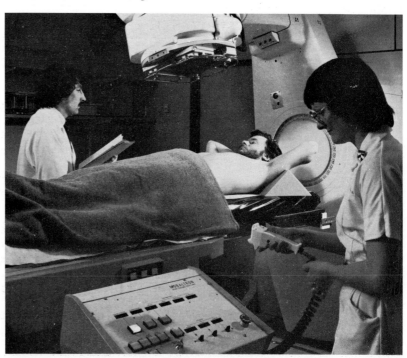

**Figure 8**  A patient being positioned on the treatment
couch before receiving radiation therapy from a
computer controlled machine.

# Investigation 1

## To find the effect of growing a seedling in darkness

1 Obtain two potted bean seedlings whose shoots have just appeared.

2 Cover one of the pots with a cardboard box. Leave the other one uncovered.

3 Water the plants occasionally so as to keep the soil moist.

4 Observe the seedlings after about two weeks.

In what ways do they differ in appearance?
Compare their overall heights and the lengths of their internodes.

# Investigation 2

## To find the effect on growth of cutting off the tip of a shoot

1 Obtain a dish containing about 12 seedlings of e.g. wheat, barley or maize. The shoots should be at least 10 mm long.

2 With small scissors cut the tip off 6 of the shoots: make your cut not more than 4 mm behind the tip.

3 Leave the dish in a uniformly lit place for several days.

4 After several days, observe the seedlings.

How does the appearance of the decapitated seedlings differ from the others?

What conclusions can you draw about how growth is controlled in the shoots?

# Investigation 3

## To find the effect of removing the apical bud from a plant

1 Obtain two potted plants which do not have any side-branches.

2 Cut off the apical bud at the top of the stem from one of the plants, but not from the other one.

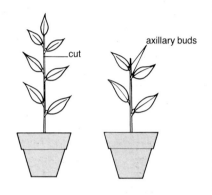

3 Observe the two plants at intervals during the next few weeks.

How do they differ in appearance?

What effect has been produced by removing the apical bud?

# Investigation 4

## To find the effect of a growth substance on cuttings

1 Cut off two healthy side-branches from a mature geranium or coleus plant. Make the cut just below a node (see page 302).

2 Obtain some rooting hormone from a gardening shop and make up a solution of it.

3 Pour the solution into a small beaker to a depth of not more than 2 cm.

4 Pour distilled water into a second beaker to the same depth.

5 Stand one of the cuttings in the beaker of hormone, and the other cutting in the beaker of water. Leave them side by side in a warm, evenly lit place and observe them at intervals during the next week or so.

Do the cuttings produce roots from the cut stem?

If so, which one produces them first?

What conclusions would you draw from this experiment?

Is it sufficient to do this experiment on only two cuttings?

# Assignments

1 Give the name of one hormone which controls growth in plants and one which controls growth in animals. In each case say where the hormone comes from.

2 Explain the reason behind each of the following:
   a) A gardener cuts the tops off a row of shrubs so as to make a thick hedge.
   b) He dips his cuttings in 'rooting powder' before he sticks them in the soil.

3 The diagram on the right shows an experiment which a scientist carried out on the shoots of three growing seedlings. In each case a thin piece of metal was placed between the tip and the rest of the shoot.
   a) What do you think the scientist was trying to prove?
   b) What do you think the effect would be in each case, and why?

4 What is the difference between a benign and a malignant tumour?

5 Which of the experiments in Figure 4 best supports the hypothesis that growth of a shoot is stimulated by a hormone produced at the tip? Give reasons for your choice.

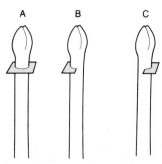

# Eggs, sperms and sexual development

*Sexual reproduction
involves the union of an
egg and a sperm. As a result,
a new individual comes into being.
In this Topic we will look at
eggs and sperms and see
when and how they
are formed.*

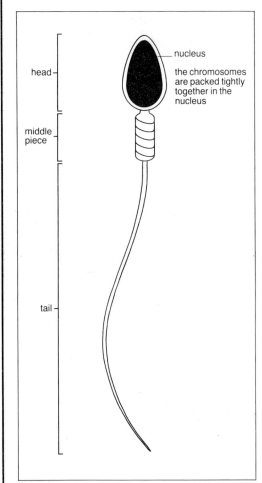

**Figure 1** A human sperm. The head is about 3 micrometres wide and the whole sperm including the tail is about 60 micrometres long.

**Figure 2** A human egg with a sperm alongside to show their relative sizes. The egg has a diameter of about a tenth of a millimetre: that is about forty times wider than the head of the sperm. Its nucleus is much larger than the sperm's nucleus and so the chromosomes are more spread out. In fact, the number of chromosomes is the same in each.

## The structure of eggs and sperms

A human **sperm** is shown in Figure 1. It is extremely small and is shaped like a tadpole with a head and tail (Investigation 1). The tail flaps from side to side, enabling it to swim. The sperm consists of only one cell, and the nucleus is in its head.

A human **egg** is shown in Figure 2. It, too, is a single cell but it is much larger than the sperm. It is shaped like a round ball and is surrounded by a thin membrane and a layer of jelly. The nucleus is situated towards the centre.

The nuclei of the sperm and egg contain chromosomes, thread-like bodies which carry genes. The genes are responsible for passing on the parents' characteristics to the offspring.

## How are eggs and sperms made?

Sperms are made in the **testes** of the male (Figure 3). Eggs are made in the **ovaries** of the female (Figure 4). If you look at thin sections of the ovary and testis under the microscope you can see the eggs and sperms developing (Investigation 2 and 3). Collectively eggs and sperms are known as **gametes**, and the ovaries and testes are called **gonads**.

## What happens to eggs and sperms?

If left on their own, eggs and sperms simply die. However, if a sperm gets close to an egg, it bumps into it repeatedly and sooner or later it penetrates it. The nuclei of the sperm and egg then join together. The process by which a sperm fuses with an egg is called **fertilisation** (Figure 5). The fertilised egg is called a **zygote**.

## Sexual development

A new-born baby has a complete set of sex organs. However, the testes of a baby boy are not yet able to make sperms, and the ovaries of a baby girl can't produce eggs although thousands of *immature* eggs are already present, ready and waiting.

Between the ages of about twelve and fourteen, the sex organs suddenly become active: the testes start making sperms, and the ovaries start producing eggs. This change constitutes **puberty**, and only when a person reaches this stage is he or she capable of producing children. A young person who has reached puberty is called an **adolescent**. The time when puberty occurs varies from person to person: it usually occurs slightly earlier in girls than in boys, and interestingly it occurs earlier now than it did about fifty years ago. Why do you think this is?

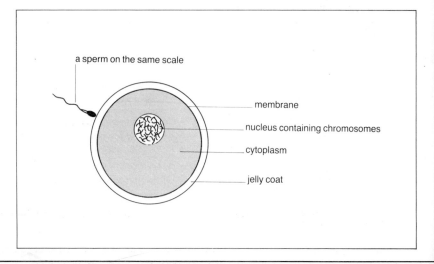

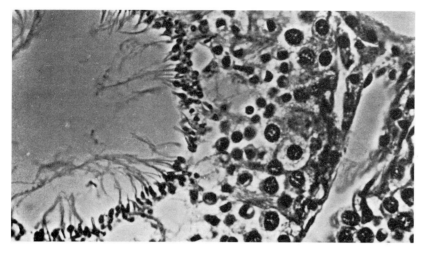

**Figure 3** A section of a testis as it appears under the microscope, highly magnified. Notice the sperm tails. They are hanging into one of the many tubules of which the testis is composed.

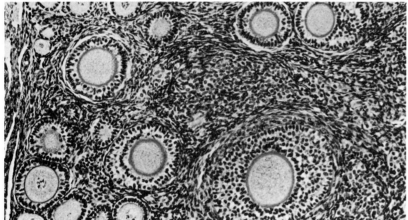

**Figure 4** A section of an ovary as seen magnified under the light microscope. The round objects are immature eggs. A human ovary, at birth, contains thousands of immature eggs.

Puberty is brought on by **sex hormones** which start being produced by the ovaries and testes themselves. The male sex hormones are called **androgens** (the main one is called **testosterone**), and the female ones are called **oestrogens**. These in turn are activated by **gonad-stimulating hormones** from the pituitary gland at the base of the brain.

The sex hormones bring about other changes as well. For example, in boys the voice breaks and hair starts growing on the legs, chest and face. A boy who has been through puberty soon finds himself having to shave. However, if a male is castrated, i.e. has his testes removed, before he reaches puberty, these changes do not take place. In medieval times choirboys were sometimes castrated to prevent their voices breaking. Such a person is called a eunuch, and in the choir they were known as castrati.

**Figure 5** These diagrams show how fertilisation occurs in the human.

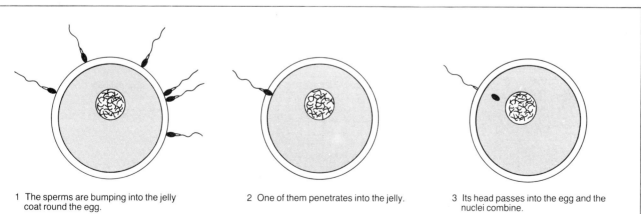

1 The sperms are bumping into the jelly coat round the egg.

2 One of them penetrates into the jelly.

3 Its head passes into the egg and the nuclei combine.

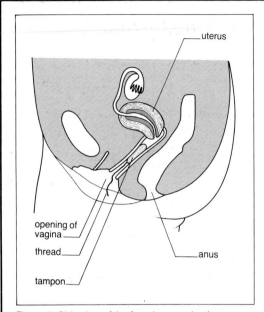

**Figure 6** Side view of the female reproductive system showing where the tampon would be inserted. It can be taken out by means of the thread.

In the female, the breasts start developing, and fat is laid down in the thighs, giving the curves characteristic of the female body.

The various changes which have just been described constitute the person's **secondary sexual characteristics**. At this stage boys and girls both become more interested in the opposite sex.

Puberty comes on quite suddenly. Boys who don't masturbate may have a 'wet dream': semen gradually builds up in the body and is discharged spontaneously during sleep. Boys who do masturbate may not have a 'wet dream'; they simply find that semen is produced when they reach a climax.

The female starts having 'periods' which are characterised by bleeding from the vagina. This bleeding is caused by the lining of the womb (uterus) breaking down, and it is known as **menstruation**. Menstrual periods tend to occur irregularly at first, but eventually they take place at fairly regular intervals of about twenty-eight days. Generally the bleeding goes on for about five days. During this time the woman wears an absorptive 'sanitary pad' or inserts a cotton wool 'tampon' (Figure 6). Some women don't feel any ill effects at these times, but others feel tense and under the weather for several days beforehand. The reason why menstruation takes place is explained on page 264.

The changes that occur at puberty are perfectly normal, but people who are worried about them should ask for help from their parents or a counsellor at school. The changes in the hormones sometimes cause depression and emotional swings during adolescence, but they are a normal part of human development.

## Growing old and sexual decline

A female will go on producing an egg every month until she reaches the age of forty-five to fifty. Her ovaries then stop producing eggs, her menstrual periods cease and she is no longer able to become pregnant. These changes occur because she stops producing sex hormones in such large amounts, and she may feel tired and run-down for some months. It is called the **menopause** or 'change of life'.

Men do not go through a change of this kind. Normally a man goes on producing some sperms for the whole of his life. However, the amount of sex hormones which he produces gradually falls, and he may experience a gradual decline in his desire for sexual activity.

**Table 1** Summary of sexual development of the human male and female.

|  | Male (♂) | Female (♀) |
|---|---|---|
| **AT BIRTH** | Testes have descended into scrotal sac but they do not make sperms yet. | Ovaries containing immature eggs are present in abdomen but they do not produce eggs yet. |
| 12–14 years **PUBERTY** | PITUITARY GLAND ↓ gonad-stimulating hormones ↓ TESTES ↓ male sex hormones (androgens) ↓ Testes start producing sperms. Secondary sexual characters develop, e.g. growth of body hair and breaking of voice. | PITUITARY GLAND ↓ gonad-stimulating hormones ↓ OVARIES ↓ female sex hormones (oestrogens) ↓ Ovaries start producing eggs. Secondary sexual characters develop, e.g. growth of breasts and laying down of fat in thighs. |
| 45–50 |  | MENOPAUSE ('change of life') Ovaries stop producing eggs |

# Investigation 1

## Looking at sperms

Your teacher will do the first three steps in this investigation.

1 Obtain a male rat which has just been killed for dissection.

2 Cut open the scrotal sac.

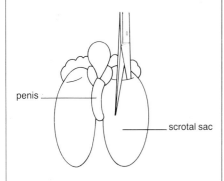

penis

scrotal sac

3 Cut into the testis and draw up a little of the milky fluid into a pipette.

4 Put two drops of the fluid on a slide, and add one drop of salt solution (0.9 per cent).

5 Put on a coverslip.

6 Observe under the microscope: low power first, then high power.

Can you see any sperms?

Which structures shown in Figure 1 can you see?

Are the sperms moving?

If not, suggest reasons for this.

Your teacher will give you some bull semen obtained from an artificial insemination centre.

7 Put a drop of the semen on a slide and put on a coverslip.

8 Observe it under the microscope: low power, then high power.

How do the bull sperms differ from those of the rat?

# Investigation 2

## Looking inside the testis

1 Obtain a prepared slide of a mature testis of a mammal (a thin section which has been cut, stained and mounted on a slide).

2 Examine it under the low power of the microscope.

3 Locate sperms with their long tails.

Which other structures shown in Figure 3 can you see?

# Investigation 3

## Looking inside the ovary

1 Obtain a prepared slide of a mature ovary of a mammal (a thin section which has been cut, stained and mounted on a slide).

2 Examine it under the low power of the microscope.

3 Locate the eggs. You will find them towards the edge of the ovary.

Which other structures shown in Figure 4 can you see?

# Assignments

1 Write down five ways in which a human sperm differs from an egg. Far more sperms are produced than eggs: why do you think this is?

2 Which of the following are associated with the ovary, which with the testis, and which with both the ovary and testis: oestrogen, sex hormones, wet dream, androgen, pituitary gland?

3 Briefly explain each of the following:

a) puberty
b) sex hormone,
c) menstruation,
d) secondary sexual characteristics,
e) menopause.

4 In a certain town in Canada there is a horizontal line by the door of buses.

If the top of the passenger's head comes below this line, he is only charged half fare. The bus company has had to raise the level of this line twice during the last thirty years. Why do you think they have had to do this?

5 The Smith family consists of father, aged 50, mother 45, John 17 and Wendy 16. During the past three years the number of family rows has increased by 30 per cent. Suggest reasons.

6 Professor J.M. Tanner has estimated the relative rates of growth of the brain, the body in general, and the reproductive organs in humans. His findings are shown in the graph below. Explain what the graph shows, and then suggest reasons why the three curves are different.

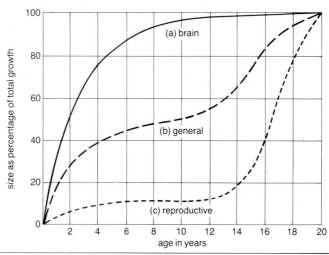

# The menstrual cycle

*Approximately once a month from puberty to the menopause the human female experiences a menstrual period. This is part of a cycle of events which occurs inside her body.*

## What happens during the cycle?

The cycle starts with menstruation, for which reason it is known as the **menstrual cycle**. During menstruation the lining of the uterus breaks down and a small amount of blood passes out through the vagina. This is what's meant by 'having a period'.

Thousands of immature eggs are present in the ovaries. Immediately after menstruation one of these eggs starts developing. As it develops, it becomes enclosed in a protective structure called a **Graafian follicle** which gradually gets larger and becomes hollow. About two weeks after the beginning of menstruation, the follicle moves to the edge of the ovary and the mature egg pops out of it into the oviduct. This process is called **ovulation** (Figure 1).

While the follicle has been developing in the ovary, the lining of the uterus has gradually been healing and building itself up again, so that when ovulation occurs it is ready to receive a fertilised egg, should one become available.

When the egg is shed from the ovary, the follicle stays behind and develops into a solid object called the **yellow body** (corpus luteum). We shall see what its job is presently. Meanwhile the lining of the uterus continues to develop: it thickens and numerous blood vessels grow into it. About two weeks after ovulation, the yellow body withers away and at the same time the lining of the uterus breaks down and menstruation occurs. The whole cycle then begins all over again.

Figure 2 shows how the changes which occur in the ovary and the uterus fit in with each other.

## How is the menstrual cycle controlled?

The menstrual cycle is controlled by hormones. The pituitary gland at the base of the brain produces a hormone which causes the follicle to develop in the ovary. The ovary in turn produces another hormone (**oestrogen**) which causes the lining of the uterus to repair itself after menstruation.

At the time of ovulation the pituitary gland starts producing a second hormone which causes the follicle to turn into the yellow body in the ovary. The yellow body in turn produces another hormone called **progesterone** which causes the lining of the uterus to become thicker and full of blood vessels.

We can sum up by saying that oestrogen and progesterone repair the uterus after menstruation and prepare it for receiving an embryo. If the egg does not get fertilised, the two hormones stop being produced: as a result the lining of the uterus breaks down and menstruation occurs.

## What happens to the menstrual cycle during pregnancy?

If a woman conceives and becomes pregnant, her menstrual periods stop until after the baby has been born. In fact the sign that the woman is pregnant is that she will miss her usual 'period'.

What causes menstruation to stop like this? The presence of an embryo in the uterus causes the yellow body to stay in the ovary and go on producing progesterone. As a result, the lining of the uterus remains intact, and continues to thicken and build itself up. So progesterone *prevents* menstruation. At the same time it stops any further eggs being produced by the ovaries.

## Breeding seasons

In the human female the sexual cycle just described goes on all the time and the female can become pregnant at any time of the year. This is true of many other animals too, including rats, mice and rabbits. However, some animals have a special breeding season when they are said to be on heat. Only at these times do their ovaries produce eggs. For example, in temperate regions dogs come on heat in the early spring, cats in the spring and autumn, and hamsters any time between March and October.

*luteinising hormone*

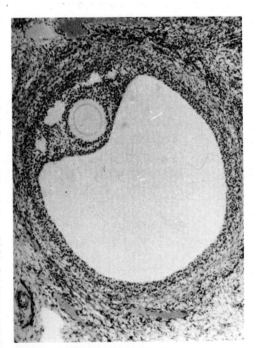

**Figure 1** A Graafian follicle in the ovary as seen under the microscope. The egg is about to be released.

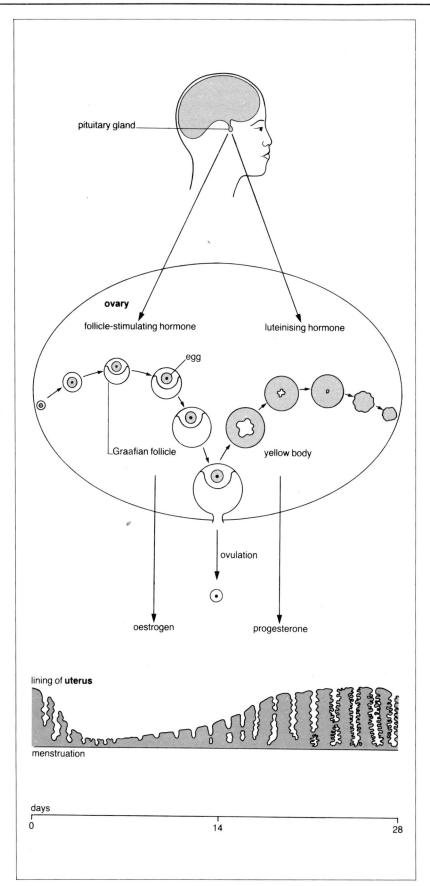

Figure 2 This diagram summarises the main things that occur during the menstrual cycle of the female.

# Assignments

1 How does the menstrual cycle get its name?

2 Explain what happens to the lining of the uterus when:
   a) a Graafian follicle develops in the ovary,
   b) the yellow body (corpus luteum) degenerates,
   c) the Graafian follicle changes into a yellow body,
   d) ovary-stimulating hormones are being produced by the pituitary gland,
   e) ovulation occurs.

3 This question is about the hormones which control the menstrual cycle.
   a) Name the hormones which prepare the uterus for pregnancy.
   b) Where is each hormone produced?
   c) How do the hormones get to the uterus from the organ which produces them?
   d) At what stage in the menstrual cycle is each hormone *most* active?
   e) At what stage in the cycle are both hormones *least* active?

4 Why is it important that a female's menstrual periods should stop when she is pregnant? What causes them to stop?

5 The graph shows the relative amounts of the hormones oestrogen and progesterone in the bloodstream of a human female during the first 14 days of the menstrual cycle.
   a) Explain the graph as fully as you can.
   b) What do you think happens to the amount of progesterone after the 14th day, and why?

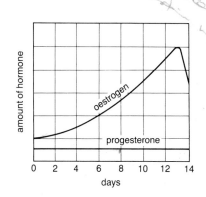

# Bringing eggs and sperms together

*In this Topic we will see how sperms and eggs are brought together. This will involve studying the reproductive system.*

## The reproductive system of the male

The reproductive system of the human male is shown in Figure 1. Many of the structures you can see for yourself by dissecting a mammal such as a rat (Investigation 1). The **testes** are suspended in the scrotal sac just behind the penis. Their job is to manufacture sperms. Because they are positioned outside the main body cavity, they are slightly cooler than the rest of the body. This is important because the testes make sperms more rapidly in cool conditions. During development of a baby boy, the testes start off in the abdominal cavity, but later they move down into the scrotal sac. Normally this has happened by the time the baby is born, but occasionally one or other testis does not come down until after birth.

Each testis is made up of a large number of narrow **sperm tubules** where the sperms are made. If they were placed end to end, these tubules would be over 500 metres long, that's long enough to go right round a football pitch. This gives the testes a high production rate.

As the sperms are produced, they move into a coiled tube called the **epididymis** where they are stored. The epididymis lies alongside the testis in the scrotal sac and it leads to the **sperm duct**. This is connected with the **urethra** which runs down the centre of the **penis**. The head of the penis, known as the **glans**, is highly sensitive and is protected by the **foreskin**. The foreskin is sometimes removed in the operation known as **circumcision**: this may be done for religious reasons (for example all Jews normally have it done), or because the foreskin is too tight. The operation is carried out at an early age, and there is no evidence that it is in any way harmful.

Various glands open into the sperm ducts and urethra. These include the **prostate gland** which is wrapped round the top of the urethra like a scarf. The

**Figure 1** The reproductive system of the human male.

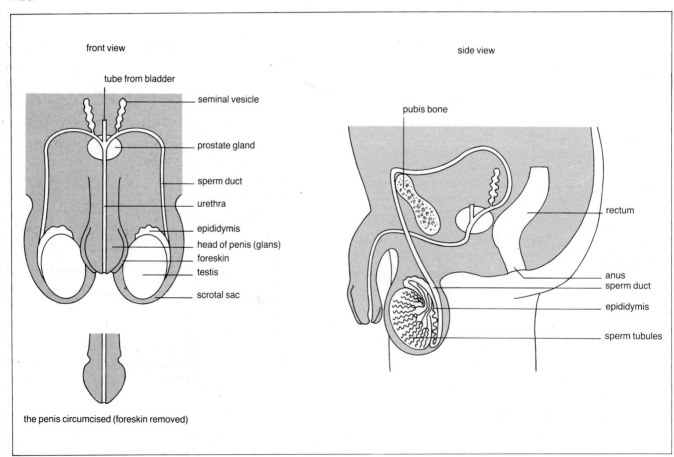

front view

tube from bladder

seminal vesicle

prostate gland

sperm duct

urethra

epididymis

head of penis (glans)

foreskin

testis

scrotal sac

the penis circumcised (foreskin removed)

side view

pubis bone

rectum

anus

sperm duct

epididymis

sperm tubules

glands produce a fluid which keeps the sperms alive and helps them to swim vigorously. This fluid, together with the sperms themselves, make up **semen**. If ejaculation does not occur, the sperms simply die and disintegrate.

If you look at Figure 1 you will see that the bladder and sperm ducts both open into the urethra. However, urine and semen never pass down the urethra at the same time. This is because it's impossible to urinate and ejaculate at the same time.

## The reproductive system of the female

The female's reproductive system is shown in Figure 2, and as with the male the various structures can be seen by dissecting a mammal such as the rat (Investigation 2). There are two **ovaries**, one on either side of the abdomen. Once every 28 days or so one or other of the ovaries produces an egg which is shed into the **oviduct**. The oviduct is also known as the **Fallopian tube**. The egg moves slowly down the oviduct towards the **uterus**. If it isn't fertilised within a day or so it will die.

The uterus, or womb, is where the baby develops. Below it is the **vagina**. The lining of the uterus and vagina secrete a lot of mucus.

In Figure 2 you will see that the vagina opens to the outside quite separately from the tube that carries urine from the bladder. Close to the urinary opening is a small protuberance called the **clitoris**. This is the female's equivalent of the penis and it can become erect during sexual excitement.

**Figure 2**  The reproductive system of the human female.

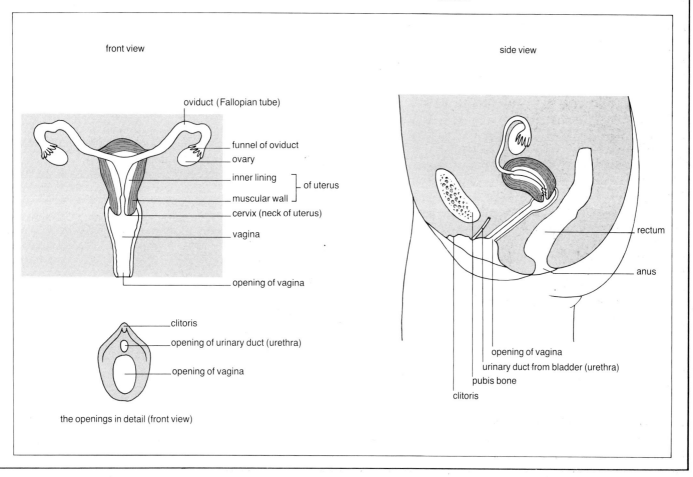

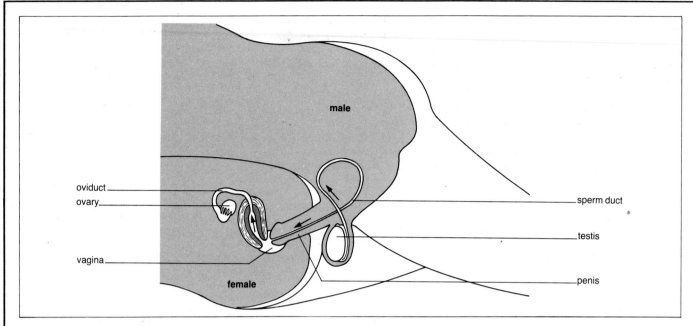

**Figure 3**  In intercourse sperms pass from the male to the female as indicated by the arrows in this diagram.

*Intercourse*

For sperms to get to the egg, **intercourse** (copulation) must take place.

First the penis of the male becomes stiff and hard. This is called an **erection**, and it's brought about by the blood pressure increasing inside the penis. The male then puts his erect penis into the vagina. Drops of fluid, secreted by the male's glands, emerge from the tip of the penis and serve as a lubricant, as does the mucus lining the vagina.

The male then moves his penis rhythmically inside the vagina. The head of the penis is very sensitive, and repeated stimulation of it results in **ejaculation**: this is a reflex in which the semen is expelled from the urethra with considerable force. It's brought about by a series of contractions which sweep down the sperm ducts and along the urethra.

Ejaculation is accompanied by a pleasurable feeling called an **orgasm**. The female may experience an orgasm too, though it usually takes longer for her to reach this point. It's brought about by stimulation of the clitoris.

Normally the male produces about 4 cm$^3$ of semen: that's about a teaspoonful. This may not seem much but it can contain as many as 500 million sperms. Once deposited in the vagina, the sperms swim through the mucus lining the uterus and up the oviducts (Figure 3).

**Figure 4**  After the egg has been fertilised it develops into a little ball of cells which becomes implanted in the lining of the uterus.

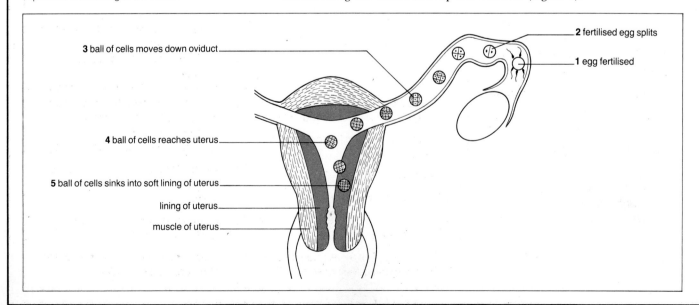

If there's an egg in the oviduct, one of the sperms may bump into it and fertilise it. Although it's only a short distance from the vagina to the top of the oviduct, the sperms are very small and the journey is not an easy one. Many never reach the egg. The reason why so many are produced is to raise the chance of one of them getting through.

What happens if there is no egg in the oviduct? The sperms can stay alive in the oviduct for as long as eight days. However, they are able to fertilise an egg for only two or three days. If an egg is shed from the ovary within this time, it may get fertilised.

What happens if an egg is produced and there are no sperms to fertilise it? The egg is capable of being fertilised for at least a day after ovulation, so if intercourse occurs within this time fertilisation may occur.

## What happens to the fertilised egg?

After fertilisation, the egg divides up into a little ball of cells which moves down the oviduct to the uterus (Figure 4). It then sinks into the soft lining of the uterus, a process called **implantation**. If this happens, we say that the woman has conceived. She is now pregnant.

# Investigation 1

**Looking at the male reproductive system**

1  Your teacher will give you a male rat which has been dissected so as to show the reproductive system.

2  Find the penis and scrotal sacs.

3  Cut into one of the scrotal sacs and locate the testis (see Investigation 1, p. 263).

    What is the coiled tube lying alongside the testis?

    Where does it lead?

    Which other structures shown in Figure 1 can you see in your dissected rat?

    The male rat differs from the human in having relatively larger seminal vesicles. They look rather like cauliflowers, one on each side of the bladder.

4  Feel the hard bone covering the top end of the urethra.

    What is this bone?

    What do you think it is for?

    *Note* Rats often carry diseases such as leptospirosis. Great care must be taken while handling them. It is better to use guinea pigs whenever possible.

# Investigation 2

**Looking at the female reproductive system**

1  Your teacher will give you a female rat which has been dissected so as to show the reproductive system.

2  Find the ovaries. These are small round organs on either side of the abdominal cavity.

3  Locate the oviduct and uterus.

    The female rat differs from the human in having a Y-shaped uterus, as shown in the illustration below.

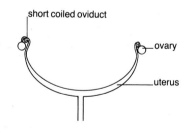

short coiled oviduct
ovary
uterus

    What other structures shown in Figure 2 can you see in your rat?

4  Feel the hard bone just posterior to the uterus.

    What is this bone?

    What do you think it is for?

5  Find the opening of the vagina to the exterior.

    There is another small opening close to the vaginal opening: what is it?

# Assignments

1  Why is it important that a very large number of sperms should be present in the semen?

2  Why is it an advantage for the testes to be situated in the scrotal sac outside the main body cavity? Can you think of any disadvantages?

3  The diagram below shows a transverse section through a penis.

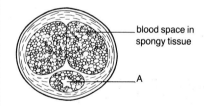

blood space in spongy tissue
A

    a) What is the name of the structure labelled A?
    b) Give two functions of this structure.
    c) At what particular times does it perform each of these functions?
    d) What is the function of the spongy tissue?
    e) Why is this function important?

4  Which structures in the female are equivalent to these structures in the male:

    (a) penis, (b) testes, (c) sperm ducts, (d) urethra?

    In each case say in what respect the structures are equivalent.

# Pregnancy and birth

*If an egg gets fertilised it divides into a ball of cells which sinks into the lining of the uterus. The woman is then pregnant.*

## What happens in the uterus?

The ball of cells is an **embryo**. An embryo is simply an early stage in the development of an organism from the egg to the adult. In the next two months the cells multiply and differentiate, and gradually the embryo grows into a **foetus**. The foetus looks like a miniature human being (Figure 1). Earlier stages are shown in Figures 2 and 3.

## The private pond of the foetus

As the embryo develops it becomes surrounded by a thin membrane called the **amnion**. You can see it in Figure 1. This membrane encloses a cavity called the **amniotic cavity** and it's filled with a watery **amniotic fluid**.

As development goes on, the amniotic cavity expands like a balloon until eventually it fills the entire uterus. The foetus floats in the middle of it, in a kind of 'private pond'. The amniotic fluid cushions the foetus, protecting it from being bumped and damaged as the mother moves around.

## How is the foetus kept alive?

Attached to the belly of the foetus is a tough strand called the **umbilical cord**. This is its lifeline, bringing it all the things it needs such as oxygen and food substances, and taking away carbon dioxide and excretory waste.

The umbilical cord runs to a structure called the **placenta**, which is attached to the lining of the uterus (Figure 4). The placenta is shaped like a plate, and it has numerous finger-like **villi** which stick into blood spaces in the wall of the uterus. The mother's blood circulates through these spaces, and the villi contain blood capillaries which are connected to the foetus by an artery and vein in the umbilical cord (Figure 5). The barrier separating the foetus's blood from the mother's blood is very thin. As the foetus's blood flows through the placenta it picks up oxygen and dissolved food substances from the mother's blood. At the same time it sheds carbon dioxide and excretory waste (urea) *into* the mother's blood.

It's not just food and oxygen that pass from the mother to the foetus. Antibodies do so too. These help to protect the new-born baby from diseases until it has had a chance to make its own antibodies.

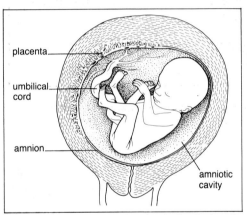

placenta

umbilical cord

amnion

amniotic cavity

**Figure 1** The foetus 14 weeks after the beginning of pregnancy.

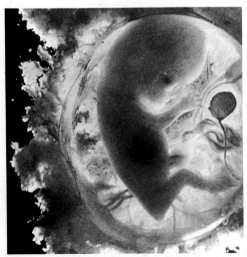

**Figure 2** A photograph of a five week-old human foetus inside the mother's uterus. Which structures in Figure 1 can you see in this photograph?

**Figure 3** (right) A human foetus at 6½ weeks and (far right) at 10 weeks. Note the formation of the fingers and toes and the development of the head.

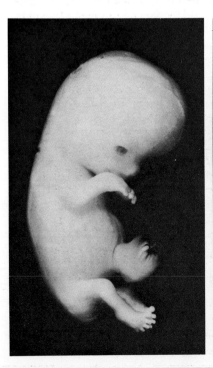

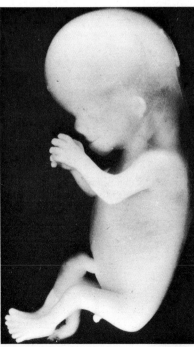

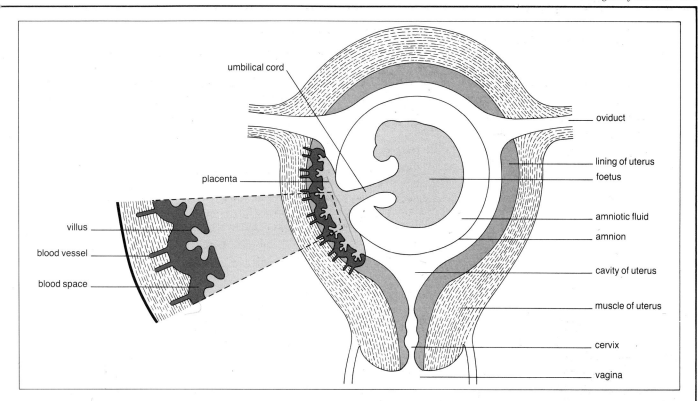

**Figure 4** This diagram shows the uterus of a pregnant woman.

So the placenta supplies the foetus with everything it needs. In addition it produces the hormones oestrogen and progesterone which stop menstruation and prevent any further eggs being produced by the ovaries. These hormones are also produced by the ovaries themselves (see page 264).

## Growth of the foetus

By the end of the third month the foetus is fully formed right down to the fingers and toes. It now grows until it fills the uterus. Meanwhile the uterus expands greatly in order to accommodate the foetus, and its wall becomes thicker and more muscular in readiness for birth. As the baby grows it gets more active: it moves its arms and legs and by the end of the fourth month the mother may feel it moving inside her.

## Care during pregnancy

During pregnancy it's important that the woman should eat the right kind of food and not do anything which might injure her baby. From time to time she visits an **ante-natal clinic** where she is examined by a doctor to make sure that everything is progressing normally, and she is given advice on how to prepare for the birth of her baby. This is called **pre-natal** care.

If the woman feels unwell during her pregnancy, the doctor may give her some medicine to help. However, doctors are cautious about prescribing new drugs, however thoroughly they have been tested beforehand. In the 1960s a number of pregnant women in Britain were given a drug called thalidomide to help them get to sleep: as a result some of them gave birth to babies with severe deformities, such as no arms or legs.

This was a tragedy which no one wants to see repeated. Even smoking and alcohol can affect the health of the foetus. The point is that the placenta is very good at supplying the foetus with the things it needs, but by the same token it may supply it with things it does *not* need.

Certain germs may also get across the placenta and harm the baby. Such is the case with the virus that causes German measles, and this is why girls who have not had this disease are always immunised against it. The germs that cause venereal diseases can also get across the placenta and damage the baby.

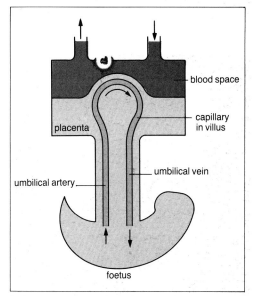

**Figure 5** This simplified diagram shows the relationship between the blood of the foetus and the mother. Although the two bloodstreams come very close to each other, they never mix. If the two systems were joined, the mother's blood pressure might burst the foetus's blood vessels. Also, if the bloods belonged to different blood groups agglutination would occur.

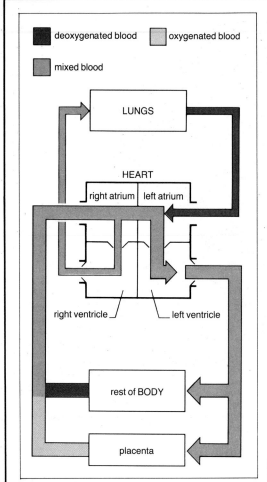

deoxygenated blood    oxygenated blood

mixed blood

LUNGS

HEART

right atrium | left atrium

right ventricle | left ventricle

rest of BODY

placenta

**Figure 6** The general plan of the foetus's circulation. Compare this with the adult circulation on page 134.

| Animal | Gestation period |
|---|---|
| hamster | 17 days |
| mouse | 18 days |
| rabbit | 1 month |
| cat | 2 months |
| dog | 2 months |
| guinea pig | 2 months |
| sheep | 5 months |
| chimpanzee | 7 months |
| cattle | 9 months |
| man | 9 months |
| horse | 11 months |
| elephant | 20 months |

**Table 1** The gestation periods of a selection of mammals.

## The circulation of the foetus

Look at the general plan of the foetus's circulation in Figure 6. Notice that the blood which enters the right atrium has been oxygenated by the placenta; very little of it goes to the lungs, which are not working at this stage. Most of the blood goes straight to the body. It bypasses the lungs by going through a hole in the partition between the two atria, or through a vessel called the 'ductus', which links the pulmonary artery and the aorta.

Immediately after birth the placenta stops functioning and the lungs take over the job of oxygenating the blood. The blood entering the right atrium now becomes deoxygenated. The hole between the atria closes and blood flows to the lungs in the usual way (see page 134).

Occasionally the hole between the atria fails to close at birth. As a result the baby's tissues suffer from lack of oxygen and the skin goes blue, giving a 'blue baby'. An emergency operation may have to be done – the famous 'hole in the heart' operation. The heart is cut open and the hole sewed up. Unless the oxygen lack is very severe, the doctors prefer to delay this kind of operation until the baby is a little older and can stand up to it.

Sometimes the 'ductus' fails to close at birth. It is easier to put this right because it can be tied off with a piece of thread.

## The gestation period

The time between conception and birth is called the **gestation period**. It lasts approximately nine months in the human, but is different in most other mammals (Table 1). At the end of the gestation period the baby is ready to be born.

## Birth

At the end of the gestation period the uterus begins to undergo occasional contractions which become steadily more frequent and powerful. This is called **labour**, and it's the first sign that the baby is about to be born. At about this time the amnion bursts and the amniotic fluid escapes through the vagina: this is called the 'breaking of the waters'. Soon afterwards the uterus starts contracting so powerfully that the foetus is pushed through the vagina. Usually the baby comes out head first (Figure 7). However, babies are sometimes born feet first or bottom first.

Once the baby has come out, it starts to breathe. If it doesn't start breathing of its own accord, the doctor or nurse may give it a tap on the backside causing it to take a quick breath in. The umbilical cord, no longer needed, is tied and cut: you can see it in Figure 8 – the scar becomes the person's navel or 'belly button'. Meanwhile the placenta comes away from the wall of the uterus and passes out through the vagina. This is called the **afterbirth**. The average mass of a newborn baby is just over 3 kg. The birth, or delivery as it's called by doctors and nurses, is now complete.

Birth is brought about by a change in the amounts of hormones produced by the placenta, and also by a hormone which starts being produced by the pituitary gland. This is called **oxytocin** and it brings about the contractions of the uterus.

A woman may have her baby either in hospital or at home, depending on circumstances. Most babies are born quite easily. Sometimes, however, the baby needs to be helped out with forceps: these are like a large pair of tongs and are used to gently grasp the baby's head as it emerges. In particularly difficult cases the medical staff may feel it's best to give the mother an anaesthetic and remove the baby by cutting open the wall of the abdomen and uterus. This operation is known as a **Caesarian section** because Julius Caesar is believed to have been born this way.

Sometimes birth occurs before the ninth month, and the baby is **premature**. If the baby is not too small and weak it will probably survive, though it may have to be kept warm in an incubator and given a special oxygen supply until it is mature enough to support itself.

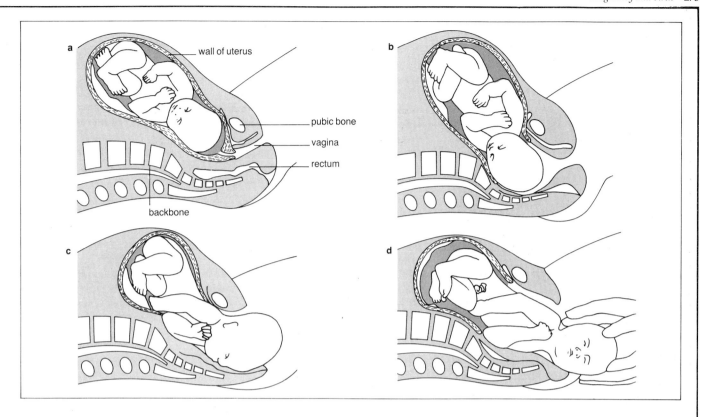

**Figure 7** These diagrams show how birth takes place.

Occasionally things go wrong at an early stage of pregnancy and the foetus is expelled from the uterus. If it's not already dead, it dies almost immediately afterwards. This is called a **miscarriage**. It is, of course, very distressing for a woman who is looking forward to the birth of her baby. However, it does not mean that she cannot become pregnant again, and during a subsequent pregnancy the doctor will give her special help to prevent it happening again.

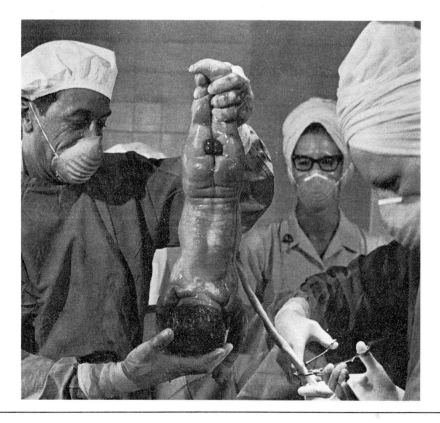

**Figure 8** This baby has just been delivered and has taken its first breath. Notice the umbilical cord on the right.

Figure 9 A mother breast-feeding her baby. The mother's milk is a perfect food, containing all the chemicals that the baby needs, and delivered at just the right temperature. It also contains antibodies which may help to protect the baby from certain diseases and allergies. Breast-feeding allows a close contact between the mother and her baby – and it's cheaper than bottle-feeding!

Figure 10 Twins! The top pair are non-identical; the bottom pair are identical.

## Caring for the newborn baby

During pregnancy the mother's breasts enlarge and the **mammary glands** inside them get ready to secrete **milk**. Soon after birth the baby starts to suck its mother's nipples. This stimulates the breasts to release the milk and make more.

Milk is the baby's food for the first few months of life. Of course it doesn't *have* to get milk from its mother: it can be fed from a bottle with a teat. However, there's a lot to be said for breast-feeding as you will see if you read the caption under Figure 9. It's not possible for the baby to take in solid food at this stage, for its digestive system would be unable to cope with solids.

Mothers wrap their babies up well, particularly in cold weather. This is necessary because the baby's ability to control its body temperature takes time to develop. Whereas adults adjust to the cold by shivering and making more heat, the baby is not yet able to do this efficiently.

These are just a few aspects of looking after one's baby. Additional advice can be found from the local clinic.

After six weeks the mother will go back to the clinic for **a post-natal** examination to make sure that her own health is satisfactory. As the baby grows older more and more foods can be added to the diet. The child must also be protected against infectitious diseases in its early years.

## Twins and multiple births

In the human, only one embryo usually develops in the uterus at a time. However, two may sometimes be present together, each with its own

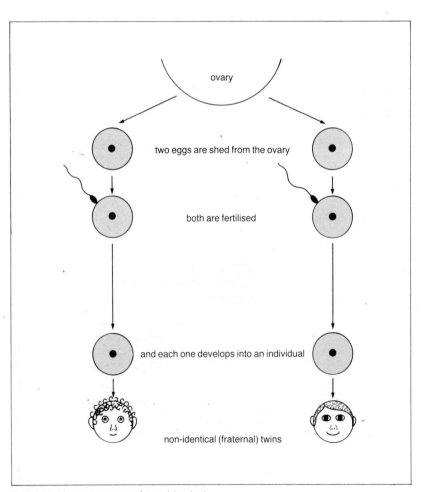

Figure 11 How twins occur. **A** non-identical

placenta and umbilical cord. These are known as **twins**.

There are two kinds of twins: non-identical and identical (Figure 10).

Non-identical twins arise if two eggs are shed from the ovaries at the same time, and both are fertilised. Although the two babies will be born together, they don't have the same genes and will be no more alike than brothers or sisters. Twins of this sort are known as fraternal twins and they may be of different sexes (Figure 11A).

Identical twins arise in a quite different way. A single egg is shed from one of the ovaries and fertilised. It then splits into two cells, *each* of which develops into an embryo. The two cells have exactly the same genes, and so the two babies will be exactly alike and will be the same sex (Figure 11B).

Sometimes the two cells into which the egg splits do not separate completely. The result is that the two embryos are joined together at some point, resulting in **Siamese twins**. If the connection is not too extensive, the two babies can be separated by an operation; but if the internal organs are intimately connected, it's very difficult to separate them and it is unlikely that both will survive.

Occasionally three or more eggs are produced by the ovaries at the same time, resulting in triplets, quadruplets or even quintuplets. Such **multiple births** tend to occur in women who have been given a fertility drug to help them get pregnant. As the foetuses grow, it becomes more and more difficult for the mother's uterus to contain them, and so she gives birth early, often around the seventh month. Very rarely do all the babies survive.

Although multiple births are unusual in man, they are quite usual in other mammals such as dogs, cats and mice. The offspring constitute a **litter**.

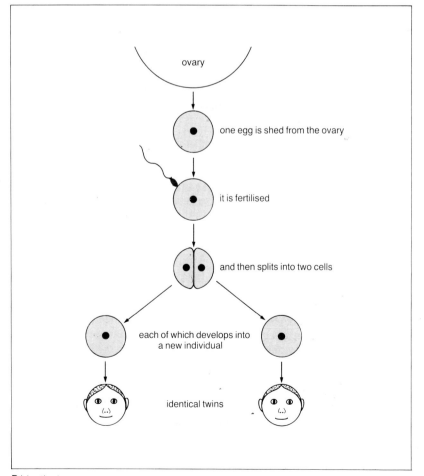

B identical.

# Assignments

1 What functions are performed by
   a) the muscle in the wall of the uterus,
   b) the amniotic fluid,
   c) the umbilical cord, and
   d) the mammary glands?

2 Name five jobs which are carried out by the placenta. What is it about the structure of the placenta which makes it ideally suited to do these jobs?

3 Babies are usually born head first. What advantages are there in being born this way? What changes take place in the baby's body soon after it is born?

4 Some of the daily food requirements of an adult woman with a body mass of 55 kg, and of the same woman in an advanced state of pregnancy are given in the following table:

|  | non-pregnant | pregnant |
|---|---|---|
| Energy | 9200 kJ | 10 700 kJ |
| Protein | 29 g | 38 g |
| Vitamin A | 750 µg | 750 µg |
| Vitamin D | 2.5 µg | 10 µg |
| Vitamin C | 30 mg | 30 mg |
| Calcium | 0.5 g | 1.2 g |
| Iron | 20 mg | 28 mg |

   a) Suggest one reason why the woman requires more energy when she is pregnant.
   b) Name two kinds of food from which she is likely to obtain most of this energy.
   c) Suggest one reason why she requires extra protein when she is pregnant.
   d) Why do you think she needs extra vitamin D and calcium when she is pregnant?
   e) What are the percentage increases in the amount of energy, protein, vitamin D and calcium which she needs when she is pregnant?
   f) Which substances in the table do not need to be increased during pregnancy?
   g) Why do you think those particular substances do not need to be increased?

# Personal aspects of sex

*Sex is not
just a bodily function.
It involves feelings, emotions and
personal choices.*

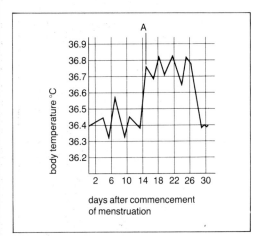

**Figure 1** This graph shows the changes in the basal body temperature of a human female during the course of her menstrual cycle. The basal body temperature is the body temperature when completely relaxed. The rise in temperature at A is when ovulation occurs.

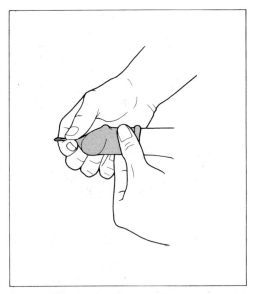

**Figure 2** The sheath is here seen being slipped onto the erect penis.

## How many children?

One of the most important decisions that faces every married couple is how many children to have. A sensible couple will want to give each child the support and love it needs, and this means not having too many. There may therefore be times when the couple wish to *prevent* pregnancy. This is called **family planning** or **birth control**.

Birth control is extremely important, particularly in over-populated countries where there isn't enough food to go round. Every couple should consider how many children they can raise, and in the light of this should use whatever birth control methods are appropriate and in keeping with their beliefs and conscience. In most countries there are family planning clinics where people can get advice about birth control methods. These methods usually involve some form of **contraception**.

## Contraception

Contraception is any procedure which prevents conception. There are many different methods, and some of them involve the use of an artificial device called a **contraceptive**. The methods fall into three groups: (1) those that stop sperms reaching the egg, (2) those that stop eggs being produced, and (3) those that stop the fertilised egg developing in the womb.

Now let's look at each method in turn, and you can decide for yourself which group each one fits into.

### Withdrawal

A commonly used way of avoiding conception is for the male to withdraw his penis from the vagina just before he ejaculates. However, the lubrication fluid which comes from the penis before ejaculation may contain some sperms, and so this is an extremely unreliable method of contraception.

### The rhythm method

A woman will only become pregnant if there is an egg in her body to be fertilised. Now there is a certain length of time in the menstrual cycle when no eggs are available: this is round about the time of menstruation. If she has intercourse at this time, it is unlikely that she will become pregnant. We call this period of time the **safe period**.

The time when intercourse is most likely to lead to pregnancy is round about the time of ovulation. This occurs about half way between one menstrual period and the next; so one should be able to work out roughly when the 'danger' period is from the time of the previous menstruation. The trouble is that the time between menstruations may vary, particularly in teenagers, and this makes the **calendar method**, as it's called, difficult to use.

However there is a more accurate method. It so happens that the body temperature rises slightly at the time of ovulation (Figure 1). By recording the body temperature and the times of menstruation over several months, one can say when ovulation has occurred in the past and when it is likely to occur in the future. This **temperature method** is better than the calendar method, but it is still difficult to be certain about the length of the safe period. It depends on (amongst other things) when exactly the woman ovulates, which can vary a lot. In some cases the safe period may last as long as three weeks, but in other cases it may only last a few days. The rhythm method is therefore unreliable, unless carried out under the expert guidance of a doctor.

### The sheath

This is a type of contraceptive, worn by the male, which stops sperms getting into the female's vagina. Known as the condom, 'rubber' or 'French letter', it consists of a rubber sheath, shaped like the finger of a glove, which fits over the erect penis (Figure 2). A little bag-like extension at the end catches the semen when ejaculation occurs. The rubber is very thin and is usually coated with a lubricant.

The sheath is quite a reliable contraceptive if used properly, and is available from pharmacies. It also has the advantage of reducing the spread of venereal diseases.

### The cap or diaphragm

This type of contraceptive also forms a barrier to sperms, but it is worn by the female. It consists of a dome-shaped piece of rubber with a metal spring round the edge. It comes in various sizes, and the correct one can be chosen by a doctor. It fits over the neck of the uterus and the woman is taught how to put it in herself (Figure 3).

The cap is a pretty good contraceptive. However, it may slip out of place if it hasn't been fitted properly, and sperms may get round it. It's best to use it with a **spermicide** and leave it in for at least six hours after intercourse.

### Spermicides

Spermicides are substances which kill sperms. They are available as sprays, creams or tablets (pessaries). The female should put the spermicide as far up her vagina as possible, not more than ten minutes before intercourse (Figure 4). The tablets dissolve in her normal vaginal secretions, forming a kind of foam.

On their own spermicides are not very effective because sperms sometimes manage to get through them. However, when used with the diaphragm or sheath, they can be very effective.

### The pill

This is a tablet which is taken by the female. It is known as the **oral contraceptive** and it prevents any eggs being produced by the ovaries: in other words it stops ovulation. One tablet has to be taken daily throughout the menstrual cycle except for about a week round about the time of menstruation. Although the tablets prevent ovulation, the woman's menstrual periods still take place at the usual times. The tablets should be prescribed by a doctor, and must be taken *regularly* according to instructions.

How does the pill work? During pregnancy the ovaries and placenta produce the hormones oestrogen and progesterone which prevent any further eggs being produced by the ovaries. The pill contains chemical substances identical with these hormones.

The pill is very effective. Since it came onto the market in the mid-1960s it has done more than any other contraceptive to reduce the number of unwanted births. If a woman who has been on the pill stops taking it, she will start producing eggs again, and can then become pregnant in the normal way.

Does the pill have any snags? Well, some women feel a bit sick for a couple of months after starting it. The pill also raises the blood pressure and, if used over many years, it may be connected with coronary thrombosis and possibly with cancer.

There is a type of pill which need not be taken until *after* intercourse. It does not prevent ovulation, but it stops the embryo becoming implanted in the uterus. Though convenient, this 'morning after' pill makes some women feel sick and so it is normally used only as an emergency measure. To be effective it must be taken within three days after intercourse.

### An injectable contraceptive

There is a substance which, when injected into the body, stops ovulation. It is called **Depo-Provera**. A single intra-muscular injection, carried out by a doctor, will prevent a woman becoming pregnant for about three months. It is a very reliable method of contraception and is used a lot in developing countries. But it is claimed that it may cause cancer, and so some countries have been reluctant to adopt it. It is very much under discussion at the present time.

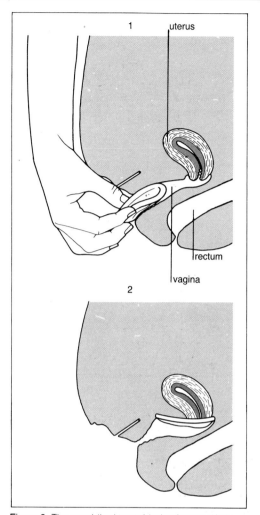

**Figure 3** The cap (diaphragm) being inserted into the vagina. Note how it fits over the neck of the uterus.

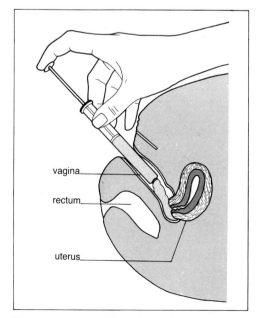

**Figure 4** A spermicidal cream being put into the vagina by means of a syringe. (Side view.)

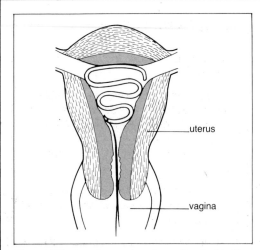

**Figure 5**  The loop is seen here in position inside the uterus, viewed from the front. The strings enable it to be taken out easily by the doctor. It is one of the most widely used intra-uterine devices.

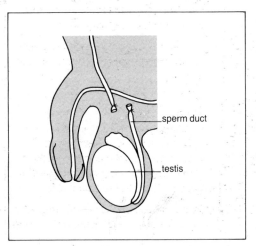

**Figure 6**  In male sterilisation the sperm ducts are cut and tied, as shown here in side view. This operation is called **vasectomy**.

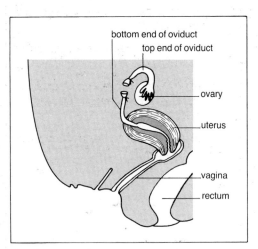

**Figure 7**  In female sterilisation the oviducts are cut and tied, as shown here in side view. This operation is called **tubal ligation**.

## *Intra-uterine devices*

These devices, called IUDs for short, are made of plastic or metal and are put into the uterus by a doctor who simply pushes them up through the vagina. They come in all sorts of shapes: one of the most widely used is shown in Figure 5.

IUDs prevent the embryo becoming implanted in the lining of the uterus. No one knows exactly how they achieve this but they certainly stop the female becoming pregnant. They don't normally cause any discomfort, and are a reliable method of contraception. If a woman with an IUD wants to become pregnant, the IUD can be taken out by a doctor.

## *Sterilisation*

In this method the person has an operation which prevents conception permanently. It can be carried out on either the male or the female. In the male the surgeon ties and cuts the sperm ducts (Figure 6). This prevents sperms getting to the urethra from the testes: the man can still ejaculate, but his semen will not contain any sperms.

In the female the surgeon ties and cuts the oviducts (Figure 7). This stops any sperms getting up the oviducts and so her eggs cannot be fertilised.

Sterilisation is the most complete method of contraception. The operation is simple and quick and there are no unpleasant consequences. Men sometimes fear that sterilisation might reduce their masculinity or change their personality in some way, but this is not true. The only snag is that once you have been sterilised, there is usually no chance of having any children in the future. So it's no use having second thoughts afterwards!

## *How good are these contraceptive methods?*

All the procedures described above are methods of birth control. Table 1 compares how effective they are. Sterilisation was not included since it was already known that in that case the number of pregnancies would have been nil. Depo-Provera and the 'morning after' pill were not investigated because of their possible danger to health.

| Method | Number of pregnancies |
|---|---|
| No method | 50 |
| Rhythm method | 14 |
| Sheath | 7 |
| Diaphragm with spermicide | 10 |
| The pill | 0 |
| IUDs | 2 |

**Table 1**  How good are the various methods of contraception? This table shows the number of pregnancies in 100 women using each method for one year. All the women were intelligent and keen to succeed with their chosen method. With less intelligent and less motivated women many more pregnancies occurred.

## *Abortion*

Despite the various contraceptive methods which are available, women may become pregnant when they don't want to. The only way to avoid giving birth to the baby is to destroy the foetus in the womb. This is known as **abortion**.

There are various ways of carrying out an abortion, and it should always be done in a clinic or hospital by a qualified doctor. It is extremely dangerous for it to be done any other way.

In many countries abortion is only allowed if the doctor considers that by continuing the pregnancy the woman's health is at risk. Some people think that the law should be changed to make abortion more easily available. Many moral and ethical issues are involved in this difficult question.

## Infertility

Some couples are unable to have children, that is, they are **infertile**. One of the commonest causes is that either the male cannot produce sperms or the female cannot produce eggs. The person is said to be **sterile**. Sometimes the male does have sperms in his semen but there simply aren't enough of them to ensure fertilisation, or he may not be able to come to a climax and ejaculate. Another possible cause of sterility is that the female's oviducts are blocked.

A couple who find that they can't produce a baby should discuss their problem with a doctor. The doctor can arrange for them to see a specialist who may be able to find out what's wrong.

A lot can be done to help childless couples these days. For example a woman who isn't producing eggs can be treated with a **fertility drug**. This is a hormone preparation and it stimulates her ovaries to start working. In the past this treatment has sometimes proved more successful than either the patient or the doctor bargained for: the woman has become pregnant and produced quadruplets, quintuplets or even sextuplets!

Scientists can now fertilise human eggs *outside* the body. The egg is taken out of the ovary in a small operation and fertilised by sperm in a test tube. The fertilised egg divides up into a tiny embryo, and this is then put into the uterus where it develops in the usual way. This technique has helped a number of childless couples to have babies.

## Masturbation

Normally an orgasm is achieved by the stimulation which accompanies the rhythmical movements of the penis inside the vagina. However, it can also be achieved by stimulating the penis or the clitoris with, for example, the hand. This is called **masturbation**. It is not in the least harmful and indeed can give considerable relief at times when intercourse is not possible. What *can* be harmful is the feeling of guilt which people sometimes have about it.

## Homosexuality

**Homosexuality** is having sexual feelings towards members of one's own sex, in contrast to **heterosexuality**, which is having sexual feelings towards members of the opposite sex. Homosexual feelings can occur between men or between women. They are quite common during adolescence, but generally only last for a short time and are a natural part of growing up.

Homosexual relationships occur quite often in places where people of the same sex are cooped up together. Such relationships develop mainly because of frustration and are not usually permanent or harmful. The people involved are generally able to form relationships with the opposite sex when the circumstances allow. However, there are people who are *only* capable of relating sexually to persons of their own sex. Such people are usually as normal in appearance and behaviour as heterosexuals, though some male homosexuals may behave in an effeminate manner.

Some individuals are sexually attracted to members of their own sex *and* members of the opposite sex. They are known as **bisexual**.

There is nothing wrong with having homosexual feelings, though a great deal of harm is sometimes done by feelings of guilt and isolation which may accompany them. If a person finds that he or she has homosexual feelings and is worried about them, it's better to talk it over with parents, a counsellor or a trusted friend than to bottle it up. Many different types of professional help are available to those who want it.

# Assignments

1  What does the word contraception mean?

   The sheath is one of the more reliable contraceptives. What do we mean by the word 'reliable' in this context? Why is the sheath so reliable, and what disadvantages do you think it might have?

2  What are the advantages and possible disadvantages of the 'pill' as a method of contraception?

3  In the rhythm method of contraception it is important to know when the safe period is.

   a)  What does 'safe period' mean?

   b)  List as many things as you can think of which might affect the time and duration of the safe period.

   c)  There are cases of women becoming pregnant having had intercourse just before, or just after, menstruation. Suggest possible reasons for this.

4  A man and his wife find that they are not managing to produce any children though they are having intercourse regularly and are not using any method of contraception. Suggest five possible reasons for their lack of success.

5  a)  Write a report on the various methods of family planning that are available in your country.

   b)  Collect data on the numbers of pregnancies in teenage girls in your country for each of the last ten years.

      Have the numbers been increasing or decreasing?

      What factors may have accounted for the changes?

   c)  What are the particular problems and dangers associated with teenage pregnancies?

      What suggestions would you make to avoid these difficulties?

# How do insects reproduce?

*In this Topic we shall see how insects reproduce, grow and develop. These three processes make up the life cycle.*

## Mating and egg-laying

All insects reproduce sexually. The male is attracted to the female by her smell or her bright colours, or by sounds which she makes. After they have met, the male and female go through a short period of **courtship**. For example, the male locust stalks the female for a short time and may make chirping noises by rubbing his hind legs against the hardened edge of his wings. This makes the female receptive to him.

Courtship is followed by **mating**. During this process the male puts his sperms into the female's body. Different insects do this in different ways. In the locust the male jumps on the female's back and grips her thorax with his legs (Figure 1). He curves his abdomen around hers, so the tip can reach her reproductive opening. Some insects, bees for example, are so agile that they can copulate while they are flying.

The sperms do not fertilise the female's eggs straight away but are taken up into **sperm sacs** in her body. There they wait until the eggs are ready. As the ripe eggs pass out of her body, each one is fertilised by a sperm. In many insects the fertilised eggs are enclosed in a horny **egg case** before they leave the female's body.

Some insects take great care where they lay their eggs, so that the young have a supply of food when they hatch. For example, the dung beetle gathers a ball of manure (Figure 2) and the female lays her eggs in it. When the eggs hatch, the youngsters (larvae) feed on the dung.

Many insects bury their eggs to protect them from the sun and enemies. For example, the locust lays her eggs in a hole in the sand. She digs the hole with her long flexible abdomen, the valves at the tip serving as little 'trowels'. The eggs are laid at the bottom. As she pulls her abdomen out, she produces a frothy liquid which hardens and forms a protective case round the eggs.

**Figure 1** Two locusts mating. The male is on top, his abdomen twisted around the female's.

## How do insects develop?

Insects are divided into two groups according to the way they develop during their life cycle. Some develop gradually, while others go through a complete change from one kind of animal to another. When an animal changes its form, we say it has undergone **metamorphosis**. This is made up of two Greek words: *meta* means 'change' and *morphé* means 'form' or 'shape'.

## Insects which develop gradually

This kind of development is shown by cockroaches, locusts, grasshoppers, bugs, termites and many other insects (Figure 4 and Investigation 1).

The egg hatches into a creature which looks like a miniature version of the adult, except that it has no wings. We call this a **nymph**. The nymph has a hard cuticle, which prevents it growing. So after a while it sheds its cuticle: that is, it **moults**. It then grows a bit bigger. This happens many times, the nymph getting bigger each time.

In the later stages small **wing buds** appear on either side of the thorax. At the final moult into the **adult**, the wings expand. By this time the sex organs have developed, so the adult insect can reproduce.

The stage of development between one moult and the next is called an **instar**. In the cockroach each instar lasts about a month, and there are thirteen altogether. So it takes the cockroach about one year to complete its development.

The change from a newly-hatched nymph to the adult takes place gradually, step by step. For this reason it is sometimes called **gradual** or **incomplete metamorphosis**.

Figure 2  A dung beetle gathering a ball of manure in which the female will lay her eggs.

Figure 3  A female cockroach. Note the egg case hanging out from the end of her abdomen. She may walk around like this for some time before depositing it.

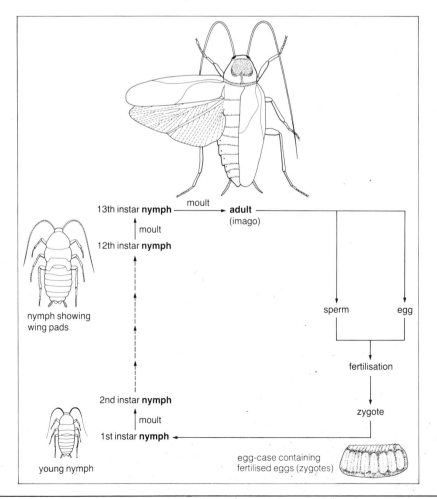

13th instar **nymph** → *moult* → **adult** (imago)
↑ *moult*
12th instar **nymph**

nymph showing wing pads

2nd instar **nymph**
↑ *moult*
1st instar **nymph**

young nymph

sperm    egg

fertilisation

zygote

egg-case containing fertilised eggs (zygotes)

Figure 4  Life cycle of the cockroach. This is an example of an insect with gradual development. After mating the female lays her eggs in an egg-case which she deposits in a dark and humid place. After about 1 to 3 months the eggs hatch out into very small colourless nymphs. These feed, turn brown and moult. Moulting occurs up to 13 times, and the nymphs are called 'teenagers'. Wing buds appear in the later instars. The nymphs feed like the adults and also avoid light and hide in dark places. The cockroach needs 1 to 1½ years to grow from egg to adult. Adult life lasts for 3 to 12 months.

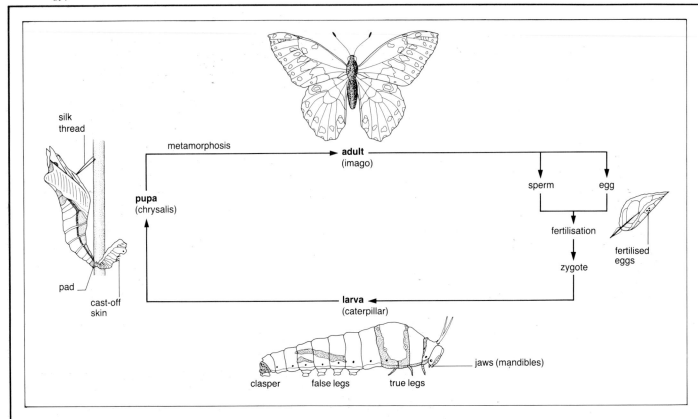

**Figure 5** Life cycle of the citrus swallowtail butterfly (*Papilio demodocus*). This is an example of an insect with complete development. Swallowtail butterflies can be seen in large numbers on bright sunny days, especially from March to May. The adults fly from flower to flower, feeding on the nectar. After mating the female lays her eggs in batches on the underside of young citrus leaves such as lemon, grapefruit and orange. The eggs are about 1 mm wide. After a few days the eggs hatch into caterpillars. The caterpillars feed on the citrus leaves, using their jaws (mandibles) for cutting off pieces. They moult several times, and grow. In the early moults the caterpillars are black and white and look like bird droppings. The older caterpillar (Figure 6) is also camouflaged. After about three weeks the caterpillar crawls to a vertical twig or leaf and turns into a pupa. The pupa is anchored by a silk thread which runs around its body and a sticky pad at the back end. In 10 or 11 days the adult is fully formed. The markings on the wings and abdomen can be seen through the pupal case. The case splits and the adult emerges. It rests on the case while its wings expand.

**Figure 6** The caterpillar (larva) of the swallowtail butterfly feeding on the leaf of an orange tree. It is well camouflaged by being green and black. It also has orange markings and a forked structure it can push out to frighten predators.

## Insects which undergo a complete change

This kind of development is shown by insects such as butterflies, moths, ants, bees, beetles and flies (Figure 5 and Investigation 2).

The egg hatches into a **larva**. The caterpillars of butterflies and moths, and the maggots of flies, are larvae (Table 1).

The larva is quite different from the adult. Its cuticle is thin and flexible, enabling it to crawl or wriggle around. As it lacks the protective armour of the adult, and is unable to move quickly, it is liable to be eaten by birds and other predators. So many of them have special ways of protecting themselves. For example, caterpillars are often covered by hairs which make them unpleasant to eat, and some are cleverly camouflaged.

Larvae have no sex organs, so they cannot reproduce. Their job is to feed and grow. In this way they build up a store of energy which enables them to develop into the adult. For example, the caterpillars of the swallowtail butterfly feed almost non-stop on citrus leaves (Figure 6).

After a time, the larva settles down and changes into a **pupa** or **chrysalis**. Sometimes the larva spins a cover of fine threads round itself. This forms a **cocoon** which surrounds and protects the pupa.

Although the pupa looks lifeless, the inside is the scene of much activity. The larval tissues break down into a kind of cream. Out of this the adult is formed. Eventually, when conditions are suitable, the wall of the pupa opens and the adult clambers out. The wings then expand and it flies away.

The adult possesses sex organs, and its main job is to reproduce. Once it has done this, it has fulfilled its purpose and can die. Sometimes the adult lives for only a day or so, just long enough to find a mate and reproduce.

In the kind of insect just described, the life cycle has two distinct types of animals: the larva and the adult. Not only do they look different, but they behave differently too. Each feeds on its own kind of food, and each lives in its own particular habitat. For example, in the swallowtail butterfly the larva moves like a worm and chews up citrus leaves, whereas the adult can fly and sucks up the nectar of flowers.

Because the larva and adult are so different, the change from one to the other is described as **complete metamorphosis**.

| Name of insect | Common name of larva | Where larva lives | Features of larva |
|---|---|---|---|
| Butterflies, moths | caterpillar | on plants | |
| Ants, wasps, bees | grub | in nest | |
| Houseflies, bluebottles | maggot | in rotting meat | |
| Mosquitoes | wriggler | in fresh water | |
| Beetles, weevils | grub | soil or grain | |

Table 1  Different kinds of insect larvae. In the pictures the head end is to the right.

# Investigation 1

**The life cycle of the cockroach**

1  Look in some dark cupboards and on clothes that have been put away for some time. See if you can find any egg-cases of cockroaches.

If they still have eggs in them keep them in a warm, dark place and watch the nymphs hatch out.

2  At night time collect as many nymphs and adult cockroaches as you can. Sweet liquid left in cups or jars may attract them.

Kill them as described on page 13.

3  Examine nymphs, from the first to last stages. Draw them, using Figure 3 to help you.

How do they differ from each other?

How does the largest nymph differ from the adult?

4  With a ruler measure the length of each nymph, and the adult, from the front of the head to the tip of the abdomen.

5  Draw a bar chart to compare their lengths.

The cockroach is an example of an insect with 'incomplete metamorphosis'. What does this mean?

# Investigation 2

**The life cycle of the swallowtail butterfly**

1  Examine the underside of young citrus leaves for the eggs of the butterfly.
Look for and collect different stages of caterpillars, from the small black and white ones to the larger green and black ones.
Bring them to the laboratory.

2  Set up an insect cage; a large container covered with mosquito netting will do.
Put the eggs and caterpillars inside, with a supply of citrus leaves.

3  Observe the feeding of the caterpillars.

What do they feed on?

What sort of mouth parts do they have?

What are the functions of the legs?

4  Keep the caterpillars until they turn into pupae.
Describe everything that happens until the adult emerges.

The butterfly is an example of an insect with 'complete metamorphosis'.

What does this mean?

# Assignments

1  Many insects bury their eggs to protect them from the sun.

What harm might the sun do to them?

2  Explain the following words, all of which are used in this Topic:

moulting
mating
metamorphosis
instar
cocoon

3  What is the difference between a nymph and a larva?

4  What happens inside a pupa?

5  Explain how an insect like the cockroach grows from the time the egg hatches until it becomes an adult.

6  How are the larva, pupa and adult of the butterfly suited to their functions?

7  Before they copulate, the male and female of a certain insect face one another and the female waves her feelers.

Someone has suggested that the male will only mount the female after it has seen her waving her feelers.

How could you find out if this is true?

# How do amphibians reproduce?

*Amphibians need water in which to reproduce. In this Topic we shall see why the common toad depends on water for its reproduction.*

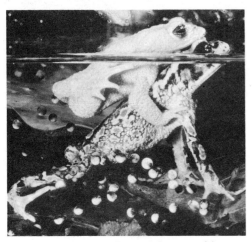

**Figure 1** Toads mating. The male is on top of the female. Notice the strings of fertilised eggs.

## Mating and egg-laying

Toads rest during the dry season amongst rocks and vegetation. When the rains begin they wake up, and the males go in search of water.

When he has found water, the male starts croaking. He does this by forcing air through his **voice box** in his throat. The croaking of the male attracts a female who by this time is loaded with eggs. By this stage the male has enlarged thumbs covered with tough black skin, like warts: they are known as **nuptial pads**.

The toads mate in the water. The male climbs onto the female's back; he places his front legs round her chest and grips her tightly (Figure 1). The skin is slippery, but his large thumbs with their swollen nuptial pads help him to get a firm grip. The pair may remain together like this for two or three days.

Eventually eggs start to pass out of the female's cloacal opening between her back legs. At the same time the male produces a stream of seminal fluid containing numerous sperms. The sperms fertilise the eggs.

Each egg is surrounded by a layer of jelly. This is a protein called **albumen**, which is the same substance that the 'white' of a hen's egg is made of. Soon after coming into contact with the water, the jelly swells up: this protects the eggs from being damaged and from drying out and it makes them join together in strings which stick to weeds and stones. This is the familiar **toad spawn**. Neither the male nor the female takes any further notice of the eggs.

## Development

After about a week the egg hatches into a small fish-like creature called a **tadpole** (Figure 2). You sometimes see tadpoles swimming about in ponds during the rainy season, and they can easily be kept in the laboratory (Investigation). The tadpole is an animal in its own right: it occurs in the development of all amphibians. It is an example of a **larva**.

The tadpole swims by flapping its tail from side to side. Its mouth is closed

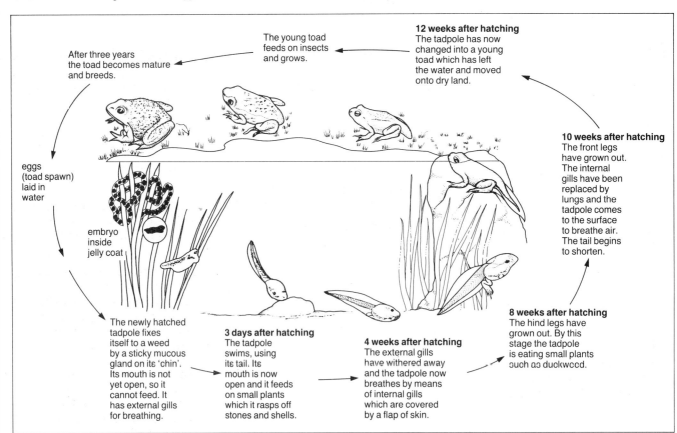

After three years the toad becomes mature and breeds.

The young toad feeds on insects and grows.

**12 weeks after hatching**
The tadpole has now changed into a young toad which has left the water and moved onto dry land.

**10 weeks after hatching**
The front legs have grown out. The internal gills have been replaced by lungs and the tadpole comes to the surface to breathe air. The tail begins to shorten.

**8 weeks after hatching**
The hind legs have grown out. By this stage the tadpole is eating small plants such as duckweed.

**4 weeks after hatching**
The external gills have withered away and the tadpole now breathes by means of internal gills which are covered by a flap of skin.

**3 days after hatching**
The tadpole swims, using its tail. Its mouth is now open and it feeds on small plants which it rasps off stones and shells.

The newly hatched tadpole fixes itself to a weed by a sticky mucous gland on its 'chin'. Its mouth is not yet open, so it cannot feed. It has external gills for breathing.

embryo inside jelly coat

eggs (toad spawn) laid in water

**Figure 2** The main stages in the development of the toad. Start at the extreme left and work your way round in an anti-clockwise direction.

at first, but as soon as it opens it feeds on small plants. To begin with it breathes by means of feathery **external gills** which stick out from the side of the head. Later these are replaced by **internal gills** which are covered by an operculum as in bony fishes (see page 58). Meanwhile it grows.

After about eight weeks the tadpole starts changing into a toad. Legs grow out and the tail shortens. Lungs develop for breathing air: they eventually take over from the gills. You often see tadpoles coming up to the surface to gulp air into their newly formed lungs.

It takes about a month for the tadpole to change completely into a miniature toad. It then leaves the water and begins its life on dry land where it feeds on small insects.

It takes about three years for the toad to become sexually mature. It then returns to the water to breed.

The tadpole and the adult toad look very different and lead quite different lives. The change from one to the other is an example of **metamorphosis**. This is similar to a caterpillar turning into a butterfly (see page 282).

In amphibians, metamorphosis is controlled by a hormone called **thyroxine** (see pages 238–9). This is produced by the thyroid gland in the neck region. For thyroxine to be made there must be iodine in the water. If the water is lacking in iodine, the tadpole cannot change into the adult. On the other hand, if you put extra iodine in the water or inject thyroxine into a tadpole, it will change into the adult more quickly. Very small miniature toads are formed.

### How do other amphibians reproduce?

It's characteristic of amphibians that they reproduce in water. However they don't all need a pond. For example, some tropical tree frogs lay their eggs in a water-filled 'nest' made out of leaves. Nor do all amphibians ignore their eggs as our common toad does. In some other tropical toads the male carries the eggs around on his back or wrapped around his hind legs, and one species of frog incubates the eggs in its mouth.

**Figure 3** Not all amphibians lay their eggs in water. This male glass frog is guarding eggs which have been laid on a leaf.

# Investigation

**Watching tadpoles develop**

1 Obtain some tadpoles from a pond (see page 13) and bring them into the laboratory.

2 Fill an aquarium tank with pond water, and put in some stones and weeds.

3 Put your tadpoles into the tank.

4 Watch them at intervals over the next few weeks.

How do they change in size and shape?

How does their behaviour change?

Do your observations agree with Figure 2?

5 At the same time as you set up your aquarium tank, set up two further tanks exactly like the first one.

6 Into one of the tanks put a tablet of thyroxine once a week throughout the time the tadpoles are developing.

7 Into the other tank put a few crystals of iodine once a week.

Do either of these treatments affect the rate at which the tadpoles develop?

Explain any observations which you are able to make.

# Assignments

1 What part does each of the following play in the reproduction of the common toad?
a) the voice box,      c) albumen,
b) the nuptial pads,   d) thyroxine.

2 Give two reasons why the common toad must breed in water.

3 Why is it an advantage to a tree frog to lay its eggs in a water-filled 'nest' in a tree rather than in a lake or pond?

4 The frog mentioned in the text which takes the eggs into its mouth is called *Rhinoderma* and comes from South America. The eggs develop right through to baby frogs in a specially large voice box.
a) Suggest four possible advantages to the young in developing in this position.
b) Why is the voice box a better place for them than the mouth cavity itself?

# How do birds reproduce?

*Birds take great care of their eggs and look after their young until they can fend for themselves.*

**Figure 1** The peacock uses his fan-like tail for displaying to the female.

**Figure 2** These two great crested grebes are courting. They have just dived into the water and have fetched some weeds.

**Figure 3** The 'lily trotter' has very long toes which enable it to walk easily over the lily leaves.

## What happens when birds reproduce?

When birds reproduce, they usually perform a particular series of actions one after the other.

**1 *The male claims a territory.***
This might be a small area of a wood, or perhaps someone's back garden. The male defends his territory by singing and displaying his feathers. If necessary, birds will fight to defend their territory.

**2 *The male's song attracts a female.***
When the female approaches, the male displays his feathers to her. The male is usually more brightly coloured than the female, as in the humming-birds. One of the most famous displays is put on by the peacock, which has a large, beautiful tail that opens like a fan (Figure 1).

Sometimes the male and female go through various actions together. For example in the great crested grebe, the males and females shake their heads, chase over the water, and occasionally dive down and fetch up weeds (Figure 2). Some birds bring bits of food or nesting material to the intended mate.

These displays are called **courtship**. They keep the male and female together and put them in the right mood for mating.

**3 *The birds build a nest.***
Often both birds do this, but sometimes the male is lazy and leaves the whole job to the female.

Various materials are used for nest-building, depending on the type of bird: sticks, grass and palm leaves are favourites, and mud is sometimes used. Many birds build their nests in trees or under the eaves of a house.

Others make their nests on the ground. As an example, the Jacana 'lily trotter' (Figure 3) builds a shallow nest at the edge of ponds. The brown pelican nests in colonies on the ground or in low trees in coastal regions.

**4 *The two birds mate.***
The male does not have a penis, just an opening. He mounts the female and presses his reproductive opening against hers. His sperms enter her body and fertilise the eggs. Each egg then passes down the female's oviduct and is coated with albumen and a shell.

**5 *The female lays her eggs in the nest.***
Usually she lays five or six eggs.

The shell is made of chalky calcium carbonate: it protects the egg and helps to stop water evaporating from it.

Figure 4 shows the structure of a hen's egg. Inside, a tiny **embryo** rests on top of a bag of yolk, the **yolk sac**. The embryo will eventually develop into a chick: the yolk nourishes it while it develops (Investigation).

The embryo and yolk sac are surrounded by a thick fluid called **albumen**. This is the 'white' of the egg: its main job is to supply the embryo with water during its development.

One end of the egg is 'blunter' than the other. At the blunt end, just under the shell, there is an **air space**. The shell has tiny holes running through it, which allow oxygen to diffuse into the air space. The oxygen is then carried via blood vessels to the embryo. Carbon dioxide passes out in the reverse direction and in this way the embryo breathes.

**6 *The female incubates the eggs.***
She does this by sitting on them: this keeps the eggs warm and is called **brooding**. Provided it is kept warm the embryo gradually develops into a chick. Figure 5 shows what the inside of the egg looks like after several days. Notice the excretory sac in which the developing embryo deposits its nitrogenous waste.

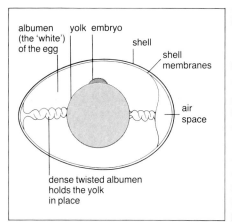

Figure 4 The inside of a fertile hen's egg just after it has been laid.

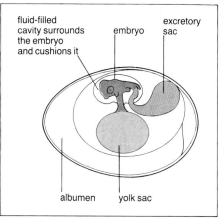

Figure 5 The inside of a fertile hen's egg about three days after it has been laid.

Figure 6 A hen's egg hatching.

## 7 The eggs hatch.

Hatching usually takes place a few weeks after the eggs have been laid. Using its beak, the chick breaks through the membranes surrounding it, and cracks open the shell (Figure 6). Then, wet and bedraggled, it clambers out.

## 8 The parents look after the chicks.

The newly-hatched chicks of most birds have no feathers and are helpless. They stay in the nest, and the mother spends some of her time sitting on top of them to keep them warm. The parents feed them on worms and other kinds of food which they collect and bring back to the nest: the chicks open their mouths and the parent bird pushes the food down their throats. (Figure 7) Some birds feed their chicks with half-digested food which they bring up from the stomach.

The chicks soon acquire a covering of downy feathers: they then leave the nest and sit on a nearby branch. Meanwhile, the parents go on feeding them and gradually the young birds grow and develop their flight feathers. Soon they start flying for short distances and eventually they fly away for good.

How long does all this take? It varies from one type of bird to another. In many birds it takes about two months from the time the parents start building the nest to the time when the young fly away. On the other hand ducklings, and the young of many other birds which make their nests on the ground, hatch out with a covering of feathers and can run or swim straight away.

Figure 7 A mother bird brings an insect to her chick in the nest..

## Investigation

**Looking at a chick embryo**

1 Your teacher will give you a fertilised hen's egg from 'free-range' chickens. Keep it warm in a small box heated with an electric light bulb for 3 to 5 days.

2 With plasticine make a 'cradle' for holding the egg.

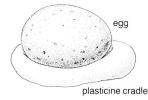

3 Let it stand for a few minutes.

4 With scissors cut away the shell, piece by piece, from the upper side of the egg.

5 Observe the embryo lying on top of the yolk.

6 Suck away the albumen with a pipette.

7 Examine the embryo under a magnifying glass. If you look carefully, you may see the heart beating.

Suggest a function for each of the structures you can see.

## Assignments

1 Why do you think it is an advantage to a pair of breeding birds to have their own piece of territory?

2 Make a list of the advantages and disadvantages of building a nest in each of these places: (a) on the ground, (b) in a tree, and (c) under the eaves of a house.

3 What part do feathers play in helping birds to produce their offspring successfully?

4 Before boiling an egg many people prick the blunt end with a pin.

Why do you think this is a good idea?

# Sexual reproduction in flowering plants

*Sexual reproduction occurs in plants as well as animals. In higher plants the part of the plant responsible for this is the flower.*

**Figure 1** A *Hibiscus* flower. The flower contains the plant's reproductive organs.

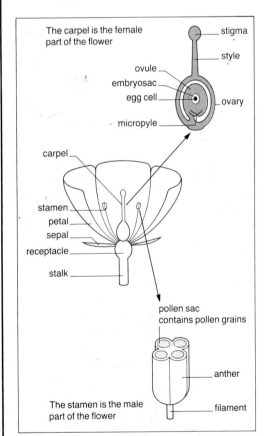

**Figure 2** The structure of a typical flower.

| | Parts separate | Parts joined |
|---|---|---|
| **Sepals** | flamboyant | hibiscus |
| **Petals** | Indian laburnum | morning glory |
| **Stamens** | sensitive plant | hibiscus |
| **Carpels** | leaf of life | orange |

**Table 1** Different kinds of flower structure.

## The structure of flowers

The basic structure of a flower can be seen in plants like Kingston buttercup and pride of Barbados (Investigation 1). This is illustrated in Figure 2.

The flower is made up of a series of rings of structures. The outermost ring consists of several small green leaf-like **sepals**; then come the **petals** which are often brightly coloured; next come the **stamens** which look rather like pins; and finally in the centre there is a club-shaped **carpel**. All these structures are situated at the end of a stalk which is slightly swollen to form the **receptacle**.

At the base of each petal you will see an area which is slightly thicker than the rest: this is called the **nectary** and it produces a sugary liquid called **nectar**.

The stamens constitute the male part of the flower. Each one has a knob at the top: this is called the **anther**, and it contains four **pollen sacs** in which pollen grains are formed. The pollen grains are equivalent to an animal's sperms. The rest of the stamen is known as the **filament**.

The carpel constitutes the female part of the flower. It consists of three parts: a slightly swollen **stigma** at the top, then a slender stalk called the **style**, and a swollen **ovary** at the bottom. Inside the ovary there are small bodies called **ovules** which are attached to the wall of the ovary by short stalks. The ovules contain a little bag called the **embryosac**, and inside this is an **egg cell**. There is a small hole in the wall of the ovule called the **micropyle**. You need a microscope to see the embryosac and the egg cell.

## Variations on the theme

You have only to look at a few flowers to realise that they aren't all exactly like the one just described although they all follow the same basic plan (Investigation 1).

Figure 3 shows two flowers to illustrate the kind of variation that one finds. Notice that the leaf of life has many carpels each containing one ovule; in contrast, the rattleweed has one carpel containing a row of ovules.

You will also notice that these two flowers differ in shape. In the leaf of life the petals are all identical as you go round the flower. Such a flower is described as **radially symmetrical**. However, in the rattleweed the petals at the top and bottom are different from those on either side. This kind of flower is described as **bilaterally symmetrical** (Figure 4).

Flowers vary in many other ways too (Table 1). The petals may be joined together to form a kind of 'trumpet' in, for example, morning glory, or the filaments may be joined together to make a tube as in hibiscus. In the canna-lily the sepals and petals look alike, while in bougainvillea there are no petals and in many grasses there are no sepals.

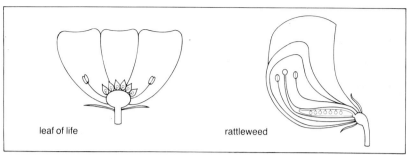

leaf of life                    rattleweed

**radial symmetry**        **bilateral symmetry**

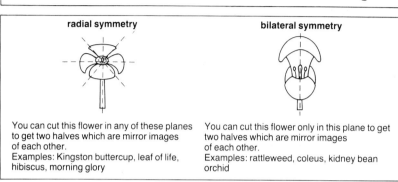

You can cut this flower in any of these planes to get two halves which are mirror images of each other.
Examples: Kingston buttercup, leaf of life, hibiscus, morning glory

You can cut this flower only in this plane to get two halves which are mirror images of each other.
Examples: rattleweed, coleus, kidney bean orchid

**Figure 3** Side views of the leaf of life and rattleweed flowers to show the kind of variety that one finds in flower structure. In both cases, the flower has been sliced down the middle so as to show the internal structure. In reality there are far more stamens than are shown here, particularly in the leaf of life.

**Figure 4** There are two ways of describing the shapes of flowers.

## How are flowers arranged on the stem?

There is a great deal of variety in the way flowers are arranged on the main stem of the plant, and in how many flowers there are altogether (Investigation 2). Some common arrangements are shown in Figure 5. The collection of flowers on the shoot is known as the **inflorescence**.

## Pollen and pollination

Pollen grains are very small bodies like specks of dust. Their job is the same as an animal's sperms: to fertilise the eggs.

The pollen grains develop inside the anthers. When the anther is mature, it splits open and the pollen grains are released. They are then conveyed to another flower of the same species, and if one of them gets onto a stigma, it sticks to it. The process by which the pollen grains are conveyed from the anthers to the stigma is called **pollination** (Figure 6).

## Fertilisation

Once a pollen grain has landed on a stigma, it sends out a snake-like outgrowth called a **pollen tube**. This grows into the stigma and down the style. It is attracted by sugar in the stigma and nourished by substances in the tissues of the style. Towards the tip of the pollen tube there is a **male nucleus** which is equivalent to the nucleus in the head of an animal's sperm.

Having reached the ovary, the pollen tube pushes its way into the ovule, usually through the micropyle. The tip of the pollen tube now grows towards the egg cell in the centre of the ovule. Then the male nucleus fuses with the egg cell. This is **fertilisation**, and is equivalent to the fertilisation of an egg by a sperm in an animal.

The fertilised egg now divides up into a ball of cells which becomes an **embryo**. This remains in the centre of the ovule, and becomes surrounded by a special tissue called the **endosperm** which supplies it with food.

Meanwhile the ovule itself becomes the **seed** and the wall around it hardens to form the tough seed coat. While this is happening the ovary develops into a **fruit**. So the seed becomes surrounded by a fruit: cut open any fruit and you will normally find seeds inside it.

Finally water is drawn out of the seeds so they become very dry. They then become dormant, and in this state they can survive bad conditions such as drought or cold.

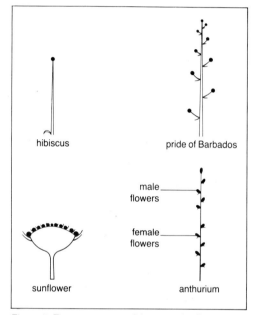

hibiscus                    pride of Barbados

male flowers

female flowers

sunflower                    anthurium

**Figure 5** These are some of the ways the flowers may be arranged on the stem of a plant. Notice that the sunflower 'flower' is not just one flower but a whole mass of very small flowers or florets sitting on top of the swollen end of the stem.

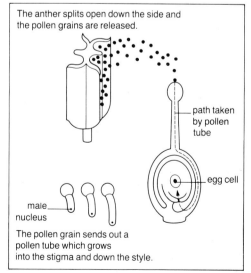

The anther splits open down the side and the pollen grains are released.

path taken by pollen tube

egg cell

male nucleus

The pollen grain sends out a pollen tube which grows into the stigma and down the style.

**Figure 6** In pollination pollen grains are transferred from an anther to a stigma. A pollen tube then grows down the style to the ovary where fertilisation occurs.

Figure 7 The 'tassel' of maize, which consists of clumps of small male flowers. The stamens have long filaments so that the anthers are easily shaken by the wind.

Figure 8 A bee collecting nectar from a flower.

The flower has now done its job, so the sepals shrivel up and the petals fall off, leaving the fruit with the seeds inside.

## Different methods of pollination

Pollination is usually carried out either by wind or by insects (Investigation 4). It can also be carried out by birds, bats and humans.

**Wind-pollinated plants** include grasses such as maize, sugar cane and rice. The familiar 'tassels' of maize (Figure 7) are clumps of very small male flowers whose pollen is blown about by the wind. The way the anthers hang out and are shaken by even a slight gust of wind ensures that the pollen is scattered over a wide area.

**Insect-pollinated plants** include rattleweed, sunflower, balsam and many others. Insects such as bees visit the flowers to feed on the nectar. As the insect pokes its head into the flower, its hairy body gets covered with pollen (Figure 8). When the insect visits other flowers, some of the pollen gets onto the stigmas, thereby pollinating them.

Experiments have shown that insects such as bees are attracted to flowers by their colour, shape and smell. Some flowers have gone to great lengths to entice the insect and make sure that it gets covered with pollen. For example, in rattleweed some of the petals form a kind of platform which the insect can land on. Marks on the petal guide the insect to the nectar, like the landing lights on an airport runway.

Some flowers are constructed in such a way that when the insect lands on it and pushes its head in, the stamens are jerked so that the insect's body gets well and truly covered with pollen.

One of the most interesting cases is an orchid whose flower looks like a female wasp. When a male wasp sees the flower, it tries to copulate with it and gets covered with pollen. It then tries the same thing with another flower, pollinating it in the process.

Wind and insect pollination are quite different and require different adaptations on the part of the flowers. You can often tell whether a particular flower is pollinated by wind or insects just by looking at it. Table 2 sums up the main differences between them.

## Cross-pollination and self-pollination

By now you must be wondering why flowers go to such lengths to spread their pollen. Why not let the pollen fall onto a stigma in the *same* flower? Actually this does sometimes happen, and we call it **self-pollination**. But it isn't good for the species. **Cross-pollination**, in which the pollen is transferred to another flower, creates variety and is really much better (see page 316).

So the various mechanisms which we have been discussing are really ways of making certain that cross-pollination takes place. There are other devices too. For example, in some flowers the stamens ripen before the carpels, so the pollen grains will have been dispersed by the time the carpels are ready. In other flowers the carpels ripen before the stamens. And some flowers are exclusively male or female and these may be found on separate plants. This is true of pawpaw, for example.

| Wind-pollinated flowers | Insect-pollinated flowers |
|---|---|
| 1 Generally small | Generally larger |
| 2 Petals green or dull coloured | Petals often brightly coloured |
| 3 Do not produce nectar | Petals have nectaries which produce nectar |
| 4 Flower hangs down for easy shaking | Flower faces upwards |
| 5 Stamens and stigma hang out of the ring of petals | Stamens and stigma inside the ring of petals |
| 6 Large number of pollen grains produced | Smaller number of pollen grains produced |
| 7 Pollen grains very light with smooth surface | Pollen grains heavier with spikes for sticking to insect |
| 8 Stigma has feathery branches for catching pollen | Stigma is like pinhead and lacks branches |

Table 2 Summary of the main differences between typical wind-pollinated and insect-pollinated flowers.

# Investigation 1

## Looking at flowers

1 Obtain a flower from e.g. Kingston buttercup or pride of Barbados.

2 Identify its parts, using Figure 2 to help you.

3 Make an accurate drawing of the flower and label its parts.

4 Pull off a sepal, petal, stamen and carpel, and lay them on a piece of paper.

5 Examine each one under a hand lens. Draw them in outline.

6 Cut open the carpel.

Can you see ovules inside it?

7 Cut open an anther.

Can you see pollen grains inside?

8 Obtain up to six different kinds of flowers.

9 Examine each one carefully and write down how it differs from the first flower which you looked at.

Suggest reasons why each kind of flower has its own characteristic shape and form.

# Investigation 2

## Looking at how flowers are arranged on the stem

1 Obtain up to four different kinds of flowering plant.

2 Make a simple sketch of each plant, showing how the flowers are arranged on the stem.

3 In each case compare the arrangement of the flowers with the diagrams in Figure 5.

Which diagram does it resemble most closely?

Suggest why each arrangement should be useful to the plant.

# Investigation 3

## To find out what makes pollen germinate

1 With a pipette put a drop of sugar solution (10% sucrose) onto a slide. Label this slide A.

2 Obtain a flower, e.g. of hibiscus, that has ripe pollen.

3 With a paintbrush pick up a few pollen grains from the anther and place them in the sugar solution. Put on a coverslip.

4 Set up a second slide, but put the pollen grains into a drop of water instead of sugar solution.

Label this slide B; it will serve as a control.

5 Place your two slides in a warm, dark place.

6 After about 30 minutes look at the slides under the microscope (low power).

How does the appearance of the pollen grains differ in the two slides?
What effect has the sugar had?

What does this suggest about the stigmas in a flower?
How could your suggestion be tested?

# Investigation 4

## Exploring the differences between wind- and insect-pollinated flowers

1 Your teacher will give you one wind-pollinated and one insect-pollinated flower.

Which do you think is which?
How do you know?

2 Look carefully at each flower.

Which features listed in Table 2 does it possess? Does it have any other adaptations for pollination besides the ones listed in the Table?

3 If possible look at flowers being visited by insects. In each case observe what the insect does, and note any special adaptations which the flower has for being pollinated.

# Assignments

1 Each of the words in the left-hand column is related to one of the words in the right-hand column. Write them down in the correct pairs.

sepal        colour
petal        egg cell
pollen       sugar
nectary      sperm
ovule        leaflet

2 Explain the difference between pollination and fertilisation.

Why do plants generally produce very large numbers of pollen grains?

3 The flower shown diagrammatically below is pollinated by wind:

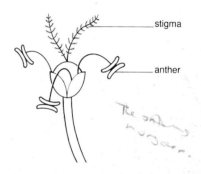

What special features can you detect which suit it to this method of pollination?

4 The flowers of some plants are of two kinds. Some flowers have their anthers high up and their stigmas low down, whilst others have their stigmas high up and their anthers low down, as shown in the illustration below. They are pollinated by bees.

In what way might this arrangement of flower parts favour cross-pollination?

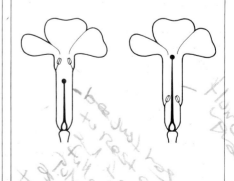

# Seeds and germination

*Flowering plants produce seeds. The seeds survive dry conditions and can later give rise to new plants.*

## The structure of seeds

If you split a pod open you will see the seeds (beans or peas) inside (Investigation 1). Each seed is attached to the pod by a short **seed stalk**, and it is surrounded by a tough **seed coat** (Figure 1). A black scar marks the position of the seed stalk. Just above this is a tiny hole, the **micropyle**.

Inside the seed coat is the **embryo**. This consists of a baby shoot (the **plumule**), a baby root (the **radicle**), and a pair of thick wing-like structures called the **seed-leaves** or **cotyledons**. They contain starch and feed the embryo when it starts to grow into a new plant.

## What happens when a seed produces a new plant?

If you put some seeds in a moist place, you can see what happens when they produce new plants (Investigation 2). The process is called **germination**. Stages in the germination of the gungo pea are shown in Figure 2.

First the seed takes up water, mainly through the micropyle. This makes it swell and increase in mass (Investigation 3). As a result, the seed coat bursts open, and the young root and shoot grow out. The root grows downwards, and the shoot upwards. The shoot is bent like a hook: this protects its delicate tip as it pushes its way up through the soil.

The tip of the root is protected by a slimy mass of loosely packed cells called the **root cap**. This prevents it being damaged as it grows down into the soil. The root gives off side-branches which help to anchor the young plant and absorb water and minerals from the soil. Slender **root hairs** increase the surface area for absorption.

The shoot eventually breaks through the surface of the soil. It then straightens, and the first green leaves open out. We now call the young plant a **seedling**.

For the embryo to grow like this, food is needed. Where does it come from? In this case it comes from the cotyledons which remain inside the seed coat beneath the soil. Starch in the cotyledons is turned into soluble sugar: this is then transported to the tips of the shoot and root where growth takes place.

Once the seedling has formed its first green leaves, it can make its own food by photosynthesis. It is then self-supporting: the cotyledons are no longer needed, and so they wither away.

## Different kinds of seeds

The gungo pea seed is an example of a **dicotyledon**. The seed has two

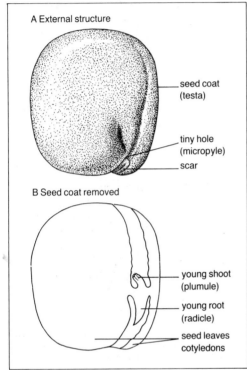

A External structure

- seed coat (testa)
- tiny hole (micropyle)
- scar

B Seed coat removed

- young shoot (plumule)
- young root (radicle)
- seed leaves cotyledons

**Figure 1** The structure of a gungo pea seed.

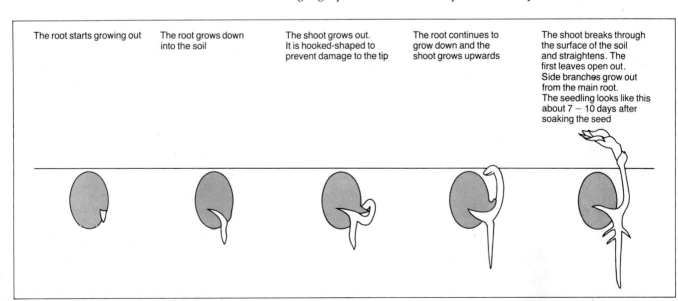

The root starts growing out

The root grows down into the soil

The shoot grows out. It is hooked-shaped to prevent damage to the tip

The root continues to grow down and the shoot grows upwards

The shoot breaks through the surface of the soil and straightens. The first leaves open out. Side branches grow out from the main root. The seedling looks like this about 7 – 10 days after soaking the seed

**Figure 2** Germination of a gungo pea seed: an example of hypogeal germination.

cotyledons. Other examples are rattleweed, black-eyed pea, kidney bean and castor oil.

**Monocotyledons** have only one cotyledon in their seed (Figure 3). Examples of monocotyledons are maize, date, coconut and rice.

Some seeds have another store of food in addition to the cotyledons. This is a special tissue called **endosperm**, which surrounds the embryo and cotyledons. It is more common in monocotyledons such as cereals, for example maize (Figure 4). It is found in some dicotyledons, for example castor oil. In most seeds the endosperm is used up before the seeds are ready to germinate.

## Different kinds of germination

When the gungo pea germinates the cotyledons stay below the ground. We call this **hypogeal** germination ('hypo' means below, 'geal' means earth). Other seeds which show hypogeal germination are the oil palm and the grasses such as maize and rice. In these the shoot, instead of being hooked, points straight up. Its delicate tip is protected by a sheath which we call the **coleoptile**. When the first leaves open out, they break through the coleoptile which then falls off.

But there are other seeds where the cotyledons come above the ground. They are said to show **epigeal** germination ('epi' means above). Seeds which show epigeal germination are castor oil, sunflower (Figure 5), kidney bean, black-eyed pea, rattleweed and flamboyant. The cotyledons are lifted out of the soil with the growing shoot. When they reach the light, they turn green and start feeding the seedling by photosynthesis.

## How long can seeds survive?

In 1933 a Japanese botanist found some lotus seeds in a dried-out lake bed in Manchuria. He sent them to the Royal Botanic Gardens at Kew. Scientists at Kew put the seeds on moist blotting paper, and they sprouted into new plants. These seeds were later found to be over a thousand years old.

More recently some viable lupin seeds were found buried in frozen soil in Canada. These were estimated to be over ten thousand years old.

Not all seeds can survive for as long as this. Many survive for up to a hundred years, others for about ten, and some last for only a few days.

Many seeds can withstand very bad weather. The seeds of desert plants can stand up to long periods of drought, sprouting into new plants as soon as

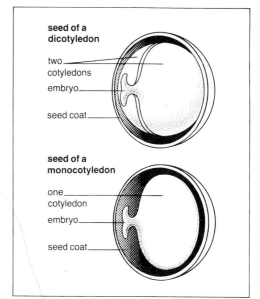

Figure 3  Dicotelydons have two cotyledons inside their seeds whereas monocotyledons have only one.

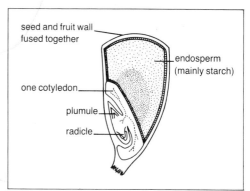

Figure 4  Endosperm is common in cereals such as maize. The maize grain is a single-seeded fruit in which the seed and fruit wall are fused together.

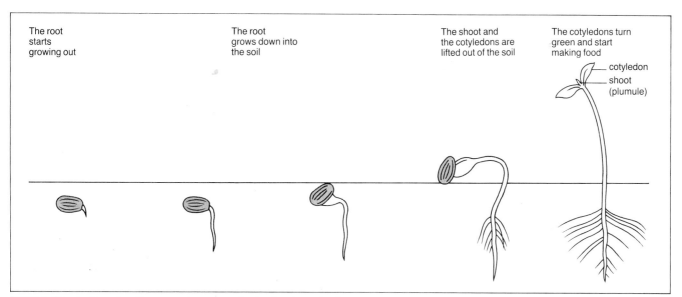

Figure 5  Germination of sunflower seed: an example of epigeal germination.

it rains. And the seeds of Arctic plants can survive extremely cold winters.

How do seeds do this? No one knows for certain. In its dried-out state, and protected within the seed coat, the embryo goes to sleep – it becomes **dormant**. In this state it *appears* to be dead, but when conditions become suitable it bursts into life.

## What conditions are needed for germination?

How annoying it is when you plant seeds in the garden and they don't grow. This is because the seed must have the right conditions in order to germinate. We can find out what these conditions are by trying to germinate seeds in different conditions (Investigation 5). From these experiments we can draw the following conclusions:

1　**Water** is essential for germination: without it seeds cannot swell up and burst open, and the embryo cannot grow.

2　A supply of **oxygen** is needed. This enables seeds to respire so they have plenty of energy for germination.

3　A **suitable temperature** is required. This varies with different plants. Usually seeds won't germinate when the temperature is below 0–5°C or above 45–50°C.

4　The effect of **light** is variable. Most seeds don't mind if it is light or dark. However some germinate only in the dark. Others require light: the amount needed may be very small – one quick flash is enough in some cases. Once the young shoot begins to grow above the soil, light is needed for the leaves to make chlorophyll and start photosynthesising.

## Man's use of seeds

Seeds contain a store of food for feeding the new plants as they develop. This makes them a good source of food for man. The food may be stored in either the cotyledons or the endosperm (Table 1).

| Plant | Storage structure | Type of food stored |
|---|---|---|
| Beans, peas | Cotyledons | Starch, protein |
| Groundnut, sunflower, castor oil | Cotyledons | Oil, protein |
| Cocoa | Cotyledons | Fat |
| Maize, rice, wheat and other cereals | Endosperm | Starch, protein |
| 'Sweet corn' | Endosperm | Cane sugar, protein |
| Coconut | Endosperm | Coconut oil |

**Table 1**　Seeds that are used as food by man.

## Investigation 1

**Looking at seeds**

1　Split open a pod of the gungo pea, and notice the row of peas inside. The peas are the seeds, and the pod is the fruit.

2　Examine the seeds of various plants. Can you explain their similarities and differences?

3　Look at the outside of a gungo pea seed. Notice the structures shown in Figure 1A.

4　Take a gungo pea seed which has been soaked in water and carefully remove the coat. Can you see the structures shown in Figure 1B?

5　Pipette a drop of iodine onto one of the cotyledons inside the seed. What colour does the cotyledon turn? What does this tell you?

## Investigation 2

**How do different seeds germinate?**

1　Lay sheets of blotting paper in the bottom of a series of dishes.

2　Moisten the blotting paper with water.

3　In each dish sprinkle some seeds of different plants, e.g. maize, rattleweed, black-eyed pea, kidney bean, etc.

4　Observe the way the seeds germinate.

How do the different seedlings obtain food?

## Investigation 3

**The effect of water on a seed**

1　Count out 20 dry seeds.

2　Weigh the dry seeds and write down their mass.

3　Put the seeds in water and leave them for 24 hours.

4　Take the soaked seeds out of the water and blot them dry.

5　Weigh the soaked seeds and write down their mass.

Which are heavier, the dry seeds or the soaked seeds?

Explain the difference.

Work out the percentage increase in mass of the soaked seeds.

$$\text{percentage increase} = \frac{\text{increase in mass} \times 100}{\text{original mass}}$$

# Investigation 4

## Watching seeds germinating

1 Put some water in the bottom of a jar.

2 Roll up a piece of blotting paper, and put it in the jar as shown in the illustration. Tilt the jar so the blotting paper is thoroughly wetted: this will make it stick to the side of the jar.

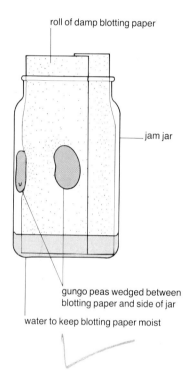

roll of damp blotting paper

jam jar

gungo peas wedged between blotting paper and side of jar

water to keep blotting paper moist

3 Push several gungo pea seeds between the blotting paper and the side of the jar. Be careful they don't fall into the water at the bottom.

4 Observe the gungo peas at intervals over the next ten days or so, and watch the stages in germination.

Do your observations agree with the diagrams in Figure 2?

Why is the shoot hook-shaped to begin with?

Where does the seedling get its food from?

What do you think makes the shoot grow upwards and the root downwards?

# Investigation 5

## To find out the conditions needed for germination

1 Push some cotton wool into the bottom of five large test tubes.

2 Pour a little water into four of the test tubes, so as to moisten the cotton wool. Leave the other one dry.

3 Sprinkle some rattleweed seeds onto the cotton wool in each test tube.

4 Set up the test tubes as shown in the illustration.

5 Observe the test tubes at intervals during the next few days.

In which tubes does germination take place, and *not* take place?

What conclusions do you draw as regards the conditions needed for germination?

Which tube serves as the control in this investigation?

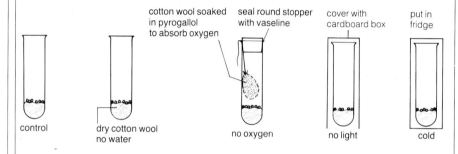

cotton wool soaked in pyrogallol to absorb oxygen

seal round stopper with vaseline

cover with cardboard box

put in fridge

control

dry cotton wool no water

no oxygen

no light

cold

# Assignments

1 Peas were placed in a retort flask which was set up as shown in the diagram below. The flask was then left for two days:

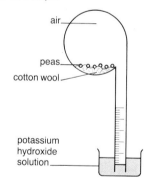

air

peas

cotton wool

potassium hydroxide solution

a) What would you expect to have happened to the level of the potassium hydroxide solution after two days?

b) What would have happened to the composition of the air in the flask?

c) What conclusion would you draw from the result of this experiment?

d) By means of diagrams show what controls are needed in this experiment.

2 Seeds which are planted too deep in the soil won't germinate. Suggest *two* possible reasons for this. Describe an experiment which you would carry out to test *one* of your suggestions.

3 The graph below shows how the dry mass of a germinating seed (and seedling) changes from the moment germination starts. (The dry mass is estimated by getting rid of all traces of water from the plant and then weighing it.)

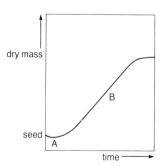

dry mass

B

seed

A

time

a) How do you think this experiment was actually carried out?

b) Explain what is happening at points A and B on the graph.

# Fruits and dispersal

*We usually think of a
fruit as something soft, juicy
and good to eat. In this Topic we will
look at different kinds of fruit, and we
shall understand why fruits are
important to plants.*

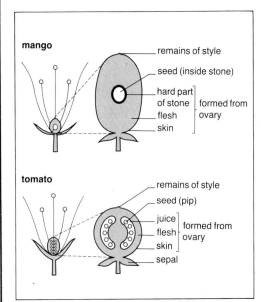

**mango**
- remains of style
- seed (inside stone)
- hard part of stone } formed from ovary
- flesh
- skin

**tomato**
- remains of style
- seed (pip)
- juice } formed from ovary
- flesh
- skin
- sepal

Figure 2 In fleshy fruits such as the mango and tomato, the ovary swells up and its wall becomes soft and succulent. The mango contains a single seed, which is inside the 'stone', whereas the tomato contains a large number of seeds (the 'pips').

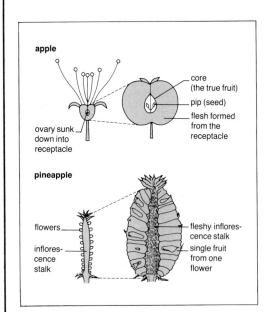

**apple**
- core (the true fruit)
- pip (seed)
- flesh formed from the receptacle
- ovary sunk down into receptacle

**pineapple**
- flowers
- inflorescence stalk
- fleshy inflorescence stalk
- single fruit from one flower

Figure 3 In the apple and pineapple, the true fruit formed from the ovary is inside the other flesh. Most of the flesh is formed from the receptacle or the inflorescence stalk.

Figure 1 Seeds being dispersed from a poppy fruit.

## What are fruits?

The fruit is the part of the plant which surrounds the seed or seeds. It is formed from the ovary in the flower. The number of seeds in a fruit depends on how many ovules were present in the ovary to start off with.

The whole purpose of the fruit is to help disperse the seeds, ensuring that they are spread over as wide an area as possible (Figure 1). The way a particular fruit helps dispersal depends on what kind of fruit it is. Looking at fruits as a whole, there are two main kinds: **fleshy** and **dry**.

## Fleshy fruits

A fleshy fruit is one in which the main part of the fruit, formed from the ovary, is soft and juicy. The seeds, which are usually hard, are located somewhere inside (Investigation 1). Examples are mangoes and tomatoes (Figure 2).

*Mango* Most of the fruit wall is fleshy and juicy. The inner part of the fruit wall (the **endocarp**) is hard and forms a protection for the single seed that is found inside. This is an example of a **drupe**. Another example is jujubes (dunks).

*Tomato* All of the fruit wall becomes fleshy and juicy. In this case the outer part of the seed (the **testa**) is hard. There are many seeds called 'pips'. This is an example of a **berry**. Other examples are pawpaw, banana, cucumber, water melon, pumpkin, guava and orange.

There is another kind of fleshy fruit in which the soft juicy part is formed, not from the ovary, but from other parts of the flower or inflorescence. Such fruits are called **false fleshy fruits**. Examples are apple and pineapple (Figure 3). Other examples are breadfruit and fig.

*Apple* In the flower the ovary is sunk down into the receptacle. After fertilisation the ovary becomes the 'core' of the apple, the true fruit containing the seeds or pips. Around this the receptacle swells to form the false fruit, the flesh of the apple.

*Pineapple* Many flowers are carried on an inflorescence stalk. Each flower forms a fleshy fruit which is one section of the pineapple. Within these are the true fruits, and sometimes seeds. The inflorescence stalk running down the centre of the fruit also becomes fleshy.

Fleshy fruits are often brightly coloured and taste good, so they attract animals such as birds, fruit-bats, monkeys and man. If the seed is very large it is usually discarded as the flesh is eaten, for example mango. If the whole fruit is eaten, for example tomato and guava, the soft part of the fruit is digested, but the seeds, protected by their hard coat, resist the action of the animal's digestive juices and pass out with its faeces. This may be a long way from where the fruits were formed, and so the seeds are dispersed.

## Dry fruits

A dry fruit is one in which the fruit is relatively hard and dry. There are many different kinds. The main ones are: the **achene** such as the grain of cereals (page 324); the **pod** or **legume** of the pea and bean family, for example Indian laburnum; and the **capsule** of, for example, balsam and Dutchman's pipe.

*Indian laburnum* The youngest flower buds are at the top of the inflorescence. Below these are the open flowers, and lower down still you may see the developing pods (Figure 4).

After fertilization the petals fall off and the sepals, style and stigma become withered. The ovary wall becomes the fruit wall (**pericarp**). The fertilised ovules become the seeds (Figure 5).

Pods are made from one carpel. When the skin dries out the pod splits open with such force that the seeds are scattered over a fairly wide area. Other examples of plants with pods are pride of Barbados, butterfly flower, rattleweed, flamboyant, crab's eye vine, groundnut and kidney bean (red pea). Fruits which throw out their seeds by splitting open are known as **dehiscent fruits**. Capsules are also dehiscent.

*Balsam* The fruit (capsule) has five parts joined together. Up the centre of the fruit is the stalk to which the seeds are attached. When the pericarp dries it suddenly breaks away, and folds over on itself. The seeds are shot out.

*Dutchman's pipe* The capsule is made of six parts (carpels) joined together. When the fruit dries the carpels partly separate from each other. The basket that is formed then swings in the wind and the seeds are shaken out (Figure 6). Other examples of capsules are mahogany, W. Indian cedar, June rose, cannon ball tree, cotton, sandbox and Mexican poppy.

The other kinds of dry fruits do not split, and they are called **indehiscent fruits**. They have various modifications to help their dispersal.

*Coconut* This is a drupe, but the middle part of the fruit wall is made of dry fibres rather than being juicy. It contains air spaces which make the fruit lighter, and able to float in the water. The inner part of the pericarp forms the hard woody cover to the seed. Other plants dispersed by water are manchineel, the seeds of some water lilies and the seedlings of red mangrove.

Wind disperal occurs with small and light seeds and fruits, or those with hairs or wings. Some examples of hairy seeds are cotton and French cotton, and of hairy fruits are railway weed, lettuce, goatweed and consumption weed. Wings are formed from the testa of seeds, as in W. Indian cedar, torchwood, and Dutchman's pipe, or from the pericarp of fruits, as in mahogany and crow.

Other plants are adapted to use animals to aid in their dispersal. The fruits of sweethearts, bur grass and Spanish needle have hooks, and hogweed has sticky drops. These cling or stick to the fur of animals and to people's clothes and hairy skin. Animals also disperse fleshy fruits as we saw at the beginning of the Topic.

Examples of the methods of dispersal are shown in Figure 7.

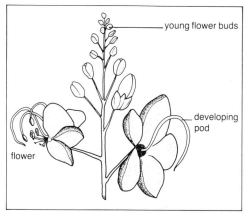

**Figure 4** Inflorescence of *Cassia* (Indian laburnum). The youngest flower buds are at the top. The flower opens, and after fertilisation the ovary develops into the pod. The petals and the sepals drop off.

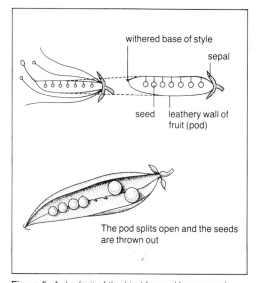

**Figure 5** A dry fruit of the kind formed by pea and bean plants. The peas themselves are the seeds.

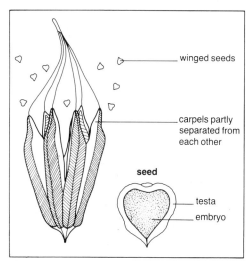

**Figure 6** Dutchman's pipe, showing the swinging basket which shakes out seeds when the wind blows. Each seed has a flattened testa which helps it to be dispersed by the wind.

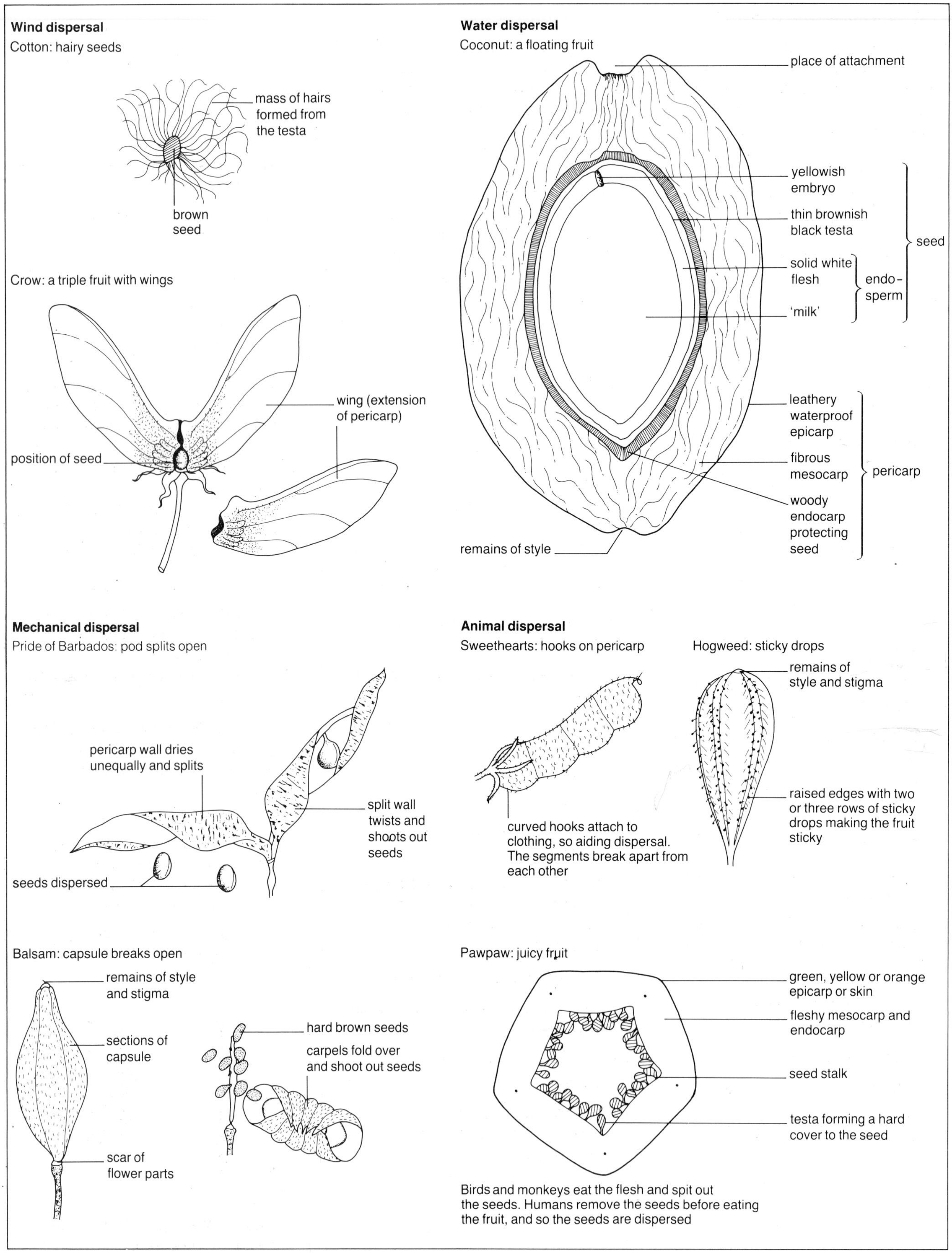

**Wind dispersal**
Cotton: hairy seeds

mass of hairs
formed from
the testa

brown
seed

Crow: a triple fruit with wings

wing (extension
of pericarp)

position of seed

**Water dispersal**
Coconut: a floating fruit

place of attachment

yellowish
embryo

thin brownish
black testa

solid white
flesh

'milk'

seed

endo-
sperm

leathery
waterproof
epicarp

fibrous
mesocarp

woody
endocarp
protecting
seed

pericarp

remains of style

**Mechanical dispersal**
Pride of Barbados: pod splits open

pericarp wall dries
unequally and splits

split wall
twists and
shoots out
seeds

seeds dispersed

Balsam: capsule breaks open

remains of style
and stigma

sections of
capsule

scar of
flower parts

hard brown seeds

carpels fold over
and shoot out seeds

**Animal dispersal**
Sweethearts: hooks on pericarp      Hogweed: sticky drops

remains of
style and stigma

raised edges with two
or three rows of sticky
drops making the fruit
sticky

curved hooks attach to
clothing, so aiding dispersal.
The segments break apart from
each other

Pawpaw: juicy fruit

green, yellow or orange
epicarp or skin

fleshy mesocarp and
endocarp

seed stalk

testa forming a hard
cover to the seed

Birds and monkeys eat the flesh and spit out
the seeds. Humans remove the seeds before eating
the fruit, and so the seeds are dispersed

**Figure 7** Different methods of dispersal.

## Why is dispersal necessary?

If all the fruits or seeds were dropped close to the parent plant the seedlings would be very close together and overcrowded. They would all be competing for the limited amount of water and mineral salts in the ground. As they grew they would also be competing for light. Those that did not get enough light would become etiolated (page 256). They would be in poor health and very likely to suffer from disease. As a result very few of them would survive to grow into healthy plants.

But when the fruits and seeds are dispersed further away from the parent they have a better chance to grow well. Some of the seeds will land on poor ground or in places where they cannot grow. Others will land on good soil where they will not be overcrowded and will be able to grow into healthy new plants. In this way the plants can **colonise** new areas and spread to new habitats.

## Investigation 1

### Looking at fleshy fruits

1 Obtain two tomatoes. These are the fruits of the tomato plant.

   What are the small leaf-like structures at the end?

2 Cut one tomato transversely, and the other longitudinally.

   How are the pips (seeds) arranged inside the fruit?

   Which structures in Figure 2 can you see?

3 Look at fruits growing on a tomato plant.

   What were they formed from originally?

   How are the seeds dispersed?

   How is the fruit adapted for this kind of dispersal?

4 Examine other examples of fleshy fruits, for example orange, mango and guava.

   Find out where the seeds are, and how they are arranged.

5 Examine an apple or pineapple.

   Where are the seeds in these fruits?

   Which structures in Figure 3 can you see?

## Investigation 2

### Looking at dry fruits

1 Obtain a pea or bean pod.

   The pod is the fruit of the pea or bean plant. It is also found in other plants belonging to the same family, e.g. flamboyant, rattleweed and butterfly flower.

2 Open the pod by splitting it down the side.

   How are the seeds arranged inside the pod?

   Which structures in Figure 5 can you see?

3 Look at pods that are still attached to the whole plant.

   What were they formed from originally?

   Describe carefully all the changes that occur from the time that the flower has been fertilised until the pod is ripe.

   How are the seeds dispersed?

   How is the pod adapted for this kind of dispersal?

4 Examine other examples of dry fruits.

   In each case locate the seeds and try to explain how they are dispersed.

## Assignments

1 What is the difference between a fruit and a seed?

2 Give an example of a fruit which is dispersed by:
   a) wind,
   b) an animal,
   c) water.
   Describe how the fruit is adapted. Why is it important that fruits should be dispersed as widely as possible?

3 Give one example of each of the following:
   a) a fleshy fruit formed from the ovary of the flower,
   b) a false fleshy fruit formed from the receptacle,
   c) a dry fruit whose seeds (but not the fruit itself) are eaten by man,
   d) a dry fruit whose seeds *and* fruit are eaten by man,
   e) a winged fruit which is dispersed by wind.

4 The seeds found inside fleshy fruits generally have a hard seed coat. Suggest two functions of the seed coat.

5 In a fleshy fruit, food substances such as carbohydrate are highly concentrated inside the seeds, but very dilute in the fleshy part of the fruit. Explain the difference.

6 Below are shown the fruits of two different plants.

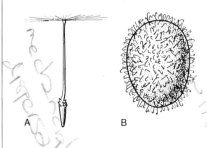

A                    B

In each case explain how you think the fruit is dispersed.

# Vegetative reproduction

*In this Topic we shall see how plants survive from one year to the next by means other than seeds, and how this gives them an alternative method of reproduction.*

## Perennating organs

You may have noticed that many garden plants die down in the dry season, but the following wet season they grow up again in the same place. This is because they form special storage organs during the wet season which they fill up with food. The organ remains dormant in the soil after the rest of the plant has died, and the next year a new plant grows out of it (Figure 1).

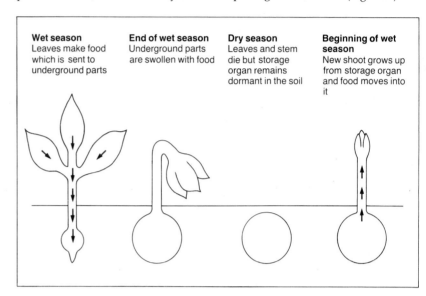

**Wet season**
Leaves make food which is sent to underground parts

**End of wet season**
Underground parts are swollen with food

**Dry season**
Leaves and stem die but storage organ remains dormant in the soil

**Beginning of wet season**
New shoot grows up from storage organ and food moves into it

**Figure 1** These diagrams show how a storage organ enables a plant to survive the dry season and come up again when the rains start.

Such organs enable plants to carry on from one year to the next, and so they are called **perennating organs**. (The word perennating means 'through the year'.) There are many examples of perennating organs, and they can be formed from different parts of the plant (Figure 2).

**Figure 2** Different kinds of underground perennating organs which store food.

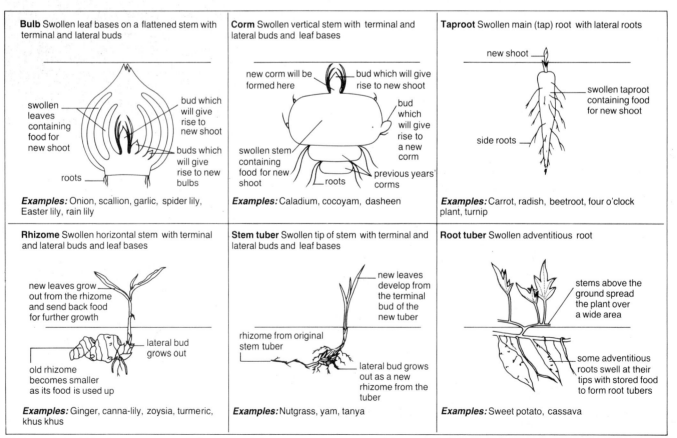

**Bulb** Swollen leaf bases on a flattened stem with terminal and lateral buds

swollen leaves containing food for new shoot

bud which will give rise to new shoot

buds which will give rise to new bulbs

roots

*Examples:* Onion, scallion, garlic, spider lily, Easter lily, rain lily

**Corm** Swollen vertical stem with terminal and lateral buds and leaf bases

new corm will be formed here

bud which will give rise to new shoot

bud which will give rise to a new corm

swollen stem containing food for new shoot

previous years' corms

roots

*Examples:* Caladium, cocoyam, dasheen

**Taproot** Swollen main (tap) root with lateral roots

new shoot

swollen taproot containing food for new shoot

side roots

*Examples:* Carrot, radish, beetroot, four o'clock plant, turnip

**Rhizome** Swollen horizontal stem with terminal and lateral buds and leaf bases

new leaves grow out from the rhizome and send back food for further growth

lateral bud grows out

old rhizome becomes smaller as its food is used up

*Examples:* Ginger, canna-lily, zoysia, turmeric, khus khus

**Stem tuber** Swollen tip of stem with terminal and lateral buds and leaf bases

new leaves develop from the terminal bud of the new tuber

rhizome from original stem tuber

lateral bud grows out as a new rhizome from the tuber

*Examples:* Nutgrass, yam, tanya

**Root tuber** Swollen adventitious root

stems above the ground spread the plant over a wide area

some adventitious roots swell at their tips with stored food to form root tubers

*Examples:* Sweet potato, cassava

## Vegetative reproduction

Consider a potato plant (Irish potato). This forms stem tubers (the potatoes) (Investigation 2). Now a single plant produces not just one tuber, but many, perhaps five or six altogether (Figure 3). These tubers rest in the soil, and each one can give rise to a new plant. This is therefore a method of reproduction as well as a way of getting through unfavourable conditions. It is known as **vegetative reproduction**.

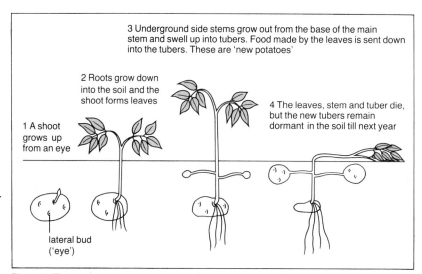

Figure 3  These diagrams show how a potato plant survives from year to year.

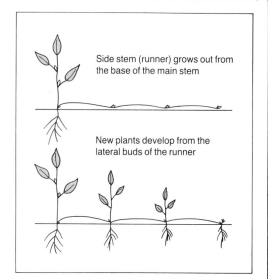

Figure 4  How plants produce runners.

Other plants, too, can reproduce by means of their perennating organs. A bulb, for example, may sprout a new bulb from the side during the growing season. Corms also produce more than one new corm. Rhizomes and stem tubers also give rise to many new plants and from one sweet potato plant many root tubers will grow. These can become new plants as the old parts rot away or man separates them.

## Other methods of vegetative reproduction

Vegetative reproduction does not necessarily involve the formation of perennating organs. Many plants reproduce vegetatively by other means. For example, some plants form **runners**. A runner is a branch of the main stem which lengthens and creeps along the surface of the ground. Roots grow down from it at intervals as shown in Figures 4 and 6.

Some plants send out stems which form roots and leaves at their ends (Figure 5). Side branches of this kind are called **stolons** and are also formed in

Figure 5  This common pot plant known as a spider plant has formed several stolons.

Figure 6  Runners, leaf buds and suckers as methods of vegetative reproduction.

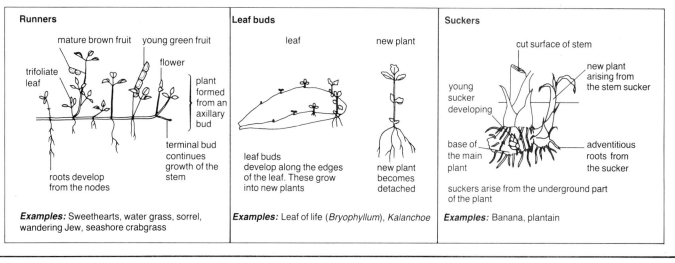

**Runners**

mature brown fruit   young green fruit

trifoliate leaf

flower

plant formed from an axillary bud

terminal bud continues growth of the stem

roots develop from the nodes

*Examples:* Sweethearts, water grass, sorrel, wandering Jew, seashore crabgrass

**Leaf buds**

leaf   new plant

leaf buds develop along the edges of the leaf. These grow into new plants

new plant becomes detached

*Examples:* Leaf of life (*Bryophyllum*), *Kalanchoe*

**Suckers**

cut surface of stem

new plant arising from the stem sucker

young sucker developing

base of the main plant

adventitious roots from the sucker

suckers arise from the underground part of the plant

*Examples:* Banana, plantain

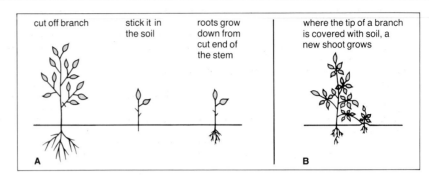

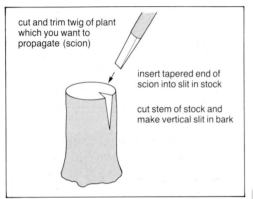

**Figure 7  A** Taking a cutting.  **B** Growing plants by layering.

**Figure 8**  Grafting one plant onto another. This particular kind of graft is called a crown graft.

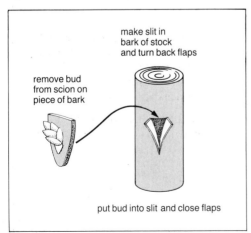

**Figure 9**  A gardener binds the scion and stock together after carrying out a crown graft.

**Figure 10**  Budding one plant onto another. The scion forms the shoot and fruits, while the stock forms the base of the tree and roots.

water hyacinth and water lettuce (page 368). Leaf buds and suckers (Figure 6) are other methods of vegetative reproduction.

## Artificial vegetative reproduction

Man can make use of the plant's ability to produce new plants by vegetative reproduction. We call this **artificial vegetative reproduction**.

People often reproduce their favourite plants by taking **cuttings** (Investigation 3). To do this you cut off a healthy young branch, preferably just below a node, and remove most of its leaves. You then stick the cut end into some good soil. With luck, roots will grow out, and the cutting becomes established as a new plant (Figure 7A). We take cuttings of sugar cane and cassava to plant the new fields.

Gardeners sometimes produce new shrubs by a process called **layering**. A young branch of a shrub is bent down and pressed into the soil. If necessary a brick can be used to hold it down. Hopefully, roots will grow out from the covered part of the branch. Once the roots are established, the branch can be cut so a new plant is produced (Figure 7B). We use layering to grow new plants of hibiscus and bougainvillea.

### Grafting

**Grafting** is a special method of reproducing trees and is used a lot by gardeners. It involves placing the cut stems of two plants in contact with each other so that the tissues join together and become continuous. Figure 8 shows one way of doing this.

A twig (the scion) is cut off the tree you want to reproduce, and it's grafted onto the cut stem (the stock) of another type of tree. Once the two cut surfaces have been brought together, the two plants should be bound with tape or raffia and the joint covered with wax to prevent evaporation and stop microbes getting into it (Figure 9). Grafting is used for tomatoes and cocoa.

### Budding

Another way of reproducing trees is by **budding** (Figure 10). In this case you cut a T-shaped slit in the bark of the stock and you cut out a bud from another plant. You then insert the bud into the slit. As with grafting, the two are then tied together and protected with wax.

Budding enables a large number of new plants to be grown on a single stock plant. Each bud grows into an individual plant and they will all be the same genetically, like identical twins. So if a gardener wants to produce a large number of, say, rose bushes of a particular kind, this is a good way of doing it. Budding is also used for citrus species such as orange and lime.

In grafting and budding the stock is chosen for its good roots and its resistance to disease. The scion is chosen for its good flowers or fruits. The new plant combines the best qualities of both the stock and the scion.

How do grafting and budding work? Just under the dead part of the bark at the surface of a woody stem is a layer of dividing cells called the **cambium** (see page 254). When the scion is attached to the stock their cambium layers are brought together. The cambium cells then form new vascular tissues which link the stock and the scion with one another.

| Advantages | Disadvantages |
|---|---|
| 1 Production of new plants is sure. (It does not depend on pollination and seed dispersal.) | 1 Improvement of quality is not possible; daughters are like the parent. |
| 2 Large food reserves are available for new plants (more than in a seed). | 2 Lack of variation means weaknesses show in offspring after several generations. |
| 3 Very rapid growth because no resting period is needed. (Seeds need a dormant period.) | 3 Diseases are automatically passed on to the offspring. |
| 4 The farmer can get daughter plants exactly like the parent (whereas seeds give variation). | 4 Overcrowding may result as daughters are close to the parent (and not dispersed as with seeds). |

**Table 1** Advantages and disadvantages of vegetative (asexual) reproduction.

# Investigation 1

## Looking at bulbs

1 With a knife slice an onion bulb down the middle.

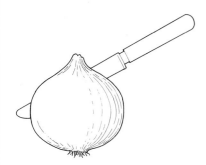

Which structures in Figure 2 can you see? Why are the inner leaves thick?

2 Look at another bulb which is beginning to sprout into a new plant.

What is the new shoot growing from? Where is the shoot getting its food from? What will happen to the bulb when the new plant is full-grown?

# Investigation 2

## Looking at other storage organs

Your teacher will give you a collection of plants with different kinds of storage organs.

1 Examine the storage organs. You may need a hand lens, and a knife to cut them in two, so that you can see inside.
Put into one group the organs which are made from swollen stems. These will have leaves or leaf scars and small buds on them.
Put into another group the ones which are made from swollen roots. These will not have leaves or buds, but they will have side roots.

2 Look at Figure 2 and try to decide what kind of storage organ each of your plants is.

3 Take one of your storage organs that you haven't cut up. Plant it in some moist soil.
Look at it every month and describe how it grows.

# Investigation 3

## Taking cuttings

1 Fill a test tube with water.

2 Cut off a side-branch from coleus or balsam. Make the cut just below a node (see page 66).

3 Remove some of the leaves. This is to prevent it losing too much water.

4 Stick the cut end of the branch in the test tube of water.

5 Place the test tube in a warm place, and observe your cutting at intervals during the next few weeks.

Do any roots grow out of it?

Suggest an experiment which could be done to find out what conditions are needed in order for roots to grow out.

# Assignments

1 Why are perennating organs also described as storage organs?

2 What, if anything, is wrong with each of these remarks?
   a) Irish potato tubers are formed at the ends of the roots.
   b) Grafting is better than budding because it produces more new plants.
   c) Lilies reproduce asexually by means of bulbs.

3 Describe how a *named* storage organ carries out vegetative reproduction.

4 How would you distinguish between
   a) a bulb and a corm,
   b) a taproot and a stem tuber,
   c) budding and grafting?

5 Irish potato tubers which are suitable for planting are called 'seed potatoes'. When a gardener plants seed potatoes he usually rubs off all but about two of the 'eyes'. Why do you think he does this?

6 What are the advantages to a gardener of propagating a plant by vegetative means?

7 When taking a cutting it is advisable:
   a) not to take a shoot which has a flower on it,
   b) to cut off some of the leaves before you plant it.

Give a possible reason for each of the above.

# Chromosomes, genes and cell division

*The nuclei of all living cells contain chromosomes. In this Topic we shall see what chromosomes are and what they do.*

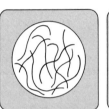

when a cell is resting the chromosomes are long, thin and thread-like

but when the cell is about to divide the chromosomes become shorter and fatter

**Figure 1** Chromosomes as they appear at different stages in the life of a cell.

**Figure 2** The full set of chromosomes of a human male as seen under the microscope just before the cell divides. At this stage each chromosome can be seen to consist of two strands joined together about half way along.

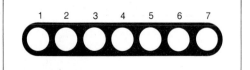

**Figure 3** In this chromosome the genes are shown as white discs. The genes at particular positions (1, 2, 3 etc.) generally control specific characteristics.

## What are chromosomes?

If you stain cells with certain dyes, the chromosomes show up under the microscope. However, if you look at an ordinary *resting* cell, you can't see the chromosomes very well. This is because they are very thin, like fine pieces of thread. To see them clearly you must look at the cell when it's about to divide: at this stage they get shorter and fatter and this makes them show up distinctly (Figure 1).

In Figure 1 notice that each chromosome has another one exactly like it. Scientists have found that in virtually all cells, both animal and plant, the chromosomes are in pairs like this. The two chromosomes belonging to a pair look exactly alike, and we call them **homologous chromosomes**: homologous comes from Greek and means 'agreeing'.

The total number of chromosomes in the cell varies from one type of organism to another. The cell in Figure 1 has only ten (five pairs). However, man has 46 (23 pairs). You can see them in Figure 2.

## What are genes?

Chromosomes contain **genes** which determine the individual's characteristics, such as eye colour and nose shape. The genes are arranged along the length of each chromosome like a string of beads (Figure 3). Each gene controls a specific characteristic, though sometimes a characteristic may be controlled by several genes acting together.

When a cell divides, it's very important that the genes should be shared out evenly between the two daughter cells, and this means that the chromosomes must behave in an orderly way.

## What happens when cells divide?

Cells divide in two different ways, by **mitosis** and **meiosis**. Mitosis is the kind of cell division that occurs during growth and asexual reproduction. Meiosis, on the other hand, takes place during the formation of eggs and sperms.

*huma*

### Mitosis

Figure 4 shows what happens to the chromosomes during mitosis. The parent cell has four chromosomes: two long ones and two short ones. Notice that the two daughter cells have exactly the same number and kinds of chromosomes as the parent cell: two long and two short.

If you study Figure 4, you will see how this is achieved. Before the cell starts to divide, each chromosome produces an exact copy or replica of itself. The original chromosome and its replica are called **chromatids**, and they are held together by a structure called the **centromere**. The chromatids now line up across the middle of the cell. Then they part company and move to opposite ends of the cell. Finally the cell splits across the middle, and the chromatids become the chromosomes of the daughter cells.

Do you agree that the chromosomes behave in such a way that the daughter cells are bound to have the same number and kinds of chromosomes as the original cell? This means that as an organism grows, all the new cells will have the same chromosome make-up. And it ensures that when an organism reproduces asexually its offspring are identical to the parent as far as their chromosomes and genes are concerned.

A good place to observe mitosis is in the tip of a developing shoot or root where rapid growth is taking place (Investigation).

### Meiosis

Figure 5 shows what happens during meiosis. The parent cell has four chromosomes as before. However, in this case each daughter cell contains only *two* chromosomes: one long one and one short one. In other words the daughter cells contain *half* the original number of chromosomes.

If you study Figure 5, you will see how this comes about. The chromosomes form chromatids as in mitosis. However, they line up across the

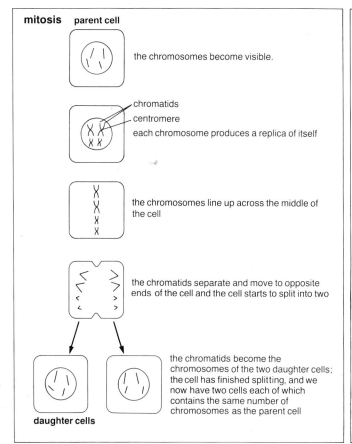

**Figure 4** These diagrams show what happens to the chromosomes when a cell divides by mitosis.

**Figure 5** These diagrams show what happens to the chromosomes when a cell divides by meiosis.

middle of the cell in a different way. In this case homologous chromosomes *come together*, and then move away from each other to opposite ends of the cell which then splits in two. There now follows a second cell division in which the chromatids part company. So in meiosis there are two cell divisions, one after the other, and the chromosomes behave in such a way that the daughter cells have half the number of chromosomes present in the original parent cell. A cell which has only half the full number of chromosomes is described as **haploid**; a cell with the full number of chromosomes is described as **diploid**.

Meiosis takes place in the ovary and testis where eggs and sperms are formed. Why is it necessary for eggs and sperms to be formed by this kind of cell division? Figure 6 will tell you.

**Figure 6** The human life cycle. The figures refer to the number of chromosomes in the cells. Meiosis takes place in the ovary and testis, and it results in the egg and sperm having half the full number of chromosomes. When fertilisation takes place the full number is restored. All the body cells of the adult have the full number of chromosomes because they are formed by repeated mitotic divisions of the original fertilised egg.

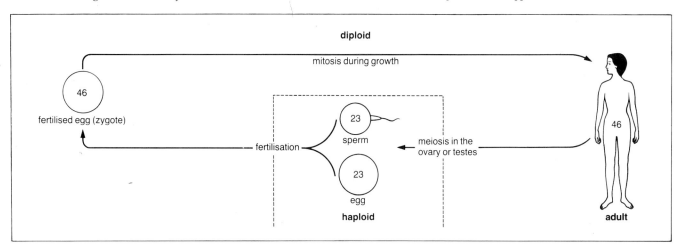

## A boy or a girl?

What determines whether the fertilised egg develops into a boy or a girl? Well, it depends on what kind of chromosomes the egg contains.

The cells of an adult human contain 46 chromosomes (23 pairs). One pair are called **sex chromosomes** because they determine the individual's sex. There are two types of sex chromosome: a long one known as the **X** chromosome, and a short one known as the **Y** chromosome. Males contain an **X** and a **Y** chromosome, whereas females contain two **X** chromosomes.

Now the sperms which a male produces in his testes contain only one of these two chromosomes, either an **X** or a **Y**. This is because they are formed by meiosis. In fact, of all the sperms formed, half will be **X** and half **Y**. On the other hand, all the eggs which the female produces in her ovaries will contain an **X** chromosome. This is shown in the top part of Figure 7.

Now when fertilisation occurs, the egg may be fertilised by either an **X** sperm or a **Y** sperm. In fact if fertilisation is random, as it's believed to be, there is an equal chance of either happening. If an **X** sperm fertilises the egg, the zygote will contain two **X** chromosomes and this will develop into a female. On the other hand if a **Y** sperm fertilises the egg, the zygote will contain an **X** and a **Y** chromosome and will develop into a male. This is shown in the bottom part of Figure 7.

## More about genes

We have seen that a chromosome is made up of a string of genes which determine the individual's characteristics. An enormous amount of research has been carried out on genes to find out what they consist of and how they work.

Genes consist of a chemical substance called **deoxyribonucleic acid**, or **DNA** for short. In the early 1950s two scientists at Cambridge, James Watson and Francis Crick, discovered the structure of the DNA molecule: they did this by working out the positions of various atoms in the molecule.

Watson and Crick found the DNA molecule to be like a twisted ladder or, more technically, a **double helix** (Figure 8). The rungs of the ladder, they discovered, are made up of pairs of organic bases. There are four such bases, and they are known by their initial letters **A**, **C**, **T** and **G**. The bases fit together as shown in Figure 8: **A** always pairs with **T**, and **C** with **G**.

So we have a series of pairs of bases along the length of the DNA molecule. Now the *order* in which the bases are arranged is variable, and this is how the genes exert their effects in the organism. For example, the order of base-pairs for producing, say, brown eyes, will be different from the order that produces green eyes, and so on. We can sum it up like this: DNA contains a set of coded instructions which tell the organism how to develop. These instructions form the **genetic code**.

How does a gene cause a particular characteristic to develop? Here is a very simple example to illustrate what is thought to happen. Suppose that brown eyes are caused by the presence of a certain pigment in the iris: the body makes this pigment because one of the genes tells it to. The gene exerts its action by making the cells produce a specific enzyme, and this in turn causes the production of the pigment.

Now the DNA is in the nuclei of the cells, but the enzymes and other proteins are made in the cytoplasm. So the message in the DNA code has to be sent to the protein-making machinery in the cytoplasm. The message is carried by another chemical very similar to DNA called **ribonucleic** acid or **RNA** for short.

The RNA is really a *copy* of the DNA and it has the same order of bases. It passes out of the nucleus to the cytoplasm. Here, in the ribosomes, amino acids are joined together in the right order to form the protein enzyme. The order of amino acids in the protein is determined by the order of bases in the DNA and RNA.

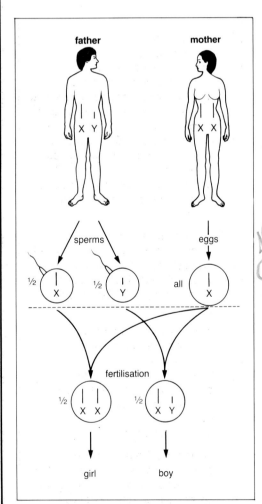

**Figure 7** A boy or a girl? It all depends on the sex chromosomes.

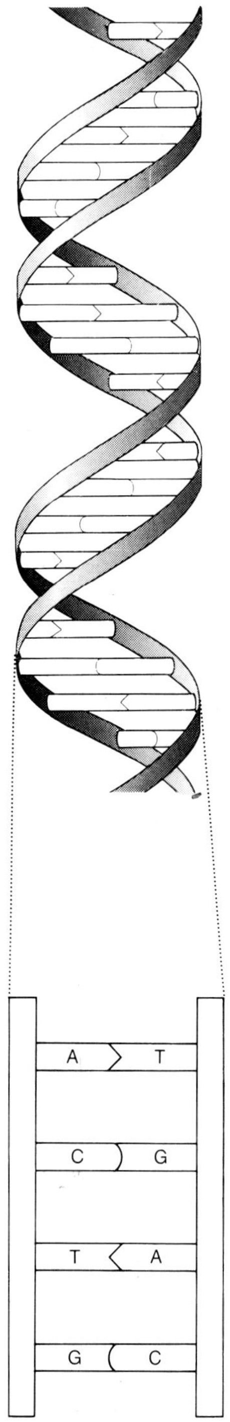

## Figure 8 (left column)

A T

C G

T A

G C

pairs of bases form the rungs of the ladder

**Figure 8** The DNA molecule is like a twisted ladder. It contains the genetic code. The code is contained in the sequence of pairs of bases which occur along the length of the molecule.

## *Investigation*

**Looking at chromosomes in dividing cells**

Obtain a prepared longitudinal section of a root tip. Alternatively make your own slide like this:

1 Cut off the end of a young root about 5 mm back from the tip.

2 Place the root tip in a watch-glass of acidified acetic orcein stain.

3 Warm the slide over a spirit burner for five minutes.

4 Place the root tip on a slide with a drop of the acetic orcein stain.

5 Break the root tip up with a needle so as to spread the cells out as much as possible.

6 Put on a coverslip, cover it with blotting paper and press down on it gently.

7 Look at your slide under the microscope: low power first, then high power.

Can you see chromosomes in any of the cells?

How are the chromosomes arranged in the different cells?

In each case try to decide if the cell is resting, about to divide, in the middle of dividing, or has just finished dividing.

## *Assignments*

1 What is the difference between a chromosome and a gene?

2 Explain the meaning of each of the following:
   a) homologous chromosomes,
   b) chromatids,
   c) gene,
   d) DNA.

3 Look at the cell shown below and then answer the questions beneath it.

   a) How many chromosomes are there altogether? 12
   b) How many pairs of homologous chromosomes are there? 6
   c) If this cell divided by mitosis, how many chromosomes would there be in each daughter cell? 12
   d) If the cell divided by meiosis, how many chromosomes would each daughter cell contain? 6
   e) If the cell divided by meiosis how many daughter cells would be formed? 4

4 The human cell whose chromosomes are shown in Figure 2 was just about to divide by mitosis. Which stage in Figure 4 does this cell correspond to? Explain your answer.

5 In a human being how many chromosomes are present in:
   a) a brain cell,
   b) a sperm cell in the testis,
   c) an egg which has just been produced in the ovary,
   d) a skin cell,
   e) a fertilised egg?

6 Mr and Mrs Cross have three children, all boys. They are sure that their next child will be a girl. Do you agree? Give the reason for your answer.

# Heredity

*Why do children look like their parents? It's because of the way genes are passed from parents to their children. This is the science of heredity or genetics.*

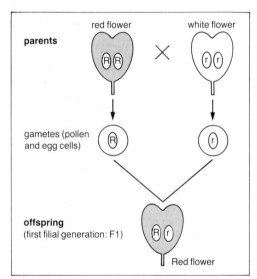

**Figure 1** The result of crossing two plants with red and white flowers. The genes are indicated by letters: R, red; r, white. The sausage-shaped objects surrounding the genes represent the chromosomes.

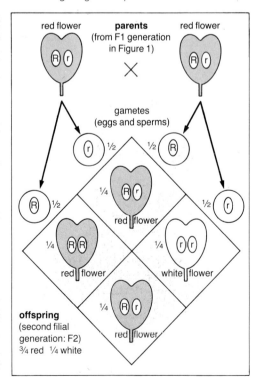

**Figure 2** The result of crossing two red-flowered plants from the offspring in Figure 1, or self-pollinating one of them.

## Crossing plants

Suppose we have a bed of plants some of which have red flowers, and others white. We take some pollen from a red flower and place it on the stigmas of a white flower: in this way we cross the two plants. When the seeds develop, we sow them in the soil.

In time new plants grow up from the seeds, and they all have red flowers:

Parents:   red × white
↓
Offspring:   all red

How can we explain this? Look at Figure 1. Each parent plant possesses in all its cells a pair of genes which control flower colour. The red-flowered parent contains two genes which make the flowers red: we can call them **RR**. The white-flowered plant contains two genes which make the flowers white: we can call them **rr**.

Now the pollen grains and egg cells (i.e. the gametes) contain only one of these genes. Each pollen grain or egg cell produced by the red-flowered parent contains one **R** gene; and each pollen grain or egg cell formed by the white-flowered plant contains one **r** gene.

When fertilisation takes place, the **R** and **r** genes are brought together; so each of the offspring contains one **R** gene and one **r** gene. We can call it **Rr**.

Now the offspring all have red flowers even though they contain an **r** gene. We can explain this by saying that the **R** gene somehow suppresses the **r** gene, so it can't exert its effect; in other words, the **R** gene is **dominant** over the **r** gene. That's why we have written it with a capital letter. The **r** gene on the other hand is **recessive**, and so it is represented by a small letter.

The genes controlling flower colour are located on a pair of homologous chromosomes, one gene on each chromosome (see page 304). The pollen grains and egg cells are formed by meiosis, in which the homologous chromosomes get separated from each other. This is why the pollen grains and egg cells contain only one of these genes instead of the normal two.

## Another plant cross

The red-flowered offspring in the previous experiment belong to the **first filial generation (F1)**. Now suppose we take two of these plants and cross them with each other. Or alternatively we might self-pollinate one of them. The resulting seeds are then planted, and the new plants grow up and bear flowers. They belong to the **second filial generation (F2)**.

This time we get a mixture of red-flowered and white-flowered plants. On counting each, we find that roughly three-quarters of them are red, and the remaining quarter white. In other words they are in a ratio of 3 to 1:

Parents:      red × red
↓
Offspring:   ¾ red ¼ white

How can we explain this? Look at Figure 2. Each parent plant contains an **R** and an **r** gene **(Rr)** as we have already seen. Now the pollen grains and egg cells produced by these plants contain *either* an **R** gene *or* an **r** gene. In fact there should be equal numbers of each type of gamete (**R** and **r**).

Fertilisation is completely random, and it's sheer chance as to which kind of pollen grain fertilises which kind of egg cell. There are three possible ways the genes might come together: two **R** genes might combine, giving **RR**; an **R** gene might combine with an **r** gene, giving **Rr**. Both these combinations will, of course, produce red flowers because, as we saw earlier, the **R** gene is dominant to the **r** gene. Alternatively two **r** genes might combine, giving **rr** which will produce white flowers.

Figure 2 shows how these combinations are brought about. If you look at the checkerboard at the bottom of the diagram, you will see that three-quarters of the offspring contain at least one **R** gene and will therefore have red flowers. The remaining quarter are all **rr** with white flowers. These are the proportions which we would *expect*, and they are confirmed when the actual cross is carried out.

## Doing a back cross

Plainly there are two kinds of red-flowered plants: those that have two **R** genes (**RR**), and those that have an **R** and an **r** gene (**Rr**). Both look exactly alike, so you can't tell which is which just by looking at them. How, then, could you tell if a given plant is **RR** or **Rr**?

One way would be to cross it with one of the original white-flowered plants. This is called a **back cross**. If the red-flowered plant is **RR**, the offspring will all be red-flowered (as in Figure 1). On the other hand if it's **Rr**, we would expect to get a mixture of red-flowered and white-flowered plants in roughly equal proportions (Figure 3).

## Producing plants with the same flower colour

Suppose you are a gardener who grows flowers and you find that your customers want mainly white-flowered plants. How could you produce nothing but white-flowered plants?

The answer would be to cross two white-flowered plants with each other, or to self-pollinate one of them. You know that these plants must be **rr**, so the offspring are bound to be **rr** too, that is white just like the parents. And if you cross two of these offspring with each other, or self-pollinate one of them, their offspring will also be white **rr**, and so on down the generations. This is called **breeding true**, and it gives us a **pure line**. In a pure line all the individuals have the same genes with respect to a particular characteristic.

Suppose your customers wanted only red-flowered plants. In that case you would have to cross two red **RR** plants with each other, or self-pollinate one of them. You'd need to make sure that these plants were **RR** and not **Rr**, because if both of them were **Rr** you would get some white plants amongst the offspring.

## The rules of genetics

On the basis of the crosses described above we can make four general statements:

1 An organism's characteristics are passed down from one generation to the next by definite objects called genes.
2 The genes normally exist in pairs, one of which may be dominant to the other.
3 In a gamete only one of the two genes is present.
4 If the dominant and recessive genes are present together in an individual, it is the dominant one which produces an effect.

These are the basic rules of genetics. They were first discovered by an Austrian monk called Gregor Mendel (1822–1884) (Figure 4). He did experiments with pea plants, studying the inheritance of such characteristics as the colour of the flowers, height of the plant, texture of the seeds, and so on.

Since Mendel's day the same rules have been found to apply to other plants and also to animals. For example, an American scientist called T.H. Morgan studied inheritance in the fruit-fly *Drosophila*. This little insect has a number of clear-cut characteristics such as the colour of its eyes and the size of its wings, and it breeds quickly. It is therefore ideal for studying heredity (Investigation 3). In more recent years scientists have found that certain human characteristics are inherited in the same kind of way.

## Some technical terms

Looking back over the crosses which we have just considered, there are two

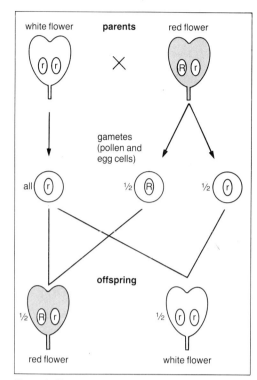

**Figure 3** The result of a back-cross between a red-flowered and white-flowered plant. Symbols as in Figure 1.

**Figure 4** Gregor Mendel, the Austrian monk who discovered the rules of genetics.

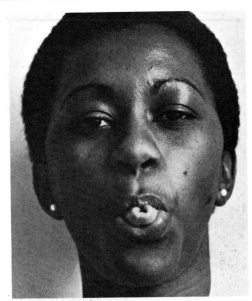

**Figure 5** This girl can roll her tongue.

ways of describing a plant. We can describe it in terms of its outward appearance, e.g. red-flowered or white-flowered. This is known as its **phenotype**. Alternatively we can describe it in terms of the genes that it contains, e.g. **RR, Rr** or **rr**. This is known as its **genotype**. When the genotype for a particular characteristic consists of two identical genes, for example **RR** or **rr**, we say that the organism is **homozygous**. If the two genes are both dominant, the organism is **homozygous dominant**; if they are both recessive, it is **homozygous recessive**.

When the genotype consists of two *contrasting* genes, for example **Rr**, we say that the organism is **heterozygous**. For example, the red-flowered offspring in Figure 1 would be described as heterozygous for flower colour.

Genes such as **R** and **r** which control the same characteristic but produce different effects are known as **alleles**. Alleles occur at the same positions on a pair of homologous chromosomes (see page 304). The term allele is commonly used by geneticists, but in this book we will keep to the word gene.

## Human genetics

Try rolling your tongue longways into a U-shape (Figure 5). Some people can do this, others can't. Tongue-rolling is caused by a dominant gene which we can call **T**. People who can roll their tongue are either homozygous dominant (**TT**) or heterozygous (**Tt**). People who can't roll their tongue are homozygous recessive (**tt**).

What happens if a non-roller mates with a heterozygous roller? The answer is given in Figure 6. Half the children should be rollers, and half non-rollers. Of course human beings don't produce large numbers of offspring like plants and fruit-flies, so it doesn't mean much to put it that way. It is more useful to say that there is an *equal chance* of any given child which they produce turning out to be a roller or non-roller.

What happens if two heterozygous rollers mate? If you look at Figure 7 you

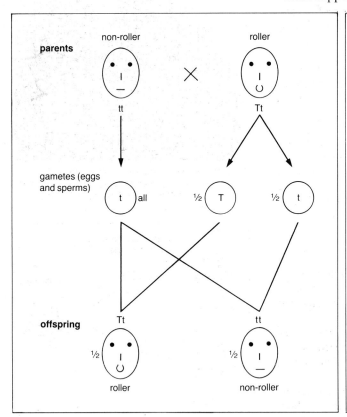

**Figure 6** The inheritance of tongue-rolling in man. The diagram shows the result of a non-roller mating with a heterozygous roller. Gene for tongue rolling: **T**; gene for non-rolling: **t**. **T** is dominant to **t**.

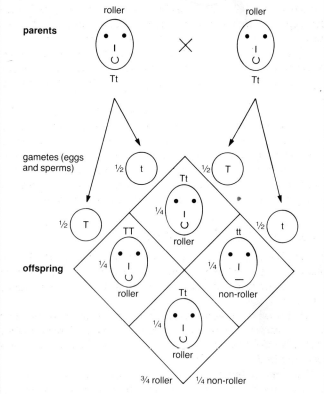

**Figure 7** The result of a mating between two heterozygous tongue rollers.

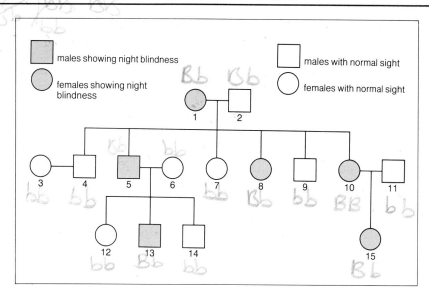

males showing night blindness

females showing night blindness

males with normal sight

females with normal sight

Figure 8 Family pedigree showing the inheritance of night-blindness, a condition in which it's difficult to see in dim light. The condition is controlled by a single pair of genes, the gene for night-blindness being dominant.

Figure 9 Two members of the Habsburg family showing the famous 'Habsburg lip'. Above: Philip IV of Spain 1605–1665. Below: Ferdinand I of Austria 1793–1875.

will see the answer: there is a three to one chance that any given child which they produce will be a roller.

What will be the outcome of matings between (1) two homozygous rollers, (2) two non-rollers, (3) a homozygous roller and a non-roller?

We have seen that a heterozygous individual can roll his tongue – indeed he can roll it just as well as a homozygous dominant individual. However, he possesses the 'non-rolling' recessive gene (**t**) which he may pass on to his children. He is therefore described as a **carrier** of the recessive gene.

## Pedigrees

A pedigree is an individual's ancestral line of descent with respect to a particular characteristic or **trait**. It involves tracing back his or her history through the parents, grandparents and so on. A pedigree can be established for any kind of organism whose ancestors are known.

A human pedigree for a particular trait is shown in Figure 8. Males are represented by squares, females by circles. Individuals showing the trait are represented by a filled-in square or circle; those not showing it are represented by an open square or circle.

Having built up a chart like this, it's possible to work out the genotypes, or *possible* genotypes, of the various individuals. From this it may be possible to work out the chance of the trait appearing in the next generation.

It's amazing how some features persist in a family. A famous example of this is the drooping lower lip of the Habsburg family (Figure 9). By looking at family portraits, this feature can be traced back through several centuries. It's thought to have been caused by a single dominant gene.

## Do genes always show dominance?

Look at Figure 10. Here a red-flowered plant is crossed with a white-flowered plant as in the first experiment described in this Topic (Figure 1). However, instead of getting red-flowered plants in the next generation, the offspring are pink!

In this case the **R** gene doesn't completely suppress the **r** gene: we say that it is only *partially* dominant over it. It is also called **incomplete dominance**. So when the flowers develop, the **r** gene is able to produce a slight effect, resulting in a pink colour.

This kind of thing occurs in both plants and animals. Petal colours are inherited in this way in balsam and the four o'clock plant; and in shorthorn cattle light red coats are found in the offspring of dark-haired bulls and white-haired cows.

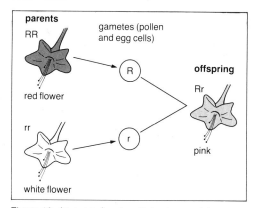

parents

gametes (pollen and egg cells)

RR

red flower

R

offspring

Rr

pink

rr

r

white flower

Figure 10 An example of partial or incomplete dominance: the gene for red flowers R is only partly dominant over the gene for white flowers r.

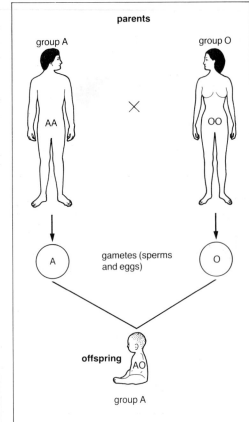

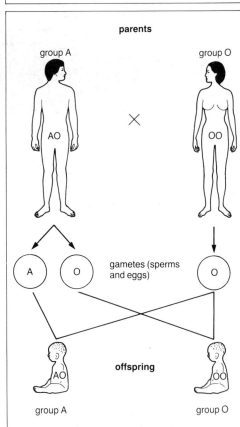

**Figure 11** These diagrams show the way the *ABO* blood groups are inherited in man.

## The inheritance of blood groups

You may remember that everyone's blood belongs to a particular group known as *A*, *B*, *AB* or *O* (see page 131). Now the particular group that a person belongs to depends on whether he possesses certain genes. There are three genes altogether, but a given individual can only have two of them.

To belong to group *A*, you must have either two **A** genes (**AA**) or an **A** gene with an **O** gene (**AO**). To belong to group *B*, you must have either two **B** genes (**BB**) or a **B** gene with an **O** gene (**BO**). To belong to group *AB*, you must have the **A** and **B** genes together. And finally, to belong to group *O*, you must have two **O** genes (**OO**). Neither the **A** nor the **B** genes are dominant over each other. However, both are dominant to the **O** gene.

Suppose a man belonging to group *A* marries a woman belonging to group *O*, and they have a child. What blood group will the child belong to? The answer depends on whether the husband's genotype is **AA** or **AO**. If it's **AA**, then the child must belong to group *A*. On the other hand, if the husband's genotype is **AO**, there's an equal chance of the child belonging to group *A* or group *O*. If you are uncertain about this have a look at Figure 11.

Blood groups are sometimes used in court cases. For example, Mrs Green claims that Mr White is the father of her child. Their bloods are tested, and it turns out that Mrs Green belongs to group *B*, the child to group *AB* and Mr White to group *O*. This shows that Mr White could not possibly be the father of the child. Not all cases are as clear-cut as this!

## Inherited diseases

Some genes produce harmful effects. Such genes may be either dominant or recessive. For example, there is a very serious defect of the pancreas called cystic fibrosis: this is caused by a recessive gene which is passed on just like the gene for non-rolling in Figure 6.

If a couple give birth to a child with an inherited disease, or if there is a history of a particular disease in either of their families, their doctor can arrange for them to see a **genetic counsellor**. The genetic counsellor will try to work out the chance of their next child being born with the disease. To do this he will need to know the parents' pedigrees.

In the case of a recessive disease, a heterozygous person will be healthy because the 'normal' gene is dominant to the gene for the disease. However, he is a carrier of the recessive gene and may hand it on to his children.

## Colour blindness: a sex-linked disease

Some genes are carried on the sex chromosomes (page 306). An example is the gene for **colour blindness**. In this condition a person is unable to see red and green: they appear as different shades of grey. The gene for normal sight (**N**) is dominant, and that for colour blindness (**n**) is recessive.

As you know, the X chromosome is longer than the Y chromosome. The gene for colour blindness is carried only on the X chromosome, and does not occur at all on the Y chromosome. This gives us three possible genotypes for females and two for males with respect to colour blindness (Figure 12).

Colour blindness is more common in men because the recessive gene on the male's X chromosome can show its effect. In a woman both X chromosomes have to carry the recessive gene for her to be colour-blind. If she has one recessive and one dominant gene she can see normally but is a carrier.

Figure 13 shows the cross between a carrier mother and a normal father. What will each of the offspring be like? Work out the offspring that might be produced by (a) a normal mother and a colour-blind father, and (b) a carrier mother and a colour-blind father.

Colour blindness is not dangerous. The worst problems are in matching one's clothes and coping with traffic lights! Other inherited diseases are more serious.

## Haemophilia

This is also a sex-linked disease caused by a gene carried on the unpaired part of the X chromosome. A person suffering from the disease is not able to clot his blood properly (page 130). If he's cut he might bleed to death.

It is inherited in just the same way as colour blindness.

## Sickle cell disease

This is an inherited disease of the blood. A person with the disease produces an abnormal kind of haemoglobin in his red blood cells. As a result, the red cells becomed sickle-shaped when oxygen is in short supply (Figure 14).

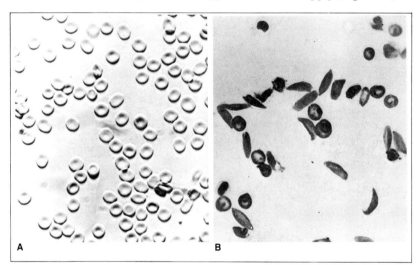

Figure 14  A Normal red blood cells. B Sickled red blood cells of a person with sickle cell disease.

Most people have genes which enable them to produce normal adult haemoglobin (**A**) and are homozygous (**AA**). Those with **sickle cell disease** have genes which make them produce the different kind of haemoglobin called sickle haemoglobin (**S**), and are homozygous (**SS**). The rest of the population have one gene for normal haemoglobin (**A**) and one for sickle haemoglobin (**S**): they are heterozygous (**AS**). They are carriers of the sickle cell gene and are said to show the **sickle cell trait** (Figure 15).

The sickle cell trait (**AS**) is much more common than the sickle cell disease (**SS**). The sickle cell trait has become common in many malarious areas of the world. This is because people with the trait have a slight immunity to malaria and therefore a greater chance of reaching adulthood and passing on their sickle cell genes (page 318).

What happens to people with sickle cell disease (**SS**)? They may have painful **crises** which can be brought on by getting cold or by taking too much exercise. They get pains, especially in the joints, which can be very severe and are usually associated with fever and red urine. The destruction of the sickled cells can cause anaemia and jaundice. The broken-down cells also obstruct blood flow in the small blood vessels, and it is this which causes the pain. The crises tend to get less frequent and less severe with age and are unusual in people over 30 years old. Because of better medical care and good nutrition, the disease, especially in the Caribbean, is now less dangerous than it used to be.

People with sickle cell trait (**AS**) are usually healthy and may not know that they have it. Trouble may develop if the blood oxygen level is low, as may occur during the use of anaesthetics or in air at high altitudes. But no special treatment is necessary.

If two people with the trait have a child there is a one in four chance that it will have the sickle cell disease (**SS**) (Figure 16). It is important that people should know if they carry the trait.

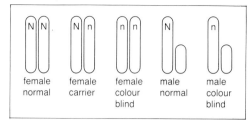

Figure 12  Various genotypes for a sex-linked disease such as colour blindness. The long chromosomes are X chromosomes, and the short ones are Y chromosomes.

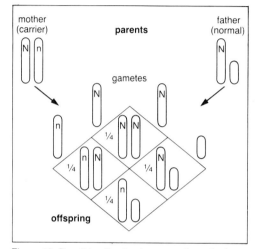

Figure 13  Possible offspring from a mother who is a carrier of a sex-linked disease such as colour blindness, and a normal father. Use Figure 12 to help you to describe each of the offspring.

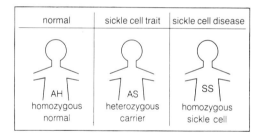

Figure 15  Various combinations of genes for normal haemoglobin (**A**) and sickle cell haemoglobin (**S**).

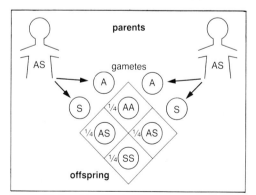

Figure 16  Possible offspring from parents both of whom are carriers, i.e. have the sickle cell trait. Use Figure 15 to help you to describe each of the offspring. What **proportion** of the offspring have sickle cell disease?

# Investigation 1

### How are genes sorted out in heredity?

### A simple situation

1  Obtain two beakers.

2  In one beaker place 50 black beads.

3  In the other beaker place 25 black beads and 25 white ones, and stir them up thoroughly.

4  Have two empty beakers in front of you, side by side.

5  Close your eyes and take a bead from each beaker. Then look at them. If they are both black, put them in the left-hand beaker, if one is black and the other white, put them in the right-hand beaker.

6  When you have used up all the beads, count the number of pairs of beads in each beaker.

How many *pairs* of black beads are there?

How many *pairs* of black and white beads are there?

What are the proportions of each combination?

In this exercise, what do the beads represent?

What do the beakers represent?

Why did you have to close your eyes when taking beads?

This exercise resembles the kind of thing that happens in one of the crosses illustrated in Figures 1–3. Which one?

In what way does the exercise differ from what really happens?

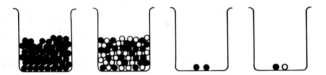

# Investigation 2

### How are genes sorted out in heredity?

### A more complex situation

1  Obtain two beakers.

2  In each beaker place a mixture of black and white beads, 25 of each colour. Stir the beads up thoroughly in each beaker.

3  Have three empty beakers in front of you, side by side.

4  Close your eyes and take a bead from each beaker. Then look at them. If they are both black put them in the left-hand beaker; if they are both white, put them in the right-hand beaker; if one is black and the other white, put them in the middle beaker.

5  When you have used up all the beads, count the number of *pairs* of beads in each beaker.

How many *pairs* of black beads are there?

How many *pairs* of white beads are there?

How many *pairs* of black and white beads are there?

What are the proportions of each?

In this exercise what do the beads represent?

What do the beakers represent?

Why did you have to close your eyes when taking the beads?

Which of the crosses illustrated in Figures 1–3 does this exercise resemble?

In what way does the exercise differ from what really happens?

# Investigation 3

**Inheritance in the fruit fly**

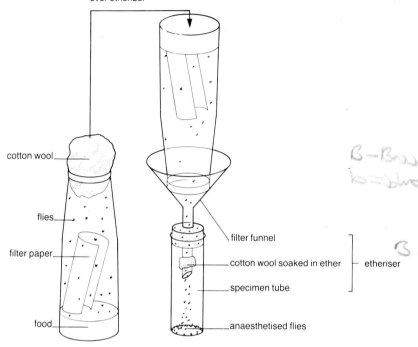

remove cotton wool and invert culture bottle over etherizer

cotton wool

flies

filter paper

food

filter funnel

cotton wool soaked in ether — etheriser

specimen tube

anaesthetised flies

1  Your teacher will give you a bottle containing male flies with short wings and another bottle containing female flies with long wings.

The bottles contain food which the fruit flies like, and a piece of rolled up filter paper for them to cling to.

2  Anaesthetise about 15 males and 10 females (see illustration). Be sure to keep them apart.

3  Put the anaesthetised flies in separate groups on a white tile.

4  With a paintbrush carefully place the flies one by one in a new bottle containing food.

5  Place the bottle on its side so the flies don't fall into the food.

6  When the flies have recovered, stand the bottle at room temperature.

7  One week later, look at the bottle.

Are there any larvae present? The larvae should form pupae.

Can you see any pupae yet?

8  Now anaesthetise the parent flies and then kill them.

Why do you think this is necessary?

9  After a further week look at the bottle again.

Are there any adult flies present? Don't proceed any further until all the adults have emerged from the pupae.

10  Anaesthetise the adult flies and put them on a white tile.

Do they have long or short wings? Which condition is dominant and which recessive?
Explain your result by writing out a genetic chart like the one in Figure 1.

11  Carry out other crosses as instructed by your teacher.

Explain your results and summarise each cross you do with a genetic chart.

# Assignments

1  A black mouse mates with a brown mouse, and all the offspring are black.

Why are no brown offspring produced? Explain your answer fully.

2  If two of the black offspring from question 1 mate with each other, what kind of offspring would you expect and in what proportions? Draw a diagram to illustrate what happens.

3  In human beings the gene for brown eyes is dominant to the gene for blue eyes. A brown-eyed man marries a blue-eyed woman and they have five children. Three of the children have brown eyes and two have blue eyes. What are the genotypes of (a) the mother, (b) the father, and (c) the children? Explain how you arrive at your answer.

4  An albino is a person who has no pigment in the skin so he is very pale. This condition is caused by a recessive gene. An albino man marries a normal woman one of whose parents was an albino. How likely is it that their first child will be an albino? Give your reasons in full. Certain individuals in this family are 'carriers'. Which ones are carriers and what does this word mean?

5  Look at the pedigree in Figure 8 and then answer these questions:
a) Using **B** as the symbol for the night-blindness gene (dominant) and **b** for the normal gene (recessive), write down the possible genotypes of all the people in the chart.
b) Explain in words how you know the genotype of person 1.
c) How are persons 13 and 15 related to each other?
d) How do you know the genotypes of 13 and 15?
e) If 13 and 15 should marry, what is the chance that any of their children will be night-blind? Explain your answer.
f) If 14 and 15 marry, what is the chance of any of their children having night-blindness? Explain your answer.

# Variation

*If you look at a group of people such as those in Figure 1, you will notice that they are all different: they vary in height, the colour of their hair, shape of the face, and so on.*

Figure 1 No two people are exactly alike.

This cell is about to form gametes. How will the four chromosomes be distributed amongst the gametes? It all depends on how the chromosomes arrange themselves before they separate in meiosis.

They might arrange themselves like this:

giving these combinations:

or they might arrange themselves like this,

giving these combinations;

Figure 2 These diagrams show the different ways two pairs of chromosomes can be distributed among the gametes.

Table 1 The percentage chance of twins suffering from the same disease.
Which diseases are likely to be
a) inherited,
b) affected by heredity, and
c) unaffected by heredity?

## Continuous variation

If you measure the heights of a whole lot of people all of the same age, you will probably find that there is a steady gradation from very short to very tall (Investigation). The same applies to body mass, hair colour, intelligence, and many other features. This kind of variation, where there is a gradual transition between the two extremes, is called **continuous variation**.

The main reason why people vary in the way just described is that each individual possesses a different combination of genes. The particular combination of genes in *your* body is probably different from that of any other human being, past or present. In other words you are unique!

What causes this uniqueness? The answer is chance. Through the egg and sperm, your parents gave you a set of genes. However, the *particular* genes which you got from your mother, and the *particular* ones you got from your father, were simply the result of chance.

The reason for this lies partly in the way your parents' chromosomes behaved during meiosis, when the egg and sperms (gametes) were formed. The genes are carried on the chromosomes, and during meiosis half the chromosomes go into one gamete and half into the other. Now it is sheer chance as to which particular chromosomes get into which gamete (Figure 2). We call this **free assortment**: it's rather like dealing out a pack of cards. Each chromosome contains its own particular set of genes, and so a great deal of variation can be brought about this way.

However, there's more to it than that. Do you remember how the chromosomes come together in meiosis (see page 304)? When this happens the homologous chromosomes get wrapped round each other, and bits of them may break off and change places. In this way genes get shifted from one chromosome to the other. This is called **crossing-over**, and it brings about further variation in the offspring.

The two processes mentioned above will make all the gametes different with respect to the genes they contain. Now it's just chance as to which particular sperm fertilises an egg: in other words fertilisation is completely random. This provides yet another source of variation.

As a result of the mechanisms just described, every individual has a unique set of genes. This kind of variation is made possible by sexual reproduction. In an organism which reproduces sexually, the offspring all have different genes, and so there is always variation in the offspring, except in the case of identical twins. This explains why brothers and sisters differ from each other, and why children differ from their parents, although they may resemble them to a certain extent.

## Discontinuous variation

Do you remember tongue-rolling? This is the ability to roll your tongue into a U-shape (see page 310). Now a person can either roll his tongue, or not; there are no 'in-betweens'.

This is called **discontinuous variation**. There aren't many examples of it in humans, but in other organisms we see it a lot: for example the different coloured flowers and different kinds of fruit flies mentioned in the Topic on heredity (pages 308–13).

| Disease | Percentage chance of twins suffering from the same disease | | Percentage risk to general population |
|---|---|---|---|
| | Identical | Non-identical | |
| Sugar diabetes | 50% | 10% | 2% |
| Gastric ulcers | 45% | 22% | 1% |
| Tuberculosis | 30% | 13% | 0.1% |
| Schizophrenia | 80% | 15% | 1% |
| Epilepsy | 80% | 20% | 3% |
| Club foot | 23% | 2% | 0.001% |
| Influenza | 30% | 28% | 25% |

This kind of variation arises as a result of a process called **mutation**. Mutation is a sudden change in the genetic make-up of an organism. It sometimes leads to people being born with a defect such as a missing arm or an extra toe (Figure 3). About two per cent of babies are born with a defect of some kind. Sometimes the defect results in the child being physically or mentally handicapped.

Mutation occurs during meiosis when the eggs and sperms are being formed. There are two main kinds: **chromosome mutation** and **gene mutation**. In a chromosome mutation a major change occurs in one or more of the chromosomes. For example the individual may lack a particular chromosome, or have an extra one. The condition known as Mongolism or Down's syndrome, for instance, is caused by the presence of an extra chromosome. Sometimes part of a chromosome gets snapped off and lost, or it may turn round the wrong way. Doctors can find out if a person has this kind of mutation by looking at his chromosomes under the microscope.

A gene mutation is caused by a chemical change occurring inside an individual gene. You cannot see this kind of mutation under the microscope, as it does not alter the appearance of the chromosome. When a gene mutation occurs, there is a change in the order of bases in the DNA molecule (page 306). The change may be very small indeed, but it may have a severe effect on the organism. An example is sickle cell disease (page 313).

What causes mutation? The answer is that nothing actually *causes* it. It just happens by chance from time to time. It can be greatly speeded up if the organism is exposed to radioactivity or certain chemical substances. This is why these things are considered dangerous. Many of the people who survived the two atom bombs which were dropped on Japan at the end of the Second World War received massive doses of atomic radiation. As a result they showed a high incidence of mutation, and many of their children were born with defects, far more than in a normal population.

Mutations aren't *always* harmful. The man in Figure 3 does not suffer because he has an extra finger and toe. Indeed, on rare occasions a mutation may even be helpful. We shall return to this in the next Topic.

### Variation and environment

How much does the environment affect variation? Let us take, as an example, the hydrangea plant which grows in temperate regions. This develops blue flowers if the plant is grown in an acid soil. If the soil is chalky, the same plant will develop pink flowers.

This is an example of variation being caused by the environment. Can you think of any other examples from plants or animals? Many of the differences between people, particularly in their behaviour, can be explained by the fact that they have been brought up in different environments. We still don't know for certain how important the environment is, compared with the genes, in making us different from one another. This particularly applies to features like intelligence and artistic ability. In seeking an answer to this difficult question, studies on identical twins can be useful (Table 1).

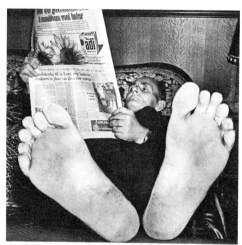

**Figure 3** What is unusual about this man? This is an example of a mutation.

## Investigation

### Looking at examples of variation

1 Measure the height of each person in your class.

  What is the height range (that is, the difference in height between the shortest and tallest pupils)?

2 Divide the heights into 5 cm groups, starting with 120 cm and finishing up with 180 cm (i.e. 120–125, 125–130, 130–135, etc.) and write down the groups in a list.

3 Work out how many people in your class fall into each group. Write the numbers alongside the groups in your list.

4 Construct a bar chart showing how height varies in your class (see page 3).

  Which group or groups contains the largest number of people?

  Which group or groups contains the fewest people?

  What is the average height in your class?

5 Join the tops of the bars in your bar chart with a smooth curve.

  What does the shape of the curve tell us about the way height varies?

  Suggest reasons why the members of your class should vary in height.

6 Make a list of other ways besides height in which the members of your class differ from each other.

## Assignments

1 Explain carefully why (a) two brothers do not look alike, and (b) why identical twins *do* look alike.

2 Explain the difference between continuous and discontinuous variation.

3 What is meant by a mutation? Whereabouts do mutations occur, and what are their consequences?

4 Which of your own features do you think you inherited, and which ones do you think were acquired from your environment? What does 'environment' mean in this context?

5 If you were a scientist what sort of studies would you carry out on identical twins to find out if intelligence is inherited or acquired?

# How do new kinds of organisms arise?

*Species do not remain the same for ever but can change in the course of time.*

Figure 1  Charles Darwin (1809-82).

## The theory of evolution

Most scientists believe that the various organisms present in the world today are descended from simpler forms which inhabited our planet in an earlier age. It is thought that these ancestors gradually changed or *evolved* into the kinds of organisms which we see today.

This theory was first put forward by the 19th-century naturalist Charles Darwin (Figure 1). In the 1830s Darwin sailed around the world in a ship called the *Beagle* (Figure 2). He visited many countries and islands and he studied the animals and plants there. He gradually became convinced that the various species which he observed had come into being by a process of slow and gradual evolution. In 1859 he published his famous book *The Origin of Species* in which he put forward evidence to support this idea. He also put forward a theory to explain *how* evolution may have taken place.

## Creation or evolution?

Darwin put forward his theory at a time when most people believed that all living things were created by God, and they found it hard to accept the theory. Today many people feel that the theory of evolution can fit in with creation if you interpret the meaning of creation flexibly. For example, it is possible that God's way of creating living things may have been through a process of evolution. Obviously this is a very difficult question to which we can never know the answer.

## Evidence for evolution

Evolution is supported by many different kinds of evidence, some more convincing than others. Here we will concentrate on three particular lines of evidence.

### 1  Distribution of sickle cell trait and malaria

Sickle cell disease (page 313) has been caused by a mutation. There is only one amino acid that is different in sickle haemoglobin (**S**) as compared with normal adult haemoglobin (**A**). The people with sickle cell disease are homozygous (**SS**). They suffer from anaemia, jaundice and painful crises, and are more likely to catch infections. They are therefore less likely to survive than other people. We might therefore expect that over a long time the gene for sickle cell disease would disappear. But it hasn't. Why is this so?

Figure 2  HMS *Beagle*, the ship that was to take Darwin round the world, lying in the Catwater at Plymouth. The ship set sail on 27 December 1831.

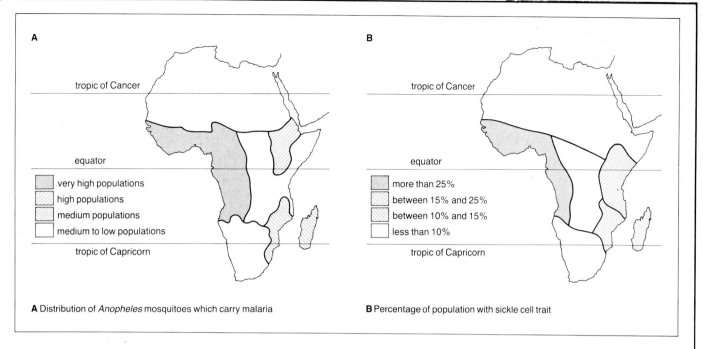

**A** Distribution of *Anopheles* mosquitoes which carry malaria

**B** Percentage of population with sickle cell trait

**Figure 3** Distribution of *Anopheles* mosquito and sickle cell trait.

Figure 3 gives us useful information. For example, on the west coast of Africa there are lots of *Anopheles* mosquitoes which carry malaria (page 340). In the same area more than 25% of the population have the sickle cell trait (**AS**). When we look at other areas on the map we see a similarity between the number of malarial mosquitoes and the sickle cell trait.

The sickle cell trait is found in other countries. In highly malarious areas of Saudi Arabia, India, Greece and Italy there are people of different races with 20–30% of the sickle cell trait. In other places where malaria is less common, the frequency of sickle cell trait is lower. For example, in the Caribbean the lowest frequency is in Barbados (7%), with 10% in Jamaica and 13–14% in Dominica and St Lucia. This compares to about 8% in the American Negro population.

It seems that the sickle cell trait in some way gives the person resistance against malaria. Especially in the past when there were no anti-malarial drugs, many people died of malaria. The people with the sickle cell trait (**HS**) had a better chance of surviving and so passing on their sickle cell genes. In this way, it is believed, the mutation spread in malarious areas.

This suggests how a mutation might spread through a population over a long period of time and lead to evolution.

## 2 *Homologous and vestigial structures*

If you compare the structure of a group of animals such as the vertebrates, you find that they are all basically similar. For instance, if you look at the limbs of amphibians, reptiles, birds and mammals, you find that they are all based on the same design, namely that of the **pentadactyl limb** (see page 371). This suggests that they may all have developed from a common ancestor which lived long ago.

Structures which are found in different animals but have the same basic design are described as **homologous**. Most biologists believe that the existence of homologous structures provides strong evidence for evolution.

Here's another interesting observation. Certain snakes, notably pythons and their relatives, have a pair of small claw-like structures about two-thirds of the way down the body, one on either side (Figure 4). They have no obvious function, and it has been suggested that they are the remains of a pair of legs which existed in an ancestor of the snakes millions of years ago. Structures which have no function today but are thought to have been important in the past, are called **vestigial structures**, and their existence would seem to support evolution.

**Figure 4** It is possible that the 'claws' of this anaconda are the relics of a pair of hind legs which were possessed by the ancestors of snakes.

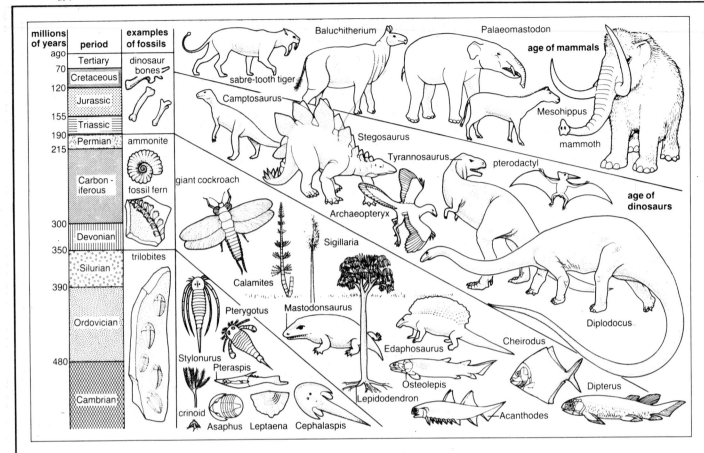

| millions of years ago | period | examples of fossils |
|---|---|---|
| 70 | Tertiary | dinosaur bones |
| 120 | Cretaceous | |
| 155 | Jurassic | |
| 190 | Triassic | |
| 215 | Permian | ammonite |
| | Carbon-iferous | fossil fern |
| 300 | | |
| 350 | Devonian | |
| 390 | Silurian | trilobites |
| | Ordovician | |
| 480 | | |
| | Cambrian | crinoid |

**Figure 5** The history of life on this planet is shown by the fossils found in the rocks. *Diplodocus* was about 30 metres long and the main part of its body was the size of a two-storey house. It ate plants and was docile. In contrast, *Tyrannosaurus* was a savage carnivore. The fossils come from different layers of sedimentary rock, and their approximate ages have been worked out by special chemical dating methods.

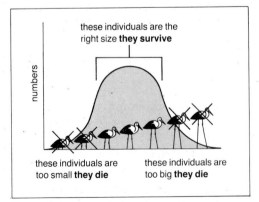

**Figure 6** This simple diagram shows how natural selection ensures the survival of the fittest. The graph shows the numbers of different sized storks in the population. The fittest individuals are those that are best adapted to the particular environment.

## 3  Fossils

Normally when an animal dies, its body decays. However, in the past dead animals sometimes became buried in mud which later hardened to form **sedimentary rock**. Meanwhile tiny particles worked their way into the animal's bones. As a result, the bones gradually got turned into rock. These are known as **fossils**.

Over the years, thousands of fossils have been discovered. They range from a few isolated bones or fragments to almost complete skeletons. By carefully piecing the bones together, scientists have been able to work out the structure of the animals which used to live on our planet. The main conclusion is that these ancient animals were basically similar to those living today, but different in detail.

To illustrate this let's go back about 150 million years. At this time there were no mammals, and the world was dominated by dinosaurs such as the ones shown in Figure 5. Many of them were much larger than, and looked very different from, any land animal living today. However, careful studies of the bones of these dinosaurs tell us that they were reptiles and were basically similar to present-day crocodiles and lizards.

Certain dinosaurs have been found whose skeletons were very similar to those of mammals, and this has led to the idea that these particular dinosaurs may have given rise to the first mammals. When sedimentary rock is formed it is laid down in layers, one above the other. The oldest layers are towards the bottom, and the most recent layers towards the top. In the sequence of fossils showing the change from reptiles to mammals, the most reptile-like fossils are found in lower layers than the mammal-like ones. This suggests that the reptiles came before the mammals and that there may have been a progression from one to the other.

This is just one change which may have taken place. Other fossils have been discovered which enable us to put the various animals and plants that used to inhabit the earth into a sequence like the one in Figure 5. All these organisms died out eventually and became **extinct**. However, most biologists believe that the animals and plants which populate the world today are their descendants.

## How has evolution taken place?

Darwin put forward an explanation of how evolution may have taken place which most biologists still believe to be correct. The explanation goes like this:

In any population of animals or plants there is usually fierce competition for food and an ever-present threat of being attacked by enemies. This creates a **struggle for existence** in which every individual is fighting desperately for survival. Now within a species there is considerable **variation** between individuals, and some individuals are better adapted to the environment than others. For example, some may be particularly strong or good at running. These individuals will be more likely to survive than the others: this is sometimes called the **survival of the fittest**. These individuals are most likely to reproduce, and when they do so they may hand on their good qualities to their offspring.

This process is called **natural selection**. Nature, as it were, *selects* the fittest individuals and *rejects* the weaker ones (Figure 6). In this way, the species as a whole is constantly tending to improve and to change into something better.

We have seen that natural selection depends on variation. The kind of variation which is important in natural selection is *genetic* variation, particularly the sort that results from **mutation** (see page 317). Mutations are usually harmful, but occasionally a mutation may occur which makes an individual *better* adapted to its environment, as with the sickle cell trait. This particular individual will win in the struggle for existence, and its useful adaptation will be passed to the offspring and will gradually spread through the population. In this way new kinds of organisms arise.

What evidence is there that natural selection really does take place? One of the clearest pieces of evidence comes from Kettlewell's studies on the peppered moth (see page 372). The black form of this moth is thought to have arisen as a result of a mutation in the 1840s. Thanks to the darkening of the trees from industrial smoke, this black form thrived in industrial areas. Its numbers increased until it eventually became the main type in those areas.

Another example of natural selection is provided by the way new kinds of germs arise. For example, new types of bacteria have been formed as a result of a mutation which makes them resistant to penicillin. In the same way new types of mosquito have arisen which are resistant to DDT, and rats now exist which are resistant to the rat-poison warfarin. Obviously these new forms are at a great advantage, and so they spread quickly.

## Artificial selection

We have seen that in bringing about evolution nature selects the fittest individuals and rejects the unfit. Now the same thing can be done by man. With a population of animals or plants at his disposal, a person can select those with good qualities and allow them to breed, whereas those with poor qualities can be killed or at any rate prevented from breeding. This is called **artificial selection** and it has been carried out by animal and plant breeders for centuries.

All our familiar breeds of farm animals, domestic animals, crop plants and garden plants have been produced this way. We now have new varieties of sugar cane and rice which grow more quickly, give a higher yield of sugar or grain and are more resistant to disease.

Man can bring together good characteristics from two different varieties and combine them in the offspring. An example is the *tenera* variety of the oil palm (Figure 7). It has the large kernel (of *dura*) and the wide mesocarp (of *pisifera*), both of which give oil. The fairly thin endocarp also allows for easy extraction of the oil from the kernel.

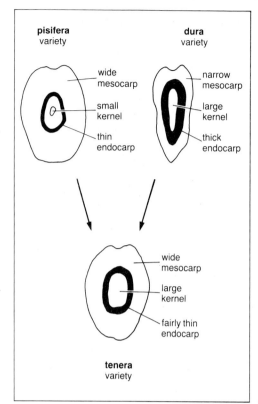

**Figure 7** How the improved variety of *tenera* oil palm was developed.

# Assignments

1 In what way do vestigial structures support the idea of evolution?

2 What are homologous structures? In what way do homologous structures provide evidence for evolution?

3 Rats are normally killed by a poison called warfarin. However, certain individuals are not affected by this poison, and they appear to be on the increase. How would you explain this?

4 In what respect is the breeding of plant crops similar to, and different from, the process of evolution as put forward by Darwin?

5 Suppose the animals in Figure 6 are antelopes in an African Game Park. Suggest reasons why it is a disadvantage for them to be (a) very short, and (b) very tall.

6 Would the *tenera* variety of oil palm 'breed true'? (See page 309.) Explain your answer.

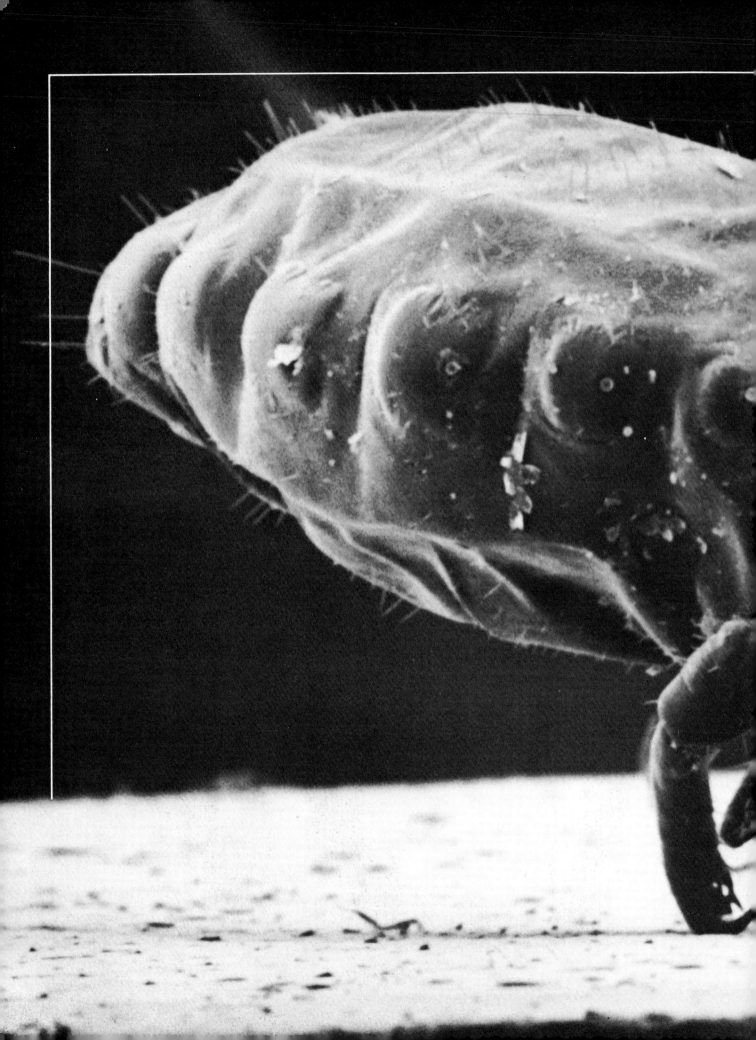

# How organisms affect humans

*The louse is
an external parasite
that sucks blood from humans.
In the next group of topics we shall
see how different kinds of
organisms affect humans*

# Organisms as food for humans

*Plants and animals store food for their own use. Man makes use of these stores as the source of his own food.*

---

**Cereals**
Rice   maize

---

**Oil seeds**
Soya bean   castor oil   sunflower seed
groundnut   cashew

---

**Vegetable fats**
Coconut   oil palm   cocoa butter

---

**Leguminous crops**
Black-eyed pea   gungo pea   soya bean
kidney bean (red pea)

---

**Starch storage crops**
Sweet potato   yam   cassava   arrowhead   carrot
Irish potato   dasheen   cocoyam   turnip

---

**Spices and flavourings**
Ginger   cinnamon   black pepper   cloves
nutmeg and mace   pimento   mint   garlic
sweet peppers and chillies   french thyme

---

**Beverages and drug plants**
Tea   coffee   cocoa   kola (cola)   tobacco   senna
red sorrel   quinine

---

**Fruits**
Banana   citrus fruits   mango   star apple   date
damson plum   pineapple   pawpaw   guava
naseberry   hog plum   otaheite apple   guinep
jujube   cerasee   gooseberry   pomegranate
W. Indian cherry   water melon

---

**Vegetables**
Pumpkin   cucumber   egg plant   tomato
ochra (okra)   avocado pear   ackee   cho-cho
breadfruit   breadnut   jackfruit   onion   scallion
calalu   lettuce   cabbage   cauliflower

---

**Table 1** Plants which we use as food in the Caribbean.

---

**Plant fibres**
Cotton   silk cotton   jute   bamboo
bowstring hemps   sisal (hemp)   raffia

---

**Timber**
W. Indian ebony (cocus wood)   laurier
bullet wood   lignum vitae   coubaril
red cedar   W. Indian cedar   balsa
blue mahoe   W. Indian elm   whitewood
mahogany   woman's tongue

---

**Other useful plants**
Indigo   logwood   annatto   turmeric   calabash
gourd   loofah   chew (chaw-) stick   khus khus

---

**Table 2** Other useful Caribbean plants.

## Plants as food for humans

We will look at each of the groups of food in turn (Table 1).

*Cereals* are those members of the grass family (*Gramineae*) which are cultivated for their fruits (grains, page 294). In the tropical regions rice and maize are the most important, and millets in Africa. They form the most important part of the food supply.

*Oil seeds* have food reserves of oil. The seeds are either eaten whole, or the oil is extracted from them.

*Vegetable fats* are similar to oils but are solid at room temperature. The fat is extracted from the seeds or, in the case of oil palms, from the fruit wall.

*Leguminous crops* all have pods or legumes. They are also called pulse crops and supply a large part of the protein of the diet. The seeds, beans and peas, are eaten. And in some cases the pod is eaten. The rest of the plant can be used as animal food. Nodules on the roots contain nitrogen-fixing bacteria (page 28).

*Starch storage crops* These are underground roots or stems which store food (pages 80 and 300). They are a basic source of starch.

*Spices and flavourings* are used to add 'taste' to food. Most of them also aid in digestion and may have medicinal properties.

*Beverages and drug plants* Tea, coffee, cocoa and kola (cola) contain **caffeine**, and tobacco contains **nicotine**. These are both mild stimulants which can be harmful if taken in excess. Marijuana contains intoxicating substances called **cannabinoids**, which can be extremely harmful (see p. 198).

*Fruits* Apart from banana and citrus fruits these are mostly grown on a small scale. In addition to water, they contain vitamins, mineral salts and roughage.

*Vegetables* Many of these are 'fruits' in the botanical sense (page 296) but we call them vegetables if they are not sweet and juicy. Others consist mainly of leaves. They supply vitamins, mineral salts and roughage.

In addition to plants that we eat, there are other plants that are useful to us (Table 2).

## Animals as food for humans

Man's animal food is mainly a source of protein. He may eat the whole soft part of the animal, as for example with snails, prawns, crabs and termites. Or he may eat just the muscles (flesh or meat) of the animal. Examples of this are fish, chicken, beef (cattle), pork (pig) and mutton (goat or sheep). He may also eat other parts of the animal such as the liver, kidney, heart, brains and bone marrow which are rich in vitamins and minerals.

Eating these foods means that the animals have to be killed. In other cases the animals are reared and some of the things which they produce are used as food. For example in the case of chickens, they are kept for the eggs which they produce; and cattle and goats are kept for their milk. The milk can also be used to make butter and cheese.

In addition to supplying food, some animals also provide us with other useful materials. For example, we get leather from the skins of cattle and pigs, and wool from sheep.

## The importance of plants and animals

You can now see that plants and animals are very important to man in providing him with food and other materials. It is therefore important that we grow or rear them with as few losses as possible from disease. We will now look in more detail at one tropical food crop and at some of the diseases which may affect it.

## Sugar cane

Sugar cane is a large perennial grass grown widely in the Caribbean. The stems (canes) grow to 3m or more in height. It is the world's most important source of sugar as well as being a source of molasses, rum and bagasse.

It is mainly grown in plantations in the wetter parts. It needs a long growing season, fertile soil of almost any kind, effective manuring, and plenty of water throughout the year. An annual rainfall of 1500 mm is preferred, but it grows well in the Caribbean with less than this. It needs a temperature of at least 25°C over most of the year, and a short dry season during the later stages of growth when the sugar is being stored.

It seldom produces seeds, and in cultivation is always propagated by cuttings from the top of the old canes. They are usually 20–25 cm long with two or three buds.

The land is cleared and the soil is ploughed to break it up and mix in the trash (old leaves). The cuttings or **setts** are usually placed at an angle in the soil, often with more than one at each position. Or the setts are laid in shallow furrows and covered over. Within two weeks the setts produce adventitious roots and some of the buds grow out as new aerial shoots (Figure 1).

The land is weeded, either by hand or by using weed killer (herbicides). Nitrogen is needed. It is given in ammonium sulphate. 'Superphosphate' is added to supply phosphates, and potash for potassium. From time to time old dead leaves are pulled off to mulch the soil (see page 380). Within 10 to 14 months the canes become mature and are ready to harvest.

The fields may first be burned to remove the sharp, saw-like leaves. But this destroys some of the sugar content and is illegal in some islands. Canes should be cut as close to ground level as possible to prevent the rotting of uncut pieces, which may damage the next crop. Also, if they are cut too high, cane and sugar will be lost. Tremendous loss of sugar occurs when cane is not sent fresh to the factory. Up to 30% is lost after eight days.

## Diseases and pests of sugar cane

*Mosaic* is caused by a virus which is spread by plant bugs. It occurs in all sugar growing areas and causes big losses from time to time. The leaves develop light and dark patches and become stunted and twisted. Resistant varieties are used, but after some time they may lose their resistance and have to be replaced.

Tobacco (see page 50), cassava and garden egg also suffer from mosaic disease.

*Chlorotic streak* is also caused by a virus. The leaves become streaked and less able to photosynthesize. It occurs especially in areas which may be flooded or are badly drained. Losses can be considerable. A variety resistant to mosaic may not be resistant to chlorotic streak. Infected plants should be burnt to prevent an attack on the next crop.

*Red rot* is caused by a fungus. The upper leaves turn red and drop off. The stems develop red internodes and the sugar content is reduced. As before, resistant varieties should be used.

*Small moth borer* is widespread in cane growing areas. Severe losses can be caused by the destruction of tissues in the stem and reduction of sugar content. Part of the damage is done by other organisms entering through the tunnels made by the borers. The pest is largely kept under control by its natural enemies.

*West Indian cane fly* has caused severe losses from time to time. This is not a true fly but a plant bug. It is a small green insect which lays eggs on the underside of leaves, in white cottony masses. The adults suck the leaves and secrete a sugary substance in which moulds can grow. The mould may cover the leaves and reduce photosynthesis.

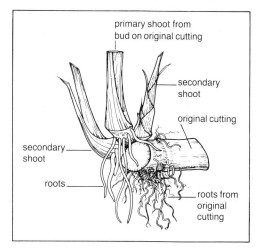

**Figure 1** Sugar cane. Secondary shoots grow out at the base of the primary shoot to form the new canes.

## Assignments

1 Go to the market and see how many of the plant foods listed in Table 1 are being sold there.

   Give different reasons why some of the plants might not be there.

2 Look back to page 72 where we discussed a balanced diet.

   List the constituents of a balanced diet.
   Choose at least three foods to supply *each* of the constituents.

3 Choose one plant from Table 1 or Table 2 and find out about its method of cultivation, economic importance and any diseases which it might suffer.
   (Do not choose sugar cane!)

4 Imagine you are a sugar cane farmer.

   List all the expenses you will have in growing and harvesting your crop.

   List all the problems you may have.

   Describe how you would solve your problems and become the best canefield owner in your country.

# Useful microbes

*Microbes, particularly bacteria and fungi, are essential in nature, and humans make use of them in many ways.*

## Decay and the cycling of matter

Bacteria and fungi play a very important part in making dead organisms decay (page 388). This is the first step in the process by which matter circulates in nature. One aspect of this circulation is the nitrogen cycle which is explained in detail on page 28. The bacteria in the **nitrogen cycle** help to make the soil rich in nitrates which are essential for the growth of plants.

## Getting rid of sewage

Sewage is got rid of in a sewage works (Figure 1). The process depends on decay bacteria.

First the sewage is pumped into a large tank. Here the solid matter sinks to the bottom, forming a sludge. This is broken down by anaerobic bacteria which give off the gas **methane**; this can be used as a fuel, supplying power to run the sewage works. When the sludge has been broken down by these bacteria, it is dried and can be used as a fertiliser.

Meanwhile the liquid part of the sewage is pumped into a long pipe with holes in it. This sprinkles the liquid onto a bed of broken stones, called a **filter bed**. The stones are coated with a slimy film of aerobic bacteria. These bacteria break up any organic matter into simple substances like carbon dioxide and nitrogen salts. The liquid is collected from underneath the filter bed, treated with chlorine to kill any harmful bacteria, then discharged into a nearby river or lake.

Figure 1 A simplified diagram of a sewage works.

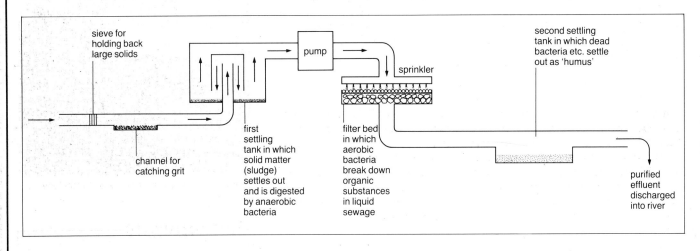

sieve for holding back large solids

pump

sprinkler

second settling tank in which dead bacteria etc. settle out as 'humus'

channel for catching grit

first settling tank in which solid matter (sludge) settles out and is digested by anaerobic bacteria

filter bed in which aerobic bacteria break down organic substances in liquid sewage

purified effluent discharged into river

Figure 2 Blue cheese is ripened by a mould which grows in it. This machine makes holes in the unripe cheese, helping the mould to spread through it.

## Making butter, yoghurt and cheese

Certain bacteria make milk go sour. They convert the milk sugar (lactose) into lactic acid (see page 124). The lactic acid makes the milk curdle and go lumpy. To make **yoghurt** all you have to do is to add a flavouring to the solidified milk. **Butter** can be made by churning sour cream.

Making **cheese** is rather more complicated. First the solid part of the curdled milk is separated from the fluid part (the whey). One way of doing this is to put the curdled milk in a muslin bag and squeeze the fluid whey out. The paste-like substance left behind is cheese.

At this stage the cheese is white and tasteless. It must now be **ripened**. This is carried out by decay microbes (Figure 2). They break the cheese down, softening it and giving it its characteristic smell and flavour.

There are many kinds of cheese, and each is ripened by particular microbes. In some cheeses the mould is visible as a network of threads. In others the microbes give off a gas which cannot get out: the result is that the cheese has cavities in it. Next time you are in a food shop, see if there are any cheeses that look like this.

Cheese should not be ripened for too long, otherwise the decay process goes too far and the cheese begins to liquefy and go very smelly.

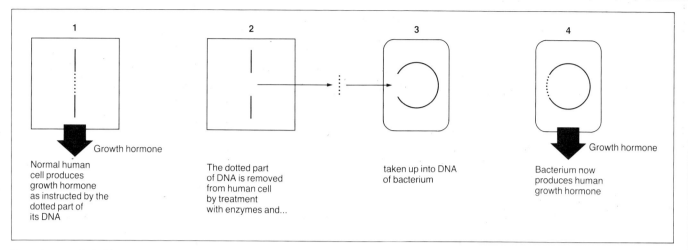

1 Normal human cell produces growth hormone as instructed by the dotted part of its DNA
Growth hormone

2 The dotted part of DNA is removed from human cell by treatment with enzymes and...

3 taken up into DNA of bacterium

4 Bacterium now produces human growth hormone
Growth hormone

## Brewing and baking

These two processes make use of yeast, a single-celled fungus. The part played by the yeast is explained on pages 122–3.

## Producing protein

It is now possible to grow bacteria and fungi in special chambers at such a rate that in the future they may become a source of protein food for farm animals and even humans. Trials have been carried out with encouraging results. In a certain restaurant the diners enjoyed 'chicken' and 'ham' which had been made with flavoured threads of a fungus!

## Making antibiotics

An **antibiotic** is a substance produced by a microbe which kills other types of microbes or prevents them multiplying. Microbes produce antibiotics so as to stop other microbes living in the same place and competing with them.

An example of an antibiotic is **penicillin**. This is produced by the fungus *Penicillium* which forms a green mould on the surface of various foods. Penicillin and many other antibiotics are now manufactured from microbes. Some of them come from fungi, others from bacteria. They are used for treating people with bacterial and fungal diseases (page 336).

## Genetic engineering

On page 257 a disease is described called dwarfism. It is caused by too little growth hormone being produced during childhood. The disease can sometimes be cured by giving the child injections of the hormone. The trouble is that for the treatment to work only *human* growth hormone will do, and it's impossible to get enough human growth hormone to go round.

What makes the human body produce growth hormone? It's produced because our cells contain a gene which tells it to do so. Now suppose we could take this gene out of a human cell and put it into a bacterium. Might the bacterium then make human growth hormone for us? Bacteria reproduce very quickly, and so we might be able to produce large amounts of the hormone this way.

Not long ago this kind of thing was just science fiction, but it has now been done. Genes consist of DNA (see page 306). Scientists have taken part of the DNA out of human cells and transferred it to bacteria (Figure 3). We call this **genetic engineering**.

Genetic engineering is part of a whole new branch of science called **biotechnology**, the application of biology to manufacturing industry. It is possible that in the future we shall be able to get bacteria to make all sorts of things including antibiotics, medical drugs and even cheap fuels.

**Figure 3** The principle behind genetic engineering. Part of the gene (DNA) for making growth hormone is transferred from a human cell to a bacterium. It is typical of bacteria that the DNA is in the form of a ring.

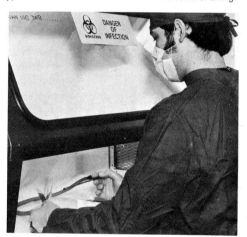

**Figure 4** A technician at work in a biotechnology laboratory.

## Assignments

1 List three useful chemicals which are made by bacteria, and one which is made by a fungus. Explain why each chemical is useful.

2 Describe two useful processes which involve decay bacteria.

3 Certain bacteria convert ethanol into acetic acid. Under what circumstances are these bacteria (a) a nuisance, and (b) useful to us?

4 A politician makes a speech in which he urges scientists to find a way of getting rid of all bacteria from the world.

Write a letter to a newspaper giving your view on this idea and explaining its probable consequences if it was carried out.

# Food spoilage and its prevention

*If you leave food out for a time it will go bad. Why does this happen and how can it be prevented?*

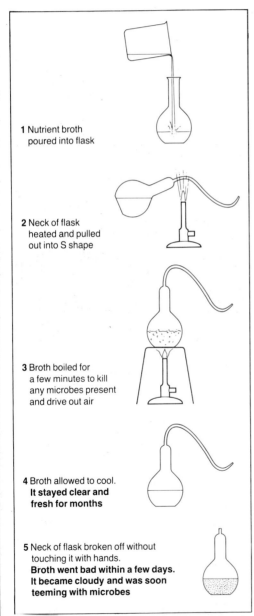

1 Nutrient broth poured into flask

2 Neck of flask heated and pulled out into S shape

3 Broth boiled for a few minutes to kill any microbes present and drive out air

4 Broth allowed to cool. **It stayed clear and fresh for months**

5 Neck of flask broken off without touching it with hands. **Broth went bad within a few days. It became cloudy and was soon teeming with microbes**

**Figure 1** What makes food go bad? This experiment, first performed by Louis Pasteur in the 1860s, shows that microbes from the air make food go bad. The narrow S-shaped neck of the flask stopped microbes getting to the broth; they got stuck on the sides of the drawn-out neck. Breaking the neck allowed microbes to enter.

## What makes food go bad?

Look at Figure 1. This shows an experiment which was carried out by the famous French scientist Louis Pasteur in the 1860s. You can do the same kind of experiment yourself in Investigation 1. Pasteur's experiment shows that there are microbes in the air around us, and if they are allowed to get into food they make it go bad. The microbes are mainly bacteria and moulds, the same kind that bring about decay.

In the course of breaking down the food the microbes give off substances which make the food smell and taste unpleasant. Some produce poisonous substances which cause **food poisoning**. When a person gets food poisoning, he usually has an upset stomach, but he soon gets better. On rare occasions the effects are more serious. Such is the case with botulism which is caused by a type of bacteria. These bacteria live in anaerobic conditions and so they can occur in canned food. The substance produced by the botulism germ is so poisonous that a spoonful of it could kill over a million people.

## How can we stop microbes getting on our food?

### Keep food clean

1  Hands should be washed before handling food. If there are any sores on the hands they should be covered before handling food.
2  Surfaces on which food is being cut should be clean. Microbes become embedded in wooden surfaces which must be scrubbed with soap and water. Food can be cut on a clean plate.
3  Utensils such as pots, pans and plates should be washed in soapy water to remove microbes and food remains. They should be rinsed and left to dry.

### Keep household pests away

*Flies*  contaminate food with bacteria carried on their bodies, and in their saliva and faeces (page 333). They lay their eggs on food, and the maggots also feed on it and make it go bad.

Flies can be kept away from food by wrapping it up or covering it with a fine net. A 'food safe' (Figure 2) can be made with fine net on the sides. When it is closed, flies cannot get to the food.

*Ants*  usually form nests in the ground close to houses. They make periodical raiding parties into the house. They are especially attracted to sweet things.

As a protection food is kept in a food safe. This should be stood in cans containing kerosene or water (Figure 2) to stop the insects crawling inside.

*Cockroaches*  live and breed in houses: under floorboards, in drawers and behind cupboards. They usually hide away during the day and come out at night. They contaminate food in the same way as flies. They eat into packaging and leave their droppings in food such as flour and milk powder, giving them a bad taste.

Protecting food against cockroaches is a constant battle. A double thickness of plastic bags tightly closed at the neck is some use, but cockroaches can eat through several kinds of packaging materials. Cupboard doors are no protection. The nymphs are very small and can get through very small spaces. It is best to store dry foods in tins with press-on lids which are air-tight.

Cockroaches can be killed by spraying insecticides into breeding places, taking care not to spray any food or utensils at the same time. The spraying needs to be repeated.

*Rats and mice*  can breed in houses and under floorboards. Houses and grain stores can be 'rat-proofed' with barriers to stop these pests from climbing into the house, but they can still run in whenever the doors are open. They contaminate food with microbes from their bodies, and from their urine and faeces.

They are able to gnaw through wood, so that many storage areas are no protection against them. All that can be done is to store dry food in tins with press-on lids, or in jars with screw-on lids. Traps and pellets can be put down to kill them.

## *How can we prevent food going bad?*

We need to kill the microbes or make conditions unsuitable for them. This is the basis of **food preservation**. There are four main ways of preserving food and they are explored in Investigation 2.

### 1  *Cold treatment*

All microbes thrive in warm conditions, and that's why food goes bad so quickly in the tropics. We can keep food cool by putting it in an insulated 'cold box' with ice. This is a useful way to transport perishable food. We can also keep things cool by covering them with a wet cloth (Figure 3). As the water evaporates it takes heat away from the food and so cools it.

But to preserve food we have to freeze it. For hundreds of years Eskimos have preserved fish by burying it in frozen ground. We do the same thing when food is frozen in a factory or in the home.

Freezing does not kill microbes, but it stops them multiplying and slows their action – and the colder it is the slower they get. However, as soon as the food thaws the microbes start up again, and the food begins to go bad. In the case of meat, decay sets in particularly quickly. This is because during freezing the cells are broken open by ice crystals, and this makes it easier for bacteria to penetrate into the food afterwards. So frozen food should be eaten as soon as possible after it has been taken out and thawed. It should not be refrozen.

It is important to freeze food quickly. This can be done by subjecting it to a very low temperature (−24°C). Once it has been frozen, it can be stored at a slightly higher temperature.

It is important to distinguish between the different parts of a refrigerator and a deep freeze (food freezer). The temperature in the main part of a refrigerator is just *above* freezing. At this temperature bacterial action is slowed down, but nothing like as much as it is when frozen. For this reason most foods can be kept safely in a fridge for only a few days.

Inside most fridges there is a small frozen food storage compartment. The temperature in here is below freezing. You should not use it to freeze food, but it can be used for storing food which is already frozen (Figure 4).

A deep freeze or food freezer works at much lower temperatures. Most deep freezes have two temperature settings: −24°C for freezing food, and −18°C for storing it. At this temperature bacterial action is slowed almost to a stop.

How long can you leave frozen food in a frozen food storage compartment or a deep freeze? It depends on the kind of food, and the temperature at which it is stored. If you look at the front of the fridge or freezer you may see a row of stars. These indicate how long food can be kept (Table 1).

Freezing food is very important nowadays, and frozen foods are transported in refrigerated lorries and ships.

### 2  *Drying*

Microbes need moisture. If food is dried they go into a state rather like hibernation. They stop multiplying and their action ceases. If spores land on dried foods they cannot germinate since moisture is needed for this (see page 52). Dried foods last indefinitely. Samples of dried food, found in Jericho, were preserved over 4000 years ago.

Removing water from an object is called **dehydration**. Nowadays food is usually dehydrated by having hot dry air blown over it. Sometimes other more complicated methods are used. Milk, eggs, potatoes, fish and meat can all be dehydrated. When water is added to dehydrated food, it quickly takes it up and can then be eaten. Of course once the dried food is made up with water it will go bad in the usual way.

Dehydrated foods are compact and light so they can be moved around easily and cheaply. They are particularly useful in wartime and in space travel. They are also useful in the tropics, for example milk powder, dried fish, beans and peas. As long as they are kept dry and free from the ravages of household pests, they can be kept safely. As soon as some is needed it can be mixed with water and used.

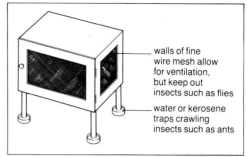

**Figure 2**  A food safe in which food can be protected against flies and ants.

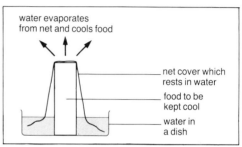

**Figure 3**  Cooling food by evaporation.

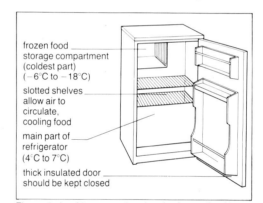

**Figure 4**  A refrigerator, showing the frozen food compartment and the main part of the refrigerator.

| Label | Temperature in food storage compartment of fridge | Temperature in deep freeze | Frozen food kept for |
|---|---|---|---|
| ✳ | −6°C | — | 1 week |
| ✳✳ | −12°C | — | 1 month |
| ✳✳✳ | −18°C | −18°C | 3 months |
| ✳ (✳✳✳) | — | −24°C | 1 year |

**Table 1**  How long frozen food can be safely kept at different temperatures.

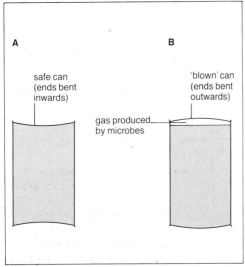

**Figure 5** A pressure cooker in action. The control valve allows steam to escape when the desired pressure has been reached.

**Figure 6** Sections through **A** perfectly sterilised and **B** 'blown' cans.

**Figure 7** A woman lays out fish to dry in the sun.

## 3   Heat treatment

Heat kills microbes. When you cook food, the heat kills many of the microbes that might otherwise make it go bad. This is especially true if a pressure cooker is used (Figure 5) in which the temperature of the steam can reach 115°C. It also cooks the food more quickly so it keeps its flavour. When drinking water is contaminated it should be boiled.

Many people preserve fruit by **bottling** it. A special bottle is used – it has a lid with a rubber rim. You fill the bottle with fruit and syrup and put the lid on. Then you heat the bottle to kill any microbes present. After that you let the bottle cool down. As it cools, the air inside it shrinks and a vacuum is created. This pulls the lid on tightly, and the rubber rim makes it airtight.

**Canning** works in the same kind of way. In a canning factory food is placed in metal cans. Air is then sucked out of the cans, after which they are sealed. They are then heated under pressure for long enough to kill any microbes.

As the contents cool a vacuum is created, so that the ends of the can curve inwards (Figure 6A). However, if any microbes are left in the can they begin to grow and respire. The gases they produce cause the ends of the can to bulge outwards (Figure 6B). Such a 'blown' can is suspicious and the contents should not be eaten.

Heat is also used for killing bacteria in milk. Milk can be completely sterilised by heating it to a very high temperature and then sealing it. Some housewives buy **sterilised milk** because it will keep for a long time. It can be packaged in cartons which can be kept outside the refrigerator until they are opened. However, sterilisation alters the flavour, and most people prefer **pasteurised milk**.

Pasteurisation is named after Louis Pasteur. He was the first person to realise that heat kills bacteria. When milk is pasteurised it is heated enough to kill dangerous germs, but not so much that it loses its flavour. In one method the milk is heated to about 70°C for 15 seconds, then quickly cooled and put into a sterilised bottle or carton, and then capped or sealed. Some dairies use a quicker method: they heat the milk to 135°C for one second, and then seal it. Some bacteria survive this treatment, but not the ones that cause disease.

## 4   Chemical treatment

The idea here is to add a chemical to the food which kills bacteria but is harmless to man.

**Pickling** is an example. When food is pickled it is put in a preservative such as vinegar. The acid in the vinegar kills the bacteria and prevents the food from going bad.

Another example is **smoking**. In this process the food is held over a wood fire. The smoke contains substances which kill the bacteria, as well as giving the food a delicious flavour.

Some foods are preserved by **salting**: the food is either soaked in a solution of salt (brine) or salt is rubbed into it. The salt pulls the water out of the bacterial cells by osmosis and kills them. This method of preservation has been used for many generations, and is very useful where there are no refrigerators. Salted fish ('salt fish') is preserved in this way. Pepper can be used in a similar way to preserve shrimps. Eventually this food will go bad, but it does stay good for some time.

In the tropics we can put fruit or fish out in the sun (Figure 7). This not only dries the food as the water in it evaporates, but also leaves a high concentration of sugar or salt. This kills any microbes present and is the reason why 'dried fruit' such as figs and dates keep for a long time.

Bacteria and other microbes can also be killed by radio-active rays, a very modern way of preserving food. However, to kill all the microbes very strong rays have to be used, and many scientists feel that this could make the food dangerous to eat. Recent information suggests that there is no danger, so radiation may eventually become a widely used method of preserving food.

# Investigation 1

**To find out what makes food go bad**

1  Make up some 'nutrient broth' as follows: put some meat juice in a test tube and add 10 cm of distilled water to it. Boil it for several minutes so as to sterilise it.

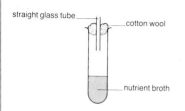

straight glass tube — cotton wool

nutrient broth

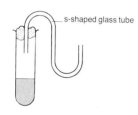

s-shaped glass tube

2  Pour half the nutrient broth into each of the two test tubes, and set the test tubes up as shown below.

3  Sterilise both tubes by heating them in an autoclave or pressure cooker for 15 minutes, then let them cool.

Alternatively boil the broth over a bunsen burner for about one minute.

4  Observe the nutrient broth in the two test tubes at intervals during the next few days or weeks.

If the nutrient broth goes cloudy, it means that bacteria have got in and are turning it bad.

Which tube goes cloudy first?

How would you explain your observations?

How does this experiment differ from the one outlined in Figure 1?

5  Place a drop of the nutrient broth from each tube on a slide and put on a coverslip.
Examine it under the microscope.

Can you see any microbes?
Which tube contains them, and why?

# Investigation 2

**Finding ways of stopping food going bad**

1  Cut six small pieces of fresh meat, about 1 cm square.

2  Obtain six large test tubes. Label them A to F.

3  Set up the six test tubes like this:

A  Put a piece of meat in a test tube and plug the tube with cotton wool. Leave it at room temperature. This is your control.

B  Put a second piece of meat in a test tube, and plug the tube with cotton wool. Place it in a refrigerator.

C  Dry another piece of meat by blowing warm air over it with a hair drier for a few minutes. Then put it in a test tube with a few crystals of silica gel, and plug the tube with cotton wool. Leave it at room temperature.

D  Put a piece of meat in a test tube, and plug the tube with cotton wool. Place the tube in an autoclave or pressure cooker, and heat it. Then cool it, and leave it at room temperature.

E  Soak a piece of meat in vinegar. Then put it in a test tube and plug the tube with cotton wool. Leave it at room temperature.

F  Rub salt into the final piece of meat. Then put it in a test tube and plug the tube with cotton wool. Leave it at room temperature.

4  Can you think of any other ways of preventing meat going bad? If you can, set up extra test tubes and label them G, H . . . etc.

5  Leave the test tubes for several days.

6  After several days look at the pieces of meat and smell them.

Which pieces of meat have gone bad, and which have not?

From this experiment, which methods appear to be good for preserving food?

# Assignments

1  Give five examples of foods which go bad within a few days if you don't keep them in a refrigerator.

2  A housewife leaves a loaf of bread, two biscuits and some pickled onions on the sideboard while she goes on holiday. When she gets home she finds that the bread has gone mouldy but the biscuits and pickled onions are unaffected. Can you explain the difference?

3  Explain each of the following:
   a)  Food left at the South Pole by Captain Scott during his expedition in 1912 was discovered many years later in perfect condition.
   b)  Sometimes the sides of a can of food bulge out and the can bursts.
   c)  Pasteurised milk eventually goes bad even if the container is not opened.

4  Here are some simple rules for freezing food.
   a)  Freeze the food as soon as possible after you have obtained it.
   b)  Handle the food as little as possible before you freeze it.
   c)  Set the freezer at its lowest temperature several hours before you put the food in.
   d)  Don't re-freeze food which has been frozen and thawed before.

Give a scientific reason for each of these rules.

5  Describe an experiment which you could do to compare the rates at which (a) dried milk powder and (b) dried milk powder that has been made up in water, go bad.

6  A fresh fish weighs 120 grams and contains 22 grams of protein. After being dried, the same fish weighs 31.5 grams.
   a)  What percentage of the fresh fish is protein?
   b)  What percentage of the dried fish is protein?
   c)  Why are the two figures different?
   d)  Why is this important in feeding mankind?

# Microbes and disease

*What causes diseases, why do they sometimes spread so quickly, and what can we do about them? In this Topic we will try to answer these questions.*

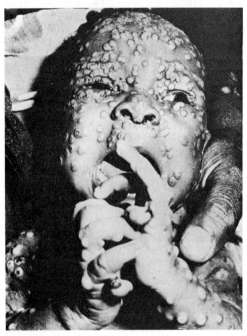

**Figure 1** Every disease has its symptoms. Smallpox is caused by a virus, and it is characterised by spots on the skin. Fortunately this terrible disease has now been successfully wiped out.

**Figure 2** Robert Koch (1843–1910) discovered the cause of many diseases. Koch took blood samples from people who had a particular disease and grew microbes from the blood on agar jelly (see page 48). He then injected the microbes into mice to see if they would get the same disease.

## What is disease?

Disease is the condition which arises when something goes wrong with the normal working of the body. As a result we become ill. There are different kinds of disease. **Deficiency** diseases can arise when we do not get the correct amounts of vitamins and minerals (see pages 76 – 9). Deficiency diseases also occur in plants (see page 142). **Physiological** diseases are when part of the body is not working properly, for example diabetes (page 181). **Inherited** diseases are caused by faulty genes, for example haemophilia and sickle cell anaemia (pages 312 – 13).

In this Topic we shall be looking at diseases which are caused by small organisms which get into our bodies or the bodies of other animals and into plants.

## What causes disease?

Many diseases are caused by **microbes**, particularly bacteria and viruses. Doctors describe them as **pathogenic**. This word comes from Greek, and literally means 'gives rise to suffering'. Here we will refer to them by their everyday name – germs. Other diseases are caused by parasitic protists, worms and fungi.

Germs get into the body mainly through the mouth and nose, or sometimes through cuts and wounds. Once inside, they may multiply very quickly. This is called the **incubation** period and several days or even weeks may go by before the person actually starts feeling ill.

Germs harm us in one of two ways. Some of them attack and destroy our cells, others release poisonous substances into the bloodstream. Our white blood cells try to destroy them, and the intense activity produces a lot of heat – this is one reason why our temperature goes up when we are ill.

The signs of the disease may include a headache, rashes on the skin, sore throat or fever. We call these the symptoms of the disease (Figure 1). When a doctor examines a sick patient he looks for these symptoms because they will probably tell him what's wrong. He can then suggest a remedy: in medical language, he prescribes some kind of **treatment**. Sometimes a doctor gives the patient a **prescription** which he then takes to a pharmacy to obtain some medicine.

## Discovering the microbes that cause disease

In the middle of the nineteenth century the French scientist Louis Pasteur discovered that there are microbes in the air around us and they are responsible for making things decay (see page 328). Pasteur suggested that microbes might also cause diseases. Some years later a German doctor called Robert Koch (Figure 2) showed that diseases such as cholera and tuberculosis are caused by certain bacteria. Similar investigations were carried out by other scientists, and by the end of the nineteenth century the particular microbes responsible for many diseases were known.

## How are germs spread?

In 1918 there was an outbreak of flu in Spain. Within a few months it had spread all over the world. Between April and November over 21 million people died of it – twice as many as were killed in the whole of the First World War. When a large number of people go down with a disease, we say there is an **epidemic**. If it's worldwide it's called a **pandemic**.

Diseases spread because germs get passed from one individual to another: a healthy person 'catches' the disease from someone else – or maybe from an animal. Diseases which are spread like this are called **infectious** diseases. Sometimes a person may have germs in his body without showing the symptoms of the disease. Such a person is called a **carrier**. There are six main ways in which germs are spread from one individual to another:

## 2 By dust

Some diseases can be spread by dust, for example diphtheria and scarlet fever. Germs stick to the dust particles and float through the air. Eventually they settle on surfaces which may be a long way from where they arose. People can catch the disease by breathing in the dust, or getting it in their mouths from infected food.

## 3 By touch

Impetigo is a skin disease which occasionally breaks out in schools. It is caused by a bacterium. You can catch it by touching an infected person, or even by brushing against his clothes or sharing his hairbrush or towel. Another skin disease, athlete's foot (caused by a fungus), can be picked up from the floor of changing rooms and showers. In both these cases infection is by contact: such diseases are said to be **contagious**.

## 1 By droplets in the air

When you cough or sneeze, thousands of tiny drops of moisture shoot out of your mouth and nose (Figure 3). If you have a disease these droplets may be swarming with germs. If they are breathed in by other people, the disease is likely to be spread to them. This can happen if an infected person breathes into someone else's face, or even talks to him. Colds and flu spread rapidly this way, particularly in crowded places.

## 4 By faeces

The faeces of an individual with a disease may be teeming with germs. If the faeces get into food or drinking water, the disease will quickly spread to other people. Epidemics of typhoid and cholera have been caused this way. Food can become contaminated with faeces if it is handled by a person with dirty hands. This is why you should always wash your hands after going to the toilet, particularly if you are about to prepare food for other people. Drinking water may become contaminated if sewage gets into it. This happens in places where sewage is not disposed of properly. In some countries the local river water is used for washing, swimming, defaecating in and drinking. Even in the most hygienic communities sewage can get into the drinking water if there is a disaster such as an earthquake or a flood.

## 5 By animals

Germs are brought onto food by animals such as rats and mice, cockroaches and flies. Take flies for example: these little animals are equally happy feeding on dung or sugar lumps (Figure 4). Their legs may be covered with germs. Moreover, they put saliva onto their food before they feed on it. In this way germs may be transferred from faeces to food.

Many diseases are spread by animals which suck blood. An example is the mosquito which transmits malaria and yellow fever.

Plague (the Black Death of the Middle Ages) is caused by bacteria which are carried from rats to man by fleas. This terrible disease still occurs in dirty places where rats are common. There were several outbreaks during the Vietnam war.

A number of diseases are spread by pets such as dogs and cats. By far the most serious is rabies, which is caused by a virus. Humans can catch it by being bitten or even licked by an infected dog. Pets also carry less serious diseases. The family dog may look innocent, but its tongue is covered with germs. It is unwise to let it lick your face.

## 6 By cuts and scratches

Suppose Jean scratches herself with a needle, and then the needle scratches Ann. Certain diseases may be passed from Jean to Ann in this way. An example is viral hepatitis. Sometimes people prick their fingers to obtain blood for observing under the microscope. If you ever do this you should use a sterilised lancet which has not been used by anyone else.

**Figure 3** In crowded places people readily infect one another with their germs.

**Figure 4** A fly feeding on a lump of sugar. The fly puts saliva onto the sugar before it sucks it up (see page 108). The saliva is likely to contain germs, and there may also be germs on the fly's feet.

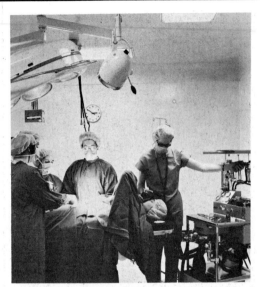

**Figure 5** A modern operating theatre – out of bounds to germs!

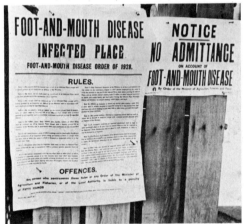

**Figure 6** When there is an outbreak of foot and mouth disease, the whole area is put in quarantine.

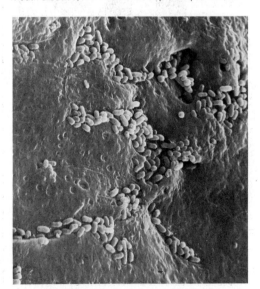

**Figure 7** This enormously magnified picture of the surface of human skin shows groups of bacteria living in the crevices

## How are we protected from germs?

Our bodies are protected from germs in many ways. Some of the ways arise from the body's own defence mechanisms (see pages 127 and 130). Others are man-made. Here we shall be concerned mainly with the man-made methods.

### 1   Germs are destroyed by sterilisation

When an object is freed of germs, it is said to be **sterilised**. One of the best ways of sterilising things is to heat them under pressure.

Why under pressure? If you heat water at ordinary atmospheric pressure, the water boils at 100°C and that's the highest temperature it will reach. Unfortunately this is not hot enough to kill all germs, particularly the spores of bacteria. However, if you raise the pressure, the water boils at a higher temperature, and the germs can be killed in the steam.

The process is carried out in a metal chamber which works in the same way as a pressure cooker in the kitchen. It is called an **autoclave**. Heating at 120°C for 15 minutes is sufficient to kill most germs. Pre-packed foods and hospital instruments are sterilised in this way.

People often try to sterilise things by cleaning them in chemicals such as Dettol. We call these chemicals **disinfectants**, and many different ones are available. The trouble is that they don't kill *all* germs. However, they are suitable for general use, particularly in the home (Investigation).

The most germ-free place is the hospital operating theatre (Figure 5). Before entering the theatre, the air passes through a special filter. The surgeons and nurses wear sterilised gowns, head covers and face masks, and all the instruments are sterilised beforehand. There is therefore no risk of the patient becoming infected.

Cooking food kills many of the germs which might infect us. Good food hygiene is one of the best ways of preventing disease.

### 2   Animals which carry diseases are exterminated

Great efforts have been made to get rid of disease-spreading animals such as rats, fleas, lice and mosquitoes. The battle against insects has been helped enormously by **insecticides**. These are chemical substances which kill insects. One of the most useful insecticides has been DDT, which was first used during the 1939–45 war to get rid of head lice. DDT has now been banned in many countries because it may be dangerous to man (see page 394). However, it has been extremely useful in the fight against diseases such as malaria and yellow fever.

### 3   Infectious individuals are isolated

A person who has a serious infectious disease, or is a carrier of it, must be kept away from other people. So he is isolated until he is no longer infectious. This is called being put in **quarantine**. Occasionally a person entering a country is placed in quarantine because it's thought he may be carrying a serious disease. This is only done if the person comes from an infected area and has not been vaccinated against the disease. Animals brought into the country have to be put in quarantine for several months. This is to make sure they don't bring in rabies. Anyone who breaks the quarantine law and smuggles a pet into the country could start a rabies epidemic.

An animal which shows signs of having rabies is destroyed immediately, to prevent the disease spreading further. This is also done with foot and mouth disease which occasionally strikes at cattle and other livestock. When there is an outbreak of foot and mouth disease on a farm, the whole area is cordoned off (Figure 6). The boots and car tyres of people leaving on essential business are disinfected. All infected animals are killed and then burned or buried in quicklime. It is one of the most distressing things that can happen to a farmer.

Most diseases have an incubation period of a week or two. In the old days a person travelling from one country to another by ship would probably show signs of the disease before docking, so he could be isolated before he had a chance to mix with other people. With modern travel, particularly by air, an infected person may arrive in a country and move about freely for quite a long time before he starts feeling ill and goes to the doctor. In the meantime he may have infected many other people.

## 4 *The skin should be kept clean*

The surface of the skin is very uneven, and thousands of tiny organisms make their homes in its nooks and crannies (Figure 7). Some of these organisms kill harmful germs, so they help to protect us against disease. However, others are harmful and can cause unpleasant skin diseases. For good health it is important to wash the skin regularly with soapy water. When you cut your skin, you open a door to germs. If germs get in the cut is likely to go **septic**. However this can be prevented by quickly applying a substance which kills germs. Such substances are called **antiseptics**; iodine is an example.

Antiseptics were discovered in the 1860s by the English surgeon Joseph Lister (Figure 8). In Lister's day more than half the people who had operations died: many of them got a bacterial infection of their wounds, called gangrene. Lister discovered that if he sprayed the patient's wound with carbolic acid during the operation, it did not go septic. Thanks to Lister, the number of people who died after operations was enormously reduced.

If you cut yourself, the wound should be cleaned and then covered with elastoplast or a bandage. These are called **dressings**. They prevent germs getting in, and bring the cut surfaces of the skin close together which speeds up the healing process. Sometimes a cut may be so large that it has to be stitched.

**Figure 8** Joseph Lister, the first person to use antiseptics.

## 5 *Being immunised*

When a particular germ gets into your bloodstream, it usually causes you to produce antibodies which kill it (see p. 130). Now suppose a small amount of fluid obtained from some dead germs is injected into your blood before you've had the disease. What effect will this have? The fluid contains antigens, so it causes you to make antibodies: you will then be protected against the disease. This is what doctors do to make people immune to various diseases. The process is called **immunisation**.

The first person to immunise someone against a disease was the English physician Edward Jenner. In 1796 he immunised a young boy against the dreaded disease smallpox. He did this by giving him serum from a girl who had a related disease called cowpox or *Vaccinia*. For this reason the process of being immunised is called **vaccination**. The material which is injected into the bloodstream is called the **vaccine**.

Since Jenner's day immunisation has been extended to many other diseases both viral and bacterial. When a doctor immunises you, he puts a small quantity of vaccine into your bloodstream. This is called **inoculation** (Figure 9). Normally it is done with a hypodermic needle or by scratching the skin, though in some cases the vaccine can be taken by mouth. The vaccine itself is made from germs which are dead or at least inactive. The germs must be in this state, otherwise they might give you the disease the doctor is trying to protect you from.

When you were a baby you were immunised against various serious diseases such as diphtheria and polio. Teenagers are usually immunised against tuberculosis unless a simple skin test shows that they are already immune to it; and young girls may be immunised against German measles (rubella): this is a mild disease but if a woman gets it in the early stages of pregnancy it may damage her baby. These immunisations should protect you for the rest of your life. However, for diseases like typhoid and cholera, protection only lasts for a limited time, and you need to be given further doses of vaccine from time to time to keep up your protection. These are called **boosters**.

## 6 *Receiving ready-made antibodies*

Tetanus is a serious bacterial disease which kills many people each year. The

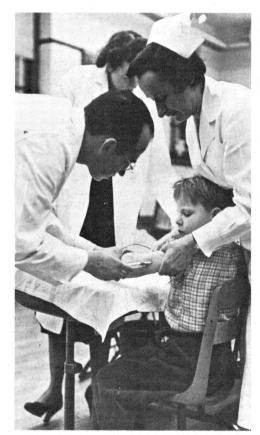

**Figure 9** Dr Jonas Salk, discoverer of the vaccine against poliomyelitis, inoculates a boy against this disease. Polio is caused by a virus which attacks the nervous system, resulting in paralysis. It is a highly infectious disease. Before the vaccine was discovered in the 1950s, it killed or crippled thousands of people. Nowadays the polio vaccine is taken by mouth.

**Figure 10** Alexander Fleming in his laboratory.

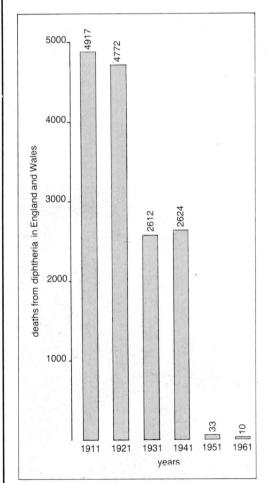

**Figure 11** In Britain between 1911 and 1961 the number of deaths each year from diphtheria fell from nearly 5000 to only 10. A bacterial disease, diphtheria used to be a major cause of death amongst children.

muscles, particularly those working the jaws, go into painful spasms – the disease is sometimes called lockjaw. Tetanus germs can be picked up if you cut yourself with a dirty instrument such as a penknife.

Suppose you cut your finger with a dirty knife; the doctor wants to make sure that you don't get tetanus. It's too late to give you an injection of antigens; by the time your body had made the necessary antibodies you would probably be dead! What can the doctor do to give you quick protection?

The answer is to give you some ready-made antibodies, that is antibodies which have already been made by someone else or by an animal. It is called **anti-tetanus serum**. The doctor injects some of this into your arm and sends you home. The serum should prevent you getting tetanus.

Giving a person ready-made antibodies is useful in an emergency. However, the protection does not last long. This is because the antibodies are gradually broken down and got rid of from the body. For long-term protection the person must make his own antibodies.

### 7    Germs are killed by antibiotics

In 1928 a Scottish bacteriologist called Alexander Fleming was working at St. Mary's Hospital, London (Figure 10). He was growing bacteria on plates of agar. The bacteria multiplied and spread over the agar, forming colonies.

Normally Fleming covered his bacteria with a lid to prevent them becoming contaminated. But one night he forgot to do this, and left one of his dishes uncovered. When he returned next morning he had a surprise. His bacterial colonies had been killed.

What had killed them? Fleming had no idea, but he was determined to find out. After a great deal of searching, Fleming discovered that his bacteria had been killed by a mould. It seemed that some spores of this mould had got into the laboratory and had landed on his bacteria; the mould had then destroyed them.

The mould was identified as *Penicillium*, a fungus related to pin mould (see page 52). Fleming realised that the mould must have produced a chemical substance which killed the bacteria. If this substance could be extracted from the mould, it might be used to cure people of bacterial diseases. It took scientists twelve years to obtain it in a usable form. In 1940 it was tried out on patients in hospital. The results were dramatic: people who were dying of bacterial diseases recovered almost immediately. This 'miracle substance' was christened **penicillin**.

Today hundreds of substances are used by doctors to treat bacterial diseases. Some, like penicillin, are obtained from moulds and other microbes: we call them **antibiotics**. Others are drugs which are made in chemical laboratories. These substances have saved countless millions of lives.

Unfortunately antibiotics only work against bacteria; viruses are unaffected by them. For this reason they are not used against the common cold and flu, both of which are virus diseases.

### Is the battle won?

Look at Figure 11. This shows the number of people in Britain who died of diphtheria each year between 1911 and 1961. You will see that there has been a tremendous fall in the number of deaths from this disease. The same is true of smallpox and many other infectious diseases. In some parts of the world these diseases are virtually extinct.

This happy state of affairs has been brought about partly by immunisation and antibiotics, but also by improvements in personal and community hygiene, and by people being better fed. If you are well fed, clean and healthy, you are less likely to succumb to disease.

Unfortunately the situation is not so good in many developing countries where infectious diseases still kill a lot of people. This is due to poor food, overcrowding and lack of hygiene and to a shortage of nurses, doctors and medical supplies.

# Investigation

## Preventing the growth of bacteria

1 Wash you hands, then obtain four petri dishes containing sterile agar. Label them A, B, C and D.

2 Your teacher will give you a tube or bottle containing a culture of harmless bacteria.

3 Transfer some of the bacteria to the agar in each petri dish, using the method shown in the illustration.

4 Cut out four pieces of filter paper, about 1 cm square.

5 Onto the agar in petri dish A, lay a piece of filter paper soaked in a disinfectant, e.g. Dettol.

6 Onto the agar in petri dish B, lay a piece of filter paper soaked in an antiseptic, e.g. iodine.

7 Onto the agar in petri dish C, lay a piece of filter paper soaked in an antibiotic, e.g. penicillin.

8 Onto the agar in petri dish D, lay a piece of filter paper which has been soaked in distilled water. This will serve as a control.

9 Cover each petri dish with a lid and fix it firmly with a piece of Sellotape.

10 Put the petri dishes in an incubator at 37°C for at least 24 hours.

11 After this time, examine each petri dish for the presence of bacteria.

Which substances, if any, prevented the growth of bacteria?

CARE Work with bacteria can be dangerous and should be carried out under strict supervision by the teacher.

**Always wash your hands after working with bacteria.**

# Assignments

1 Make a list of all the diseases mentioned in this Topic. By each one write the name of the organism which causes it, how it is spread, and how it can be controlled.

2 Give five examples of places where diseases are likely to spread by people coughing and sneezing.

3 What part is played by each of the following in spreading disease:
a) flies,
b) rats,
c) mosquitoes,
d) needles,
e) aeroplanes?

4 Explain the reason for each of the following:
a) A pet which is brought from overseas is put into quarantine for several months.
b) If you graze your knee it is sensible to wash it immediately and put iodine on it.
c) A surgeon wears a mask over his mouth and nose.
d) Many of the food items in a supermarket are wrapped in cellophane.
e) Chlorine is sometimes added to drinking water.

5 Mr X makes hamburgers in a small town. Though he does not know it, he is a carrier of typhoid. Mr X is usually very clean, but one morning he is late for work so he does not bother to wash his hands after going to the toilet. That day he makes 600 hamburgers, all of which are sold in his shop. Two weeks later several hundred people in the town go down with typhoid.
a) There were germs on Mr X's hands. Where might they have come from?
b) Name two other ways this disease might be spread round a town.
c) Suppose you were the Health Officer for the area in which this town is situated. What steps would you take to prevent the disease spreading further?

6 In the Middle Ages soldiers used to rub mould on their wounds. Why do you think they did this?

7 Why is it particularly important that the following places should be as free of germs as possible:
a) operating theatres,
b) public lavatories,
c) hotel kitchens,
d) swimming pools,
e) doctors' surgeries?

8 'Disease can cause loss of man hours and productivity and loss of human life, livestock and agricultural crops.'
   Illustrate the statement made above by reference to four different diseases.

9 During the influenza epidemic of 1918 people in Britain were given face masks like the one in the picture below to protect them from breathing in the influenza germs. These masks proved to be useless. Why do you think they were of no use?

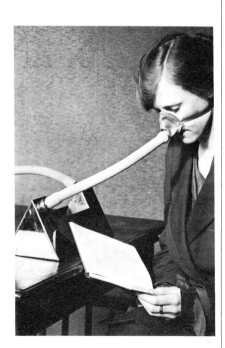

# Sexually transmitted diseases

*Sex involves close contact between two people. It is therefore an easy way of passing germs from one person to another.*

Any infectious disease is liable to be passed from one person to another during sexual intercourse. However, certain diseases are normally *only* passed this way. These are called **sexually transmitted diseases** (**STD**) or **venereal diseases** (**VD**). The germs which cause them cannot survive even for a short time outside the body, so it's impossible to pick them up from towels or lavatory seats.

Sexually transmitted diseases can be very serious, in some cases deadly. The trouble is that in the early stages the symptoms may be very slight, and the person may not know that there's anything wrong. For this reason they are sometimes called 'hidden diseases'. They occur in all sections of society, and are as common amongst homosexuals as heterosexuals.

## Syphilis

This is caused by a certain kind of bacterium (Figure 1). The first sign of the disease usually appears about two to four weeks after intercourse, and consists of a sore on, or near, the genital organs: usually just inside the vagina in the female, and on the end of the penis (the glans) in the male. The sore doesn't hurt and it usually lasts for only a week or two at the most, so the person may not notice it. The germs then move to other parts of the body, causing a mild fever and spots on the skin (Figure 3). After a few weeks these symptoms dissapear and the person seems to recover. However, the germs are still in the bloodstream and eventually they may attack the brain, making the person go blind and insane. The final stage of the disease may not occur until many years after the original infection.

If a pregnant woman has syphilis, the germs are likely to pass across the placenta into the baby's bloodstream. As a result the baby may be born dead ('stillborn'), or it may be born with the disease and become crippled with it later. Nowadays all pregnant women have their blood tested to make sure that it does not contain any syphilis germs.

## Gonorrhoea

This is also caused by a bacterium (Figure 2). The first sign of the disease usually appears a few days after intercourse, and consists of a burning sensation when urinating. This happens because the tube down which the urine passes, the urethra, becomes inflamed. There may also be a yellowish discharge from the reproductive opening: this is easily seen in the male, but the female may not notice it because it is mixed with her normal secretions. Sometimes the germs spread to other parts of the body, and the person may feel ill and get swollen and painful joints. Gonorrhoea can cause sterility, making it impossible to have children.

If a pregnant woman gets gonorrhoea, her baby may become infected as it passes through the vagina during birth. As a result it may develop very sore eyes which, if untreated, can lead quickly to blindness.

## Other sexually transmitted diseases

A number of other diseases can be passed from one person to another by intercourse or close sexual contact. However, they can be spread in other ways as well, so strictly speaking they aren't sexually transmitted diseases.

### Urethritis
In this disease the urethra gets inflamed, much as it does in gonorrhoea, causing pain and irritation when urinating. The kind of urethritis associated with sex is caused by a virus, and in rare cases it may lead to another condition called Reiter's disease which is characterised by aching joints (arthritis), painful feet and sore eyes (conjunctivitis).

### Genital herpes
This is caused by a virus similar to the kind that causes chicken pox and cold

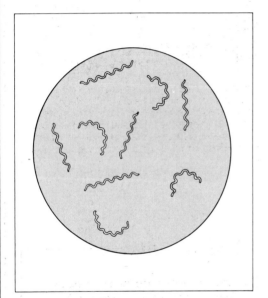

**Figure 1** This is the germ that causes syphilis. It is a spiral-shaped bacterium called a spirochaete. It is magnified here about 3000 times.

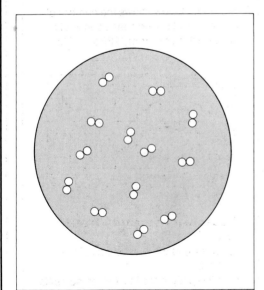

**Figure 2** This is the germ that causes gonorrhoea. It is a ball-shaped bacterium called a coccus, and normally occurs in pairs. It is magnified here about 7000 times.

sores. The symptoms include blisters on the genital organs, usually inside the vagina in the female and on the head of the penis (the glans) in the male. In some cases the person may get an attack of skin irritation and muscle pains. Once the virus is in your body it remains there for life and further attacks of the disease may occur from time to time. A pregnant woman with herpes may pass it on to her baby.

### Viral hepatitis

In this disease the liver gets infected by a virus. The patient has repeated bouts of sickness, fever and abdominal pains, sometimes accompanied by jaundice, which may go on for many months. It can take several years to recover completely from this unpleasant disease.

### Thrush

This is caused by a fungus which may make the mouth cavity and genital organs sore and inflamed. In the female there is a white or yellowish discharge from the vagina.

### Trichomoniasis

This is caused by a protist. The symptoms may be hardly noticeable, but sometimes it causes discomfort when urinating and in the female there may be a discharge from the vagina.

### Acquired immune deficiency disease (AIDS)

This disease was discovered around 1980 amongst homosexuals. Since then it has spread to heterosexuals. The person's natural immunity to disease breaks down with the result that he succumbs much more readily to diseases like pneumonia and a certain kind of skin cancer. It is caused by a particular virus and has an incubation period of about two years. A lot of research is going on into this new disease.

### How to avoid sexually transmitted diseases

The only *sure* way of avoiding sexually transmitted diseases is to make certain that one's sexual partner is not infected. Obviously this is not easy, but having casual sexual relations with many different people is asking for trouble.

The wearing of a contraceptive sheath by the male helps to prevent the spread of most sexually transmitted diseases, but it doesn't give complete protection. Sexually transmitted diseases are much more common now than they were thirty years ago, and the reason may be that the sheath has been replaced by 'the pill' as the main means of contraception.

### Curing sexually transmitted diseases

Syphilis and gonorrhoea can be cured with antibiotics such as penicillin *provided that a full course of treatment is carried out at an early enough stage.* The trouble is that often people don't realise they have got the disease, and so they do nothing about it until it's too late. Thrush and trichomoniasis can also be cured with drugs.

Virus diseases such as urethritis and hepatitis are more difficult to cure, because they don't respond to antibiotics. This means that the patient must wait for them to clear up of their own accord though anti-viral drugs may help. AIDS is particularly difficult to treat.

Most large hospitals have a special clinic where people can be examined to find out if they have got any sexually transmitted diseases. The examination takes only a short time, and includes a urine and blood test. When the results are known treatment can, if necessary, be given. If possible, the person's sexual contacts should be traced and treated also.

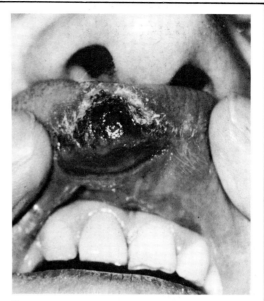

**Figure 3** A painless sore on the genital organs characterises the first stage of syphilis. Very occasionally the sore may appear in other places such as on the lips, as in the case shown here. The sore is like an ulcer but it does not hurt. Fortunately this person went to the clinic soon enough and was cured.

## Assignments

1 Why is syphilis described as a 'hidden disease', and why is it so serious?

2 Why is gonorrhoea easier to cure than herpes?

3 The graph below shows the number of new cases of gonorrhoea seen in VD clinics each year from 1936 to 1970:

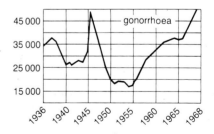

Suggest reasons why the number of cases
a) rose rapidly in the first half of the 1940s,
b) fell rapidly in the last half of the 1940s,
c) rose steadily from the mid-1950s onwards.

# Harmful protists

*Many protists live inside other animals. Some of them live in the human bloodstream. Others live in the gut or amongst the cells. They are parasites, and can do a lot of harm.*

## The malarial parasite

Every year about 200 million people get malaria, and about two million die of it. It is carried from person to person by a certain type of mosquito called *Anopheles*. This mosquito is found mainly in hot countries. Malaria only occurs in places where the mosquito is found.

### What happens when you get malaria?

John is camping in West Africa. During the night he is bitten by an *Anopheles* mosquito (Figure 1). During the next two weeks John feels poorly, but he doesn't realise he has malaria.

One night he wakes up with a terrible fever (Figure 2). His temperature soars up. He sweats, shivers and becomes delirious. Then suddenly the fever dies down and he feels better. Exhausted, he falls asleep.

Several days later he has another attack of fever. He goes on having attacks every few days.

What has been happening in John's body? To understand this we must study the life cycle of the parasite (Figure 3).

### Life cycle of the malarial parasite

When the mosquito bit John, it injected a drop of saliva into his bloodstream (see page 108). The saliva contained tiny worm-like parasites.

Once in the bloodstream, the parasites made for John's liver. They stayed in the liver for the next two weeks, feeding and multiplying. This was when John felt poorly.

After two weeks, the parasites left the liver and got into John's bloodstream. They then invaded his red blood cells. Each little worm-like parasite bored its way into a red blood cell. Once inside it changed its shape. It became like a little amoeba, and it fed like an amoeba on the contents of the cell. Gradually it grew, until it just about filled the cell. Then it split into lots of tiny offspring. Finally the red blood cell burst, releasing the new batch of parasites (Investigation 1).

This grisly procedure was undergone not just by one parasite, but by thousands of them all at the same time. John's temperature gradually went up while the parasites were inside his red blood cells. His fever reached its height when his blood cells burst and the parasites were released.

After being set free, the new parasites invaded more red blood cells, and the cycle was repeated. This is why the attacks of fever kept coming back.

### What happens inside the mosquito?

When a mosquito bites you, it sucks up your blood. If malarial parasites are present in your bloodstream, the mosquito takes these up too.

Inside the mosquito's stomach the parasites multiply. They then make their way to the salivary glands. Here they wait until the mosquito bites another person. They are then injected into that person's bloodstream with the mosquito's saliva.

So the mosquito carries the malarial parasite from one person to another. We call it a **vector**. The word vector means 'carrier'. It is applied to any animal which transmits parasites or germs from one individual to another. Vectors play an important part in spreading disease.

### How does the malarial parasite reproduce?

The malarial parasite reproduces at three stages in its life cycle: in the liver, in the red blood cells, and in the stomach of the mosquito.

The main method is **asexual**. The parasite grows and then splits into lots of offspring. The nucleus divides first, then the rest of the cell. This process is called **multiple fission**.

**Figure 1** A mosquito sucking blood from a person's arm. This type of mosquito carries malaria.

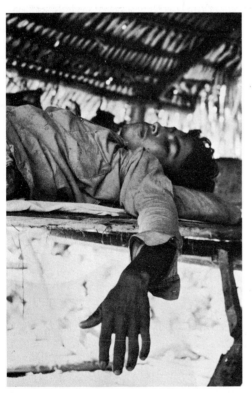

**Figure 2** Malaria is characterised by recurring bouts of fever.

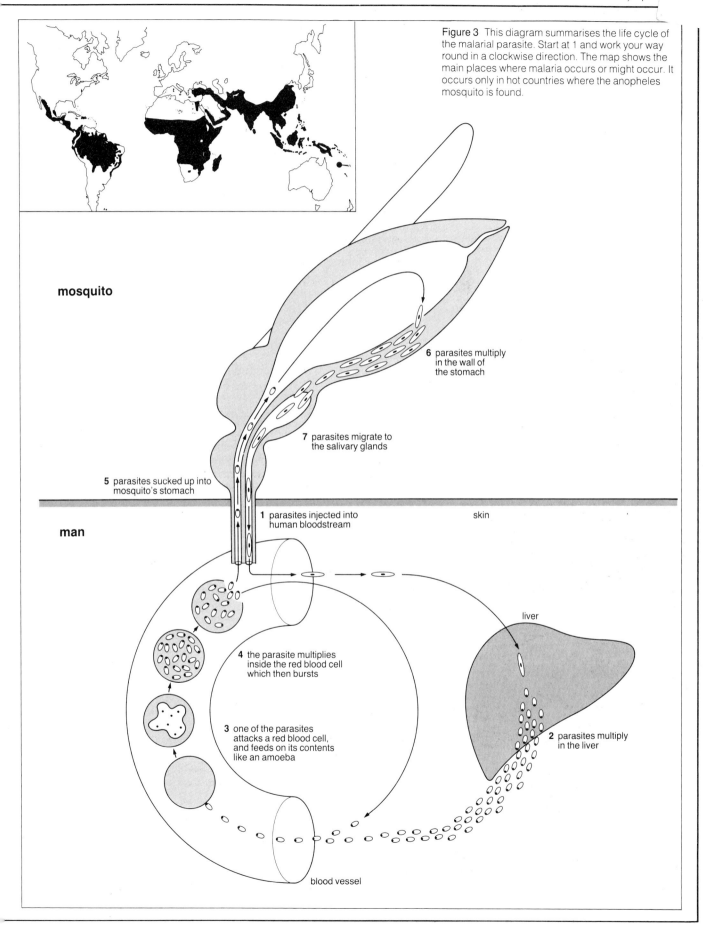

**Figure 3** This diagram summarises the life cycle of the malarial parasite. Start at 1 and work your way round in a clockwise direction. The map shows the main places where malaria occurs or might occur. It occurs only in hot countries where the anopheles mosquito is found.

**mosquito**

**6** parasites multiply in the wall of the stomach

**7** parasites migrate to the salivary glands

**5** parasites sucked up into mosquito's stomach

**1** parasites injected into human bloodstream

skin

**man**

liver

**4** the parasite multiplies inside the red blood cell which then bursts

**3** one of the parasites attacks a red blood cell, and feeds on its contents like an amoeba

**2** parasites multiply in the liver

blood vessel

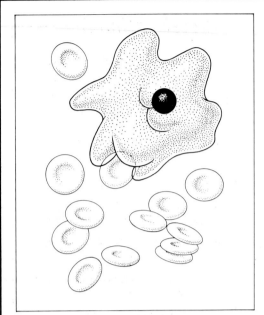

**Figure 4** The dysentery amoeba is here seen feeding on a red blood cell in the lining of the large intestine. It is called *Entamoeba histolytica*.

Vast numbers of offspring are produced quickly by this method. In the liver, for example, as many as a thousand offspring may be formed every time one of the parasites undergoes multiple fission.

The malarial parasite also reproduces **sexually**. Male and female reproductive forms are produced, and these unite with each other. This takes place in the stomach of the mosquito.

### How can malaria be controlled?

John was eventually cured of malaria by being treated with certain **drugs**. These killed the parasites in his body.

Such drugs can save lives, but obviously it is better not to get the disease in the first place. If you are going into an infected area, you can protect yourself by taking **anti-malarial tablets** beforehand. Some of the drugs can be taken daily or weekly in a 'preventive dose'. If you get malaria anyway, a larger 'cure dose' can be taken. The drugs used against malaria are quinine or drugs based on quinine, for example Chloroquine, Carmaquine, and Nivaquine. Unfortunately the malaria parasite has become resistant to some drugs, so new ones have to be introduced. In malarial areas people should sleep under a mosquito net or have netting placed over the windows.

The best way of conquering malaria would be to get rid of the parasite altogether. How could this be done? We know that malaria is spread by mosquitoes, so if we could get rid of mosquitoes we would get rid of malaria. Of course this is easier said than done. It is discussed on page 351.

## Other harmful protists

### The dysentery amoeba

This is like the ordinary amoeba, but instead of living in ponds and streams it lives in the human large intestine (Figure 4). It feeds on the lining, and causes bleeding and diarrhoea. If severe it also causes vomiting and fever and can cause death. The disease is called **amoebic dysentery**. It is a cause of 'runny belly', and is especially dangerous in young babies.

Occasionally the parasites pass out with the person's faeces. If they get into food or drinking water, other people can become infected. The dysentery amoeba is spread if people eat infected food. In many places it has been brought under control by improvements in community health and personal cleanliness. Sulphur drugs and ematine are used to treat it.

### The sleeping sickness parasite

Sleeping sickness afflicts many people in tropical Africa. It is caused by a little worm-like parasite called a trypanosome. This lives in the bloodstream of human beings, cattle, and wild animals (Investigation 2). The parasite moves around by flapping a membrane which sticks out from the side of the body (Figure 5). Unlike the malarial parasite, the sleeping sickness parasites do not attack the blood cells. Instead they wriggle around in the fluid part of the blood (the plasma), soaking up its food substances. They release poisonous substances which get to the brain and cause the person to become unconscious, hence the name of the disease. Human sleeping sickness can be fatal. It is treated with drugs such as Pentamidine.

The sleeping sickness parasite is passed from one individual to another by the blood-sucking tsetse fly (pronounced 'tetsy fly'). A lot of progress has been made in controlling this disease by getting rid of tsetse flies. The trouble is that the parasites live in wild animals such as buffalo without causing them any ill effects. These animals serve as a kind of 'reservoir' from which the parasites are carried to humans by the tsetse fly.

In addition, trypanosomes can cause animal sleeping sickness or nagana. Infected cattle die in large numbers. Certain areas called 'fly belts' cannot be used at all for rearing cattle.

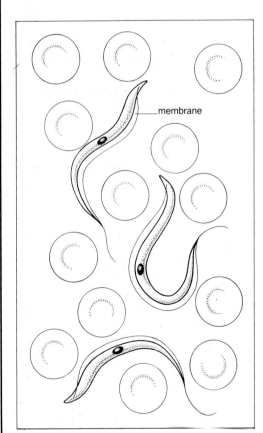

membrane

**Figure 5** The sleeping sickness parasite *Trypanosoma* has a worm-like shape with a membrane down one side. It moves by flapping the membrane.

## Investigation 1

**Looking at the malarial parasite**

1 Obtain a prepared slide of blood taken from an individual suffering from malaria.

2 Examine the slide under the high power of the microscope.

3 Observe normal red blood cells first, so you know what they look like (see page 126).

4 Now look for red blood cells which appear to have something unusual inside them.

Can you see anything which might correspond to stages 3 and 4 in the life cycle in Figure 2?

## Investigation 2

**Looking at the sleeping sickness parasite**

1 Obtain a prepared slide of blood taken from an individual suffering from sleeping sickness.

2 Examine the slide under the microscope: low power first, then high power.

3 Find some sleeping sickness parasites (trypanosomes) amongst the red blood cells.

4 Make a simple outline drawing of a parasite and a red blood cell side by side to show how they compare in size.

What do the parasites feed on?

Why does this parasite cause such a serious disease?

## Investigation 3

**Looking at live parasitic protists**

Your teacher will give you a watch glass containing the contents of the rectum of a toad or frog, mixed with dilute salt solution.

1 With a pipette, place a drop of the material on a microscope slide.

2 Cover it with a coverslip.

3 Examine it under the microscope: low power first, then high power.

4 Look out for small protists covered with beating cilia.

What can you say about their shape and the way they move?

What adaptations would these protists need to have for their mode of life?

## Assignments

1 The following words are used in this Topic. What does each one mean?

parasite
fever
delirious
life cycle
fission

2 Why does malaria occur mainly in tropical countries?

Occasional cases of malaria occur in colder countries; how would you explain this?

3 Why do you think the body temperature of a person suffering from malaria goes up during the disease?

4 What do the malarial parasite, the sleeping sickness parasite, and the dysentery amoeba feed on? Be as exact as you can.

5 What precautions could John have taken to prevent himself getting malaria?

6 The malarial parasite has been likened to 'Dr Jekyll and Mr Hyde', the characters in the famous horror story by Robert Louis Stevenson.

In what respect does the malarial parasite resemble them?

7 The graph below shows the body temperature of a person suffering from a certain kind of malaria.

Explain what the malarial parasite is doing in the person's body at point A on the graph.

Why does the temperature keep going up and down?

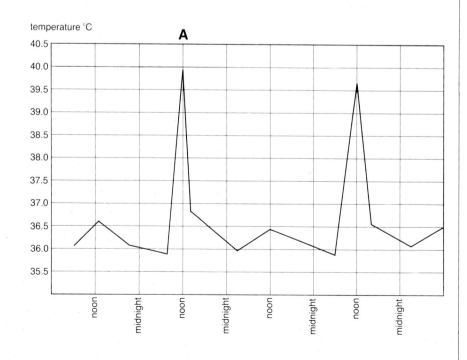

# Parasitic worms

*Many people are
infected with 'worms.'
These worms are parasites which
make their home inside human beings
and other organisms. Some of
them make people very ill.*

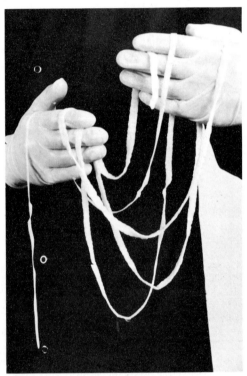

**Figure 1** A beef tapeworm from the intestine of a human being.

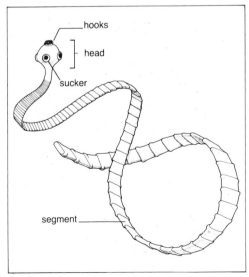

**Figure 2** The pork tapeworm. The beef tapeworm is similar except that its head has no hooks.

## The tapeworm

The animal in Figure 1 is the beef tapeworm. It is a type of flatworm (see page 16). You can get it by eating infected beef, hence its name. It has a close relative which can be got by eating infected pork: the pork tapeworm.

These two worms both belong to the genus *Taenia*. They live in man's small intestine where they soak up his digested food. Although they look alarming, they don't actually do much harm.

The structure of the tapeworm is shown in Figure 2. It is flat, like a long piece of ribbon, and can reach a length of 5 metres. It hangs onto the wall of the intestine by its head. To give it a firm grip, the head has four **suckers**, and, in the pork tapeworm, **hooks** as well (Investigation 1).

The body is divided up into a series of segments, about a thousand in all. The youngest segments are at the head end, the oldest ones at the back.

The worm constantly produces new segments just behind the head. As new ones are produced, the older ones get pushed further and further back, and grow larger. The largest ones are about 2 cm long and 1.5 cm wide.

### Life cycle of the tapeworm

The life cycle of the beef tapeworm is summarised in Figure 3. Each mature segment contains a full set of sex organs. Two segments can mate with each other by the worm doubling back on itself. By the time the segments reach the rear end of the worm, they are full of eggs.

The segments at the extreme back end drop off and pass out with the host's faeces, taking their eggs with them.

A person with a single worm may pass eight or nine segments a day, releasing a total of three quarters of a million eggs.

To continue their development the eggs must be eaten by a cow. The cow is called the **intermediate host**. In the case of the pork tapeworm the intermediate host is a pig.

The tapeworm's eggs get into the intermediate host if it eats food which is contaminated by human faeces. In the animal's gut the egg shell dissolves and a tiny **embryo** emerges. This bores through the gut wall and gets into the muscles. Here it forms a **bladder**, about the size of a pea.

No further development takes place unless the bladders are eaten by man. This can happen if a person eats infected meat which hasn't been cooked properly. In the person's intestine, the bladder turns inside out and a young tapeworm pops out. This buries its head in the wall of the intestine, and grows to full size.

### How is the tapeworm adapted to its parasitic life?

The tapeworm is well adapted to its parasitic life. Its hooks and suckers allow it to hold on tightly to the wall of the intestine. Its flat body gives it a large surface area for absorbing its host's digested food. Of course it does not need a mouth or gut of its own. It is not itself digested by the host's digestive juices because it produces a substance which stops this happening.

Spreading from one host to another is difficult for a parasite. The tapeworm gets round this by producing vast numbers of eggs and by having an intermediate host to 'carry' it from one human to another.

### How can we get rid of tapeworms?

To avoid getting these tapeworms people should make sure that they don't eat infected meat. In many countries meat is inspected to make sure it does not contain tapeworm bladders. In such countries tapeworms are rare. Proper disposal of sewage is also important in preventing these worms from spreading. To some extent infection can be avoided by cooking meat thoroughly: prolonged heating destroys the tapeworm bladders.

If a person does get a tapeworm he can be given doses of medicine which

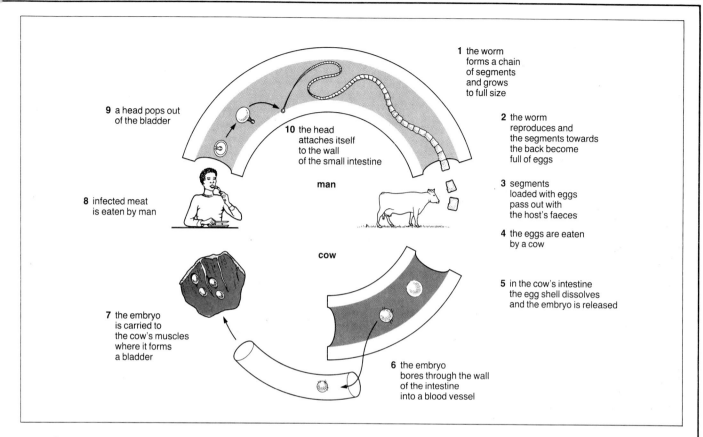

**1** the worm forms a chain of segments and grows to full size

**2** the worm reproduces and the segments towards the back become full of eggs

**3** segments loaded with eggs pass out with the host's faeces

**4** the eggs are eaten by a cow

**5** in the cow's intestine the egg shell dissolves and the embryo is released

**6** the embryo bores through the wall of the intestine into a blood vessel

**7** the embryo is carried to the cow's muscles where it forms a bladder

**8** infected meat is eaten by man

**9** a head pops out of the bladder

**10** the head attaches itself to the wall of the small intestine

**man**

**cow**

cause the worm to let go of the wall of the intestine. The worm is then flushed out with the faeces. It is essential that the head doesn't get left behind. If it does, a new worm will grow from it.

**Figure 3** This diagram summarises the life cycle of the beef tapeworm. The life cycle of the pork tapeworm is similar, except that the intermediate host is a pig.

## The blood fluke

This is another kind of flatworm, and it causes 'snail fever' (the proper name is **bilharzia** or **schistosomiasis**). People with this disease suffer from sickness, diarrhoea and loss of blood. It makes the people feel ill and unable to work properly. Sometimes the body swells up with fluid. The people become weak, and if they are not treated they usually die.

There are several kinds of blood fluke. In the Caribbean the commonest one is *Schistoma mansoni* and this is spread by a water snail *Planorbis*, which has a flattened, coiled shell. The worms occur in St Lucia, Martinique, Guadeloupe and Puerto Rico. The intermediate host, the snail, is found in several other islands. It is therefore very important that the worms do not spread to these islands.

In the Far East the commonest blood fluke is *Schistosoma japonicum*; this is spread by a water snail *Oncomelania*, which has a tall, pointed shell.

Most blood flukes live in the blood vessels in the wall of the intestine. The worms are one or two centimetres long. There may be so many of them that they block the blood vessels.

They have a flat body, rather like a curled-up leaf. There is a **sucker** near the front for holding onto the sides of the blood vessels. They feed by sucking blood through the mouth.

### Life cycle of the blood fluke

The blood fluke's life cycle is summarised in Figure 4. The worms mate in the host's blood vessels. A single female may lay over 3000 eggs a day. Eventually the blood vessels burst, and the eggs are released into the intestine. They then pass out of the host with the faeces.

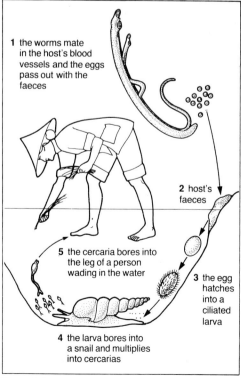

**1** the worms mate in the host's blood vessels and the eggs pass out with the faeces

**2** host's faeces

**3** the egg hatches into a ciliated larva

**4** the larva bores into a snail and multiplies into cercarias

**5** the cercaria bores into the leg of a person wading in the water

**Figure 4** This diagram summarises the life cycle of the blood fluke.

Figure 5   A bare-footed worker planting rice seedlings. When human dung is used as manure, this is a sure way to get bilharzia.

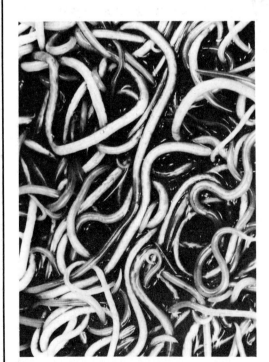

Figure 6   *Ascaris*. A roundworm that lives in the small intestine of man. This collection was removed from one child (×0.2).

The eggs will only hatch in water. The egg opens, and a tiny **larva** comes out. The larva is covered with beating cilia which enable it to swim through the water in search of a particular kind of water snail, the intermediate host. If it finds one, it bores into its soft body. Inside the snail the larva reproduces asexually to form thousands of little organisms called **cercarias** – these move by means of a muscular tail which bends from side to side.

The cercarias creep out of the snail into the water. If someone is bathing or paddling in the water, the cercarias attach themselves to the skin and bore through it into the bloodstream. They are then taken to the blood vessels of the intestine. Here they feed and grow into adult flukes. The cycle is then repeated.

### How can we get rid of the blood fluke?

Drugs can be used to cure people of bilharzia. However, they are not very successful, and some of them have unpleasant side effects.

A better approach is to get rid of the parasite altogether. This can be done by killing the snails. People have tried putting chemicals in the water to kill the snails, but this has not been very successful; and it also kills the fish.

The best solution is to stop people drinking, or paddling in, water which contains human faeces. In places where sewage is got rid of properly, there is no problem. But in some parts of the world, particularly the Far East, human dung is used as manure in the rice fields. The fields are flooded, and the rice seedlings are planted by farm workers who wade through the water in bare feet. In such places the chances of infection are very high (Figure 5).

## Roundworms

There are many different roundworms (page 16) parasitic in man and in plants.

*Threadworms* are common in children. They look like little bits of white thread, a few centimetres long. They live in the rectum, and can cause itching of the anus.

The worms mate in the host's rectum, and the eggs pass out with the faeces. It is very easy for other people to get infected. This is the sort of thing that happens: the child's bottom itches, he scratches it, and gets some eggs on his fingers; later his mother holds his hands, then puts her finger in her mouth; she swallows some eggs and they hatch in her gut. It's quite common for an entire family to become infected.

*Ascaris* is a large worm that lives in the small intestine of man. It is pinkish white and can grow to 30 centimetres. One person can be infected with many worms (Figure 6). Up to 200 000 eggs are produced *daily* by a female worm and pass out in the faeces. They can survive for about 5 years in moist soil.

Another person may become infected by eating unwashed food with the eggs on it. *Ascaris* causes loss of appetite, slowness and general weakness.

*Hookworms* are similar to *Ascaris* and although they are much smaller, only 1 centimetre long, they are more dangerous. They attach themselves to the lining of the intestine and suck blood. Eggs are passed out with the faeces and hatch in moist soil. People walking on the soil may become infected, because the larvae bore into the feet. In the Caribbean this is called 'ground itch'. The spread of hookworms can be reduced by proper disposal of faeces and by wearing shoes.

The roundworms that live in the alimentary canal can be treated by drugs taken as tablets or in a flavoured drink. These drugs kill the worms, and they are then passed out of the alimentary canal with the faeces. But there are other worms which are more difficult to treat.

Filarial worms cause several diseases in the tropics. One kind causes **elephantiasis**. The worms live in the lymph vessels of man, which they block. The lymph cannot escape and so the affected parts, often the legs, become very large (Figure 7). Tiny larvae are released into the blood where they are sucked up by the intermediate host, which is a mosquito or blood-sucking fly. They can then be injected into new hosts.

Another kind of filarial worm causes **river blindness** or onchocerciasis. These worms also live in the lymph vessels, in this case in the eye, where they cause blindness. The intermediate host is a blood-sucking fly which breeds in rivers and marshy areas near lakes or reservoirs. The number of cases of river blindness increased markedly when the Volta River Dam was developed in Ghana, West Africa.

## Plant parasites.

Some nematode worms are parasites of plants. They attack the roots especially of vegetable crops such as tomatoes and potatoes. They cause the development of swellings or galls on the roots and stop them from working properly. Such plants may appear to suffer from deficiency of minerals (page 142) and become stunted. Some nematodes attack the shoots of vegetables, causing the production of distorted buds or flowers.

Crop rotation helps to reduce the incidence of the disease. A nematode killer such as 'Nemagon' can be used if infection is severe.

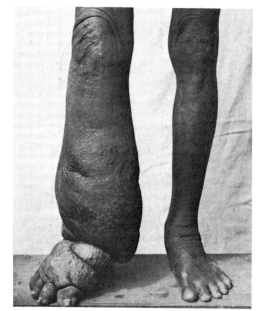

Figure 7 Elephantiasis. The filarial worms block the lymph vessels, causing the leg to swell.

# Investigation 1

### The front and back of a tapeworm

1 Look at a prepared slide of the head of a tapeworm under the microscope.

   What structures help it to cling to the wall of the host's intestine?

2 Now look at a prepared slide of a mature segment from the back end of the tapeworm.

   It is full of small round objects: what are they?

3 Make a sketch of the head and a mature segment. Label them.

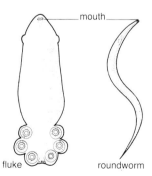

mouth

fluke          roundworm

# Investigation 2

### Looking at live flukes and roundworms

Your teacher will dissect a frog and take out the lungs.

1 Put the lungs in a watch glass with some 1 per cent salt solution.

2 With needles pull the lungs to pieces.

3 With luck, two kinds of worms may be released from the lungs: a fluke and a roundworm. They are illustrated on the left. Both can be as much as a centimetre long, so they should be visible.

4 With a pipette transfer a few of these parasites from the watch glass to a slide.

5 Add a little salt solution and cover them with a coverslip.

6 Examine them under the microscope.

In what ways do these two worms appear to be adapted to a parasitic life?

What might they feed on?

Do you think they harm the frog?

# Assignments

1 Imagine you are a tapeworm living in the intestine of a human being.

   What difficulties might you encounter living in such a place?

2 Tapeworms have no gut and no sense organs.

   How do you think they manage without them?

3 What advice would you give to people to prevent them becoming infected with (a) the beef tapeworm, and (b) bilharzia?

4 Parasites usually produce very large numbers of eggs. Why is this necessary?

5 Make a list of the ways that either the tapeworm or the blood fluke are adapted to a parasitic life.

6 In Africa, bilharzia is common in lowland areas, but absent from mountainous regions.

   Suggest two reasons why bilharzia does not occur in mountainous regions.

7 'Nearness to streams eats the eyes' – Upper Volta proverb. What does this mean?

# Parasitic fungi

*A number of fungi
are parasites and cause
diseases in plants and animals.
Here we shall study just
a few of them.*

**Figure 1** The leaves of an Irish potato plant infected with potato blight disease.

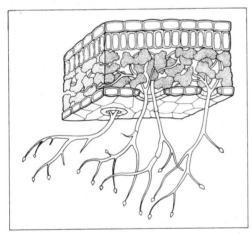

**Figure 2** Hyphae have grown out of the underside of this leaf. They are forming spores which may be blown onto other potato plants.

**Figure 3** Cocoa pods infected by *Phytophthora palmivora*. The pods gradually turn black as they are rotted away by the fungus.

## Introduction

Fungi are either parasites or saprotrophs. We looked at saprotrophs when we studied pin mould (page 52) and yeast (page 122).

Most of the parasitic fungi are parasites of plants. Different species of fungi attack different species of plant. Crops and trees of economic importance are particularly likely to be attacked. This is because it is easy for a fungal disease to spread where plants of the same species are growing close together. This causes loss to the farmer.

Let us now look at a fungal disease in detail.

## Potato blight

Potato blight occurs wherever Irish potatoes are grown. It is particularly remembered because of an outbreak in Ireland in 1845 which destroyed the potato crop. Thousands of people starved and more than a million emigrated to America. The disease is caused by the fungus *Phytophthora infestans*.

### The disease

Look at Figure 1. This shows the leaves of a plant with potato blight. They are covered with brown patches. If you looked at the tubers you would find that they were soft and rotten. The fungus lives inside the potato plant and destroys its cells.

### The fungus

If you examined a small piece of an infected potato plant under the microscope, you would see lots of fine threads amongst the cells. These are called **hyphae** and they are similar to the threads of pin mould (see page 52). How did they come to be inside the potato plant?

The potato blight fungus is spread by tiny air-borne **spores**. If a spore lands on a leaf it bursts open and sends out a hypha. The hypha gets into the leaf either by growing through a stoma or by boring through the epidermis. Once inside, the hypha sends out branches which penetrate the leaf cells and feed on the contents. The tips of the hyphae produce enzymes which break down the cytoplasm into soluble substances. These are then absorbed by the fungus. Not content with feeding on the leaves alone, the hyphae grow down the stem to the tubers where they continue to invade the cells.

### How does the fungus reproduce?

One of the reasons why potato blight is so serious is that it spreads extremely quickly. This is because of the way the fungus reproduces. In damp weather some of the hyphae in the leaf grow out through the stomata and form branches. At the tips of the branches spores are formed (Figure 2). When ripe they break off and are blown by the wind to other potato plants. If a spore lands on a leaf, the plant may become infected. If it lands on the soil it may infect a tuber.

### How is potato blight controlled?

Potato blight is far less common now than it used to be. This is because we now understand the life cycle of the fungus and have learned how to control it.

To prevent infection, potato crops are sprayed with a **fungicide**, that is, a chemical substance which kills fungi. Copper sulphate is particularly effective; it kills the spores.

Other ways of controlling the disease are to avoid growing potatoes in warm, humid areas, and not to plant them down the prevailing wind. If there is a serious outbreak, all infected crops should be burned. The fungus can become dormant in the tubers during the dry season and it is important not to plant infected tubers the next year.

By cross-breeding potatoes, scientists have developed special varieties of potato plants which are resistant to the fungus.

## Black pod of cocoa

This is caused by a related species, *Phytophthora palmivora*. The spores germinate on the young cocoa pods. As the hyphae grow they push their way inside the tissues. They affect both the tissues of the pod and the developing seeds (cocoa beans). The pod turns dark brown and then black as the tissues are rotted by the fungus (Figure 3). Some of the hyphae on the surface produce spores which can infect other plants. The disease causes widespread destruction of cocoa pods. The disease is controlled by the removal of all affected pods, by weeding, and by regular spraying with copper fungicides.

## Other fungal diseases

*Rusts* belong to the genus *Puccinia*. They attack maize, rice and other cereals. The fungus causes red or brown spots and rusty stripes on the leaves. This reduces photosynthesis, and the leaves may die. The spores are shot out and may travel some distance to infect other plants. After harvesting, the spores can rest in the soil and infect the next year's crop. The use of resistant varieties and early planting help to stop attacks by this fungus.

*Smuts* belong to several genera in the order *Ustilaginales*. They also attack maize, rice and other cereals. The fungus grows on the leaves, stems, cobs or other fruiting bodies. Maize smut fungus causes maize grains to swell to many times their normal size (Figure 4). The fungus destroys the plant and produces black spore sacs which open to spread the infection. Affected plants must be burned.

*Black root rot* attacks tobacco roots. It also causes the roots of groundnut and black-eyed pea to rot. The soil should be sterilised to kill the spores.

*Damping-off disease* mostly affects seedlings, which up to then appear to have been growing well. The stems dry up at ground level and die, causing the seedlings to fall over. The disease is made worse by over-watering and sowing the seeds too close together; so both of these things should be avoided.

## Summary of how fungal diseases are controlled

First we need to know the general characteristics of fungal diseases. Then we can devise control measures, such as the following:
1 Try to use varieties of plant which are resistant to disease.
2 If sowing seeds, first cover them with chemicals which will kill the fungus.
3 Don't sow the plants too close together so disease can spread.
4 Spray with copper sulphate solution or modern fungicides.
5 Destroy affected plants by heating to kill the spores.
6 Rotate crops on the same field because any spores in the soil will not be able to attack the different crop.

## Fungal diseases of animals

These are not very common, and not as important as the crop diseases.

### Ringworm

This is the name of a human disease. It is caused by a fungus that lives just under the surface of the skin. Often the infected areas are circular, hence the name ringworm. One kind attacks the skin of the head, causing the hair to fall out in clumps so bald patches develop. Another kind lives between the toes where it causes itching: this is known as **athlete's foot**.

As with other fungi, ringworm forms spores. These quickly spread from person to person. Athlete's foot can be picked up by walking in bare feet on a changing-room floor which has been contaminated by the feet of an infected person. Ringworm can be cured by antibiotics, and fungicides on the skin.

**Figure 4** Maize cob infected by smut, a fungus which causes the grains to swell to a large size.

## Investigation

### Looking at a fungal disease

1 Obtain a plant whose leaves have coloured spots or are covered with white threads. Maize, rice or other cereals are often infected.

2 Look at the leaves under a hand lens or binocular microscope.
What can you say about the structure of the fungus?
What part of the fungus are you looking at?

3 With needles tease some of the fungus away from the leaf. Mount it in a drop of water on a slide and put on a coverslip.

4 Examine the fungus under high power. What can you see of its structure?

5 Obtain a prepared section of a leaf that is infected with a fungus. Examine it under high power and look for hyphae. Can you see any hyphae inside the leaf cells?

How does the fungus get its food?
How does it reproduce?

## Assignments

1 In what ways is a named parasitic fungus adapted to its mode of life?

2 In what ways, *without using chemicals*, could you reduce the spread of fungal diseases?

3 The Irish potato famine of 1845 was followed by another one in the following year.
What reasons can you give for this?

# Insects, harmful and helpful

*The locust is one of the world's most serious pests. It is just one of many insects which are harmful to man. Many other insects are helpful.*

Figure 1 A swarm of locusts in North Africa. A swarm like this may contain ten thousand million locusts.

## The locust

Locusts thrive in warm parts of the world such as Africa, the Middle East and South America. There are several types of locust but they all lead the same kind of life. Much of the time they live singly or in small groups, feeding on grass and leaves. But sometimes their numbers build up, and then they do a great deal of damage to man's crops. Locusts have enormous appetites and a few of them can strip a plant very quickly (Figure 2).

The female locust lays her eggs in the sand. The eggs hatch into nymphs, which are called **hoppers**. They have no wings, and cannot fly. As their numbers build up, they crowd together. Food begins to run out, and this causes them to start 'marching' in bands.

They march during the day, eating the leaves of plants as they go. They move about a kilometre a day. At night they rest in shrubs and small trees. Every week or so they moult and grow. After about six weeks they undergo their final moult, their wings expand, and they become adults.

They now start to fly. They move across the country in a vast **swarm**, like the one in Figure 1. A single swarm may contain ten thousand million locusts. With the aid of the wind, the locusts fly about 80 km a day. They may travel several thousand kilometres before settling down to breed.

The swarming locusts will strip a vast area of all its vegetation. A large swarm may eat 160 000 tonnes of food each day. This amount of corn would feed 800 000 people for a whole year.

At one time, locust swarms occurred regularly in many parts of the world. They caused widespread famine and did millions of pounds-worth of damage. Fortunately man is now learning how to control them.

### How are locusts controlled?

In the old days farmers tried to drive locusts away by lighting fires or beating drums. The hoppers were driven into trenches, then buried or burned, or they were killed by putting poisoned bait in their path. Where possible, the eggs were dug up and burned.

Nowadays crops are sprayed with powerful insecticides which kill the locusts. The insecticide is sprayed from vehicles or aeroplanes. Spray from an aeroplane on one flight can kill as many as 180 million locusts.

Constant watch is kept on locusts and in this way scientists can forecast when and where swarming is likely to occur, so the crops can be sprayed in good time. This requires co-operation between different countries, and much of this work is co-ordinated by the United Nations.

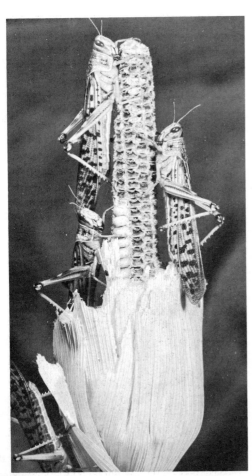

Figure 2 This corn cob is being eaten by locusts.

# The mosquito

There are many different kinds of mosquitoes. They carry serious diseases, such as malaria and yellow fever (Table 1). The female mosquito sucks blood, and carries the parasites which cause these diseases from one person to another.

| Mosquito | Organism that it spreads | Disease caused |
|---|---|---|
| *Anopheles* | *Plasmodium* (protist) | Malaria (page 340) |
| *Culex* | Filarial worm (nematode) | Elephantiasis (page 346) |
| *Aedes* | Dengue virus<br>Yellow fever virus | Dengue fever<br>Yellow fever |

Table 1  Diseases spread by different kinds of mosquitoes.

Mosquitoes need water for breeding: ponds, lakes, water-tanks, tin cans, old car tyres – any place where the water is still. The swamp shown in Figure 5 is ideal.

The female mosquito lays her eggs on the surface of water. The eggs hatch into small wriggling larvae. The larva lives in the water; it has a **breathing tube** at the back end, by which it hangs onto the surface film. The end of the breathing tube is open, so air can get in.

After several weeks the larva pupates. The pupa hangs onto the surface film by a pair of breathing tubes on the head. After a few days, the pupa splits open and the adult mosquito emerges. Stages in the life cycles are shown in Figures 3 and 4.

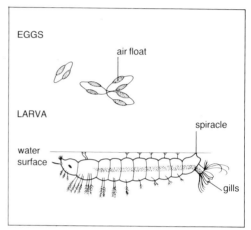

Figure 4  *Anopheles* eggs and larvae. The eggs are laid singly and each has air floats that keep it on the surface of the water. The larvae lie parallel to the surface of the water and breathe through a breathing tube. The pupae are similar to those of other mosquitoes.

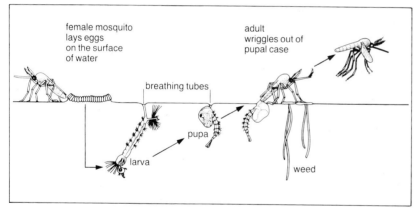

Figure 3  The life cycle of *Culex* and *Aedes* mosquitoes.

## How can we get rid of mosquitoes?

The adult mosquito can be killed by spraying with insecticides such as DDT. However, DDT is a hazard to health, so it is better to use other methods.

The larvae can be destroyed by spraying oil onto the water (Figure 5 and Investigation 1.) The oil lowers the surface tension of the water, causing the larvae to let go. Water then enters their breathing tubes and they drown. Pupae are destroyed in the same way. Usually the oil is mixed with insecticide so as to make absolutely sure they die.

Another way of getting rid of mosquitoes is to stock up lakes and ponds with fish, such as *Tilapia*, that eat the larvae or pupae. Or one can drain swamps, so as to get rid of the mosquito's breeding areas.

None of these methods on its own is much good, but together they are quite effective. However, the mosquito is still a major pest in many parts of the world, and the diseases which it carries have not yet been wiped out. In the tropics windows are usually covered with a fine-mesh screen to keep mosquitoes out, and campers should always use tents with mosquito nets.

Figure 5  This swamp is just the kind of place where mosquitoes breed. The men are spraying oil onto the surface of the water to kill the larvae and pupae.

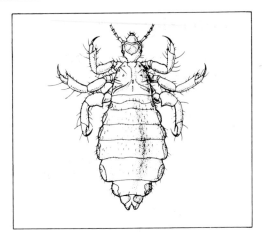

**Figure 6** The head louse has sharp claws for clinging onto the skin while it sucks blood. Outbreaks of this insect pest occur in schools.

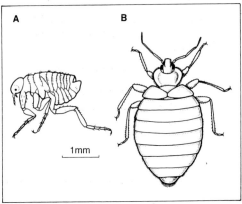

**Figure 7** **A** A flea **B** A bedbug. Both cling onto the human skin and suck blood.

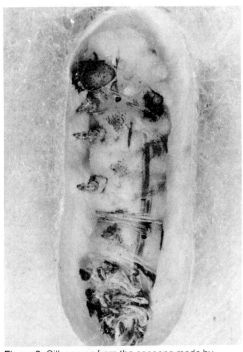

**Figure 8** Silk comes from the cocoons made by 'silkworms', which are the caterpillars of the silkworm moth, *Bombyx mori*. The photograph shows a caterpillar in its cocoon.

# Summary of how insects affect man

*Here are some ways that insects are harmful:*

**1  *They eat and destroy crops.***
Insects like the locust will eat just about anything with leaves on it. Other insects are more fussy; for example, caterpillars of the citrus swallowtail butterfly eat nothing but citrus leaves and closely related plants. They can be killed by spraying or dusting the leaves with an insecticide before the caterpillars start eating them. Grain weevils do damage to man's stored crops. They eat grains such as rice, maize and beans.

**2  *They spread diseases.***
Many insects, besides the mosquito, spread diseases from person to person. Blood-sucking flies, houseflies, fleas and lice are all guilty (see page 333). Some insects spread diseases amongst plants. One reason why greenflies (aphids) are such a nuisance to gardeners is that they carry harmful viruses from one plant to another.

**3  *They spoil food.***
The housefly and blue-bottle lay their eggs on food, particularly meat. Because of their dirty habits, these insects also bring germs onto our food, thereby spreading diseases such as cholera.

**4  *They destroy buildings and furniture.***
A major culprit here is the termite which eats wood. In the tropics termites can completely destroy a wooden building.

**5  *They ruin clothes.***
The larva of the clothes-moth eats the fibres of woollen garments, making holes in them. You can protect clothes from this insect by means of 'moth balls'. They contain a chemical substance which kills the larvae.

**6  *They are irritating.***
The head louse occurs in schools and other places where people live or work close together (Figure 6). It clings to the skin and sucks blood, and can cause intense itching. The eggs, known as nits, stick to the person's hair. Head lice can be got rid of by rubbing an insecticide preparation into the hair, and washing it later. Any remaining nits are then combed out. Fleas and bed bugs (Figure 7) are also pests of humans, and suck blood.

*Here are some ways that insects are helpful:*

**1  *They pollinate plants.***
Insects such as butterflies, bees, moths and flies carry pollen from one flower to another (page 290). The insects may visit hundreds of flowers in one day.

**2  *They kill harmful pests.***
You have probably heard that ladybirds are useful insects. This is because their larvae eat greenflies, thus helping to get rid of this garden pest. The praying mantis eats several insects which destroy crops.

**3  *Bees make honey.***
Honey bees are reared by man to make honey. Before sugar was discovered it was the only way of sweetening things.

**4  *Some insects produce silk.***
The caterpillar of the silkworm moth makes its cocoon from a single strand of silk (Figure 8). This may be over a kilometre long. At one time these insects were cultivated to obtain silk, but nowadays its place has largely been taken by synthetic fibres.

# Investigation 1

## Getting rid of mosquitoes

1 Half fill a tin can with water (preferably rain water or pondwater, but tap water will do).

2 Put in some rotting leaves or stalks.

3 Leave the tin outside in a place where it will not be knocked over, and examine it each day.

 Within one to two weeks you will probably find mosquito larvae and pupae in the water.
 Where do you think they came from? Describe what they are like.

4 Take the container to the laboratory. Notice that the larvae and pupae hang on the surface film. The slightest disturbance causes them to let go and wriggle down into the water.

5 Wait till the larvae and pupae have settled at the surface. Then very gently run some oil or paraffin onto the surface of the water.

What happens to the larvae and pupae?

Do you think this is a good way of getting rid of mosquitoes from the world?

Can you think of any disadvantages?

Why do you think oil and paraffin have this effect on the larvae and pupae?

Suggest two other ways the larvae and pupae of mosquitoes might be destroyed.

Find out about the methods used in your country for controlling mosquitoes.

6 Obtain a preserved adult mosquito, and put it on a piece of white paper.

7 Measure its length, and width with wings outstretched.

What advice would you give to the manufacturers of mosquito netting to make sure their product is effective?

# Investigation 2

## A look at some harmful insects

1 Examine the head of a female mosquito under the microscope.

 What does the mosquito feed on?

 Why is it harmful?

 What adaptations can you see which enable it to live in the way it does?

2 Examine a louse under the microscope.

 Where does the louse live?

 What adaptations can you see which enable it to live in such a place?

3 Examine the head of a caterpillar of a swallowtail butterfly under the microscope.

 What does this caterpillar feed on?

 What structures can you see which enable it to feed efficiently?

# Assignments

1 Why are the following insects regarded as pests:

 locust,        bed bug,
 mosquito,      housefly?
 head louse,

2 Which is best, to spray locusts with an insecticide from an aeroplane or from a vehicle on the ground?

3 a) Which diseases do mosquitoes spread?
 b) List five ways in which mosquitoes can be controlled. For each method describe any precautions which need to be taken into account.

4 Each word in the left-hand column is related to one of the words in the right-hand column.

 Write them down in correct pairs.

 locust        pollination
 termites      insecticide
 ladybirds     swarms
 bees          greenflies
 DDT           wood

5 Why do head lice occur particularly in schools?

6 An insect pest may be controlled either by spraying it with an insecticide or by bringing in another insect which eats it.

 Put forward arguments for and against each method.

7 Below is a map of Northern Africa. The crosses show the occurrence of swarms of the desert locust during a particular year.

a) From an up-to-date map of Africa, list the names of the countries in which swarming was observed.
b) Suggest reasons why swarming occurred in these particular parts of Africa and not elsewhere.
c) The information shown on the map was obtained some years ago, and swarms of locusts in these areas are less common now. Why do you think this is?

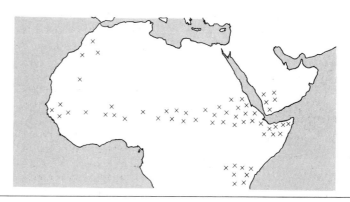

# Living things and their environment

*The grasshopper is
feeding on the plant.
In the next group of topics
we shall see that organisms are dependent
on their environment for many
things besides
food.*

# Finding out where organisms live

*The places where
a particular kind of organism
is found make up its distribution.
This Topic is about how we can
investigate distribution.*

| Description | Meaning |
|---|---|
| Dominant | has the greatest effect |
| Abundant | hardly ever out of sight |
| Frequent | constantly found |
| Occasional | seldom found |
| Rare | hardly ever found |

**Table 1** This scale is used for describing the occurrence of plants or animals in a habitat. It is called the DAFOR scale from the initial letters of the words.

**Figure 1** These students are using a quadrat on the seashore.

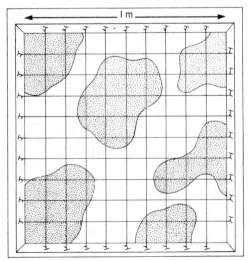

**Figure 2** A grid made by dividing a one-metre quadrat into 100 squares. The stippled areas represent patches of grass. Grids can be made any size to suit the particular habitat being studied.

## Investigating an organisms's distribution

To study an organism's distribution we need to know roughly how many individuals occur in different places. There are three main ways of doing this: by just looking at the organisms, by counting them, or by working out the area which they occupy.

### The looking method

You simply look at the habitat and describe in words how many organisms are present. Each plant or animal species is given one of the descriptions listed in Table 1. Dominant does not mean the most numerous species; it is the one that has the greatest effect on the environment. For example, if you were looking at an area under a tree, the tree itself would be the dominant species. Grass would probably be abundant, various weeds would be abundant, frequent or occasional, depending on how many there were; and an odd plant of a particular species would be called rare.

This is the simplest method of describing distribution, and the least accurate. But it may help you to spot something interesting which you can then investigate more carefully.

### The counting method

Suppose you want to find out how many weeds of a particular kind grow in a field. How could you do it? One way would be to count all the weeds in the field. However, this would probably drive you mad. So what you do is to count the number of weeds in a series of small areas in the field, then work out the average. We call this process **sampling**. As many areas as possible are sampled, and they are selected at random so that the figures are not biased in favour of a particular result. Obviously if you were to deliberately choose areas where there were lots of weeds, the results could be totally misleading.

One of the simplest ways of sampling a habitat is to use a **quadrat**. This is a square frame made of wood or metal which is laid on the ground (Figure 1). Quadrats come in many different sizes, but for counting weeds in a field, a quadrat with a side of one metre would be suitable. You simply count up the number of weeds inside the frame, repeating the process in, say, ten different parts of the field. You then work out the average number of weeds per square metre. We call this the **density** of the weeds (Investigation 1).

### The area method

Suppose you want to find out how much grass is growing on a piece of waste ground. In this case you cannot count the plants individually because it's impossible to tell where one ends and the next one begins. Instead you estimate the area of the ground covered by grass.

To do this you use a **grid**. This is a quadrat which has been divided by string into 100 small squares (Figure 2). You lay the grid on the ground and estimate the number of squares which the grass covers. Say grass fills a total of 15 squares. This means that the area inside the quadrat occupied by grass is $\frac{15}{100} = 15$ per cent. We call this the **percentage cover**.

You repeat this randomly in different parts of the waste ground, and then you work out the average percentage cover (Investigation 2).

*Note* This same grid can be used to find the **frequency** of plants. Frequency is the *number* of small squares, out of a 100, in which the plant is found.

## Other ways of investigating distribution

You may have noticed that in some places the types of organisms gradually change as you go across a habitat. This is particularly noticeable at the edge of a pond or between the high and low tide marks on the seashore. In such cases it is useful to record exactly where each kind of organism occurs. You can do this by making a **line transect**. A length of string or a plastic clothes-line is marked with a felt tip pen at regular intervals. It is then stretched across the habitat which you want to examine. You then list all the plants (and animals,

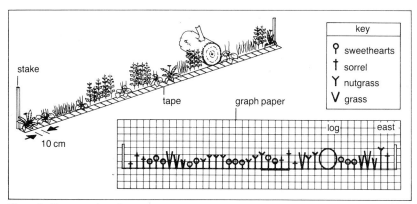

**Figure 3** How to make a line transect.

too, if you wish) which are touching the line and record their positions.

An example of a line transect is shown in Figure 3. Notice that some plants which occur at one end of the transect are completely absent at the other. Investigating the reason for such a difference is one of the most important aspects of ecology.

The trouble with a line transect is that it only gives you the organisms that are right on the line. A better method is to lay out two parallel strings a metre apart and record the plants between them. We call this a **belt transect**. If you lay a grid between the two lines it will help you to put the different plants in their right positions. You could also estimate the frequency or percentage cover of particular species along the length of the transect.

## Investigation 1

### To find out the density of weeds in a field

1 Obtain a quadrat, 1 metre square.

2 Select a field, and decide what particular weed you wish to investigate.

3 Lay the quadrat on the ground, and count the number of weeds inside it.

   If a weed is touching the frame, include it in your count if more than half of it is inside the quadrat.

4 Repeat the above procedure with the quadrat in at least five different places, chosen at random.

5 Work out the average number of weeds per square metre in the field. This is the **density** of weeds.

Do you think this is a good method of finding out how many weeds there are in the field? If not, why not?

What are the main reasons for any inaccuracies in the results?

What could be done to improve the method?

## Investigation 2

### Estimating the frequency and percentage cover of a weed

1 Obtain a grid. This should be a one-metre quadrat that has been divided into 100 squares.

2 Lay the grid on the ground, and count up the *number* of squares, out of a hundred, which contain the weed. This is the **frequency**.

3 Now find the **percentage cover**, which is the *area* covered by the weed. Estimate the number of squares that would be filled by the weed. If a square is only partly filled with the weed, take this into account in making your estimate. For example, four squares that are each a quarter full count as one square.

   The final figure you arrive at is the percentage cover.

4 Repeat steps 2 and 3 with the grid in at least five different places, chosen at random.

5 Work out the average frequency and percentage cover of the weed.

## Assignments

1 Why is the scale in Table 1 an inaccurate way of describing the occurrence of different species of animals or plants in an area? Write down as many reasons as you can think of.

2 Explain the difference between
   a) quadrat and grid,
   b) line transect and belt transect.

3 A grid was used to find the distribution of plants V, W, X, Y and Z.

For each plant:
   a) describe it, using the DAFOR scale.
   b) work out the frequency,
   c) work out the percentage cover.

4 A student counted the number of seedlings in 13 quadrats on a lawn. Here is a summary of her results:

| Number of seedlings | 4 | 5 | 6 | 7 | 8 | 9 |
|---|---|---|---|---|---|---|
| Number of quadrats in which the above number of seedlings occurred | 1 | 2 | 4 | 3 | 2 | 1 |

   a) Plot these results as a bar chart (histogram) (see page 3).

   b) Calculate the average number of seedlings per square metre. (This is called the **mean**.)

   c) What is the most common number of seedlings in a square metre? (This is called the **mode**.)

   d) Which is the best way to express the density of seedlings in the lawn: as the mean or as the mode? Explain your answer.

# What controls where organisms live?

*In this Topic
we shall ask why certain
organisms are restricted to
particular places.*

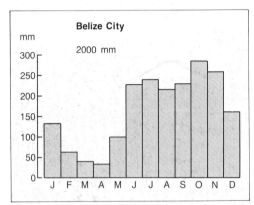

**Belize City**

Figure 1  Rainfall for Belize City, Belize.

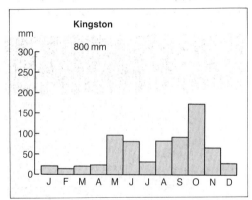

**Kingston**

Figure 2  Rainfall for Kingston, Jamaica.

Figure 3  Tropical rain forest. Notice the epiphyte on the left, and the large number of lianes hanging from the trees.

## What is the environment?

Every habitat has certain conditions which make it suitable for some organisms but not for others. These conditions make up the **environment**. An organism's environment consists of two parts: the physical environment and the biological (biotic) environment.

The **physical environment** includes temperature, rainfall, light, humidity and so on. The precise features which make up an organism's physical environment depend on whether it lives on land or in water. For land organisms temperature, rainfall and humidity are particularly important. For water-dwellers (aquatic organisms) the most important features are how salty the water is, and how rapidly it flows.

The **biological environment** is made up of all the other organisms in the habitat. One of the most important examples of an organism's biological environment is the presence of another organism which it feeds on.

## The Caribbean

Let us now look more closely at the effect of some of these features on the plants and animals occurring in the Caribbean.

Is *temperature* important? Yes it is, but it doesn't change very much from month to month. This is because all the Caribbean countries lie in the tropics between 23°N and the equator and so they all have an average monthly temperature which varies between about 20°C and 30°C throughout the year.

The *annual rainfall* however varies a great deal from country to country and from one part of a country to another. What determines this is the position of the country in relation to the rain-bearing *winds*, and also the presence or absence of *mountains*. The other important point is that the rain does not fall in the same amounts each month. There are wet and dry seasons, which are more marked in some countries than others.

Let us now take a 4000 km journey from the westernmost country of the Caribbean, Belize, to the easternmost one, Guyana. The maps at the front of the book will help you to see where we are going. As we pass over these countries we will note their major characteristics and some ways in which these affect the vegetation. After this we will be able to summarise the different kinds of vegetation and the factors that are important in controlling where organisms live.

Fasten your seat belts!

## Belize

The northern half of the country has 1500–2000 mm of rain a year and most of the land is less than 60 metres above sea level. It is therefore a swampy plateau that is mostly covered by **tropical rain forests** from which logwood is cut and exported. The rainfall for Belize City (Figure 1) shows the alternating wet and dry seasons.

Rainfall is even heavier in the south: from 2500 mm to 4500 mm on the Maya Mountains. The forests are even thicker, with a lot of logwood and mahogany. Chicle, sugar cane, citrus fruits and tobacco are grown.

## The Greater Antilles

This includes Jamaica and the Turks and Caicos Islands. Parts of them have less rain than the other Caribbean countries. They also have a more marked dry season, with many parts receiving very little rainfall for several months. This is especially true of the southern part of Jamaica.

The annual rainfall for Kingston, Jamaica, is 800 mm (Figure 2). Rainfall is heavier on the higher north-eastern end of the island, and on the Blue Mountain Range more than 3000 mm of rain are recorded. In these areas rainfall is more than 2000 mm throughout the year and a tropical rain forest of evergreen trees is found (Figure 3). This occurs on the mountains all over the Caribbean where rainfall and humidity are high. On the higher mountains it is cooler and the vegetation is more characteristic of temperate regions.

## The Lesser Antilles

The Lesser Antilles have more rain, a less marked dry season and less change in temperature during the year than the Greater Antilles. Usually the larger and higher the island in the Lesser Antilles, the wetter it is. Most of the islands, except for Barbados, still have a lot of tropical rain forest.

## Leeward Islands

These are the British Virgin Islands, St Kitts, Nevis, Anguilla, Montserrat, Antigua, Barbuda and Dominica. On the whole the Leeward Islands tend to be drier than the Windward Islands. A progression is also seen from the north to the south, with the British Virgin Islands being the driest, and Dominica being very rainy (Figure 4). In Dominica large areas of its original tropical rain forest remain. There are also areas where the forests have been cut down and replaced by tracts of grassland and trees, called **savannas**.

## Windward Islands

These are St Lucia, St Vincent, the Grenadines, Grenada and Barbados. St Lucia, St Vincent and Grenada get more than 1800 mm of rain. This rises to more than 2000 mm on the windward sides of higher mountains where most of the tropical rain forests remain. Grenada especially is renowed for its production of spices.

Barbados has an average rainfall of 1500 mm, although it may rise to 2000 mm in the north. Most of the original tropical rain forest has been removed, especially for the growing of sugar cane. However, **tropical deciduous forests** can be found which contain deciduous trees. In other parts of the Caribbean similar deciduous forests may be found in valleys. The Grenadines have considerably less rainfall than 1500 mm and are the driest of the Windward Islands. As in Greater Antilles, thorny shrubs, spiky succulents and cacti are part of the tropical scrub vegetation (Figure 5).

## Trinidad and Tobago

In the Caribbean these are the islands with the greatest rainfall.

*Trinidad*  The northern range traps rain-bearing winds and so these mountains have over 3500 mm of rain and bear thick tropical rain forests. In the central part of Trinidad on the low-lying east and west coastal areas are found the extensive Nariva and Caroni **mangrove swamps** (see page 362). Where forests have been cleared, or cannot grow, there is the development of savannas such as the Aripo savanna (Figure 6).

*Tobago*  This is a long, narrow island with a volcanic mountain ridge running along its length. Predictably, therefore, the rainfall is high and the island is heavily forested. The dry season runs from January to May.

## Guyana

The rainfall of Guyana is mostly over 2000 mm, for example Georgetown (Figure 7), and even the 'dry' months are quite well supplied with rain. In some areas, such as parts of the Pakaraima Mountains, the rainfall is over 3000 mm. The high rainfall and the closeness to the equator account for over three-quarters of the country being covered with **equatorial rain forest**. This is the only place in the Caribbean where such forest is found. A drier region with less than 2000 mm rainfall is found in the south-west where there is a savanna, with grass for the raising of cattle. The coastland is swampy. The beautiful nuisance, the water hyacinth, thrives in the numerous **aquatic habitats** and drainage canals.

# Different types of vegetation

In our 'island hopping' we have seen many kinds of vegetation. They are actually of two main types – *forests* and *savannas*.

Forests are dominated by trees and savannas are dominated by grasses.

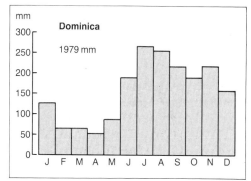

**Figure 4**  Rainfall for Dominica.

**Figure 5**  Tropical scrub. On dry, sandy ground thorny shrubs and succulents are found.

**Figure 6**  Savanna grassland is widespread in dry areas. The vegetation is mainly grass, with scattered trees.

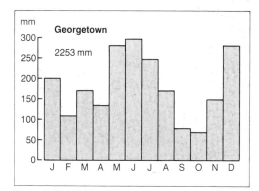

**Figure 7**  Rainfall for Georgetown, Guyana.

| Type | Where found | Important environmental factors | Notes | |
|------|-------------|--------------------------------|-------|--|
| **Equatorial rain forest** (evergreen) | Guyana | Within 10° of the equator. Continuously hot and has plenty of rainfall at least 10 months of the year. | Both types of rain forest have trees arranged in a series of layers. The dense canopies shade the ground so few plants can grow there. Epiphytes (p.372) are abundant. More plant species and climbers are found in equatorial rain forests than in tropical rain forests. | |
| **Tropical rain forest** (evergreen) | Belize, Trinidad, Dominica, Jamaica. Windward locations and mountains in most countries. | Roughly from 10° to 23°. Long, hot wet season alternates with cooler season with reduced rainfall. | | |
| **Mangrove swamp** | Trinidad, Guyana, Belize, Jamaica. Some on most coastal regions. | Develop on tropical coasts which receive mud from river mouths, and where water is shallow. | A succession of plants develop with zones of various kinds of mangrove (page 362). | |
| **Tropical deciduous forest** (mainly deciduous) | Barbados, Jamaica. Some in other countries in valleys. | Long wet season with a lot of rain alternates with a definite, rather cool dry season. | Trees less close together than in rain forests so there is more light and more vegetation on the ground. Climbers and epiphytes common. | |
| **Savanna woodland** | Widespread in the Caribbean. | Wet season alternates with dry season. Not enough rain to allow trees to form a closed canopy. | More trees than in savanna grassland. Dense lower layers of shrubs and grasses. | Trees xerophytic with small leaves or thorns, or may be deciduous in dry season. Fires in dry season. Trees fire-resistant, and grasses regrow from underground parts. |
| **Savanna grassland** | Widespread in drier areas. | Severe drought in the cooler dry season. Great heat before the onset of the rains. | Less trees than in savanna woodland. More or less continuous grass on the ground. | |
| **Tropical scrub** | The Grenadines, Jamaica. Widespread, especially on sandy and stony coasts. | Very long dry season with short, intensive rainy season. Found, for example, above sandy shores. | Low woody shrubs, often with thorns and largely deciduous. Cacti often present. Bare ground or scattered clumps of grass. | |

**Table 1**  Different types of vegetation in the Caribbean.

The main kinds of forests and savannas are shown in Table 1.

Man often interferes with the type of vegetation that *could* grow in a particular place. The temperature and rainfall may allow tropical rain forests to grow, but man wants the timber to sell, or he wants to use the land to build a town. And so the forest disappears.

In many parts of the country trees are cut down and the ground is burned. This causes the development of savannas in places where forests might be able to grow.

## What kinds of vegetation do you have in your country?

Apart from the equatorial rain forest you probably have all the kinds of vegetation listed in the table, as well as some aquatic habitats like that shown in Figure 8. Try to find out the different places in your country where each kind of vegetation is found.

What causes the differences? You should look through the descriptions of the countries and the table to identify the various factors which control the distribution of vegetation.

Use the information on the next page to set up a weather station in your school and keep records for an entire year of, for example, rainfall and temperature. This will help you to find out what kind of vegetation you may have in your area. If you live in a town or city you may have to go to the nearby countryside to see the vegetation in its natural condition.

## The physical environment

### Climatic factors

*Temperature*  is measured with a 0–110°C **thermometer**. The thermometer should be left in position in the habitat for 3 minutes in order to give a correct reading. Different habitats can be compared. A double thermometer, called a **maximum-mimimum** thermometer, is used to find the range of temperatures during a period of time.

**Figure 8**  An aquatic habitat. Living in water has its own special problems.

Organisms which are especially affected by changes in temperature are cold-blooded (poikilothermic) animals (see pages 58–61).

*Light intensity* is measured with a **light meter** such as photographers use. Different habitats can be compared. Plants have different light requirements; for example hibiscus and morning glory grow in bright light, while ferns, many orchids and elephant's ear (*Alocasia*) prefer shady conditions.

Many animals such as earthworms, blowfly larvae, woodlice and bats avoid light, while plants and green protists grow or move towards the light (Investigations 1 and 2).

*Rainfall* is measured with a **rain gauge** (Figure 9). At intervals the amount of water in the measuring cylinder is found and the rainfall is worked out.

The regular alternation of wet and dry seasons in the tropics has a great effect on the organisms (see page 364). Where rainfall is very limited, or it is difficult to get water out of the soil or sand, the plants show modifications called **xerophytic** characteristics. For example, leaves are reduced in willow and prickly pear and stomata are buried in pits in oleander.

*Relative humidity* describes the amount of moisture in the air. It is measured with a **wet and dry bulb hygrometer** (Figure 10). Readings are made on the two thermometers and converted to relative humidity by means of special tables. To *compare* the relative humidity in different parts of a habitat, cobalt chloride paper can be used. The times taken for it to change from blue (when dry) to pink (when damp) are compared.

Invertebrates such as blowfly larvae, woodlice and termites need air with a high relative humidity otherwise they may dry out (Investigation 3).

*Wind* The *direction* from which the wind is blowing is found with a **wind vane**.

The *speed at which the wind is blowing is found with an* **anemometer** (Figure 11). We count the number of times the wind makes the cups swing round in a given period of time.

Wind is important in pollination and dispersal, and in the movement of rain clouds. It also increases the rates of evaporation and transpiration.

## Special factors in aquatic habitats

*Speed of flow* is measured by timing how long it takes for a **float**, such as a piece of wood, to travel a certain distance.

*Depth* is measured with a vertical metre stick.

*pH* (degree of acidity or alkalinity) is measured with universal indicator.

*Muddiness or turbidity* is compared by lowering a weighted white plate (held by strings) into the water. The depths at which it just cannot be seen are compared.

*Oxygen concentration and salinity* also affect the distribution of organisms. Oxygen concentration is higher in a swift moving stream than in a stagnant pool. Salinity (amount of salt) varies from low values in fresh water, to high values in sea water, with in-between values in estuaries and mangrove swamps.

## Physical features (physiographic)

These are the variations in the earth's surface such as hills, mountains and valleys, which affect the vegetation and the rainfall. The *angle of slope* of a hill is measured with a **slope gauge** (Figure 12). Note that in the figure the angle of slope is 20°. The *aspect* is the direction in which the hill is facing. It is found with a **compass**.

## Soil factors (edaphic) These are described fully on pages 378–80.

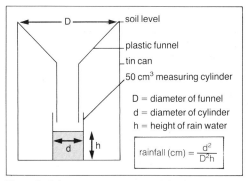

Figure 9 Rain gauge to measure rainfall.

D = diameter of funnel
d = diameter of cylinder
h = height of rain water

$$\text{rainfall (cm)} = \frac{d^2}{D^2 h}$$

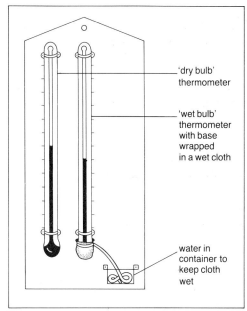

Figure 10 Wet and dry bulb hygrometer to measure relative humidity.

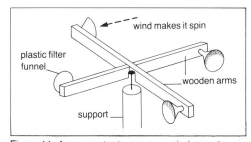

Figure 11 Anemometer to compare wind speeds.

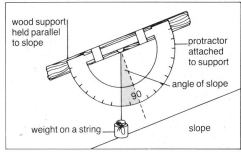

Figure 12 Slope gauge to measure the angle of slope of a hill.

Figure 13 A caterpillar feeding on a leaf.

Figure 14 Seedlings of the red mangrove. The seeds germinate on the parent plant to form droppers (see left of photograph). These then fall down into the mud and continue growing.

Figure 15 The prop roots of the red mangrove.

# The biological environment

Look at the caterpillar in Figure 13. It is feeding on the leaves. Without them the caterpillar could not survive. Organisms are found close to their source of food: this is a most important aspect of their biological environment.

Feeding is one of the most important ways in which organisms affect each other. We only have to think of predators and their prey, or parasites and their hosts, and of plants growing in a forest trying to get enough light.

There are also examples of co-operation between different kinds of organisms. For example, butterflies and moths need flowers because they get nectar and pollen from them, and flowers need insects for pollination.

Animals may compete for mates or breeding grounds and so chase away other animals of the same kind. Competition may also occur between animals as they try to find sufficient space and shelter. Man himself is the most important biological factor in the lives of many plants and animals.

These are just a few examples of the way one organism's distribution is related to that of another.

## A mangrove swamp: an example of plant succession

Mangrove swamps occur in river estuaries and coastal bays in the tropics. They are common around the coasts in the Caribbean wherever mud is being deposited. We shall see how the plants affect each other.

A new mud surface is a difficult and constantly changing place. It is affected by the river, which brings down more mud and lowers the salinity. It is also affected by the sea which raises the salinity and causes a change in water level with the tides. The water and mud are also very poor in oxygen.

There is, however, a plant which can **colonise** these areas. The red mangrove has seeds which begin development on the parent. These **droppers** (Figure 14) float in the water and already have well-developed roots to establish themselves in any mud deposits.

The red mangrove is a **pioneer** species which forms the outermost zone near to the sea. It has extensive **prop roots** (Figure 15) which reduce tidal currents and cause more mud to be deposited. It also provides surfaces for snails and barnacles to grow, and the mud is colonised by crabs and mudskippers.

Once the mud becomes stabilised and the level is raised to near high tide level, seeds of the black mangrove can germinate. The plants send up numerous small breathing roots called **pneumatophores** (Figure 16), which further help to stabilize the swamp. At this stage the white mangrove can also develop. It too has pneumatophores to help it to get oxygen.

As the ground is raised further and a more normal soil develops from decaying remains, the button mangrove, dogwood, screwpine, sea grape, French cotton, and wild sage can grow.

There is thus a series of changes, one after the other. We call this a **succession**. The plants·present at one stage alter the habitat in such a way that new species can move in. In other words each lot of plants *prepares* the habitat for the next lot. The area further develops as a terrestrial environment with its characteristic plants. This final community is called the **climax** of the succession.

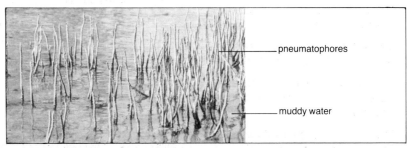

Figure 16 The breathing roots of the black mangrove. These are able to take in oxygen from the air.

# Investigation 1

## To see if Euglena is attracted towards light

1 Set up three tubes of *Euglena* like this:

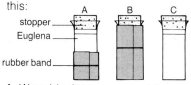

A Wrap black paper around the bottom half of tube.
B Wrap black paper around the entire tube.
C Leave uncovered.

2 Place the three tubes under a lamp (not too bright) for about 24 hours.

3 After 24 hours remove the black paper from the tubes, and examine the distribution of euglenas in each. Whereabouts are the euglenas? What is the reason for setting up tubes B and C?

What would be the use of this experiment?

# Investigation 3

## To find out how woodlice react to humidity

Woodlice normally live under logs and stones in damp places.

How do you think they would react to dry conditions?

You can find out by setting up a 'choice-chamber' containing a dry area and a moist area.

1 Set up the choice chamber as shown in the illustration below.

Anhydrous calcium chloride powder absorbs water, so the air on this side

of the choice chamber will become very dry. In contrast, the air above the water will become relatively humid. Wait at least ten minutes to allow time for these conditions to develop.

2 Place about ten woodlice in the choice chamber.

3 Observe the woodlice at intervals during the next half hour or so.

Which end of the choice chamber do woodlice seem to prefer?

On what observation do you base your answer?

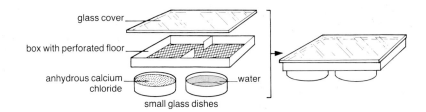

# Investigation 2

## To find out how blowfly larvae react to light

Blowflies lay their eggs on dung, and the larvae live *inside* it.

1 Obtain a sheet of white paper approximately 24 cm long.

2 Direct a lamp towards one end of the sheet of paper.

3 Switch the lamp off and darken the room.

4 Place about 6 blowfly larvae at the end of the sheet of paper where the lamp is.

5 Switch the lamp on and observe the blowfly larvae.

How do they react to your switching on the lamp? Is this what you expected?

What could you do to make sure their response is not caused by heat from the lamp?

Repeat the experiment with woodlice. Do you get the same result? Why?

# Investigation 4

## What controls where organisms live?

1 Choose a shady and a sunny place on the ground or on a wall.

2 Mark out a plot in each place with sides 50 cm.

3 Use the methods on page 356 to describe the percentage cover of the various plants present in the two plots.

4 Measure the various factors in the two plots.
a) Light intensity   b) Temperature
c) Relative humidity

5 Compare the soil in the two plots. Use the methods on pages 382–3. Compare:
a) The amount of leaf litter
b) The amount of humus
c) The water content

Describe your results.
What might be the reasons for the differences? What effects might the differences have?

# Assignments

1 Name one organism which forms the biological environment of each of the following:
a) an adult mosquito
b) a butterfly
c) a tadpole

2 A brick wall runs east-west. There are mosses on the north side but not on the south side. Suggest two possible reasons for this.

3 A forester notices that in a certain area young seedlings die after reaching a height of about 6 cm, whereas in another area a short distance away the same seedlings grow successfully to a large size. Suggest possible reasons why the seedlings do badly in the first area.

4 Use an atlas and draw a map of your country. Mark in the hills and mountains. Find out as much as you can about the amount of rain in the different parts. See if you can relate these differences to the various kinds of vegetation that are found.

# Changes through the year

*There are great differences between the wet and dry season. How do organisms respond to these differences?*

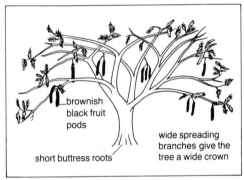

**Figure 1** *Delonix regia*. The flamboyant tree during the dry season, when it loses its leaves.

**Figure 2** The flamboyant tree during the wet season, a mass of leaves and red flowers.

**Figure 3** These diagrams show what happens when a leaf falls off a tree or shrub.

## Climatic changes through the year

The main climatic factors which change throughout the year are temperature, light and rainfall. In the Caribbean it is always warm enough for plants and animals to remain active and continue their growth. The amount of light also does not change very much from month to month. For example, in temperate countries the shorter day lengths associated with autumn and winter cause the **short-day** chrysanthemum plants to flower. In the Caribbean, gardeners have to shorten the days artificially to get these plants to flower.

Many garden plants such as hibiscus and bougainvillea flower throughout the year, while others such as mango have definite seasons.

In the Caribbean the major change during the year is the amount of rainfall, with the characteristic dry and wet seasons.

## The dry season

When there is a marked dry season which is long and severe there is little water in the soil and the air is dry and hot. The plants may then rest or become **dormant**, and they reduce water loss from their leaves:
a) Some of the trees will be **deciduous**, that is, they will lose all their leaves at the same time (Figure 1).
b) The above-ground parts of grasses and other plants may die. There will be stem tubers, corms, bulbs and so on which survive under the ground.
c) Many herbaceous plants survive the dry season in the form of seeds.
d) For most animals the dry season is a time when they are less active. If it is very dry, animals such as the lungfish may **aestivate** by burying themselves in the mud.

## The wet season

This is the active growing season.
a) New flower buds and leaf buds are formed on the deciduous trees (Figure 2). In fact several trees flower towards the end of the dry season before the leaves are formed.
b) Fresh new grass begins to grow, and the lawn needs mowing again. Shoots with leaves and flowers grow up from storage organs.
c) Gardeners and farmers sow their seeds.
d) Many animals, such as termites, toads and frogs begin to reproduce.

## Losing leaves

As we have seen, losing all the leaves at one time can be a response to the dry season. But even evergreen trees lose their leaves. It just happens a few at a time and so we don't notice it.

What makes the leaves fall off?

A layer of cells grows across the leaf stalk at the point where it's attached to the main stem or branch: the cells form a partition, leaving only the veins (vascular bundles) running through (Figure 3). This creates a region of weakness at the base of the stalk, and eventually it breaks and the leaf falls off. A layer of cork then grows over the cut surface, creating a **leaf scar** in which the marks left by the veins can be seen (see Figure 3).

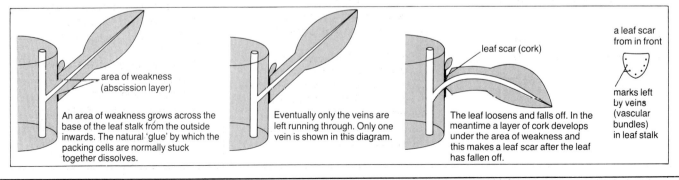

An area of weakness grows across the base of the leaf stalk from the outside inwards. The natural 'glue' by which the packing cells are normally stuck together dissolves.

Eventually only the veins are left running through. Only one vein is shown in this diagram.

The leaf loosens and falls off. In the meantime a layer of cork develops under the area of weakness and this makes a leaf scar after the leaf has fallen off.

a leaf scar from in front

marks left by veins (vascular bundles) in leaf stalk

# Investigation 1

## To find the changes that take place throughout the year

1 Choose one of the following plants: An herbaceous weed such as nutgrass, a shrub such as June rose, and a tree such as flamboyant, silk cotton tree or mango tree.

2 Find an example of your plant growing near to your home or school which you can observe easily.

3 Make a table in your book like the one shown below.

4 In the first week of each month observe your plant and record by ticks opposite each description what your plant looks like.

5 Under 'Climatic conditions' record the average temperature and rainfall for each month as recorded at your weather station (see page 361). From the readings identify which is the wet season and which is the dry season.

6 Try to relate changes in your plant to changes in the climatic conditions. If your plant is deciduous:
a) When do the leaves fall?
b) When are the flowers formed?
c) When are new leaves formed?

If your plant is not deciduous:
d) Why do you think this is so?
e) Does your plant flower more than once in the year?

| Observation | Months of the year | | | | | | | | | | | |
|---|---|---|---|---|---|---|---|---|---|---|---|---|
| | J | F | M | A | M | J | J | A | S | O | N | D |
| **Leaves:** | | | | | | | | | | | | |
| No leaves | | | | | | | | | | | | |
| New young leaves | | | | | | | | | | | | |
| Many leaves | | | | | | | | | | | | |
| **Flowers:** | | | | | | | | | | | | |
| No flowers | | | | | | | | | | | | |
| New flower buds | | | | | | | | | | | | |
| Open flowers | | | | | | | | | | | | |
| **Fruits:** | | | | | | | | | | | | |
| Young fruits | | | | | | | | | | | | |
| Ripe fruits | | | | | | | | | | | | |
| **Climatic conditions:** | | | | | | | | | | | | |
| Temperature | | | | | | | | | | | | |
| Rainfall | | | | | | | | | | | | |

# Investigation 2

## What is the effect of the dry and wet seasons?

*This investigation should be done in the dry season.*

1 Mark out two plots of ground, each with sides 50 cm long.

2 Make the following observations for each plot and record them:
a) Appearance and feel of the soil.
b) Colour and appearance of the grass.
c) The number of different species present.
d) The average height of the plants.
e) The number of plants that are flowering.
f) Any animals such as ants or earthworms.

3 Water one of the plots every day.

4 At the end of each week repeat the observations listed in 2 above.

5 At the end of one month compare the two plots.

(The observations you make on the unwatered plot would be like those in the dry season).
(The observations you make at the end of the watering exercise are similar to those you find when the wet season begins.)

6 What effect has the water had on:
a) the appearance and feel of the soil?
What other effects would this have?
b) the colour and appearance of the grass?
Why do you think this has happened?
c) the number of different species growing there?
Where did these come from?
d) the heights of the plants?
What have the plants been doing?
e) the number of plants that are flowering?
Why is this important?
f) the activity of animals such as ants, earthworms, termites, slugs, grasshoppers etc?

# Assignments

1 A mango tree is covered with leaves all through the year. Does it lose any leaves at all? How could you find out?

2 What does *deciduous* mean?

3 How do the following plants survive the dry season?
a) Flamboyant
b) Nutgrass
c) Sweet potato
d) Hibiscus

4 At what time of year would you
a) plant your crops?
b) expect to eat mangoes?
c) expect to see termites flying?
d) not find earthworms easily?

5 There are two flamboyant trees, one at the school and one in the middle of town. The first one was covered in red flowers at the beginning of May, but the other one didn't flower until June. What possible reasons can you suggest for this?

# A look at some habitats

*We shall look at three different habitats and some of the organisms that live in them.*

**Figure 1** A ghost crab. A familiar sight on sandy shores.

## Different kinds of habitats

Apart from our study of the mangrove swamp, we have so far been mostly concerned with *terrestrial* habitats.

In this Topic we will consider *aquatic* habitats: a fresh-water pond, and the habitats that lie between the sea and the land.

## Between the sea and the land

Below the low tide mark the organisms are always covered by the sea. We call this the **sublittoral** zone. But those organisms, such as the crab (Figure 1), that live between the low and high tide marks are covered by the sea for only part of the day. We call this the **intertidal** zone. Those near the top of the shore are exposed for the longest time to the dry, hot air.

Further up the shore is the **splash** zone; this receives sea spray but is not covered at all by the tide. Above this there may be a **pioneer** zone where the sand shifts and moves in the wind. This grades into fully terrestrial habitats.

## A sandy shore

We will first look at the organisms we can expect to find in the different zones on a sandy shore (Figure 2). We will then look in more detail at a few organisms to see how they are adapted to their habitats (Figure 3).

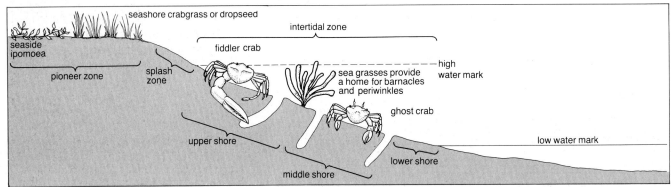

**Figure 2** A cross-section of a sandy shore, showing some of the organisms living in the different zones.

*(Figure 3 labels: seashore crabgrass; fiddler crab; seaside ipomoea; ghost crab)*

**Figure 3** Some of the organisms that live on sandy shores.

### Seashore crabgrass or dropseed
'Crabgrass' refers to the creeping habit of the stems, which spread over the sand, with clumps of upright leaves at intervals. The leaves are rolled, with the stomata on the inside. This keeps moist air near to the stomata and so less water is lost. The roots are deep and widespread, and help to hold the sand steady so it is not blown away.

### Seaside ipomoea
The stems are also creeping, and form a mat lying close to the ground where it is more sheltered from the wind and the drying effect of the sun. Being close together, the stems also keep the air around them more humid. The leaves are large, thick and fleshy, and they store water. The roots are deep and help to hold the sand.

### Fiddler crab
The fiddler crab lives on the shore between the high and low tide marks. It digs burrows in the sand into which it retreats when the tide comes in. When the tide goes out it emerges to eat the minute organisms left behind by the water. One of the front legs in the male is enlarged as a huge claw with which it can fight.

### Ghost crab
This is almost transparent (ghost-like), which makes it very difficult to see against the sand – until it scurries away with its sideways run. It has eyes on the top of stalks to see its predators and prey. It lives in burrows which

protect it from enemies and from changes in temperature and salinity. It emerges to attack any small creatures that venture too close.

## A rocky shore: many habitats in one

On a rocky shore we find all the zones from the sublittoral to the splash zone, each with its own characteristic collection of organisms.

In addition we find a special habitat: the **rock pools**. These are found anywhere on the shore where the hollow rocks become filled with sea water that is trapped when the tide goes out. Animals can live here that cannot survive on the open rocks: for example, starfish, sea urchins, sea anemones, sponges and even small fish. And on the rocky slopes and in the crevices leading into the pool we find periwinkles, sponges and small crabs.

A visitor to the rock pool is the hermit crab (Figure 4). This is a crab which is living in an empty shell which usually has a sea anemone on top of it. This gives the crab camouflage. And it is also protected against enemies by the tentacles of the sea anemone. This is an example of **commensalism**. The anemone may also benefit by getting transportation and leftover food from the crab.

We will now look at the different zones on a rocky shore (Figure 5) and at the adaptations of selected organisms (Figure 6).

**Figure 4** A hermit crab inside an old shell. The shell is also the home of a periwinkle and a sea anemone.

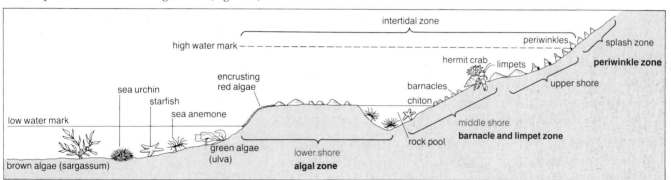

**Figure 5** A cross-section of a rocky shore, showing some of the organisms living in the different zones.

### Periwinkles

Different kinds of periwinkles are found in all the zones of the shore. These are small snails which have a multi-purpose muscular foot. They can use it for clinging firmly onto the rocks or for wandering around in search of their food, microscopic algae. They have a shell and a lid or **operculum** which they can close and so are protected from the air.

### Limpets

Limpets move about only a little on the rocks, searching for microscopic algae. When they are relaxed there is a space between the rock and the bottom of their shell. But if they are disturbed, for example by a collector, they pull down with their muscular foot and are extremely difficult to get off the rock. This tight fit to the rock also protects them from drying out.

### Sea anemone

This is a soft-bodied animal which does not have any shell to protect it against the dry air and so it cannot survive on the open shore. It is found in rock pools and in the sublittoral zone. It is firmly attached to the rock surface. Its tentacles are supplied with sting cells which shoot out threads that paralyse its food, such as small fish.

### Sargassum

This has a **holdfast** by which it is firmly attached to the rock. This helps it to withstand the movements of the sea; dead sargassum is often washed up onto the shore. Its 'leaves' have small air bladders which help them to float upright in the water and this helps in photosynthesis. It has a thin covering and absorbs water, carbon dioxide and salts from the sea water.

**Figure 6** Some of the organisms that live on rocky shores.

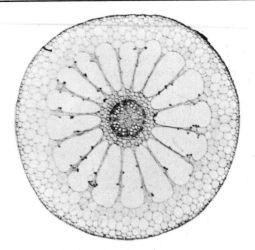

**Figure 7** Cross-section of a leaf stalk of an aquatic plant, showing the large air spaces that help it to float in the water.

# A fresh-water pond

Living in water is very different from living on land. For the *plants*, they no longer have to rely on their roots to get water and mineral salts from the ground; they can just take them in all over their surface. This also means that they do not need conducting tissue. They can also exchange gases with the water and so their leaves do not need stomata. Because they are supported by the water they do not need the strengthening tissues found in land plants. Instead they have many air spaces in their stems or leaves (Figure 7) which help them to float in the water so that they can carry out photosynthesis.

For the *animals*, there is no danger of drying out, and so there are many soft-skinned forms, including the young stages of many insects. The animals show various adaptations for breathing. Small organisms exchange gases through their skins, while larger ones often have gills. Others have breathing tubes for taking in air at the surface, while some bring down a bubble of air into the water with them. Many water animals feed by filtering small organisms from the water, while others are notorious carnivores.

We will now look at a cross-section of the habitat (Figure 8) and then at some of the adaptions of selected plants and animals.

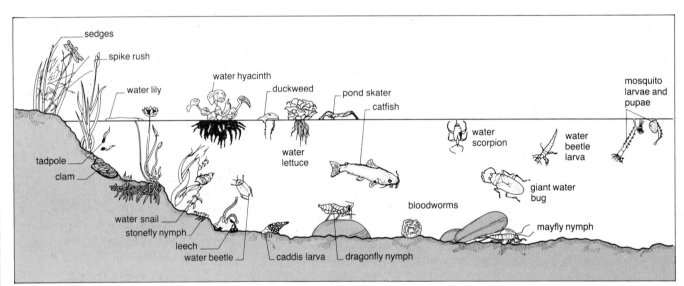

**Figure 8** A cross-section of part of a fresh-water pond, and the organisms that live there.

**Figure 9** Water hyacinth: a weed of fresh water and drainage canals. Notice the swollen leaf bases which help it to float.

## Water lily

This has a rhizome which is buried in the mud and from which the floating leaves and flowers grow. It does not have well developed roots because it can absorb the water and gases that it needs through its entire surface, which has only a thin cuticle. Also it does not have well developed transporting tissues, or strengthening material to hold it upright. It is held up by the water and by air spaces in the stems, which also supply oxygen to the underground parts. The large leaves which lie flat on the surface of the water carry out photosynthesis. They have a waxy cuticle on the upper surface so that water runs off easily. The lower epidermis has no stomata, only a thin permeable cuticle.

## Water hyacinth

Depending on the depth of water, this is either rooted or free floating (Figure 9). It has inflated leaf stalks to help it to float. It forms extensive mats and can be a serious nuisance. This is because it reproduces vegetatively very quickly; 20 plants can produce a solid hectare of plants in eight months.

## Water lettuce

This is also a weed. It has rosettes of spongy green leaves which float on the water surface with bunches of roots hanging down in the water. The upper epidermis of the leaves is covered with hairs so that the water runs off. The plant reproduces by stolons which grow out to produce new rosettes.

## Animals in a freshwater pond

The particular animals found in a pond will depend on whether the water flows through or whether it is stagnant, and whether the bottom is rocky, stony or muddy. Some common animals are described in the account below.
 Animals are found in different locations in the pond.

### On or close to the surface of the water

*Pond skaters* are slender brown insects which use four long legs to skate over the pond. The legs do not break the surface film of the water. If it goes under water to escape enemies the animal quickly bobs up again and is kept quite dry by a coating of hairs on its undersurface. Its front pair of legs is shorter, and it uses these to hold its food, dead or dying insects floating on the water. The skater sucks juices out of them.

*Mosquito larvae and pupae* hang from the water surface by hairs so that they can get air through their breathing tubes. They also have flattened anal gills to help them breathe under water. They can wriggle or jerk around in the water. They are less common where ponds and streams have been oiled, or where mosquito-eating fish have been introduced to control them.

### Floating or swimming in the water

*Water beetles* are shiny, black or brown, oval-shaped animals about 3 cm long. The stout hind legs are flattened and bear stiff bristles which help in swimming. Their wing cases enclose an air space which is filled with air when the beetle goes to the surface. Like their larvae (see page 22) they are carnivorous, using their biting jaws on soft-bodied organisms.

*Giant water bugs* can be 8 cm long. The front legs are modified into powerful claws which hold the prey while the strong, pointed beak sucks up the juices. They have flattened fringed legs and an air space like the water beetles, and from the tip of the abdomen they can put out a tube to draw in air.

*Catfish or mudfish* is common in muddy waters. It has a long, slippery body and a flat head with eight slender feelers round its mouth. Its shape and its smooth skin adapt it well for swimming. It is coloured black above and lighter below, which helps to camouflage it from enemies. It can remain alive out of water for a long time because it has an extra breathing organ in the throat above the gills.

### Under stones or in the mud at the bottom

*Bloodworms* are the larvae of a kind of fly called a 'midge'. Their red colour is due to the presence of haemoglobin which helps them to extract oxygen from the water. They can therefore live in stagnant water. They move by wriggling and are herbivorous. They mostly live in soft tubes of silk in which they pupate, rising to the surface only when the adult is ready to emerge.

*Dragonfly nymphs* are short and stout. They are notorious carnivores with a grasping lower lip with pincers, with which they attack insect larvae, tadpoles and small fish. They have an internal gill chamber at the end of the body through which gas exchange can take place. Water squirted out from this chamber also helps them to move forward quickly. They may grow for up to three years before the adult dragonfly emerges. This lives near the water and is also a carnivore.

*Mayfly nymphs* are elongated, with three long 'tails'. They also have seven pairs of breathing 'gills' on their abdomen and are mainly herbivorous.

*Caddis worms* are the larvae of the caddis fly, which is a moth-like insect. They live in the mud in portable cases which they make from sticks, small stones and leaves stuck together with silk. Only the head and thorax come out of the tube, the abdomen being held inside by two hooks. Some caddis fly larvae spin a silk net around their front end in which they trap small organisms and debris from the water.

## Investigation

**To observe the organisms in a habitat and their adaptations**

1 Visit your chosen habitat. If it is a shore you should arrange to go when the tide is going out so the organisms will be exposed. Or choose a pond or stream.

2 Describe the habitat, especially the slope and the kind of material of which it is made.
 Describe variations in the surface such as crab holes on a sandy shore, rock pools on a rocky shore or the sloping sides of a pond.

3 Use a line transect through the habitat and identify and collect the organisms. (Refer to pages 12 and 13, and pages 356 and 357.)

4 Observe the exact position of the organisms within the habitat and try to relate these to any adaptations that they show.

## Assignments

1 Choose one named plant and one named animal and describe the ways in which each is adapted to its particular habitat.

2 In what ways is living in a rock pool different from living on the upper shore?

3 If you were a snail that couldn't live in water but didn't want to dry out in the sun, whereabouts on the shore would you live?

4 What is commensalism? Describe one example.

5 Do you think it is 'easier' or 'harder' for a plant to live in water than live on land? Explain your answer.

6 Describe, with named examples, four different methods of breathing shown by aquatic animals.

7 Plants in the pioneer zone live not far from the sea, so there should be plenty of water. Why then do they show so many adaptations for cutting down on water loss?

# Adaptation and survival

*Figure 1 shows a caterpillar which looks like a twig. In this way the animal is camouflaged so it cannot be seen by its enemies. This is an example of adaptation.*

Figure 1  This is not a twig but the caterpillar of the peppered moth.

Figure 2  This praying mantis is disguised as a flower.

Figure 3  The false 'eyes' on the wings of this moth help to protect it from its enemies.

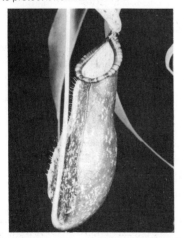
Figure 4  A pitcher plant. Insects fall into the 'jar' and cannot escape.

## What is meant by adaptation?

When we say that an organism is **adapted**, we mean that its appearance, behaviour, structure and mode of life make it well-suited to survive in a particular habitat.

**Appearance** will include ways in which it is camouflaged from its enemies. **Behaviour** will include not only the ways in which it hides from enemies but also, for example, ways in which it avoids extremes of temperature. **Structure** covers all the various parts of the organism – both its internal structure and the parts that we can see. And **mode of life** is concerned with how it feeds, breathes, moves, reproduces, etc. All of the adaptations help it to survive in its habitat – to live with the particular environmental factors and to make its food if it is a plant, or to get its food and escape its predators if it is an animal.

The habitat of the organism may, for example be a mangrove swamp, a sandy shore, a rocky shore or a fresh-water pond. Or, in the case of parasites, the habitat might be inside another organism. In each habitat there will be particular factors at work, and the organism will have to be adapted to them in order to survive. The caterpillar in Figure 1 is a particularly striking example of adaptation. However, *all* living things are adapted, though it may not always be obvious (Investigation 1). Every organism must be adapted if it is to survive.

## Shape, colour and pattern

Most animals are clearly adapted in their external appearance, but none more so than insects. Some insects are wonderfully camouflaged. Many of them are the same colour as their background. Others have the same colour and shape as objects like leaves, twigs, thorns and even flowers (Figure 2). In this way they avoid being seen by other animals.

Some moths have false 'eyes' on their wings (Figure 3). These markings frighten other animals away. Do you think they have any other function?

Some insects with distinctive markings taste unpleasant. Animals such as birds learn to recognise these markings, and they avoid eating these particular insects. Some insects which taste nice have the same markings as those that do not. So predators will avoid *these* insects too. This is known as **mimicry**, and it is a good means of defence.

## Plants that feed on animals

We usually think that animals feed on plants, but there are some plants that feed on animals. The plants are adapted in different ways to capture small animals, especially insects. The plants may have leaves with sticky hairs, as in sundew, or leaves which close over and trap the insects, as in the Venus fly trap. There are also leaves that are shaped like jars, as in the pitcher plant

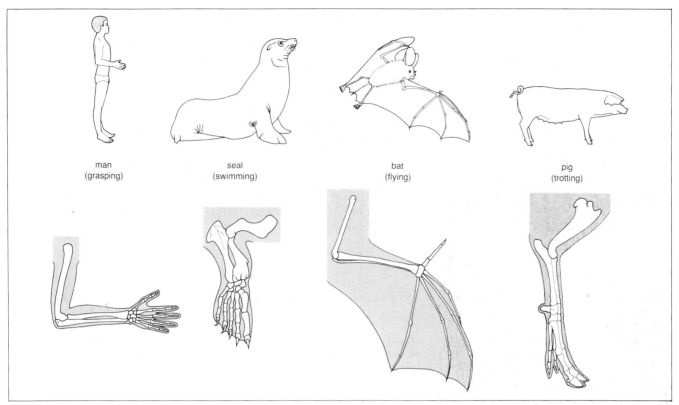

man
(grasping)

seal
(swimming)

bat
(flying)

pig
(trotting)

**Figure 5** These diagrams show how the forelimbs of four different mammals are adapted to carry out different functions.

(Figure 4). The insects fall into the 'jar' and cannot escape again.

The plants pour digestive juices over their prey. Then they absorb the dissolved substances, which are mostly broken-down proteins. The plants are green so that they can make their own carbohydrate food. They may have become adapted to this way of feeding on animals because many of them live in swampy places where the soil is poor in nitrogen-containing substances.

## A detailed look at adaptation: the vertebrate limb

In Figure 5 you can see the forelimbs of four mammals including man. Notice how they differ. In each case, the limb is adapted to do a particular job. For example, in the bat the fingers are greatly lengthened to support the wing, which is used for flying. In contrast the seal has short, flat fingers to support the flipper, which is used in swimming.

Although the limbs illustrated in Figure 5 are all different and are used in different ways, they are all built on the same basic plan. This is illustrated in Figure 6; it is known as the **pentadactyl limb** – the word pentadactyl comes from Greek and literally means 'having five digits' (fingers or toes). This kind of limb is found in amphibians, reptiles, birds and mammals, though in different groups it is adapted to serve different purposes.

Structures which have the same fundamental design, though they may be used for different purposes, are described as **homologous**. The limbs of vertebrates provide a particularly good example of homologous structures, though there are many other examples (Investigation 2).

## Living together as a means of survival

Many organisms are adapted to living inside, or sometimes on the surface of, another organism. The latter is called the **host**. Sometimes the host is harmed in some way, in which case we call the organism a **parasite**. The blood fluke and many fungi are examples of parasites. They feed on the host's tissues and damage them. The blood fluke is an example of a parasite that lives inside its host: we call it an **endoparasite**. Other parasites, such as the head louse, live

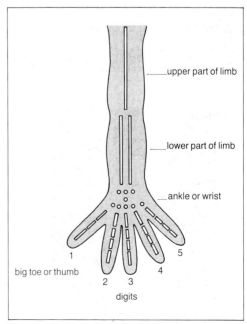

upper part of limb

lower part of limb

ankle or wrist

big toe or thumb

1

5

2

3

4

digits

**Figure 6** The pentadactyl limb with its five digits. The legs of all land-dwelling vertebrates are variations on the basic theme.

**Figure 7A** (upper) White and black peppered moths resting on a light coloured tree trunk.

**Figure 7B** (lower) White and black peppered moths resting on a dark coloured tree trunk.

on the surface of the host: they are called **ectoparasites**. Every parasite is specially adapted to live in or on its particular host, and to spread from one host to another.

A common example of a plant parasite is love-bush. This is adapted in many ways to its parasitic way of life. It consists of long, pinkish-orange threads which twine around bushes and garden shrubs. The stems have suction pads or **haustoria** that actually grow inside the stem of the host and take away food. The parasite depends entirely on its host for food materials and water; the adult plant does not have roots in the soil. It has no chlorophyll and its leaves are very small and do not carry out photosynthesis.

It reproduces by making a large number of small seeds which are dispersed by the wind. When they germinate the new shoots can twist round in a circle and so have a better chance of finding a new host. If a shoot does not find a host, it soon dies because it cannot make its own food. If the seedling is successful it begins to twine around the host and develops haustoria.

Organisms which live in or on the bodies of other organisms don't always harm their hosts. For instance, mosses and lichens grow on the trunks and branches of trees. However, they don't feed on the tree's tissues and they don't damage it in any way. We call these organisms **epiphytes**.

In some cases the organism may actually help its host in some way. For example, a single-celled protist called *Chlorella* lives in the cells of some kinds of coral. The protist gives the coral sugar which it makes by photosynthesis. In return it receives shelter and carbon dioxide from the coral. This kind of relationship is called **symbiosis**. There is no doubt that it can help organisms to survive.

Another example of symbiosis is lichens. A lichen consists of a photosynthetic protist and a fungus living together. The threads of the fungus make up the main part of the lichen, and the protist cells are packed in amongst them. The fungus gains oxygen and food from the photosynthesis of the protist. The protist gains protection from the fungal threads, together with carbon dioxide, water and mineral salts. The association is so intimate that the two partners are regarded as a single organism. It enables lichens to survive in very dry conditions on rocks and tree trunks. The lichens can grow in these places, but neither the fungus nor the protist could grow there separately.

## Does adaptation work?

When you look at an organism you can usually see certain features which *appear* to be useful adaptations. But how can we be sure that a particular feature actually helps the organism to survive?

To answer this let's look at an example from Britain: the peppered moth. There are two forms of this moth: a white form and a black form. In the 1950s a scientist called Bernard Kettlewell studied the distribution of the peppered moth in Britain, and he found that in industrial areas the black form was the more common, whereas in non-industrial areas the white form was the more common.

How can we explain these observations? The peppered moth rests on tree trunks and is fed on by thrushes which peck them off the trees. In non-industrial areas, the tree trunks are usually covered in lichens which are light in colour: against this background the white form of the moth is well camouflaged, whereas the black form shows up clearly (Figure 7A). As a result, the thrushes take mainly the black moths, and the white ones survive. However, in industrial areas the tree trunks are darkened by soot: here the black form of the moth is camouflaged, whereas the white form shows up (Figure 7B). The result is that in these areas the thrushes take mainly the white ones and the black ones survive.

We can sum this up by saying that in industrial areas the black colour is a useful adaptation. On the other hand, in non-industrial areas the white colour is a useful adaptation. So adaptation does work.

# Investigation 1

**Some examples of adaptation**

1 Collect organisms from the environment that appear to show adaptations to their surroundings. You will have to look closely because they may be well camouflaged!

   Good places to look are in leaf litter, under stones and amongst flowering shrubs. At night you may also be able to catch night-flying moths.

2 Examine the various organisms, and pictures of organisms, provided by your teacher.

3 Use the classification on pages 14–19 to find out what group each organism belongs to.

4 Examine each organism carefully, and write down one way in which it appears to be well adapted to its environment.

   In each case explain how you think the adaptation may help it to survive.

# Investigation 2

**An example of homology**

1 Obtain preserved specimens of a grasshopper, butterfly, beetle and housefly.

2 Examine the wings of these animals, the forewings first, and then the hindwings.

3 Draw this table into your notebook:

4 In each box describe the shape and form of each wing, and say what it is used for.

How is the structure of each wing adapted to perform its function?

What other homologous structures can you see in these four insects?

|  | grasshopper | butterfly | beetle | housefly |
|---|---|---|---|---|
| forewing |  |  |  |  |
| hindwing |  |  |  |  |

# Investigation 3

**How are weeds adapted?**

Weeds are wild plants growing where they are not wanted.

1 Find some weeds growing at school or near your home. Look at the way in which the leaves are arranged. Notice that some of them are arranged as rosettes close to the ground. How might this help them to survive?

2 Trace the extent of a single plant. Does it have just one set of roots? If not, how would this help the plant?

3 Look at the flowers and fruits. What are they like?
How would they help to spread the weeds?

4 Try to pull a weed out of the ground. What happens?
Is it easy to pull out the root?
What does this tell you about the way the root is in the soil?

5 Dig up several different kinds of weeds.
What do you notice about their roots, and the other parts that are underneath the ground?
How might they help the plant to survive?

6 Summarise in your own words how weeds are well adapted to survive unfavourable conditions and to produce many new plants.

# Assignments

1 Give one example of how a named animal or plant is adapted to its environment, *excluding* any of the examples given in this Topic.

2 Why is it an advantage to an insect to taste unpleasant?

3 Write down *one* special adaptation which would be needed to enable:
   a) a small mammal to feed on the fruits from the top of a tree,
   b) a lizard to avoid being seen by birds in a sandy desert,
   c) a parasitic worm to live on the gills of a fish,
   d) the leaves of a plant to avoid being eaten by cows,
   e) a fish to be equally at home in fresh water and the sea.

4 Hover flies have yellow stripes and look very like wasps, but they are not wasps at all, they are flies and do not sting.

   Why is it useful to hover flies to look like wasps?

5 The illustration below shows the appearance of a certain moth, viewed from above when at rest. Of what possible value might its shape and markings be?

Describe further observations which could be carried out to test your suggestion.

6 Fifty black mice and fifty white mice were released into an area inhabited by a pair of owls. After four months the mice in the area were recaptured: only 38 black and 9 white mice remained.

   How would you explain this result?
What further experiments could you do to find out if your explanation is correct?

   Suggest two ways in which owls are well adapted for hunting.

# Social insects

*Certain insects live together in an organised society or colony. This helps them to survive in their environment. We call them social insects.*

Figure 1 Termites living in wood. On the right is a worker. At the top is a soldier. At the left is a reproductive with wing pads. Eggs and nymphs can also be seen.

## Termites

A large termite nest can contain over a million termites. At the head of it is the **queen**, who is very much larger than the others and is best described as an egg-laying machine. Queen termites have been observed to lay 30 000 to 80 000 eggs in one day.

The queen has a consort, the **king**, who is much smaller. He mates with her at the founding of the colony and at regular intervals afterwards. The colony is therefore one enormous family (Figures 1 and 4).

Many of the termites have wing pads (developing wings) on their backs. These are the **reproductives**, males and females who will be able to found new colonies (Figures 1 and 4).

The majority of termites are wingless workers. These may be either male or female, but they are not able to mate or reproduce. Their job is to build and repair the nest, feed all the other termites, and rear the young; in short, to do all the work.

There are also large numbers of soldiers which protect the nest. They either squirt out a sticky liquid to entrap intruders, or they attack them with their huge mandibles.

Figure 2 These termites have built their nest in a tree. Notice the covered tunnels coming from the nest.

### The structure of the nest

Different kinds of termites live in different kinds of nests. Some simply burrow underground or tunnel out cavities inside timber or wood. Others make their nests in trees (Figure 2) or build elaborate **termitaria** (Figure 5). These are common in Africa and Australia and in parts of Central and South America.

The nests provide protection against enemies and a controlled environment with a fairly constant temperature and humidity. This is an advantage to the community and to the developing young. The nest consists of a labyrinth of galleries (Figure 3). It is made of soil which is cemented together with saliva and sets to a rock-like consistency which is hard to break even with a pick-axe or spade.

Figure 3 These termites have built a mound, which has been opened. You can see the galleries, with the queen in the centre.

### What do termites eat?

The majority of termites eat wood in one form or another, others eat grass or plant debris, while a few set up **fungus gardens** where they grow fungi which they use as food.

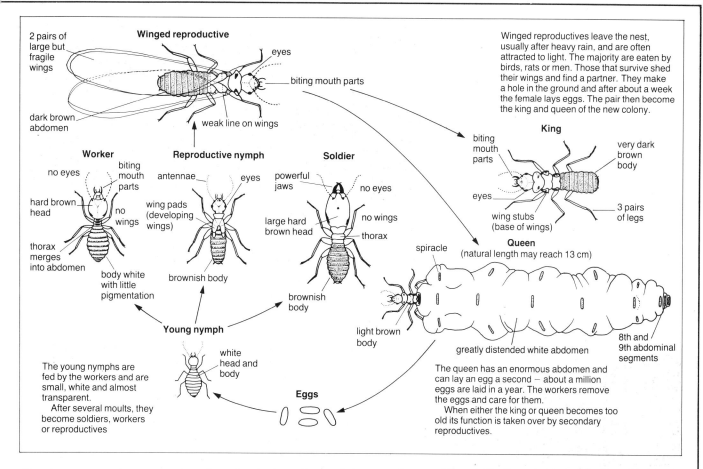

**Figure 4** The life cycle of a termite. Start with the king and queen and work round, the cycle in a clockwise direction.

Termites are poorly protected against the drying effects of the sun. So when the workers go in search of food they avoid the daylight and build covered tunnels in which they travel.

The main constituent of wood is cellulose, but this the termites cannot digest. Within the intestine of the workers lives the protist *Trichonympha* which assists in the digestion of the cellulose. The workers then feed the other termites in the nest.

## Producing new colonies

The foundation of new termite colonies starts at the beginning of the wet season. At this time the soil will be soft and damp. Some of the winged reproductives escape and fly off. When their flight is over they shed their wings and find a partner. They can often be caught in water under a light, and as they walk around the floor they look like a pair of walking sausages. The pair find a suitable location and set up home (Figure 4).

Unlike other social insects, such as bees, wasps and ants, what hatches out from the egg is a **nymph** (see page 281). This is a miniature version of the adult. The nymphs grow and moult, and become either workers, soldiers or reproductives. At the next wet season the cycle is repeated.

## Economic importance

Termites feed on wood and do great damage to wooden parts of houses and to trees. But they do also feed on fallen leaves and dead tree trunks and help to change these into humus which enriches the soil. And as they tunnel through the ground they help to aerate it. In addition, the soil from abandoned nests can be used in farming and for making bricks.

**Figure 5** Some termites live in large mounds which stick up from the surface of the ground.

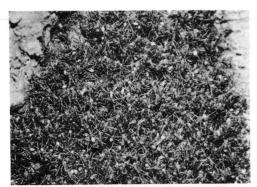

**Figure 6** A bivouac or temporary nest of driver ants. It is made up of living ants.

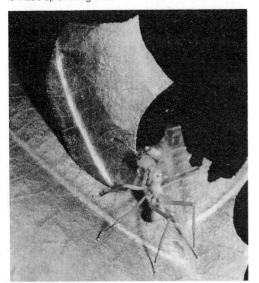

**Figure 7** Leaf-cutting ant, Maracas bay, Trinidad.

**Figure 8** Pastoral ants tending their small aphid 'cows'. The ant strokes an aphid which produces a drop of honeydew.

# Ants

There is a great variety of ants, from the sugar ants to the biting red ants and the carnivorous driver ants. They live in different kinds of nests: in the ground, in old termite nests, or in trees. Some of them, for example the tailor ants, join leaves together to form their nest.

They all form colonies, and they have the most complex social system of all insects. The head of the colony is the **queen**, and she lays the eggs. She is mated once by a male when the colony is first set up and these sperms last her for ten years or more. The **workers** usually are of two sizes. The larger ones have large, strong mandibles and are called **soldiers**. They guard the nest, and workers coming in must first be recognised by the touching of antennae.

The nest has several chambers. The queen lives in one and lays eggs. These are taken by workers to be hatched and then moved to the nursery. They become larvae and then pupae. Other chambers have stores of food such as seeds which the workers have collected. If the nest is disturbed the workers pick up the eggs and larvae in their jaws and move them to safety.

## Driver ants or army ants

These ants are nomads which make a temporary nest or **bivouac** (Figure 6). The bivouac is made in a hollow tree or on the ground underneath a fallen branch. It consists mainly of living ants linked to each other to form layers. Inside are the queen and the larvae.

In the daytime some of the ants form into a column and set out into the countryside. They are feared, because they will eat any animals which get in their way. They put down chemicals so that they can slavishly follow the same direction of the column. They retrace their steps in the evening.

The bivouac stays in place for about three weeks while the queen may lay up to 300 000 eggs and a new generation is produced. By then the nearby countryside has also been exhausted. Scouts go ahead to seek out a new home and then the column sets off. The queen leaves last, protected by a crowd of soldiers. Young queens and males are produced and these may go off with a group of ants to set up a new colony.

## Leaf-cutter ants

These ants are farmers. First they set up their farm. A trail of ants sets out for a nearby mango or orange tree. The ants divide into working parties which cut up each leaf in turn into small pieces that can be carried (Figure 7). These are taken back to the nest where they are cut into smaller pieces and chewed so as to help them to decay more quickly.

The smaller pieces of leaf are added to the layer of rotting leaves which forms the vegetable plot. On this the ants grow a fungus, some of which was brought by their queen from the last colony. As the fungus grows it produces tiny swellings on which the ants feed. Extra-small worker ants look after the gardens, keeping them clean and removing any unwanted materials.

## Pastoral ants

These ants keep 'cows' and 'milk' them. Their 'cows' are aphids which feed on plant juices. The aphids produce a milk called **honeydew**. An ant goes up to an aphid which is full of honeydew and strokes it with her antennae. The aphid responds by passing out a droplet of honeydew which the ant eats (Figure 8). This continues until the ant is satisfied and returns to its nest.

The aphids also benefit because they are protected from enemies by the presence of the ants. If there is danger the ants drive away the intruders with a spray of formic acid, and may pick up and carry the aphids to safety.

The greatest extreme is found in some ants that take aphids into their underground nests. These aphids feed on the roots of plants while the ants regularly milk them of their honeydew.

Now you can see how advanced the colonies of ants are!

# The honey bee

A large hive may contain more than 50 000 bees. As with termites, they are all descended from the **queen**. Her only job is to lay eggs.

Several hundred male bees may be present in the hive. These are called **drones**. Their only job is to mate with a queen.

The remaining bees are **workers**. They are sterile females which cannot reproduce. Their job is to look after the hive, feed the queen and the drones, rear the young and protect the hive.

## What is honey?

Honey is the main food that bees live on. It is made by the workers from **nectar**, the sugary fluid found in flowers (see page 288). When a worker visits a flower, it sucks up the nectar with its tongue-like proboscis, and stores it in its stomach. In the stomach the nectar is turned into honey.

When the bee returns to the hive, it regurgitates the honey into one of the cells of the comb. The worker then closes the cell with a wax lid. Honey is stored in the comb for use later on.

Man can take honey from bees because they normally make far more than they need. In a man-made hive, the bees construct their combs inside wooden frames. The top ones, where the honey is stored, can be taken out.

## Defending the hive

A worker on guard duty stands at the entrance of the hive, looking out for wasps, mice and other animals which might come to the hive to steal honey.

The worker's main weapon is its sting. This is a sharp needle-like tube with a poison sac at the base. The sting has tiny barbs sticking out of it, like a fish hook, so when the bee has used its sting it cannot pull it out. The result is that when the bee flies away, the sting gets left behind. Unfortunately for the bee, part of its gut gets left behind too, so it dies soon afterwards.

The queen bee has no barbs on her sting, so it does not stay in the victim's body and can be used again. The same applies to wasp stings.

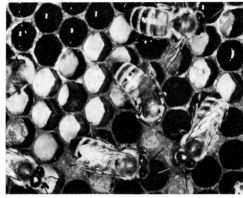

Figure 9 Worker bees in a hive.

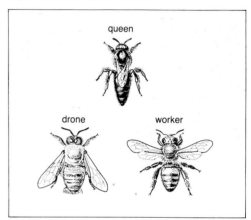

Figure 10 The three types of individual found in a bee colony. Each has its own job to do.

# Investigation 1

**Looking at termites**

1 Search for where termites live. Good places to look are up in trees, near rotting wood and in termite mounds.

2 Do *not* break open or destroy the whole nest.
Simply find some of the covered passage ways leading from the nest and break open a part of this.

3 Collect some of the termites in a plastic bag and return them to the laboratory.

4 Identify the workers and soldiers. Describe the ways in which they are adapted for the jobs they have to perform.

5 If available, examine preserved specimens of the queen termite. How is she adapted for her job?

# Investigation 2

**Looking at ants**

1 In the evening leave out a small bowl containing some sugar.
In the morning collect some of the sugar ants and describe their appearance.

2 Search in the garden, especially in places where the soil is moist or has been recently dug up. You may see a place where the soil looks more 'crumbly' and loose. This may be an ant nest.

3 Proceed with care. Some ants can give a nasty bite.
Collect some ants in a plastic bag and return them to the laboratory. Describe how the ants behaved when they were disturbed.

4 Set up a display area for your ants which includes some soft earth and a source of food.
Describe how the ants behave.

# Assignments

1 Explain each of the following:

reproductives
termitaria
nymph
bivouac

2 How does the organisation of a termite nest compare with the organisation of a human society such as a town?

3 Choose one kind of ant. Compare how it carries out its activities with humans carrying out similar activities.

4 Drone bees have been described as 'lazy, stupid, fat and greedy'.

Do you think this is a fair description?

5 Give *three* examples of how social insects are adapted to survive in their environment.

# What is soil?

*Soil is the surface of the earth's crust where plants have their roots and where many small animals make their homes. As the soil directly affects the growth of plants, it is of the utmost importance to man.*

**Figure 1** The way the soil is made up of layers can be seen from this photograph. The depth shown is about 1 metre.

## How is soil formed?

Thousands of millions of years ago, the land was covered with bare rock. Gradually the surface of the rock was broken up by rain, wind, snow and frost into small particles. These particles were gradually piled up on top of the rock to form soil.

If you look at a cliff or a new motorway cutting, you will see that the soil is made up of layers (Figure 1). At the top is a dark layer where plants and other organisms live. We call this the **topsoil**: it is formed by surface weathering and the activities of the many organisms which live in it, and it contains the decaying remains of dead organisms. It may be covered with dead leaves; this is called **leaf litter**.

Beneath the topsoil is a lighter-coloured layer of gravel, stones, clay and so on. This is called the **subsoil**. It contains the deeper roots of large plants, like trees, but otherwise not much lives there.

Further down still is solid **rock**. This is non-porous and won't let rain through, so water tends to gather above it. The surface of this water is called the **water table**.

These three layers are shown diagrammatically in Figure 2. Their relative thicknesses, and the position of the water table, vary a great deal from place to place.

## What does soil consist of?

### Rock particles

These vary in size. Depending on their size, they are classified into clay, silt, sand and gravel (Figure 3). Clay particles are so small that they can only be seen properly under the microscope. At the other extreme, gravel consists of small stones which can be separated from the rest of the soil by sieving.

The smaller soil particles can be separated from each other by shaking up a sample of soil with some water and letting it stand (Investigation 1). The sand sinks to the bottom, but the tiny clay particles remain suspended in the water above the sand.

Rock particles make up the framework of the soil, its 'skeleton' as it were. Both clay and sand are important in this respect. Clay holds on to water better than sand, thus making it sticky and helping to bind the rest of the soil together. On the other hand, sand is looser and more easily penetrated by air and water. Good soil consists of a mixture of the two: this is called **loam**. Loam contains roughly twice as much sand as clay.

If you look at some good garden soil you will notice that the particles are stuck together in small clumps (Investigation 2). These are called **soil crumbs**: they make the soil coarser, helping air to get into it and water to drain through it.

### Humus

When animals and plants die in the soil, their dead bodies gradually decay into a sticky jam-like liquid called **humus**. The layer of soil where most humus is found is the topsoil. Much of it comes from the leaf litter on the surface. Humus is black, so soil that contains a lot of it tends to be a dark colour. For the gardener one of the best sources of humus is compost (see page 389).

Humus makes the soil rich in nutrients which are needed for plant growth. It also forms a sticky coating round the soil particles, helping them to clump together into soil crumbs. Humus stores water and prevents valuable nutrients being washed out of the soil when it rains. It also helps to insulate the soil against extremes of heat and cold. In good soil humus takes up about a tenth of the total volume (Investigation 6).

For material to rot completely, oxygen is needed. If there is not enough oxygen, it accumulates into a thick carpet of half-decayed material called **peat**. If peat is added to well-aerated soil it will decay into humus.

## Soil water

Soil particles are normally surrounded by a thin film of water. It is from these films that plant roots take up all the water they need. Unless the soil is excessively dry, these films are always present. What ensures that this is so? Let's answer this by thinking what happens after a heavy shower of rain.

The rain sinks down into the soil, wetting the soil particles. Eventually it reaches the water table. The roots of plants absorb water from the films surrounding the soil particles, and some water also evaporates from the surface of the soil. But as quickly as water is lost this way, more is drawn up from lower down. If you don't believe this, try doing Investigation 3.

The process which causes this is **capillary action**. It is the same process that causes water, or ink, to spread through a piece of blotting paper, or to rise in a narrow capillary tube.

For water to move through the soil like this, the soil particles must be the right size. If they are too large, water will sink straight through and will not be pulled up. Such soil is useless: not only does it fail to hold water, but useful nutrients are washed out of it as the water sinks through. This is called **leaching**. On the other hand, if the soil particles are too small and tightly packed, water cannot get through – it just stays on top or flows off the surface.

You can find out how much water is present in a sample of soil by doing Investigation 4. In good, well-watered soil the water should take up about a quarter of the total volume.

If there is very heavy rain and the drainage is poor, the soil may become full of water. It is then **waterlogged**. Waterlogged soil is short of oxygen, so roots cannot breathe properly. In swamps and bogs the soil is waterlogged all the time. Only certain kinds of plants will grow in these conditions.

## Mineral salts

Dissolved in the soil water are various mineral salts. These provide plants with important elements such as nitrogen, phosphorus and potassium, and they are essential for growth.

Some mineral salts come from the rock which formed the soil. They may give the soil a particular colour: for example, bauxite soils usually appear red because they also contain iron salts. Other minerals, such as nitrogen salts, are formed when humus breaks down. This is why humus is so good for plants.

## Lime

Lime comes from limestone, a type of rock which contains **chalk**. Chalk is calcium carbonate. All good soil contains a certain amount of this important chemical substance. You can find out if a sample of soil contains chalk by adding acid to it; bubbles of carbon dioxide will be formed.

Lime is important for three main reasons: (1) Calcium is one of the elements which all plants need for proper growth and development. (2) Lime helps soil particles to clump together into soil crumbs. (3) Lime is alkaline, and this prevents the soil being too acidic: in gardeners' language it prevents the soil being 'sour'.

We can express how acidic or alkaline the soil is by a number called the pH. These numbers are arranged in a scale running from 0 to 14. A pH of 7.0 is neutral – neither acidic nor alkaline. A pH of less than 7.0 indicates acidity, and above 7.0 indicates alkalinity. You can do a simple test on samples of soil to find out their pH (Investigation 5).

Most plants grow best in soil which is round about neutral. However, some plants like alkaline soil, and others like acidic soil.

## Soil air

In good soil there are plenty of spaces between the soil particles and crumbs. These spaces are filled with air. The oxygen in this air is needed for respiration by plant roots and the other organisms which live in the soil.

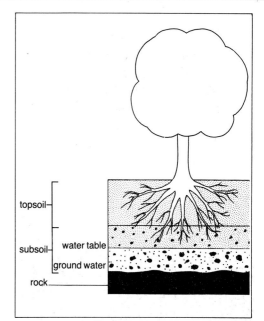

**Figure 2** Sectional view of the earth's crust to show the different layers of soil and other materials.

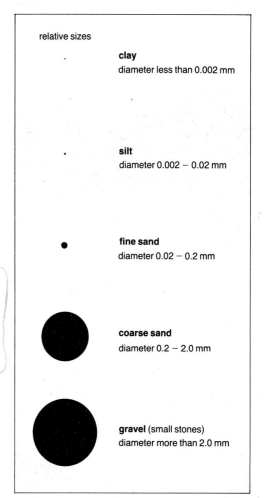

**Figure 3** The different kinds of particles which make up soil.

**Figure 4** Sheet erosion. A layer of soil is removed from all over the surface of the soil.

**Figure 5** Gully erosion. Water has gradually removed more and more soil to form deep gullies.

Oxygen is also needed for material to decay into humus – this is because the microbes responsible for decay are aerobic.

You can find out how much air is present in a sample of soil by the method given in Investigation 8. In good soil about a quarter of the volume is taken up by air.

If the soil particles are too tightly packed together, or if the soil is waterlogged, the amount of oxygen will be lowered, and few organisms will be able to live there.

## Different kinds of soil

You often hear people say that the soil in their garden is dreadful. There are many different types of soil, some good, some bad. Here are the main types:

### Sandy soil

As the name implies, this kind of soil contains mainly sand. Sandy soil is loose, light and easy to dig: think how easy it is to dig sand on a beach. It contains plenty of air, and it drains well. However, it is a cold type of soil because it readily loses heat. It dries up quickly in hot weather, and useful chemicals are washed out of it when it rains. So sandy soil is not very fertile.

If you have a garden with sandy soil you should add humus to it. As well as putting goodness into the soil, the humus helps to bind the sand together. It also holds on to water when it rains.

You can prevent sandy soil from drying up by spreading a layer of dead leaves, peat or manure over the surface. This is called **mulching** and it also helps to keep the soil warm.

### Clay soil

This kind of soil contains a lot of clay. It holds on to water and nutrients very well, so it tends to be rich in plant food. However, it is extremely heavy and difficult to dig, being sticky when wet and hard when dry. The soil particles are held together so tightly that there is little room for air in between. Rain, rather than draining through it, runs off the top.

If you have a lot of clay in your garden, you should add lime to it. This causes the particles of clay to clump together into soil crumbs, a process known as **flocculation**. This breaks up the soil, making the particles bigger, getting air to it and draining it. Clay soils can also be improved by the addition of humus, which is spongy and helps air to get into the soil. It also adds nutrients to the soil and improves its texture.

### Chalky soil

This kind of soil contains a lot of lime. It is therefore very alkaline. As chalky soil comes from calcareous rock, it looks rather white.

Chalky soil is usually rather clayey and therefore difficult to cultivate. If you have chalky soil in your garden, the best thing is to add humus to it. This makes it more acidic, and helps to break it up. Although most garden plants dislike a lot of chalk, many wild flowers thrive on it.

### Peaty soil

This kind of soil contains a lot of peat. Although peat is useful, too much of it can make the soil acidic. Most plants dislike this kind of soil, though some like it. If you have this sort of soil in your garden you should add plenty of lime to it.

### The ideal soil

The best soil is a balanced mixture of sand, clay, humus and lime. What should their proportions be? Good garden soil should contain roughly: 50 per cent sand, 30 per cent clay, 12 per cent humus, and 8 per cent lime.

## Soil erosion

The washing away of the surface layers of the soil is called **soil erosion**. It is caused when heavy rains fall onto unprotected ground.

When plants are present their roots hold the soil together. Their leaves also break up the rain drops so that they do not fall with as much force onto the ground. Soil with plants also contains humus which can absorb a lot of water.

Plants are removed by man cutting them down for timber or by harvesting his crops. Animals such as cows and goats may eat the plants more quickly than they can grow back again. This is called **overgrazing**. When plants are removed the earth is unprotected from the drying effect of the sun and becomes hard and cracked.

Especially during the dry season the unprotected ground is affected by the wind. Strong winds can blow away part of the surface soil. When the rains come a lot of water falls at once and with a lot of force. It falls faster than it can be absorbed by the soil. It therefore runs off the surface, and takes part of the soil with it.

Erosion usually begins as a shallow layer of soil is removed all over the surface. This is called **sheet erosion** (Figure 4). As more rain falls it accumulates in furrows at the sides of paths, down ridges and where the soil is softer. These furrows become deeper and deeper as the rain runs down them. More soil is removed, and so fewer plants can grow. And so more soil is removed. This goes on and on and we eventually get **gully erosion** (Figure 5).

## Soil conservation

How can we stop erosion occurring? There are several ways.

### Cover the ground with plants
We have seen how important the plants are. The advice is never to leave the ground uncovered. If a crop has been planted in rows and there is bare ground in between, another plant should be put there. This is called **inter-cropping**. For example cassava, which has deep roots, can be grown in amongst maize, which has shallow roots.

When a crop is harvested the ground must not be left exposed. Uncovered ground will be affected by the rain and the wind (page 396). There must be a **rotation of crops** with different ones being grown each year. This has the advantage of covering the ground, and also making use of the different nutrients in the soil. A leguminous crop such as groundnuts is especially useful. This has root nodules and increases the amount of nitrogenous substances in the soil (page 29). The crop may also be ploughed into the ground as green manure.

The earth between plants in the garden should be covered with dried grass. This stops erosion. It also reduces the number of weeds and helps to keep moisture in the ground.

### Build terraces on sloping ground
Erosion occurs particularly easily on the side of a hill. The water quickly makes furrows and runs down, taking the soil with it.

One method of protection is to make **terraces** (Figure 6). Piles of stones are laid along the side of the hill, and behind them the soil is built up. The surface of the soil is now in many flat parts and the crop can be planted. If water tries to run down the hill it is taken up by the soil and the plants in the top terraces and cannot cause so much damage.

### Use contour ploughing
Look at Figure 7. The top part shows that the ploughing has been done so that ridges run *down* the hill. You can imagine what will happen! (see Investigation 7.) In the bottom part of Figure 7 the ploughing has been done *around* the hill. It has followed the contours of the land and is called **contour ploughing.** As water runs down the hill it is stopped by the rows of plants that are put in along the contours. Figure 8 is a photograph that shows how contour ploughing can be used.

Figure 6 Terracing has converted this hillside into a series of flat farmlands which can be used more easily.

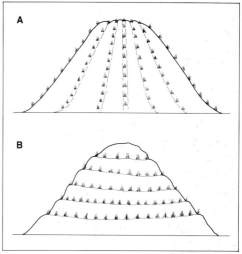

Figure 7 Two ways of ploughing a hillside. A increases erosion of the soil, B is contour ploughing.

Figure 8 Contour ploughing.

# Investigation 1

## Separating the components of soil

1 Quarter fill a large test tube with soil.

2 Add water until the tube is three-quarters full. Notice that air bubbles are given off: what does this tell you?

3 Put your hand over the open end of the tube, and shake well.

4 Put the tube in a rack, and let the soil settle. The heaviest components of the soil will sink to the bottom, the lighter ones will float at various levels.

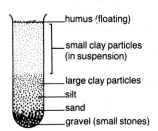

humus (floating)

small clay particles (in suspension)

large clay particles
silt
sand
gravel (small stones)

Does the appearance of your test tube agree with the illustration?

5 Repeat this experiment with different kinds of soil and compare the amounts of the different components in each.

# Investigation 2

## Looking at soil crumbs

1 Obtain some good garden topsoil. Look at it, and feel it with your fingers, then describe it as fully as you can.

2 Notice that the soil is composed of numerous small particles. Some of the particles may be separate, but others are clumped together into soil crumbs.

3 Put a soil crumb on a sheet of paper, and squash it with your finger. What

makes the particles stick together?

4 Look at the roots of a plant which has been pulled out of the soil. What causes the soil to cling to the roots? How are the roots connected to the soil crumbs?

Soil crumbs make the soil better for plant growth – why?

Make a list of all the features of the soil which, directly or indirectly, help plants to grow in it.

# Investigation 3

## To see if water moves upwards through soil

1 Obtain a wide glass tube, about 20 cm long.

2 Plug one end of the tube with glass wool.

3 Hold the tube upright with the glass wool end downwards.

4 Fill the tube with dry soil above the glass wool.

5 Scatter some seeds on the surface of the soil at the top of the tube (rattleweed seeds will do).

6 Set the tube up so that the lower end is dipping into a dish of water. Note the time.

7 Observe the tube at intervals, watching to see if the water rises through the soil.

8 Note the time when the seeds start germinating.

How long after setting up the apparatus do the seeds start to germinate?

Do they germinate as soon as the water reaches them?

9 Repeat this experiment with different kinds of soil, and compare how long it takes for water to rise through them.

What should the control be in this experiment?

# Investigation 4

## To find out how much water there is in soil

1 Half fill a small crucible with soil.

2 Weigh the soil and crucible.

3 Put the soil and crucible in an oven at about 100°C for at least 30 minutes. The water in the soil should evaporate.

4 Put the soil in a desiccator and let it cool down.

5 Re-weigh the soil and crucible.

6 Repeat steps 3 to 5 until you get no further change in mass.

What is the difference in the mass of the soil before and after drying it?

Do you agree that this is the mass of the water in the soil sample?

What percentage of the soil is taken up by water?

7 Repeat this experiment with two soil samples, one taken after a period of dry weather, the other after heavy rain.

# Investigation 5

## To find out how acidic or alkaline soil is

1 Put a little soil in a test tube and cover it with distilled water.

2 Put your thumb over the end of the test tube, and shake it vigorously.

3 Obtain a piece of pH paper.

4 Dip the pH paper into the water. What colour does it go?

5 Compare the colour of the paper with the colour code supplied by the manufacturer.

6 What is the pH of the soil sample?

Is the soil sample acidic, alkaline or neutral?

7 Repeat this experiment with different kinds of soil and compare their pH.

# Investigation 6

**To find out how much humus there is in soil**

1 Half fill a small crucible with soil.

2 Dry the soil by putting it in an oven at about 100°C for at least 30 minutes.

3 Put the soil in a desiccator and let it cool down.

4 Weigh the dry soil and crucible.

5 Repeat steps 2 to 4 until you get no further change in mass.

6 Place the crucible of soil on a wire gauze on a tripod, and put a bunsen burner underneath.

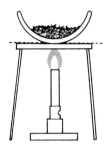

7 Light the bunsen burner and heat the crucible with a strong flame for 15–20 minutes. The humus will burn up into carbon dioxide gas and water vapour.

8 Put the soil back in a desiccator and let it cool down.

9 Re-weigh the soil and crucible.

10 Repeat steps 6 to 8 until you find no further change in mass.

What is the difference in the mass of the dry soil before and after burning it?

Do you agree that this is the mass of the humus in the soil sample?

What percentage of the soil consists of humus?

11 Repeat this experiment with different kinds of soil, and compare the percentages of humus in them.

# Investigation 7

**To find ways to reduce soil erosion**

*Method 1*

1 Fill a flat tin with soil.
Into a similar tin put a block of turf (soil which has a covering of grass).

2 Lift up one side of each tin so that they are slanted.

3 Pour water onto the raised end of each tin so that it runs downwards over the soil.
Describe what happens in each case.

What conditions might cause erosion and how could it be reduced?

*Method 2*

1 Stick some long pieces of paper towelling on the blackboard.

2 Dash some water onto the blackboard above the top piece of paper.

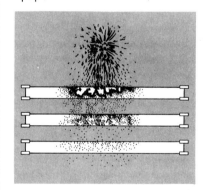

The paper strips represent terraces or ridges of plants that absorb water. How could they help to reduce erosion?

*Method 3*

1 Build up several mounds of topsoil of about the same size.
Pack them down tightly.

2 Now make lines or furrows in them as shown in Figure 7. In some mounds make furrows that run downwards, and in others make them run around in circles.

3 Pour equal amounts of water on the mounds.
Describe what happens.

Which arrangement is the way to do contour ploughing?

# Investigation 8

**To find out how much air there is in soil**

1 Use a 100 cm³ measuring cylinder.

2 Put soil into the cylinder up to the 50 cm³ mark.

3 Tap the cylinder on the bench so that the soil is bedded down.

4 Run water slowly into the cylinder from a tap until it reaches the 100 cm³ mark.

5 Stir the soil and water gently so as to dislodge all the air bubbles from between the soil particles.

6 Note the new level of the water.

What is the difference between the new level of the water, and the original level?

Do you agree that this is the amount of air in the sample of soil?

What percentage of the soil consists of air?

In what ways is this method of measuring soil air inaccurate?
How could the method be improved?

# Assignments

1  a) You put a potted plant on a saucer and pour some water onto the surface of the soil, but none of the water comes through. What has happened to it?
   b) Some people water their potted plants by standing the pots in a saucer of water. Will this work? Explain your answer fully.

2  On a certain mountain top the soil is only a few centimetres thick, whereas in a forest at the foot of the mountain the soil is about twenty metres thick.
Suggest two reasons for the difference.

3  a) Describe the causes of erosion.
   b) Describe, with the help of diagrams, *two* ways in which man can reduce the chance of erosion.
   c) What advice would you give to a farmer who has a field on the side of a steep hill?

# Life in the soil

*The soil
provides a home
for many different organisms and
they can greatly affect
its quality.*

## Organisms in the soil

When we look at soil, the organisms that we notice first are the plants. The main effect which plants have on the soil is to hold it together. We can see that this is the case, because if the plants are removed the soil is washed away and erosion occurs. The plants also provide a home for insect larvae and for parasitic fungi and worms.

The soil contains numerous organisms that we cannot see with the naked eye. It contains vast numbers of bacteria and fungi which help it to support life. These bacteria cause decay and enable carbon and nitrogen compounds to circulate in nature (see pages 27 and 28). Some soil bacteria and fungi are harmful because they use materials in the soil that the plants need.

Some quite large animals live in the soil, for example earthworms, caterpillars, beetle larvae and adults, millipedes and centipedes. However, most soil animals are small and you have to use special methods for collecting them. One commonly used method depends on the fact that soil animals do not like light and move away from it. You obtain some soil and shine a light on it so as to drive out the animals (Investigation 1).

Having got the animals out of the soil, you can look at them in detail and use a key to identify them (Figure 1).

**Figure 1** Key to invertebrate animals found in the soil.

| Identification | | Appearance, habitat and feeding | | | Identification | | Appearance, habitat and feeding | | |
|---|---|---|---|---|---|---|---|---|---|
| Three pairs of true legs | Insect larvae | No false legs on abdomen | **Beetle larvae** 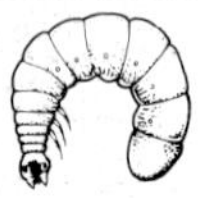 | Active burrowers Many feed on plants, some scavengers | No legs | No segments | No shell Small, long and thin | **Nematodes** | In soil water Parasites, predators and decomposers |
| | | False legs on abdomen | **Caterpillars** 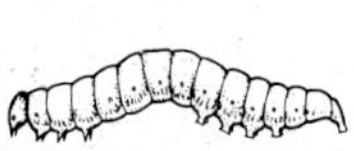 | Spaces in soil Mainly non-feeding pupae in soil | | Segments | Less than 14 segments | **Fly larvae** | Pore spaces Many parasitic, others decomposers |
| | | Less than 0.5cm long with 'spring' | **Springtails** 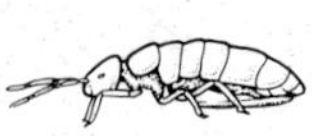 | Pore spaces Eat decomposing plants | | | 14 or more segments | **Earthworms** | Active burrowers Eat decaying plant material |
| | Insect adults | Hard head, Pale body Workers white | **Termites** 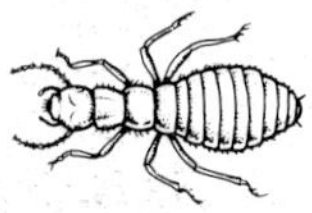 | Active burrowers Eat decaying wood | 4 pairs of legs | | Body not clearly divided into two parts | **Mites** | Pore spaces Attack earthworms and nematodes |
| | | Hard wing covers meet in middle | **Beetles** 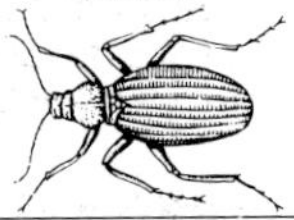 | Active burrowers Attack plants and animals | | | Body clearly divided into two parts | **Spiders** | Leaf litter, soil spaces & under stones Scavenge dead material |
| | | 'Waist' between thorax and abdomen | **Ants** 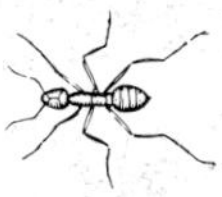 | Active burrowers Feed on small animals, and plants | 7 pairs of legs | | Flattened body | **Woodlice** | Leaf litter, soil spaces & under stones Scavenge dead material |
| No legs | No segments | Shell. Body with tentacles | **Snails**  | Leaf litter, upper soil or under stones Feed on leaf litter | Many pairs of legs | | Each segment with 2 pairs of legs | **Millipedes**  | Leaf litter & spaces Eat decaying plants, break down humus |
| | | No shell. Body with tentacles | **Slugs** | Leaf litter, upper soil or under stones Feed on leaf litter | | | Each segment with 1 pair of legs | **Centipedes**  | Leaf litter & spaces Feed on small animals |

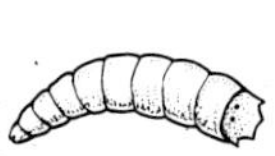

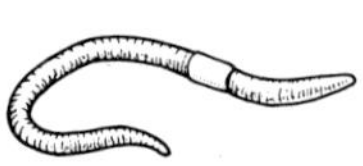

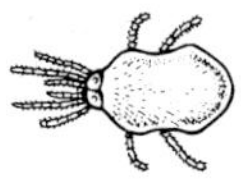

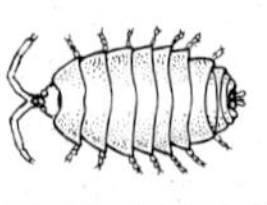

## A helpful animal: the earthworm

There may be over two million earthworms in a hectare of good garden soil.

Like other soil animals earthworms don't like light, so during the day they live underground in their burrows (Figure 2). Here they eat soil, grinding it up in their gut. Any undigested particles are then passed out through the anus onto the surface of the ground as **worm castings**.

At night worms come out of their burrows and feed on dead leaves which they pull down into the soil. If you go out into a garden with a torch, you may see the worms lying on the ground. Tread softly because the slightest vibration will make them jerk back into their burrows.

Earthworms are rare in places that have droughts and so they are often difficult to find in hard, dry soils in the tropics. They are also rare in waterlogged or acid soils, and are most plentiful in moist, loose soil.

The earthworm that is found in tropical and subtropical soils is *Pheretima*, which is pink in colour with a dark mid-dorsal stripe (its dorsal blood vessel). It is about 15 cm long when mature.

You can find out the effect which earthworms have on the soil by building a wormery (Investigation 2).

## How do earthworms improve the soil?

### 1 They turn it over

By constantly burrowing through the soil, they loosen it and mix it up. This helps to drain and aerate it, and it ensures that the various nutrients are evenly spread out. In this way worms do what a gardener does when he digs his garden. It has been estimated that in one hectare, worms may turn over as much as 50 tonnes of soil in a year.

### 2 They fertilise it

Worm castings contain nitrogenous waste which makes them very fertile. They also contain calcium carbonate which helps to make the soil less acidic. Worms also help to fertilise the soil by pulling leaves into it: once buried the leaves quickly decay and useful nutrients are released from them. The worms add further goodness to the soil when they themselves die and decay.

### 3 They make it finer

Having been ground up in the worm's gut, worm castings are very fine. Seeds get covered with this fine soil, which protects them and helps them to germinate successfully. And when the young roots emerge they can push their way easily through it.

## Some harmful soil organisms

Unfortunately the soil contains a number of organisms which are a nuisance to farmers and gardeners. Various insect larvae eat the roots of plants and do a lot of damage. These include the larvae of certain beetles (Figure 3) and weevils. Millipedes can also be harmful, and so can certain nematodes (page 347). Spores of parasitic fungi (page 349) also rest in the soil and attack plants.

Various poisons can be used to kill these pests. These are available as powders which can be dug into the soil before planting, or they can be dissolved in water and sprayed onto the soil.

## Termites and the soil

It is sometimes difficult to decide whether an animal is useful or harmful. Take the termite, for example. Like earthworms they burrow in the soil and help to turn it over, keeping it loose and aerated. They also break down decaying wood and so assist in the formation of humus. The disadvantage comes when they turn their attention to living plants such as young trees. And they also eat wood which man does not wish to have eaten – like that which forms the framework of his house.

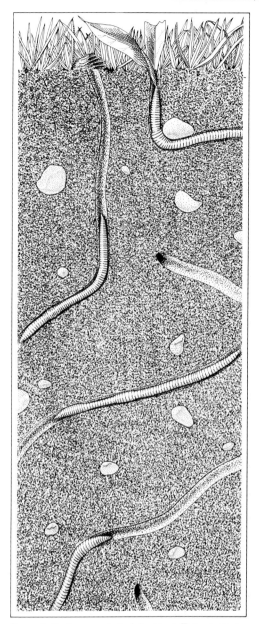

Figure 2 Earthworms in their burrows. The worm on the left has just deposited a cast on the surface. The one on the right is pulling a leaf into its burrow.

Figure 3 The larva of a beetle which lives in the soil. It has three pairs of true legs and no false legs.

# Investigation 1

## Collecting organisms from the soil

### Method 1

This method is used for larger soil animals such as earthworms, caterpillars, beetles (larvae and adults), millipedes and centipedes. Snails, slugs, spiders and woodlice may also be found in the leaf litter.

1 Collect a quantity of loose soil and leaf litter with a garden fork. A good place to sample is the ground near some rotting wood or under stones.

2 Spread it out on a white sheet or newspapers.

3 As soon as you see any movement pick up the animal with a spoon, pooter or forceps and put it in a plastic bag.
*Note* Centipedes bite and should be treated with caution.

4 Put some of the soil in a wide-meshed kitchen sieve and shake it. Some other animals may then come through.

Use the key on page 384 to identify the animals.

### Method 2

This method is used for collecting small arthropods such as ants, termites, woodlice and insect larvae.

1 Make up a 25 per cent salt solution by dissolving 25 g of common salt in 100 cm³ of water.

2 Pour the solution into a plastic bowl.

3 Add some soil and stir it around.

4 Small arthropods will float to the surface.
Pick them up with a spoon or paintbrush and transfer them to an empty bowl.

5 Use the salt solution to sort out another sample of soil.
Use the key on page 384 to identify the animals.

### Method 3

This method is used for collecting small arthropods such as ants, termites, woodlice and insect larvae.

1 Obtain a sample of good garden soil.

2 Set up the apparatus shown in the illustration, spreading the soil out on the perforated tray. (This apparatus is called a **Tullgren funnel**.)

3 Switch the lamp on, and leave the apparatus for between one and three days. The light and heat from the lamp should drive the animals downwards out of the soil into the beaker.
If the beaker contains ethanol this will preserve the animals.

4 Observe the contents of the beaker.

Are there any animals in it?

What kind of animals are they?

Use the key on page 384 to identify them.

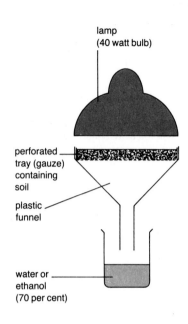

lamp
(40 watt bulb)

perforated
tray (gauze)
containing
soil

plastic
funnel

water or
ethanol
(70 per cent)

### Method 4

This method is mainly used for collecting roundworms that live in the soil water.

1 Obtain a sample of good garden soil.

2 Wrap the soil up in a bag made out of cheesecloth or mosquito netting, and set it up as shown in the illustration.

3 Switch the lamp on, and leave the apparatus for several days. The light and heat should drive any small animals living in the soil water out of the bag.

4 Open the clip and run a little water from the funnel into the beaker.

5 With a pipette transfer a drop of the water to a microscope slide, and cover it with a coverslip.

6 Examine the slide under the microscope: low power first, then high power.

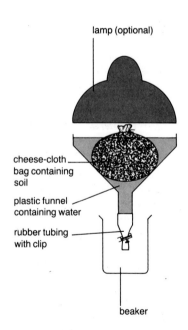

lamp (optional)

cheese-cloth
bag containing
soil

plastic funnel
containing water

rubber tubing
with clip

beaker

Can you see any slender worms with pointed ends? These are roundworms (see page 16).

Can you see any other organisms on your slide? If so, try to identify them. Use the key on page 384.

# Investigation 2

## To find the effect of earthworms on the soil

1 Set up the wormery shown in the illustration.

2 Place about 10 worms on the surface of the soil.

3 Watch the worms burrowing.

4 Observe the wormery at intervals during the next week or so.

What happens to the leaves at the surface?

What happens to the two chalk-sand layers?

(Disturbance of these layers is an indication of the extent to which the worms are mixing up the soil.)

Make a list of the effects the worms have on the soil *which you can see for yourself.*

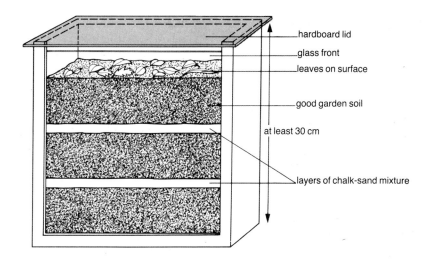

- hardboard lid
- glass front
- leaves on surface
- good garden soil
- at least 30 cm
- layers of chalk-sand mixture

### Catching worms

1 Make some soapy water from 50 cm³ washing up fluid in 10 litres of water.

2 Pour this solution on a square metre of good garden or farm soil.

3 Any worms should come up in a few minutes, and they should be gently rinsed in fresh water before putting them in the wormery.

# Assignments

1 Name two soil animals which are useful to man, and two which are harmful. Explain why each animal is useful or harmful.

2 The apparatus shown on the right was set up to find out if there were any microbes in a sample of soil:

After 48 hours the level of the water had risen in the left-hand side of the U-tube and dropped in the right-hand side.
a) Suggest an explanation for this result.
b) What should the control be in this experiment?

3 While digging the soil, a gardener notices that there are lots of earthworms in one part of his garden but none in another part. Suggest *one* possible reason for this. Describe an experiment which you could do to find out if your suggestion is right.

4 You suspect that worms prefer one kind of leaf to another. Describe an experiment which you could do to find out if you are right.

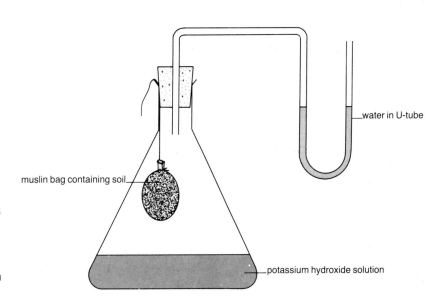

- water in U-tube
- muslin bag containing soil
- potassium hydroxide solution

5 Why are (a) soil water and (b) soil air important to organisms which live in the soil?

6 Look at Figure 1. Use the information to list the organisms which

a) would probably loosen and mix up the soil,
b) might be found under stones,
c) might damage living plants,
d) eat decaying plant material,
e) are predators.

# Decay

*It is said that
if no decay had occurred
during the last 400 years, the
bodies of dead organisms
would cover the earth
to a depth of a
kilometre!*

## What happens during decay?

When something decays – a dead animal if you like – it is gradually turned into a liquid. Three main things cause this to happen:

1  Immediately after death, enzymes start breaking down the body. The organism literally digests itself. This may happen remarkably quickly: an animal's gut, for example, may become as thin as tissue paper within a day after death.
2  Various natural processes help to break the body up. Birds peck at it, worms and maggots wriggle through it, rain softens it, and alternate freezing and thawing breaks it up into pieces.
3  Certain **microbes**, mainly moulds and bacteria, feed on the dead remains and break it down. They are **decomposers**, and they are the main agents of decay.

You can see some of the organisms that bring about decay in Investigation 1.

## How do microbes bring about decay?

When an animal or plant dies, it isn't long before some spores of moulds and bacteria land on it. They burst open, giving rise to new individuals. These grow and multiply, spreading quickly through the dead material. A teaspoonful of rotting vegetation may contain over a thousand million bacteria.

To feed on the dead material the microbes must first break it down into a liquid, just as we have to digest our food before we can absorb it. They do this by producing digestive enzymes which break down the solid material into soluble substances (Figure 1). They then soak up all the nutrients they need. Soft remains like skin and flesh decay more quickly than hard structures like bone and wood (Investigation 2). A skeleton may remain intact for years after the rest of the body has decomposed (see page 320).

Decay does not occur all at once: it happens step by step. A dead body is attacked by one kind of microbe first. This works its way in, and prepares the way for another organism and so on. As decay gets underway the rotting material may get warm, because of the heat given out by the millions of microbes (Figure 2). It may also have an unpleasant smell, due to certain gases being given off.

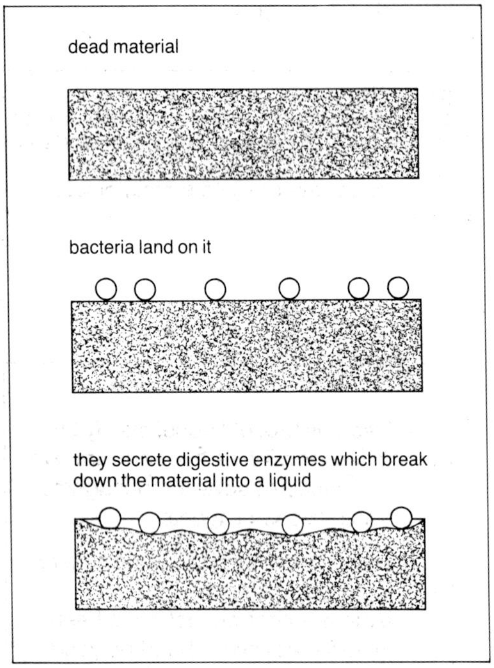

## What conditions are needed for decay to occur?

Experiments tell us that the following conditions are needed for decay to occur:

### 1  There must be plenty of moisture
This is needed for the spores to germinate, and for the microbes to grow and multiply. If a dead body is kept dry it loses moisture and the skin shrinks, but it does not decay. This process is called **mummification**: the ancient Egyptians used it to preserve the bodies of their kings.

### 2  It must be warm enough
Most microbes which bring about decay thrive in a warm environment. If it is cold, decay is slowed down; and if it is well below freezing, it will not happen at all. Extinct mammoths, which died in Siberia thousands of years ago, have been dug out of the ice with their flesh intact: the intense cold had stopped their bodies decaying.

### 3  Oxygen must be present
The microbes which bring about decay need oxygen for respiration. If oxygen is lacking they respire without it, i.e. they respire anaerobically. The end-product of this is lactic acid (see page 124). The lactic acid *prevents* further decay from taking place. So when there is no oxygen present decay is incomplete. This is how **peat** is formed (see p. 378).

dead material

bacteria land on it

they secrete digestive enzymes which break down the material into a liquid

**Figure 1** These diagrams summarise how microbes bring about decay.

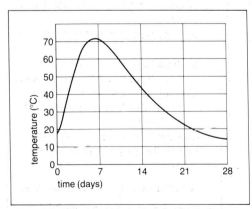

**Figure 2** The graph shows how the temperature inside a heap of dead vegetation changed after it had been piled up.

**4 Chemicals must not be present which kill the microbes**

This sometimes happens when poisonous substances are discharged into lakes and rivers from factories. It also happens when a biologist puts a specimen in alcohol or formalin to preserve it. In the past it has happened when animals have fallen into tar pits: a tar pit is a lake full of an oily liquid. In California there are tar pits containing the undecayed skeletons of extinct sabre-toothed tigers which died there about a million years ago.

### How can we make decay occur?

To bring about decay all we need to do is to put some dead material in a place where microbes can flourish. This is what a gardener does when he makes a **compost heap** (Figure 3).

Any rottable material can be used to make compost: old cabbages, potato peelings, tea leaves – you name it. In making a compost heap you must make sure that the conditions listed in the previous section are present, otherwise decay won't occur.

Sometimes we want to stop decay taking place. For example a farmer may want to store grass cuttings for feeding his livestock during the dry season. So he packs the grass tightly in a pit or container so that air cannot get into it. Without oxygen the microbes form lactic acid and the grass is prevented from decaying any further. The result is **silage.**

### Why is decay important?

If it wasn't for decay, the dead remains of organisms would simply pile up. However, decay is important for another reason: it helps chemicals such as carbon and nitrogen to circulate in nature so that they can be used over and over again. This cycling of matter is explained on pages 27 and 28.

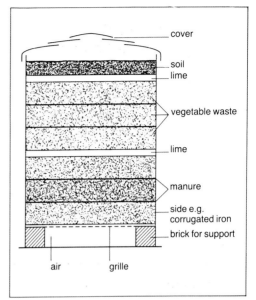

**Figure 3** Diagram of a compost heap seen in sectional view. The space at the bottom lets air in so the microbes can get oxygen. The lime prevents the heap getting too acidic. The manure contains microbes and so helps to get the decay process started.

## Investigation 1

### Looking at organisms which bring about decay

1 Pull off a *small* piece of mould from some stale bread with forceps. Put it on a slide. Add a drop of water, and cover it with a coverslip.

2 Pull off a piece of decaying earthworm with forceps, and put it on another slide. Add a drop of water and cover it with a coverslip.

3 Examine your slides under a microscope. You may see three types of organisms which help to bring about decay:

| | |
|---|---|
| Bacteria | look like tiny dots |
| Moulds | look like fine threads |
| Roundworms | are slender with pointed ends |

In what ways are these organisms suited to living on dead material?

## Investigation 2

### To find out how quickly different things decay

1 Fill a plant pot with damp soil. Make sure there are no earthworms in it.

2 Put different objects on the surface of the soil, e.g. a dead earthworm, dead insect, leaf, stick, bone, and plastic.

3 Cover the pot with a polythene bag.

4 Put the pot in a warm place.

5 Examine the objects at intervals for the next 2–3 weeks.

How does the appearance of each object change during the 2–3 week period?

Explain your observations.

Why was it necessary to make sure there were no live earthworms in the soil?

## Assignments

1 Decay is brought about mainly by microbes such as bacteria. However it is helped by several other agents. Name *five* such agents.

2 A body was found in a remote cave in the Sahara desert. Forensic experts estimated that it had been there for well over a hundred years. The skin, though dry and shrivelled, was still intact. Suggest reasons why it had not decayed.

3 When making a compost heap, you should
   a) support it on bricks or large stones,
   b) break up old cabbage stalks before you put them on the heap,
   c) mix grass cuttings with bulkier materials when you put them on the heap,
   d) keep it moist but not saturated,
   e) turn the heap occasionally with a fork.

   Give reasons for each of the above.

4 Study Figure 2. Explain why the temperature rises and then falls.

# Populations

*People, people everywhere! This Topic is about populations: how they grow and what happens if they get too big.*

Figure 1 A crowded scene in Kingstown, St Vincent.

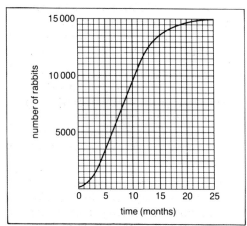

Figure 2 This graph shows how a population of rabbits may increase with time.

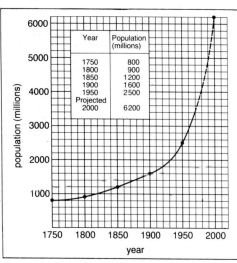

Figure 3 World population: the past, and a projection for the future.

## How do populations grow?

Suppose you introduce a hundred rabbits onto an unpopulated island. The rabbits reproduce and gradually the population increases. If you were to count the number of rabbits at intervals and plot them against time, you would find that the population rises as shown in Figure 2.

One of the most noticeable things about populations is that they increase very quickly. This is because the numbers go up by *multiplication*, like this:

$$100 \xrightarrow{\times 2} 200 \xrightarrow{\times 2} 400 \xrightarrow{\times 2} 800 \xrightarrow{\times 2} 1600 \xrightarrow{\times 2} 3200 \longrightarrow$$

In other words the total number *doubles* at regular intervals of time. This type of increase is described as **exponential**, and it is how populations grow, whether it is rabbits, flies or human beings.

## Why do populations grow?

In any population new individuals are born and older ones die. The rate at which new individuals are born is called the **birth rate**, and the rate at which older individuals die is called the **death rate**. The birth rate and death rate are expressed as percentages. If the birth rate is 10 per cent, it means that for every 100 individuals at the beginning of the year there would be 10 more (i.e. 110) at the end. If the death rate is 3 per cent, it means that for every 100 individuals at the beginning of the year there would be 3 less (i.e. 97) at the end. The whole population would show a net increase of 10 − 3 = 7 per cent. This means that for every 100 individuals at the beginning of the year the actual number at the end would be 107.

Populations increase because new individuals are born at a faster rate than older ones die, in other words the *birth rate* is greater than the *death rate*.

## What stops a population growing?

Look again at the graph in Figure 2. Notice that once a certain number of individuals has been produced, the curve gradually flattens out: in other words the population growth slows down and levels off.

Why does this happen? In the case of our rabbits there are several possible reasons. Here are some of them:

1 The food (grass and so on) begins to run out, so some rabbits starve.
2 There are so many rabbits that there is no room for any more burrows.
3 The rabbits are so overcrowded that diseases spread rapidly and many die.
4 Being overcrowded the rabbits fight each other, resulting in many deaths.

These are the kinds of 'checks' which normally stop populations growing for ever. This may seem harsh and cruel, but it is a normal and important aspect of the balance of nature. In the case of the rabbits there may be **predators** such as foxes or hawks to prevent the population from getting too large.

If there are no predators, man may step in and take control. Australia used not to have any rabbits, but in 1859 some domestic rabbits ran wild and bred at such a rate that parts of Australia soon became overrun with them and they did a great deal of damage to crops and gardens. Unfortunately there were not enough predators to keep them under control. Eventually a virus disease called **myxomatosis** was deliberately introduced to destroy them. The disease swept through the rabbit population very quickly, and their numbers dropped dramatically. This shows us how man can reduce the population of a pest by introducing an organism which kills it. We call this **biological control** (page 392).

## Human population

Figure 3 shows the world population at various times from 1750 to 1975, and a projection for the year 2000. Notice that it is an exponential curve as is shown in Figure 2 and that it has not yet 'flattened off'. The world population as a whole is increasing by about 80 million people each year, that's 9000 an hour, or 150 a minute. Someone has worked out that if this were to go on indefinitely, the whole of the earth's surface would be covered with people standing shoulder to shoulder in less than 600 years' time!

## Population increase in different countries

Populations increase when the birth rate is greater than the death rate. Let's see how this works out in four different countries (Table 1).

| | Country | | | |
|---|---|---|---|---|
| | A | B | C | D |
| Birth rate | 5% | 5% | 3.5% | 2% |
| Death rate | 3% | 2% | 1.5% | 1% |
| Overall population growth | 2% | 3% | 2% | 1% |

**Table 1** Birth rates, death rates and overall population growth in four countries.

*Country A* has a birth rate of 5 per cent and a death rate of 3 per cent, giving an overall population growth of 2 per cent per year. This describes the situation as it was in many parts of the world at the beginning of this century. There was a high birth rate, but there was also a high death rate, with many children dying under one year of age (**infant mortality**) and adults dying quite young (**low life expectancy**).

*Country B* shows what happens when the death rate is lowered by better food and medical services but the birth rate remains high. This has happened in many developing countries, where more children have survived childhood but the parents still have large families. The improved medical care has actually *increased* the population growth to 3 per cent. A growth rate of 3 per cent per year means that the population will double in only 23–24 years. That is twice as many mouths to feed, twice as many people to clothe, house, educate and provide employment for.

*Country C* shows what happens when birth control methods are introduced so that the birth rate is lowered to 3.5 per cent. At the same time further improvements occur in living conditions, and the death rate decreases. This is the stage in which many developing countries presently find themselves. A growth rate of 2 per cent per year means that the population will double in about 35 years.

*Country D* shows a further reduction in birth rate and death rate to give an overall population growth of 1 per cent. In the USA and several countries in Europe the growth rate is now less than 1 per cent per year.

If the population growth is not too rapid it gives the country more chance to develop and to take better care of its people.

## Assignments

1 Study Figure 2, then suggest two reasons why the population rises slowly to begin with and then speeds up.

2 If all its offspring survived, a single greenfly could produce 600 000 000 000 offspring in one season, with a mass of over 600 000 kg – roughly equivalent to 10 000 men. What prevents this happening?

3 It was suggested that in order to protect the deer in a nature reserve in the United States, the deer's predators (wolves and coyotes) should be killed. What do you think the consequences of doing this would be?

4 Suppose that a certain island becomes overrun with rabbits. Suggest three different ways by which the people living on the island might try to reduce the rabbit population. Briefly mention the advantages and disadvantages of each method.

5 a) How many of the checks and balances suggested in the Topic for controlling the rabbit population also apply to the human population?
   b) What additional checks do humans have in controlling their population size?

6 The table shows the birth and death rates for four countries.
   Calculate the percentage increase in the population of each country.

   Suggest reasons why the population is increasing at different rates in the four countries.

| Country | Birth rate % | Death rate % |
|---|---|---|
| UK | 1.71 | 1.19 |
| USA | 1.76 | 0.96 |
| China | 2.9 | 1.3 |
| India | 4.2 | 1.7 |

7 What is the effect on population size of
   i) increasing the birth rate;
   ii) decreasing the birth rate;
   iii) increasing the death rate;
   iv) decreasing the death rate?

# Man and the environment

*Man alters the environment in almost everything he does, from farming to industry.*

## Man's effect on the environment

Early man was part of the balance of nature. He hunted wild animals and collected grains and other fruits. But then he began to shape the world to suit his own needs. He found he could save himself trouble by rearing the animals and growing the plants that he ate. He began to use fire to cook his food. He cut down the forests for firewood and to provide land to grow his crops. More food was available and human populations increased in size.

As time went by, hand tools gave way to industrialisation. The amount of pollution increased. By his actions, man began to control which plants and animals should multiply and which ones should be killed.

This Topic describes some ways in which man controls his environment, how he pollutes it and some of the steps he needs to take to conserve it for future generations.

## Controlling pests

Some animals and plants are called **pests**. They are harmful to man in some way. They may affect his health, for example houseflies and rats and the biting of mosquitoes. Or they may affect his crops by causing disease or, in the case of weeds, competing for nutrients from the soil.

Man gets rid of pests in two main ways:
1 By spraying the ground with a chemical substance which kills the pests. We call this **chemical control**.
2 By making use of another organism which kills the pests. We call this **biological control**.

### Biological control

Greenflies (aphids) suck plant juices. They can damage crops and are therefore a nuisance to humans. Now greenflies are eaten by ladybird larvae, and so if ladybirds are released in an area they will help to get rid of the greenflies. The ladybirds are serving as agents of biological control. Another biological control agent is *Tilapia* which is used because it eats mosquito larvae and pupae.

The advantage of biological control is that it does not involve putting artificial substances into the environment. Nature is doing the job for us. However, not every pest has a predator that will keep its numbers down sufficiently, and so chemical methods are more often used.

### Chemical control

A chemical substance which kills pests is called a **pesticide**. Those which are used against weeds (herbs) are called **herbicides**; those which are used against insects are called **insecticides**. Some of these chemicals are taken directly from plants. An example is quinine, which is extracted from the bark of *Cinchona* trees. It is still used to kill the malarial parasite *Plasmodium* (page 342). Another chemical, extracted from semi-contra or wormweed, is used to kill intestinal worms.

Other chemicals, such as DDT (whose full name is **d**ichloro**d**iphenyl**t**richloroethane!) are made by man. DDT is an insecticide which has been used in the past against mosquitoes and many other insect pests (but see below, pages 394–5).

The trouble with pesticides is that they may damage the environment. Spraying the countryside with herbicides may get rid of weeds but it also kills many wild flowers; and insecticides may destroy harmful pests but they also kill beautiful insects such as butterflies and moths, and may even be a hazard to humans. This is an aspect of **pollution**.

## Pollution

Pollution is any process which leads to a harmful increase in the amount of a chemical substance in the environment (Figure 1). These harmful substances

**Figure 1** The air around this cement works is heavily polluted.

or **pollutants** accumulate more quickly than they can be recycled by the processes of nature, if, indeed, they can be recycled at all.

It is often difficult to know for certain whether a particular substance is harmful or not. Its effects may not appear straight away, but only after a long period of time. Also a pollutant may affect some organisms more than others. For example, certain gases from factories may not affect man in the concentrations in which they normally occur, but they may damage plants. Some pollutants which are harmful to certain organisms may actually *help* others. For instance, a high concentration of carbon dioxide in the air, though harmful to animals, is useful to plants because it enables them to photosynthesise faster.

## Air pollution

A widespread air pollutant is **smoke** from the burning of fossil fuel such as coal and gasoline (Figure 2). The smoke contains particles of carbon which float through the air and settle on the surface of buildings and trees, turning them black. If breathed in, the particles irritate the breathing passages and can cause bronchitis. A simple method of finding out how much smoke pollution there is in different places is given in Investigation 2.

Smoke contains two main gases: carbon dioxide and sulphur dioxide. The effects of carbon dioxide are discussed on page 398. Sulphur dioxide is a poisonous gas, but fortunately it is not normally produced in sufficient quantities to endanger man. However, it certainly affects plants, either killing them or reducing their yield. In industrial areas the concentration of sulphur dioxide in the air may reach 4 ppm.* Concentrations as low as 0.3 ppm may damage plants.

Lichens are particularly sensitive to sulphur dioxide and in polluted regions you do not find lichens growing on the tree trunks. In fact the number of lichens in an area can be used to indicate the amount of pollution there.

Sulphur dioxide reacts with oxygen and water in the atmosphere to form sulphuric acid. This aggravates bronchitis and other breathing complaints. The sulphuric acid is washed down into the soil as **acid rain**. It may make the soil highly acidic, harming the growth of plants. It also eats into the surface of buildings, eroding the stone and brickwork.

One of the main causes of air pollution is the motor car. The exhaust contains carbon monoxide and lead. Carbon monoxide poisoning is described on page 126. Even quite small amounts may make one feel faint. Lead affects the brain and in extreme cases may cause mental retardation.

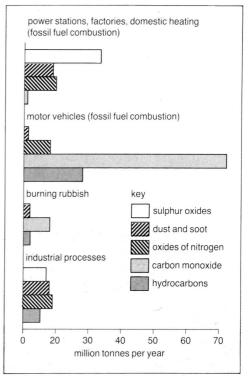

Figure 2 The chart shows how much air pollution is produced each year in America. The same kinds of pollutants are produced all over the world.

* ppm means parts per million. This is the number of cubic millimetres of sulphur dioxide in one million cubic millimetres (i.e. one cubic metre) of air.

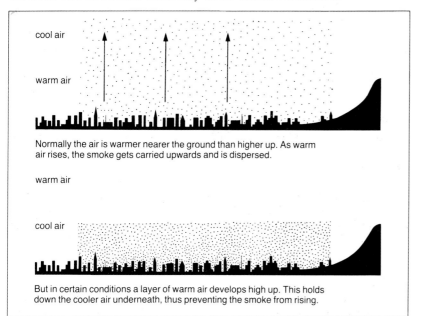

Normally the air is warmer nearer the ground than higher up. As warm air rises, the smoke gets carried upwards and is dispersed.

But in certain conditions a layer of warm air develops high up. This holds down the cooler air underneath, thus preventing the smoke from rising.

Figure 3 These diagrams show how smog can build up as a result of temperature inversion.

**Figure 4** This bird, was the victim of the spillage of oil from a damaged oil tanker. Notice the lumps of tar on the badly polluted beach.

Eutrophication

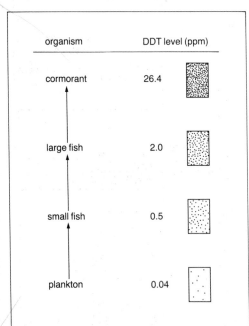

| organism | DDT level (ppm) | |
|---|---|---|
| cormorant | 26.4 | |
| large fish | 2.0 | |
| small fish | 0.5 | |
| plankton | 0.04 | |

**Figure 5** This diagram shows the amounts of DDT in four organisms belonging to a food chain. Notice how the DDT gets more and more concentrated as it goes up the chain. This is because it is kept in the animals' bodies and not excreted.

## Smog

Normally smoke from factories goes straight up into the atmosphere and is blown away by wind and air currents. However, in certain conditions it stays close to the ground where it builds up to form **smog**. Smog is a mixture of smoke and fog, and it is caused by a layer of warm air developing above a region of colder air. The warm layer prevents the colder air from escaping. This is called **temperature inversion** (Figure 3).

Smog is not only unpleasant but it can be dangerous. In December 1952 there was a particularly bad smog in London. It lasted five days, and is said to have caused 4000 deaths. Street lamps had to be put on in the middle of the day, and in cinemas it was impossible to see the screen clearly from the back of the theatre.

Although smoky smogs have largely disappeared, there is another kind of smog which is still a problem. This is the type which you get in sunny places like Los Angeles and Tokyo. It is caused by the action of sunlight on the chemicals in motor vehicle exhaust, for which reason it is called **photochemical smog**. Temperature inversions are frequent in these areas, and the result is a brown haze which makes people's eyes sting and can cause severe headaches. In Tokyo many car drivers wear masks, and there are 'fresh air dispensers' in offices. The smog also damages plants and is said to have reduced the yield of citrus fruits (oranges and lemons) in the Los Angeles area.

In summary, air pollution is a nuisance because it:
a) causes ill-health and affects plant life,
b) discourages people from living and working in polluted areas and
c) damages buildings etc. by dirt and corrosion.

## Water pollution

From time to time **oil** is spilled into the sea from a tanker or an off-shore oil rig. The oil forms a thick layer, or slick, which floats on the surface of the sea. The slick may then be carried by ocean currents to the coast, where it is deposited on the shore (Figure 4).

The oil ruins the beaches for the local residents and tourists. It also kills fish and sea birds. In the past, attempts have been made to get rid of oil slicks by spraying them with **detergents** which break the oil up into drops. The trouble is that the detergents are even more deadly than the oil and they kill many organisms that might have escaped the oil. Nowadays less destructive methods are used.

Another water pollutant is **sewage**. If untreated sewage is put into a river or lake, it is decomposed by bacteria which quickly multiply. The bacteria use up so much oxygen that there is not enough for the fish and other animals, which suffocate and die. The same thing happens when excessive amounts of **fertiliser** or farm waste are drained into a river from the surrounding farmland. With so much nitrate to feed on, the algae multiply and the water turns green. This great growth of algae is called **eutrophication**. When the algae die the bacteria multiply, using up all the oxygen. Matters are made even worse if hot water from a local power station is discharged into the river. This is called **thermal pollution**. The extra warmth makes the organisms multiply even faster.

The insecticide DDT has a cloud hanging over it. It gets into rivers and lakes and is taken up by small organisms at the beginning of various food chains. It is then passed along the chains, becoming more and more concentrated as it goes from one stage to the next (Figure 5). DDT is known to damage animal tissues, and may be a danger to man. For this reason it has been banned in many countries. Here we have an example of a useful substance turning out to be a pollutant. Another example is dioxin, a powerful herbicide used for killing weeds in conifer plantations. This chemical, which was used by the Americans to defoliate the jungle during the Vietnam war, is now known to be highly dangerous to man.

Finally **chemical waste products** from factories are sometimes discharged into seas and rivers. They may be so concentrated that the fish are killed straight away. But sometimes they are taken up into food chains just like DDT. Some years ago over 60 people died in Japan from eating fish whose bodies contained mercury. The mercury had been discharged into the sea from a local factory and had then passed right through the food chains.

You can test the effects of some water pollutants on various animals in Investigation 4.

## Land pollution

There are many examples in the Caribbean of land that has been stripped of vegetation for housing, industrial development or mining. These activities may give rise to land pollution.

Let us take the mining and processing of bauxite as an example. In order to get the bauxite (impure aluminium oxide) the vegetation cover has to be removed, and this can lead to soil erosion. The bauxite is then treated with caustic soda in which the alumina (pure aluminium oxide) dissolves. The residue, which contains iron oxide and some caustic soda, is separated off and dumped in storage lakes as 'red mud'. The caustic fumes of the sodium hydroxide affect the nearby atmosphere and there could be seepage of chemicals from the lake. These dangers are monitored by the bauxite companies. The trouble is that we just don't know the long-term effects which this kind of thing might have on people's health.

Have you ever thought what happens to all the rubbish which people throw away? Much of it will decay: this includes bits of left-over food and discarded parts of fruits and vegetables – in fact anything which can be broken down by microbes. We call this sort of rubbish **biodegradable**. Thanks to microbes, the chemicals in these materials can be set free and used again: in other words they are recycled in nature.

Other kinds of rubbish will not decay, because they are made of substances which microbes cannot live on. They are called **non-biodegradable**. They include plastic, polythene and many other man-made materials. This rubbish can cause a special problem if it is dumped at the sides of roads.

Some man-made materials can of course be used again: for example paper, and scrap metal from used cars. But the majority cannot be re-used and must be got rid of somehow. Getting rid of this kind of rubbish is a major problem in modern society.

## Noise pollution

We have defined pollution as an increase in a harmful chemical substance in the environment. However, other things besides chemicals may be harmful, and these too can be regarded as pollutants. An example is **noise**.

Noise can be measured by a sound meter and is expressed in a unit called the decibel (dB) (Investigation 5). The quietest sound that the human ear can detect (zero decibels) is called the **threshold of hearing**. Figure 6 relates the loudness of sounds as measured in decibels to a series of everyday situations. Notice that a sound of 120 dB is on the **threshold of pain**: sounds louder than this actually hurt your ears and can give you a headache. If they go on continuously they may damage the sensory cells in the inner ear, causing permanent deafness. People who work close to machinery in foundries and mills are at a particular risk, and they normally wear ear-plugs.

## Radiation pollution

Another type of pollution to which we are all exposed is **radiation** from radio-active materials. Radiation affects dividing cells, damaging the genes. It can cause leukaemia, which is cancer of the blood. It also causes mutations in the sex cells in the ovary and testis, and this can result in babies being born with deformities. The offspring of survivors of the atom bomb raids on Japan at the end of the second World War showed a high incidence of mutations.

Most of the radiation to which we are exposed comes from the sun and outer space and is a natural part of our environment. However, man adds to this natural radiation by nuclear power stations, medical equipment such as X-ray machines, and of course atomic explosions (Figure 7). The total amount

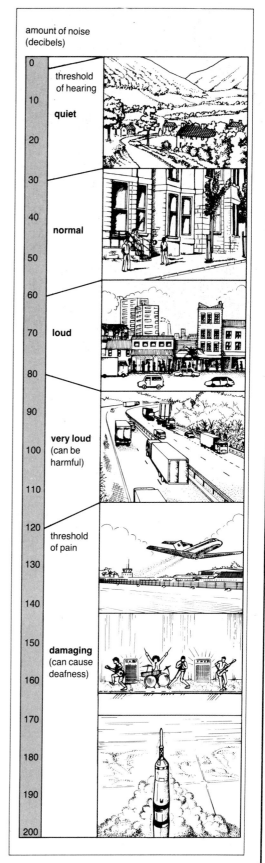

amount of noise (decibels)

| | |
|---|---|
| 0 | threshold of hearing |
| 10 | **quiet** |
| 40 | **normal** |
| 70 | **loud** |
| 100 | **very loud** (can be harmful) |
| 120 | threshold of pain |
| 150 | **damaging** (can cause deafness) |

**Figure 6** This illustration shows the noise scale as expressed in decibels, the standard unit of noise as measured with a sound meter.

**Figure 7** A test explosion of an atomic bomb carried out in the South Pacific in the early 1950s. Atomic explosions add to the amount of radiation in the atmosphere.

heavy rains

topsoil washed away

Leaching occurs as chemical nutrients are washed out of the soil. Soil becomes impoverished and is less useful for growing plants.

hot, dry weather

dry soil blown away

Evaporation draws minerals to the surface. These make a hard crust on the surface. The soil again loses its minerals and becomes poorer.

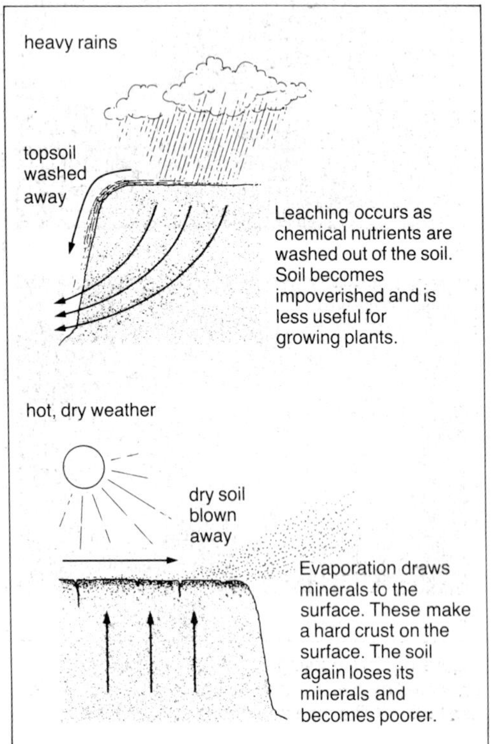

**Figure 8** How erosion occurs on bare soil.

of radiation which an average person receives from all these man-made sources is about half the natural radiation. This is not considered a hazard to health. However, people who work in places where radiation levels are particularly high, such as nuclear power stations, are at a greater risk than the rest of us, and so special precautions are taken to protect them.

Obviously an atomic war poses a particular threat to man. After an atomic explosion radioactive materials get into the atmosphere and come down to the earth as **fallout**. Many atomic tests were carried out in the 1950s, but test ban treaties since then have greatly reduced the number of tests. Fortunately the atomic tests carried out so far have increased the amount of radiation by only two per cent, but this figure could be raised drastically by an atomic war.

## Conservation

To *conserve* something means to protect it and keep it in a healthy condition. This is especially important because of all the ways in which humans pollute their world. And the more humans there are, the greater are the problems of pollution, damage to the environment and reduction of our natural resources.

Applied to our environment, conservation means protecting the natural resources: water, soil, air, other organisms and the natural scenery. We may need to use our natural resources, but these should not be wasted. We will need to control the chemicals and waste materials that are put into the water, the soil and the air. We must protect animals and plants from being harmed and we must conserve the natural beauty of the environment round about us. These are some of the things that we can do:

1  We must reduce pollution as much as possible, particularly those kinds which are liable to damage natural habitats and harm the organisms that live there.

This will involve finding out, for example, which factories are polluting the water or the air with their waste materials. Then action must be taken to reduce these problems. Another major way to reduce pollution is to stop burning fossil fuels such as coal and gasoline. Instead, non-polluting forms of energy, such as solar energy, should be used whenever possible.

2  We must conserve our natural resources by recycling as many useful materials as possible.

To take a simple example, everyone could sort out the rubbish which they produce in their homes. At the moment most of this is collected and, literally, 'goes up in smoke'. Instead, used glass, metal tin cans and newspapers could be recycled. This would save having to use more of our natural resources of metals or trees. All bio-degradable food materials could be put into a compost heap and their nutrients would be released by microbes. The compost could then be used to increase the fertility of the soil without having to use so many artificial fertilisers.

3  We must practise methods of soil conservation so as to reduce soil erosion.

We looked at this problem on page 381. The soil must be kept covered by plants so that they can reduce the effects of the sun and rain (Figure 8). The plant roots also hold the soil together, and the decaying organisms return nutrients to the soil.

It is also necessary to practise **crop rotation**. Each kind of crop in the soil takes out certain nutrients. It is therefore better if you grow *different* crops on the soil from year to year. It is especially important to include leguminous plants, such as beans and peas, in the rotation cycle. Leguminous plants have nodules on their roots (page 28) which contain bacteria that produce nitrogenous compounds. These nitrogenous compounds are then added to the soil when the roots decay. These enrich the soil for other crops.

A | B

Figure 9 **A** In bauxite mining large quantities of earth have to be removed. **B** As a conservation measure the land is filled and used for farming or to grow trees.

4   We must improve land that has been made use of for mining.

In the case of bauxite, this means trying to reduce the amount of red mud that is dumped, as well as trying to find methods of recovering the useful materials that it contains. Also, vegetation is removed during the process of mining, and the earth is disturbed. This could lead to serious soil eroison. So, it is important to fill in the spaces and allow the soil to be used, for farming or growing trees (Figure 9).

5   We must prevent an upset in the balance of nature.

In a natural habitat the numbers of the different kinds of organisms tend to stay about the same. However, if man were to kill off one of the predators this could result in a large increase in the numbers of its prey. The prey may then compete with each other for food. If they are grass-eaters, then this can lead to **overgrazing**. Grass no longer covers the soil and erosion can occur. Overgrazing can also occur, for example, when man tries to support too large a number of cattle on a piece of land.

Another way in which the balance of nature can be upset is when man cuts down tropical forests. This removes the trees which have taken a very long time to grow. It also removes the habitats of many animals and plants which may therefore also be in danger. It is better to rely on plantations in which the felled trees are replaced by new seedlings, especially of quicker-growing species. This procedure is called **reafforestation**. It helps us to replace, for future generations, some of the trees which we are making use of now.

6   We must protect endangered species.

Animals that are killed for food, or any other purpose, must not be used up so quickly that their numbers start falling to the point that they might die out. Two examples are the sea turtle and the W. Indian manatee (sea cow) (Figure 10) which are now considered to be **endangered species**. One way of overcoming this problem is to set up breeding programmes to build up the numbers. This is done for turtles in some of the islands. Even more widespread is the setting up of man-made **fish farms** where fish are reared for food. Some fish are removed from time to time, and more small fish introduced. This avoids the possible problem of **over-fishing** which could occur if too many fish were taken from their natural habitats.

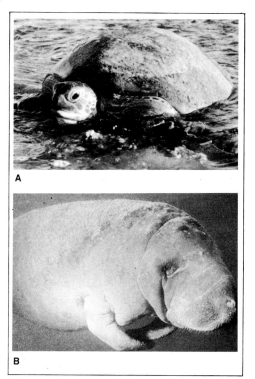

A

B

Figure 10 Two endangered species which are protected by law in many Caribbean countries. **A** The sea turtle. **B** The manatee or sea cow.

In many countries certain areas have been set aside where the animals and plants are protected. These are often called **National Parks** and they contain an abundance of wildlife and natural scenery which everyone can enjoy. Because of man, most of the wild animals which used to roam the earth have long since died out. However, in places such as East and South Africa there are large game parks with lions, giraffes, elephants, zebras and many other animals.

7   We must respect our countryside.

This means not leaving litter around, not destroying natural habitats, and not taking birds' eggs out of their nests. We have a responsibility to look after our environment so that it can be enjoyed by future generations.

## Man's long-term effects on the environment

When we are thinking of the effects of man's activities on the environment, we must look ahead. What will be the effects in a hundred years' time, or even a thousand years? Let's take an example: the air around us.

The amounts of oxygen and carbon dioxide in the air are delicately balanced. However, man does two things which *might* lower the amount of oxygen and raise the amount of carbon dioxide:

1   He cuts down trees for timber and destroys vegetation to make room for towns.
2   He burns fuel, which uses up oxygen and produces carbon dioxide.

How could we find out if doing these things affects the amount of oxygen and carbon dioxide in the atmosphere? We would have to make measurements over many years of the amounts of these two gases in our atmosphere. This has been done in several parts of the world during the last hundred years.

In the case of oxygen, there has been no detectable change. Even if we burned all the coal and other fuels that exist in the whole world, the oxygen content of the atmosphere would decrease by only a fraction of one per cent. Also we should have to destroy an awful lot of plants to lower the amount of oxygen in the atmosphere, and even then any changes would take place very slowly.

What about carbon dioxide? Look at the graph in Figure 11. If carbon dioxide goes on increasing in the atmosphere, what might its effects be? It is unlikely to increase so much that our health would be affected. However, some scientists believe that it could bring about a change in climate by making the temperature go up. Why do you think this might happen and what could its consequences be?

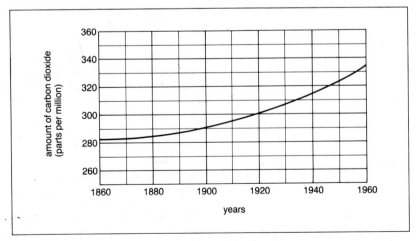

**Figure 11**  This graph shows how the amount of carbon dioxide in the air has increased during the last hundred years. The measurements were made in Vienna. Similar figures have been recorded in other parts of the world.

# Investigation 3

**Estimating the amount of pollution in rainwater**

1 Obtain a jar about 15 cm tall, a funnel and filter paper.

2 Set them up as shown in the illustration.

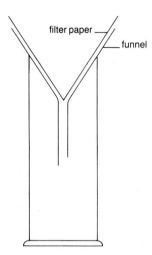

filter paper

funnel

3 When it is raining, place the apparatus in a safe place out of doors and leave it there for at least 30 minutes.

4 Examine the filter paper for particles of dust which have been brought down by the rain.

5 Using universal indicator paper, measure the pH of the rainwater in the jar.

You will probably find that the pH is round about neutral.

However, if the air is badly polluted the pH may be acidic.

What is the acidity caused by?

If you have the chance, try doing this experiment in different parts of the country and compare the results.

# Investigation 4

**Finding the effect of chemical pollutants on organisms**

1 Set up a series of jars all containing the same amount of clean water.

2 Into each jar place a small selection of living organisms such as tadpoles, water fleas and mosquito larvae.

3 Put a substance which you suspect may be a pollutant into each jar. You might try oil, detergent, paraffin, acid and so on.

4 Observe the behaviour of the organisms straight away and, if necessary, over a number of days.

Is the behaviour of any of the organisms abnormal?

Do any of them die? If so, which ones?

What conclusions do you draw?

Describe an experiment which you could do to find out the maximum concentration of a chemical substance a particular species of animal can tolerate without being visibly harmed.

# Investigation 5

**Measuring the noise level in different places**

1 Using a sound meter, measure the maximum amount of noise in different places such as: a street corner, a railway station, an airport, a children's playground, a school dining hall, a reference library, a factory, a park, a disco.

2 Compare your results with Figure 6, and state whether the noise level in each place is quiet, normal, loud, very loud or dangerous.

How could you find the *average* noise level in a particular place?

# Assignments

1 How did the word 'smog' get its name?

What causes smog to develop over a city?

2 Suggest one reason for each of the following:
a) Discharging sewage into a river may kill the fish.
b) The Los Angeles smog is worse on bright days than cloudy days.
c) The use of the insecticide DDT has been stopped in many countries.

3 Certain lichens are never found in industrial areas, though they are abundant in non-industrial areas. Suggest one possible reason for this.

Describe an experiment which you could do to find out if your suggestion is correct.

4 The following figures show the concentration of mercury in sea water and of various organisms expressed in parts per million:

| | | |
|---|---|---|
| sea water | 0.00003 | ppm |
| algae | 0.03 | ppm |
| fish | 0.3 | ppm |
| water birds | 2.0 | ppm |

Suggest an explanation for these figures. What do they tell us about mercury as a pollutant?

5 It is intended to build a new factory close to where you live. Discuss with a few friends the possible advantages and disadvantages of such an idea. What advice would you give to the factory manager?

6 The amount of nitrates in drinking water has increased in recent years. Politicians are concerned about this because nitrates are believed to cause stomach cancer.
a) Why do you think the amount of nitrates in drinking water has increased?
b) How would you test the suggestion that nitrates cause stomach cancer *without* experimenting on animals?
c) What might be done to reduce the nitrate content of drinking water?

# Appendix

Common names and scientific names of flowering plants
mentioned in the text.

| Most used name | Other names | Scientific name | Family |
|---|---|---|---|
| acacia bush | wild popanax | Acacia tortuosa | Mimosaceae |
| ackee (Barbados) | guinep in Jamaica | Melicoccus bijugatus | Sapindaceae |
| ackee (Jamaica) | akee | Blighia sapida | Sapindaceae |
| alligator apple | bobwood, corkwood | Annona glabra | Annonaceae |
| annatto | bija, achiote, atta | Bixa orellana | Bixaceae |
| anthurium | | Anthurium spp. | Araceae |
| apple | English apple | Malus pumila | Rosaceae |
| arrowhead | | Sagittaria sagittifolia | Alismataceae |
| avocado pear | pear, aguacate | Persea americana | Lauraceae |
| balsam | busy Lizzie | Impatiens balsamina | Balsaminaceae |
| bamboo | | Bambusa spp. | Gramineae |
| banana | guineo | Musa sapientum | Musaceae |
| baobab | corn tree | Adansonia digitata | Bombacaceae |
| Barbados gooseberry | W. Indian gooseberry | Pereskia aculeata | Cactaceae |
| beetroot | | Beta vulgaris | Chenopodiaceae |
| bougainvillea | | Bougainvillea spp. | Nyctaginaceae |
| black bead shrub | bread-and-cheese | Pithecellobium unguis-cati | Mimosaceae |
| black-eyed pea | cow pea, black eyes | Vigna unguiculata | Papilionaceae |
| black mangrove | mangle negro | Avicennia germinans | Avicenniaceae |
| black pepper | | Piper nigrum | Piperaceae |
| blue mahoe | Cuba bark | Hibiscus elatus | Malvaceae |
| blue shak shak | virgin flower | Crotalaria verrucosa | Papilionaceae |
| bottle-cod root | mabouya, devil's bean | Capparis flexuosa | Capparaceae |
| breadfruit | | Artocarpus altilis | Moraceae |
| breadnut | seeded form: chataignes | Artocarpus altilis | Moraceae |
| bowstring hemp | | Sansevieria spp. | Agavaceae |
| bur grass | sandbur | Cenchrus spp. | Gramineae |
| butterfly flower | poor man's orchid | Bauhinia spp. | Caesalpiniaceae |
| button mangrove | buttonwood, button bush | Conocarpus erectus | Combretaceae |
| cabbage | | Brassica oleracea | Cruciferae |
| calabash (tree) | gourd | Crescentia cujete | Bignoniaceae |
| caladium | variegated coco | Caladium spp. | Araceae |
| calalu | spinach | Amaranthus spp. | Amaranthaceae |
| Canadian pondweed | | Elodea spp. | Hydrocharitaceae |
| canna-lily | Indian shot | Canna indica | Cannaceae |
| cannon ball tree | | Couroupita guianensis | Lecythidaceae |
| carrot | | Daucus carota | Umbelliferae |
| cassava | tapioca, manioc | Manihot esculenta | Euphorbiaceae |
| cashew (nut) | | Anacardium occidentale | Anacardiaceae |
| castor oil | higuerilla | Ricinus communis | Euphorbiaceae |
| cauliflower | | Brassica oleracea | Cruciferae |
| cerasee | carilla, coolie pawpaw | Momordia charantia | Cucurbitaceae |
| chew (chaw)-stick | cho-bush | Gouania lupuloides | Rhamnaceae |
| cho-cho | christophine, chayote | Sechium edule | Cucurbitaceae |
| cinnamon | | Cinnamomum zeylanicum | Lauraceae |
| climbing coco | Barbados ivy | Philodendron spp. | Araceae |
| cloves | | Syzygium aromaticum | Myrtaceae |
| cocoa | cacao, chocolate tree | Theobroma cacao | Sterculiaceae |
| coconut (palm) | cocos | Cocos nucifera | Palmae |
| cocoyam | white eddo, coco | Colocasia esculenta | Araceae |
| coffee | café | Coffea arabica | Rubiaceae |
| coleus | Joseph's coat | Coleus blumei | Labiatae |

| Most used name | Other names | Scientific name | Family |
|---|---|---|---|
| consumption weed | Cupid's paint brush | Emilia spp. | Compositae |
| coralita | coralilla, San Diego flower | Antigonon leptopus | Polygonaceae |
| cotton | sea island cotton | Gossypium spp. | Malvaceae |
| cow-itch | pica pica | Mucuna pruriens | Papilionaceae |
| crab's eye vine | jumbie beads | Abrus precatorius | Papilionaceae |
| crow | | Stigmaphyllon emarginatum | Malpighiaceae |
| crown-of-thorns | | Euphorbia milii | Euphorbiaceae |
| cucumber | pepino | Cucumis sativus | Cucurbitaceae |
| custard apple | golden apple, cashimar, coeur de boeuf | Annona reticulata | Annonaceae |
| damson plum | damsel, wild star apple | Chrysophyllum oliviforme | Sapotaceae |
| dandelion | piss-a-bed | Cassia occidentalis | Caesalpiniaceae |
| dasheen | eddo, cocoyam | Colocasia antiquorum | Araceae |
| date palm | | Phoenix dactylifera | Palmae |
| duckweed | | Lemna spp. | Lemnaceae |
| dutchman's pipe | dolly basket, guaco | Aristolochia spp. | Aristolochiaceae |
| egg plant | aubergine, garden egg, melongene | Solanum melongena | Solanaceae |
| fig | edible fig | Ficus carica | Moraceae |
| flamboyant | poinciana, flame tree | Delonix regia | Caesalpiniaceae |
| fleabane | | Vernonia spp. | Compositae |
| four o'clock plant | marvel of Peru | Mirabilis jalapa | Nyctaginaceae |
| French cotton | mudar, madar | Calotropis procera | Asclepiadaceae |
| French thyme | Spanish thyme, country borage | Coleus aromaticus | Labiatae |
| garlic | | Allium sativum | Amaryllidaceae |
| ginger | | Zingiber officinale | Zingiberaceae |
| goatweed | herbe à femme | Ageratum spp. | Compositae |
| gooseberry | wild plum | Phyllanthus acidus | Euphorbiaceae |
| gourd | bottle gourd | Lagenaria vulgaris | Cucurbitaceae |
| groundnut | peanut, mani | Arachis hypogaea | Papilionaceae |
| guava | guayaba | Psidium guajava | Myrtaceae |
| guinep (Jamaica) | ackee or akee in Barbados | Melicoccus bijugatus | Sapindaceae |
| gungo pea | pigeon pea, no-eye pea | Cajanus cajan | Papilionaceae |
| hibiscus | shoeblack | Hibiscus rosa-sinensis | Malvaceae |
| hog plum | gully plum, jobo | Spondias mombin | Anacardiaceae |
| hogweed | easy-to-bruk | Boerhavia spp. | Nyctaginaceae |
| Indian laburnum | cassia-stick tree, purging cassia | Cassia fistula | Caesalpiniaceae |
| Irish potato | English potato | Solanum tuberosum | Solanaceae |
| jackfruit | jak fruit | Artocarpus heterophyllus | Moraceae |
| Job's tears | Christ's tears | Coix lachryma-jobi | Gramineae |
| jujube | dunk, mangustine | Ziziphus mauritiana | Rhamnaceae |
| June rose | Queen of flowers | Lagerstroemia speciosa | Lythraceae |
| jute | | Corchorus olitorius | Tiliaceae |
| khus khus | khas khas | Vetiveria zizanioides | Gramineae |
| kidney bean | bush bean, red pea, French bean, frijol | Phaseolus vulgaris | Papilionaceae |
| Kingston buttercup | | Tribulus cistoides | Zygophyllaceae |
| kola (cola) nut | bissy | Cola acuminata | Sterculiaceae |
| leaf of life | love leaf, resurrection plant | Bryophyllum pinnatum syn. Kalanchoe pinnata | Crassulaceae |

| Most used name | Other names | Scientific name | Family |
|---|---|---|---|
| lettuce | lechuga | *Lactuca sativa* | Compositae |
| lignum vitae | | *Guaiacum officinale* | Zygophyllaceae |
| logwood | campeche, tinta | *Haematoxylon campechianum* | Caesalpiniaceae |
| loofah | sponge gourd | *Luffa aegyptiaca* | Cucurbitaceae |
| love bush (vine) | dodder, devil's guts | *Cuscuta* spp. | Convolvulaceae |
| mahogany | | *Swietenia* spp. | Meliaceae |
| maize | corn, Indian corn, maiz | *Zea mays* | Gramineae |
| manchineel (manchioneel) | | *Hippomane mancinella* | Euphorbiaceae |
| mango | | *Mangifera indica* | Anacardiaceae |
| maraval lily | | *Spathiphyllum cannifolium* | Araceae |
| marijuana | ganja, hashish, Indian hemp | *Cannabis sativa* | Cannabaceae |
| Mexican poppy (thistle) | yellow hock | *Argemone mexicana* | Papaveraceae |
| mint | | *Mentha* spp. | Labiatae |
| morning glory | | *Ipomoea purpurea* | Convolvulaceae |
| Moses-in-the-bulrushes | two-men-in-a-boat | *Rhoeo spathacea* | Commelinaceae |
| naseberry | nispero, sapodilla | *Manilkara zapota* | Sapotaceae |
| night blooming cactus | | *Epiphyllum* spp. | Cactaceae |
| nutgrass | | *Cyperus rotundus* | Cyperaceae |
| nutmeg and mace | | *Myristica fragrans* | Myristicaceae |
| ochra (okra) | | *Hibiscus esculentus* | Malvaceae |
| oil palm | | *Elaeis guineensis* | Palmae |
| old man's beard | currant cactus | *Rhipsalis baccifera* | Cactaceae |
| old man's beard | Spanish moss | *Tillandsia usneoides* | Bromeliaceae |
| oleander | | *Nerium oleander* | Apocynaceae |
| onion | | *Allium cepa* | Amaryllidaceae |
| orange, lime etc | | *Citrus* spp. | Rutaceae |
| orchid | | *Orchis* spp. | Orchidaceae |
| otaheite apple | etiote apple, pommerac | *Eugenia malaccensis* | Myrtaceae |
| pawpaw | papaya | *Carica papaya* | Caricaceae |
| periwinkle | ramgoat rose | *Catharanthus roseus* | Apocynaceae |
| physic nut | Barbados nut | *Jatropha curcas* | Euphorbiaceae |
| pimento | allspice | *Pimenta dioica* | Myrtaceae |
| pineapple | | *Ananas comosus* | Bromeliaceae |
| pitcher plant | | *Nepenthes* spp. | Nepenthaceae |
| plantain | platano | *Musa paradisiaca* | Musaceae |
| poinsettia | Christmas flower | *Euphorbia pulcherrima* | Euphorbiaceae |
| prickly pear | tuna, flat hand dildo | *Opuntia* spp. | Cactaceae |
| pride of Barbados | flower fence, flambeau flower | *Caesalpinia pulcherrima* | Caesalpiniaceae |
| pumpkin | squash | *Cucurbita pepo* | Cucurbitaceae |
| quinine | | *Cinchona* spp. | Rubiaceae |
| radish | | *Raphanus sativus* | Cruciferae |
| railway weed | goatweed | *Tridax procumbens* | Compositae |
| rain lily | crocus | *Zephyranthes* spp. | Amaryllidaceae |
| rattleweed | shak shak | *Crotalaria* spp. | Papilionaceae |
| reed | common reed, wild cane | *Phragmites australis* | Gramineae |
| red mangrove | | *Rhizophora mangle, R. harrisonii* | Rhizophoraceae |
| red sorrel | sorrel, roselle | *Hibiscus sabdariffa* | Malvaceae |
| rice | arroz | *Oryza sativa* | Gramineae |
| rose | | *Rosa* spp. | Rosaceae |
| scallion | escallion | *Allium fistulosum* | Amaryllidaceae |
| screwpine | | *Pandanus* spp. | Pandanaceae |
| sedge | | *Cyperus* spp. | Cyperaceae |
| sea bean | purple seaside bean | *Canavalia maritima* | Papilionaceae |
| sea grape | mangrove grape tree | *Coccoloba uvifera* | Polygonaceae |
| seashore crabgrass | dropseed | *Sporobolus virginicus* | Gramineae |
| seaside ipomoea | goat's foot, morning glory | *Ipomoea pes-caprae* | Convolvulaceae |
| seaside mahoe | bark tree | *Hibiscus tiliaceus* | Malvaceae |
| semi-contra | worm weed, bitter weed | *Chenopodium ambrosioides* | Chenopodiaceae |
| senna | Indian senna | *Cassia italica* | Caesalpiniaceae |
| sensitive plant | shame weed, ti marie | *Mimosa pudica* | Mimosaceae |
| sensitive plant (Barbados) | | *Aeschynomene* spp. | Papilionaceae |
| silk cotton tree | kapok tree, fromager | *Ceiba pentandra* | Bombacaceae |
| sisal (hemp) | | *Agave sisalana* | Agavaceae |
| sourgrass | beardgrass | *Andropogon* spp. | Gramineae |
| soursop | | *Annona muricata* | Annonaceae |
| sow thistle | | *Sonchus* spp. | Compositae |
| soya bean | | *Glycine max* | Papilionaceae |
| Spanish needle (nettle) | duppy needle, mozote | *Bidens* spp. | Compositae |
| spider-plant | | *Chlorophytum comosum* | Liliaceae |
| spurge | milkweed | *Euphorbia hirta* | Euphorbiaceae |
| star apple | caimite | *Chrysophyllum cainito* | Sapotaceae |
| strangling fig | | *Ficus* spp. | Moraceae |
| sugar cane | cana de azucar | *Saccharum officinarum* | Gramineae |
| sundew | | *Drosera capillaris* | Droseraceae |
| sunflower | | *Helianthus annuus* | Compositae |
| sweethearts | dog tick | *Desmodium* spp. | Papilionaceae |
| sweet peppers and chillies | | *Capsicum* spp. | Solanaceae |
| sweet potato | camote | *Ipomoea batatas* | Convolvulaceae |
| sweet sop | sugar apple, pomme canelle | *Annona squamosa* | Annonaceae |
| tamarind | tamarindo | *Tamarindus indica* | Caesalpiniaceae |
| tea | | *Camellia sinensis* | Theaceae |
| thorn apple | devil's trumpets | *Datura stramonium* | Solanaceae |
| tobacco | tabaco | *Nicotiana tabacum* | Solanaceae |
| tomato | love apple, tomate | *Lycopersicon esculentum* | Solanaceae |
| turk's cap cactus | melon thick | *Melocactus communis* | Cactaceae |
| turmeric | | *Curcuma domestica* | Zingiberaceae |
| turnip | | *Brassica campestris* | Cruciferae |
| Venus fly trap | | *Dionaea muscipula* | Droseraceae |
| wandering Jew | creeping jenny | *Zebrina pendula* | Commelinaceae |
| water grass | pond grass | *Commelina* spp. | Commelinaceae |
| water hyacinth | | *Eichhornia crassipes* | Pontederiaceae |
| water lettuce | | *Pistia stratiotes* | Araceae |
| water lily | white water lily | *Nymphaea ampla* | Nymphaeaceae |
| water melon | sandia | *Citrullus linatus* | Cucurbitaceae |
| W. Indian cedar | cedar | *Cedrela odorata* | Meliaceae |
| W. Indian cherry | Barbados cherry, cherry | *Malpighia punicifolia* | Malpighiaceae |
| W. Indian ebony | cocus wood | *Brya ebenus* | Papilionaceae |
| W. Indian elm | bastard cedar, bois d'orme | *Guazuma ulmifolia* | Sterculiaceae |
| white mangrove | mangle blanco | *Laguncularia racemosa* | Combretaceae |
| whitewood | poirier | *Tabebuia pallida* | Bignoniaceae |
| wild sage | yellow sage | *Lantana* spp. | Verbenaceae |
| willow | whistling pine, mile tree | *Casuarina equisetifolia* | Casuarinaceae |
| woman's tongue | shak-shak | *Albizia lebbeck* | Mimosaceae |
| yam | | *Dioscorea* spp. | Dioscoreaceae |
| yellow sorrel | shamrock | *Oxalis* spp. | Oxalidaceae |
| zoysia | | *Zoysia* spp. | Gramineae |

# Index

*Past-into-Present Series*

# THE
# LIBERAL PARTY

## Peter Lane

Principal Lecturer in History,
Coloma College of Education

B T BATSFORD LTD London

First published 1973
© Peter Lane, 1973

Typeset and printed in Great Britain by
REDWOOD BURN LIMITED
Trowbridge & Esher
for the publishers
B T Batsford Ltd, 4 Fitzhardinge Street, London W1H 0AH
ISBN 0 7134 1791 9

# Acknowledgments

The Author and Publishers wish to thank the following for illustrations used in this book:
Baron Studios for fig. 61; *Country Life* for fig. 15; Fox Photos for fig. 62; The Greater
London Council for fig. 52; the Liberal Party Organisation for fig. 60; the Mansell
Collection for figs 3, 5, 8, 12, 13, 16, 18–22, 27, 33, 39–42, 47, 51, 53, 54, 56–59; the
Trustees of the National Maritime Museum for figs 17, 23; the Trustees of the National
Portrait Gallery for figs 6, 25; Radio Times Hulton Picture Library for figs 2, 11, 14,
31, 34, 37, 46, 55; the Trustees of the Victoria and Albert Museum for fig. 24; the
Walker Art Gallery, Liverpool for fig. 4. Fig. 30 is reproduced by gracious permission
of H M The Queen. Other pictures are from the publisher's collection.

# Contents

# The Illustrations

# Introduction

In 1882 a popular song went:

> *I often think it's comical*
> *How Nature always does contrive*
> *That every boy and every gal,*
> *That's born into the world alive,*
> *Is either a little Liberal*
> *Or else a little Conservative*

These words were written by W. S. Gilbert and, set to Sir Arthur Sullivan's music, form part of *Iolanthe*, one of the many successful operas which Gilbert and Sullivan wrote.

Gilbert was commenting on the political situation of the early 1880s—Gladstone and the Liberals had been in power from 1868 to 1874; Disraeli and the Conservatives had taken over in 1874 only to be displaced by the Liberals after the 1880 election. To Gilbert, and most of those who went to see *Iolanthe*, it seemed that, like Tweedledum and Tweedledee, there were two parties to one of which every voter owed allegiance.

But although *Iolanthe* is still produced to-day, Gilbert's words are obviously no longer true. In less than one hundred years the once-great Liberal Party has declined, and the Labour Party, which had not even been formed in 1882, has become the alternative to the Conservative Party. Why did this decline take place? Could it have been avoided, or was it inevitable? These are some of the questions which will be examined in Chapters 7 to 10.

1 A *Punch* cartoon of January 1886 shows Gladstone addressing the MPs who have entered the Commons for the first time after the 1886 election. He had first entered Parliament in 1832 and had earned the title of Grand Old Man as a sign of the respect in which he was held by his colleagues

THE GRAND OLD HAND AND THE YOUNG 'UNS.

**2** Gladstone (Picture 1) was the first Prime Minister who can be called a Liberal. Lloyd George (on the far left) was the last Liberal Prime Minister. In this picture he is talking to Orlando (of Italy) while Clemenceau (France) and President Wilson (USA) wait to restart their negotiations over the Peace Conference at Versailles, 1919

Gilbert wrote his words in 1882. If he had been writing a hundred years before, in 1782, he would not have used the same words, since the term 'Conservative' only came into popular political use after 1834, while the name 'Liberal' was not applied to a political party until the 1860s. In 1782 men may have been Whigs or Tories—or more likely of no political party at all. Those who were Whigs have some claim to be the forerunners of the later Liberal Party. Why did the Whigs change their name? Was this change merely one of title, or did it signify deeper and more fundamental changes of policies and ideas? These are among the questions to be examined in the course of this book.

Finally Gilbert says that 'every boy and every gal' was interested in the political life of the country. This was certainly untrue in the 1880s when only a minority of the men and none of the women in the country had a vote. But perhaps the non-voters did tend to support a political idea even though they did not have a vote—just as many thousands of people who have never been to either Oxford or Cambridge Universities still take a close interest in the annual Boat Race. But Gilbert's stress on 'every' one being involved in the country's political life is important. It reminds us that a political party is more than the handful of people who sit as MPs in the House of Commons. A political party is an organisation which includes MPs, national agents and officers, local constituency committee members, ward officials and rank-and-file members. Why do these people join a particular political party? What drives people out to canvass at election time? How do MPs and their opponents persuade the electorate to 'Vote for Bloggs' and not to 'Vote for Cloggs'?

6

# 1 The Seventeenth-century Roots of the Liberal Party

## The power of the Monarch 1660

In 1660 England was governed by politicians who had lived through the period of the Civil War (1640–6), had seen Charles I beheaded and had experimented with the republican government established by Oliver Cromwell. They restored the Monarchy in 1660 and gave it again almost supreme political power. Certainly Charles II ruled with a Parliament; but he alone decided when Parliament was to be summoned, prorogued and dissolved for an election to be held. The King could grant a borough the right to elect an MP—and could take away that right if it chose someone he disliked. Through his friendship with the more important landowners the King could influence the election results in the few places where elections were held and could persuade many of the landowners to nominate 'sympathetic' people for the many constituencies where elections were never held.

**3** The execution of Charles I in 1648 was a stage along the road to the formation of political parties. If you look carefully you can see the signature of Oliver Cromwell (left hand column)

FAC-SIMILE OF THE WARRANT FOR THE EXECUTION OF CHARLES I.
A.D. 1648.

The King chose his Ministers and, sitting in the Council, he determined the policies which his government should follow. Parliament might criticise a certain policy, but there seemed to be no way in which Parliament could challenge the power of the Monarch. 'God', it was said 'was the only ruler of princes'.

In this situation there was no room for political parties to develop. A political party exists so that people of similar ideas (Liberal, Conservative, Labour, Communist, etc) may try to gain control of the government of the country in order that they can put their ideas into practice. When the government of the country consisted of the Monarch and his friends, the Ministers whom he appointed and dismissed as he willed, there was no opportunity for any grouping of politicians to take place.

### The Stuarts and the Monarch's power

Between 1640 and 1646 there were the first glimmerings of two political parties; some MPs supported the claims of Charles I while others opposed him, claiming that the King should be subject to control by Parliament. But this was settled by war, and not by political argument. In the 1670s the same dispute arose again—was Parliament to have increased control over the King or not? This time the issue was settled without a war.

On 15 March 1672 Charles II issued a Declaration of Indulgence by which he proposed to grant freedom to Catholics and Nonconformists to practise their religion. To some this was merely a step towards religious toleration. To others it seemed part of a Stuart plan to restore Catholicism to the place it had held before Henry VIII's reign. Other parts of this plan were his own marriage to the Catholic Princess Catherine, the marriage of his brother, James, to a Catholic Princess, Mary of Modena, and Charles's friendship with the Catholic King Louis XIV. This religious issue was the one on which British political parties were founded.

As Charles was issuing the Declaration of Indulgence, French troops were pouring into Holland, while the English fleet was being defeated by the Dutch.

**4** (*Left*) Charles II painted by Kneller. It was Charles II's policies which drove politicians into forming the first political parties

**5** (*Right*) Anthony Ashley, the first Earl of Shaftesbury, one of Charles II's Ministers who became increasingly suspicious of the King's Catholic policies. He gathered a group of sympathisers in Parliament (the Whigs) and used various means to whip up support outside Parliament

This war had been declared while Parliament was not sitting and only France and Catholicism stood to gain from it.

The Parliament which reassembled in February 1673 had first been elected in 1662. At first it had been a very friendly Parliament—elected in the happy cavalier mood of the early 1660s. Time had changed this; by-elections caused by deaths or resignations had brought in a sprinkling of new members without the old memories and loyalties. Some Ministers—notably the first Earl of Shaftesbury—were now among those who distrusted Charles.

They could try to persuade Parliament to refuse to vote the King the taxes or 'supplies' he needed to carry on the unpopular war unless he first listened to their criticisms. But Charles had the power to dismiss Parliament and call for new elections—and his opponents were not at all sure that they would then win enough seats to constitute a threat to the Monarch's power.

## The Protestant challenge to Charles II

When Charles met his Parliament in March 1673 he declared: 'I will deal plainly with you. I am resolved to stick to my Declaration.' Parliament replied that 'Penal statutes in matters ecclesiastical cannot be suspended except by Acts of Parliament'. They refused to grant him the money he needed until the Declaration was withdrawn and in April 1673 Charles was forced to withdraw his Declaration.

This was a humiliation; but an even greater one was to follow. Parliament went on to pass a Test Act which required that every office-holder under the Crown had to take communion in the Anglican Church. Shaftesbury, later the leader of the Protestant Whigs, opposed this intolerant Act which was aimed at those Catholics whom Charles had appointed; MPs waited to see which of them would be driven from positions of power back into private life. One of Charles's Ministers was Clifford. Many suspected that he was a Catholic but could not confirm this until the doors of his carriage were accidentally flung open one day to reveal the

**6** Mary of Modena, the wife of the future James II; this Catholic Princess was a major factor in the formation of the Whig Party

9

figure of Clifford's Catholic chaplain in his priestly robes. Clifford resigned from his office of Treasurer.

But the Protestant MPs who led the opposition to Charles had a much more important victim in mind than Clifford. James, Duke of York, was the heir to the throne. He had become a Catholic in 1668 or 1669 and under the terms of the Test Act, he was obliged to give up his office of Lord High Admiral. This showed the strength of his Catholicism while at the same time alarmed those who were worried about the danger of a Catholic successor to Charles II. In November 1673 he re-married, choosing Mary of Modena—a Catholic who had wanted to become a nun. When she arrived in England the Lord Mayor of London refused to receive her—an indication of popular dislike for this Catholic marriage.

### The French Alliance
The fear of Catholicism was bound up in the opposition's mind with fear of France and its Catholic King. Early in 1674 Charles addressed Parliament:

> I cannot conclude without showing the entire confidence I have in you. I know you have heard much of my alliance with France; and I believe it hath been very strangely represented to you, as if there were certain secret Articles of dangerous consequence; but I will make no difficulty of letting the Treaties and all the Articles of them, without any the least reserve, to be seen by a small Committee of both Houses, who may report to you the true scope of them; and I assure you, there is no other Treaty with France, either before or since, not already printed, which shall not be made known.

This was untrue because Charles had made a secret Treaty of Dover with Louis, which bound him to the French King in return for financial aid. Parliament refused to give Charles the money he needed, so he dismissed the Parliament. He also dismissed Shaftesbury, still one of his Ministers, but now openly the leader of the opposition to Charles's pro-French and pro-Catholic policies.

### The Tories and the Whigs
Charles appointed Thomas Osborne, the Earl of Danby, to be one of his ministers. Danby was an Anglican and responsible for the Test Act, and disliked the French alliance. He was, however, loyal to the King. By using bribery and other means of persuasion he built up support among MPs so that the King could usually rely on a majority in the Commons. This Court party was nicknamed the Tory Party—a name given to Irish thieves and rebels.

Opposed to Danby was Shaftesbury who worked against the power of the King, the danger of the succession of the Catholic Duke of York and for the Protestant Dutch whom he thought should be helped in their war against Catholic France. His supporters were known as the Country or Whig Party. If there is one person who can lay claim to be the founder of modern political activity it is Shaftesbury.

**7** The interior of a London coffee house in the seventeenth century. Some of these were centres for merchants and financiers and from them developed some London financial institutions such as Lloyds. Other coffee houses were well-known as centres of political activity. In these the political leaders, such as Shaftesbury (Picture 5) could meet MPs, members of the House of Lords and other influential people. The coffee houses were the first political clubs and as such, were closed on Charles's orders.

## Political activity

Shaftesbury's aim, like that of all subsequent politicians, was to persuade other MPs and the electorate at large to support his policy of opposing the King and his policies. To do so Shaftesbury employed all the techniques of propaganda so that he tried to influence not only 'every boy' who was directly involved in political life, but the mob outside, who had no vote but who could be relied on to create an atmosphere of fear which, in turn, would influence the small number of those directly involved in elections or votes in the House of Commons. The London mob could always be relied on to rally under a 'No Popery' banner; the middle and upper classes could be reached in the coffee houses where those concerned with politics met to exchange plans and pamphlets. Shaftesbury himself presided over the Green Ribbon Club, whose members wore their colours to show their allegiance. Through the two daily newspapers then on sale in London Shaftesbury tried to influence the reading public. The wider reading public in the country as a whole was also offered a constant supply of news sheets and weekly or monthly journals, such as the *Tatler* and *Spectator*.

Among his main supporters were the clergy of the Anglican Church who exercised a great deal of influence in their village communities. Sermons by the clergy, poems, cartoons and plays were all used as media for the spread of Shaftesbury's Protestant propaganda. This was so successful that in 1675 Charles was refused supplies by an angry Parliament which he then prorogued without calling for a fresh election. He recalled this same Parliament in February 1677, after he had closed London's coffee houses where so much of the opposition gathered.

In the recalled Parliament, Shaftesbury demanded fresh elections—hoping that his supporters would triumph and his hand would be strengthened. The House of Lords sided with the King and sentenced Shaftesbury to imprisonment in the Tower of London. During Shaftesbury's imprisonment Charles managed to handle Parliament which insisted, however, that he should take account of the anti-French feeling. In the summer of 1678 he prorogued Parliament once again —just in time for the start of the 'Popish plot season'.

### Titus Oates and political activity

Titus Oates was a small, bow-legged man who claimed to be a biologist. He was also a cleric, having been at one time an Anglican clergyman and at another, a Jesuit priest. In 1678 he was a good Anglican again, eager to denounce his former Catholic colleagues. He claimed to have evidence of a Catholic plot to murder the King and put James on the throne. On 28 September, Oates was examined by the Privy Council, to whom he told a marvellous tale. The Pope was in the plot, as were the King of France, the General of the Jesuits and the Archbishop of Dublin. In England, five Catholic peers—Arundel, Powis, Petre, Stafford and Bellassis—were named as leaders, and he said that at a given signal thousands of Catholic fanatics were to rise and murder the honest Protestant citizens of London while the capital would be burned to the ground by an army of incendiaries.

S.r E. B. Godfree takeing D.r
Oates his depositions.

**8** One of a set of playing cards issued in 1684 by the Whigs who wanted to whip up opposition to James II. Titus Oates (with his back to the artist) is giving his evidence about the Popish Plot to the magistrate, Sir Edmund Berry Godfrey. Godfrey's death in suspicious circumstances merely strengthened the opposition to the King

**9** On the anniversary of Queen Elizabeth I's accession, 17 November 1679, Shaftesbury organised a massive anti-Catholic procession to march through the City of London. The scene reconstructs the Popish Plot showing the Pope, Jesuits with knives at the ready, and other Catholic plotters, following the magistrate Godfrey (Picture 8). This was one example of the way in which Shaftesbury and his Whigs whipped up support for their anti-Catholic policies. Today politicians can use radio, television and newspapers to achieve the same object—although mass processions through London are still used as political propaganda

The King was to be waylaid by Irish ruffians; stabbed to death by Jesuits; shot with silver bullets in St James's park and poisoned by the Queen's physician. Charles laughed at the idea of such a plot. However, on 12 October the magistrate who had first heard Oates's testimony disappeared and five days later was found dead on Primrose Hill. Although there was some evidence that it was suicide, the majority preferred to believe that he had been killed by the Catholics. The magistrate's name, Sir Edmund Berry Godfrey, was turned into 'Dy'd by Rome's reveng'd fury' and overnight London was in the grip of anti-Catholic hysteria. People barricaded their houses; ladies carried pistols; Catholic houses were searched for weapons; priests were hunted down and suspects dragged off to prison. A cutler who made 'Godfrey' knives sold three thousand in one day. Throughout London the mob marched with the slogan of 'No Popery'. From his headquarters at the King's Head Tavern, Shaftesbury and the other members of the Green Ribbon Club made the most of their opportunity to attack the Duke of York, the friendship with France and the King's Catholic policies.

In 1679 Charles dismissed Parliament and called for new elections—the first for eighteen years. The well-organised Country (Whig) Party set out to ensure by persuasion, bribery and intimidation that when the new Parliament met it would be dominated by their supporters. To try to cool the atmosphere Charles sent the Duke of York to Brussels and made Shaftesbury a member of the Council again. However, the Country Party was not to be bought off in this way. In April the Commons debated that: 'The Duke of York being a Papist and the hope of his coming soon to the Crown have given the greatest countenance and encouragement to the present conspiracies and designs of Papists against the King and the Protestant religion.' In May the Commons carried a resolution that: 'a bill be brought to disable the Duke of York to inherit the Imperial Crown of this realm'. Charles dismissed this Parliament, saying: 'I will submit to anything rather than endure the gentlemen of the Commons any longer'.

On 17 November, the anniversary of the accession of Queen Elizabeth I, Shaftesbury and the Green Ribbon Club organised a massive show of strength. This was followed by the parliamentary debate on the Exclusion Bill which was finally defeated by Charles's friends. Charles then dissolved this Parliament and announced that after elections a new Parliament would meet in Oxford, away from London's coffee houses, mobs and demonstrations.

**Reaction**
Shaftesbury's attempts to form what we would call a political party with himself as leader, alarmed many people who had previously been willing to agree with his opposition to the autocratic Charles. This alarm was reflected in the pro-Stuart pamphlets, the refusal of juries to bring in verdicts against people accused by Titus Oates and the election of MPs opposed to the Exclusion Bill.

In March 1681 Charles went to meet his last Parliament, knowing that the French King had renewed his money subsidy so that Charles did not need Parliament's approval and note of supplies. The Whigs, on the other hand, having lost the battle over Exclusion were determined to have a final throw.

**10** James II. When he was Duke of York he had aroused the suspicions and fears of many people because of his Catholicism. His policies after his accession led to the 1688 rebellion and marked a major step along the road to the development of political parties

Shaftesbury lined the roads to Oxford with his armed supporters: opposed to them were the King's men. This seemed, for a while, the prelude to yet another civil war: but, unlike 1640, the opposing groups tried to settle the argument in Parliament, without fighting.

In Oxford Shaftesbury demanded that James be excluded from the succession. Charles replied that to do this was against divine justice and the law of the land; the Earl told him that Parliament would attend to the alteration of the law. The King's reply was emphatic:

> My Lord [he said] let there be no self-delusion. I will never yield and will not let myself be intimidated. Men ordinarily become more timid as they grow old; as for me, I shall be, on the contrary, bolder and firmer and I will not stain my life and reputation in the little time that perhaps remains for me to live. I do not fear the dangers and calamities which people try to frighten me with. I have the law and reason on my side.

A few days later, on 28 March, Charles summoned the Commons to assemble, led by the confident Exclusionists. To their surprise Charles announced that Parliament was dissolved.

The reaction in Charles's favour now gathered pace. On 2 July Shaftesbury was again arrested and sent to the Tower; boroughs were forced to give up their charters; Whig Mayors and Sheriffs were replaced by Royalists, and everywhere the Crown was victorious. Shaftesbury, acquitted by a London jury, fled to Holland where he died, broken in spirit and crippled in body.

## Conclusion

This first step along the road to the formation of political parties is important, not only because it was a first step, but because it tells us a good deal about the roots of liberalism. Then, as later, liberals opposed the autocrat and campaigned for some popular control over the King's power: then, as later, liberalism stood for religious toleration—but was very suspicious of Roman Catholicism: then, as later, liberals were supporters of small national movements (e.g. in Holland) and opponents of despotic Monarchs such as Louis XIV. These liberal seeds flowered in the eighteenth and nineteenth centuries.

# 2  The Eighteenth-century Whig Party

**James II's overthrow**

The reaction to the Rye House Plot to kill the King was used by the Court (or Tory) Party to whip up support for Charles II. Many towns were deprived of their charters and the right to elect an MP. When James II came to the throne in 1685 the Commons contained a majority of MPs who were either active members of the Tory Party or passively willing to allow that Party to have its way. However, James II's Catholic policies were such that by 1688 even many Tories had become convinced that he could not continue to govern. An informal alliance between leading Whigs and leading Tories led to an invitation being sent to the Stuart Queen Mary and her husband, William of Orange; they arrived in England in 1688 and, after a brief war fought mainly in Ireland, James II was driven into exile, while William and Mary became joint rulers of the country.

**The Glorious Revolution**

1688 is one of the most significant dates in British history. Parliament, under the leadership of both Tory and Whig politicians, asserted its right to throw one King off the throne—so that Monarchs could no longer claim that 'God was the

**11**  The coronation of William III and Mary II who ascended the throne at the invitation of Whig and Tory politicians. This marked a weakening of the power of Monarchs and a growth in the power of Parliament and the politicians

only ruler of princes'. Parliament also invited William and Mary to become Monarchs—so indicating that the throne was Parliament's to dispose of as it wished. One of the main planks of Whiggery had been attained.

When Parliament invited William and Mary to take the throne it also drew up a series of documents for the Monarchs to sign. In these, Parliament tried to ensure that no future Monarch would be able to behave as James II had done; Parliament had to be summoned each year at least; the Monarch was not allowed a permanent army which might be used to overawe Parliament and people; Catholics were forbidden to become Monarchs. Parliament also tried to deal with the problem of who was to govern the country in future—but here it was less successful.

Briefly, the Settlement agreed that the Monarch had the right to appoint the Ministers and to decide government policy. In this the Settlement made very little change from the past. However, it was also made clear that both the Ministers and their policies would have to be acceptable to Parliament. What was not clear was which of the two were supposed to be the more important—the throne or Parliament? The Settlement did not try to assert that Parliament was supreme. The new form of power was to be the King–in–Parliament—which was a step along the road to parliamentary power and government—but only a step, and not the final one.

## The political power of the Monarch

We have already seen that Shaftesbury formed a sort of political party in the 1670s. His aim, and that of every other party leader since then, was to try to gain enough support both in Parliament and in the country as a whole to ensure that his policies would be carried out by the government. This is what political parties are about—men want to control the government (or executive) and the Parliament (or legislative) to get their policies into operation.

Today we are accustomed to this. In the late seventeenth and early eighteenth centuries it was not quite so clear. In the first place it was generally agreed that it was the Monarch's job to govern—even after 1688. Most MPs, even at the end of the eighteenth century, did not represent a political party; they were independent MPs whose main aim was to represent the interests of the constituency from which they came. Provided that the Monarch got on with his job and was seen to be doing it effectively, these MPs were normally prepared to vote for the government's policies.

Then there was the great influence exercised by the Crown over the Lords (one of the Houses of Parliament), the Commons and the electorate. The Lords are, in one sense, the second rung in the social ladder on top of which sits the Monarch—from whom they get their titles. The Lords usually acted as a House on which the Monarch could depend. It was the Lords, for example, which threw out the India Bill proposed by Fox and North in 1783 although this Bill had been

**12** The British electoral system in the days of open voting when although few people had the vote, almost everyone took part in the long period of disturbance which accompanied the election. If you examine the picture you will understand why a King's agent, an influential landowner or an influential Minister would be able to 'fix' an election

passed by the Commons against the wishes of King George III (see Chapter 3).

There were 513 MPs elected for English and Welsh constituencies in 1740. About one-fifth of them were civil servants, legal advisers to one of the government departments, Army or Navy officers or MPs representing Crown properties in Cornwall and other counties. These MPs would be bound to vote as the Monarch wished—whether the government was a Whig one, as under Walpole, or a mainly Tory one, as under the Younger Pitt. Apart from these 'tied' MPs, the Crown could also exercise a good deal of influence over other MPs; one might be promised a title or one of the many well-paid but undemanding jobs which the Crown had to give out; another could be offered a place in the government with all the financial rewards that this could bring. There might be contracts for that merchant or a promotion for that soldier. There were so many ways in which the Crown could ensure that many of the apparently independent MPs were influenced in the way in which they cast their votes.

**Landowning politicians**

Sometimes supporting and sometimes opposing the Monarch were the very wealthy landowning families who exercised almost a Monarch's power in the areas where they owned the land. When looking at the origins of parties we have to remember that in the eighteenth century only about 160,000 men were qualified to vote. The most democratic qualification was that which allowed everyone who owned the freehold of land worth an annual rent of forty shillings (£2) to vote in the county (or non-borough) constituencies. This gave the vote to about 15,000 men in Yorkshire and about 600 in Rutland. There were various ways in which these county elections could be influenced; one landowner might buy up all the freeholds in his area so that only he had the vote; another might use his social influence to persuade his less-wealthy colleagues to vote as he wished. In an open system of voting he would know how they had voted and could ensure that only those who had voted as he wished would get that coveted invitation to the castle, or that promised post for a son or relative.

Much less democratic were the boroughs; in some every ratepayer had the right to vote; in others only those who owned certain houses; in others only the freemen; in others only the members of the local council or corporation. In many there was no-one who had the right to vote and a local patron would himself nominate the two MPs for the borough. In these constituencies it was fairly easy for an MP to bribe his way to success. This was often expensive—as Gladstone found as late as 1832 when his election at Newark cost him £30,000. This expense helps to explain why there were so many uncontested seats, even in 1860; rather than spend this sort of money, and fail to win (as one of the parties obviously had to fail), the various interests involved would often agree that Lord x should have the right to name the MP for borough y, while Lord A should have the same right for borough B. Sometimes the bribery went wrong, as Pitt discovered.

19

A by-election was impending in Yorkshire, and Pitt, paying a social visit to the famous Mrs B—one of the Whig Queens of the West Riding—said banteringly: 'Well, the election is all right for us. Ten thousand guineas for the use of our side go down to Yorkshire tonight by a sure hand.'

'The devil they do!' responded Mrs B, and that night the bearer of the precious burden was stopped by a highwayman on the Great North Road, and the ten thousand guineas were used to procure the return of the Whig candidate.

## Voters and MPs

It was not only the electorate which was small and select; to become a candidate one had to own land worth £600. These candidates were drawn from a small

**13** Thomas Pelham, the Duke of Newcastle, the great 'borough monger' who 'ran' the electoral system in the first half of the eighteenth century on behalf of the Whig Party

class of wealthy people—able to afford the time away from their estates or able to combine the task of being an MP with their job as lawyer or officer.

Since the candidates and the MPs came from a small social class they tended to have the same ideas—about taxation, trade, the rights of property and so on—so that it was fairly easy for the government of the day to know what sorts of things would please and what would offend them.

Whilst there were 513 MPs for England and Wales, few of these were interested in being Ministers in the government. Many MPs did not go to London at all in the winter, when travel was dangerous; others were absent on service in the Army or Navy. The small group of regular attenders were those who were really interested in the art of government and ambitious enough to want to share in this interesting and financially rewarding work. As with the candidates, so with these active politicians; they were drawn from a very small social class nearly all of whom had been to the same schools and many of whom were related by marriage.

These inter-related politicians tended to group themselves around one or other of the more talented or influential of their set, so that we find that Lord Townshend had his followers while the Duke of Grafton had his. When a Monarch wanted to form a government he was restricted in his choice by the existence of this sort of grouping; would the Duke of Portland's supporters enter into a Ministry led by the Earl of Chatham? If not, could Chatham get others who would support him? If he could not, then Chatham could not form a Ministry and the King would have to try someone else.

This helps to explain the long dominance of the Whigs as the governing party in the early and mid-eighteenth century. Between 1688 and 1713 first William and Mary, then Queen Anne, had appointed both Whigs and Tories as Ministers. Broadly it was true that the Tories were appointed to look after home affairs while the Whigs were appointed to look after foreign affairs; they were more likely to be anti-French and pro-Dutch than the Tories who had once supported Charles II's policies.

But when Queen Anne died in 1714 the Tories, then in power, tried to set aside the Act of Settlement (by which the Elector of Hanover was to be invited to become King in succession to the childless Anne), and to invite a Stuart (who would have been James III) back to the throne again. Their attempt failed, and when Elector George became King George I, he naturally turned to those politicians who had opposed this plot to keep him off the throne in favour of a Stuart. He turned to the Whigs in 1714 and so began nearly a half century of one-party government.

### Whig principles and policies
This long period of Whig government gives us a chance to see what Whiggery meant and to see whether it provided any more 'roots' for later liberalism. The most famous of the Whig Ministers was Sir Robert Walpole and if we examine his

**14** This print appeared in 1737. Captain Jenkins (with wig being removed) is trying to show his ear—in his left hand—to Walpole, who refuses to see it. A merchant with complaints about Spanish attacks on British shipping is being pushed out through the door, whilst a complaint from another is being chewed up by Walpole's dog. Through one door you can see a British ship being attacked by the Spaniards, and through the other, money being poured into the Sinking Fund—Walpole's scheme for paying off the National Debt. 'Peace at any price' seemed to be Walpole's policy

long period of rule (1721–42) we find that his policies were concerned mainly with taxation, trade, religious toleration and peace. It is almost impossible to separate these policies from one another since each influenced the other; if Walpole had pursued a warlike policy then he would also have had to implement a different policy on taxation in order to raise the money needed to fight his wars.

Walpole tried to lower the levels of every tax; in the case of the land tax which was paid by the country gentlemen he succeeded in lowering this from 4 shillings (20p) to 1 shilling (5p) an acre. This considerable reduction meant that the land-owner kept more of his money than he had previously done. This was important because the country gentlemen might have been the supporters of the Stuarts in 1715 and 1745, when the Jacobites tried to overthrow the Hanoverian Monarchy.

**15** The Gallery in Horace Walpole's house at Strawberry Hill, Twickenham. This son of the Prime Minister made enough money out of the corrupt political system to build himself this magnificent house

This principle of lowering taxes is certainly one which was inherited by the Liberals who, under Gladstone in the late nineteenth century, claimed that the abolition of income tax was the main plank in their electoral platform (see Chapters 5, 6 and 7).

Walpole also tried to lower indirect taxes, particularly taxes paid on imports and exports. He lived long before Adam Smith, who is sometimes called the 'Father of Free Trade' because he called for the total abolition of import duties (or tariffs). Walpole believed that a reduction in tariffs would lead to a fall in prices, which would lead to an increase in demand. Here is another root which flowered in the Liberal Party in the nineteenth century.

Intimately connected with this policy of low taxation was Walpole's policy of peace abroad. This led him to ignore the successful attempts by the American colonists to develop their own trade—even though this meant breaking his own Molasses Act (1733) and led to wholesale smuggling. Walpole had the sense to see that the choice lay between adopting this 'blind-eye' attitude to what was happening, or going to war with the growing colonies. Later Liberals would adopt the same attitude towards British colonies, being prepared to accept the case for greater colonial freedom and the development of what had once been subject races in Asia and Africa.

In foreign, as distinct from colonial, affairs Walpole maintained a peaceful policy. When he was finally forced by popular demand to declare war against Spain in 1739, he listened to the sound of London rejoicing at this opportunity to attack its trading enemy and then declared: 'They now ring the bells but they will soon wring their hands'. Here again, Walpole was the fore-runner to the nineteenth–century tradition of a peaceful foreign policy (see Chapters 5 and 6). In one sense this was a departure from Whiggery which had supported the war against France on the side of the Protestant Dutch; it had been the Tories who stood for peace with the Continent.

Walpole is perhaps best known for his remark 'Let sleeping dogs lie' which indicated his policy of not doing anything which would upset the people as a whole. This later developed into the policy of *laissez faire* which was adopted by the Liberals in the nineteenth century (see Chapters 4–6). This policy of non-activity or non-interference made the Whigs, and later the Liberals, popular with those people who had a good life, but it allowed conditions to develop in towns, factories, schools and so on, which made life very harsh for the majority of the population and led to a demand for government interference in the nation's economic and social life.

# 3  Fox, the Whigs and Liberalism

## The political system in 1760

George III came to the throne in 1760 when he was only 22 years old. He had been taught by his mother, and his tutor—the Earl of Bute—to believe that the Whigs had taken away power from the first two Georges. They were wrong. King George II had been an independent King—as was allowed him by the Settlement of 1688. In his *Memoirs of the Reign of George II*, Lord Hervey recalls:

> The Queen [Caroline] had in five years changed his Majesty's first plan of government . . . . He intended to have all his Ministers in the nature of clerks,

**16**  George III was the first Hanoverian King to be born in Britain. He wanted to end the domination of the political system by the Whigs by reclaiming for the Monarchy the power that had been given it by the Revolutionary Settlement which followed the overthrow of James II. This displeased the Whigs who claimed that George was trying to overthrow the constitution

not to give advice, but to receive orders; and proposed to distribute favours through no principal channel, but to hear from all quarters ... the Queen possessed his Majesty that it was necessary that he should have but one Minister; and that it was equally necessary, from Sir Robert's superior abilities, that he should be that one .... His way of thinking, and his behaviour towards Sir Robert Walpole was visibly changed; for ... instead of hating him whilst he employed him, he very apparently now took all occasions to declare him his first Minister.

This is only one of many examples that could be used to show that the first two Georges were aware of their power and frequently used it. They knew also that their Ministers had to win the support of Parliament. The political system was a balance of power between the King and his Ministers, on the one hand, and Parliament on the other. In 1760 most leading politicians were Whigs—even Bute called himself a Whig when he was attacking the policies of the Ministers of George I and II. Many of the independent country MPs were Tories, suspected of hankering after the return of the Stuarts, resentful of the upstart Hanoverian Monarchy, in favour of High Anglicanism and opposed to Nonconformity.

### George acts as King

In 1761 George III appointed Bute as one of the Secretaries of State—the other was Pitt. Bute and George III were anxious to end the war with France and Spain; Pitt was in favour of continuing the war. Horace Walpole, the son of the former Prime Minister, described Pitt's attack on the proposed Peace Treaty. 'The doors opened, and at the head of a large, acclaiming concourse was seen Mr Pitt, borne in the arms of his servants; he crawled by the help of a crutch .... He allowed the prerogative of the Crown in making peace or war. The Crown might finally sign the Treaty; but at the same time it was a fundamental right of the House of Commons to offer their opinion'.

Pitt, the war-hero, acknowledged in this speech the King's right to govern. One of the King's Ministers was Henry Fox, who was anxious to get Parliamentary approval for the proposed peace treaty. Horace Walpole recalled:

[Fox] set himself to work at the root; he directly attacked the separate members of the House of Commons; a shop was publicly opened at the Pay Office, whither the members flocked, and received the wages of their venality in bank-bills. Twenty-five thousand pounds, as Martin, Secretary of the Treasury, afterwards owned, were issued in one morning; and in a single fortnight a vast majority was purchased to approve the peace.

'The King', it was given out, '*would* be King ... great lords must be humbled!' The Peace Bill was passed by 223 votes to 63. Whoever, holding a place, had voted against the preliminaries, was instantly dismissed.

**17** The taking of Quebec, September 1759. Britain's success in wars against France led to the creation of an American and Indian Empire as well as to major colonial possessions in the West Indies. These successes not only made the Whigs popular; they also helped to create the conditions which were favourable to the so-called Industrial Revolution of the late eighteenth century. This, in turn, was a major factor in the development of a new political framework in which Liberalism developed

The Honourable
Roger North Esq.ʳ
Ætatis cir. 30.

**18** Lord North, George III's Chief Minister, 1770–1783. In spite of the opposition of Fox and the Whigs, North could govern because of the support he got from the majority of MPs and their patrons. When his policies led to defeat in the American War, the Commons withdrew their support and North had to resign in spite of the King's wish that he should continue. Power was still shared between the King who had the right to appoint Ministers, and Parliament which had the right to support or oppose Ministers

## Power of Parliament

The King had the right to govern; he had the assistance of the patronage system to help him get his own way. But as the 1688 Settlement had made clear, the King still had to get Parliament to approve his policies. George's favourite, Bute, soon became unpopular with Parliament, owing to his wish to increase taxation, and was resented because of his treatment of John Wilkes. Bute was forced to resign. In his place George III appointed George Grenville, a brother-in-law to Pitt. He proposed that the American colonists should pay part of the cost of their own future defence against Indian, French, or Spanish attacks. His Stamp Act (1765) was the first of a series of Acts proposing ways of raising money in the American colonies; this Act, like the others, was ineffective and had to be dropped after rousing great opposition in the colonies and in Parliament, and Grenville was forced to resign. There followed a rapid succession of weak Whig Ministries, led in turn by Rockingham, Pitt (now Lord Chatham) and Grafton. All of them were short-lived since Parliament refused to agree to the American policies which each proposed.

This rapid succession of weak Ministries worried some MPs. A group of them met to declare: 'His Majesty should have the free choice of his own servants and that he should not put the management of his affairs unconditionally into the hands of the leader of any party'. They hoped that there would be enough MPs who 'have always hitherto acted upon the sole principle of attachment to the Crown' to ensure that a stable government could be formed. These MPs became known as the King's Friends; some of them were ambitious politicians; others were independent MPs who merely wanted to see an efficient government in power.

## Lord North

In 1770 George III appointed Lord North as his leading Minister. The North government was as unsuccessful at dealing with American colonies as previous governments had been. In 1775 war broke out, much to the annoyance of many Whig politicians. As Chatham said in 1777: 'As to conquest, therefore, my lords, I repeat, it is impossible. If I were an American, as I am an Englishman, while a foreign troop was landed in my country, I never would lay down my arms, —never—never—never!' A rising member of the Rockingham Whigs was an Irish lawyer, Edmund Burke, who said of the American struggles: 'An Englishman is the unfittest person on earth to argue another Englishman into slavery'.

## Edmund Burke

It was Edmund Burke who, in 1770, first wrote about the benefits of party government. In *Thoughts on the Cause of the Present Discontents* he examined why the Americans were threatening to revolt. He claimed that the root of the trouble lay in George III's attempts to govern without a party. Burke claimed that the King's Friends, who were not a political party, could not produce a workable policy.

**19** Edmund Burke, MP, painted by one of Reynold's pupils. Burke was a follower of Rockingham, one of the leading Whigs who wanted to lessen George III's influence. His *Thoughts on the causes of the present discontents* was the first serious attempt to argue in favour of party government. In this book Burke was looking ahead to the future; few of his contemporaries shared his opinion

On the other hand he believed that government by a political party could produce successful policies, since a party is 'a body of men united for promoting by their joint endeavours the national interest upon some particular principle in which they are all agreed'.

Burke was wrong; there were no political parties in his sense of the word—only loose alliances around the leading politicians. George III's apparently increased power was mainly due to the break-up of the Whigs into warring factions so that no King and no Minister could form a stable government.

As one method of limiting what he thought of as increased royal power, Burke proposed a modest parliamentary reform. Under his 'economical reform' many of the useless offices in the royal household would be abolished, many Crown officials would not be allowed either to vote or to sit in Parliament. This would save taxpayers' money; it would also lessen the influence of the King over the

**20** Fox brings Pitt's head to the French revolutionary leader Dumourier, who dined at St James's on 15 May 1793

commons. Charles Fox supported this and in 1782 the Civil Establishment Act was passed, carrying out many of Burke's proposals. One of those who were affected by it was Edward Gibbon, the historian. He recalled:

> I was appointed one of the Lords Commissioners of Trade and Plantations [1779]: and my private income was enlarged by a clear addition of between seven and eight hundred pounds a year. . . . It must be allowed that our duty was not intolerably severe and that I enjoyed many days and weeks of repose, without being called away from my library to the office. . . . The Board itself was abolished by [this] bill, which decency compelled the patriots to revive; and I was stripped of a convenient salary, after having enjoyed it about three years.

## Fox and the King

In March 1782 the country gentlemen in the Commons made it clear that Lord North's government was no longer going to get their support; following continual defeats in the American War, the King sent once again for Rockingham, who died after only three months in office, to be succeeded by another Whig, Shelburne. He negotiated the Treaty of Versailles which brought the American War to an end. This roused the anger of North and his followers, and because of the concessions that were made to France, Fox and the Rockingham Whigs were also annoyed. In February 1783 an alliance of the old enemies, Fox and North, defeated Shelburne.

The King disliked Fox intensely, believing that he intended to destroy the royal power. But since Parliament approved of the alliance, the King had to accept a Fox-North Coalition government. Many people were critical of this alliance; some thought that Fox had given up his ideas of limiting the King's power and of Parliamentary reform: others attacked him because he signed the Treaty of Versailles which he had so vigorously opposed. Others saw in the alliance a cynical grasping for political power—why else should Fox ally with his enemy, North?

In December 1783 Fox brought in an India Bill to try to deal with the problems of British rule in that country. The measure was passed by the Commons where Fox and North had a majority. The King, however, used his influence with the Lords to ensure that the Bill was defeated. Less than a week before Christmas he dismissed the Coalition and appointed William Pitt, then only twenty-three, as First Lord of the Treasury.

## Fox versus the King

Since Fox and North had a majority in the Commons it is easy to understand that they were angered by the King's attempt to foist Pitt on the nation. After all, if the King had the right to appoint Ministers, Parliament had the right to approve or disapprove of his choice. For four months Pitt faced violent opposition in the Commons; all his proposals were defeated by the stronger alliance. The 'schoolboy minister' of the 'mince-pie administration', which was expected to fall once Christmas was out of the way, held on.

George III used the wide powers of royal patronage to persuade some MPs to support Pitt and to persuade the Lords to advise their nominees to do so. Pitt himself knew what it was to be a nominee: he had been elected to Parliament in 1780 as the MP for one of the nine boroughs which a friend of his controlled. Pitt's courage in standing up to the continual attack aroused a certain sympathy, and his refusal to take any of the usual sinecure offices which would have enriched him won him even wider support. By March 1784 Fox had a majority of one over Pitt in the Commons. Pitt's opponents, demanded that the King should listen to the voice of the Commons and dismiss Pitt in favour of Fox. George III refused to do so. In March 1784 he dissolved Parliament and called a general election.

21 Adam Smith—a painting by John Kay, 1790. Smith has been called the father of economics, the subject which tries to explain how money is earned and spent, how businesses are run and why taxes have to be paid. His work and that of other economists, such as Nassau Senior and Ricardo, was a great influence on the development of Liberal ideas on Free Trade, *laissez faire*, taxation, overseas trade and peace

Pitt and the King, between them, won a great victory: between 100 and 120 of Fox's followers lost their seats and earned the nickname 'Fox's martyrs'. The power of politicians was still limited.

### The French Revolution

In 1789 the French King was forced to call his States General and it seemed that France was going to develop some sort of constitutional government on the British model. The attack on the Bastille symbolised the French people's determination to end the days of royal tyranny. Fox, who had welcomed the prospect of a democratic France, endorsed the attack on the Bastille, saying: 'How much the greatest event it is that ever happened in the world! And how much the best!' He described the draft of the proposed French constitution as 'the most stupendous and glorious edifice of liberty which has been erected on the foundation of human integrity in any time or country.'

But his former ally, Edmund Burke, was the first to see that the French Revolution had little in common with England's 'Glorious Revolution' of 1688. Burke had upheld the rights of the Americans: he had proposed parliamentary reform and the limiting of the power of George III. But he was totally opposed to the French Revolution which did nothing to amend the past but to destroy it, and which was trying to produce an 'equality' which could never accompany 'liberty'. Burke's *Reflections on the Revolution in France* was published in 1790. Opposition to Burke's point of view came from radicals such as Tom Paine, from dissenters such as Dr Price and Joseph Priestley. But the mass of political opinion and the greater part of popular opinion sided with Burke. Most of the leading Whig politicians became anti-French, leaving Fox with only a handful of supporters to oppose Britain's entry into the war against France in 1793.

With the onset of war, the Pitt government became steadily more repressive, fearing that British radicals—demanding parliamentary and other reform—might easily bring about the British counterpart of the bloody French Revolution.

Amongst the victims of the reactionary backlash was the Corresponding Society movement. A Corresponding Society was a political group which encouraged members in different parts of the country to exchange pamphlets and views. Many of them were working class in origin, demanding universal suffrage and annual Parliaments. One such was the *Society of the Friends of the People* which was founded by a young Whig nobleman, Charles Grey. Burke and other Whigs repudiated such developments; Fox, true to his principles, sided with the young Grey.

### Fox in government, 1806

Pitt died in 1806 and George III was forced to appoint a Ministry of 'all the talents', including Fox. The Ministry was very short-lived since George III worked for its overthrow. Fox himself was dead before the year was out. But in that short time he did manage to get Parliament to pass one major piece of legislation which

22  Fox and his friends bemoan the success of Nelson and the defeat of the French

**23** The Battle of Trafalgar, 1805. This victory kept England safe from the danger of a French invasion, ensured the freedom of the seas for British traders and reflected the growing power of the small island nation of 'shopkeepers' who were soon to become the world's leading traders and industrialists. Liberalism flourished in the climate of industrial progress

abolished British participation in the slave trade. This was a step along the road to the abolition of slavery (see Chapter 4).

### Fox's heritage

Fox and the Whigs held office for only two short periods and in the 1790s he saw the former reformers like Burke become supporters of Pitt and the Tories. In one sense he left little behind him—a broken party with his own supporters driven from public life by a mob which equated the Whigs with revolution and massacre. But in another sense he had left a good deal behind. He had campaigned for the growth of parliamentary control over the Crown; he had succeeded in passing a modest Reform Act which limited the political power of George III; he sided with Grey and his Whig friends in their demand for reform; he taught that foreigners—whether American or black—had rights as great as those of an Englishman; he had claimed the right for foreigners—whether American or French—to determine their own political future. These were valuable contributions to the development of Whig-Liberalism.

# 4  The Last of the Aristocratic Whigs, 1832

**The changing industrial scene**

If Shaftesbury had fallen asleep in 1670 and woken up again in 1770 he would have recognised the country in which he found himself. There was a King arguing with Whig politicians as to his power and their claim to control it; there were arguments about foreign wars with France and Spain; there was the aristocratic upper class exercising political power in the House of Lords and, through its nominees, in the House of Commons. The country was still predominantly agricultural; most people lived in small villages and London was the only town of any real size.

But if someone had fallen asleep in 1780 to wake up again in 1880 their reaction would have been totally different. Britain was, by 1880, the workshop of the world, the pioneer of industrial change which had produced the steam engine, the railway system, massive factories, sprawling towns and a tremendous growth in population. In 1780 the nation's life revolved around an axis running from London through Oxford to Bristol—with the agricultural South and South West dominating life.

**24** *Work on the Tyne*—a painting which illustrates the changes that took place in the nineteenth century. Heavy equipment, such as the crane (on the left), coal, iron and steel were used by British craftsmen to build and run ships, engines, textile machinery and mills in the new industrial towns of the 'new Britain'. Liberalism had firm roots in these industrial centres

By 1880 the centre of activity had changed and the axis now ran from London through Birmingham to Manchester and Liverpool, with the industrial areas of Lancashire and Yorkshire, the Midlands and South Wales dominating the nation's economic life.

## Changing political problems

This evolution in the industrial and economic scene was accompanied by many other changes. There was the growth of an industrial middle class—of factory-owners, merchants, financiers—and the growth of a professionally qualified middle class—of engineers, surveyors, doctors, accountants and so on. These were the products of the industrial change which started in the middle of the eighteenth century but gathered pace in the nineteenth.

There had always been a middle class—below the landed gentry and above the working people. But before the Industrial Revolution its members had been relatively few in number, and the landed gentry would either admit them to their ranks—particularly if they bought country estates and tried to get titles for themselves—or they could ignore them. But with the growth of industry there were so many more of them that they became impossible to ignore. They became so wealthy and influential that they began to challenge the aristocrats' claim to be the most powerful in the land.

Moreover, a man who had developed his cotton, woollen, iron or railway firm, was not only wealthy and successful; he was also very confident of his own ability and of his claims to be considered any man's equal.

**25** John Wilkes, a portrait by R. Earlam

## Political reform

The political system as it existed in 1830 was that which had existed when Shaftesbury was starting his anti-Stuart campaign. Most MPs represented constituencies in South and South West England; the new towns such as Manchester, Birmingham, Bradford, etc were unrepresented in the Commons in 1830. Similarly the qualification for the vote was what it had been, (Chapter 2), so that there was no provision for most of the new, rich, tax-paying middle class even to vote, or to stand for election.

The demand for political reform had started in the late eighteenth century when Wyvill, Wilkes, the Duke of Bedford, Burke and the Younger Pitt had proposed changes which would have abolished some constituencies in the now less-important agricultural South, and given representation to the more populous new towns of the industrial Midlands and North. Changes in the qualifications for the vote had been suggested by which more of the new middle class might have had a share in the electoral process.

But these demands had been turned down, and with the onset of the French Revolution reform was made to appear as synonymous with revolution. It was the aristocratic Whigs who resurrected this idea of reform in the 1820s. Slowly they came out of their country palaces and returned to an active political life and as

26  A cartoon by Cruikshank, 1819, which reflects the fears of the ruling class when faced with demands for reform. Reform is seen here as a wicked force attacking an almost helpless maiden (Britain) who is busy defending, with the aid of 'Laws', the religion of the country. The loyal 'Lion' is seen rushing to her aid. In fact, the Liberals who wanted reform were opposed to violence, revolution and mob activity

they did so, picked up again the threads that Fox had left dangling. One of these was parliamentary reform. It was Lord John Russell, son of the wealthy and landed Duke of Bedford, who proposed in the 1820s that some of the more notorious rotten boroughs should lose their right to be represented, while some of the new towns should be given that right.

This demand was continually turned down by the Tory governments of Perceval, Liverpool, Canning and Wellington. Perhaps they really were convinced that reform would lead to revolution. The Whigs, on the other hand, agreed with Macaulay who said that revolution would be the result of trying to exclude the middle classes from a share in the political system:

> But, Sir, every argument which would induce me to oppose universal suffrage induces me to support the plan which is now before us. I am opposed to universal suffrage, because it would produce a destructive revolution. I support this plan; I am sure it is our best security against a revolution.
>
> That we may exclude those whom it is necessary to exclude, we must admit those whom it may be safe to admit. At present we oppose the schemes of revolutionaries with only one quarter of our proper force. We say that it is not by mere numbers, but by property and intelligence, that the nation ought to be governed. Yet, saying this, we exclude great masses of property and intelligence. We do more. We drive over to the side of revolution those whom we shut out from power.
>
> History is full of revolutions, produced by causes similar to those which are now operating in England. A portion of the community which had been of no account expands and becomes strong. It demands a place in the system, suited to its present power. If this is granted, all is well. If this is refused, then comes the struggle between the young energy of one class and the ancient privileges of another. Such is the struggle which the middle classes in England are maintaining against an aristocracy. [House of Commons, 2 March 1831.]

However, it would be a mistake to think of the Whigs as being ardent radicals, eager to overthrow the existing system. They were in fact very moderate reformers. After all, the Reform Bill was introduced in 1831 by Lord John Russell, the son of the Duke of Bedford. He was a member of the aristocratic Cabinet presided over by Earl Grey which produced a moderate Reform Bill, by which 143 seats were to be taken away from the more glaringly rotten boroughs and given instead to some of the more populated new towns. This part of the Bill helps to show how the face of the country was changing while industry replaced agriculture as the main occupation and while the industrial Midlands and North replaced the South and South West as the main centres of population. But this was a very modest attack on the system. Even after 1832 there were still plenty of rotten boroughs where candidates could be nominated by a patron; even after the redistribution of 143 seats, the South and West were still more heavily represented than the larger

**27** Gladstone being chaired after winning the seat at Newark in the 1832 election. The issue was never in doubt since Newark was one of the rotten boroughs which escaped the Reform Act; the young Tory MP had spent £30,000 to ensure his victory which returned him to a Reformed Parliament where he soon attracted the attention of Peel and other Tory leaders

towns of the North and Midlands. The Reform Act was a modest change but hardly a revolutionary one.

For the borough franchise (or the right to vote) the Reform Bill proposed that all the old-fashioned and so-varying qualifications (Chapter 2) should be done away with and in their place a uniform qualification introduced. In future anyone who owned a house worth more than £10 a year qualified for the borough vote. We have to remember that Peel's Metropolitan Police (formed in 1829) were paid twelve shillings and six pence (62½p) a week; today's policemen are paid at least 60 times that. If the voting qualifications today were the same as those proposed in the 1831 Reform Bill, only the owners of property worth £600 a year would have the vote.

For the county franchise the Bill proposed to retain the forty-shilling (£2) freehold franchise but to add to this by allowing leasehold tenants of larger farms to have the vote also.

Here again the Bill proposed modest changes; in addition to the 200,000 or so who voted in 1830 the Bill proposed that another 217,000 or so should be allowed to vote. These would all be people of substance and wealth, the owners of valuable property in towns or the wealthier tenants in the countryside. The emphasis here, as in Macaulay's speech, was on property, wealth, substance, and not on democracy, numbers, the people or the mob.

## People versus Peers

The Reform Bill was finally passed through the Commons and the Lords only after a great struggle, three elections in two years, and the real threat of a civil war. Wellington and the Tories seemed prepared to use the power of the Lords to prevent the Bill becoming law—in the hope that the Bill might then be postponed indefinitely; Wellington, claiming that he would 'rule the country by the sword', had second thoughts and, after consulting his fellow politicians, reported to the King that he could not hope to form a government which would meet with the approval of the House of Commons. When the Lords still threatened to throw the Bill out, Grey persuaded King William to promise that he would create as many new Whig Peers as might be required to get a favourable vote through the Lords. In the face of this dilution of their House, the Lords climbed down and the Bill was finally passed in 1832.

## Whig policies

Once the excitement over the Reform Act had died down the aristocratic Whigs got on with governing. They produced a number of moderate reforms. The first effective Factory Act was passed in 1833—but it was a very modest reform which still permitted employers to use child labour in most factories. The first government grant towards education was made in 1833—but only £20,000 was given for this purpose as compared with £50,000 which was set aside for the cleansing of the stables at Windsor Castle. Slavery was abolished in the British Empire and slave owners were compensated by £20,000,000. The Poor Law system was reformed by the Poor Law Amendment Act, 1834 which set up the first modern administrative system. The Poor Law Commissioners in Whitehall were to supervise the work of elected Guardians of the Poor in each district of the country and they in

**28** A memorial to the Tolpuddle martyrs who were sentenced to be transported to Australia in 1834 for their share in trying to organise a trade union in their Dorset village. The Whig government, and in particular the Home Secretary, Lord Melbourne, approved of the sentence. The Whigs were not radicals

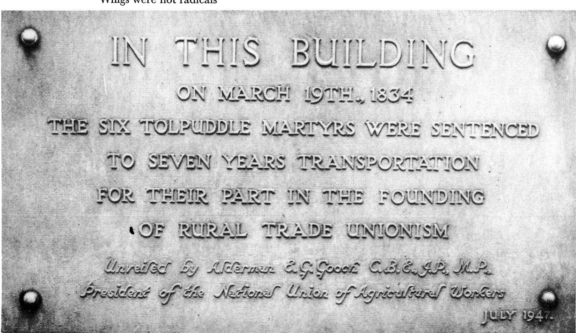

**29** A woodcut of 1874 representing the labourer starving at the expense of the fat landowner

turn were to administer the Poor Law through their workhouses and overseers. Today we are accustomed to this system of Civil Service supervision of locally elected boards or committees; this is how we run our State education system as well as subsidised housing, the health service and so on.

The reforming Whigs were prepared to listen to the advice of the experts of the time—Jeremy Bentham, Nassau Senior, John Stuart Mill and others—who argued that the nation's institutions (poor law, prisons, local government etc), should be examined by Royal Commissions which should present reports to Parliament which in turn might pass an Act to reform the institution concerned and appoint Inspectors to see that the Act was carried out. The Whigs did this for factories and the Poor Law; later governments have imitated them and most reforms that have taken place have been the result of Commissions on the Whig model.

This process—of examination, legislation and supervision—is a very tidy way of clearing away old-fashioned and out-dated habits and the Whigs were prepared to do this—provided that it did not cost much to do so. The Whigs in the 1830s, like Walpole before them (Chapter 3), and Gladstone after them, were concerned to keep taxation as low as possible. This helps to explain their reluctance to appoint more than four factory Inspectors or to spend more than £20,000 on popular education.

The Whigs were also following the Walpole line in believing that the government

should interfere as little as possible in the social and economic life of the nation. This explains their reluctance to get involved in the question of factory laws. Was it the duty of the government to stop women going to work if they wanted to go? Was the government supposed to tell employers whom they could employ and for how many hours they should open their factories? The Whigs supported the idea of *laissez faire*—that it was the duty of government to interfere as little as possible.

This helps to explain why, after a surge of reforming activity between 1833 and 1835, the Whigs seem to have run out of steam. They continued to govern until 1841, Melbourne becoming Prime Minister in 1835; but they passed very little legislation of any importance after 1835, preferring to do nothing rather than get involved in attempting to solve the problems of the early nineteenth-century towns—housing, poverty, sickness and so on. Neither did they think it was any of their business to try to improve Britain's trading position, which went from bad to worse in the late 1830s. Indeed, it was this failure to help the country's economy that explains their defeat in the election of 1841 when Peel and the Tories came to power—and went to tackle in a most un-liberal way the various problems facing the country. Melbourne was prepared to allow the Tories to get on with this; for himself and the Whigs, all this was a quite un-English interference with life.

# 5  Middle-class Liberalism, 1840–1860

**The continuing Industrial Revolution**

In many history books the term 'Industrial Revolution' is used to explain the changes that had taken place in Britain between about 1750 and 1830. The reader is given the impression that there was very little industry before 1750 and very little change after 1830. In fact, as we know, the industrial inventions of the late eighteenth century—the steam engine, the 'Spinning Jenny' and others—were only the beginnings of that technological revolution which is still going on. We also know that the rate of change is greater today than it was in, say, 1830—when the so-called Industrial Revolution was thought to have ended.

The development of a nation–wide railway system between 1830 and 1860 created a boom in the coal, iron and engineering industries and also helped to provide national markets for manufacturers of almost every type of commodity— from candles to fish, from soap to soup. As a result of the continued growth in British industry there was also the continued growth in British towns; in 1851 the census showed that for the first time there were more people living in large towns (with populations over 50,000) than were living in small towns or villages. This process of urbanisation went on until, by the end of the century, over two-thirds of the British people were living in large towns or cities.

**The growing middle classes**

Those who profited most from this increasingly rapid industrialisation were the continually-growing number of middle-class families. The men who owned the railways and canals, the factories and mines, iron and steelworks, cotton and woollen mills, engineering and chemical factories, grew richer as the country became more industrialised. Many of them spent part of their new wealth on investments in their own or other industries, and so laid the basis for their descendants' well-being. Many of them spent part of these riches on improving their own living standards—they paid for the building of the large houses which encircle the older parts of our industrial towns and form suburbs in our industrial cities. In these large, well-furnished houses the new middle class employed an army of domestic servants of whom there were over one million in 1870. With their carriages, clubs, servants, homes and seemingly ever-increasing wealth, many members of this group saw themselves as the most important people in the country. The Reform Act of 1832 was a recognition by the upper class of their emergence as well as a first step along the road to their take-over (see Chapter 4).

**31** A middle-class couple sit with the family in the garden of their new home. The rich industrialists, merchants and financiers could afford these houses—which can still be seen in the older parts of Britain's industrial towns and cities. Men of property such as this were eager to play their part in the government of the country

## Middle-class politicians

In the years immediately following the Reform Act there was very little change in the composition of the House of Commons. Even as late as 1846 the majority of MPs were sons or relatives of members of the House of Lords. In part this can be explained by the continued existence of many rotten boroughs where the influence of the local landowner was very important; in such boroughs the landowner could nominate his son or nephew to a seat in the Commons. In part the reluctance of the middle class to get themselves elected can be explained on personal grounds; many of them were so engaged in their businesses that they did not feel they had the time to spare. If they were busy at Parliament in London, who was going to look after the factory in Rochdale, the engineering shop in Darlington or the ironworks in Merthyr?

But even in these years there were some middle-class men who were prepared to take an active part in political life. Before a person could use his vote he had to be on the electoral register—a list kept by the constituency's Returning Officer (usually the Mayor of the borough). When the number qualified to vote was very small it was not difficult to keep a check on which of one's neighbours were entitled to vote. But as the number grew after 1832, the leaders of the Whig and Tory Parties realised the importance of ensuring that their supporters' names were on the register. This led the Whigs to set up a National Party Headquarters at the Reform Club in London, where full-time officials were employed to supervise the work of local Associations whose job it was to look after this question of registration of voters.

At first this machinery was used by the aristocratic Whigs. But the leaders of middle-class opinion soon learned to use the system. Speaking to the Committee of the Anti-Corn Law League in 1839, Cobden said:

**32** The Industrial Revolution gave a boost to many people's aspirations. This illustration from a working-class men's magazine of 1861 shows an idealised Lancashire working man and his family enjoying life 'rent free' in their 'own home'. As people's living standards gradually rose, so they too became interested in government policies

We propose to provide a copy of every registration for every borough and county in the United Kingdom. . . . We propose to correspond with these electors. . . . We propose to keep people well informed as to the progress of our question by means of the penny postage. . . . [We] propose to send them one letter a week, and that will cost twopence for the stamp and the enclosure. That will be £2,500. . . . We intend to visit every borough in the kingdom. . . . We will specially invite the electors to meet such deputations without distinction of party. . . . We shall urge upon our friends to organise themselves, and to commence a canvass of their boroughs to ascertain the number of Free Traders, and in every case where it is possible to obtain a majority of the electors in favour of Free Trade . . . the League will pledge itself, where a borough finds itself at a loss for a candidate, to furnish it with one.

## Individualism

In the same speech, Richard Cobden also said: '[Ours] is not a party move, to serve any existing political organisation; we care nothing for political parties. As they at present stand, there is very little indeed to choose between the two great Parties. Let a statesman of established reputation, of whatever side in politics, take the step for perfect freedom of trade, he shall have the support of the League.'

It is important to realise that the Whig and Tory Parties were still led by a handful of landed aristocrats. While the middle class wanted to imitate this class in their life style, the new, pushing, ambitious industrialists were different to the old, landed, farming class. One of the major differences was in their attitudes to their fellow men. The older class, brought up in the Anglican religion and living in

47

small villages, had a sense of community; the rich man certainly lived 'in his castle' while the poor man waited 'at the gate' but they did worship in the same church, attend the same fairs, live in the same area. The squire had been brought up to realise that while he had power over the lower classes, he also had duties towards them. In the new industrial towns the middle class felt none of that sense of community, nor any of that sense of responsibility which the older class had felt. On the contrary they were conscious of having made their way by their own efforts and saw no reason why everyone else should not do so. Samuel Smiles, in *Self Help* (1857) was writing for all his middle-class contemporaries:

> The spirit of self-help is the root of all genuine growth in the individual; and ... it constitutes the true source of national vigour and strength. Help from without is often enfeebling in its effects, but help from within invariably invigorates. Whatever is done for men or classes, to a certain extent takes away the stimulus and necessity of doing for themselves; and where men are subjected to over-guidance and over-government, the inevitable tendency is to render them comparatively helpless ... it is every day becoming more clearly understood that the function of government is negative ... being resolvable principally into protection of life, liberty and property.

### Laissez faire

This is the expression of that individualism—or concern for self—which is one of the marks of the mid-Victorian middle class who opposed any attempts by governments to set any limit to the freedom of a man to help himself. This partly explains the middle-class opposition to the early Factory Acts and their refusal to consider making improvements in their towns. In *Victorian Cities* Asa Briggs praises the men who built the new harbours and docks, the railways and bridges, the town halls and their own splendid houses; he then goes on to contrast these successes with the failure, by the same men, to build decent towns.

Another writer who expressed the ideas of this new class was Jeremy Bentham. He claimed that the test of a law or an institution (such as Parliament) was whether it brought the 'greatest happiness for the greatest possible number' of people. Bentham, like Adam Smith, believed that if men were set free from government regulation each man would work for his own betterment and this in turn would lead to the betterment of the community as a whole. There is a good deal in this. For example, William Morris (later Lord Nuffield) was allowed to seek his own betterment by developing a motor car. The Morris Company became part of what is now known as British Leyland Motor Corporation. Morris made a fortune for himself but also provided employment for millions of people as well as providing cars for millions of others. This was good. But by the end of the century the idea of freedom was being challenged (Chapters 6 to 8).

## Anti-Corn Law League

This belief in freedom lay behind the demand for the abolition of government regulations which interfered with people's freedom to do what they wanted to with their businesses. One of the most important campaigns waged by the new

**34** Cobden addressing the meeting of the Council of the Anti-Corn Law League, a painting by Herbert. These merchants, industrialists and financiers were creating the new Britain in which they were also making their own fortunes; they demanded an equal share in the government of their country which brought them into conflict with the older, aristocratic and landed upper class

middle-class politicians was the Anti-Corn Law League. Formed by the manufacturers of the northern counties in 1838, the League was, in part, a battle for
Free Trade. Walpole had been among the first to realise the benefits of lower
customs duties (Chapter 2). As Britain became the world's leading industrial
nation, so the need for customs duties diminished. If there were no duties on
imports of raw materials, and no duties on the exports of finished products, then
the price would be lowered and everyone—from manufacturer through workmen to
consumer—would benefit. This helps to explain the continued lowering of British
tariffs in the 1830s, 1840s, and 1850s.

But if this were true for raw materials and finished goods, why wasn't it also
true for food? This was the question posed by the new middle class through their
League. The upper-class answer was given by Disraeli and others who believed that
the importing of cheap foreign food would lead to a decline of British farming,
lower incomes for the landowning upper class and their eventual disappearance
from the social, economic and political scene.

Cobden and the League believed that the abolition of the Corn Laws had more
than economic aspects. Of course, cheap foreign food would lead to a fall in the
cost of living and so to a rise in the standard of living. But more than this it would,
so Cobden believed, see the end of the dominant position of the old upper class,
since their income would fall. This explains why Peel's Conservative government
opposed Cobden's pleas in 1842 and 1843. But the logical argument of the League,
plus the onset of the Irish famine of 1845–6, caused Peel to change his mind.
In February 1846 he addressed the Commons:

> I admit that a natural consequence of the course I have pursued, is to . . . alien-
> ate a great Party. I know what would have conciliated temporary confidence.
> It would have been to under-rate the danger in Ireland, to invite a united
> combination for the maintainance of the existing Corn Law . . . by such a
> course I should have been sure to animate and please a Party.

## Universal peace

1832 marked the emergence of this middle class as a political factor; 1846 marked
their emergence as the most powerful economic and social group in the country.
Cobden, the League's leader, had always argued that if the world entered on an
era of Free Trade it would also have to enter on an era of universal peace. This
belief in the virtue of peace was carried to extreme lengths by the middle-class
politicians; many of them opposed the war-like policies of the Whig Foreign
Secretary, Lord Palmerston. As Cobden said:

> Free Trade! What is it? Why, breaking down the barriers that separate nations;
> those barriers behind which nestle the feelings of pride, revenge, hatred and
> jealousy, which every now and then burst their bounds, and deluge whole

# NEW POLITICAL CATECHISM.

## THIRD EDITION.

### WITH EMENDATIONS AND CORRECTIONS BY "TRUTH."

Granted that the Expenditure of the Liberals in 1861 was £73,000,000, what was it in 1865 - £66,000,000

What was the Income Tax when the Liberals took Office in 1861? - - 10d. in the £

What was it in 1865 when they left Office? - - - - 4d. in the £

What is it now under Tory management? - - - - - 6d. in the £

Who are the men that proposed to charter a Roman Catholic University in Ireland by a } **THE TORIES**
further grant of Money?

Who are they that seek to perpetuate an injustice like the Irish Church - **THE TORIES**

Who opposed the admission of Dissenters to the Universities? - **THE TORIES**

Who abolished the Compound Rating Clause, thus compelling personal payment of Rates? **THE TORIES**

Who gave the Nation a uniform Penny Postage? - - - **THE LIBERALS**

Who reduced the National Debt £12,000,000? - - - **THE LIBERALS**

Who reduced the Duty on Tea from 2s. 2d. to 6d. per lb.? - - **THE LIBERALS**

Who reduced the Duties on Sugar, Wine, and Hops? - - **THE LIBERALS**

Who reduced the Duty on Coffee from 6d. to 3d. per lb.? - - **THE LIBERALS**

Who reduced the Duty on Fire Insurance from 3s. to 1s. 6d. per cent., and intend to }
abolish it altogether - - - - - - **THE LIBERALS**

Who repealed the Duties on Soap, Bricks, Timber and Paper? - **THE LIBERALS**

Who abolished compulsory Church Rates? (Gladstone) - - **THE LIBERALS**

Who amended and improved the so far good, but still imperfect, measure of Reform, }
and carried it too? - - - - - - **THE LIBERALS**

From these facts and many others, which could be quoted, it must be clear to all, }
that the true friends of the Country are - - - - **THE LIBERALS**

And to them only can we look for any reduction of Taxation, or removal of Burdens from the People.

☞ Electors! ponder on these things, talk them over amongst yourselves when you meet **together, and by your own firesides, and you must come to the conclusion that the Conservatives are not the men you ought to support, but THE LIBERALS!**

35 An election bill issued by the Liberals in 1868 to attract the support of the newly enfranchised working-class voters. Notice the Liberal emphasis on lower taxation and lower government expenditure—designed to appeal to taxpayers. One of the costs of this lower taxation was the absence of any policies about housing, poverty and other social problems. Notice also the lower duties paid on imports—which led to a fall in the cost of living. This fall was one of the main reasons for the rise in living standards in mid-Victorian Britain; more people could afford to buy more of the cheaper goods

countries with blood; those feelings which nourish the poison of war and conquest, which assert that without conquest we can have no trade, which foster
that lust for conquest and dominion which sends forth your warrior chiefs to
scatter devastation through other lands, and then calls them back that they may
be enthroned securely in your passions, but only to harass and oppress you
at home. It is because I think I have a full apprehension of the moral bearing
of this question, that I take a pride and gratification in forming one in the
present agitation; and I invite you all to take a part in it, for there is room and
glory and fame enough for all as soon as we have achieved the great triumph
of the downfall of the Corn Laws.

This is another important strand in the Liberal fabric. Walpole had started
spinning this strand, Cobden and Bright continued the policy which was later
that of Gladstone and Lloyd George (Chapters 6 to 8).

**Taxation**
One of the reasons for having a peaceful policy is that it allows governments to
keep taxation down. If a country goes to war then taxation has to go up, to pay
for ammunition, etc. Low taxation was a very important part of Liberal policy.
The new, middle-class Liberals believed that taxation was an interference with
the freedom of the individual to spend his money as he thought best. Their
Benthamite beliefs taught them that if a man were allowed to spend his money
as he wanted he would first seek his own happiness and so produce the greatest
happiness for the rest of the community. This was what Gladstone meant when
he said that 'Money should be allowed to fructify in the pockets of the people'.

# 6 Gladstonian Liberalism, 1860–1890

**Wider democracy**

The aristocratic Whigs had widened the franchise to take in the rich middle class (Chapter 4) but they had no intention of encouraging the growth of a democracy in which even all the adult males had the right to vote. There was no room, it seemed, for the working class in the political process. By 1860 this belief was being challenged; many members of this class had shared in the increasing prosperity of industrialised Britain, now the workshop of the world. The skilled engineers, boilermakers, carpenters, bricklayers, shipwrights and members of other craft unions shared in the self-help confidence of their middle-class employers. Through their unions they had persuaded their employers to increase their wages; in their unions they organised welfare schemes to provide for the sick, unemployed, injured or retired members of their unions. Many of them had joined one of the many building societies and owned their own homes. Others could afford the rent of one of the thousands of small but solid houses which were springing up around the industrial towns and cities.

These skilled, confident, well-off members of the working class were also self-educated in one of the Mechanics' Institutes or Workingmen's Clubs which provided classes, libraries and learned societies where the ambitious could 'get on'.

Above these in the social scale were the ever-increasing number of employees who could be called lower middle class. The clerks in offices and government departments, the foremen and apprentice surveyors, accountants, the slowly increasing number of qualified industrial technologists (e.g. chemists, mechanical and civil engineers) as well as the administrative staffs of the growing railway companies—all these began to demand a share in the political process. This demand came to a head in the mid-1860s. John Bright, one of the more radical members of the Anti-Corn Law League, speaking in Birmingham in 1865, said:

> Perhaps our friends who oppose us will say, 'We do not fear elections and order. What we fear is this—the legislative results of this wide extension of the franchise'.
>
> It is not democracy that is the peril of this country. It was not democracy in 1832 that was the peril. It was the desperate antagonism of the class that then had power to the just claims and rights of the people. And at this moment I tell them that Conservatism, be it Tory or be it Whig, is the true national peril which we have to face. They may dam the stream, they may keep back the waters, but the volume is ever increasing, and it descends with accelerated

**36** If you only read certain sections of Dickens' books you may get the impression that throughout the nineteenth century the workers were badly paid, ill fed and poorly clothed. In fact, by the middle of the century a section of the working class—men with a craft and certain skills—were well paid and enjoying quite a high standard of living. Here you can see some of them relaxing in one of their clubs, where they had a games room and a library as well as classrooms and debating halls

**37** Gladstone was the son of a Liverpool shipowner who had made a fortune in the slave trade. He was an Anglican and had once been a leading Tory. He had followed Peel in 1846 and so had won the support of Cobden and his Free Traders who also liked Gladstone's opposition to Palmerston's vigorous foreign policy. He held high office from 1841 onwards and when Palmerston died in 1865, Gladstone was a natural second in line of succession to the leadership of the Liberal Party

force, and the time will come when, if wisdom does not take the place of folly, the waters will burst their banks, and these men, who fancy they are stemming this imaginary apparition of democracy, will be swept away by the resolute will of a united and determined people.

## Gladstone

In 1846 Gladstone was a member of the Peel government which repealed the Corn Laws. On the split of the Peelite Party, Gladstone followed his leader and, along with other Peelites, joined with the Whigs to form governments in the 1850s and 1860s. Gladstone's period as Chancellor of the Exchequer had seen Britain become a Free Trade country while at the same time taxation fell. Gladstone continually opposed the more war-like policies of his colleague and sometime leader, Palmerston, who died in 1865 leaving the Whig-Peelite Party to be led by the ageing Lord John Russell.

By 1865 there were more middle-class MPs in the Commons and they saw Gladstone as their leader. He had pleased them by supporting Free Trade and lower taxation, as well as by his desire for peace. In 1866 Gladstone led these middle-class MPs in their demand for an extension of the franchise. However, the less radical Whigs in his party resisted this change. Robert Lowe led the Opposition. Speaking in the Commons in March 1866, Lowe said:

The government is proposing to enfranchise one class of men who have been disfranchised heretofore . . . I ask the House to consider what good we are to get for the country at large by this extension of the franchise? The effect will be to add a large number of persons to our constituencies, of the class from which,

55

if there is to be anything wrong going on, we may naturally expect to find it. It will increase the expenses of candidates . . . the management of elections. You must look for more bribery and corruption than you have hitherto had; the working men of England, finding themselves in a full majority of the whole constituency, will awake to a full sense of their power. They will say 'We can do better for ourselves. Don't let us any longer be cajoled at elections. Let us set up shop for ourselves. We have machinery, we have our trade unions, we have our leaders all ready. We have the power of combination and when we have a prize to fight for we will bring it to bear with tenfold more force than ever before'.

## Disraeli

Gladstone's proposal for reform was defeated by an alliance of Lowe's followers

**38** *The Colossus of Words*, a *Punch* cartoon of 1879 which well illustrates the main features of Gladstonian Liberalism. Its main planks were Retrenchment (left), which meant spending as little as possible, Peace (right) and, very low down the scale, Reform (sailing into harbour). Not much hope here for the many millions of badly-housed, unemployed or homeless people

with the Conservatives led by Disraeli who then introduced his own Reform Bill in 1867. Disraeli's proposals were amended in debate and when the Reform Act was finally passed in July 1867 the right to vote had been given to every male over twenty-one who was a householder—i.e. who paid rates. This added about two million to the electoral register and so forced the parties to think again about the question of organisation.

The increase in the number of voters was accompanied by a redistribution of seats, so that many of the older, more corrupt constituencies were abolished while the industrial towns were given more representatives. This led to a decline in the influence of the landowning class and a rise in the political influence of the middle-class employers.

While the number of voters had been small it had always been possible to use bribery to gain a political result. However, with much larger numbers, this was more difficult—and more expensive. The open system of voting allowed land-owners and employers the chance of influencing the way in which their tenants or employees voted. But the 1872 Ballot Act brought this system to an end—and political leaders had to think of some other way of influencing the voters.

As in 1832 and 1838 (Chapter 5) political leaders thought that registration was important; if the potential voter did not have his name on the Register in the mid-1860s then he could not vote. To register voters was essential and so Liberal Associations were set up in many towns. In addition to registering their possible supporters, these Associations were also involved in getting their supporters to the polling booths at election time. When many voters lived miles away from the booth this was a complicated business which involved letter-writing, personal canvassing and the provision of carriages to get people to the booths.

**Gladstonian Liberalism**

Disraeli hoped that the enlarged electorate would return the Conservatives to power in the 1868 election. However, the new voters—lower middle class and working class—thought that they had more in common with the nonconformist liberals than with the Anglican Tories. Gladstone became Prime Minister for the first time in 1868 and, for the first time, men described the government as a 'Liberal' one and not a 'Whig' one. The aristocratic influence had declined and the Party was now led by a member of the rich middle classes, supported by voters from that class and from the working class.

Gladstone's first Ministry (1868–74) is often called 'the great reforming Ministry'. This government brought to an end the old system of recruitment and promotion in the Civil Service, which had favoured the relatives of the aristocracy; instead they set up the present system of examinations by which promotion and recruit-ment are dependent on ability. Similarly, promotion in the Army was to be on merit since the buying of commissions was abolished. These two reforms were welcomed by the middle class, whose sons were now coming from the new public

57

**39** A meeting of the London School Board at their new offices on the Thames Embankment, London, 1875. Such Boards were called into existence by the Education Act, 1870, and elections to the Boards led to the formation of loose-knit party organisations such as that started in Birmingham by Chamberlain

boarding schools, eager for a share in the running of the country and its Army. The middle class also welcomed the university reform which abolished the rule that one had to be an Anglican in order to be an undergraduate at Oxford or Cambridge.

Godwin Smith was a contemporary of Gladstone's. In *My Memory of Gladstone* he wrote:

> Wonderful improvements in finance, great administrative reforms, the opening of the Civil Service, the Postal Savings Bank, the liberation of the newspaper press from the paper duty, the abolition of purchase in the Army, the reform of the universities followed by that of the endowed schools, the disestablishment of the Irish Church, and the Commercial Treaty with France, make up a mighty harvest of good work.

## Limited reform

Certainly the Ministry deserves to be remembered as one which set about making many efforts to create the administrative machinery required by a modern, industrialised country. This, we might remember, is one of the features of Liberal and Labour governments. In general it is fair to say that most major reforms have been introduced by either Liberal or Labour governments; they seem to be more conscious of the need for change and more willing to make the changes required (Chapters 4 and 8).

This, of course, tends to make them unpopular with people who are opposed to the changes. It even exposes them to being unpopular with those whom they hoped to help. Gladstone, for example, helped the trade unions by passing a law which made them legal bodies, entitled to own property and to sue in the courts. This annoyed the employing middle classes, who resented this growth in the power of their employees; meanwhile, Gladstone was losing the support of the working classes by passing a law which made picketing illegal so that strikes were made less effective.

Similar repercussions followed his Licensing Bill the Education Act and his attempts to deal with the Irish problem. There was also the accusation that the reforms were not wide-ranging or extensive enough. Morley, a colleague of Gladstone's, wrote:

> The most marked administrative performance of Mr Gladstone's great government was the reform and organisation of the Army. In Mr Cardwell he was fortunate enough to have a public servant of the first order; Before he had been a month at the War Office the new Secretary of State submitted his ideas of a plan that would give us an effective force for defence at a greatly reduced cost.

Now Army reform was obviously important, particularly after the humiliations of the Crimean War. But there were other reforms that might have been considered more important. The Liberal government did little, if anything, to make industrial

**40** Seven Dials, London (an area where many old clothes were sold): a Doré drawing of 1872. The wretched lives lived by millions of people in the overcrowded slums of Britain's major cities and towns is illustrated by this drawing. Liberalism had little to offer these people—who needed council housing, old-age pensions, a medical service, unemployment benefit, family allowances and other benefits from a Welfare State

towns healthier places in which to live; they did little to try to deal with the problem of housing the lower-paid workers, condemned to live in overcrowded slums; nothing was done for the poor, the sick or the unemployed. So while the Ministry was one of reforms, it cannot be considered a Ministry of social reforms.

## Taxation

One of the reasons for this failure to deal with social problems was that the Liberals believed in liberalism—or freedom. They did not think that governments should interfere overmuch in the economic or social life of the country. Indeed, by their Free Trade policy they were specifically saying that the government should withdraw from these spheres of activity. They were also concerned, as good Liberals, with keeping taxation as low as possible. To say that trade unions shall be legal bodies, or that Nonconformists shall be allowed to go to Oxford doesn't cost the government or the taxpayer much money. But if slums are cleared, or the unemployed given some help, this will lead to an increase in taxation.

## Pacifism

In keeping with this ambition to keep taxation as low as possible, the Gladstone government adopted a very pacific foreign policy. Coming as it did after the long era of Palmerston this was welcomed by many people who had opposed the way in which he had thrown England's weight around. When the French and Prussians went to war in 1870 Britain remained neutral; when, in 1871, the Russians broke the Treaty of Paris by fortifying the Crimean Ports, Gladstone did nothing; when the Americans claimed damages from Britain—because of the activities of British-built ships during the American Civil War—Britain paid up.

Peace abroad and low taxation at home should have been popular. Yet J.A. Froude, writing after the election of 1874, noted:

The Washington Treaty and the Alabama arbitration are supposed to have lowered England in its status as a great power. We did not wish to maintain a

**41** Rudyard Kipling, the poet of the British Empire, with some of his famous characters, painted by Cunes. Kipling's work is a memorial to the late-Victorian belief in the Empire—on which the sun never set and in which British soldiers were constantly involved in wars

quarrel with Russia, yet we were sore and resentful when the Treaty of Paris was torn to pieces and flung in our faces. We had no desire to meddle in the French and German War, yet we did not like to see England unconsulted when the map of Europe was remodelled. Internally the Ministry made enemies whether they did well or ill. The Irish Land Bill alarmed the owners of property; the Education Bill offended the dissenters. The abolition of purchase in the Army, though welcome in itself to most reasonable persons, yet shocked us all. The Licensing Bill exasperated the brewer and the publican.

## Imperialism

During the last quarter of the nineteenth century, Britain and other European nations enlarged their Empires. For Britain this was not a new development. Gladstone and the Liberals were opposed to this sort of acquisition. It tended to lead to an increase in taxation—since wars had to be fought against reluctant people, unwilling to accept domination by the white man. It also ran counter to the Liberal idea of equality; there was little point in Bright and others claiming that British working men were equal to British aristocrats if, at the same time, they were to support the claim that any Britisher had the right to rule foreigners. Finally, there was always the danger that the enlargements of Empire might lead to war between the Great Powers.

Disraeli and the Conservatives, on the other hand, took advantage of this European movement for acquiring larger Empires. The Transvaal was annexed, parts of the East and West coasts of Africa were acquired, as was Cyprus. For many British voters this was a welcome development—they were happy at the thought of so much more red (the colour usually used to show British territories) on the maps of the world. Other voters, however, believed that this was a costly, wasteful and unnecessary development from which only a few rich industrialists might gain.

Gladstone had retired from an active part in politics after his defeat in the 1874 election. However, Disraeli's active foreign and imperial policy drew Gladstone back into the fray again. In 1879 and 1880 he conducted a vigorous campaign against Disraeli, touring Scotland and the North of England in what became known as the Midlothian campaign. This was an important development; it was the first time that a political leader had gone out to 'meet the people' in an attempt to get them to support his policy and to oppose that of his rival. He was successful and won the 1880 election—only to find that the political scene had been very much affected by the growth of a new force centred in Birmingham. (Chapter 7.)

**42** Joseph Chamberlain, who always wore an orchid in his button-hole and was equally well known for his monocle. Chamberlain was much more radical than Gladstone the 'Old Hen' and refused to be treated as a little 'un (Picture 1); he was anxious that the Liberal Party should become socially conscious and should pass laws to help the poor, badly housed and unemployed. Liberal failure to follow this socialist path left room for the Labour Party to develop

THE DARING DUCKLING.

# 7 Liberalism: the Beginning of the End

## High tide

Gladstone had won the election of 1868 and was successful again in 1880, replacing Disraeli's imperialist Conservatives. Supported by the majority of the borough constituencies, Gladstone and the Liberals seemed all set for yet another great reforming Ministry. Supported by the powerful and growing National Liberal Federation, Gladstone looked forward to a long period of office. Yet 1880 was, in fact, the high tide of Gladstonian Liberalism; by 1886 the Party had been split and the Conservatives were back in office again, where they remained for the greater part of the next twenty years. What went wrong?

## Organisation

During the 1860s and 1870s most large towns developed their own Liberal Associations which soon set up branches outside their own immediate boundaries. Perhaps the most important of these was the Birmingham Liberal Association founded in 1865. This, and other Associations, tried to bring together middle-class and working–class Liberals, voters and non-voters. It was important for the Liberals that they should win the town constituencies since the Conservatives could usually depend on winning the county seats.

The Education Act of 1870 had divided the Liberal Party into those who wanted

**43** In 1891 the Liberal Party finally adopted a policy of social reform. This 'Newcastle programme' was intended to win the support of the infant Independent Labour Party whose leader, Hardie, is portrayed leading the Liberal horse along the new road. However, when the Party did get back to power in 1892 it failed to put the Newcastle programme into practice. This caused George Bernard Shaw, on behalf of the Fabians, to write a long article in which he invited the trade unions to give their support to Hardie. This led to a Conference in 1900 at which the Labour Representation Committee was formed. The Liberal conversion to radicalism was too late to have free, compulsory, State education with no religious teaching in schools, and those who supported the compromise that was finally reached by which Church schools were supported with government grants, while State schools were set up in places where there were not enough Church schools. The Act said that the country was to be divided into school districts, in each of which there were to be elected School Boards. Each elector had as many votes as there were members of the board; he could give any number of his votes to a particular candidate or candidates. This meant that someone had to organise the electors to distribute their votes so that they did not all give their total votes to one or two Liberals, so allowing the Conservatives to defeat other, less well-known Liberals.

The Birmingham National Education League was set up to fight against Church schools but also to organise voters after 1870. In 1873 the League's candidates won the Birmingham School Board elections and Joseph Chamberlain, its leading spokesman, became Chairman of the School Board. The organisation that had ensured this victory was also used by the Birmingham Liberal Association, which had been formed in 1865 by William Harris. He had hoped to organise the city so that Liberals would be returned for all three parliamentary seats. In 1873 this Association was taken over by two remarkable men: Francis Schnadhorst, a draper and a Nonconformist who became Secretary of the Birmingham Liberal Association in 1873, and Joseph Chamberlain, a Unitarian and a rich manufacturer. Under these two men the Association became highly organised and efficient. It was based on the wards and every resident could become a member of a ward Association for a shilling (5p) per year. The ward members elected a ward committee which had the power to co-opt other members. The ward committee officers plus three other members of the ward committee went on to the city executive committee, and since there were 16 wards this meant that there were 80 members. These were allowed to co-opt another 30 members. This executive committee, plus 30 members from each of the 16 wards, (a total of 480), made a general committee of 590, so that the committee was usually known as 'The Six Hundred'. Finally, this committee elected four people to join seven persons nominated by the executive committee as a committee of management, popularly nicknamed 'The Council of Ten'. On the surface this was a democratic organisation. In fact, Schnadhorst, Chamberlain and their friends always managed to get their supporters either elected or co-opted, so that they exercised a tight control over the machine.

In 1877 Schnadhorst and Chamberlain called a meeting of about 100 other Liberal organisations and set up the National Federation of Liberal Associations, which declared that:

The essential feature of the proposed federation is the principle which must henceforth govern the action of Liberals as a political party—namely, the direct participation of all members of the Party in the direction of its policy,

44 Saturday night at the pawnbrokers, 1901, as people crowd in; some have come to get back the best clothes which they bring in each Monday but will want for Sunday; others have come to put in the few household goods they own in return for a few coppers to buy food for the weekend. There were thousands of pawnbrokers even as late as the 1930s; their disappearance in modern Britain is an indication of the change in the quality of life now being led, even by the poorest

and in the selection of those particular measures of reform and of progress to which priority shall be given. This object can be secured only by the organisation of the Party upon a representative basis; that is, by popularly elected committees of local Associations, and by the union of such local Associations, by means of their freely chosen representatives, in a general federation.

### Chamberlain, the radical democrat

Chamberlain claimed that he wanted the Party leaders to take account of the wishes of their supporters as represented in the Association. Certainly a political leader has always to be aware of his supporters' wishes; usually the leader spent his time ensuring that their wishes were his—and for this purpose they used the various techniques of propaganda to win the support of their potential followers. This, after all, was what Shaftesbury had done in the beginning.

Chamberlain was claiming something more than this. He wanted the policies to be decided by the membership. The job of the political leaders was to be simple; they were to listen to the Association and then carry out the policies which it laid down. This was a radical change. The original attempts at forming political

**45** *Sowing tares* in the field of Labour, a *Punch* drawing of 1886 when Chamberlain was arguing with Gladstone. Chamberlain believed that socialism would lead to a better life for the majority; Gladstone and his followers preferred to believe, along with *Punch*, that socialism was an evil thing which would foul up the economic and social scene

parties had been made by MPs who wanted support from people outside Parliament. Chamberlain was claiming that men outside Parliament had the right to dictate policy to MPs. This was a complete reversal of roles.

This was not the only way in which Chamberlain differed from Gladstone. Chamberlain was much more interested in social reform than Gladstone had been. As Mayor of Birmingham between 1873 and 1876 Chamberlain had taken advantage of laws passed by the Conservatives to make Birmingham a healthier town. It was the first British city to try to come to terms with the results of the Industrial Revolution: an active local council spent money on parks, street lighting, slum clearance, refuse collection, town drainage—and all the other amenities that today we accept as normal.

As we saw in Chapter 6, this was not Gladstone's idea of reform; nor did he support the idea of spending the public's money in this way. However, Gladstone had approved of the setting up of the National Liberal Federation and when Chamberlain was elected MP, he welcomed this newcomer to the House. In 1880 Gladstone offered Chamberlain a place in the Cabinet—a recognition of the newcomer's importance.

### Chamberlain, the socialist

Chamberlain had been a very successful businessman, creating a monopoly in the profitable production of screws and nuts and bolts. He brought the businessman's approach to his political life; this helps to explain the successful way in which he helped organise first Birmingham, then other neighbouring constituencies in which his supporters were then elected. It was his business acumen that also helped him to realise that British towns did not have to be dirty, unhealthy, slum-ridden places, where the majority of the population died at a very early age. He saw that the town could be organised to be a better place in which to live. This helps to explain his success as a reforming Mayor.

When he entered the national scene after 1876, and particularly after he entered the Cabinet in 1880, Chamberlain again applied this same business sense to a consideration of national matters. Was it inevitable that so many people should be unemployed in Britain's industrial towns? Why should old or sick people have to rely on charity to get enough to keep themselves alive? Was it not possible to organise the nation's life so that it produced enough good things to allow the government to pay old age pensions, unemployment relief and other of the welfare benefits that Bismarck was already introducing in Germany.

Chamberlain the politician also realised that such policies would be, at one and the same time, both popular and unpopular. They would be popular with a large section of the working class who stood to gain most from such policies. They would, however, be unpopular with the richer section of the population—the upper and middle classes who would have to pay increased taxes in order to finance these proposed reforms.

## Chamberlain and Gladstone

Gladstone had first entered Parliament in the 1830s, Chamberlain in the late 1870s. There was a great gulf between the two, not only of age but of outlook. There was also the ambition of both men. Gladstone had been Prime Minister in 1868, was appointed again in 1880, was to become Prime Minister for the third time in 1886 and for the fourth time in 1892. He had played an increasingly important part in the country's political life since 1841 when Peel first gave him office. Chamberlain had been a dominant businessman, a successful Mayor of Birmingham and founder of the influential Federation. He was unwilling to take second place to anyone for very long.

So a clash between the two men was probably inevitable because of their different ages and ambitions, because of their different policies and attitudes to reform. Gladstone condemned Chamberlain's proposals as 'socialism'—which in the 1880s was a very serious accusation. Chamberlain, on the other hand, called Gladstone a 'Rip Van Winkle come down from the mountain', who did not understand the needs of the late-nineteenth century and the demands of the enlarged electorate.

## The middle class and radicalism

The continuing industrialisation of Britain had helped many people to become

**46** Gladstone introducing the Home Rule for Ireland Bill in the Commons, April 1886. Behind him, with a monocle in one eye, you can see Joseph Chamberlain who was soon to cross the floor of the House to join the Conservatives. This was a major step along the road to the destruction of the Liberal Party, and also to the rise of the Labour Party

very rich. There were industrialists and bankers whose fortunes were counted in millions; there were shopkeepers like Thomas Lipton who were welcomed into the circle of friends surrounding Edward, Prince of Wales. These very rich, upper middle-class men imitated their social superiors in their life style—and by the 1880s were beginning to imitate them in their politics. Having started off as Nonconformist Liberals, many of these had now become Anglican Conservatives.

Other less well-off members of the middle class began to suspect that Liberalism under Chamberlain's influence would prove to be a very different animal from that which they had known when Gladstone and Cobden were the leaders. These, too, began to leave the more democratic Liberal Party for the more aristocratic Conservative Party.

### The split, 1886

Gladstone had tried to deal with the problem of Ireland in his first Ministry (1868—74) and again brought in many reforms favourable to the Irish in his second Ministry (1880–85). But in the last days of that second Ministry, the Irish MPs, led by Parnell, had allied with the Conservatives to defeat Gladstone. In the ensuing election (1885) Gladstone and the Liberals won 335 seats; the Conservatives won 249—a majority of 86 which was the number of seats controlled by Parnell. Which way would Parnell order his MP supporters to vote when Parliament met again? Gladstone feared that the Conservatives might bribe Parnell with promises of reform. To forestall this Gladstone announced that his first reform would be an Irish Home Rule Bill. This, he hoped, would be enough to win him the support of that important group of Parnellite MPs.

**47** The Old Age Pension Act, 1908 provided the first of the modern Welfare State's payments to the less well-off members of society. This picture shows one of the earliest recipients in London. Many old people thought of Lloyd George, who introduced the Act, as a generous nobleman dispensing charity

But he made this announcement without first consulting his Cabinet colleagues. Chamberlain felt insulted by this announcement made on his behalf without any consultation. He also felt that if the government were going to spend their time on Irish Home Rule they obviously would not be able to spend time on what he considered more important things—reform of a socialist nature. Finally, he believed that the Irish policy would not be popular in the country so that the Liberals would lose the next election, and with it any hopes of carrying out a socialist policy.

Another group of Ministers was led by the ageing Hartington, who had led the Liberal Party after 1875 when Gladstone had appeared to have retired from politics. Hartington's followers believed that the Irish Home Rule Bill was a mistake; they believed that the Catholics in Ireland would take revenge on the English who owned a good deal of land in Ireland. They feared that these land-owners would be driven out, either by high taxation or by force. This, they believed, would be a betrayal of their own class.

Hartington and his followers also believed that this Home Rule Bill would lead to similar demands for Home Rule from other parts of the Empire, which would then split into a number of independent countries to the detriment of British trade and influence.

And so Chamberlain, for his reasons, and Hartington for others, led their followers out of the Cabinet and into Opposition. Gladstone's Home Rule Bill was defeated in 1886 and Salisbury and the Conservatives took over. In the 1890s Chamberlain and his friends formally joined the Conservative Party. Since they had voted to retain the Union with Ireland they had been called Unionists and so the Conservative Party became known as the Conservative and Unionist Party.

Chamberlain had hoped to take with him all the money, organisation and influence of the National Liberal Federation. He barely managed to hold on to the Birmingham branches. The rest remained loyal to the Liberal Party and the headquarters of the Federation moved from Birmingham to London, where it became the co-ordinating agency for all Liberal Associations in England and Wales. Chamberlain's attempt to take over the Liberal Party had failed. More significantly, the Liberal Party had turned its back on socialism—and so left a partial vacuum in the political world, a vacuum which the infant Labour Party came along to fill.

# 8  New Liberalism, 1906–1914

## Challenge from Labour

The origins, rise and growth of the Labour Party are dealt with in another book in this series, *The Labour Party*. Robert Lowe had foreseen the probability of the emergence of a working-class political party (page 55) during the debates on the 1867 Reform Act. Events proved him right; working men with a vote began to be influenced by the propaganda put out by a variety of socialist societies which taught them that life could be much better if only a more active social policy was pursued by governments. The unskilled, low-paid workers were the first to take a positive step towards the formation of a working-class political party which came into being in 1900.

As one of its early leaders recalled, it did not get off to a flying start:

> The new movement did not begin auspiciously. At the end of the first year only 40 trade unions out of about 1200 then existing had affiliated, with a membership of 353,000. The great organisations of the miners and the textile workers stood aloof, looking on the new movement with suspicion and regarding it with undisguised hostility. The first Annual Conference was held in Manchester in February 1901, and I well remember the feeling of despondency which prevailed. . . . During the previous year (1900) a general election had taken place. It came before the new Committee had had time to get into its work. The ILP had nine candidates in the field, and the trade unions four. Of these only two were successful—Keir Hardie at Merthyr and Mr Richard Bell at Derby. (From '*Viscount Snowden: An Autobiography*', *published by Ivor Nicholson and Watson.*)

## Small challenge

Snowden was right in remembering that the first years of the Labour Party were not very auspicious. But leading Liberals at the time were less pessimistic than he was. They realised that if the Labour Party was to grow, it could only do so by capturing support now being given by working men to either Liberal or Conservative candidates.

In the main this transfer of support would affect the Liberal Party more than the Conservative. We know today that this is what, in fact, did happen; the Liberal strength lay in the old industrial towns and cities—which is where the Labour Party is strongest today.

Evidence shows that people's voting habits follow certain fairly defined lines. For example, a young person tends to vote for the party which his parents have

**48** The giant Lloyd Georgibuster in a *Punch* cartoon 1909, saying: 'Fee, Fi, Fo, Fat, I smell the blood of a Plutocrat: Be he alive, or be he dead, I'll grind his bones, to make my bread'. The cudgel (Budget) is going to be used to force taxes out of the rich man who is hiding under the table

voted for; this is not surprising and it only confirms what we already know about the influence of the home on our development generally. There is also plenty of evidence that over three-quarters of us continue to vote throughout our lives for the party we voted for when we voted first. Taking both of these 'rules' together, we see why the Labour Party could not expect much support in 1900. Most voters had been brought up in Liberal or Conservative homes, and had, in the past, only been able to vote for candidates from one or other of these older parties.

Labour voters in 1900 were the small number of 'rebels' who were not following a family pattern. In time, of course, they would tend to influence their own families so that the number of Labour voters would tend to grow. The Liberals had to try to stop this development by making their Party more attractive to the potential Labour voter.

## Social benefits

In 1906 the Liberals won a massive electoral victory, gaining 397 seats to 157 for the Conservatives, 53 for Labour members (of whom 29 belonged officially to the Labour Party, the rest being Liberals), and 83 for the Irish Nationalists. Although the Prime Minister was Campbell-Bannerman, the leading figures in this Ministry were Asquith, who became Prime Minister in 1908, Lloyd George, who became Chancellor in 1908 and Winston Churchill, a former Conservative.

Between 1908 and 1911 this Liberal government produced three Acts which provided old age pensions for people over seventy, unemployment benefit for some of the workers and the beginnings of a National Health Service. Most of the skilled workers were already paying towards their own pensions, unemployment and sick benefits, through their trade unions. The State system which Lloyd George introduced was meant to help the less well-off who, before 1911, did not belong to some private insurance scheme. Speaking in Parliament, he said:

What is the explanation that only a portion of the working classes have made provision against sickness and unemployment? Because very few can afford to pay the premiums at a rate of 1s 6d [7½p] or 2s [10p] per week at the very lowest. There are a multitude of the working classes who cannot spare that, because it involves the deprivation of children of the necessaries of life. Therefore the vast majority choose to insure against death alone. Those who can afford to take up two policies insure against death, sickness and unemployment, but only in that order. Why not insure against all three? Their wages are too low to enable them to insure against all three. The second difficulty is that during a period of sickness or unemployment, when they are earning nothing, they cannot keep up the premiums, so, in circumstances over which they have no control, [they] abandon their policies. That is the reason why not one-half of the workmen have made any provision for sickness and not one-tenth for unemployment. There is a real need for some system which would aid the workmen over these difficulties. A system of national insurance which would invoke the

**49** Lloyd George in a *Punch* cartoon 1912, after the passage of the National Insurance Act which laid the foundations for the modern schemes of unemployment benefit and a health service. The arrows are a reminder of the opposition that his proposals had roused —from Tory Opposition, the House of Lords, doctors and employers. The halo round his hat is a reminder that many people thought Lloyd George was a good man

74

aid of the State and of the employer to enable the workman to get over these difficulties and make provision for himself against sickness, and, as far as the most precarious trades are concerned, against unemployment.

## Taxation

These new schemes had, of course, to be paid for. The government set up a National Sickness and Unemployment Fund. Every insured employee had to pay 4d a week (about $1\frac{1}{2}$p) while his employer paid 3d and the government 2d. This was described by Lloyd George as '9d for 4d'.

The old age pensions were paid for directly out of taxation. This, together with the payment which the government had to make into the Sickness and Unemployment Fund meant that taxation had to be increased. In 1909 Lloyd George introduced his 'People's Budget'. Philip Snowden, a young Labour MP remembered:

No Budget in pre-war days ever exposed so many vulnerable points of attack. It was bound to excite the bitter opposition of a large number of vested interests. The opposition of the income-tax payers would be incurred by the proposed increase in the tax. The liquor interests would fight the increase in the licence duties to the utmost of their powers. One brewer asserted that these increased licences would mean ruin to half the brewers in the country! The City was up in arms against the increases in the stamp duties, and, of course, the landed interests were infuriated by the proposed land taxes.

**50** *Punch* 1909, showing Shepherd Lloyd George saying to his pet lamb: 'You're too beautiful to die'; the Budget lamb replies, 'But perhaps the butcher will think so too, and then perhaps he won't kill me'. To which the crafty Chancellor-Shepherd replies; 'Hush, don't talk such nonsense'. This is a reminder that many people believed that Lloyd George's Budget was a put-up job meant to rouse the opposition of the Lord's so that the Liberals could appeal to the country on the issue of the 'Peers *versus* the People' and so end the power of the Lords

**51** The rejection of the Budget led to the passage of the Parliament Act which ended the power of the Lords; the Liberal Party is carrying off the new baby 'Veto' (or the Lords' power to obstruct) and is leaving the old baby—or Budget—to itself. Maybe the Budget had been a put-up job after all

Here we have a major departure in Liberal philosophy. Gladstone had based his electoral campaign on the theme of lower taxes; he had hoped to live to see the day when income tax in particular would be abolished—and had managed to reduce it to 2d (about 1p) in the £.

But the new Liberal policy was going to lead to large increases in taxation—with income tax rising from 1s (5p) in the £ to 1s 2d (about 6p), with a new super-tax to be paid on incomes of over £3,000 a year.

### Freedom defined

Gladstone and his Liberal followers had argued that government interference with men's lives—through taxation or legislation—was an interference with their freedom to do as they wished (see Chapters 5 and 6). Lloyd George and the new Liberals argued that this freedom from government regulation had produced a good life for the few rich, successful people—but had produced a very poor quality of life for a large portion of the British people. Over one-third of the population lived in a state of dire poverty; often unemployed, when working they were low-paid. They lived in squalid hovels or were homeless and lived on the streets; for their families life was bleak and dismal. As one writer of the time said:

How does a working man bring up a family on 20s [£1] a week? Assuming that there are four children and that it costs 4s [20p] a week to feed a child, there would be but 4s left on which to feed both parents. Four shillings is allowed for food for a child boarded out by Boards of Guardians; it would seem to be a justifiable figure to reckon upon. For a woman with 20s a week it is ridiculously high. If the calculation were made upon half this, the food for the children would amount to 8s [40p]. To allow the same amount to each parent as to each child would not be an extravagance, and we should arrive at the sum of 12s [60p] a week for the food of six people. That would leave 8s for all other expenses. But rent alone may come to 6s or 7s, and how could the woman on 20s a week manage with 1s, or perhaps 2s, for coal, gas, insurance, clothes, cleaning materials and thrift? (From 'Round About a Pound a Week' by Mrs Pember Reeves, 1913.)

Lloyd George and his followers argued that these poor people were not really enjoying true freedom; they certainly were not free to eat well, to dress properly, become better educated, travel, visit a theatre and so on. New Liberalism proposed to change the emphasis which had once been on *freedom from* (from taxation, regulation, interference and so on) into *freedom to* (to enjoy a better standard of living). Obviously this change meant that some people had to enjoy less freedom—from taxation etc. But it also meant that more people would enjoy freedom—to eat, dress, and live.

## Opposition
There was a good deal of opposition to Lloyd George's ideas inside the Liberal government and Parliamentary Party (Chapter 9); there was also opposition from many Liberal supporters in the country outside. The rich, upper middle class had begun to drift away from their Liberal base even in the 1880s. Lloyd George's policies only increased the flow of these people towards the Conservative Party, which was totally opposed to these policies and used its power in the House of Lords to throw out the Budget in 1909. This led to an election (in January 1910). During the election campaign Lloyd George said:

**52** A medical inspection at Holland Street, 1911—a stage in the development of our modern Welfare State. This was one of the results of Liberal legislation

They have slain the Budget. In doing so they have killed the Bill which . . . had in it more promise of better things for the people of this country than most Bills that have been submitted to the House of Commons. It made provision against the inevitable evils which befall such large masses of our poor population —their old age, infirmity, sickness and unemployment. . . . And yet here you have an order of men blessed with every fortune . . . grudging a small pittance out of their super-abundance in order to protect those who have built up their wealth against the haunting terrors of misery and despair.

Well now, we are on the eve of a general election, which will decide this great question—who are the guardians of this mighty people? . . . They are men who have neither the training, the qualifications, nor the experience which would fit them for such a gigantic task . . . they are simply men whose sole qualification is that they are the first-born of persons who had just as little qualifications as themselves.

### Democracy

The Liberals were the heirs of the Whigs who, in 1832, had started off the process of democratising the political system. Under the influence of John Bright they carried this process further in 1867 and again in 1884–85. Lloyd George realised that while the House of Lords remained as an equal partner in Parliament there could be no true democracy. In 1911 the Liberals passed the Parliament Act which effectively truncated the powers of the House of Lords and set the seal on a process which had started in 1832:

Be it therefore enacted by the King's most excellent Majesty, etc.

I (i) If a Money Bill having been passed by the House of Commons, and sent up to the House of Lords at least one month before the end of the session, is not passed by the House of Lords without amendment within one month after it is so sent up to that House, the Bill shall . . . be presented to His Majesty and become an Act of Parliament on the Royal Assent being signified. . . .

II (i) If any Public Bill (other than a Money Bill or a Bill containing any provision to extend the maximum duration of Parliament beyond five years) is passed by the House of Commons in three successive sessions . . . and having been sent up to the House of Lords at least one month before the end of the session, is rejected by the House of Lords . . . that Bill shall on its rejection for the third time by the House of Lords . . . be presented to His Majesty and become an Act of Parliament. . . .

### Problems

In one sense it seemed as if the new Liberalism had triumphed; the pension, health and unemployment schemes were on the statute book; a number of laws had been passed which were meant to help young children in school and in employment; low-paid workers were helped by the Trade Boards Act; unemployed workers by the new Labour Exchanges. The first Town and Country Planning Act was intended to ensure the healthy growth of British towns and cities. This was indeed a reforming Ministry, far more so than was Gladstone's (Chapter 6).

And yet Liberalism still seemed fragile. There were the many problems that it did not seem capable of coping with—the problem of women's rights, of Irish Home Rule, of militant trade unionism, of rising unemployment. There was also the evidence that support for the Labour Party was not diminishing, as the new Liberals had hoped. Finally, there was the evidence of the 1910 elections in which the Liberals won only 273 seats—only one more than the Conservatives; the electorate was not being won over to new Liberalism, as Lloyd George had hoped.

# 9 The Break-up of the Liberal Party after 1914

### Seeming success 1906–14

We have already seen that the Liberal government (1906–14) deserved the title of 'the great reforming Ministry' in a way that Gladstone's so-called Ministry of 1868–74 never did. This was due to the work of Lloyd George with his ideas on social welfare and taxation, the energy of his Cabinet colleague, Winston Churchill, and the determination of Prime Minister Asquith and all his colleagues not to let the aristocratic House of Lords act as a block to this new Liberalism.

However, 'all that glisters is not gold', and the apparent success of this Liberal government disguised the fact that the Liberal Party was an uneasy alliance of people of different views. There were for example, the old Liberal Imperialists who in 1900 under the then Liberal leader, Lord Rosebery, had supported the Conservative government's policy in South Africa. Opposed to them were the 'little Englanders' or 'pro-Boers' who had vigorously opposed the invasion of the Transvaal, The Boer War, and the disasters which that involved. Lloyd George, a notable pro-Boer, saw the Boers as somehow like his own people—eager to be free from English domination, a small nation with their own culture and way of life.

The earlier rift had been healed by two unexpected events. The first was the passage by the Conservative government of the 1902 Education Act which allowed Local Education Authorities to pay part of the cost of building, maintaining and staffing the Church schools. Liberal Nonconformists saw this as a case of 'Rome on the Rates' since the Catholic and Anglican schools were going to be maintained by the ratepayers—most of whom were neither Catholic nor Anglican. The outcry

**53** Paul Kruger, the President of the Boer Republic, enemy of the British in the Cape

**54** Asquith, portrayed in his role of Chancellor of the Exchequer in 1907. He was responsible for the Old Age Pensions Act (1908) and as Prime Minister supported Lloyd George in his social reforms. He was violently attacked by the Conservatives because of his proposals to reform the House of Lords and this opposition was one of the reasons for his overthrow in 1916 when the Conservatives supported Lloyd George, who became Prime Minister

over this proposal helped the Liberals to sink their other differences. They were further helped in this by Joseph Chamberlain, the former Liberal. He resigned from the Conservative government in 1903 to set out on a tariff reform campaign. This attack on Free Trade was enough to cement the warring factions together in an alliance to try to defeat the Church Education Act and the danger of tariff reform.

## Precarious unity

So, in 1906 Asquith, Sir Edward Grey, Haldane and other Liberal imperialists entered a government along with pro-Boers such as Lloyd George, and John Burns, the former Labour leader. But the apparent unity was then further threatened by the vigorous policies pursued by Lloyd George and Churchill. Was increased taxation and greater government activity part of the Liberal tradition? Lloyd George had made it clear that he wanted a new liberalism; but the Liberal imperialists favoured the older, more traditional, Gladstonian *laissez faire* sort of Liberalism. Whereas Lloyd George wanted the Party to come to terms with the twentieth century, many of his colleagues seemed anxious to return to the more staid, slower pace of the nineteenth. Here were the makings of a new clash.

And this clash seemed more likely because of the personalities involved; there were on the one hand highly-educated, well-trained, fairly rich men such as Asquith, Grey, Haldane and others who were the product of public schools and universities; on the other hand there was Lloyd George who had been brought up by his cobbler uncle in relative poverty, articled as a fourteen-year old to a solicitor, self-educated, ambitious and successful. One of his Liberal colleagues was Herbert Samuel. In his *Memoirs* he wrote of Lloyd George:

Not having had the opportunity of close study of public affairs, he had picked up his history, economics and politics as he went along ... His fixed points were those which had been set in his mind when he was a poor lad in a Welsh village—a lively sympathy for all who suffered from poverty and social injustice; and a fervent Welsh nationalism, which afterwards expanded into a championship of all small nationalities. Beyond that he was frankly an opportunist ... He was never anxious or fearful; his courage never flagged in face of the most formidable dangers. 'The battle was his pastime' and he seemed to be marching through life, head high, to the strains of *Men of Harlech*.

## The war 1914–18

There was yet another reason why the uneasy alliance inside the Liberal government might have come to grief. Lloyd George and his radical supporters were pacifists—having opposed the Boer War, they were eager that any increased taxation should be spent on social development and not on wasteful armaments.

An international crisis developed with the murder of the Archduke Ferdinand in Sarajevo in June 1914. Austria declared war on Serbia; Russia mobilised her forces; Germany declared war on Russia; France, as Russia's ally, was drawn into the war and Germany invaded Belgium in order to attack France. What would Britain, under a Liberal government, do in this situation? Winston Churchill recalled:

> The Cabinet was overwhelmingly pacific. At least three-quarters of its members were determined not be be drawn into a European quarrel unless Great Britain were herself attacked, which was not likely ... It was not until ... 3 August that the direct appeal from the King of the Belgians for French and British aid raised an issue which united the ... Ministers and enabled Sir Edward Grey to make his speech in the House of Commons.

## Liberals and war

The declaration of war led to the resignation of John Morley from the Cabinet; his Liberal pacifism could not countenance even the declaration of war. Other Liberals were prepared to stomach this much—but were quite unprepared to fight a modern war which involved millions of men and women in the armed forces, submarine warfare with the consequent shortages of goods at home, the demands from the services for vast quantities of munitions and equipment. Asquith and many of his colleagues were quite unwilling to see that in such a war the government had to involve itself in the life of the country as no previous government had ever done. If we look at just two of the main problems, we will understand both Asquith's dilemma and the reasons why Liberalism fell apart.

The first involved the question of recruitment to the Services, and in particular, to the Army. In 1914 there was a small professional Army of men who had voluntarily joined. Lord Kitchener, the hero of the Sudan and of South Africa, was brought into the government as Secretary for War. He claimed, and most Liberals agreed with him, that the Army's needs would be met quite easily by encouraging young men to volunteer for service. For a time this seemed to work. But the slaughter of 1914, 1915 and 1916, and the continued demands by the generals for even more soldiers, soon proved too much for this voluntary system. There were not enough men coming forward to meet the demand. Now what was the government to do? Today, it seems a ridiculous question; we would expect the government to announce a system of compulsory service for all men between the ages of, say, 18 and 40. But in 1916 many Liberals were unable to bring themselves to do this; they had a tradition that men should be left as free as possible, that governments should not step in and say 'You must do this or that'. The long debate over conscription lasted from June 1915 to May 1916. It divided the Liberal government and led 27 Liberals to vote against their own Party.

An equally long, bitter and divisive debate took place over the problems of munitions. Was the government going to allow industry to carry on more or less as it had in peacetime, or was there to be greater government control so that steel-makers and others were told what they had to produce? The soldiers knew what they wanted—more ammunition and weapons; the industrialists were unwilling to produce the extra required—unless the price was right; contracts had been negotiated, and so on. Lloyd George was made Minister of Munitions in August 1914 and was responsible for the Munitions of War Act, 1915. No private interest was to be permitted to obstruct the service, or imperil the safety of the State. Trade union regulations must be suspended; employers' profits must be limited, skilled men must fight, if not in the trenches, in the factories; man-power must be economised by the dilution of labour and the employment of women; private factories must pass under the control of the State, and new national factories be set up. Results justified the new policy: the output was prodigious; the goods were at last delivered.

But was this Liberalism? Were industrialists going to be told what profits they could make, what prices they could charge? Were trade unionists not to be allowed to demand higher wages to meet the rising prices of scarce goods in the shops?

## Asquith's fall

Industrialists resented interference, labourers resented attempts to restrain their wages, soldiers resented the failure to provide enough material, the nation as a whole resented the failure to prosecute the war vigorously and mourned the loss of its dead. In May 1915 Asquith invited the Conservatives to join him in a Coalition government; there seemed to be no point in playing at party politics when the nation was in peril. But by December 1916 many of the Conservative and Liberal members of the Coalition were not satisfied at the way in which Asquith was running the government. Lloyd George asked Asquith to set up a small War Cabinet of four members, of whom Asquith was not to be one. When he refused,

Lloyd George resigned. On 5 December Asquith himself resigned and suggested to the King that the Conservative leader, Bonar Law, should be invited to form a government. As Lloyd George recalled: 'Mr Bonar Law then refused to undertake the responsibility of forming a Ministry and recommended the King to send for me'.

## Resentment

The Lloyd George Coalition government was a great success, largely because of the energy and determination of Lloyd George who proved as war-like as he had once been pacific.

Lord Beaverbrook served with him in 1917–18. In *Men and Power* he wrote:

Many will say that Lloyd George's greatest days, his most splendid efforts, were in times of peace, when he put upon the Statute Book more social legislation than any single statesman in our history; but I do not hold that view. To me his greatest hour came as late as the Spring of 1918, when our line of defence had been broken, our troops were in retreat, the Russian Armies were out of the war, and the American Armies had not yet come in ... It was at that moment that Lloyd George penetrated the gloom of doubt and indecision. It was the hour of our peril that he refused to contemplate any plan for retreat. He would talk only of counter-attacks. It was then his leadership showed itself supreme, his courage untarnished. No other moment in Britain's recurring story of escape from disaster can surpass it, save only the decision of the summer nights after the defeat of France in 1940.

But the Asquithians remembered only the betrayal of their leader. Their bitter resentment of the way in which the suave Asquith had been treated by the pushing Lloyd George never died down.

55 Lloyd George, now Prime Minister in a Coalition government, walking towards the hall at Versailles where the Peace Conference was being held, 1919. He had succeeded in smashing the Lords, and had led the country to victory over the Germans. He was also in the process of smashing the Liberal Party

## Election, 1918

In April 1918 a debate took place on whether Lloyd George's government was doing enough to help the soldiers fighting on the Western Front in France. Some generals, notably Robertson, thought that they should be given more help and more power. Lloyd George believed that most generals were inefficient and he wanted to get more power over them. Robertson's chief assistant, Sir Frederick Maurice, wrote a letter to the *Morning Post* in which he accused Lloyd George of starving the Western Front of men and material as a way of getting at the generals. Asquith demanded a debate on the Maurice letter; Lloyd George defended himself with a brilliant speech and most Conservatives voted for him—but the Liberal Party was divided equally between those who supported Lloyd George and those who supported their old leader, Asquith.

In November 1918 the Germans sued for peace; the war came to an end and Lloyd George and his Coalition colleagues decided to call an immediate general election. Lloyd George, the war hero, sent a letter (later called a coupon) to every candidate whom he wanted elected. Not one of those who had voted against him in the Maurice Debate received a coupon. In the hectic fervour of the time, most of those whom Lloyd George supported were elected, and the Asquithian Liberals were decimated. 338 Conservatives and 140 of Lloyd George's Liberals made up the Coalition side, faced by 59 Labour MPs and a mere 27 Asquithian Liberals. For the first time the Labour Party became the official Opposition; for the last time a Liberal entered Number 10 Downing Street as Prime Minister.

## Lloyd George's downfall

Lloyd George was, in fact, a prisoner of the Conservatives who had a majority in the Coalition and a majority in the House. Asquith himself was no longer an MP; along with most of his leading followers he had been defeated by a Coalition candidate. But Lloyd George's position was far from secure. By 1922, Lord Beaverbrook recalled: 'unemployment was widespread . . . agriculture declined; the public disliked Lloyd George's busy and impulsive foreign policy. But the immediate cause of his fall was his arrogance, coupled with the decline of the

**56** Bonar Law who had become leader of the Conservative Party in in 1911. By 1921 it seemed as if Lloyd George and Law were on the way to forming a Centre Party which would oppose the Socialist (Labour) Party. However, in 1922 Bonar Law was persuaded to lead the Conservatives in an election.

confidence which he had inspired during the war... At the very height of his popularity he became impatient, critical and dictatorial in manner'.

In 1922 the leading Conservatives were still quite prepared to go along with Lloyd George as their leader; but the back bench Conservatives decided that they had had enough. At a meeting of all Conservative MPs at the Carlton Club, they voted that the Conservative Party should withdraw its support from the Coalition, and again fight as an independent Party under Bonar Law. In the ensuing election the Conservatives won a majority of the seats, Lloyd George's Liberals won 60, Asquith's supporters won 57 and the Labour Party won 142. Once again, the Labour Party was the official Opposition. Once again, the Liberals had shown the truth of the adage 'divided we fall'.

**Lloyd George—a man without a party**

Lord Beaverbrook noted that Lloyd George was a political leader without a political party—'a source', said Beaverbrook, 'of great weakness'. It is important to remember the dominant role which the political party plays in the fortunes of politicians. Some, like Lloyd George and Ramsay MacDonald, have thought that they could get along without a party. The majority of politicians realise how unimportant they are personally and how important the party is. It has a nation-wide organisation which pays for pamphlets and posters, speakers and researchers. At the constituency level it has its own organisation to keep the active supporters together, to work at election times and to distribute party propaganda.

We have already seen that there are 'rules' which guide people's voting habits (Chapter 8). It is important to notice that in both 'rules' it is the party and not the individual politicians who count. Few individual politicians are worth more than about 500 votes; most voters support a party—and the lucky politician is the one who represents the popular party of the moment.

Another of the 'rules' we saw shows that people tend to continue to vote as they had voted first. In 1900 few people voted Labour; this number slowly grew—as some people came to the vote for the first time, while older voters changed their voting habits. We saw that such a growth could only be at the expense of the Liberal Party.

**57** Lloyd George, no longer leader of a Coalition government, appealing once again as a Liberal leader for the voters' support. Here he is reminding them of his wartime success.

WE MOBILISED *for* WAR —— LET US MOBILISE *for* PROSPERITY!
VOTE
LIBERAL

87

OUT OF THE SHADOWS

UNEMPLOYMENT **CAN** BE CONQUERED
VOTE
LIBERAL

**58** (*Left*) Unemployment was a major feature of British life in the 1920s and 1930s. Lloyd George was the only leading politician to produce any constructive ideas on how to cope with this problem.

**59** (*Right*) A Conservative poster warning people against voting for Lloyd George and the Liberals. The voters are being warned that a vote for the Liberals would be a vote for MacDonald and the Labour Party. There is no evidence that this was so; indeed, it seems likely that when people stop voting Liberal, they tend —like Chamberlain—to vote for the Conservatives

ANOTHER LEG-UP FROM THE LIBERALS

NATIONALISATION CONFISCATION

VOTE CONSERVATIVE AND STOP IT!

## Attempt to re-unite the Liberals

In 1922 the Conservatives got rid of Lloyd George and under Bonar Law called for an election. The result of this and other, later elections can be seen in the table at the end of this Chapter. Lloyd George and his Liberal supporters gained 57 seats, Asquith and his Liberal supporters another 60. Stanley Baldwin became Conservative Prime Minister in 1923 on Bonar Law's retirement and announced his conversion to tariff reform. As with the 1903 campaign (Chapter 8), this attempt to end Free Trade tended to unite the divided Liberals. But the bitter memories of the fall of Asquith in 1916, Lloyd George's memories of the harsh things said about him in the Maurice debate of 1918 and their mutual memories of what had happened in the election campaign of 1918 made such unity a very uneasy thing. In any case, who was to be the leader—Asquith or Lloyd George? In the 1923 election they scored a limited success—but still remained the third party in the House, with Labour once again the official Opposition. This was important because it not only made Labour supporters more confident, it also made many new voters believe that Labour and not Liberal was the natural alternative to Conservative and so affected their voting habits.

The limited nature of the attempts to unite in the 1920s can be seen in the election figures for 1924 and 1929 when, under Lloyd George, the Liberals won less than 60 seats. In 1931 the country entered upon a period of economic crisis which involved the break-up of the Labour Party, the introduction of a system of tariffs and the beginnings of long-term, large-scale unemployment. In the political upheavals of the 1930s the Liberals split into three groups; there were some, led by Sir John Simon, who were prepared to accept tariffs; they finally joined the Conservatives, and Sir John Simon became a Minister in the Chamberlain government. There were others, under Herbert Samuel, who were unwilling to accept tariff reform; finally, there was a small group of Lloyd George's own family— who remained separated from the other two groups. The Samuelite Free Traders slowly disappeared. The defection of Lloyd George's daughter—Lady Megan— to the Labour Party in 1955 was a sign that she at least believed that the radicalism for which her father had once stood was better represented by the new Labour Party than the modern Conservative Party.

## Some revivals

At fairly regular intervals in the 1950s and 1960s political writers spoke about 'the Liberal revival'. This usually happened during those periods when governments were unpopular and the Opposition only slightly more popular. Then, in opinion polls or by-elections, people supported the third party—saying, as it were, 'a plague on both your houses'. However, each of these regular revivals was usually of a short-lived nature; by the time of the next general election the voters had swung back to their traditional voting habits, so that the Liberals continued to win very few seats.

The most notable of the revivals was connected with Eric Lubbock who, in 1962, changed a Conservative majority of 15,211 into a Liberal majority of 7,496 when he captured Orpington in a by-election. People talked about 'Orpington Man' as some sort of new class of voter—not rich enough to be a Conservative, not working class enough to be a Labour supporter, but well-paid, educated, technically or professionally qualified—representative of a new middle class which emerged in the changing world of the 1950s and 1960s. These, many believed, would tend to be Liberal—and there was an influx of bright young TV stars, actors and actresses into the ranks of the Liberals. But again the revival was short-lived; in the 1970 election the Liberals were back again to their 6 seats and Orpington was again Conservative.

Two other factors have helped the Liberals to remain more active than their numbers warrant. One was the quality of their former leader, Jo Grimond, who seemed to be a more honest, intelligent and pleasant man than the leaders of the two main Parties. It was easier for him to appear so—he was not burdened by office or the thought of office; he could afford to promise this and that, knowing that he would not be called upon to prove his words. Nonetheless, he attracted a good deal of personal support, which kept the Liberal name in front of people.

The other factor has been the relatively small majorities which one or other of the major parties has been able to win. In 1964, for example, the Labour Party had a majority of only 4 in the House of Commons. In this situation even the 9 Liberal votes were important; for a time Jo Grimond spoke about a Labour-Liberal alliance. This has never happened—but the fact that it was talked about kept the Liberals in the forefront of politics.

## Liberal weakness

The major weaknesses now affecting the Liberal Party have already been considered. The first is people's voting habits; very few families are Liberal as they were in Gilbert's time (page 5); there are fewer Liberals with a Liberal voting habit. Another major difficulty is a psychological one; few people expect the Liberals to win, so few people are willing to 'waste' their vote on the Liberal. A third weakness is that the Liberals have less money than the other two Parties; they have no natural supply of money as have the Conservatives from big business and the Labour Party from the trade unions: this affects their national organisation.

Some young voters, dissatisfied with the two major Parties—have joined the Liberals in the hope that they can turn it into a more active and more democratic party. They see the Conservatives as representing big business, the Labour Party as representing only the larger trade unions, so that no-one represents 'people'. These radical Liberals have scored some successes; it was they who spearheaded the Anti-Apartheid Campaign to keep the South African Cricket team out of Britain in 1970. But this very success is in one sense a weakness because their more violent, more direct methods tend to frighten off people who might otherwise vote Liberal in their despair at the failure of other Parties.

## Liberal contributions

However, the Liberal Party has been more significant than its numbers would warrant. It is the Liberals who have produced most of the original ideas in British politics in the last twenty years. They were the first Party to support the idea of

**60** (*Left*) Jo Grimond, the Liberal Party leader in the 1950s and 1960s

**61** (*Right*) Jeremy Thorpe who succeeded Jo Grimond as leader of the Liberals

**62** The interior of the House of Commons. The two-sided nature of the Commons and of the voting system have, between them, squeezed out the Liberals

British entry into the Common Market—an idea which, with limitations, is now the policy of both the major Parties. They were the first to work out a scheme for helping the low-paid through a system of negative income tax—which has been adopted by each of the other Parties since. On these, and on many other issues, the Liberals have acted as a 'think-tank' for the political body as a whole. But this is not what a political party is supposed to be about. As Shaftesbury and later politicians realised, 'politics is about power' and there does not seem to be much chance of the modern Liberals exercising that power as did Walpole, Gladstone, Asquith or Lloyd George.

| | CONSERVATIVE | LIBERAL | | LABOUR |
|------|--------------|---------|---------|--------|
| 1885 | 249 | 335 | | — |
| 1886 | 316 + 78 Unionists | 191 | | — |
| 1892 | 269 + 46 | 273 | | 1 |
| 1895 | 340 + 71 | 177 | | 0 |
| 1900 | 402 | 268 | | 2 |
| 1906 | 157 | 377 | | 53 |
| 1910 | 273 | 274 | | 40 |
| | | *Lloyd George* | *Asquith* | |
| 1918 | 338 | 116 | 26 | 57 |
| 1922 | 347 | 57 | 60 | 142 |
| 1923 | 258 | 158 | | 191 |
| 1924 | 415 | 40 | | 152 |
| 1929 | 260 | 59 | | 288 |

| 1931 | 472 | 4 | 33 | 35 | 46 |
| 1935 | 357 | 4 |    | 13 | 154 |
|      |     |   | |  |     |     |
| 1945 | 213 |   | 12 |   | 393 |
| 1950 | 297 |   | 9  |   | 315 |
| 1951 | 326 |   | 6  |   | 295 |

Seats won at general elections 1885–1951.

*Note:*

1 1886. 78 Liberal Unionists tended to vote with the Conservatives; by 1900 they had become totally assimilated.

2 1918. The Liberals split into supporters of Lloyd George and Asquith; in 1923 they came together in an uneasy alliance which split into three in 1931; one wing became assimilated into the Conservative Party and the Samuelites tended to fuse with Lloyd George's family group.

# Further Reading

**General studies of the history of political parties**

| | | |
|---|---|---|
| THOMAS, IVOR BULMER | *The Growth of the British Party System* | Baker |
| MACKENZIE, R. T. | *British Political Parties* | Heinemann |
| JENNINGS, SIR IVOR | *Party Politics—the Growth of Parties, Vol. 2* | C.U.P. |

**The Liberal Party**

| | | |
|---|---|---|
| RASMUSSEN, J. S. | *The Liberal Party* | Constable |
| MACCALLUM, R. B. | *The Liberal Party from Earl Grey to Asquith* | |
| WILSON, T. | *The Downfall of the Liberal Party* | Collins |

**Memoirs or Autobiographies**

| | | |
|---|---|---|
| BONHAM-CARTER, M. (ed.) | *Autobiography of Margot Asquith* | Eyre & Spottiswoode |
| GORE, J. (ed.) | *The Creevey Papers* | Batsford |
| FULFORD, (ed.) | *The Greville Memoirs* | Batsford |

**Biographies**

| | | |
|---|---|---|
| FALKUS, C. | *Charles II* | Weidenfeld & Nicolson |
| PLUMB, J. H. | *Walpole* | Cresset |
| TREVELYAN, G. M. | *Lord Grey of the Reform Bill* | Longman |
| LORD DAVID CECIL | *Lord Melbourne* | Constable |
| MAGNUS, P. | *Gladstone* | John Murray |
| JAMES, R. R. | *Rosebery* | Weidenfeld & Nicolson |
| JENKINS, R. | *Asquith* | Collins |
| BEAVERBROOK, LORD | *The Decline and Fall of Lloyd George* | Cassell |
| | *The Dictionary of National Biography* | |

**Topics**

For general background, see the Pelican *History of England* Series for each of the Seventeenth, Eighteenth and Nineteenth Centuries.

| | | |
|---|---|---|
| HILL, C. | *A Century of Revolution, 1603–1714* | Nelson |

| | | |
|---|---|---|
| MARSHALL, D. | *English People in the Eighteenth Century* | Longman |
| READER, W. J. | *Life in Victorian England* | Batsford |
| MARLOWE, J. | *The Peterloo Massacre* | André Deutsch |
| BRIGGS, ASA | *Victorian People* | Odhams |
| BRUCE, M. | *The Coming of the Welfare State* | Batsford |
| MARWICK, A. | *Britain in a Century of Total War* | Bodley Head |

# Index